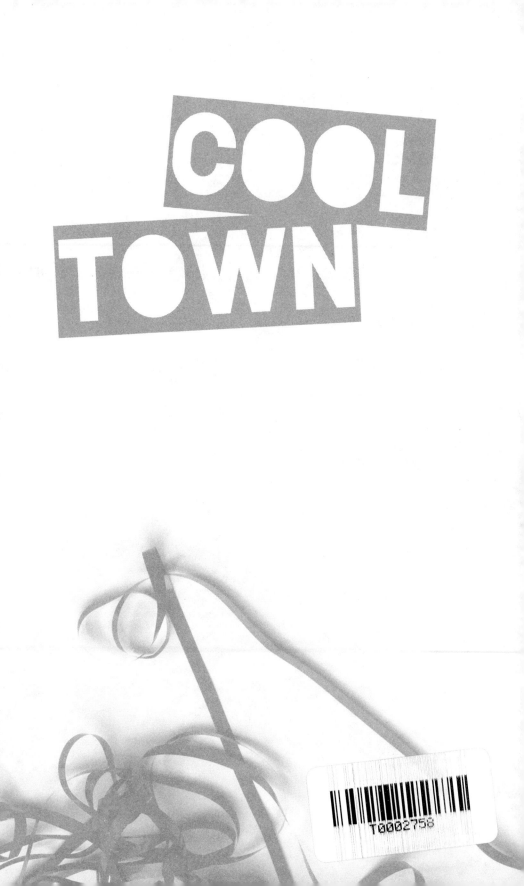

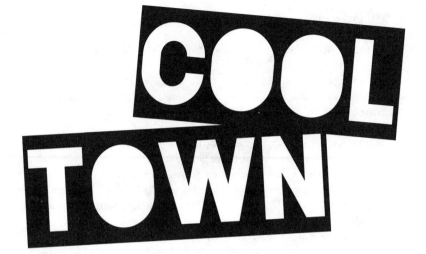

COOL TOWN

**How Athens, Georgia,
Launched Alternative Music
and Changed American Culture**

Grace Elizabeth Hale

A Ferris and Ferris Book

THE UNIVERSITY OF NORTH CAROLINA PRESS

Chapel Hill

This book was published under the Marcie Cohen Ferris and
William R. Ferris Imprint of the University of North Carolina Press.

Designed by Jamison Cockerham
Set in Arno, Biro, Blackout, and Cooper
by Tseng Information Systems, Inc.

The University of North Carolina
Press has been a member of the
Green Press Initiative since 2003.

LIBRARY OF CONGRESS CATALOGING-IN-PUBLICATION DATA
Names: Hale, Grace Elizabeth, author.
Title: Cool town : how Athens, Georgia, launched alternative music
and changed American culture / Grace Elizabeth Hale.
Description: Chapel Hill : The University of North Carolina Press, [2020] | Includes index.
Identifiers: LCCN 2019035107 | ISBN 9781469654874 (cloth : alk. paper) |
ISBN 9781469664057 (pbk. : alk. paper) | ISBN 9781469654881 (ebook)
Subjects: LCSH: Alternative rock music — Social aspects — Georgia — Athens —
History — 20th century. | Alternative rock music — Georgia — Athens — History and
criticism. | Bohemianism — Georgia — Athens — History — 20th century. | Youth,
White — Georgia — Athens — History — 20th century. | Nineteen eighties.
Classification: LCC ML3918.R63 H33 2020 | DDC 306.4/84260975818 — dc23
LC record available at https://lccn.loc.gov/2019035107

For Bill

Contents

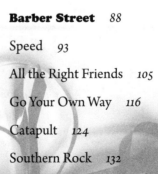

Figures

An Unlikely Bohemia

We are hope despite the times.

R.E.M., "These Days" (1986)

In Athens, Georgia, in the 1980s, if you were young and willing to live without much money, anything seemed possible. Magic sparkled like sweat on the skin of dancers at a party or a club. Promise winked underfoot like the bits of broken glass embedded in the downtown sidewalks. A new world seemed to be emerging out of our creativity, our music and art, and our politics, but also the way we understood ourselves and related to each other.

In my memory, the weight of the air on summer nights made possibility seem like a substance I could hold in my hand. Always, local bands played and people listened—at practice spaces and house parties and venues like the 40 Watt. People went to hear their roommate or boyfriend or coworker play one night and urged everyone to come and see their group the next. Easy to make and easy to hear, live music was everywhere. We used it to reinvent and express ourselves and connect with each other. We used it to live.

After the clubs let out, the scene kept moving until dawn. Small groups climbed the fences at apartment complexes—no one would admit to living in one—and went skinny-dipping. Sometimes people walked to a big Victorian house on Hill Street and danced to mix-tapes in the hall between the rolled-back pocket doors until their clothes dripped with sweat and their heads spun. Occasionally, at midnight, a small drama troupe would perform an original play up and down the aisles of the twenty-four-hour Kroger. Film buffs too young to see movies like *Sleeper*, *Raging Bull*, and *Paper Moon* when they came out watched them for free in the air-conditioned quiet of the seventh floor of the University of Georgia's library. Often, people paired up, going home with the person they were seeing or an acquaintance or someone they had just met. One perfect July night, I lay naked with a friend on the cool cement floor of a screen porch as the wet heat thinned and the crickets rasped and we talked about music until dawn. Possibility proved more addictive than the beer everyone drank and the drugs many people took.

We were unlikely people in an unlikely place. No one expected us to do these creative things. No one who mattered thought that we could make a new kind of American bohemia. Yet Athens kids built the first important small-town American music scene and the key early site of what would become alternative or indie culture.

We had grown up anything but alternative. Home was a new version of the South created by desegregation, interstates, air-conditioning, and airports. Our parents had mostly enjoyed the rewards, a hard-earned success that had been knocked back in the last decade by the oil crisis, stagflation, and the Reagan recession. Our schools practiced a form of neglect that suggested racial integration was easy, feminism unnecessary, and gay sexuality nonexistent. None of that was true, of course, but white, middle-class kids often skated over the consequences.

On some vague level, we sensed that we were living in a changed and changing world, yet the adults around us seemed to be in denial, clinging to old ideas about life and work and community. The most visible alternative, the hippies and peace activists left over from an earlier generation's counterculture, appeared to have degenerated into caricature. Reading books and music magazines and talking to older Athens artists and University of Georgia professors, we learned about creative communities in Paris and London and New York, places that had nurtured earlier rebels from the Beats and the jazz musicians and the abstract painters to the rockers and the drag queens and the punks. Some of us even got to know nearby "folk" artists and musicians, people who followed their own visions right here at home. We longed to send our yawp over the roofs of the world, too, to live for music and art and sex, to be daring and original and important. Why the hell not? We did not want to be rednecks or racists or conservative Christians or live in subdivisions or work as middle managers. We dreamed not of the Reagan-era Sunbelt but of a different world, a new, new, new South. And in the university's libraries and archives and studios and galleries and concert halls and the town's old buildings, we found resources to try to make that world a reality.

The scene was our answer to what we understood as the failures and limits of our America. And our participation in this collective creativity transformed us. In my case, the scene took in an unhappy accounting major confused about politics and about six years later spit out a feminist and anti-racist scholar determined to live her life as art. Along the way, I waited tables and catered, made rugs and wall-hangings out of old clothes, took up painting and the cello, earned a master's degree in history, and cofounded and ran a local venue. When I left Athens to start a history PhD program elsewhere, I took that magical sense of possibility with me and used it to weather the perils of graduate school and the academic job market. My story was not unique. The scene changed everyone I knew. Middle-aged now, a historian and the mother of college kids myself, I can see how the things we learned — question the givens, find something to do that engages your passions, build community into whatever you do, and stop often for beauty and pleasure — radically transformed the trajectory of our lives.

From the late-seventies origins of bohemian Athens to the early nineties when Seattle became the center of American alternative culture, the Athens scene produced amazingly good music, from famous groups like the B-52's, R.E.M., and Widespread Panic to critics' darlings like Pylon and Vic Chesnutt and acts that built a grassroots fan base one show at a time, like the Squalls and Mercyland. But the scene also transformed the punk idea that anyone could start a band into the even more radical idea that people in unlikely places could make a new culture and imagine new ways of thinking about the meaning of the good life and the ties that bind humans to each other. The history of the Athens scene proves that people you would not expect in places you have not thought about can create a better world. It also reveals how cultural rebellion can transform human experience.

Of course, the music mattered. Athens musicians combined an arty, avant-garde approach that prized originality with its seeming opposite, a commitment to the pleasures of pop culture, rhythms that made you feel and move, and spectacle that made you stare. Reimagining the structures of rock music went hand in hand with having fun. Athens bands helped make this pop-art fusion an important part of the new overlapping music genres of college and alternative and indie rock. Because the Athens scene emerged so early in the transition between punk and indie, it also served as a model for kids trying to make their own music in other places not previously understood as having underground potential. If punk taught people that anyone could play, Athens taught them that this music making could happen anywhere, even in the South, even in small-town America.[1]

While bands created the most widely circulated forms of eighties alternative culture, the point was never only to make our own music. People in Athens and in other outposts of indie America were working on something

Members of R.E.M., the most successful band from the Athens scene, goof around in a patch of kudzu. *Left to right:* **Bill Berry, Mike Mills, Michael Stipe, and Peter Buck. (Photograph © Laura Levine)**

more. We were trying to build authentic and meaningful lives in opposition to what we understood as the stifling conventions, false idols, and emptiness of modern middle-class American life. We were trying to save popular music, sure, but we were also attempting to create real places in which real people interacted with each other in order to boost real human flourishing. Surrounded by New Right politics, evangelical social conservatism, and corporate-dominated life, we worked to preserve the very idea of culture as a space of freedom and play and pleasure. And our efforts helped move the ideals we valued—a much more open and tolerant society, an appreciation for and investment in the local, a commitment to beauty and pleasure in everyday life, and a belief that what you do for a living does not define your identity—from the margins to the mainstream of contemporary life.

It is easy to scoff at our naivete and our ignorance—and even our arrogance—and to argue that the DIY notions we imagined as utopia gave way instead to today's start-up mentality, the gig economy, and ballooning inequality. Many people whose opinions I value want the story of Athens to follow a rise and fall arc. But this story distorts and simplifies the history of this scene and ignores the facts. And I am not ready to give up on the promise of alternative culture yet, not in my Athens of the past or in any possible Athens of the future.

Unlike many other places where eighties and nineties alternative culture flourished, contemporary Athens has not become a bohemian stage set for the top 10 percent of Americans, with a little bit of genuine creative culture clawing for survival among the rising rents. It has not been taken over by tech culture and "creative" entrepreneurship like Seattle, Brooklyn, and Austin. And it has not turned slick and rich with retirees and people with "family" money like many other college towns. Gentrification is occurring, but the area remains relatively cheap, isolated, hard to get to, and modest, especially outside the historic districts and areas close to campus. And somehow, within and even on the margins of the scene, wealth is still not something you want to brag about or display unless you want to be considered an idiot or a racist or a Republican. The currency remains DIY culture, and while you can buy other people's creativity and aesthetic sensibility, nothing is as cool as cultivating your own. While the scene is still too white, events like Hot Corner Hip Hop and venues like the World Famous have stretched the boundaries of Athens alternative culture to include African American musicians and fans of indie hip-hop. Today, bohemian Athens still works about as well as it ever did, nurturing a famous band here or there but always churning away at the less glamorous but arguably more important work of transforming the lives of suburban and small-town southern kids and giving them a vision of a bigger and more creative, open, and tolerant world.[2]

In 1977, when the B-52's played their first party, the only people who thought Athens was special were the Dawg fans who overran the town on football Saturdays. The big roads bypassed the area. It took more than half an hour driving north to reach I-85 and almost an hour in the opposite direction to reach I-20. Amtrak's Southern Crescent came no closer than Gainesville. The airport was so small and expensive that few people ever flew. If you wanted to visit, you had to drive or ride the Greyhound.

Either way, you probably came into town on the Atlanta Highway, a thick sprawl of a road heavy with traffic lights and fast-food outlets, discount stores, car dealerships, and a mall. The rolling red-clay hills and pine trees might have been pretty once, but now you had to look past a Howard Johnson, a Mexican restaurant that kept changing names, and an apartment complex if you wanted to catch a glimpse of the Oconee River. Driving into town from any direction other than west, the roads were smaller, but sooner or later you hit little pockets of the same unplanned development, Golden Pantry convenience stores, Waffle Houses, and old motels. Fewer than 75,000 people lived in Clarke County then, about 42,000 of them within the city limits of Athens. Before GDOT, the state highway department, finished building GA 316 to Atlanta in the 1990s, the edge of that city's suburbs ended about an hour and a half west and a little south of the college town, far enough away to be a completely separate world. More than anything, the town and its outskirts were modest and ordinary. Some patches were even ugly.[3]

Moving east, the Atlanta Highway turned without fanfare into Broad Street, Athens's version of "Main." Past what remained of a historic African American neighborhood after the small-town version of urban renewal "improved" it, a public housing development, and a couple of hotels catering to the university trade, you finally reached what actually looked and felt like a town. A traditional nineteenth- and early twentieth-century commercial landscape, Athens's historic downtown survived the strips and the malls only because it sat next to the University of Georgia. Arrayed over about twenty-four small blocks, mostly two-storied buildings with storefronts at street level and very little upstairs besides storage lined four main streets — Broad, Clayton, Washington, and Hancock — that ran parallel to the original entrance to UGA and the smaller side streets that connected them. On corners sometimes and more rarely at mid-block, taller buildings that had formerly housed hotels or department stores or still functioned as banks broke the skyline. A three-story, yellow brick, Beaux Arts–style city hall took up half of one block. On the northern edge away from the university, a three-story post office with classical columns and lots of marble covered half of another. On the west end, the old storefronts gave way to buildings that were a mix of styles and ages, a furniture store, a restaurant equipment salesroom, the venerable Snow Tire, and other automotive businesses. On the east end, the old Farmer's Hardware and a historic firehouse marked the start of an area of old brick warehouses sloping downhill to the river. To the south, on the other side of Broad and separated from downtown by a wrought iron fence, the oldest college buildings and ancient trees of the original campus quads unrolled toward the more modern landscape of the nation's first public university.[4]

West of downtown, historic neighborhoods struggled to survive the combined onslaught of a growing university and the local middle class's move to the suburbs. The large antebellum and Victorian houses on Milledge Avenue had been converted into sorority and fraternity houses or torn down and replaced with mid-twentieth-century copies of their former selves so Greeks could enjoy modern floorplans. On Prince Avenue, a sprinkling of once-grand historic homes survived, subdivided into rental apartments or repurposed as church classrooms or bank offices. One columned antebellum mansion, owned by the Junior League of Athens, could be rented for weddings and other events. Another served as the University of Georgia president's home. Between these structures on lots where other old houses had once stood, a Krystal, a Dunkin Donuts, a pharmacy, a cleaners, and assorted medical supply stores and gas stations made clear how far the neighborhood had fallen. Northwest of downtown, the residents of the Cobbham district were fighting Prince Avenue Baptist Church at one end and Athens Regional Hospital and its affiliated doctors at the other, struggling to preserve their curved streets of bungalows and Victorians. In the Boulevard district, the biggest enemy was deferred maintenance. Little remained of an antebellum vision of Athens as an American version of that ancient site of learning and culture except references to the "classic" city and the existence of the college.

When journalists started coming to town to ask locals what made the place special, early scene participants did not talk much about this landscape. Instead, they focused on expenses. Michael Lachowski, the bass player for Pylon, told a reporter, "Athens is a cheap place to live. That influences the scene, the dress, the music and the recreation in this town." The members of Pylon could live off what they made playing music. Juan Molina confessed to a reporter that his day job, baking cookies, paid only $3.50 an hour. The son of a Cuban immigrant to the United States, he had originally moved to Athens from Atlanta to go to UGA, but he stayed in town to play in a band called the Little Tigers. He and his bandmates rented a huge practice space in the basement of the Morton Theater for $50 a month. "Can you imagine," he asked, "what this space would cost in New York City?" Curtis Crowe, Pylon's drummer and the cofounder of the legendary venue the 40 Watt Club, echoed his bandmate: "You've got the intellectual movement of a city with small-town quiet. And it's cheap. You can afford to be a goof-off musician. You can come up with a band that is so avant-garde nobody will like it, and you'll make money. It's tested all the time. Anything goes. Everyone will pay to see anything once."[5]

When outsiders asked "Why Athens?," the low cost of living and the isolation coupled with the presence of the university became the standard answer. And without these conditions, Athens could never have nurtured the nation's first small-town bohemia. But many other college towns and college neighborhoods of larger cities had low living costs, little-used historic buildings, big public universities, and large populations of bored young people. Very few of them developed world-famous music scenes.

It also helped that Athens was in the South, a region many journalists, music critics, and fans from elsewhere only understood through stereotypes. How could people from a place no one had really heard of actually be avant-garde? Lachowski put it bluntly: "They're freaked out, especially in the states, that bands with any measure of sophistication should come from a small southern town." Being from Athens was a novelty, a great backstory that made a group of musicians stand out among all the New York bands clamoring for attention. According to Crowe, the B-52's got a lot of mileage out of their hometown. When they played New York, "people asked, 'How could anything that good possibly come out of Athens, Ga.?'" Peter Buck, the guitar player for R.E.M., also described this element of surprise. Being from Athens "definitely helps. . . . You won't get a second job some place just because you're from Athens if you're not good. But people will say, 'They're from Athens, let's give them a chance.'"[6]

Yet neither the material conditions nor the regional stereotypes can fully explain the outpouring of creativity, the collective practice of making art out of nothing and everything. Vic Varney, a member of early Athens bands the Tone Tones and the Method Actors, got closer to an answer when he told a reporter in the early years of the scene: "There's this absolutely incredible naivete here about the possibilities about life on Earth. I don't know why we're so arrogant or stupid to think we can do the things we do, but we do." Artist April Chapman described how rare it was for a place in the South to be "so open to anything new." "You could see alternatives," she told me. "You could think, 'I can live like this, too.'" Even an exasperated Pete Buck, tired of being asked in 1982 about the place R.E.M. originated, admitted that in Athens "you are really encouraged to express your art—in poems or painting or music."[7]

About three and a half decades after he talked to that reporter, I interviewed Varney. And he told me that even before Ricky Wilson started the B-52's with his friends, he had the idea: "Let's make a scene." Varney made explicit what I had pieced together from other sources. Athens did not just happen. The earliest participants were trying to build their own version of New York City bohemia in their small southern town.[8]

In particular, Ricky Wilson and other early participants were inspired by New York gay and queer culture in the years when the closet was beginning to break down. From the performance practices and rituals associated with drag, these Athens kids learned how to experiment. Conventional understandings of what made someone a man or a woman did not have to define them. A person could be one thing and its seeming opposite simultaneously. Yet few people in the scene talked explicitly about the queer sources of their sense of openness and fluidity. Some people "forgot." A lot of participants never really knew. Part of the problem was homophobia, which only became stronger in the eighties with the emergence of the AIDS epidemic. Another, related reason was a different understanding of the boundaries between public and private. Few Americans then felt compelled to talk publicly about their private lives.

In the early twenty-first century, we believe that the fight against homophobia and other forms of discrimination requires recognition of multiple categories of gender and sexuality, an expanding array of identities referred to by the acronym LGBTQA+. In contrast, Athens bohemians in the late seventies and eighties understood categories of gender and sexuality as bourgeois conventions, as part of the very structure of discrimination. Drawing on drag's refusal to pick a team or answer the either/or question, they were more interested in living outside the boxes "man" or "woman" and "queer" or "straight" than in creating more. From a contemporary perspective, this way of living could look like cowardice, a refusal to "come out," a way to have it both ways. And some scene participants like Ricky Wilson and Mark Cline were out as we understand that term today. But for many of the people who created and expanded the scene over the years, having it both ways was the point. This fluidity, rare not just in small towns but in much of America, made Athens special. The blurred lines between men and women, gender and sexuality, and anatomy and identity became a model for thinking about everything else, too. Suddenly other seemingly opposed categories like amateur or professional, southern or avant-garde, and even making your own culture versus remaking *the* culture looked more permeable. That characteristic Athens sense that anything was possible grew out of this fluidity.[9]

That Ricky Wilson had the courage to come out around 1970 while he was still a student at Athens High School makes it clear that he would have been a radical visionary in any town. But Wilson had something a lot of kids then did not have: access to a local queer community. Through an older gay friend, Ricky and his best friend, Keith Strickland, also gay, met members of a network of gay and bisexual and queer Athens residents connected to the UGA art school. Some of them were professors. Others were current or former undergraduate and graduate students or adjunct instructors or people who worked at the university in other capacities. Many of them were fully or partially closeted, but all found work and friends and lovers in Athens because of the university.[10]

The University of Georgia hovers underneath my story here, a given in the town where the university had long been the largest employer and the reason so many young people lived there. In 1977, when Wilson, his sister Cindy Wilson, and Strickland and their friends Kate Pierson and Fred Schneider formed the first "new music" band in Athens, the B-52's, UGA already enrolled almost 22,000 students, and it was growing. By 1991, when R.E.M.'s album *Out of Time* made the longtime indie darlings into an internationally famous rock band, UGA had over 28,000 students. Indirectly, this is a story about how big, non-elite public universities in the postwar period created conditions that enabled many Americans to thrive in new ways. The people who built the Athens scene took advantage of what the University of Georgia had to offer, whether they were enrolled or not: the classes, talks, exhibitions, concerts, and interactions with professors, but also the spaces and the collections, the studios, practice rooms, common areas in dorms, and exhibition areas and the freely available books, audio recordings, magazines, newspapers, and films.[11]

As the writer Marilynne Robinson has argued, Americans created public colleges and universities, the nation's "best idea," to democratize privilege. Most visibly, public higher education expanded access to the professions, to careers in fields like medicine, the law, applied sciences, and education that require lengthy training and formal qualifications. But public colleges also opened up access to knowledge in a less instrumental and arguably even more important way. They suggested that everyone had a right to study what other humans have thought about the answers to big questions like the nature of the good life. And at their best, they prepared students to ask and answer those big questions for themselves. In Athens, UGA gave the young people who created the Athens scene resources we could use to question the mostly white, mostly middle-class, and mostly southern culture from which we had come and create our own definition of a meaningful life.[12]

In practice, that questioning took the form of endless conversations. Through coffee-soaked afternoons and beer-buzzed nights, we used what we had learned from books and from our experiences to think about the meaning of bohemia or what we increasingly called alternative culture and its relationship to "the mainstream," an America dominated by the white middle class and massive corporations. Early on in the history of the scene, this theorizing occurred at what was jokingly called the "Cobbham Institute," a house on Cobb Street where Vic Varney, John Seawright, and others held forth at all hours in a kind of unofficial intellectual salon, and at the Gyro Wrap, a café that served pitas packed with what other places called doner or shawarma along with the area's first cappuccino and espresso. Later, it flourished in venues like the Grit and the Downstairs, spaces open during the afternoon and late-night hours when people were not listening to live music and where patrons could sit all day over a cup of coffee that cost less than a dollar.

When we weren't talking about particular bands or sex, we often argued about what I would later learn to call "cultural politics." What makes something or someone cool? What is the relationship between the scene and the mainstream? We also debated the terms under which a person or a band got to count as a part of our scene. After a few years, musicians and even fully formed bands began to migrate to town, and this debate about who was a local became particularly fierce. Some participants thought anyone who intentionally moved to a place to "make it" could never authentically belong, while others conjured exceptions for lovers or friends or bands whose music they liked. Commitment helped, and people who stayed around long enough and became generous members of the community earned local status as other participants ceased to know or to care why they had arrived.

The more nerdy of us even debated terminology. "Bohemian" felt too French and too pretentious to many participants. Some frat boys and rednecks favored another label for people in the scene: faggots. Early on, we flipped the meaning of the term "townie," historically a pejorative in college towns and college neighborhoods of cities, and used it to identify ourselves, whether we were students at UGA or not, as not Greek or otherwise part of the conventional student population. "Townie" emphasized the localness of our attempt to create a new culture and its rootedness in a particular place.

In Athens and other outposts of alternative culture, being a part of the scene meant you had to question conventional ideas about everything, from sex to citizenship. DIY theorizing, though few people would have called it that, was as important as all our other forms of DIY culture. When books about new bohemias, alternative culture, and indie music began to appear in the mid-nineties, it made sense that the best of them were written by participants like Gina Arnold, Barry Shank, Michael Azerrad, and Ann Powers. What I love about these authors is how they stay true to the worlds they describe by blurring the boundaries between their roles as critics and scholars and their experiences as participants.[13]

More recently, the study of alternative or indie culture has become an academic subfield. And I want to give credit to fellow scholars who have produced a lot of smart thinking about punk and alternative/indie music and alternative culture over the last two decades. But like many scene participants in Athens and elsewhere, I already understood the arguments, even when I did not know all the particulars. Participants in indie culture argued endlessly about how cultural resistance worked and how it also often failed. And the best answer we could come up with was cultural autonomy imagined as a local and egalitarian and everyday practice.[14]

Historically, bohemia originated in mid-nineteenth century Paris as a middle-class revolt against the limits of middle-class experience. In other words, bohemians have worked to create greater freedoms, rather than political revolutions. They have shaped society not by overthrowing political regimes but by reimagining what art can do in particular times and places.[15]

In twentieth-century America, the imported possibilities of bohemia expanded right alongside the ranks of the middle class. When punk fused avant-garde ideas about what it meant to be an artist and popular musical forms in the 1970s, it opened up this kind of cultural rebellion even further. If "everyone" could be middle class, then everyone could also be an artist, a rebel musician kicking at the corpse of mass culture, a bohemian. We certainly can and should ask the questions: what exactly is this freedom and who gets to have it? But we should not stop dreaming of and working toward a free life.[16]

In 1992 in the *Village Voice*, the cultural critic C. Carr coined the phrase "bohemian diaspora" to describe a world in which, "for the first time in 150 years, bohemia can't be pinpointed on a map." Seventeen years after the B-52's played their first party, bohemian emphasis on life as art, its celebration of beauty and pleasure over work, and its dogged repudiation of commercialism and consumption existed everywhere and no particular where: in gritty, unrenovated urban lofts, in ramshackle old houses on small-town streets, and in sections of seedy strip malls turned into suburban clubs. On one level, place mattered—you used what was on hand to create your own art and music and community, your own alternative to big, corporate culture in your own particular locality. In Athens, those resources were the gay community, the art school and other spaces and libraries on offer at the University of Georgia, the rich culture of the rural South, a low cost of living, and old houses and other buildings that could be rented for cheap. But the larger message was that place did not matter, that it did not determine who you had to be. With a few like-minded friends, you could make a more free and authentic life anywhere.[17]

In retrospect, this moored unmooring was the sweet spot. Earlier rebels had to move to Paris or New York. Later rebels found anything and everything, including other weirdos, on the internet and did not have to make face-to-face community. The Athens, Georgia, scene was one of the earliest, most important, and most lasting sources of this bohemian diaspora. If young people could create their own alternative culture there, they could make one anywhere. We can't write bohemia's epitaph any more than we can write its history by standing in a few big American cities.

David Levitt, my roommate and later husband, my business partner, and the leader of Cordy Lon, the Athens band in which I played, never liked to be pinned down on the meaning of his lyrics. But I always thought his song "Hunting Divine" explored the same paradox that Ernst Bloch, a philosopher I read in graduate school, wrestled with in his work *The Principle of Hope*. "I used to think this / I used to think that. / This is the road that's ever more new / While hunting divine," David would sing in a voice that started in melancholy and ended in peace. Utopia is impossible, but necessary. Or as Bloch put, "That which is coming up is not yet decided. . . . Through a combination of courage and knowledge, the future does not come over man as fate."[18]

As a historian, I know that people can only dream inside history, within the structures and webs of meaning that have accumulated up through the present. When we attempt to make a new world, we stand in and start from the old. It is easy to understand why utopia is not achieved. Instead, I want to ask a different question. What exactly is it that makes us try?[19]

The Factory

If you're in outer space
Don't feel out of place

'cause there are others like you
others like you
others like you.

The B-52's, "There's a Moon in the Sky" (1979)

Jeremy Ayers wore ragged layers in 1986 when I first met him — dark trousers, the coat from an old suit, a vest, multiple button-up shirts, and a worn fedora. Bits of lint and leaves seemed to spill out of his seams where a pegged pants-leg met a flapping brogan or a thin wrist poked out from a collage of sleeves. Sipping espresso at the Grit and showing up, late and quiet, at a party or an art show or, more rarely, a gig, he scared off the conventional. Jeremy's presence made a place as part of the scene, and he radiated an aura that made other people circle like planets. Close to him, the air buzzed. The light dazzled. He seemed more like a piece of art than a person — he was that beautiful. He was a star.[1]

In a college town where people flowed in and out with the semesters, Jeremy was an old-timer, genuine Athens royalty. His father, Robert Ayers, had joined the University of Georgia faculty as chaplain and professor of religion in 1949. Jeremy knew Keith Strickland and Ricky Wilson when they were still in high school, before they formed the B-52's, and he invited them to visit him in New York in the early 1970s when he was writing and acting there. He used the nickname Jerry then, and he remained close friends with Strickland and Wilson after moving back to Athens in the mid-1970s. As Jerry, he shared a writing credit on the B-52's song "52 Girls," the B side of the band's first single and a cut on their first album.[2]

When the B-52's relocated to New York, Ayers remained in Athens. Like a hipster Forrest Gump, he seemed to pop up wherever anything arty and interesting was happening. Sometime between Halloween 1979 and early 1980, he and Michael Stipe started hanging out together. People who were in town then remember Stipe quitting his cover band, cutting off his white-boy fro, and copying Ayers's scarecrow style, the look he worked in the early years of R.E.M. They became friends and briefly lovers — the line was a carefully maintained blur in a network of beautiful men, not out but not in the closet and not always strictly gay or straight. Around 1981, Ayers formed the avant-garde noise band Limbo District with Craig Woodall, Dominique Amet, David Stevenson, and later Tim Lacy. The group played locally for a few years, toured a little, and made a film with University of Georgia art professor Jim Herbert. In 1985, Ayers earned another cowriting credit, this time on the R.E.M. song "Old Man Kensey" released on their third album, *Fables of the Reconstruction*.[3]

Jerry Ayers was not the only person in those early years with a New York connection. Other people also moved between Athens and the city, including Maureen McLaughlin, the first manager of the B-52's, and Teresa Randolph, who also knew Wilson and Strickland in high school. Magazines and papers also circulated New York news. Stipe devoured the *Village Voice* every week after he got a subscription through Publishers Clearing House while a high school student in Illinois. Michael Lachowski and Randy Bewley, future founders of Pylon, read about punk and other new music bands in the magazine *New York Rocker* as young University of Georgia art students. But Ayers was different, a living connection to the New York underground.[4]

For suburban and small-town kids who filled this university town, he modeled the essential bohemian act — he made his life into art. He played in the most avant-garde band in town, wrote, painted, took photographs, and decorated his run-down, turn-of-the-century house with secondhand furniture and his own and his friends' art. He also befriended and mentored many androgynous and beautiful young men, from Wilson, Strickland, and Stipe to Love Tractor's Mark Cline and the Chickasaw Mudd Puppies' Brant Slay and Ben Reynolds. Life, he suggested by example, gained its meaning not from work or school but from aesthetic expression. In this way, Jerry/Jeremy was more than a local star. He made Athens the place *to be* a star.

It should have been obvious, but unlike most people who were around when the scene started, Ayers did not talk much about his past. He participated in the mythmaking, not by telling stories but by being present as a mystery. Only a few people knew that Ayers had not just lived in New York.

No other single figure did more to nurture the Athens scene than Jerry Ayers, who changed his name to Jeremy Ayers in the mid-eighties. (Photograph by John Lee Matney)

In the early 1970s, he had been a part of the Factory, Andy Warhol's studio and bohemian hangout, a central hub of New York's underground art world. He had used a "stage" name which he adopted from a cigarette brand whose ads proclaimed "cigarettes are like women. The best ones are thin and rich." As "Silva Thin," Ayers had already been a star, a Warhol superstar.

In Athens, our man as metaphor presented himself as the opposite of

In New York in the early seventies, Jerry Ayers became
a part of Andy Warhol's Factory and transformed
himself into the superstar Silva Thin.
(Photograph © 2019 The Andy Warhol Foundation for
the Visual Arts, Inc. / Licensed by Artists Rights Society
[ARS], New York; Andy Warhol, photographer)

a glamorous celebrity. But in New York around 1970, Andy Warhol photographed him working the Greta Garbo end of 1940s stardom. In a small Polaroid, Thin's pose is jaunty, a brash kind of feminine. He has combed his longish natural hair loosely back, and he wears a two-toned, feminine jacket with high-waisted pants held up by suspenders. A brown scarf knotted at the neck tops a dark blouse that ties close to reveal a dagger of bare skin. Deep red lipstick traces a heart shaped mouth. Faked brows arch high above eyelids covered in dark shadow. White eyeliner underneath adds a touch of theater. His left hand in his pocket cocks his right hip forward. Chest up, he bends his right hand at the elbow and again at the wrist, holding a cigarette sexily in his long, thin fingers. As Silva Thin, Ayers embraced what people at the time were beginning to call "genderfuck," a form of drag in which people made their cross-dressing obvious in order to call attention to the fact that men could be women and women could be men.[5]

Historically, the practice of drag or dressing up in ways that self-consciously played with broadly shared ideas about what made a person a man or a woman worked as a powerful means of challenging those conceptions. Because gender and sexuality were central to understandings of social order, this questioning often spiraled outward, from bodies and intimacies to politics and culture. Pretending, embracing illusion and artifice, paradoxically created an opening for examining the very meaning of reality. Drag performers used characters and styles that seemed out of date or fake or trashy to imagine new sexualities, new ways of living, and even new kinds of art.[6]

In the late 1960s and early 1970s in downtown New York, artists, musicians, playwrights, and filmmakers incorporated the forms and aesthetics of this cross-dressing into their work. Drag fused high and low, the avant-garde art world and the sexual and musical undergrounds. It taught artists how to use artifacts of old popular culture, including movies, magazines, and cast-off clothes, to make art that questioned contemporary popular culture. Yet drag was more than an inspiration for pop art; it was also a performance practice. Cross-dressing enabled artists to explore ideas about gender and identity across creative mediums, including theater and music, and to take their questioning of norms out into the world. All this acting, in turn, helped people create alternative ways of living in their bodies and creating intimate relationships. Drag dragged all the diversity of identities represented by the acronym LGBTQA+ into the light.[7]

At the Factory, transvestites Holly Woodlawn, Jackie Curtis, and Candy Darling starred in happenings and Warhol films, and the Velvet Underground, named after a paperback about suburban spouse swapping, became the house band. In 1968, Warhol moved his studio to Union Square West, right around the corner from the nightclub Max's Kansas City, where the Velvets played regularly and the Factory crowd took over the back room. By the early seventies, Max's had become the center of a heady mix of music, art, and drag. Glitter boy David Bowie, androgynously sexy Iggy Pop, the New York Dolls in their tutus and combat boots, then-lovers Patti Smith and Robert Mapplethorpe, the transgender punk pioneer from Georgia named Wayne County, and former Velvet Lou Reed all hung out and often also performed there. In the fertile scene that developed between Max's and the Factory, drag and other forms of dress-up inspired new kinds of performance art and filmmaking as well as the music that would become punk. The drag stars, Reed made clear in his David Bowie–produced recording "Walk on the Wild Side," helped create and radicalize this scene:

> Holly came from Miami, F.L.A.
> Hitchhiked her way across the U.S.A.
> Plucked her eyebrows on the way
> Shaved her legs and then he was a she.

The mere act of dressing up could upend the world.[8]

It is unclear exactly when Ayers moved to New York, but he was there around 1970, when Warhol took his photograph. As Silva Thin, he interviewed the San Francisco drag troupe the Cockettes—a group of gay and straight men and women who invented a kind of psychedelic Victorian gender-bending—about their visit to New York for the February 1972 issue of Warhol's *Interview* magazine. Trading makeup tips—he shaved rather than waxed his eyebrows—Thin set the members of the group at ease. Their act, they admitted, confused their audiences, who labeled the performers transvestites, freaks, or dykes depending on the situation. They also talked about Thin's performance in Jackie Curtis's play *Vain Victory*, featuring Warhol superstar Candy Darling. Curtis, Thin told them, had recently changed her name to James Dean, an act of drag play that also made it into Reed's "Walk on the Wild Side." Rumors put Ayers in all kinds of interesting places in this period, from modeling tuxedos for French *Vogue* to riding on John and Yoko's wedding plane. He might not have been a major Warhol superstar, but he was part of New York's downtown scene.[9]

When Warhol traded the drag queens and Max's for wealthy New Yorkers and Studio 54, Ayers moved back home and replaced his glam superstar act with a different form of drag. In opposition to hippie excess and yuppie success, he modeled ragged and flapping failure, a style the *Village Voice* called "Boho as hobo" more than a decade later when it was still an alternative culture staple. Ayers was an early adopter, even an inventor of this aesthetic. He looked like a copy of a copy, a contemporary version of a sixties folk-music fan's fantasy of a Depression-era working-class man. Somehow, his scarecrow act conjured and questioned the whole journey from the sixties to the eighties, the curdling of once idealistic political and cultural critiques into a new conservatism.[10]

Drag as gender play was still there, though, in the clothes but more powerfully in his affect. Cool and constrained, Ayers hung back at the edges. He whispered, and people had to lean in to hear. He made self-effacement sexy. Emotionally, he played "the girl." Jeremy, as he called himself then, was our straw man, the thing we pushed against, our cypher. Without exerting a straight masculine privilege that undermined old countercultural claims, he made the still radical and unfulfilled demands. Fuck anyone. Be anyone. Question all the givens.

In 2013, when I asked him for an interview, he nicely, sweetly even, refused. He said he simply did not remember his past. Or maybe, just maybe, the master of ambiguity was even then working the mystery, still provoking questions about his intentions and refusing to reveal or even acknowledge the boundary between his personality and his performance, his art and his life.

Through Jerry Ayers, the Factory's pop art performance practices came to Athens. Around Warhol, drag had mashed together avant-garde and burlesque, the art world and the emerging punk scene, men and women, gay and straight and trans, and glam and trash. It also conjured childhood dress-up games, Halloween costumes, school theatricals, and other forms of play. In Athens, drag worked as a solvent, a playful way of dissolving conventions and categories, a "fun" form of rebellion. It pushed what happened in apartments, art-school classrooms, and studios into the streets. It sent people digging through the piles at thrift stores, the castoffs of popular cultures now past, for ideas and materials. And it connected Athens residents who were not necessarily students but were interested in exploring nonstraight sexualities to the art students and their friends.

In the middle of the seventies, a small circle of Athens friends discovered the pleasures and transgressions of genderfuck, even if they were too "southern" to use the term. They wanted to make performance art. They wanted to have fun. They wanted to create their own versions of what was happening in New York.

Small-Town Drag

The college kids split then. On one side were preps sipping bourbons and Cokes and wearing what might as well have been their grandparents' clothes. On the other were hippies wearing jeans and tees, barefoot, long-haired, and high. Keith Strickland, a local, a nineteen-year-old graduate of Athens High but not a UGA student, had the day off work loading bags at the bus station. A band was playing in the plaza in front of Memorial Hall, then the University of Georgia's student center, and he decided to walk to campus. Maybe the music or even the people would be interesting. The concert was free, and Strickland was looking for fun.[11]

It is hard now to imagine, in a town transformed by everything that followed, how radical Strickland looked then, walking across Broad Street and through the campus in a costume that would have turned heads on Halloween. In Rodger Lyle Brown's account, he wore a gold lamé jacket, stacked heels, a pair of cat-eye sunglasses, and lipstick. His hair, stiffened with hairspray, stuck up high in a trashed approximation of a down-rent beauty-shop style. A Mack truck mirror hung like a pendant around his neck. Others remember Strickland wearing knee-high boots and a Christmas garland instead on this cross-campus romp. All agree that somewhere along the way he pulled a bag of pillow fill out of the trash. In the plaza, the event turned out to be less an open-air party than a failed attempt at campus programming. Only two people were dancing. Still, the man in the pair might be interesting — neither preppies nor hippies wore loud Hawaiian shirts then. Glitter boy Strickland danced up to the pair, smiled, and rained the stuffing down on their heads. The man was Fred Schneider, future member of the B-52's.[12]

Strickland had moved from the country to Athens when he was in ninth grade and his father got a job managing the Athens bus station. He met Ricky Wilson, a year ahead of him, at Athens High School. They tracked down information on their adolescent obsessions, including extraterrestrials, and they talked about art and music together. As Beatles fans, they followed the band into Eastern religion and mediation. In the late sixties and early seventies, Athens had a small folk-music scene organized around the venue the Last Resort where Georgia musicians and even stars like Odetta and Doc Martin played, a network Strickland and Wilson learned about through Strickland's older brother Kenneth. Wilson bought a Silvertone guitar at a pawnshop and taught himself to play the instrument by watching a how-to program on public television. After school, he listened to Joni Mitchell and began writing songs. His younger sister, Cindy Wilson, would listen to the songs he had recorded on his reel-to-reel and learn to sing the lyrics. With another high school friend and Strickland, who took up the drums, Ricky Wilson formed a band called Black Narcissus that played Jimi Hendrix covers at a high school concert.[13]

In their last years in high school, Wilson and Strickland often hung out with an older crowd, including Jerry Ayers, a mix of college students, professors, and locals interested in art and music. According to Strickland, when they were sixteen or seventeen, Wilson asked his friend to sit down so he could tell him something important, and then he made a formal, third-person pronouncement: "Ricky Wilson is gay." Strickland was shocked, not at the news—he believed everyone close to them both knew they were gay—but at the fact that Wilson had the courage to state his sexuality out loud, even to his best friend. Yet Wilson's example was not enough to get Strickland to speak out, and he spent months working up the nerve to say what his friend clearly already knew. Despite the emergence of a gay rights movement and openly gay enclaves in New York and San Francisco, very few people then lived completely out of the closet. Strickland and Wilson were fortunate to live in a town that had a gay community. They were also lucky enough to find it. As Strickland remembered this local network was still "fairly closeted. It depended on who you knew." Vic Varney, a member of early Athens bands the Tone Tones and the Method Actors, described Athens this way: "There's a lot of queers in the South but there aren't a lot of communities where they had a culture." A university with an ambitious art school made Athens different from other small southern towns. Strickland and Wilson's heterosexual friends, Strickland insisted later, were also "very supportive, even in high school."[14]

Ayers had already moved to New York City when Strickland and Wilson rode the Greyhound up in the summer of 1972, after Strickland graduated from high school. In the city, they toured the sights, met Ayers's friends, and observed the mix of sex, drag, performance, and music on offer around the Factory. Warhol superstars including Holly Woodlawn and Jackie Curtis taught them how to buy glamorous 1940s-era fashions at thrift stores and dress up like Hollywood starlets. Back in Athens, Wilson and Strickland lived together and continued experimenting with drag. Wilson took a night class or two at UGA, and they both worked at the bus station. In 1973, Strickland played in the Athens glitter-rock band Zambo Flirts. At some point, the two friends saved enough money to travel to Europe where they worked odd jobs and backpacked and lived for a while on the beach in Greece. In Europe, they fell in love with the street musicians. Back home, they made a plan to go back and work as buskers with Cindy Wilson in tow, and they began practicing. Around this time, Strickland also started hanging out with Fred Schneider.[15]

Schneider had moved from New Jersey to Athens in 1969 to study forestry at the University of Georgia and avoid the draft. On his first day at UGA, Schneider met William Orten Carlton praising an obscure brand of potato chips in a booming, backwoods voice in the dining hall. An Athens native, Carlton, around twenty and already a local character, went by the nickname Ort and stomped around town with his wild, almost black hair, waving his big hands in exclamation. In the mid-1960s, he had been part of what he remembered as a crowd of would-be bohemians at Athens High School. Schneider shared Ort's goofy sense of humor and loved his new friend's redneck savant routine.[16]

In 1972, trying to turn his obsession with obscure old records into some income, Ort opened a store downtown. Though the place moved through multiple locations, Ort's Oldies's motto remained the same: "If Ort doesn't have it, he'll sing it for you." Behind the counter, he shared his passion for rare records with everyone who wandered in. Soon, Schneider started showing up there wearing a Little Richard mustache, in homage to the fifties rock-and-roll star who teased his hair high and wore makeup in a carryover from his drag performer past. While Ort scavenged roadside junk stores for more inventory, Schneider ran the shop, listening to and looking at the old records and playing them for his friends. In those predigital days, recordings of popular music of the past were hard to hear unless an older relative or friend owned the disc. Access to Ort's collection was like having the keys to a Library of Congress listening room dedicated to archiving half a century of old popular rather than folk culture.[17]

In the early seventies, Strickland and Wilson shared what they had learned from Ayers and other Warhol superstars with their Athens friends, including Schneider. Hanging out, they listening to David Bowie, Alice Cooper, and the New York Dolls and looked at the photographs on the album sleeves. Then they headed to the Potter's House Thrift Store on Washington Street to poke through the used clothing piles. Back at home, at Schneider's house on Barrow Street or Wilson and Strickland's house on Pulaski, they constructed their own costumes out of the clothes, jewelry, wigs, and fabric they found and practiced their album art poses. Like many of the Factory folks, they were not interested in creating a seamless illusion. They were not trying to "pass." Instead, embracing the space where male and female visually met, the guys put on vintage dresses and makeup without shaving their faces or their legs. A few women sometimes joined in, wearing old over-sized suit jackets and dress shirts or their own versions of their male friends' drag looks. Wilson and Strickland's friend and UGA art grad John Martin Taylor, for example, took a photograph of two young painting students Margaret Katz and Debbie McMahon looking almost like boys in identical white shirts and ties. Still a teenager, Cindy Wilson started shopping at thrift stores and raiding her brother's closet. One day she wore an outfit he had gotten from Jackie Curtis to high school.[18]

Like Strickland the day he met Schneider, these friends often took their act out into the streets. They called themselves "freaks" in opposition to the hippies and "straight" people they loved to shock. Piling into someone's big old car, handed down from a grandparent or bought on the cheap, they drove around looking for parties and crashed them, scaring the hosts with their clothes and crazy dancing. Sometimes, their friend and future member of many Athens bands Dana Downs remembered, they hit the local disco the Circus, across the kudzu-covered field from Schneider's house, and people threw drinks at them. Other nights, they drank quarter beers at the redneck bar Allen's and scared the bubbas. On one particularly memorable Halloween party, Schneider dressed up as Ginger from *Gilligan's Island*, Wilson went as a nurse, and Strickland wore his infamous purple yak wig, a purple dress, and purple eyeliner. After the party wound down in the wee hours, they took their drag show out of the house and down the street to the Five Points all-night laundromat, a self-consciously lowbrow choice of venue. There, lit by fluorescents and backed by washers and dryers, they performed in front of the plate glass windows for a handful of customers and the few people who wandered by. It might not have been Max's, but it was fun.[19]

Kate Pierson met this cross-dressing crowd through Jerry Ayers. By the time she moved to Athens in 1973, she had already gone to college, performed as a folksinger, and traveled around Europe. On the outskirts of Athens down Jefferson River Road, Pierson and her British husband rented an old, run-down farm for $15 a month. Old hippies and "back to the land" folks lived in falling-in farmhouses and old tenant shacks on rented parcels scattered throughout the area, in between the established farms where rural families raised cattle. The young people planted big gardens, raised chickens and other animals, and hiked into the woods to cultivate pot in isolated openings between the trees. Shaped by the folk music revival, they also rejected much of the commercialized popular culture of the moment. Instead, they took up weaving, taught themselves to play guitars and banjos and other instruments, baked their own breads, skinny-dipped in nearby creeks and ponds, and hosted potlucks and sing-alongs that lasted until dawn. Locally, with the materials at hand, they made their own culture. And they shared these habits with their country neighbors, longtime residents whose self-reliance made them masters of recycling and reuse and well-practiced in the art of making their own fun. In this way, long before punk rock reached Georgia, folkies and hippies there created a powerful do-it-yourself model. They created the Athens Folk Music and Dance Society and its annual North Georgia Folk Festival to celebrate the music and other arts they loved.[20]

Pierson lived this back-to-the-land life. She heated her house with a wood-burning stove, collected her own water in rain barrels under the eaves, and milked her four goats. Taylor remembers Pierson biking the six miles into town with a quart of fresh milk that the two friends put in their coffee. Pierson brought this do-it-yourself approach to life with her when she started hanging out with Wilson, Strickland, and Schneider, who had learned their own scavenger ethic from drag queens and record collectors.[21]

Despite the myth created later, Athens was not the isolated edge of nowhere in the mid-1970s. An hour and a half away, Atlanta had a large and visible hippie scene on the Strip, along Tenth Street from Peachtree Street toward Piedmont Park and along Fourteenth Street, and a widely read alternative paper, *The Great Speckled Bird*. Many UGA students grew up in the Atlanta suburbs and returned home on weekends, during winter and summer breaks, and after graduation. Along with Athens people who were not students, they visited the Strip and the park, read the *Bird*, hung out at Atlanta Rising, a market and tearoom; Middle Earth, a head shop; and clubs like Twelfth Gate and the Catacombs. Georgia kids, too, grew up with southern rock and bands like the Allman Brothers and Lynyrd Skynyrd. They already knew a powerful "up from the sticks" backstory of how the small, conservative Georgia city of Macon became the center of an internationally successful musical genre. They might even have voted as Jimmy Carter traced his own version of this journey, from southern Georgia peanut farmer via the Navy and the governor's mansion to the presidency.[22]

Together, Ricky and Cindy Wilson, Strickland, Schneider, and Pierson built a small, bohemian beachhead in Athens with the aid of a shifting group of current and former art students, closeted gays, and other friends. Sure, as they would tell reporters later, they were fighting small-town boredom. But they were also connected to the wider world. Ayers had lived in New York. Strickland and Wilson had traveled there and to Europe. Pierson, too, had traveled widely, lived in England, and played in a folk group in Boston called the Sun Donuts. She told people she moved to Georgia because she read too much Flannery O'Connor and Carson McCullers. Pushing back against the preppies and the hippies, these friends created a little bit of that Factory-Max's mix right in their own little town. They knew what they were doing. The point was to perform and attract attention and create their own little alternative world.[23]

Historically, small-town eccentrics moved to the city, to New York especially and to other large cities like San Francisco. If they stayed home, they learned to adapt and do their partying in private. Many southern college towns, for example, tolerated unconventional behavior as long as the rebels were white and kept their sexuality to themselves. As Strickland remembered, "There were always eccentrics in Athens, but we took it into the streets." Like the little knots of art and music obsessed kids in the late seventies in other unlikely places like Akron (Ohio), Louisville (Kentucky), and Austin (Texas), these Athens friends were not moving, and they were not hiding. By staying where they were, they invented something that had not existed before, a new kind of small town bohemia.[24]

The earliest manifestation of this new scene in Athens was an art-house theater that someone ran at the Station, an old railroad freight train depot on the edge of downtown, for about a month in 1975. Called Locomotion, the venue showed one film, Mick Jagger's *Performance*, and hosted other happenings. The owner knew Schneider wrote poetry and experimented with sound, and he gave him a slot opening for a poetry reading. Schneider quickly wrote and rehearsed some songs with Wilson, Strickland, and other friends. Calling themselves Night Soil, a euphemism for human excrement, they crowded their friends onto the stage. Some played instruments, including a violin and three saxophones. Others performed as go-go dancers or screamed along to the rush of sound. A slideshow of Canadian tourist attractions played behind them. Schneider, wearing a dress and blue lipstick, grinned from the middle of the chaos. The audience stared back, confused.[25]

That same year, Cindy Wilson graduated from high school. She enrolled in a typing class at Athens Tech and worked at Kress's lunch counter downtown. The next year, Schneider, sick of Athens, moved to Atlanta. On an October trip back to see friends, he went out to eat Chinese food with both Wilsons, Strickland, Pierson, and Strickland and Wilson's high school friend Owen Scott, then a graduate student at UGA. Scott and Wilson had briefly played together in Zambo Flirts. Scott had also been a member of Black Narcissus. Riding a bit of a buzz from too many flaming drinks, they went to Scott's house. He stayed upstairs, while the rest of the crowd played around on the instruments in his basement and hammered out a rough version of a song they called "Killer B's." Early the next year, Schneider asked his friends the art students Julia Stimpson and Gray Lippett if the new band could play at their Valentine's Day party.[26]

In Athens, UGA students and other residents collected and distributed news about parties friend to friend in the dining halls, classes, and dorms. They passed along locations and addresses and news of any free alcohol on offer at work and at restaurants. Some people simply cruised neighborhoods where young people lived looking for cars and crowds. On the edges of campus, along Milledge Avenue and Lumpkin Street where the fraternity houses clustered, parties raged many nights of the week, but the Greeks did not have a monopoly on kegs and grain punch. Athens was a party town.[27]

Wilson, Schneider, Strickland, and Pierson knew lots of current and former art students and professors, and their house parties offered an alternative to the frat events on campus and the hippie bashes in the countryside. Ayers threw legendary themed parties for the overlapping art-school and gay crowds. At John Martin Taylor's house, the attraction was food: "I was always feeding the masses. My place was one of the salons and people were always going there." Taylor remembered, "We were typical twenty-something pot-smoking, beer-drinking students, though we were mostly involved in the arts. . . . Yet in other ways, we were special: curious, well-read, and knowledgeable about painting, film, and contemporary music." Unlike most UGA students and recent graduates, these kids listened to Brian Eno, the Ramones, and Patti Smith, as well as Booker T., Aretha, and James Brown. They watched foreign films, especially Fellini, and they made and exhibited art. They devoured what a few of their art, film, and literature professors taught them and made use of the university's resources, like the main library's seventh-floor film archive, to explore the avant-garde culture completely absent from their suburban and small-town upbringings. Whether or not they graduated from UGA or ever even took classes, they learned about the larger world. They were educated.[28]

The turn-of-the-century house at 653 North Milledge sat at the very visible corner of that street and Prince Avenue. On Valentine's Day, lucky friends and acquaintances, a few people with fourth-hand directions, and anyone with the sense to know that all those cars did not belong to the residents stumbled into a new kind of Athens party. With the exception of African American musicians playing a form of R & B called beach music and, increasingly, funk at fraternity houses, live bands did not play at local parties; a few friends strumming guitars and awkwardly singing by a backyard bonfire did not count. Right away, the fact that the front door was blocked and guests had to enter through the back suggested something was different. In-

**Fred Schneider, Cindy Wilson (*middle*), and Kate Pierson
of the B-52's perform during the band's debut
at an Athens, Georgia, Valentine party.
(Photograph by Kelly Bugden, courtesy of Keith Bennett)**

side, instruments including bongos and Wilson's tape recorder were set up in the front room. An eclectic group of people mingled, many of them current and former UGA art-school students. Kelly Bugden hung a Barbie doll from the chandelier, where it swayed overhead as people walked past. MFA student Zeke Addison loaned his giant speakers. John Martin Taylor wore a shirt he had made at a county fair with the head of a woman with a beehive hairdo on the front and the phrase "B-52's" written on the back. Sally Stafford, doing her best *Sound of Music* imitation, wrapped a patterned 1950s curtain around her waist as a skirt. This crowd dressed up for parties, and the five performers fussed with their costumes in a back room, working to upstage their friends. When they came out, Strickland had on his crazy purple wig. Schneider wore a wifebeater and white jacket and sported a thin mustache, reworking a Halloween costume in which he had dressed as a hangover. Guitarist Ricky Wilson provided a kind of preppy contrast, looking out at the crowd from underneath his long blonde bangs. Worried that people would not understand that the band's name referred to a hair-style, not a bomber, Strickland and Schneider bought fake fur muffs for Cindy Wilson and Pierson to wear on their heads. In the muffs, cat-eye sunglasses, dark blouses, and silky pants, the two women looked like drag queens.[29]

After they took their places in a little alcove-turned-stage, Schneider started bleeping his walkie-talkie, and the five friends launched into "Planet Claire," a routine that would become standard in early gigs. Much of the music came out of Ricky Wilson's tape machine. In those first performances, the five friends danced and sang and added beats and sound effects to music they had previously recorded, not sure enough yet of their act to put on their show and play their instruments simultaneously. Strickland did not even own a drum kit. People in the audience mostly remembered what the performers looked like and how they moved, not what they sounded like beyond the danceable beat and the three voices alternately singing and shouting the absurd lyrics. The B-52's played everything they knew, six original songs, including "Killer B's" and "Rock Lobster." Then, because everyone was having so much fun, they performed the whole set again.[30]

The audience, buzzed on alcohol and pot, danced madly. The Barbie doll bounced on its string. Steve Hollis, then a coworker of Pierson's, remembered, "It was very wild, just wonderful. I literally thought that whole downstairs was about to cave in. The floor was coming away from the walls." Cindy Wilson later recalled, "People were dancing so hard the floor was like a trampoline." Almost as soon as the party ended, people started talking. Stimpson and Lippett's Valentine's Day bash quickly became a legend. But it was not until the B-52's played a second gig, a week later at Wilson and Strickland's friend Teresa Randolph's place, that anyone remembers someone saying it. As Pierson recalled, Randolph, riding someone's shoulders through the dancing crowd, screamed over and over, "I can't believe this is happening in Athens, Georgia."[31]

Townies in the City

Setting their drag review to music and putting it on display was wild and fun, but the B-52's playing local parties was not enough to make Athens a scene. In 1977 New York City was the new music center of the United States. The Velvet Underground and the New York Dolls started it. Television formed in 1973. The Ramones, the Patti Smith Group, and Blondie all debuted in 1974. Talking Heads formed the next year. Playing at CBGB's, which opened in the East Village on the Bowery in 1973, and Max's, which reopened in

1975 northwest of the East Village near Union Square, these and other bands invented an American punk, more formally eclectic and more tied to the avant-garde art world than British punk yet linked through their shared rejection of middle-class culture.[32]

By the second half of the 1970s, these New York punk bands were touring and putting out albums. As the critic Tom Carson has argued, a sense of generational competition with older siblings and friends animated their fans. Kids in high school and college in the late 1970s were mad that they had missed the sixties, the radical politics and the parties, the commitment to causes, the new hair and clothes and the new rock. They wanted to know what it felt like to believe that young people and their music could change the world. In punk, they heard their own contradictory feelings of longing for both the innocence and the excess of the period that had just passed. And they found a post-sixties way to live, a "let's just fuck it and have fun" attitude perfect for people with an ambivalent relationship to politics. In response to bands like the Patti Smith Group and the Ramones, alienated kids all over the country, in small towns and suburbs as well as cities, formed their own bands. Like earlier generations of would-be artists and bohemians, many punk fans moved to the city be closer to the scene. Others practiced their music in suburban garages and basements and dreamed of New York gigs.[33]

The Ramones in particular, a band that started in a place as unlikely as Athens—the suburban New York neighborhood of Forest Hills, Queens—inspired punk fans everywhere to try to make their own music. Wearing black leather jackets and ripped jeans like midcentury working-class rebels, the all-male quartet used exaggerated swagger to rework the sounds and themes of girl-group pop. And they performed this revival so straight that fans could not tell if their act was serious or a joke. Together, their sound and their look made early rock and pop, cast aside as lacking in seriousness after the Beatles, cool again. Richard Hell, a member of Television, explained the Ramones' appeal as "a great combination of stripping rock and roll to its essence—in a cartoon-like way, which was really calculated to succeed, like Andy Warhol or something—[and at the same time] pure, real street emotion and narrative." As Tom Carson put it, the Ramones practiced a form of parody that achieved its emotional impact through "a moving flippancy, a sense of the cartoon as real life that comes straight out of the everyday surrealism of growing up with Batman on TV, Herman's Hermits on the radio, and Green Berets parachuting into the backyard."[34]

In Atlanta, a group of young male musicians created their own punk band, the Fans. They made their first trip to New York in January 1977, a slot opening for Talking Heads at CBGB's. Dana Downs, a UGA philosophy student, got to know the members of this Atlanta group when she took a year off college and lived in Atlanta. Back in Athens to finish her degree, she hung out with the art-school crowd and lived with Teresa Randolph. Downs, a future member of the first band to form in Athens after the B-52's, the Tone Tones, told Mike Green of the Fans about the B-52's Valentine's Day debut and urged him to come see the second show at Randolph's new place. By the end of the summer, Strickland and Wilson were riding along to New York for the Fans' second CBGB's show to share their homemade tape. Before the B-52's had ever played a club anywhere, they were trying to get their own New York date.[35]

By the mid-1980s, what was happening in Athens proved that people did not have to move to the big city to live an alternative life. In the late 1970s, though, that scene emerged out of the very direct movement of musicians and ideas back and forth between Athens and New York. Disagreement about who got the B-52's their Max's gig makes clear that many people in Athens had connections in the New York scene. Conflicting memories also reveal how participants understood this trip as a key moment in the scene's origins.[36]

Maureen McLaughlin, the B-52's manager for part of 1978 and 1979, remembered that she got the band the date through her boyfriend Moe Slotin. Slotin left Atlanta, where he worked on the staff of the *Great Speckled Bird*, and moved to New York, where he got a job as a roadie for Blue Oyster Cult. Allen Lanier, a member of that band, was dating Patti Smith then, and around 1976, Slotin started working for the Patti Smith Group. Through Slotin, McLaughlin met Smith and the members of her band, including Lenny Kaye and Ivan Kral, and went with them to Max's and CBGB's. In her memory, because she got the Fans their first New York gig (she remembers it as Max's, not CBGB's) the B-52's asked her to get them a date as well. She did, and they debuted in New York opening for Teenage Jesus and the Jerks on a Sunday night.[37]

According to others, Curtis Knapp, who moved to Athens after he saw the Fans perform and met Teresa Randolph in the city, got the B-52's their first Max's gig. Ricky Wilson went to the UGA library to research audio recording techniques and more general information about the music industry. Using what Wilson had learned, members of the band made a tape and created a little fake press kit with help from their art-school friends. Ricky Wilson, Fred Schneider, and Keith Strickland, along with their Athens friends Dana Downs, Betty Alice Fowler, and Sean Bourne, road-tripped to New York to see the Fans play at CBGB's. Knapp, who was living in Athens that summer, tagged along to get his stuff out of storage. Fowler's surviving Super 8 films of this visit depicted them all partying at the Iroquois Hotel and acting goofy in the subway. At CBGB's for the Fans' show, members of the B-52's gave the soundman the press kit. After he said no, Knapp suggested they try Max's. Before moving to Athens, he had painted a mural there, and he knew many of the club's employees. After they all returned to Athens, Knapp worked the pay phone at the bus station while Strickland and Wilson unloaded suitcases and packages. After a week of calling, he got the band a gig on a Monday in December as part of Max's showcase night. John Martin Taylor, who knew Ayers, Strickland, Wilson, and McLaughlin well, remembered yet another version of this story, that Ayers got the band the Max's gig through his connections.[38]

In a December 1979 profile of the B-52's in *Creem*, band members remembered taking a tape to CBGB's, being turned down, and then going to Max's where they were offered a show. Schneider told *Rolling Stone* writer James Henke a similar version of this story in 1980: "A friend of ours who had done the mural or something at Max's Kansas City said, 'Y'all sound at least as good as some of the bands in New York.' So we drove up there with this tape we had made in someone's living room, and they let us play on an audition night with two other bands." Schneider's account leaves out the Fans entirely, however, and exaggerates the outsider angle. Knapp, a recent transplant to Athens, probably did not say "y'all." Max's ad in the December 12, 1977, *Village Voice* listed the B-52's opening for Gizzmo and Nylon on a Monday night.[39]

To get ready for their New York gig, the B-52's lined up another house party, this time hosted by Curtis Crowe, future Pylon drummer, and Bill Tabor. The two friends would later create the first Athens venue for this kind of music, the 40 Watt Club. They lived then off the Atlanta Highway in what seemed like the middle of nowhere, a small house surrounded by pecan trees down a long driveway behind Poss's Bar-B-Que. At the time, Danny Beard, a UGA graduate, had moved back to Atlanta to found a version of Ort's Oldies there, the record store Wax 'n' Facts. He heard the B-52's play at Crowe and Tabor's party and liked them so much he asked if he could go to New York as their roadie. The band used the Wilson family's big old station wagon and "borrowed" Strickland's parents' charge card. Friends, including Downs and Randolph, came along too. The Athens drag party was on the road.[40]

"We thought it was exciting, that we were able to come to New York City and do this," Ricky Wilson told *Creem* in 1979, "cause like in Athens there are no clubs we could play at." The reporter made Wilson sound like a hick, and it is likely Wilson was playing up a "rube in the city" routine, band members' stories of their origins in the nowhere town, Kate's goats, and the bored kids (the oldest was then twenty-nine) just trying to have fun. Schneider remembered, "Max's had such an aura." Cindy Wilson confessed, "I'd hide behind the curtain and peak out." Pierson recalled, "I didn't really know whether the audience liked us or not because a lot of our friends came up from Athens, so they were dancing and screaming and everything." Cindy told *Rolling Stone* three years later, "We were so nervous." At Max's, the three bands split the door, and the B-52's made $17. As they were leaving the club, Pierson recalled, "A friend of ours just ran back and asked the booker if she wanted us back and she said 'Yes!'" Ricky Wilson told Tom Carson, who wrote a long piece about the band for *New York Rocker* in July 1979, "I was amazed that we got such a good reaction that first time we played at Max's." Strickland confessed, "We didn't know what to expect."[41]

Back home, band members worked hard just to find places to play. In January, Cindy Wilson, her boyfriend Keith Bennett, and other Athens people went to see the Sex Pistols perform their first U.S. date, a sold-out show at Atlanta's Great Southeast Music Hall. About a week later, the B-52's took the stage at the first Atlanta Punk Festival, quickly organized to take advantage of the Sex Pistols' buzz. Friends helped persuade the tiny Athens folk club the Last Resort to let the band play a date, and an article appeared in the local paper, impressing Strickland's parents even if their friend Taylor wrote the piece. "This is an opportunity to enjoy some dance music without disco banality or romantic overtones," Taylor told readers, and he invented the phrase that would be repeated by many future critics to describe the B-52's music, "thrift store rock." Danny Beard came from Atlanta. Despite the fact that WUOG broadcast the concert on the radio and confused listeners called in to see if the music was a joke, Beard could see that people in the club, like the crowd at that party in the country, loved it. He offered to pay for the band to record a single and booked time at Stone Mountain Studio near Atlanta. He also worked with Emory University student Pete Buck, future member of R.E.M., to book a room for a performance at that university just outside Atlanta to showcase the band. A few UGA students and future scene participants, including Sam Seawright and Mark Cline, drove over from Athens to see the B-52's play. UGA student Kurt Wood, future host of a punk show on UGA's college radio station WUOG, covered the gig for the *Red and Black*, the student newspaper. In an article titled "Punk Rock Plays Emory," he asked,

"Who knows? The group may return with a contract, in addition to future experiences in the Northlands."[42]

In response to all this attention, Strickland, Pierson, Schneider, and the Wilsons began practicing seriously, in secret, at Pierson's place in the country, and in town. Their downtown Athens practice space, they frequently told reporters, had previously served as the bloodletting room in an old funeral home located in the run-down, turn-of-the-century Morton building that also housed the vegetarian restaurant El Dorado where Fred worked. Band members also went to the UGA library to look at old *Harper's Bazaar* and *Vogue* magazines for ideas about style, something they would do until they left Athens. By late February, they were in New York City again with Athens friends in tow for dates at both Max's and CBGB's.[43]

Maureen McLaughlin remembered getting the band a second gig in the city, a Tuesday night at Max's. People like Lou Reed came, and music critic Lester Bangs told her that Ivan Kral of the Patti Smith Group had called every music critic, musician, and photographer he knew. While key people in the New York scene saw the band on their second trip to New York, *Village Voice* ads put the band at Max's, opening for the Fast, on Friday and Saturday nights February 24 and 25, and then at CBGB's, opening for the Rudies, on Sunday February 26. Critic Tom Carson said they played a Wednesday night at CBGB's too, and it is possible they were added to the bill after the ad was printed. According to Carson, John Rockwell from the *New York Times* and Robert Christgau from the *Village Voice* went to the show. *Rolling Stone* described the B-52's as "the hottest club band in New York" that winter. Andy Schwartz, in an editorial for the first issue of *New York Rocker* under his ownership, was giddy: "When an unknown quantity of a band like ... the B-52's can blow me away on a chance visit to CBGB's, then I know that 1978 is a great time to be alive and in love with rock 'n' roll."[44]

Pop Art Rock

From the late spring of 1978 through the summer of 1979 when the B-52's released their first album, the New York underground scene fell hard for the Athens band that managed somehow to be both southern and avant-garde, silly and serious. According to critic Tom Carson, when the B-52's headlined four nights in a row at Max's one week and three at CBGB's the next in late May and early June, "the word was out and everybody went to see them." The critic John Rockwell was there, in Carson's telling, "lurching around in a black leather jacket with day-glo racing stripes on the sleeve, clutching a broken bottle of Lowenbrau and bellowing, 'Fan-fucking-tastic! I'll fight anybody in the house who says no!'" In his own piece on the band, John Rockwell got right to the point: "Anyone who thinks the CBGB's-Max's underground-rock club [scene] in New York has stopped introducing exciting new bands hasn't heard the B-52's. This eccentric, downright loveable quintet from Athens, Georgia was at Max's last weekend and is at CBGB's through tonight, and provides about the most amusing danceable experience in town." Strickland and Wilson had come full circle. Having brought the Factory and Max's scene to Athens, now, with help from Schneider, Cindy Wilson, and Pierson, they brought their Athens to Max's and CBGB's.[45]

Like good pop artists, they created that world and their art out of pieces of pop culture, history as recorded on the shelves of thrift stores and junk shops. "Planet Claire" was an adaption of Henry Mancini's "Peter Gunn Theme," a song written for the late-fifties and early-sixties television show. Other lyrics, sonic and visual gestures, and melodies, whether deliberate or not, reference musicians including the early Kinks, the Shangri-Las, and Duane Eddy, the instrumental song "Telstar" by the Tornados, the Ventures' song "Pipeline," the teen movie *Beach Blanket Bingo,* and the television show *Star Trek.* One critic called their live performance "the Theater of the Big Surf in a Mr. Ed World." Somehow, critic Van Gosse wrote in *Village Voice,* the band "opened up the process so that all the different models from the junkyard of twenty-five years' *Big Beat* and *TV Eye* could collide and synthesize to create New Sound." The B-52's, Gosse argued, drew "their power from cuisinarting shards of association and ambience and rhythm that date from 1955–1965." The contrast of pop past and present often played as funny but could also be biting. The B-52's' cover of "Downtown," a song recorded in the 1960s by Petula Clark, took on different meaning in an era when punks and bohemians were moved into parts of central commercial districts abandoned by businesses in the wake of the civil rights movement.[46]

Often, in early B-52's performances, in a gesture that evoked "bubblegum" rock, Schneider would introduce the members of the band. Sometimes he called Strickland "the former Pebbles," a reference to a popular cartoon daughter of Fred and Wilma Flintstone. Both fans and critics then often referred to the band's cartoon-like style. Taylor, in his Athens *Observer* piece advertising the B-52's Last Resort show, described how his friends turned "the dance floor into something out of a Saturday morning cartoon." A later *Observer* piece compared the band's performances to "cartoon sock hops." The British music critic Jon Savage asked in a piece on the B-52's in

Melody Maker, "Why do all these new American groups come on like cartoons?" For Americans growing up in the 1960s, the Flintstones (and to a lesser degree the Jetsons) modeled how pop culture could remix conventional images and plots and characters into comic critique. The Flintstones mimicked and twisted the popular show *The Honeymooners,* with its lineage that ran through radio and vaudeville back to the blackface minstrel show. "Cartoonlike" referred to the band's playful, even childlike performances, but it also suggested the multiple layers of play-acting and reenactment at work. At a time when rock was a fairly dark and serious affair, the B-52's made the music fun again.[47]

Members of the B-52's also played to and with their New York audiences' expectations about southerners. Their southern accents, the license plate on their station wagon, and the stories the band told about their love for "dance music; soul, people like Junior Walker and James Brown" all announced their place of origins. Critics responded by looking for qualities that they associated with the South. In the *Village Voice* in June 1978, Tom Carson, a Virginia native, found an "undeniably Southern spookiness" in their music: "As in Cindy Wilson's wailing, cat-on-a-hot-tin-roof vocal on 'Hero Worship,' or the whole premise of 'Devil in My Car,' inspired by a gospel show on the radio; when Cindy and Kate Pierson ask, 'Where you takin' me, devil?' they sound as snippety as a grandmother in a Flannery O'Connor story." A reporter for the *Washington Post* insisted that before the B-52's, New Wave had emerged from "urban sprawl" but this band, "from of all places Athens, Georgia" broke the mold. A critic for the British magazine *New Musical Express* wrote that Kate Pierson (who was actually a New Jersey native) peeked around a door and asked, "Y'AHL WANT gumbo?" and that "her deep southern accent tells ahl [*sic*] that her deep southern dish is ready." The same critic described Cindy Wilson's voice as "a sassy southern lilt that adds 'h's rather than drops them, the complement to her blonde belle looks." Sometimes, members of the band seemed to ham it up with journalists, laying their regional identity on thick.[48]

In May, Beard launched his own label, DB Records, to sell the B-52's' first single, "Rock Lobster," backed with "52 Girls." The photograph on the sleeve featured the five band members, their names typed in all caps attached to their legs to identify them, a visual representation of the introductions Schneider always performed during their show. The contact address in Athens on the front connected the band and their sound to the town. Reviews praised the band's sense of rhythm. "Another genius single of the month is The B-52's 'Rock Lobster/52 Girls.'" Glenn O'Brien wrote in his review of the single for *Interview*, "The B-52's are the fastest rising group in America today. This is not because they are from the South and unheard of, but because of a remarkable talent, which this self-produced single proves handily. . . . The B-52's are the most important rhythm band since, uh, Talking Heads." On both cuts of the single, Strickland's propulsive fatback drums laid the foundation, and the toy instruments parts, repeated words, squeals, screeches, and organ riffs built up in percussive layers. In the late 1970s, serious rock critics were an overwhelmingly white male group, and they tended to divide the music worth listening to into danceable and fun "black" genres like soul-influenced R & B and funk and serious "white" genres like rock and punk. However they understood the B-52's genealogy, critics often followed long-established trends that labeled music by whites that sounded "black" as "southern." A few critics including Tom Carson linked the B-52's danceable rhythms to disco, but band members and most critics gave funk and soul music the credit for the band's danceable beat.[49]

The B-52's' singing sounded southern, too. Nailing what became his characteristic deadpan dissonance, Schneider performed "Rock Lobster" in alternating accents. He sang "rock" like a downhome southern boy and then he sang "lobster" like a kid from the Jersey Shore, losing the "r." He also delivered lyrics like "his air hose broke" like a character from the *Andy Griffith Show* and dragged out the final syllable of his lines, turning words like "jam," "clam," and "fish" into two syllables, a vocal characteristic common across his adopted region. Yet because he could turn his accents on and off like his walkie-talkie, his southern sound seemed like a costume, a sonic version of Pierson and Wilson's wigs.

In the summer of 1978, the "Rock Lobster" single sold out fast in New York at record shops like Bleecker Bob's, and after his initial two pressings of 1,000 copies, Beard produced 5,000 more. And as the summer wore on, fans got into the B side too, a song called "52 Girls." On the surface, the lyrics, written by Jerry Ayers, sounded like a list of women's names, old starlets, TV characters, country stars, and the women in the band. But who, besides "Kate" and "Cindy," were these girls? Were they women under their skirts, because they were biologically born that way? Or were they women because they were wearing skirts, because they had women's names? Were these the stage names of drag queens? "52 Girls" played hide and seek like a drag act.[50]

Live, in downtown New York with its history of drag cabarets and performances, audience members easily picked up on the queerness of the song lyrics and the way all the band members danced and dressed against type. What could be more drag than cross-dressers like Strickland and Wilson deciding to impersonate 1950s college students like UGA frat boys were still doing back home? Than New Jersey Fred doing his "character from a Tennessee Williams play" routine? Than Pierson and Cindy Wilson dressing up like transvestite Warhol superstars who also happened to look like the women who worked with Cindy at a downtown Athens lunch counter? The B-52's employed an aesthetic that was transgressive in both its content and its forms. But even outside of New York, many people who saw the band perform understood. Once the album came out, even high school kids got it. I know, because I was one of those high school kids. You had to be a pretty dumb heterosexual not to get it—you had to want not to get it.[51]

By the time their second album *Wild Planet* came out in 1980, the B-52's had bucked a growing conservatism that was shutting down the seventies sexual revolution and taken their drag act right into the center of American culture. The ambiguity, the disjuncture, the questioning of the categories kept gay, transgender, and queer identities in circulation in a period when the tiny gains of the seventies were under assault from all sides. The "tacky little dance band from Athens, Georgia," the group New York critic Glenn O'Brien called "the greatest white dance band in the world," had learned the lesson of drag well. Acting could be the same as telling the truth.[52]

Dance This Mess Around

In late March 1978, a little over a year after their 1977 Valentine's Day house-party debut, the B-52's had played three parties and two gigs in Athens, three nights at Max's Kansas City and two at CBGB's in New York, and two Atlanta gigs. Buzz about the band had Atlanta fans of the music that critics had started calling New Wave talking. "They were heroes to us," Georgia State student Kelly Mills remembered. "We were all into the idea of the stripped-down sound and that anyone could be an artist." When Mills and his friends heard the band was playing Atlanta again at a club in Virginia Highlands called the Downtown Café, they took equipment from the Georgia State closed-circuit television station where they worked to the show. Using two video cameras on tripods, they plugged into the soundboard and shot the Athens band on black-and-white half-inch tape. Surviving footage shows the B-52's performing "Rock Lobster" and "52 Girls" as well as other songs that would appear on the band's first two albums, "Dance This Mess Around," "Hero Worship," "Devil's in My Car," "Downtown," and "Runnin' Around." With clear audio and visuals that flicker out of but mostly into focus, this video may not be a time machine, but it is the next best thing, an artifact that captures something of the sound, look, and feel of a live performance as the band, on the cusp of becoming famous, began to attract an audience and record label attention in Georgia and New York. In fact, Seymour Stein, the head of Sire Records, the label that had signed both Talking Heads and the Ramones, attended this show.[53]

Live, the B-52's in 1978 revealed their origins as "expatriates in their own briar patch," a homegrown "rock cabaret" with southern accents and origins stories to hide their New York genderfuck roots, as much theater as music. They were out of place—from the small-town South and yet making "new" music—and out of time—performing in the present sounds and moves borrowed self-consciously from the past. They were also out of time in a musical sense, occasionally off the beat and out of tune. This musical amateurism, too often cleaned up in the recording process, was essential to their live appeal. Polished, the band's sound came across as retro, as a mere copy, rather than as an avant-garde art commenting on the relationship of pop cultures past to the pop culture present. Live, they revealed the layers of disjuncture and disconnection at work in their lyrics, sound, dance moves, and dress, a multi-layered dissonance at once visual, aural, and symbolic. Schneider, Cindy Wilson, and Pierson in particular, demonstrated the drag-show origins of their costumes and moves. Lit up on stage, framed by the dancing of the crowd, the B-52's produced an art which highlighted the gaps: between expectation and execution, the meaning of the words and the flow of the moves and the feeling of the sound.[54]

The best song on the B-52's video shot by the Georgia State students is "Dance This Mess Around." With Ricky Wilson's sixties surf-rock guitar providing the melody, Cindy Wilson, her southern accent in overdrive, is free to scream more than sing her lines. Her raw, hurt voice—a mashup of Patti Smith, Yoko Ono, and Peggy Lee—expresses feelings that seem real enough as she asks her question, "Why don't you dance with me?" Yet the rest of the line, "I'm not no Limburger," uses absurdity to undercut its revelation of rage, vulnerability, and desire. If the man she is addressing thinks she is a piece of meat, she'll tell him! She is *not* a piece of cheese. Schneider's dissonant and flat repeated rejoinder—"dance this mess around"—cuts against any expectation of a harmonizing backup vocal. The echo—human-made reverb—threads through Pierson's pan-flute-from-another-planet keyboard part. Hints of science-fiction-movie sound effects thrust past visions of the future into a present in which they are not the time to come but already the past.[55]

At the most powerful point in this performance, Cindy Wilson asks another question, part snarl and part sexy come-on: "Hey, didn' that make you feel 'lot better, huh?" Schneider offers an instant answer in the form of another question: "Huh?" And Wilson asks again, and Schneider has to lay his answer "Yeah" right over her sassy line, "What you say? I'm just askin'." Schneider comes right back, his shouted vocal "Come on!" slightly off, not the harmony pop songs make listeners expect. As Ricky Wilson's fuzzy guitar lays in, Wilson yells "Shake!" A measure behind where you would expect it, Schneider answers with "Bake." The shake and bake chant repeats, transforming the iconic meat coating, first introduced in 1965, into a dance and, like the sugar in the coffee of old blues songs, a double entendre for sex.[56]

All this dancing and all this messing suggest to listeners with a keen sense of pop music history not just the 1965 Motown hit "Stop in the Name of Love" but also one of Ray Charles's first hits, "Mess Around," released in 1953, the kind of record that would have been available at a thrift store or even at Ort's Oldies. The B-52's song is not a cover and not even any kind of straightforward homage, yet Schneider's call and response with Cindy Wilson sounds like it should be with Ray. "Dance This Mess Around" creates a collage of pop culture allusions and time periods in which Schneider in the present sings and dances and messes with Ray in the past.[57]

The B-52's had learned from New York drag queens that retro could be radical. But context mattered, too. In Athens in the late seventies, some white women still wore fifties-style shirtwaist dresses and worked their hair or their wigs—purchased at Lee's downtown—into beehive styles. Band members knew and loved both the "originals," women passing through the bus station or working at lunch counters who dressed this way, and the New York drag versions. Cindy Wilson and Pierson's costumes were their vision of Ricky Wilson and Strickland's take on New York drag queens' version of these women. But they were also a more direct translation of these styles and a commentary on how much had not changed as middle-class fashions moved on. Despite the civil rights movement and feminism and gay liberation, the midcentury past remained all too contemporary in much of America. I am not sure how much he knew about drag queens, but Ronald Reagan, too, understood the power of retro, and he used it to create a new kind of American conservatism.

Birth of a Scene

In May, what would become the Athens scene was still so new it lacked a venue. In order to perform for record company representatives interested in signing the band and to celebrate the launch of their single with their home town friends, the B-52's rented a space called the Georgia Theater, an old downtown movie house that showed second-run films and staged occasional southern rock concerts. The performance was not a particularly important event in the history of the B-52's — the band eventually rejected the contract offer from Virgin. Locally, though, the Georgia Theater show proved that there was more going on in town than just one band. The Georgia Theater might have been shabby, but it had lights, a PA, and an actual stage. The local drag party crowd turned out and mingled with students who worked at WUOG, the art-school students, and their friends.[58]

"The Incredible Phyllis," an art student and coworker of Schneider's named Phyllis Stapler, opened the evening with a performance piece in which she marched and kicked her high school drill team boots high to recordings like "These Boots Are Made for Walking." The Tone Tones, the second new music band to form in town, took the stage next. Former UGA art student Nicky Giannaris had known the members of the B-52's in Athens. After seeing this band made up of what he approvingly called "sissies and girls" blow everyone away at the Atlanta Punk Festival, he had moved back to town to start his own group. David Gamble joined him on drums. Dana Downs could sing a little, and she convinced Giannaris that she could learn to play the bass. When the B-52's asked the new band to open for them at the Georgia Theater, the keyboard player quit. Vic Varney, who played guitar, not keyboards, spent the next two weeks learning a new instrument. Downs recalled her first time on stage performing: "A roar came up from the audience. Well, that was *it*. Throw those college degrees to the wind! I was smitten." Then the B-52's took the stage, and some audience members who had broken into the closed balcony turned a spotlight on Schneider's crotch.[59]

One band playing dancing parties and filling a tiny folk club in downtown Athens with their friends was a fluke, an exception that proved interesting and creative people could turn up anywhere. A band written about positively in *New York Rocker, Interview,* and the *Village Voice* with a single out and major-label interest, a second new band making its debut, a piece of performance art, and a wildly enthusiastic audience suggested these locals could make their own scene.

After their late May and early June string of dates, the B-52's spent the fall commuting to New York City, where they played at CBGB's, the rock disco Hurrah, and the Mudd Club, which opened that year. In Atlanta, they opened for Talking Heads and Elvis Costello at the Agora Ballroom. In November, they played the University of Georgia's Memorial Hall, near the plaza where Strickland met Schneider. The next spring, the B-52's set out on

**The B-52's perform at Memorial Hall on the campus
of the University of Georgia in November 1978.
(Photograph by Terry Allen, courtesy of Keith Bennett)**

their first tour and performed in Philadelphia, Buffalo, Toronto, Minneapolis, and Chicago before ending up back in New York.[60]

While the B-52's were away, the Tone Tones played Athens. The parties got bigger. In February, a group of current and former art students formed another new band, Pylon, and in March, they debuted at a party in a second-floor downtown space. *New York Rocker*'s editor Andy Schwartz caught up with some of the members of the B-52's in Athens in April, and Cindy Wilson told him, "It's nice to be able to go back here after all this." Still, what Wilson meant when she said that at home "we're no big deal" was that they were not stopped on the streets or recognized at the grocery store. To people in the art-school party world, they were stars. Even a few people in the fraternity and sorority crowd had noticed. Schneider had stopped working at the El Dorado, where he had some sometimes waited tables wearing a speedo, but the Greeks who went looking for him ate the whole-wheat biscuits and grits and gawked instead at the odd attire of the current servers. Some even bought the B-52's single or went to a show.[61]

By late April, after turning down Virgin and Radar in addition to Sire, the B-52's signed an offer with Warner Brothers. In the process, they fired their friend Maureen McLaughlin, who had been serving as their manager, and hired Talking Heads' Gary Kurfirst. Their first album, recorded in the Bahamas, came out early that summer. In late June, interviews and reviews began to come out in *Melody Maker, New York Rocker*, the *Village Voice*, and elsewhere. *New Musical Express* put bluntly what other critics said less directly: "This is the best debut album of the year. No conditions, no exceptions."[62]

Before some white musicians and critics in the 1960s tried to turn the genre into art, rock had been exuberant and joyful. Following the model of the Ramones, the B-52's also dressed up like fifties characters and reminded fans that rock could be art and yet also fun. Drag, as both a practice and an aesthetic, taught the members of the band how to turn playing with conventions into a performance. Drag sent them to thrift stores and other secondhand shops and the UGA library for both ideas and materials. And drag connected them to pop art. The critic Stephen Holden, writing in the *Village Voice*, coined the phrase "pop art rock" to describe the B-52's method and their magic: "Urbane, funny, and sharp, they use *American Graffiti*–era trash with the precision and purpose of 'serious' artists," nudging rock back toward its original "wise-ass attitude toward official culture."[63]

The B-52's made music fans could dance to, but they also made music that asked big questions. Glam rock and disco, in different ways, were already suggesting that gender and sexuality were fluid. The B-52's were different because members were "amateurs," men and women from a small town in the South, and because they made this fluidity seem like something anyone could try. In an era when many Americans could barely conceive of, much less accept, "gay," "bisexual," "queer," and "transgender" as identities, this band acknowledged the possibility that people's clothes, sexual organs, and sense of themselves might not match. All that partying was on a deep level not just fun. It was political.[64]

In the *Village Voice*, Van Gosse described the B-52's as "the first modernist objectification of rock 'n' roll and its associated pop culture." By objectification, he meant parody, the "distanced recreation of original forms." This type of copying, he insisted, was not new. It happened anytime anyone tried to sing like Elvis. What was new about the B-52's was the way they referenced not just specific musicians or even musical genres but broad trends, fads, popular plots, and stock characters, the very structure and grammar of mass-produced popular culture. For Gosse, the B-52's had become the first postmodern rock band. The irony was that the members of a band so critical of the concept of authenticity started a local scene that helped rehabilitate the very possibility of authentic culture. More than any other single place, Athens provided the model for the small, deeply local bohemias that together formed eighties indie culture.[65]

When the members of the B-52's moved together to a big Victorian house outside Mahopac, a small town north of New York City, in the late spring of 1979, nobody could blame them. Three of them had grown up in Athens, and Schneider, who had been there since 1969, had a boyfriend in New York. The southern college town did not have a single new music club. When a record company wanted to see the B-52's perform there with a professional sound system, band members had to rent a venue and produce as well as play the show. New York, where they were the darlings of the downtown scene, was nineteen long hours away. It had all happened so fast. A year after they played their first gig that was not an Athens party—at Max's in New York—their fans jammed the 1,000-seat Irving Plaza. They met Debbie Harry of Blondie, became friends with the members of Talking Heads, and stayed at Brian Eno's apartment. They were barely home anyway. How could Athens compare?[66]

Nobody could blame them, but music critic Tom Carson did. In his interview with the band, he asked if they felt "any special loyalty to Athens as their original home base." Strickland replied, "I've lived there all my life. I feel ready to go somewhere else." Pierson insisted, "People were interested that we were from Georgia, but I don't think it matters at this point whether we stay there or not." Pressed, Pierson did express some ambivalence: "I'd like to stay just because I like my place—but there isn't anything happening there, and it didn't seem possible to build anything up there." Carson was bothered by this answer, and added in parentheses that "only a few minutes later she was telling me about all the bands that have sprung up in the Athens area in the wake of the B-52's success." Carson clearly loved the band:

> If there is any justice in this world, their album is going to be one of the biggest hits of the year, not just because it is good, but because in the B-52's music there is something that strikes an elemental nerve, a rhythm and a feel for certain kinds of experience that have always been there but which have never been converted into art before and which, as soon as you've heard the band, seem so undeniable and so automatic a part of your life that you can't imagine it not being there.

He ended his long interview with a prediction: "They might change the face of popular music in the Eighties and then again they might turn into the Village People." Pierson, of course, was wrong about Athens. Carson was wrong, too, but only in proposing an either/or framework for the B-52's' future.[67]

As Warner Brothers released the B-52's' eponymous first album in mid-July 1979, Glenn O'Brien, a music critic who was a part of the Factory scene and wrote for Warhol's magazine *Interview*, also dared to describe the future. The B-52's would "change everything, starting with a lot of late July and early August parties, many of them outdoors under the stars. There, vital young people will thrill to the exotic, unexpected, hypnotic rock rapture of dancing with the B-52's. Many will fall in love. Many more will just fuck later. But seriously, this one is required. It will change everything—including moods, and dancing on a large scale." Here, O'Brien hinted at not just the musical but the social impact of the music, how the band from Athens made it cool for punks and bohemians everywhere to dance but also how they made it okay for everyone who felt like a freak to step into the light.[68]

Maybe you wanted to kiss the kid you shared a bunk with at summer camp or have sex with another member of your high school basketball team. Maybe you wanted to ditch your jeans and t-shirts and wear dresses. Maybe you did not know what gay or bisexual or trans or even freak really meant, but you knew somehow that you did not fit into your community's religion or its culture or its vision of what you should do with your future. Whether you understood the B-52's' queerness explicitly or not—and after the album came out the band drew increasing numbers of high-school-aged fans—the music and style conveyed the message that it was simply fabulous to be.

"We were always an art band," Wilson told me. Yet over time, the band's very success made it harder for listeners to hear their originality, their punk comment on the way popular culture could rework the relationship of the past and the present. As they became more polished, listeners could understand their music as retro, as a copy of rather than a comment on popular culture past. At times, their music lost its exquisite balance, the way their early performances danced on the head of the pin at the intersection between silly and serious, celebration and critique, nostalgia and a suggestion of what was wrong with the past.

Yet what did that matter in those years when LGBTQA+ people experienced so much discrimination and felt so much shame? In 2016 and 2017, Cindy Wilson toured smaller venues in support of her solo recordings and made a point to talk to audience members after her performances. At every stop, older fans lined up to talk to her. And time and time again, they told her the same thing. The B-52's had literally saved them.[69]

2

The Art School

There are these forms I like to watch
There are these shapes which talk to me

I like forms, and forms like me
The more you look, the more you see

Pure

Everything is cool

Pylon, "Cool" (1979)

In Athens, people got into bands the way people everywhere get into most things: through their friends. Vanessa Briscoe Hay—then Vanessa Ellison— was finishing her last year in the University of Georgia's art school when the B-52's started playing around town. Originally from the small Georgia town of Dacula, she had enrolled at UGA in 1973 as an arts education major before switching to drawing and painting without telling her parents. At first, she thought Athens was boring and conservative, but after Jimmy Carter became president, people across the country began to pay more attention to the state. Important artists began to give lectures at the UGA art museum and even donate works. UGA students started to have "more chances to see beyond the sleepy town."[1]

Briscoe Hay missed the B-52's 1977 Valentine's Day party debut, but she heard people talking about it the next day at the art school. Like other studio majors, she knew the members of the B-52's from the party circuit. "Anytime they showed up at a party," she remembered, "they had to take things up a notch. Everything had to be a little wilder and crazier." Because she did not have a car, she also missed the Sex Pistols' Atlanta concert in January 1978 and the B-52's' early shows there. She finally caught the new band when they played their first gig at an actual Athens club, the folk venue the Last Resort.[2]

After graduation, Briscoe Hay stayed in Athens while her husband Jimmy Ellison finished his degree. Through word of mouth at the art school, she got a job at DuPont, a nylon factory nearby. The next Christmas, she landed a second job in the catalog department at J.C. Penney downtown. In February 1979, her good friend Randy Bewley, still working on his degree in painting, stopped by there to talk to her about a performance-art project he and art student Michael Lachowski had created that involved making music. Another art student, Curtis Crowe, had already joined them to play drums. Bewley wanted Briscoe Hay to try out for the role of singer. Though she had played flute in the high school marching band and loved singing in her church choir and high school chorus, she told him she wasn't really a musician and was too shy to sing alone. Bewley insisted they were all amateurs. What mattered was they respected her as an artist.[3]

Lachowski had moved to town a year behind Briscoe Hay. More than a little precocious, as a high school student in suburban Atlanta he had taught himself photography by reading the *Time/Life* photography series and building a darkroom in his parents' house. He had chosen UGA over private art colleges because he wanted to escape the "sheltered environment" of St. Pius, his Catholic high school, and actually learn something about the real South. When he moved into Russell Hall, he set up his quadraphonic stereo and decorated his side of the dorm room with a painted mannequin head. His roommate from Moultrie, Georgia, countered with a huge Confederate flag.[4]

In the UGA photography studio that first year, Lachowski met Bewley, a shy sculpture major from suburban Atlanta. Bewley had a work-study job in the studio to help pay his tuition. As they took classes, worked in the open studios, and looked at the exhibitions in the art-school galleries together, they grew close. Outside class, Lachowski made drawings, prints, Super 8 films, and sculptures, as well as photographs. Bewley made photographs and other two-dimensional work, as well as sculptures, and later switched his major to drawing and painting. As Lachowski remembered, this kind of experimenting with genre just seemed normal in Athens: "We had an exuberant group of people; creativity was prized above all else; everybody was just putting out work. It led to us going out of the boundaries of our disciplines. A lot of us in the art school were trying out different media with a punk rock message, which is just go in there and do it. You don't need training, or authority or legitimacy. Just figure it out."[5]

In the late seventies and eighties, the University of Georgia's art school introduced suburban and small-town Georgia kids like Briscoe Hay, Bewley, and Lachowski to the possibilities of a creative life. They studied a little art history, but mostly they took classes in their mediums. They attended critiques and exhibitions of student and faculty work as well as shows at the Georgia Museum of Art. And they made things. Increasingly, students staged their own shows, like Margaret Katz and Debbie McMahon's September 1977 exhibition of their paintings, drawings, and prints at the local nonprofit Lyndon House Galleries and the May 1978 exhibition at UGA's Memorial Hall Gallery by a collective of painters and printmakers who worked in studios above the downtown art supply store the Loft.[6]

Both in class and at off-campus studios, parties, and performances, students got to know professors including Robert Croker, James Herbert, Judy McWillie, Richard Olsen, and Art Rosenbaum, as well as visiting artist Elaine De Kooning. These professors exposed students to contemporary artists and to ideas being worked out in the larger art world. They also modeled how to work as artists and teachers, how to weave questions of aesthetics, form, experience, and expression into everyday life. Away from urban art scenes with their important museums and galleries, UGA art students experienced a combination of education and isolation. What they did not know could not intimidate them. What they learned inspired them to try to make their own work.[7]

If drag pushed some people in Athens to dress up and perform, art school taught people to make things. In the 1970s, performance art brought these practices together. The turn toward performance had roots in Romanticism and in the Dada movement of early twentieth-century Europe, but it exploded at the end of the 1950s as artists began to stage what Allan Kaprow, then an art professor at Rutgers, called "happenings." Inspired by John Cage and his focus on the act of creating rather than the result, avant-garde composers and artists experimented with combining mediums and producing immersive experiences. They also took the ideas developed by artists at Black Mountain College like Josef Albers and Merce Cunningham—that making and learning about art and everyday life were not separate activities—out of school and into the world. In the 1960s and 1970s, the art movement Fluxus promoted artists interested in erasing the boundaries between life and art, like Yoko Ono whose *Cut Piece* (1964) was celebrated as a major work. These developments paralleled punk's 1970s dismantling of the divisions between performers and audience members. Part avant-garde theater, part pedagogical exercise, and part temporary and living installation, performance art flourished in this period and developed into a recognized practice. Unlike other art forms, it demanded the participation of viewers and produced unrepeatable, ephemeral experiences rather than displayable objects or scripted productions. It also challenged audience members' ideas about art itself.[8]

These trends inspired young artists who loved punk to experiment with music-making. At UGA, some art students learned about the rise of performance art in their classes. In the periodicals room at the UGA library and at Barnett's Newsstand downtown, they read art and underground music news in publications like *Artforum*, the *Village Voice*, and the *New York Times* as well as British music magazines *Melody Maker* and *New Musical Express*. At local record stores like Chapter Three and Wuxtry, they bought records by bands like Devo, inspired in part by an experimental art class at Kent State University; Talking Heads, a group created by former art students; and the Mekons, formed in England as an art collective.[9]

Lachowski and Bewley fell hard for the new music. They read the papers and magazines and also relied on recommendations from John Underwood and Chris Rasmussen who ran Chapter Three Records on Broad Street right across from the UGA campus. When the two friends had money, they bought discs by the Ramones, David Bowie, Talking Heads, and Kraftwerk. But what really got them excited was a fanzine that began appearing in 1976, the *New York Rocker*. It did not look like much, a cheap tabloid sitting in small stacks on the counter or a rack in the record stores. Repeated thumbings smudged the pictures and print and softened the pages. Inside, however, was a whole new world.[10]

Like Briscoe Hay, Bewley and Lachowski went to parties with other current and former UGA art students, art professors, local artists, and their assorted friends, a loose and overlapping network of students and Athens residents who were gay or connected to the arts or both that included members of the B-52's. As Bewley told *New Musical Express* in 1980, "Back in '77, you'd go around to some art shows in Athens and see these guys with purple wigs and really weird clothes. Everyone in the B's wore wigs in those days, the men and the women. It was crazy." Lachowski remembered seeing the B-52's play in the kitchen of a friend's house. "It seemed really clear that they really did not know what they were doing," but the music was "really fresh" and "inspiring." Artists and musicians seemed to be mixing right in their own little town, too.[11]

Just about the time the B-52's started playing New York City regularly, *New York Rocker* increased its coverage of non–New York bands. Suddenly,

The Art School

Bewley and Lachowski could read about people they actually knew in their favorite music magazine. Back in Athens, the B-52's began performing in venues where "real" musicians played, like the Georgia Theater and UGA's Memorial Hall Ballroom. When they put out a single and celebrated their success with a record-release party at the El Dorado late in the year, Kate Pierson and Cindy Wilson autographed copies with lipstick by kissing the sleeves.[12]

Bewley wanted to form a band, too. With the B-52's on the road to New York all the time, the Tone Tones were the only local new-music group. Lachowski resisted. The problem was not that they were not musicians. The fact that they had no experience playing instruments was no different from the fact that they had no experience making prints or installation art before they went to art school. They could learn. Instead, Lachowski hesitated because making music seemed unoriginal: "I thought it had been done already and that it was way behind the curve. . . . It seemed like such an obvious thing." But then the friends had an idea. Briscoe Hay told the story that became an essential part of the Athens myth, "They'd been reading New York Rocker and it seemed like it would be an easy thing to have a band and go to New York and get some press and come back. And that would be it." Then they would quit. Instead of a band, they would create a kind of performance art.[13]

Though the artists who created Pylon tried to be different, the group benefited from the B-52's' success. Glenn O'Brien, the first critic to write about Pylon, was friends with the members of that first Athens group. After the B-52's released two major-label albums and outgrew the New York underground, Pylon was there to step into their slot. Village Voice critic Van Gosse wrote, "My pal Danny voices the common hipster sentiment when he says, 'Pylon, they're like the B-52s, but they mean it.'" It was as if the members of Pylon had set out to fulfill what the beloved underground rock critic Lester Bangs had written almost a decade before: "the magic promise eternally made and occasionally fulfilled by rock that a band can start out bone-primitive, untutored and uncertain, and evolve into a powerful and eloquent ensemble." But unlike the B-52's, Pylon stayed in Athens rather than moving to New York.[14]

It may have started as performance art, but the band Lachowski and Bewley created with Briscoe Hay and Crowe did more than any other local group to transform a network of gay and queer artists and their friends into a real bohemia. As Curtis Crowe told the Red and Black in 1981, the B-52's "came along and punched a great big hole and made it a whole lot easier" for people to think they could make their own music. Pylon confirmed this

Through their commitment to remaining in Athens and their understanding of musical performance as a kind of performance art, Pylon did more than any other early band to transform a group of friends centered on the University of Georgia art school into a scene. Here, Vanessa Briscoe Hay stands above Michael Lachowski, Curtis Crowe, and Randy Bewley. (Photograph © Laura Levine)

faith in hometown creativity and also did something more. Collectively, the band members launched a story about musical amateurism, the importance of pleasure, and the elevation of art — formal originality as well as self-expression — over commerce. These ideas shaped how the people creating the scene understood themselves as different from other Americans.[15]

When in 1987 *Rolling Stone* named R.E.M. "America's best rock and roll band," drummer Bill Berry denied it. The best band in America, he said, was Pylon. Without this group, Athens might have remained an interesting detail in the B-52's' biography rather than becoming the most important model for the new alternative culture rooted in unlikely places that offered a refuge from an increasingly conservative America.[16]

In its first life — the band broke up and reformed twice over its thirty-year history — Pylon expanded the B-52's' fusion of pop art ideas and performance art practices. Without the explicit use of drag, Pylon made music that commented on popular culture, on rock conventions, images, and stories, and on the relation of art and life. Members bravely flaunted a lack of professional technique that the B-52's worked to hide, and used it to create a sound that was fun to dance to without being in any way easy. Their songs were angular, dissonant, and difficult, full of minor-key progressions and staccato rhythms. Jangle alternated with funk. The bass throbbed and the drums boomed as guitar licks cut across the rhythm section without being leads. The vocals varied from deadpan recitations of short phrases to howls, and Briscoe Hay rarely flirted with the audience. Instead, she sometimes blew a shrill whistle mid-song, like a referee or a cop.

Pylon's act could be shocking or jolting or heavy. It could also be deep. In fusing pop and rock forms with an avant-garde sensibility, the band members asked what art could mean in the midst of industrial decline, production-line mass culture, and rising political conservatism. And they tentatively offered an answer. "Be careful, be cautious, be prepared," the lyrics of their song "Danger" warned. But be creative, too. "Everything is cool." "Turn up the volume." "Turn off the TV." "Now, rock and roll, now." "Read a book, don't be afraid." "Function precedes form. Things happen." Pylon pushed people to think as well as dance, to put their minds and bodies back together. Playing live, the four art students could pound their awkwardness and their amateurism and their artistic vision into something transcendent. If people in Athens revived on a local scale that old dream that music could make a new world, it was because they were living it.[17]

By the time I became a part of the scene in the mid-eighties, Pylon had already broken up and become a legend. You might snag a rare single at Wuxtry or hear their songs on WUOG's local music program *Sound of the City*. You might even have a friend with a better record collection than yours who would make you a tape. But locals who had seen them play agreed that none of Pylon's recordings captured the magic of the band's live performances. If you asked them to explain, they would go all glassy-eyed and sigh and then fall silent before mumbling that you just had to be there. Before Pylon re-formed in 1988, the best you could do was make your band flyers at Kinko's and bask in Vanessa Briscoe Hay's aura as she fixed your jammed machine or rang up your bill.

Performance Art Rock

It was not a promising beginning. A few gigs in, Lachowski wrote his former professor Robert Croker: "In Athens they receive us politely—they have to like us since 'we're all in this (town) together.' We're all in this (music sub-culture scene) together." People talked, however, and he added a list of comments he had heard after their first few gigs: "too art oriented," "conceptual," "they sound like a bunch of artists who got together and decided to have a band," "Michael, your music sounds just like your art," and "they'll like what you're doing in New York (as if to imply that they don't really in Athens)."

Once Bewley and Lachowski decided in the fall of 1978 to create a piece of musical performance art, they actually had to learn to play instruments. Bewley started out on drums, but Lachowski couldn't decide what to play. Bewley, trying to help, asked him, "What do you listen to when you hear music—the melody, the guitar line?" Lachowski replied that he was not sure, that he "always heard it as a mix, a texture." Listening again to his favorite albums, he realized the bass "was the thing that kind of grabbed my attention." As an added bonus, it had two fewer strings to master than a guitar. Bewley bought Lachowski a bass at a pawn shop, and Lachowski plugged it into his stereo. Then Bewley found a guitar and amp for cheap at a flea market.[18]

With Bewley alternating between guitar and drums and Lachowski on bass, the two friends began getting together and just making sounds at Lachowski's off-campus studio. Two UGA students, Curtis Crowe and his friend Bill Tabor, had rented the two floors above Schlotzsky's sandwich shop in a commercial building on College Avenue right across from the university. They rigged some plumbing and wiring, hauled out decades of trash, dust, and dead pigeons, and moved in on the third floor, with its fourteen-foot ceilings and three arched windows overlooking the street. To cover the rent, they sublet the roughed-out small spaces on the second floor as studios to art students Sean Bourne, Neil McArthur, Sam Seawright, and Lachowski, and to Chapter Three's Chris Rasmussen who kept his record collection there. It was an easy walk from the UGA art building down Jackson and across on Broad to College. Soon, Lachowski's studio doubled as a practice space. Bourne remembers waiting for them to finish playing many nights so he could watch *The Rockford Files* on the TV Lachowski used to create feedback with his bass.[19]

When Crowe and Tabor moved to Athens in 1976 to go to school, they first rented a house in the country where they hosted legendary parties, like an early B-52's gig. Their new third-floor loft downtown, they believed, was a perfect place to continue the tradition, and the two friends spent much of the fall just trying to get the place clean. Sometime during the process, dirty and tired, they looked up and noticed that a single bulb dangling overhead lit the space, and Tabor said it looked like a "goddamn forty-watt club." The name stuck. Since it was almost Halloween, they decided to have a party. Crowe and Tabor ripped pictures out of *Interview* and *Cosmopolitan* and copied them with an added talk bubble, "I know where I'm going to be on Halloween, the 40-Watt Club." Then they hung the flyers, which included no address or directions, all over town. They bought a keg and some liquor and asked some women they knew to work the bar. Other friends decorated the space with balloons containing joints of bad pot and took donations at the door. On Halloween night, the room was packed. Bewley arrived wearing an inflatable space suit that he kept filled with a hair dryer attached to a long extension cord. He had also rigged a tube running from his mouth down his arm to his finger. All night, he floated around the loft, stealing his buzz by sticking his finger in other peoples' drinks. Crowe met Bewley that night, when the future guitar player won the party's costume contest.[20]

Sometime that winter, Bewley and Lachowski began practicing regularly. Briscoe Hay remembered, "They didn't know anything about playing these instruments . . . and they learned how to play just doing the same thing over and over and over again." Lachowski worked from a bass instruction book. Bewley played his guitar with an alternate tuning because he did not know the standard one. Plugged into little Pignose amps, they practiced by alternating positions, with one holding the groove and repeating a phrase while the other experimented. In time, these long jams gave birth to a remarkable independence between the bass and the guitar parts. Then, the "endless riffs," what Crowe later called "a never-ending series of hooks — no bridges or chorus, just hooks," echoed and vibrated right up through the floor of Curtis and Tabor's loft. There, the two landlords huddled around a single space heater in their huge room during that miserable winter, skipping their classes and listening to a taped version of *King Lear* because Tabor was too lazy to read the book for his literature class. "They'd *do it* and *do it* and *do it*," Crowe told a critic in 1981. "I had every song memorized before I ever went down." [21]

Lachowski and Bewley did not know Crowe very well. Like them, he was from the Atlanta area, and they saw him at the art school and parties and paid him rent, but they were not really friends. One day Crowe reached his breaking point: "So I kinda went ahead and knocked on the door lookin' real timid and said, 'Hey, mind if I drag these drums in here for a little bit?'" Crowe, as it turned out, knew what he was doing. He already played in a band with friends from his hometown, Marietta, a small city rapidly becoming an Atlanta suburb. [22]

Two years earlier, Crowe had bought an old bass, snare, and tom combo, then painted a lumpy, lacquered black, while he was home for winter break. Back in Athens, he slammed out beats inspired by the records he started buying by the Sex Pistols and the Ramones. Sometime in 1978, he and his old friends formed a group they called Strictly American, and this band performed at his and Tabor's Halloween party. When Crowe began playing with Bewley and Lachowski, he told them he was only sitting in for fun as his priority was his other band. Later, Lachowski and Bewley decided to get serious and put up flyers looking for a permanent drummer. An offended Crowe finally committed. According to Briscoe Hay, the three men then began writing "actual songs that had a beginning, middle, and end, and Michael was writing lyrics." Whatever their intentions, the trio began to sound like a band. [23]

Despite their lack of musical experience, Bewley and Lachowski started out confident. While BFA students, they had already successfully crossed mediums. Nancy Lukasiewicz, the director of the Lyndon House, remembered that in May 1977 Lachowski used black tubing and a hose to turn an outdoor light on the house gallery's lawn into a giant water sprinkler-like sculpture. The juror for the Georgia Sculpture Exhibition, brought in from up north—no one seems to remember his name—awarded Lachowski's sculpture first prize over the more traditional works made of wood, marble, and clay. That same month, in an annual photography show and competition run by UGA's Visual Arts Division and hung on campus in the Memorial Hall Gallery, Bewley, then a painting major, entered a series of mounted Polaroids that Lachowski helped him with and won an honorable mention. Their successes made them trust their ideas over technique and training. Lachowski, in particular, impressed other art students with his talent. Sam Seawright remembered that Lachowski "always had a posse"; he attracted a crowd. In Briscoe Hay's words, "everybody looked up to him like he was on the level of, like, a real artist," rather than a student. "Michael was just really cool. . . . Everything he did was cool. The way he dressed, the music he listened to, his art."[24]

When Bewley and Lachowski decided to find a singer, it made sense to them to ask art students whose work they liked. One day they gave Sam Seawright a cassette and a piece of paper with typed lyrics "for this art project we are working on; it's a band." When he said no, claiming he was "too shy and awkward," they said, "That's why we want you." Next, they asked another art student, Neil McArthur, but they did not like the way he sounded singing Lachowski's lyrics or the fact that he bought an electric guitar from art professor Jim Herbert and wanted to write songs. Frustrated, they hit upon the idea of using found lyrics, such as passages from the record Bourne played in his studio next to Lachowski's, *How to Teach Your Parrot to Talk*, and broadcasts from Lachowski's weather radio. Maybe they could record this material and play behind it like the B-52's had used a tape player in their early gigs to provide a bass line and other parts. The B-52's, in fact, had played Bourne's parrot instruction record before the start of their May 1978 show at the Georgia Theater. After a while, though, the found-lyrics approach felt constraining, and Bewley suggested they ask Briscoe Hay.[25]

Briscoe Hay knew Bewley and Lachowski from art school and Lachowski from working at DuPont. For Athens art students trying to pay their way through school or support themselves after they graduated, the Factory meant not Warhol's studio but the nylon plant in Athens where they worked weekends. College students and graduates could earn good wages pulling long shifts when working people with families wanted off. Briscoe Hay was surprised when Bewley showed up at her other job at Penney's and asked her to try out for their band. Like many in her art-school crowd, she loved the new music coming out of New York—the Ramones, Blondie, and Talking Heads—as well as bands from elsewhere like Pere Ubu, Devo, Elvis Costello, and the Wire. By the time she graduated in the spring of 1978, she was also a huge B-52's fan. As she recalled, all the art students loved them.[26]

Post-graduation, Briscoe Hay found Athens a little boring, and when Bewley asked her to try out, she thought being in a band might be fun. After her shift at DuPont, she picked up cookies at A & A Bakery—it was Valentine's Day—and headed to Lachowski's studio. The audition turned out to be oddly formal. On a music stand, her future bandmates had placed an orange vinyl notebook full of typed lyrics. They would play a song, and she would try to make the lyrics fit, sometimes cracking up in the attempt. When she finished they said, "Great. Thank you for coming by." She left wondering what it was all about. The next day, they called her and announced, "We've decided you're going to be our vocalist." She remembered, "They couldn't really hear what I was doing," but "they liked the fact that I put forth some honest effort and they liked the way I looked, and they liked me as a human being." Learning the lyrics over the next few weeks, she recalled, was "like doing homework."[27]

When the band debuted on March 9, 1979, in the second-floor space downtown above Chapter Three Records, it was hard to imagine its members would soon be local stars. At this performance and at their second, at Crowe and Tabor's loft, Pylon opened for the Tone Tones. As Lachowski wrote a former professor, they played "all original songs, except for 'Batman,' which includes Sean Bourne the Artist." Briscoe Hay stood on a mirror with her back to the big windows that looked out on old campus and concentrated on the words. While she and her friends performed, Watt King, an MFA student who described himself as "a poor man's Dan Flavin," produced a light show.[28]

In Athens, everyone danced at parties, and yet the audience at Pylon's early shows stood strangely still. As Crowe told a critic in 1981, "Nobody knew what to do, so they were real polite." A surviving photograph of the second show at Crowe and Tabor's place suggested the scene. Briscoe Hay stood stiffly in a sleeveless vintage dress as she sang, a tambourine and what looked like a notebook propped on a stepladder to her right. Bewley's hands and guitar were blurred, but his face was serious and focused. Lachowski also concentrated, staring down at his hands as he played his bass. Only Crowe, set up in the open window of his own loft and wearing a baseball hat, smiled. The image captured the bohemian setting: old curtains flanking the open window, plaster walls artfully mottled and flaking, and a thin, framed column of collaged Warhol-like headshots hanging over an amp. What the photograph did not suggest was fun.[29]

At their third gig in an old brick house out in Oglethorpe County, everything changed. "Up until that point, people just kind of stood there and stared at us. They didn't know what to make of us," Briscoe Hay recalled. Then "the B-52s showed up at that party, and they started dancing and running around like crazy and everybody else did too." As Schneider wrote later in the liner notes for the 2007 reissue of Pylon's 1980 album *Gyrate*, "I saw Pylon's third public gig. . . . In someone's backyard, I partied with the rest of the crowd on the grass right in front of the band." They were "totally original" and "totally danceable," "minimal, yet powerful, and driving." After the show, as Briscoe Hay remembered, Schneider and Pierson "were very supportive." They said, "You've got to play New York." Briscoe Hay told Schneider, "We saw you guys and figured if you could do it, so could we."[30]

The quartet rounded out their busy spring by playing their first club date at Tyrone's O.C., an Athens bar located in an old railroad depot on the corner of Oconee and Foundry Streets that had just started to book the new bands. But to get what they really wanted, a New York date, Pylon needed to make a demo. Someone bought some Kmart cassette tapes, and the four art students recorded themselves playing a few songs at Lachowski's studio. Schneider, Briscoe Hay recalled, took them to New York and gave one to Jim Fouratt at Hurrah, the new punk dance club where the B-52's had been playing lately. The timing was perfect. "Rock Lobster" was a huge New York hit, and the B-52's reached the peak of their underground fame in the weeks before the release of their first album that July. Fouratt actually called the members of Pylon, in Athens, read through a list of coming bands, and asked them who they wanted to open for. Bewley and Lachowski picked Gang of Four.[31]

For a group of art students who were just learning to play, it was hard to believe: after playing just three Athens parties and one local club, the members of Pylon were taking their art project to New York.[32]

Art in the Dark

It was not hard to find the University of Georgia's art school then. In the late 1970s, even Karen Stinnett's dog, Zak, could do it, running all the way from her apartment on Baxter to the white modernist building on Jackson Street with wings on one end of the roof that instead of suggesting flight somehow pushed the whole structure back down to earth. Even though Stinnett never walked the young German shepherd there, he seemed to learn the directions by watching the route from her car.[33]

After Stinnett went to one of art professor Robert Croker's "epic" mixers in October 1977 to try to meet people and took Zak along, the dog seemed to know everybody. At parties, he sat on the furniture with his legs dangling and begged for potato chips. He ran happily into the middle of wildly dancing crowds. Sometimes, he hid from Stinnett when she tried to take him home. Left alone in her apartment, the canine Houdini often escaped and made his way to the UGA campus. He wasn't snobby—Stinnett's friends reported they saw the dog playing Frisbee with frat boys—but he seemed to like the art school the best. Showing up alone at the Jackson Street building, he would convince someone to open the door for him. Some days he "took inventory" of the work in the sculpture and painting studios, as art professor Richard Olsen put it, getting color on his fur in the process. Other days he drew laughing crowds into the hallway with antics like stalking wind-up toys art student Sean Bourne let loose on the floor.[34]

Before Croker left Athens and moved to New York, the students in his circle organized an exhibition of works called the Zak MFA show as a way of honoring their professor's teaching. Croker reserved a gallery in the visual art building and opened the door at a prearranged time. BFA and MFA students did the rest, filling the space with their unattributed work. Some students took the opportunity to show outside the boundaries of their primary mediums. Lachowski created an installation by hanging a hot pink float over a kiddie pool filled with Styrofoam balls. Printmaking MFA student Michael Paxton hung photographs he had made with a strobe light in his back yard as he ran around naked with his wife. Because someone had to represent the anonymous works, to go on record as "the artist," the students chose the German shepherd. At a time when the art school functioned as a kind of creative clubhouse, Zak became an art-student alternative to Georgia's bulldog mascot.[35]

The Zak MFA show proved controversial on campus. The art-school establishment may not have "gotten" the work, but they picked up on the not-so-subtle gesture of defiance. The nude photographs offended the secretaries. More than one person remembered some professors ripping some pieces off the walls and breaking some sculptures. And the problem went beyond individual works of art. Student artists had taken over the space, produced a show of what they felt was important, and forced their professors to look. They seemed to think the art school belonged to them.[36]

It is difficult to imagine from the wired and connected present just how hard it was in the late seventies and early eighties for young people in southern suburbs and small towns to find places in which people engaged in intellectual and aesthetic experimentation. Sean Bourne spent his high school years in suburban Atlanta wanting to be a hippie, and he looked like a flower child in his embroidered jeans and long hair when he left for college in the fall of 1973. Surely, he would find his people at Georgia's largest public university. In Athens, many students he met smoked pot and wanted to have as much sex as possible—who wouldn't?—but they were politically conservative. In his memory, there were only "ten real hippies" at Georgia. But the art school, he remembered, "blew [his] mind."[37]

Four years later, Mark Cline also moved to Athens to go to art school. St. Pius, his Catholic high school in Atlanta, measured its male students' hair until his last year there. By then, Cline had discovered the Ramones and "buzzed off" his own long locks. For him, hippie was over. Yet he, too, found UGA students conservative, "all Greeks and rednecks, business majors and agricultural students." The art majors and a few other liberal arts majors, he remembered, formed a small group of "freaks against the world" in a place that was "very backwards," very "small-town."[38]

Sam Seawright, who arrived at the University of Georgia the same year as his future best friend Cline, recalled, "If you were the odd kid, or the nerdy or the arty kid in your little small town in Georgia, you kind of aspired to go to Athens." Jennifer Hartley, who started as an art student during winter quarter 1980, remembered a huge divide between the regular college students on one side and all the alternative types. The unconventional kids might disagree sometimes — in her first painting class, a hippie who wanted to listen to the Grateful Dead while they worked argued with a punk who wanted to listen to Talking Heads. But they also recognized each other as allies. It was not unusual to see Walter Dunderville, an openly gay and eccentric painter who wore his hair in little ponytails, sitting on a bench rolling Drum cigarettes with Sunny Baumgartner, a red-haired earth mother. In the Greek-dominated undergrad culture of UGA, the hippies and the new music fans were really just two ends of a relatively small group. Many of these kids would increasingly think of themselves as bohemians.[39]

The art school was not just open in terms of being relatively accepting of difference. It was also physically open, the classrooms, studios, hallways, balconies, and backyard of its Jackson Street building easy to access and use. The classrooms had tall ceilings and big sliding glass doors that opened onto the street and made it possible, in nice weather, for people to come and go. While the place was technically locked at night, anyone who tried seemed to be able to get a key. As MFA printmaking student Andrew Krieger recalled, "the great thing about the studios and about being a studio artist at the University of Georgia . . . was that the art building was open 24–7. It was back when nobody was worried over security, theft, property, and your well-being for the most part, and people were coming and going all the time, working at all hours of the night if they wanted to." People smoked cigarettes openly everywhere. No one had their own space except the professors, and the open design of the building meant everyone could see who was working. Grad students painted and printed and built sculptures and installations right alongside undergraduates in the big open studios, some of which had glass walls. People were "willing to share their skills and advise you, even if it was two o'clock in the morning." Some professors would stop by at night, too. The fact that professors outside of class and other students were interested in each other's art-making and eager to help was inspiring. Krieger remembers "great camaraderie" and "peer encouragement": "People bonded in little groups, and there were a lot of interactions. From those interactions, a lot of skills and a lot of techniques and a lot of visual discussions got passed around so you felt like everybody was growing too in the process." There was an "electricity," "a vibe in the air that people felt."[40]

This feeling that anything was possible, that they needed to act on their creative ideas, took concrete form in local happenings. When faculty members told Krieger that UGA could not afford a letter press, the printmaking grad student toured small towns around Athens visiting newspaper offices and persuaded one to donate its old Chandler and Price press and type to UGA for a tax deduction. Once the press was up and running in the art building, Krieger and another grad student came up with the idea for the Edible Art show. On the day of the exhibition, faculty members, students, and even the local A & A Bakery brought their $1 entry fees and their pieces to the UGA Visual Arts Gallery. The money collected funded the prizes. Lachowski painted fruit safety orange, black, and pink, cut and peeled it open, and wrapped it in black licorice "string." He won first prize. Art professor Jim Herbert, not to be left out after people started setting up, ran and got a raisin and displayed it on the end of a spyglass-like tube. The bakery sent a Barbie doll wearing an antebellum dress made out of frosting and cake. Krieger cut the crust off white bread, ran it through the letter press, and spread the result, which looked like toilet paper, with Nutella. Croker entered a "desiccated cabbage," bought to make slaw for the first of his parties and forgotten so long in his fridge that the judges debated whether it qualified as edible. After the reception, people were encouraged to participate in the event by eating the art. Only Zak had broad enough taste to try most of the work.[41]

It's not clear anyone got the irony of tax dollars supporting nonconformity, but UGA's art school worked as an incubator of creativity, a local, state-funded, and slightly more structured version of Warhol's Factory. It brought the rebels, thinkers, and "the others" together, provided some ideas and materials, and inspired everyone to experiment. It also gave these young people a place to hang out and display the results of their efforts. With the notable exception of the B-52's, almost all of the early Athens bands included cur-

EDIBLE ART EXHIBITION

Tuesday March 6th----Visual Arts Gallery U.G.A.

Entries from faculty, students and other Athens cooks are welcomed with a $1.00 entry fee per work. --------------------

Exhibition will be set-up March 6th, at 6p.m. -sharp-. Opening from 7p.m. to 9p.m. that evening - Consumption of the ART after show --- Cash awards based on visual and culinary aspects - Have entries in on time.!!!!!!!!!!!!!!--!!

For additional information call Thommes-Krieger at 542-2144

Art students organized their own shows in the galleries of the Jackson Street art building. Andrew Krieger designed and printed this poster, "Essen Die Kunst," for the Edible Art Exhibition that he also helped organize. (Courtesy of Andrew Krieger)

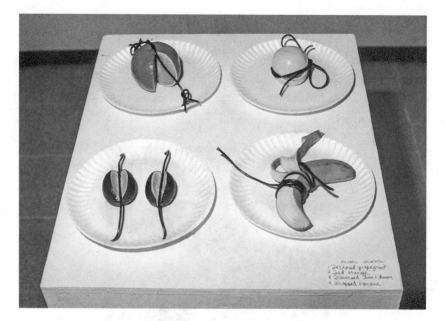

Michael Lachowski entered four pieces, including one called "Whipped Banana," in the Edible Art show and won first prize. (Photograph by Michael Lachowski)

rent or former art students, and even the B-52's had important art-school connections. Art majors Robert Waldrop, who formed an inseparable foursome with Keith Strickland, Ricky Wilson, and Jerry Ayers, and Keith Bennett, Cindy Wilson's boyfriend, tied the art-school crowd to the band and shaped its visual image. When, inspired by the B-52's, art students began to create their own bands, they drew on what they had learned about playing with forms and questioning conventions in the art school. As Mark Cline, a founder of the Athens band Love Tractor, remembered, "people took what they were learning in visual aesthetics and applied it to aural aesthetics."[42]

For an institution in the Deep South far from any art-world centers, the University of Georgia's art school had a surprisingly experimental curriculum in the postwar years, driven by the ambition and fundraising of the long-term head of the program, the painter Lamar Dodd. Beginning in the early 1950s, Dodd used grant money to create an advisory committee charged with reimagining art education and creating a new design department. The committee, led by the well-known designer George Nelson and also including Charles Eames, produced an experimental, multimedia sample art lesson that combined slide and film projectors, multiple screens, tape recorders, recorded music, and odor-producing chemicals dumped in the air conditioning vents. The idea was to produce an immersive visual and aural experience — a pioneering example of what would later be called virtual reality — that would simultaneously teach students the art and design of the past and new ways of thinking about and seeing the present. Widely exhibited in the fifties, Art X reimagined arts education as a kind of performance art.[43]

Around the same time, UGA art professors were also experimenting with the ideas and teaching techniques of Ohio State art professor Hoyt Sherman to create a new kind of introductory art class. During World War II, Sherman had adapted scientific theories about visual perception, gestalt psychology, and the painter Rembrandt's account of learning to see by looking through the strobe-like effects of a windmill into a program to teach naval aviators to identify enemy aircraft. While still working for the U.S. military, he adapted his training methods to create a course for teaching undergraduates with no art experience how to draw. The "Flash Lab" used a special projector to flash shapes and forms for a fraction of a second while a tape recorder played music. Sitting in the dark, students watched and listened and drew what they had seen. In 1947, Sherman published *Drawing by Seeing* to circulate his teaching methods.[44]

By the late 1950s, art professors at Georgia had combined features of the Flash Lab and Art X into a radical new introductory sequence called Art in the Dark. Pedagogically, the program broke down the boundaries between art mediums by focusing on abstract forms. Henry Fran described a class he took as an undergraduate then: "An image was projected on a screen. But, first, we were instructed to 'feel' the surface of our paper with the palms of our hands while looking at the image on the screen. Then, the image was turned off. The instructor asked us to try to capture our impression of that image (in the darkness) with our charcoal or other drawing materials. Sometimes, we were required to do this in clay." Chatham Murray took Art in the Dark over a decade later, and she remembered "producing piles of 'drawings' on newsprint paper using big chunks of charcoal and producing shapes and marks in varying values of black." Over the first year, the courses moved from black-and-white to color images and from two- to three-dimensional forms, but students did not actually make any art.[45]

When Dodd convinced the university to construct a new visual-arts building, professors had the opportunity to design classrooms especially for this program. After the Jackson Street art building opened in 1962, students took their introductory classes in square, windowless rooms that looked like a cross between an avant-garde theater and a lab. Red "safe" lights like those used in a darkroom forced students to focus on shape rather than color.

Spotlights illuminated installations, and speakers flooded the room with sound. Multiple retractable screens filled the walls and ceilings, and a high equipment booth, like a movie theater projection room, held slide and film projectors and tape recorders. A catwalk ran around the ceiling, enabling professors to access the equipment and watch students working below. In some courses in the early days, professors referred to students by numbers instead of names. Self-consciously modern in its use of technology and its patina of science, Art in the Dark worked to tear down students' preconceived ideas about art. It trained them to use their eyes and ears, stripped of the past and grounded instead in their direct experience of the present, the image flashed on the screen and the sound coming out of the speaker. It tried to teach them a new way to see.[46]

Richard Olsen was still teaching Art in the Dark classes in the 1970s. A typical day in his class, he recalled, was constructed to challenge students' expectations. "They don't know when it is going to happen—here it comes . . . and then it doesn't come. And then it does come, and [students say], 'I wasn't looking! I was asking a neighbor!' But, whatever happened, happened. And you're responsible for leaving some reaction to the image on your paper." The trick was to suspend any idea of what something looked like and relax instead into the sound of the music and the feel of the paper and the charcoal and the friction of an arm moving against the page. Before class, Olsen created a sequence of slides, choosing from the hundreds available, "just a huge series of marks" that he could organize as he wished. On each four-by-four-inch flash slide, one to three marks made shapes, "lozenges," "cylinder shapes," "vertical, maybe a slight tilt—a one o'clock tilt." The teacher's job, according to Olsen, was to create the order: "You could pick slides that had to do with building complexity, then turn around and use marks of less complexity. . . . You could keep the suspense going, the anticipation going, and you never gave them what they expected. . . . When I would pick slides I would always set up the class to have the rug pulled out from under them so that no one ever could trust me at all. They had to learn to trust themselves." In other sessions, the professor illuminated an object with a spotlight for a fraction of a second, and students sat in the dark with X-Acto knives and carved the shape into pieces of balsa wood. Students called the class "Thirty Cuts," and around campus people identified the art majors by the scars on their hands.[47]

In parallel with many midcentury art movements, the Art in the Dark program blurred the boundaries between art and life. It might have been mechanistic and abstract, but it was also psychological and experiential.

Drawing and other art making became a matter of perception and repetitive practice, rather than rarified talent. In this sense the program, for all its rigidity, was freeing. It demystified craft and devalued an older model in which skills were acquired through careful study. And it taught students, including future scene musicians, a lesson that punk would increasingly reinforce: pick up a tool, look and listen, ignore the burden of the past, and follow your own vision, even if you bleed.

By the late 1970s, the art school no longer ran the formal Art in the Dark intro sequence, but professors still taught in the lab rooms and incorporated some of the exercises into their curriculums "a la carte." Judy McWillie, who did her MFA at Ohio State, already knew about Sherman's methods when she arrived at UGA in 1974 as the first woman hired at Georgia to teach studio art. In one of her favorite activities, she projected a "totally blurred" image for ten seconds as standing students used charcoal to draw what they saw. Gradually, in ten-second intervals, the image grew increasingly focused as students continued drawing. After about a minute, the image on the screen was sharp and students had produced "a fully fleshed out black and white tonal drawing." Many professors, including McWillie and Croker, also taught "gesture drawing," a method that joined the body and the eye and understood drawing as a physical activity, even a dance.[48]

Professors also kept the curriculum's use of music. While the old program had relied on classical music, the younger professors often mixed in folk music, rock, and, by the late seventies, punk. McWillie, Croker remembered, "came into the painting studio one day with something called 'White Punks on Dope,'" a song by the Tubes released in 1975, and introduced them all to the new sound. In this way, some art professors taught their students that looking at and making visual art and listening to and making music were "parallel experiences."[49]

Mark Cline and Sam Seawright met in the fall of 1977 in Robert Olsen's Art 101 class and then enrolled together in Croker's drawing class Art 130 the next quarter. Croker based the course on Kimon Nicolaides's *The Natural Way to Draw*, and according to Mark Cline, "you were a fool if you didn't take it from him." Like the art in the dark format, the Nicolaides curriculum assumed that anyone could learn to draw and that a cosmopolitan understanding of art was not only not required but also possibly harmful. Before he moved to New York at the end of spring quarter in 1978, Croker taught all the members of Pylon — Briscoe Hay, Bewley, Lachowski, and Crowe — as well as Mark Cline, Keith Bennett, and other future scene participants.[50]

In Croker's classroom, students stood up and drew on a pad of paper clamped to their easels. A model—Vanessa Briscoe Hay worked at this job for a while—would hold a pose for a few minutes. Then Croker would yell "fire" and hit play on his tape player, and the students would draw for ten to fifteen seconds as the Ramones, the Velvet Underground, the Beatles, or Blondie blasted through the room, until Croker hollered "cease fire." According to Cline, "you just didn't hear this stuff" then, and Croker "wanted to expose us to music that equaled the level of the art he wanted us to make." Once a quarter, he devoted class to a "two-hour pose," delighting all the students who wanted to "get really precious" about "all the detail work." Then at the end of the period, he had students put their drawings on the floor and dance on them. In another class activity, "transit surfing," students rode buses around town and drew what they saw. Sometimes he threw away his plans for the day to take his students to draw something happening nearby, like a burning building. Outside of class, Croker would bring however many students he could cram in his Volkswagen Thing to the local disco to draw the dancers. "Record what you see," he always repeated; "get it down."[51]

In all his lessons, Croker taught students to work fast rather than fuss, to capture a scene with bold, quick gestures, and to use drawing to interact with and understand the world. He also showed them how to recognize "the good mistakes," the times when an artist unintentionally made something interesting. Croker's teaching transformed drawing into a kind of visual version of gonzo journalism, a way to document experience. According to Cline, Croker's classes "had a great effect on how we approached music."[52]

The one thing professors were not teaching much of was technique. In Bourne's memory, "the program did not teach you how to manipulate the mediums" but instead offered a "post-hippie education," with instruction that pushed the motto, "if it felt good, do it." Cline remembered drawing and painting classes rooted in "abstract expressionism," in the idea of art as a means of self-expression. Jim Herbert, who taught filmmaking classes as well as painting, told his students not to plan their films but instead, to go out and "provoke the image." McWillie painting and color theory classes were rare exceptions. Vanessa Briscoe Hay remembered taping off a section of the studio's linoleum floor and painstakingly rendered every scruff, speck, and scratch for a photorealist exercise assigned by McWillie. More common was Jennifer Hartley's experience. Art classes were often "a big, crazy guessing game" in which students struggled to figure out what the professors wanted. Only once did she experience a teacher carefully demonstrating a technique, how to paint on unprimed canvas with thinned acrylic paint that stained the canvas and could be layered in thin washes to create effects. Like a lot of art professors in this era, UGA faculty members did not teach their students to think about technique as skills acquired through careful, disciplined, time-consuming practice. It was not much of a leap to think about musical instruments in the same way they understood paintbrushes, etching tools, or cameras — as tools anybody could pick up and use.[53]

Students also learned from their professors outside of class. Art Rosenbaum taught drawing and painting, but he was also a traditional banjo player with skill on other instruments as well, an active folk music collector, and an organizer of events like the North Georgia Folk Festival. In Athens, the folk music revival flourished long past its national peak in the late sixties and early seventies, and the revivalist community in and around the town functioned as a concrete, visible example of community that blurred the distinctions between performers and audiences. Rosenbaum was easy enough to find at concerts and monthly song swaps hosted by the Athens Folk Music and Dance Society. His large, mural-like figurative paintings often incorporated folk musicians, students, and other local subjects.[54]

Jim Herbert rented rooms in his huge old house on Dearing Street to current and former UGA students like Sam Seawright, his older brother John Seawright, Sally Speed, and Keith Bennett. He also rented studio space to current and former students like Lachowski and Speed in old commercial buildings where he kept his own studios. In his art, Herbert explored erotic desire and youth, and he filled his paintings and films with intimate scenes of young people, often current or former students, in various stages of undress and arousal. Awkwardness in front of the camera, he believed, made films "intimate" and "real." A winner of Guggenheim fellowships in both painting and film whose 1970 work *Porch Glider* premiered at MOMA, Herbert modeled what it meant to be a working artist. He also treated students like they were all already artists, talking to them about their own work in progress and asking for their feedback. What one participant called "porch culture" flourished in warmer weather as Dearing Street residents and friends sat outside on the gliders and talked when the weather was nice in a kind of informal art salon. One perfect night, Sally Speed and Sam Seawright drank gin and tonics in silence and listened to the rain on the magnolia leaves. The world around them had become an art film.[55]

About once a quarter, Croker invited everyone he knew to invite everyone they knew to his house in the country for a party. People brought musical instruments, split into acoustic and electric camps, and played. They also drank, of course, and smoked pot and, around the edges, took other drugs. Performance pieces seemed to emerge out of the revelry, run their course, and subside back into the general merry-making. At one party, someone sat in a tree naked and gave an art lecture. At another, Olsen drew diagrams of Cézanne compositions on the window shades. More than once, partygoers projected an old print of *The Incredible Shrinking Man* on the side of Croker's van. The drawing professor also gave dramatic readings from *Gravity's Rainbow* or, in his Georgia-accented Middle English, "The Miller's Tale." People took turns playing deejay in the living room, and the dancing went on without stop.[56]

In their interactions outside the classroom, art professors modeled alternative ways to live. Some were part of a network of mostly gay and queer locals that Jerry Ayers had helped Keith Strickland and Ricky Wilson discover when they were still in high school. It was not easy to be a young man interested in the arts in the South, even in the seventies. "Art was sissy. If you were arty, you were queer," Croker, who was a generation older than his students, recalled. This understanding—as well as the way queer meant both gay and odd—remained powerful into the eighties in the South.[57]

In the face of these gendered conventions, some young people abandoned any serious interest in the arts or they shifted into the "safer" subjects of arts education or graphic design. Yet for those who wanted to explore non-normative genders and sexualities, these assumptions made a life in art even more attractive. Others muddled along, following their artistic passions while trying to defend or deny or determine their sexual ones. The idea that art was queer or gay worked as both a blessing and a curse. If you were not strictly heterosexual, it gave you cover. If you were straight and male, you could adopt a kind of heterosexual hypermasculinity like the abstract expressionists and the earth artists or you could live with the emasculation. If you were a woman, you could make all the art you wanted but few people would take your work seriously.[58]

The relatively small number of women who were studio art, rather than arts education or design, majors did not experience the art school in quite the same way as their male counterparts. All of the studio professors, with the exception of Judy McWillie, were white men, although later an African American man held a teaching position at the art school briefly. In the seventies, in fact, the University of Georgia had very few women professors. The art school had only hired McWillie because the federal Office of Equal Opportunity forced the university to diversify its faculty. UGA, like many other southern universities, she recalled, "went into it kicking and screaming." For years, her position was probationary, subject to a yearly assessment. Sally Speed, who returned to school to work on an MFA in painting at age thirty, remembered it was "very hard to be a woman in art school." The never-spoken "mantra" was "you had to paint like a man." Some women students recalled the lack of boundaries between students and faculty members as a problem that allowed professors to abuse their power and act inappropriately, in ways that ranged from merely inappropriate — like dating students — and offensive to demeaning and arguably illegal. Neither the university nor the art school held professors accountable for their behavior. Some women dropped out for a quarter or two and struggled to recover from critiques that moved beyond a focus on the work and became personal. Art student Annelies Mondi, for example, left school for a while after being harassed by a visiting artist. Others changed majors or quit the university altogether.[59]

McWillie, who arrived as a single twenty-eight-year-old, survived the "serious sexism" in the art school by trying to support her female students and by focusing on her work. She lived with a great deal of what was not then but now would be called sexual harassment by telling herself some of her male colleagues were just crazy. When she started teaching at UGA, one beloved male art teacher decided that they should be a couple and showed up uninvited at her apartment at odd hours for months. One day when McWillie went to the art office to talk to the secretary about making an appointment with the director, another colleague came in — years later she still did not want to name him — and yelled, "You're the last person I want to see." Then he knocked her against the wall and walked out. The secretary, a woman of course, immediately said he did not mean it. Shaken, McWillie decided the attack was "leverage": "I spread it around among the men, and they told him." In this way, she figured, she had something to hold over him to prevent him from bothering her again. She only stayed at UGA because she loved the town.[60]

Many art students remembered that they were amazingly naive about the range of human sexuality when they moved to Athens to go to college. At a party with friends as a first-year student, Keith Bennett was thrilled to find an attractive woman staring at him, until Margaret Katz laughed and informed him that the woman was actually a man in drag, Keith Strickland. Armistead Wellford remembered being awed by his future bandmate Mark Cline's ability to flirt with women at parties before he grasped the fact that Cline was gay. After the members of the B-52's and their friends started the scene, people came "out" as bohemians, with all the openness and experimentation that category implied, more frequently and more publicly than they came out as gay or bisexual or trans or queer. The fluidity enabled people comfortable with ambiguity to experience same-sex intimacies without having to face homophobia. Others remember less space for women in a world in which men could be bandmates and friends and also lovers.[61]

In the art crowd, sexuality and gender did not map easily onto conventional dichotomies like "gay versus straight" and "out versus closeted." Some former students and colleagues remember art professor Bill Marriott as one of the first "out" people they knew, but this quiet man was not publicly gay in the ways possible today. Another art professor, Jim Herbert, lived with former art student Jackie Slayton even as he made paintings and films that explored the play of eroticism—including homoeroticism and the naked bodies of androgynous young men—and desire. Years later, he began having relationships with men.[62]

Art student and R.E.M. singer Michael Stipe, who arrived in Athens in 1978, spent his early years in town having emotional and sexual relationships with both men and women. Later, he came out as queer and bisexual and then finally as gay. Michael Lachowski did not talk publicly about his sexuality and instead created a style and way of being in the world that many people would have read as gay or queer. Mark Cline, in contrast, was completely out as gay in a way that was rare then, and he laughed as he told me, "That was what made me so popular."[63]

Women, too, experimented across a spectrum of gender identities and sexual partners. In the early eighties, Laura Carter, singer for the Athens hardcore band the Bar-B-Q Killers, often dressed like a man and dated women as well as men. Lauren Fancher, an art student and member of the country-flavored band the El Caminos, also had relationships with men and women, while her bandmate Gwen Carter was an out lesbian. In retrospect, the fluidity of the emerging Athens scene worked liked a reticent, nonconfessional version of the current-day explosion of genders and sexualities. Art students did not just make art. They made what often seemed to them like new identities by trying everything, by playing with a huge variety of partners just like they played with multiple mediums of artistic expression.[64]

In the end, it did not matter so much for the art students creating the scene whether individual professors or fellow students were "really" gay or bi or transsexual. The rumors and the gossip, given the absence of public outings, worked as well as the truth in making what was then a revolutionary point. In a place and time when very few people were talking about sex, gender, and desire, the community that grew up around the art school offered young people a wide array of alternatives. In their classes and the big open studios, students learned to trust themselves and express their visions. And they learned, in their interactions with their professors and other students, a then rare and radical perspective: people who were not straight and con-formist could experience friendship, desire, pleasure, and even love. They could live and even, possibly, thrive.

Gang of Four

In April 1979, Lachowski wrote his former professor Robert Croker about his new band:

> Our only goal is to play in NYC at least once. After we play there, we will decide on the basis of the response (esp. if the press writes a mention) whether to quit or continue. But after NY, it won't hurt me at all to sell my amp and hang my guitar on the wall and mount the pics in an album and save the posters and make copies of the tapes. I mean, we are not musicians, we do not like to "jam" or even practice, we only want to perform . . . the experience of playing in public is very intense, very pleasurable.

Pylon's name, he told Croker, refers to "the kind in the road, not the architec-tural one or the ones that hold up electricity" and not, as some critics wrongly reported, the Faulkner novel. "We chose Pylon because it is severe, indus-trial, monolithic, functional. We subscribe to a modern techno-industrial aesthetic. Our message is 'Go for it!, but be careful.'" "Three of the 4 of us work @ DuPont so we are safety conscious." The steel-toed boots, safety goggles, yellow and black striped tape, and signs announcing the rules at their weekend jobs at the nylon factory had shaped their musical aesthetic.[65]

In making their performance-art rock, the four members of Pylon drew on what they had learned in art school. As Briscoe Hay recalled, they ap-plied concepts like "form follows function," "everything that we're doing, all the time, is going on in a 'space,'" and "with the first line you make, the drawing could be finished" to their new band. They also employed what they had learned about the ways that tensions between materials, mediums, and expectations could animate art. Middle-class kids holding down working-class jobs, they turned the factory into a style. Posters featuring orange safety cones and music full of machine-like repetition punctured by whistles and screams contradicted audience assumptions that small southern towns pro-duced only country and folk sounds and handmade things. Band members also understood that artists working in the ephemeral format of performance art needed to be disciplined about documentation. Still, Lachowski's admission of pleasure foreshadowed the future of his band and the Athens scene. What started as art continued for many reasons, but fun was always part of the mix, mostly because it was true but also because it worked to mask or deny less artistic ambitions like money and fame.[66]

In August, Crowe, Briscoe Hay and her then-husband Jimmy Ellison, and friends Lori Shipp and Kurt Wood piled into Wood's old Volvo and drove north. Lachowski and their friend Vic Varney—formerly of the Tone Tones and about to form the Method Actors—came separately in Lachowski's early-sixties whale of a sedan. In Washington, D.C., they met Bewley, who had spent the summer at his dad's house there. After practicing for several days—they had not played together since June—they drove on to Philadelphia. Varney had helped them use their Hurrah date opening for the Gang of Four to get gigs at the Hot Club in Philadelphia and the Rat in Boston. And easy as that, a half-year-old band had a New York gig, a connection to an up-and-coming British act, and a mini three-city tour.[67]

In Philly, Pylon faced a tough crowd. The members of Gang of Four had flown from Britain to New York with plans to drive to their first show in Philadelphia, but their vehicle broke down in the Holland Tunnel. The club kept announcing that the headliners were on the way, but people were mad, and the Pylon struggled to win the audience over by playing every song the band knew. Then, as Briscoe Hay recalled, "the Gang of Four blew into the club . . . wearing leather jackets. They put a bottle of liquor in the middle of the table in the dressing room and ran onto the stage. Then they proceeded to play one of the best shows I have seen by *anybody*, anywhere . . . their on-stage chemistry was amazing."[68]

The next night, Pylon made their New York debut opening for the Gang of Four in front of a huge crowd at Hurrah. Briscoe Hay remembered borrowing a whistle from the doorman for the song "Danger" and that Gang of Four members Hugo Burnham and Jon King told her afterwards how much they liked the song. The audience was full of musicians. Briscoe Hay saw people in the front shake Bewley's hand after the set, and from that show on, young guitar players badgered him with questions about how he came up with his strange tunings and original chords.[69]

A day or two later, Pylon performed at the Rat, and then band members and their friends returned home so everyone could get back to their day jobs. They brought a copy of the not-yet-released Gang of Four album

Entertainment! with them, and the album became the soundtrack of Athens parties before most people had even heard it in New York. Then the September 1979 issue of *Interview* arrived, with O'Brien's review of the show that gave as much space to Pylon as to the Gang of Four:

> Pylon, the first Athens band to hit the town since the B-52s. A tough act to follow—but Pylon is also a credit to their community. There's not much resemblance to the Bs. Although the guitarist has real classy taste in licks that is sometimes reminiscent of RICKY WILSON's. Pylon has a charming chanteuse up-front—sort of Georgia Georgie Girl who manages to carry off several difficult postures, including kooky, endearing, sincere and wry. And not all the songs sound the same. These kids listen to dub for breakfast. Recommended.

Interview was not *New York Rocker*, but O'Brien's coverage was better than Pylon's wildest dreams, even if they had to look up the meaning of the word "dub." Their art project was a success. They did not want to quit now. They were having too much fun.[70]

With O'Brien's review in hand, Briscoe Hay and Lachowski drove to Atlanta to the record store Wax 'n' Facts to give one of their homemade tapes and a poster to Danny Beard, who had put out the first B-52's single. Later that fall, Pylon got to open for both the B-52's and Talking Heads, who were on tour together but split up in Atlanta to play separate nights at the Agora.[71]

On Halloween, Pylon packed Tyrone's with costumed partiers, and Vic Varney's new band the Method Actors debuted as the opening act. Watt King created another light show, this time using neon rods to "translate" the buzz of bass and guitar into the sight of light in the dark. Pylon played their sixteen original songs and then covered the Batman theme for an encore. At the hip Halloween party afterwards, film and painting professor Jim Herbert came as an Oscar, painting his chiseled chest gold above his jeans. Jerry Ayers dressed as a scarecrow, a version of his new boho-hobo style.[72]

As the art-school crowd embraced Pylon that fall and winter, Briscoe Hay's marriage to Jimmy Ellison fell apart, and she moved in with her friends Edna Lori Shipp and Craig Woodall. Woodall was a member of yet another new Athens band, Limbo District, which also included Jerry Ayers and his partner Davey Stevenson, French exchange student Dominique Amet, and a changing cast of guitar players. They practiced at the apartment, creating a kind of "fun, arty, international" salon there. Listening to the group, more an avant-garde art noise project than a band, shaped Briscoe Hay's emerging style.[73]

After their Hurrah date, Fouratt had told the members of Pylon that they sounded good but their stage performance—they stood completely still as they played—needed some work. He urged them to practice more and to move. Briscoe Hay took this advice and began belting out vocals in a southern-accented fusion of Yoko Ono and Patti Smith, bouncing up and down and shaking her head like a dancer in a Charlie Brown television special. She told a local paper that when she sang, she thought about "trying to get the idea across, the emotions, the sound. Sometimes the words are not as important as to use my voice as another instrument in the band." Becoming more at home on the stage, at Tyrone's she bantered casually with audience members between songs. At the end of the year, the group opened for the California band the Cramps at the former movie palace the Georgia Theater, the same venue the B-52's had been required to rent a year and a half earlier just to be able to play for record executives in Athens.[74]

Around the same time, Pylon began recording their first single at Stone Mountain Studios, the same Atlanta facility used by other groups Beard worked with, including the B-52's and the Atlanta band the Fans. The band had, in Lachowski's words, "rehearsed the shit out of" the two songs they planned to record, "Feast on My Heart" and "The Human Body." After a day in the studio, everyone took a cassette of the rough mix home with them as they went their separate ways to stay with parents and friends. Somehow, the songs just sounded "trite." The next day, against the advice of Beard, they quickly recorded "Cool," a song they had written about three days before they started recording, and "Dub," another new song written in response to O'Brien's review. On these cuts, the "freshness," the spontaneous feel and the lack of polish, seemed to capture the way Pylon sounded live. With Danny Beard's support and money, they released the two new songs as a single in January 1980 on their own Caution Records. Having a record made bookings much easier, and Pylon used the 45 to get gigs opening for Lene Lovich and P.I.L.

Selling singles was easy then because new music fans tried out new acts by purchasing inexpensive 45s from independent record stores. As Curtis Crowe recalled, bands would take their 45s with them when they played out of town: "You could go to a record store in any town and they'd go, 'New 45? We'll take 5 of 'em.' They'd throw them into the store and it didn't cost them anything. They thought somebody'd buy them even if they were terrible." Pylon sold "Cool"/"Dub" this way through New York's 99 Records and other stores across the country.[75]

In New York, underground music critics fell in love with this first single by "the other great band from Athens." Glenn O'Brien raved about both sides of "Cool"/"Dub" in *Interview* that June. On "Cool," "drummer CURTIS has a micro-lag that poses problems for some but interesting opportunities for good dancers. Vocalist VANESSA's job here is to scream and shout and moan which she does beautifully, on key and in control but singeing the edges of her voice." O'Brien liked "Dub," "a hypnotic rhythm work out crescendorama," even better: "one bass note plunks out clock time. In the interval, drummer and guitar scratcher go berserk, exchanging attacks of hyper-rhythm variations" while Briscoe Hay "chants plenty vociferously, 'We eat dub for breakfast,'" the line from O'Brien's own review. Bewley's "rapid rhythm attack style," "equally influenced by ARTO LINDSAY, big chords, and JB [James Brown] style guitar groove" was "shockingly cool." Robert Christgau, music critic for the *Village Voice*, liked Pylon so much he began writing about the band whenever they played in the city. At the end of the year, he named Pylon's record the "best independent single of the year."[76]

When Pylon played New York's Hurrah that winter, "the audience consisted of wildly gyrating B-52s, other members of the Georgia mafia [former Athens residents living in the city], a handful of critics, and the curious." The next day, on a sidewalk in the East Village, someone carrying a boom box walked by Lachowski, playing a style of music he had never heard before. Asking around, he learned name of the artist and the song, Afrika Bambaataa's "Planet Rock," and discovered what he learned then to call rap, a new kind of music emerging out of a scene centered in the Bronx. The intricate wordplay over the repetitive beat created just the kind of aesthetic, formal contrast Lachowski loved in any art form. As far as anyone can remember, he became the first hip-hop fan in the mostly white Athens scene, pushing everyone he knew to listen to Bambaataa and Grandmaster Flash and the Furious Five. Over the next few years, the rhythms of this new genre shaped Pylon's sound as the band helped create a kind of punk-disco dance music. In New York, deejays played their second single "Crazy"/"M-Train" in dance clubs. Meanwhile, back in Athens, Lachowski started working as a deejay.[77]

No one then missed the fact that region and race divided these musicians in Athens and the Bronx, but they were linked, too. In both these places, young people were creating new sounds and new cultures by mining what was already out there and turning the fragments — characters, images, and gestures, licks, chord progressions, and beats — into something new.

And observers from outside these scenes could not talk about the musics that would become hip-hop and alternative rock, respectively, and the broad alternative cultures growing up around these emerging genres without mentioning the unlikeliness of it all, that these people in these places might make anything new. Yet class differences pushed these unexpected innovators in different directions. Early hip-hop musicians sourced their borrowings from the African diaspora and contemporary popular music. Coming from mostly working-class families, they had little interest in the kind of kind of self-consciously retro, down-market and amateur aesthetic that inspired Athens musicians. And they did not deny their desire to find success in the music business. In contrast, early Athens bands repurposed what they thought of as bits of the pop-culture past, a sonic and visual form of thrifting that made sense to middle-class participants. They took a previous generation's folk romanticism and applied it to outdated and discarded pop artifacts. Even their words had a non-narrative, nonlinear, found-lyric feel. In this way, Athens bands and other new-music groups like the Cramps and Talking Heads helped "gentrify" punk, making it less gritty and urban and angry and setting up its transformation into college rock, a genre characterized by romanticism and stylistic recycling.[78]

As Pylon matured, band members settled into their roles—the fearless and frenetic singer, the wholly original guitar player, the bouncing, affectless bass player, and the hard hitting, dance-beat drummer. In February 1980, the group opened for former Velvet Underground member John Cale at the Georgia Theater. A few months later, they headed back to New York without having played any of the places in between, like Washington, D.C., and Atlanta. That spring and summer, three new bands, R.E.M., the Side Effects, and Love Tractor, debuted in Athens.

Around the same time, Curtis Crowe turned the parties he had been throwing in his loft apartment into a business by opening the small 40 Watt Club East. He and another former UGA student named Paul Scales stripped a second-floor downtown bar at the corner of Broad and College right across from the main entrance to the university of its lounge décor. Then the partners built a small stage and "borrowed" the beer license of the Sub and Steak sandwich shop below. On May 16, 1980, the first in a long line of clubs named after Crowe's old party loft opened, featuring music by Jimmy Ellison's new band the Side Effects and $1 cans of beer.[79]

While new-music fans loved Tyrone's, where their bands played some nights, with the opening of the official 40 Watt they finally had their own place. Less a club than a clubhouse, the small venue was difficult to find.

No sign marked the entrance to the stairway. When the place was closed, it looked abandoned, like most of the other upstairs spaces downtown. But on nights when the venue was open, the music coming through the opened windows announced something was happening. To enter, you walked up the dark stairs to a landing where someone collected the dollar or so cover. If you were a newcomer, you felt like that person was deciding whether you were cool enough to be admitted. If you were a regular, you felt like you were being welcomed. That summer and fall, the small space could and frequently did hold everyone in the emerging scene and then some, around seventy-five people.[80]

The members of Pylon took what the B-52's and their friends had started and made the happenings and performances and parties into a scene. Lachowski lived then in a shabby Victorian divided into apartments on Barber Street where N. Pope Street dwindled down to an alley. The housemates named the empty lot next door, with towering bamboo at the back, Pylon Park. Parties there grew increasingly elaborate — named, sometimes themed, and advertised on flyers and on "the Party Line," which operated off Lachowski's answering machine as a kind of automated calendar of events. Watt King ran his light shows, and Lachowski created art installations. One night he hung a huge sheet of clear plastic with the word "RAIN" spray-painted on it twenty feet up in the trees and positioned an oscillating sprinkler to spray drops of water that sparkled against the sheet like stars. On the fourth of July, the party moved into the non-air-conditioned 40 Watt Club. Pylon packed the tiny place, and someone measured the temperature inside at more than one hundred degrees. Between sets, partiers washed down the steps and outside, gasping for air as their clothes dripped sweat onto the sidewalk. Downtown Athens could be so dead at that time of the year that you could lie down in the middle of Broad Street, but everyone remembered that summer as special.[81]

That same month, Pylon played for their biggest crowd yet, opening for the B-52's in New York's Central Park as last-minute replacements for the Plastics. Vanessa Briscoe Hay had to quit her job at DuPont to do the gig because she had not asked ahead of time for those days off. Bewley and Lachowski soon stopped working too. Band members found they could live two to three months in Athens on what they earned on their New York City guarantees. At the end of the year, Crowe got out of the club business, when the not entirely official beer license and other problems forced him and Scales to close the 40 Watt. Pylon had become their job.[82]

By then, the June/July issue of *New York Rocker* had reached the empty college town. "Something is happening in Athens, Georgia, and we don't

know what it is," a one-page piece on Pylon and the Method Actors began. In text that snaked around photographs of both bands, the magazine that had inspired Lachowski and Bewley to form a band in the first place tried to figure out what the B-52's, Pylon, and the Method Actors shared, besides that fact that they all knew each other. Vic Varney, contacted for an interview, had an answer: "We all use strange guitar tunings that we stumbled on independently. Also, almost no one played an instrument before they started a band." Athens, *New York Rocker* told its readers, was "full of empty buildings, cheaply rented. . . . Go South and create a scene!" It was like New York City, only safer and cheaper.[83]

Over the next few years, as Crowe put it, "each time the band got mentioned, the town got mentioned." As *Village Voice, Trouser Press, New York Rocker*, and later *Rolling Stone, New Musical Express*, and even the *New York Times* wrote about Pylon, a kind of geographic branding emerged. Asked by an Atlanta journalist why where the band was from had become as important as what they were playing, Lachowski answered "surprise": "They're freaked out, especially in the states, that bands with any measure of sophistication should come from a small Southern town." For self-consciously bohemian music fans and critics, especially in New York, "avant-garde" and "southern" were mutually exclusive cultural categories. Yet the shock drew critical attention and eased the way for wild experimentation. As Briscoe Hay told a critic, at a New York show a blond woman stood watching them and laughing. "People from Athens can get away with anything," she yelled. The scene and the band grew up together.[84]

Working Is No Problem

Sonically and visually, Pylon worked the contrast between flat, machine-like minimalism and ragged, southern-accented amateurism. Their songs used a four-on-the-floor disco beat to mash together punk's emotional excess and industrial repetition and detachment. The band may have been "safety conscious," but the raw, pounding sound did not make anyone feel safe. Band members turned uneven development—the collision between Athens as a small southern town and Athens as the home of a modern university and Athens as a peripheral industrial site—into a startlingly original sound, an audio portrait of postmodernity.

After Jim Fouratt left Hurrah, he and a partner opened Danceteria, a New York dance club that also showcased live bands. Video artists Emily Armstrong and Pat Ivers programmed the video lounge there, and they recorded one of Pylon's shows. The surviving footage revealed what Pylon looked and sounded like at the height of their power.[85]

The song "Danger" begins with a bass drum beat and Briscoe Hay quietly alternating between making a "ssssss" sound and chanting words like "the sound of danger." Drum and voice hold the line as the bass rings out and a scattering of guitar notes compete with a clanging cymbal. Someone thinks to turn up the stage light, and Briscoe Hay's head and upper torso emerge from the dark. Lachowski's bass builds, repeating a bouncing five-note phrase again and again, and the guitar and symbol clang repeatedly. Briscoe Hay stares straight ahead at the audience, her eyes barely visible under a thatch of brown bangs, and hisses into the mic, impersonating a snake or a valve letting off steam, the sound equivalent of the machine in the garden.[86]

On stage, Briscoe Hay and Lachowski's bodies and clothes create a kind of visual dissonance. Briscoe Hay wears a church dress gone wrong, its color a bit faded and its shape a little soft. As she shakes and twirls her head, a limp lace sleeve slips down her shoulder. Instead of a necklace, she wears her whistle. Her facial expressions alternate between lack and excess, an underplaying that suggests choked amateurism and an overplaying that evokes the entwined histories of blackface and drag.[87]

As the song builds, Briscoe Hay spins like a windup whirling dervish, slowing down and speeding up according to the tension in her spring. As she dances, her moves accentuate her curves. The only sharp things here are her cheekbones. Her accent is somehow flat and yet also lushly southern. Like Cindy Wilson in the B-52's, Briscoe Hay both conjures and contradicts the multiple meanings of performing like a girl. In contrast, Lachowski is tall, hard, and thin, a pole of a man with slow, repressed gestures. He sticks out his tongue, and he turns his head a little, looking away from the crowd on one side and then the other. At times, he seems a little scared. His t-shirt and jeans refuse notice. In the critic Van Gosse's words, Lachowski and Bewley look "like bike mechanics or sculptors" who perform a kind of "abstract hopping around, cute yet unposed."[88]

About a minute in, Briscoe Hay shakes her brown bangs from her brown eyes and half smiles, half grimaces at the audience as she increases the volume and the emotional intensity of her voice. "Dannnne . . . gerrrr," she sings, like a southern girl struggling to speak a foreign tongue, "Be careful. Be caw . . . tious." Drawing out the "caw" until it mimics the sound of a crow, she over-enunciates and turns her head for emphasis, like a teacher trying to force her students to pay attention. A delay effect sends the vocals echoing in all directions and conjures the large space of a factory or a church. With Briscoe Hay's vocal shift, the song explodes. The drums become fat and big and bullying. Sprays of a few guitar and bass notes and shouted words form achingly simple hooks. Then Briscoe Hay blows a long blast on her whistle right into the mic, and the sound of a safety alert at a factory or a foul in a gym rings out an elementary need. The serial riffs convey both the repetition of machinery and a growing urgency as volume and tempo slowly build. At the end, the guitar and bass sound like they are unwinding. Briscoe Hay begins to scream and moan, and the delay effect unravels her voice. The creamy skin of her chest shows just above her breast where her dress has slipped off her shoulder. Decreasing the volume and cutting the speed, she winds listeners out of the song on a wash of emotions that refuse to coalesce into any coherent form.

In person, Briscoe Hay *sounded* like a girl—she spoke in a soft, high voice with a deep Southern accent. On stage, she developed a grown-up and powerful roar. Part beauty queen and part drag queen, she worked the intersections of white southern conventions of femininity and drag performance, Patti Smith's androgyny and Yoko Ono's arty shock and awe. The Danceteria video conveyed the charisma of the maturing band's live performances, an allure never quite captured on their recordings. Back in Athens, Vanessa's performances made other women think that if a sweet southern girl could do *this*, then they too might dare to dream.

That November, DB Records released *Gyrate*, Pylon's first album, recorded the previous spring in a three-day session at Stone Mountain Studios and produced by Kevin Dunn, a former member of Atlanta punk band the Fans who had also helped with the B-52's and Pylon's singles. In December, Armageddon Records released the album in England. Critics raved. *New Musical Express* named the record "one of the year's most fundamental rock and roll celebrations." *Melody Maker* worked the unlikeliness angle: "Buried deep in the land of rednecks, peanut farms and wave-yer-hat-and-shoutyeehaw boogie bands, there's something stirring." Pylon made its first over-seas tour, playing across England and a few dates in Europe in November and December. Back in New York, John Lennon was murdered. Briscoe Hay remembered getting out of a car in Liverpool and accidently stepping into a pile of flowers left as a makeshift memorial.[89]

Reagan had been elected president just as the album came out, and many critics heard something political in the band's unique sound. Glenn O'Brien prefaced his positive review of *Gyrate* with a rant about the new po-litical moment. He agreed with the president that America still believed in "those great ideals, those hopes and dreams." The problem for O'Brien was that collectively, Americans had lost "our national ability to identify facts, to absorb information and correlate it; in short, our ability to *know* anything." By really making you feel like dancing, by moving listeners and making them think, Pylon worked as an antidote to this know-nothingness.[90]

For critic Van Gosse, writing in the *Village Voice*, Pylon's new album was not just great; as the Reagan era began amidst "imperial decline and the sound of cowboy bluster," it was essential. "If there is any conceivable 'rock 'n' roll future,'" he argued, it lay "in the intrinsic values of a music that is kept blindingly simple, unsentimental, uncomfortable: that which embodies the particular contradictions of its historical epoch in three minutes of glorious noise." For Gosse, rock and roll meant "nothing more or less than controlled rhythmsmack, an exquisite tension and release embodied in sound." Pylon embodied "this formal truth right now in a way that only the Rolling Stones ever have before." After lovingly describing their sound and raving about the "hypnotic" Briscoe Hay, "shoeless with whistle," he returned to the impor-tance of this kind of band in this kind of time. Before Pylon, "the class acts of post-everything modernism" came from "the most ancient bowels of de-cayed industrial capitalist, the dreary olde U.K." While many young Ameri-cans loved this music, "we're not really rotted enough yet ourselves. What was needed was something with a little frontier chutzpah, some rooty-toot-toot all-American get-up-an-go, to sing of *our* bodies electric and alone." Pylon, from "the proverbial sleepy college town," was that band.[91]

New York Rocker's March 1981 Pylon cover story and interview "From Athens, Georgia: New Sounds of the New South" did not so much argue as gush. The band's "utter lack of attitude" offered an antidote to big city jaded-ness: "Aren't y'all tired of patronizing arty-fartiness pawned off as enter-tainment?" Pushed to describe Pylon's sound, Lachowski called the band's music "temporary," in contrast to contemporary, rock. In the same issue, Vic Varney explained the new Athens scene under the headline "Nineteen Hours

**Pylon broke up for the first time in late 1983 at what
seemed to their local fans like the height of their fame.
(Polaroid photograph by Curtis Knapp)**

from New York," and *New York Rocker* printed photos of the next wave of
bands: R.E.M., Love Tractor, and the Side Effects.[92]

When the 40 Watt Club reopened with new ownership on West Clayton near the old Last Resort space, Pylon was the obvious choice to headline.
Varney had exaggerated when he told *New York Rocker* that Pylon was essentially "commuting to New York." Despite touring with the Gang of Four in
the Midwest and Canada and recording a new single, "Crazy"/"M-train,"
and a second album, *Chomp*, band members still lived in Athens and spent
a lot of time there. In January 1982, the group played a now-legendary show
on campus, selling out the large Memorial Hall ballroom. That fall, Pylon
packed the i and i, a warehouse-sized club that for a short time booked the
new bands. In April of 1983, when the 40 Watt moved from Clayton Street to

a bigger venue on Broad Street, only Pylon could headline the back-to-back closing and then opening shows and pack both rooms. Pylon ruled the scene that the band had done so much to create.[93]

In contrast, the New York–based B-52's hit something of a slump. After following up their debut album with 1980's successful *Wild Planet*, the group finally released *Mesopotamia* in early 1982, a David Byrne–produced recording that ended up being an EP because the band simply did not have enough new material. Most critics panned it. *New York Rocker* captured the prevailing sentiment: "This best-dressed act doesn't know what to do for an encore." Still, a lot of Athens folks headed down to Atlanta to catch the B-52's at the Fox, and Schneider plugged his friend Jerry Ayers's band Limbo District, playing later that night at the Atlanta club 688. The next spring, the B-52's released *Whammy!*, a new album that returned to their original sound and did better commercially than the EP without generating any hits.[94]

Pylon, too, hit a wall. From an underground perspective, the band seemed wildly successful. In Athens, New York, a few other American cities, and in England, they packed the clubs. Elsewhere, audiences did not seem to know what to make of the group. And while the members of Pylon made enough money to live cheaply in Athens, they weren't exactly comfortable. To reach the next level, they hired a professional booking agent. He landed them a gig most bands would have been giddy to get: the opening slot for U2's U.S. tour in support of their recently released album *War*. At first, band members said no, but eventually they compromised and agreed to play the first several dates. When they took the stage, crowds impatient to see the Irish band ignored them. As Briscoe Hay recalled, "People were heckling . . . 'Where's U2?' and 'Get off the stage.'" What everyone said was great felt instead like failure. It certainly was not fun. Maybe they did not really want this kind of success. Maybe their music was not for everybody. Maybe their performance-art-turned-band was exactly what they said it was, "temporary rock."[95]

In January 1983, Briscoe Hay told the *Athens Observer*, "I think if it ever became miserable, we would just disband," and in retrospect she was hinting at what was to come. Band members decided around this time to break up at the end of the year, after they fulfilled their bookings, but they kept their decision secret. In Athens, most people found out when posters went up for "Pylon's Last Show" with opening act Love Tractor. The gig took place in a huge venue known more for its cheap drink nights than live music so everyone could come.[96]

A live recording of that farewell show released in 2016 finally gave those of us who missed it a chance to listen in on this essential moment in Athens history. From the opening note of the first song, "Working Is No Problem," Pylon lays out what a critic fittingly describes as "an all-business, no-banter set" of twenty-two songs with hair-on-fire intensity that does not let up until the five-song encore finishes. Over the course of approximately an hour and a quarter of music, the crowd roars out its encouragement. Sometimes, the fans sing along to lyrics like "everything is cool" and even occasionally to guitar hooks, like the woo-woo of "M-Train." At other times, they just yell. No one wants the evening to stop. When it does, Pylon ends with a song that only their earliest fans would get and an homage to their origins in La-chowski's loft studio, their version of the *Batman* theme song. Superheroes fight evil. To resist the way the market strips away every meaning but money, maybe you just have to refuse to play.[97]

Interviewed about the breakup, band members reflected on why they had started making music "as another form of artistic expression." "We accomplished what we set out to do," Lachowski said. "It's not that we are miserable, it's just that we've seen all we're going to see and don't want to put any more time into it." "Our whole reason for doing it was for fun," Crowe argued, "and when the fun wears out and it starts turning into a serious type of job — there's no reason to do it anymore." Briscoe Hay captured the purity and the privilege of the band's attitude: "We wanted to do what we wanted to do when we wanted to do it." As Lachowski explained, "What was frustrating was not trying to live like other bands, but trying to convince everybody that we didn't want to do it that way. . . . We were the only ones that understood why we were not out there with the other bands trying to make it big." But for all the talk about fun, at least one band member was still thinking about the importance of form. "We'll become a cult band now," Bewley predicted on the eve of Pylon's last show. "This is a type of suicide that'll make us more popular in the long run." And he was right.[98]

I t was a tiny crowd really, fewer people than belonged to a single average-sized fraternity. Cline remembered about sixty people plus hangers on, a hundred tops. Briscoe Hay recalled a tight core of about one hundred people. Lachowski, comparing Athens to the early CBGB's days, argued that both scenes were "so vibrant because they were so tight." Proximity and personal relationships were key. Yet closeness alone was not enough. To be a scene, you needed a story. You needed a narrative to connect what was happening in Athens to a larger vision of the good life. You needed a myth.[99]

With their attention to "form" and their decision to quit at the height of their fame, Pylon provided this story, doing more than any other single group to fuse the loose, downtown-based network of art students, artists, other outsiders, and their friends that the B-52's had helped spark into what became known as the Athens scene. Performing their music, they also shared their bohemian vision. Life should be about making art for and with friends, combining creativity and pleasure and personal relationships, and living within and sharing a culture that you made yourself. Money and fame were not necessary. They might even be lethal, killing the experience of creative pleasure.

The B-52's had turned pop art and drag into a form of punk music and proved a little bit of bohemia could flower even in as unlikely a location as a Georgia college town. Pylon, too, started with art and ratcheted up the intensity. Performance art depended on presence to offer messy truths. Pylon made performance art people could dance to, delivering a punk comment on the survival of originality in the machine-made future in a southern drawl more commonly associated with the handmade past. Live, the band's raw, intense music worked the contradictory meanings of repetition, how duplicated sounds and acts could evoke expansiveness or constriction, pleasure or boredom, play or work, and the body or the machine. Critics' darlings, repeatedly named the best band in Athens, Pylon carried their art piece so far that they broke up on the cusp of stardom. The members of Pylon might not have had the language to describe resistance to what people by the end of the century would be calling neoliberalism, but they had the sound.

Barber Street

chronic town
poster torn
reaping wheel
stranger, stranger to these parts

R.E.M., "Carnival of Sorts" (1982)

Michael Stipe called it a "good slum-dump." Sometime in the previous decade, someone had constructed a two-story plywood shell of an apartment within the sanctuary of the former St. Mary's Episcopal Church on Oconee Street, like a stage set for a slacker sitcom. Inside the box, the one-time hippie squat offered impossible-to-heat rooms and a functional bathroom and kitchen. Outside the box, reached through a hole in the back of a bedroom closet, some of the old space of worship still existed — open, dusty, damp, and beckoning. You had to be young and broke to even think about renting it. You had to like the story. Years later, Peter Buck told *Rolling Stone* that the place had "been romanticized beyond belief. It was a rotten, dumpy little shit hole where college kids, only college kids, could be convinced to live."[1]

When people showed up for Kathleen O'Brien's birthday party at what locals called simply "the church" on an April evening in 1980, they did not know they were making history. Some were friends of the birthday girl or her roommates Buck and Stipe. Others were looking for free beer or for a current or former resident of the apartment who sold drugs. Some people had listened that afternoon as deejay and station music director Kurt Wood, who started the first punk show on the college radio station WUOG, interviewed members of the two new bands that would perform for the first time at the party. Buck played guitar and Stipe sang with one of these groups, a quartet too new to have a name. Neither the radio program nor the posters the other band made mentioned an address. To know where to go, you had to know someone.[2]

Wanting more than the usual keg party, O'Brien had lined up the bands. She knew the drummer Bill Berry from Reed Hall, the dorm where they both lived the year before, and from the radio station where she and Berry had performed with a loose group of musicians called the WUOGerz. In late 1979, O'Brien had introduced Buck, whom she first met back in Atlanta when she was in high school and he clerked at a record store near Emory University, and Stipe to Berry, and the drummer had introduced the other guys to his friend from Macon, Mike Mills. By the spring, they were practicing regularly in the old sanctuary, and O'Brien and Berry were dating. O'Brien also knew Paul Butchart, the drummer in the Side Effects, from Atlanta, where they had met at a high school German conference.[3]

Somehow hundreds of people heard about the party and packed the place, crawling through the hole in the back of O'Brien's closet and into the soaring space of the old sanctuary where the raised platform that had formerly held the altar made a perfect stage. A local jam band called Men in Trees played first, and hippies and hipsters mingled, united by the fact that they were not Greeks. Brand new group the Side Effects went on next, fumbling through nine or ten nerdy originals and a couple of covers. Besides the drummer Butchart, the trio featured Kit Swartz on guitar and Jimmy Ellison, who started playing the bass to cheer himself up after his marriage to Pylon singer Vanessa Briscoe failed. All of them were still learning their instruments. Then another group of local guys climbed onto the stage to make their debut. Playing a set of around twenty songs, Buck, Stipe, Berry, and Mills alternated between rough covers, including the Sex Pistols' "God Save the Queen," and ragged originals like "A Different Girl." They even came back for a sloppy, multiple-song encore that included audience members singing along to their cover of Patti Smith's version of "Gloria." Art major Sandi Phipps, another of O'Brien's friends from Reed Hall, took photographs. Pot and other drugs circulated as party goers drained the kegs. People got smashed and paired off. Miraculously—maybe the space was still sacred—no one fell through the rotten floorboards. Crazy and a little out of control—it was a typical Athens party. A few weeks later, after Michael Stipe found the abbreviation for a phase of sleep called "rapid eye movement" in a dictionary, the unnamed quartet decided to call themselves R.E.M.[4]

As the new decade opened, the UGA art school taught that anyone could be an artist, and punk and other new music broadcast on WUOG announced that anyone could be a musician. These ideas eroded the traditional bound-

Peter Buck, Michael Stipe, Bill Berry, and Mike Mills play their first gig together at Kathleen O'Brien's birthday party at the church. They had not yet decided to call themselves R.E.M. Stipe already has an eye for the camera. Buck is behind him in profile, and Mike Mills has his back to the camera. (Photograph by Sandra-Lee Phipps)

aries between cultural producers and consumers, a process made concrete in the small space of downtown Athens. While the members of the B-52's moved away in the spring of 1979, they often returned to town to visit friends and family. Other musicians — the members of the short-lived Tone Tones, the Method Actors which formed out of that breakup, and mighty Pylon — and their friends and fans continued to live and work in town. They ate breakfast at the El Dorado, drank beer at Allen's, and sipped espressos at Russo's Gyro Wrap and the 11:11 Kaffee Klub, so named because that was the time of night the venue opened. If, as Pete Buck explained later, "the whole punk thing pointed out in Athens that anybody can do it," locally that anybody was likely to be a coworker, classmate, or friend. Curtis Crowe, the drummer for Pylon, recalled a shared sense that "you were a member of some sort of revolution." Rock and roll "wasn't completely dominated by corporations anymore. It was something individuals could do after all. Part of the fun of it was feeling like we were in a tidewater and that we also belonged to a larger culture. . . . It was a real heady time."[5]

The emergence of a music underground in Athens was also part of a trend. Writing in the *Village Voice* about another unlikely scene in Louis-ville, Kentucky, critic Tom Carson called this development "regional rock." "The same thing" was happening "in dozens, maybe hundreds of towns." For Carson, these tiny openings marked "the beginnings of a radical realign-ment in the ways popular art [was] created and disseminated in this coun-try." Popular music, he predicted, did not have to be part of mass culture, recorded and distributed by the music industry. Instead, people could make and distribute their own music to their friends. In this way, they would nur-ture not just their own creativity but also their own system of valuing and rewarding. They would make their own popular culture.[6]

Carson's regional rock offered one way of thinking about a larger shift in which a new generation rejected the older forms of political organizing and turned instead to cultural rebellion. Growing up with defeat in Vietnam, the Watergate scandal, and a growing conservative backlash against sixties and early seventies social and political movements, many young people were looking for different ways to shape the world. "Politics are kind of passé and nobody really wants to get involved with it," Curtis Crowe told a reporter for UGA's student paper the *Red and Black* in 1981. "What better time than now," he insisted, to build an alternative culture? But what looked like a rejection of an earlier generation's choices and values masked a borrowing of key ideals. Back-to-the-landers living outside Athens and other college towns making bread, milking goats, and smoking homegrown weed had taken the "participatory democracy" of sixties politics and applied it to their everyday lives. Kids in the eighties took up this participatory ideal and used it to make their own music scenes.[7]

Though few of these cultural rebels in Athens and elsewhere used the term, participants in these new scenes adapted for their own purposes a model of cultural rebellion with a long history. Bohemianism originated in Europe in the early 1800s along with the development of the modern bourgeoisie as some people with middle-class educations and incomes re-jected middle-class values and norms. From the Left Bank in Paris in the mid-nineteenth century to Greenwich Village in New York City in the mid-twentieth century, this kind of oppositional culture flourished in a handful of large cities in the United States and Europe. Bohemians built lives centered on the cultivation of aesthetics and experiences in place of a middle-class focus on work and family. They openly embraced the pleasures of the body, violating middle-class norms of sexual restraint. And they congregated in working-class and low-income neighborhoods instead of living at "respect-able" addresses. Some bohemians worked as artists, writers, and musicians, and their interest in formal originality made them part of the avant-garde. Others understood crafting their own identities as a kind of artistic practice.[8]

Before the late 1970s, would-be American bohemians moved to areas of New York City like Greenwich Village and, to a lesser extent, to particular neighborhoods in smaller cities like San Francisco and Boston. Then suddenly that pattern changed. *Rocky Horror Picture Show* reenactments and the Sex Pistols' U.S. tour helped introduce punks and other outsiders to each other in places like Atlanta. Instead of retracing the paths of earlier rebels, young people who wanted to be bohemians began cultivating an intense localism and attachment to the quirks of secondary cities or college towns. What could be more radical than creating outposts of revolt against middle-class culture in unexpected places? As Tom Carson argued in his piece about Louisville, "The message of punk, wasn't only that anyone could do it: the other half was that anyone who wanted to try had to," no matter where they lived. Punk's democratic promise extended to both places and people. In time, these decisions "not to move to New York" created what the critic C. Carr called a "bohemian diaspora," a national network of local, place-based scenes that people in the eighties began to call "alternative culture." Together, these new bohemians reclaimed a kind of sixties optimism that young people and their music could change the world by replacing their older siblings' participatory politics with their own do-it-yourself local cultures.[9]

Yet Athens was not just a part of this trend of unlikely bohemias. It was one of the first and the most important model for what was happening in places like Louisville. By the end of 1980, Athens already had a new music infrastructure: two clubs—the 40 Watt Club and Tyrone's; a record label, DB, even if it was located in Atlanta; record stores like Wuxtry, where local acts could sell their recordings; and a college radio station, WUOG, which played local music and announced upcoming gigs. The first wave of Athens bohemians had also developed an understanding of how to create a band. If anyone had tried to write it down, that manual would have looked something like this:

> Step 1: Assemble a group of your friends, preferably including at least one art-school student, one woman and/or one gay or queer person, and multiple people with no musical experience.
> Step 2: Borrow some instruments and try to make interesting sounds together.
> Step 3: Draw on your amateurism to write your own original songs.

Step 4: Play a party at a friend's apartment in an old house.

Step 5: Open for other friends who have an established enough band to get a gig at a local club.

Step 6: Use your connection to a more established Athens band to get a gig in New York.

The other thing that Athens had that other new bohemias did not was R.E.M., the one local band then that did not follow this pattern. Instead, R.E.M. drew on the fluidity that had characterized the Athens scene from the start to build a new model. In making an alternative way of being a band, Buck, Stipe, Berry, and Mills reworked the relationship between amateurism and professionalism and autonomy and support. In their first few years as a band, they broke open the small network of friends that had originally created the Athens scene by drawing in wave after wave of new participants. Ironically, the least bohemian of the early Athens bands made more young people into bohemians than any other new-music group in town. And R.E.M. had this same effect on the road. Playing everywhere from small-town discos and pizza parlors to clubs in other unlikely cities and towns, they served as ambassadors for their own scene and for the entire emerging network of scenes in other unlikely places that would become alternative culture.[10]

Speed

If Athens was an unlikely bohemia, Buck, Stipe, Berry, and Mills were an unlikely band. Growing up in Macon, Berry and Mills were, in Berry's words, "arch-enemies in school . . . exact opposites. I was a rebel and he was a studious nerd. We hated each [other] on sight." In Athens, Buck did not think he had the talent. "I'd always loved music and worked in record stores," Buck told a journalist in 1983, "but I'd never formed a band, because I always thought you had to have some great gift to do it. . . . Michael talked me into it." Through the decades, band members have provided varying accounts of how the four of them met, but one detail remained constant. Buck and Stipe liked Berry. Mills, wasted during their first encounter, seemed like a jerk, and yet Berry insisted the two of them came as a set. Stipe remembered thinking, "No fucking way am I going to be in a band with those guys." Somehow they started playing music together anyway. As Mike Mills said on the MTV program *The Cutting Edge* in 1984, "All it took was a party."[11]

In the beginning, Buck, Stipe, Berry, and Mills were all college students. After graduating from high school in Roswell, just outside Atlanta, Peter

Buck went to Emory University, where some people remember he joined a fraternity. He also clerked at a record store on the edge of the campus. Buck remembered buying Patti Smith's record *Horses* the day it came out in December 1975 because he liked the poet and singer's "arty" look. Later, he had his hair cut like hers and started wearing "a Patti Smith jacket." "I don't think Georgia was ready," he recalled, "for men to dress like their favorite woman artist." About two years later, he took off in the middle of the term for California, where he was born and spent his early childhood, without withdrawing from his classes. Back in Atlanta months later with Fs on his transcript that prevented him from reenrolling at Emory, he worked as a record distributor. Tired of driving, he applied for a job at an Atlanta independent record store called Wuxtry, which also had two stores in Athens. Whether he asked to work in the college town or Wuxtry just sent him there, Buck remembered moving around New Year's Day 1978 because he had to drive back to Atlanta to see the Sex Pistols show January 5. Other Athens people recall meeting him when the B-52's played at Emory that February and that he helped Danny Beard arrange a performance space on campus. In Athens, Buck worked mostly at Wuxtry on Baxter, near the UGA dorms, although he occasionally worked at the downtown branch. He also enrolled in night courses at UGA.[12]

Like Buck, Michael Stipe did not move to Athens for college. Born in Georgia, he grew up near military bases in Germany, Texas, Alabama, and Illinois as his father served in the U.S. Army. At around fifteen, he signed up for a subscription to the *Village Voice* without really knowing what the paper was about. Inside its tabloid pages, in the grainy photographs and opinionated reviews of shows and recordings, he discovered punk. He, too, bought Patti Smith's album *Horses* in 1975 and stayed up all night listening to it. For Stipe, punk's "whole Zeitgeist was that anybody could do it. And I took it very literally." Stipe decided he wanted to be a rock star.[13]

Around the time Stipe graduated from high school in Collinsville, Illinois, his dad retired from the army and moved with his mom and two sisters to a small town outside of Athens. Stipe stayed behind in the St. Louis area to continue playing in a local punk band and attend the University of Illinois at Edwardsville. Sometime before the end of the year, Stipe quit college and that band and reluctantly followed his family to what he thought of then as a "this cowpoke, hippie town in rural Georgia." In early 1979, he enrolled at the university. In classes and in the Jackson Street building, he met art students like Mark Cline, Linda Hopper, Sandi Phipps, and Armistead Wellford and decided to major in art. Art Rosenbaum, an art professor and painter as well as folk-music collector and accomplished musician, taught Stipe in an intro art course. Rosenbaum tried to interest the young art major in southern folk art and music but "all he cared about was Warhol."[14]

Mark Cline remembered Stipe telling him when they first met that he wanted to be a singer in a famous band like Roger Daltrey. Around the same time, Stipe met Buck at Wuxtry. "I was buying all the records that he was saving for himself," the future R.E.M. member recalled. Buck was "funny, smart, curmudgeonly, and a little off putting, and we instantly bonded." When Buck moved into the church, Stipe started staying there instead of driving back to his parents' house outside of town. That fall, Stipe and Buck followed Pylon to New York City. Stipe recalled, "We spent a week living out of a van on the street in front of a club in the W[est] 60s called Hurrah." They saw Pylon and shows by other bands. At a party someone threw for the Athens group, they even met the rock critic Lester Bangs. It was Stipe's first trip to the city, and "everything was so romantic and sexy."[15]

Mike Mills and Bill Berry followed the more common route when they moved to Athens in early 1979 to go to the university. Neither was from Georgia — Mills was born in Orange County, California, and Berry in Minnesota — but they both ended up in Macon. They stopped hating each other and became friends as they performed together in the high school band and a "lounge trio" organized by their band teacher to do paying gigs. As Berry later recalled, "We'd dress up in suits and ties and play country clubs, weddings and the like. Hell, that was good money, too. I was 17 years old and making 60 bucks a night. That's when I became addicted to playing." Berry and Mills also helped form a local group called Shadowfax and then the Back Door Band that performed some originals along with covers at parties and at Moe's, an all-ages place.[16]

While still in high school, Berry got a dream job driving rock stars to and from the Atlanta airport and running errands for the Paragon Booking Agency, a management company affiliated with Macon's Capricorn Records. After graduation, Berry and Mills rented an apartment near Paragon's office, where Berry continued to work, and Mills got a job at Sears. When Paragon hired Ian Copeland to diversify the agency's southern rock–heavy roster, Copeland turned Berry and Mills onto punk and new-wave music, including the Police, his brother Stewart Copeland's band, and the Ramones. As their high school friend Diana Crowe, who later married Pylon's Curtis Crowe, remembered, Mills and Berry continued to play music: "They would practice in a little space behind the Paragon.... It might even have been a garage." Copeland sometimes jammed with them there.[17]

After a year or so, Mills's dad asked his son, who had been a good student in high school, what he actually planned to do with his life. The two friends decided they had to get out of Macon, and they applied to UGA. Inspired by Copeland and Paragon, Berry had decided to study law and become a music industry lawyer or manager. Mills thought he might become a journalist. Like Stipe, they started in the middle of the 1978–79 academic year.[18]

By the fall of 1979, as Buck and O'Brien moved into the church, new-music nights at Tyrone's were drawing punk fans, art students, WUOG DJs, and what was left of a group of friends that had coalesced around the B-52's. On Halloween, after the Method Actors debuted and Pylon played, the hip, costumed crowd stumbled down the hill to a party in the old sanctuary space behind the apartment that lasted into the morning. It may have been the night, after missing the show at Tyrone's because of a competing gig, that Stipe decided to quit singing for local cover band Gangster. And it may have been the early morning in which he met his future friend and mentor Jeremy Ayers and his future friend and lover Carol Levy. A few months after that party, around January, Buck, Stipe, Berry, and Mills finally got together to jam at the church, and the session went well enough that the four guys started practicing regularly, rehearsing covers and then writing their own songs. Kathleen O'Brien and other friends began crawling into the sanctuary space to listen, dance, and drink as the guys practiced. Not yet officially a band, the four guys already had fans.[19]

Right away, after they played O'Brien's birthday party, the talk started. Locals noticed that the group did not quite fit the pattern established by earlier Athens new music groups. Passionate enthusiasm mixed with critique. "There was something in the air that night," but Mike Green, a former member of pioneering Atlanta punk band the Fans who had moved to Athens, did not like R.E.M. He "was much more impressed with the Side Effects." R.E.M. was "50 percent covers but they sounded like a garage band and everything they played sounded like a cover." According to Green, "they were the 'digestible-by-frat-boys' version of the Athens sound." Curtis Crowe, the drummer for Pylon, was there too, and he also remembers a lot of covers. "At the time, the whole art school party crowd had this thing about cover songs. We were on the 'leading edge of a musical revolution' and we thought playing cover songs was taking two steps back and everyone kind of put their nose in the air about it." Playing another band's music seemed as unoriginal as copying another artist's painting. How could real bohemians play in a cover band? Yet Crowe also remembered being so impressed that he wrote a review of the show and got his friend Green to type it. "It just felt like something had happened. It needed to be documented." The music "had a lot of energy about it."[20]

Because the guy who booked Tyrone's liked the group at the church party, he arranged for the newly named R.E.M. to open for Atlanta band the Brains. In the spring of 1980, the Brains had an underground hit single, "Money Changes Everything" and a new album on Mercury. Supporting them at the major Athens venue for the new music was a big gig. To practice, R.E.M. played a show at the 11:11 Kaffee Klub, a late-night venue on Hull Street where patrons put their name on their coffee cups and left them in a cabinet. A local hippie entrepreneur, "Rick the Printer" Hawkins, owned both the Kaffee Klub and the Print Shop, a combination bike and car repair garage, printing facility, and hangout next door to the church. The police shut down R.E.M.'s short set at the unlicensed venue, but UGA law student Bertis Downs, who knew Berry from the university's student-run Contemporary Concerts Committee and Buck from Wuxtry, heard enough to become a fan and later the band's lawyer and manager.[21]

The Brains should have found a supportive audience in a nearby college town full of Atlanta kids. Yet former art student Sean Bourne, who had moved to Atlanta after graduation and worked at Danny Beard's record store as well as for the Brains, was worried when he heard R.E.M. was opening. "I knew from being in the klatch in Athens," Bourne recalled, "that there was this weird Athens/Atlanta rivalry thing that Athens had." About a year earlier, the WUOGerz, "a group of campus radio station amateur musicians" including Bill Berry on drums, had opened for the Brains in the Memorial Hall Ballroom, and a *Red and Black* reporter claimed the amateurs "upstaged" the headlining band. Now the Brains were back, paired with another amateur band with Berry again on drums. It did not help that the Brains had sound problems, a murky, sludgy mix that made it impossible to understand the lyrics. In contrast, R.E.M. sounded like "James Brown fronting the Dave Clark Five," a reporter for the *Red and Black* wrote in a fawning review, the band's first press coverage. "R.E.M.'s original material was even more amazing than their excellent cover choices. They switched tracks from funky R and B to pulsing reggae with an ease and speed that belied their short history." About R.E.M.'s encore, the Monkees' "(I'm Not Your) Steppin' Stone," the reporter simply gushed, "Enough said." The night "really belonged to R.E.M. . . . The Brains may have two years of clubbing and a record contract under their belts, but R.E.M. won the hearts and feet of the crowd at Tyrone's." R.E.M. even got paid. It was hard to imagine a better start.[22]

While earlier Athens bands like the B-52's and Pylon had taken breaks after their first few gigs to work on new songs and polish their acts, R.E.M. just kept playing, headlining Tyrone's on May 13 for a "standing room audience" and then opening for the Brains again at the Memorial Hall Ballroom. It was hard not to feel bad for the Atlanta band as yet another *Red and Black* review announced "the score" for the two concerts in two weeks as "R.E.M. 2, Brains 0." "Buck's guitar style" blended "surf music, the British Invasion, and power pop," the student reporter raved, and yet still sounded "unique." Stipe's vocals seemed "learned from Buddy Holly's hiccups." "Call it a miracle, but the band, on their fourth appearance after being together only two months, took Memorial by storm, turning in their finest performance to date. Right now, the group is the best in Athens, and they just keep getting better."[23]

However difficult it might be for fans of R.E.M.'s early albums to imagine Stipe singing like either James Brown or Buddy Holly or hear the band's sound as a combination of "raunch" and "punch," these student journalists were not bad critics. Instead, they were learning to write by describing four young musicians learning to perform as a band. The sixties garage-rock bands early R.E.M. sometimes covered and often sounded like featured young musicians who learned to play early rock and roll in their parents' basements or garages by playing along to records. The R.E.M. guys were copying amateurs who were copying the rock stars of an earlier era. In this music, attitude, intensity, and speed mattered more than craft.[24]

Like other punk rock fans, the members of R.E.M. discovered this and other sixties music like the Velvet Underground by following musicians like Patti Smith, Lou Reed, the Sex Pistols, and the Ramones back to their respective influences, to earlier bands these seventies artists played in, covered, or praised. Buck, especially, read rock critics including Robert Christgau and Lester Bangs regularly and may well have encountered Greil Marcus's 1979 collection *Stranded: Rock and Roll for A Desert Island*, with Ellen Willis's piece on the Velvet Underground and Tom Carson's piece on the Ramones. Buck was also a collector in a period in which old records were about the only way to listen to the popular music of earlier eras. Lenny Kaye, Patti Smith's guitarist, called garage rock "punk" in the liner notes for the influential 1972 *Nuggets* collection, an anthology of reissues of this music that he edited and that Buck probably owned. Buck used "punk" this way when he described his band's early efforts to find a unique niche in Athens: "Nobody sounded like a punk band. There were the B-52s, who made their own rules. Pylon was a weird, angular dance band. The Method Actors were a two-piece psycho-funk band. And then there was us."[25]

A surviving recording of a 40 Watt show less than two months after O'Brien's party preserves R.E.M.'s sound that first year, playing original compositions and covers later dropped in favor of newer material. Berry pounds the drums and frequently hits the cymbals, setting a manic tempo. Mills's bouncing bass supports the rhythm and fills in the otherwise sparse texture. Buck's guitar phrases switch back and forth between power chords and high and feathery fills. At times, Buck sounds as if he is playing speeded-up versions of guitar parts ripped from the Patti Smith Group. Stipe pops and chants his lyrics as much as he sings them. On the bridge of the band's cover of "Route 66," he channels Elvis Presley. On an adaption of a Velvet Underground and later Lou Reed song, "Lisa Says," he emphasizes each word in his last phrase, turning "That's what Lisa says" into a cheer. On many songs, Mills struggles to sing sometimes charmingly awkward backing vocals. The band even plays a reggae-like original, "I've Got a Charm." On all the songs, the fast tempo mostly holds the ragged parts together and produces a danceable sound. Background noises audible on the recording suggest the audience is having as much fun as the band. Years later, Stipe confessed the source of band members' frenetic energy: they were all taking speed.[26]

People who saw R.E.M. then remembered Stipe employing a low and throaty catch in his voice and other stylings that reminded them of Elvis Presley. Stipe probably got some of his mid-fifties sound from the Cramps' singer Lux Interior, who in turn modeled his approach on old rockabilly stars like the young Elvis. The Cramps had been scheduled to play the Georgia Theater on December 1, 1979, with former Big Star leader Alex Chilton and Pylon opening. During Pylon's set, the manager of the theater told the Cramps he was closing down the show because of the poor turnout. Chris Rasmussen, co-owner of Chapter Three, and other audience members quickly organized an alternative venue. They borrowed some mics and Vic Varney's PA and bought some beer. Soon the show was back on in the room above the record store. Chilton, tripping on acid, marched around in a dog collar. Lux got naked. Locally, the canceled and resurrected show became legendary. If Stipe did not see the Cramps play in Athens in late 1979, he certainly heard about the show, and he later cited the band, originally from California, as a major influence. On surviving recordings of R.E.M. made in 1980, Stipe sounds like Lux Interior as he switches a rockabilly style southern-accent off and on like an effect.[27]

Not just in Athens, but across the punk-influenced underground popping up all over the bohemian diaspora, new-music bands proudly displayed their musical amateurism. Here, too, R.E.M. did not quite fit the mold established by earlier Athens groups the B-52's, Pylon, and the Method Actors. To an experienced musician like John Keane, who later recorded many R.E.M. demos and side projects as well as other local bands at his Athens studio, the four guys lacked technique: "I used to go see R.E.M. at Tyrone's . . . for a dollar cover. Back then, they were really raw. I didn't really like them much because I was a musician at the time and had been playing in several bands and was more into seeing musicians who were accomplished." DB Records had already put out recordings by the B-52's, Pylon, and the Method Actors when Danny Beard caught the band that first summer in Atlanta: "The only thing I liked was Michael's voice, but the songs weren't that good. Pete couldn't play very well."[28]

But some Athens bohemians believed R.E.M. suffered from the opposite problem, members with too much musicianship who produced a predictable sound. Mills and Berry had enough experience that they actually functioned as a rhythm section. According to Mark Cline, an art student and member of Love Tractor, "we were the little art fags" and R.E.M. was "really rock 'n' roll." As an early scene participant recalled, "it became trendy to be bitchy about R.E.M." In his piece for the March 1981 *New York Rocker* with the Pylon cover story, Vic Varney included subtle digs at "the most conservative" of the new Athens bands and described their music as "American Fast." "They do a lot of mid-sixties sounding stuff, kind of rockabilly, 3½ minute, bam-bam-bam, hook line and sinker, 30 songs, three-fourths original. That's why the people who love them so much do and the few who don't don't." In August 1981, Lachowski told a reporter for an Atlanta paper, "They built up a huge following of college students and brought new wave weekends to Tyrone's by packing 'em in. They are by far the biggest local draw. They bridge the gap between the more experimental stuff and the college crowd." Varney, too, talked to this reporter: "They're the only band in this milieu that also appeals to people outside it. . . . They're a pop band."[29]

Even visitors noticed the tensions. Anthony DeCurtis, then an Atlanta-based freelance writer on his way to becoming a music journalist, drove to Athens in early June 1981 to research a story about the town that *Rolling Stone* ultimately killed. Pylon's Michael Lachowski served as his host, introducing him to scene participants and taking him to the must-see local shows. In a spirit of "fairness," Lachowski took the writer to see R.E.M.'s first set at Tyrone's, before they went to the 40 Watt to see a "serious" Atlanta band called Vietnam. Just about everyone DeCurtis met in town dismissed R.E.M. as a "pop band" rather than an "art band." The journalist remembered being "afraid to make my enthusiasm too obvious for fear of embarrassing myself." Later, he saw R.E.M. play often at 688, an Atlanta new-music club, and found the shows there "spellbinding": "I thought the fucking place was going to levitate." Jim Fouratt, a New York City music promoter and an early supporter of the B-52's and Pylon, remembered traveling to Athens late that same summer with his boyfriend as well as the music critic Tom Carson and his wife. Their unnamed Athens hosts took them to Atlanta to see Stipe's sister Lynda's band open for R.E.M. at 688 and were ready to leave as soon as Oh-OK finished their set. Fouratt decided to stay and loved the headliners. Back in Athens, the club owner's hosts made it clear that he "was not hip."[30]

In a small-town scene, this mix of critique and jealousy had to hurt. In response, the R.E.M. guys played down their ambitions. Asked by a student journalist in 1981 what R.E.M., "Athens' most popular band," had to offer, Stipe answered, "Unadulterated fun. . . . I put tape on the bottom of my shoes to make sure I don't fall down (from dancing)." Buck told the same reporter: "We're serious about what we do, but we're doing it for fun. This really isn't a big career for us." Band members also exaggerated their lack of experience. As Stipe told a journalist in 1983, "Peter had never played before. I had a band in St. Louis, just a bad punk band, Bad Habits. We played like twice in public. . . . Mike and Bill had both played in country club trios and marching bands, stuff like that, playing Glenn Miller's greatest hits or something. . . . We were all rank amateurs, and still are to this day."[31]

Buck, Stipe, Berry, and Mills also broke with other early Athens bands by hiding a surprisingly serious work ethic beneath their stories of amateurism and fun. "They decided very early on before they even started making money that it was going to be a business, and they were going to treat it like a business," Kathleen O'Brien, Berry's girlfriend and roommate in the early days of the band, remembered. Berry left school first, flunking out around the time the band debuted. For him, drumming for R.E.M. "was a sink-or-swim situation. If he didn't make it, then what was he going to do?" Before Jefferson Holt became R.E.M.'s roadie and then manager in the spring of 1981, Berry booked and ran the band, assisted by O'Brien. As Cline remembered, he "was really tough" on Mills, Buck, and Stipe. He wanted them to quit college to focus on music. Berry also encouraged them to think seriously about how the band should function. According to DeCurtis, "they all worked their asses off." Buck, in particular, "ate, slept, and breathed R.E.M. twenty-four hours a day." To avoid fights that broke up other groups, Buck, Stipe, Mills, and Berry decided to split songwriting credits equally. They also made decisions by consensus, through long, hard discussions that in their own later descriptions sounded like the opposite of fun.[32]

In Macon, Berry had learned a lot about music as a business from Ian Copeland, his boss at Paragon. Major labels had developed a model of spending enormous sums promoting bands through magazine and record store advertising, radio, and expensive tours. In contrast, Ian and his other brother, Miles, founder of the record company I.R.S., had pioneered an alternative strategy of breaking British acts like the Police in the United States by creating inexpensive tours so bands could travel without record-company support. Berry and later Jefferson Holt followed this model in booking R.E.M. anywhere that might draw a paying audience. From the start, rather than house parties, R.E.M. played places where they at least had a chance of being paid like the Mad Hatter, the kind of venue that was the opposite of in-crowd clubhouse the 40 Watt. Berry remembered after one of their early shows, "standing under the stage and counting the money" — $343 dollars — "which seemed like a fortune." R.E.M. members then used the money they made in Athens to subsidize their touring. That first year and a half, the band played an astonishing range of out-of-town venues, from an Augusta, Georgia, disco named New York, New York to Phrank 'n' Steins, a basement beer and hot dog stand in Nashville that booked punk bands for a $100 guarantee, to Fridays, a Greensboro, North Carolina, pizza parlor whose manager charged a $1 cover and gave bands the door.[33]

All this touring through other unlikely towns and cities not only made R.E.M. a tighter, better band; it also gave curious residents alienated from southern rock and the pop charts a rare chance to see a live alternative. In some of these places, knots of music fans began to think they, too, might make their own music and create their own scenes.

Berry also actively worked his connection to Ian Copeland, who by then was running his own New York–based management and promotion company, Frontier Booking International or F.B.I., which specialized in representing post punk and new wave bands. When Gang of Four, represented by F.B.I., headlined two dates at Atlanta's 688 in the summer of 1980, R.E.M. got the opening slots. In December, Copeland gave his friend a huge break, booking R.E.M. to open for the Police at Atlanta's 4,000-seat Fox Theater. Throughout 1981, R.E.M. continued to open for F.B.I. bands, including Wishbone Ash, Bow Wow Wow, Oingo Boingo, and Siouxsie and the Banshees. Buck seemed to forget this history in 1983 when R.E.M. turned down the chance to support U2 and the Go-Go's, and he told *Rolling Stone* that "opening for other bands is just the rankest sort of masochism." Yet here, too, the members of R.E.M. had learned from Copeland, who always said that playing for a band's own audience, even if it was small, was better than perform-ing for another band's fans.[34]

Back home, Berry tried for a while to establish the Athens Agency to book other local bands in the same kind of places that R.E.M. played, but he found Athens musicians were not that interested. "We were quite an anomaly in that we were in a bar band that could play pizza parlors and pool halls," Buck remembered, "and we did that for about a year and a half. We kind of established a circuit of places where no one else would have played." A Kerouac fan, Buck talked about the early days as an *On the Road*–style ad-venture, four broke guys driving their battered '75 Dodge Tradesman from dive to dive, sleeping on fans' floors and sharing a communal stash of clothes and cassettes. "We'd play, go to a party, drink, steal food from the fridge," Buck remembered, "and then at four in the morning go, 'Ok, time to go to the next town.'" Once there, they would park the van behind the club and sleep until five in the afternoon, get up, sound check, and then wait to play again.[35]

New-music bands in this period actually had good reasons to avoid play-ing venues in out-of-the-way places. In the late seventies and early eighties, rednecks and frat boys everywhere threatened to beat up "faggots," any man at all different. Much of the deep South remained culturally as well as politi-cally conservative, especially outside a handful of bigger cities. Racial ten-sions remained high, and in some places, including Athens, working-class African American men occasionally threatened bohemian white and black men as well. Atlanta—at least in some close-in commercial areas and his-toric neighborhoods, functioned as something of an oasis. A large hippie counterculture flourished in the late sixties and seventies along a section of Peachtree near 10th Street and in nearby Piedmont Park. By the early eighties, parts of midtown nurtured an increasingly out gay scene. Yet even in Atlanta, people had to be careful. New-music bands and their fans were easy targets, even when they seemed straight, and the B-52's, Pylon, and Love Tractor, formed in the summer of 1980, all had members who did not. Even in Athens, bohemians faced this problem. Scene participants remem-bered Michael Stipe being called a faggot and having beer cans thrown at him while walking down Baxter Street.[36]

"It was pretty adventurous leaving Athens in a van and touring at that time because the first major stop out of Athens going north was Washington, D.C., and that was kind of like the frontier," Curtis Crowe, Pylon's drum-mer, remembered. "From there the next stop was New York City. It wasn't an uncommon thing to jump in a van and head to New York City where you could actually play a venue where they wouldn't throw beer bottles at you." "The difference between Pylon and R.E.M.," Crowe argued, was "that we were completely unwilling to explore any of these places in between." Yet R.E.M.'s endless road trip enabled band members to hone their chops and practice their songs outside the view of their inside-the-scene critics. It also broadened their fan base and gave them a sense of how their sound might fit within the broader landscape of underground music.[37]

At home, R.E.M.'s critics were not wrong about the new band's appeal beyond the small, close-knit network of bohemians that had nurtured the B-52's and Pylon. At their gigs, record buyers who knew Buck from Wuxtry and Stipe's art-school classmates mixed with UGA students Berry and Mills met in classes and the dorms or students who Berry knew from WUOG or the University Union. As Woody Nuss, who sometimes worked sound for local bands, remembered, by the time R.E.M. had played at Tyrone's two or three times, "it was *the* thing. At the end of every two months or so, R.E.M. would have both weekend nights, and it would sell out. It was a $3.00 cover, and they were making $2,000. Nobody was making that much." "Those shows were amazing," Nuss recalled. "People would dance unbelievably. . . . Then there was the stuck-up neo-bohemian factor standing toward the back," not wanting to miss anything but not entirely willing to join in the fun.[38]

The more inclusive atmosphere at Tyrone's O.C. operated in contrast to the 40 Watt, which functioned then as a kind of bohemian clubhouse. When local eccentric and record collector Ort worked the door at the 40 Watt's first official location, he kept fraternity guys and "anyone who looked like they had money" out. Many bohemians, raised in middle-class homes, looked poor by choice. Still, what people wore served as a declaration of where they belonged. Ort's actions and the generally exclusive atmosphere of the tiny club policed the boundaries of the scene. R.E.M.'s shows at Tyrone's had the opposite effect. They opened up the underground to all kinds of UGA students not connected to the art school, including Greeks, scholarship kids, and even law students.[39]

As a *Red and Black* reporter described R.E.M.'s live act around this time, the band's "dense, powerful and utterly kinetic" sound produced a singular effect, "moving people onto the dance floor." Stipe would step "away from the mic between verses to urge on the crowd with a jerky, rag-doll brand of dancing that's a wonder to watch." Chuck Reece, who moved to Athens from the small, north Georgia town of Ellijay in the fall of 1979 to go to UGA, remembered seeing Pylon and the Method Actors perform his first year there.

Their music was "the weirdest shit I ever heard." Then he caught R.E.M.'s first show at Tyrone's, opening for the Brains, and fell hard for the band. Dancing like a wild man as R.E.M. played covers like "Route 66" and "Does Your Mother Know," "I began to feel like I was a part of the scene." Julie House, who moved to Athens in the fall of 1980 to go to the university, recalls that dancing and "singing along with whatever we thought Michael was singing" made the audience at R.E.M.'s early shows feel "like family." Dancing gave people a way to be a part of the performance, and this participation in turn helped build a sense of community.[40]

As Stipe began to do odd things like climbing up in the rafters or lying down on the dance floor while singing, he pulled the Tyrone's crowd along with him. Before one show, Stipe put dry red henna powder in his hair. As he sang, scene participant April Chapman remembered, he shook his head with such force that henna flew everywhere. The powder mixed with the perspiration of the dancers. By the end of the show, people near the front looked like they were sweating blood. The members of R.E.M. pulled their fans into the scene and broadened what it meant to be a bohemian.[41]

All the Right Friends

When I moved to Athens in 1982 to attend the University of Georgia on an academic scholarship, among the possessions I hauled up to the sixth floor of Brumby Hall were a sailor dress picked out by my mother and a poster of a chimp playing tennis. Before school even started, I put on an add-a-bead necklace, washed my bad perm, and went out for sorority rush. Supported by my father's job as an airline pilot, my family had survived the oil shortages, rising inflation, and airline deregulation of the 1970s with some stringent budget-cutting. Other middle-class families in Jonesboro, a modest, conservative town rapidly becoming a south-side Atlanta suburb, had not been so lucky. When a recession began during my junior year of high school, young people with degrees started moving back in with their parents. At UGA, I signed up for the business school because I wanted to graduate with a job.

Like a lot of students not connected to the art school, I discovered the Athens scene over the years by hanging out downtown. Athens scene-makers used their thrift-store clothes to mark their difference in public spaces like the graffiti artists marking the hip-hop scene onto New York's boroughs by tagging trains. The El Dorado, where Fred Schneider waited tables, had turned into the Bluebird by then, but the breakfast-and-lunch place kept its most popular dishes, its mixed hippie and bohemian staff, and its location in the once-elegant Morton building that had previously housed a black vaude-ville theater. Bohemians still sat outside drinking espressos where everyone could see them, but by then new sidewalk cafés at places like True Confec-tions and Rocky's Pizzeria had replaced old haunts like the Kaffee Klub. The city had made College Avenue near Broad one-way by the time I came to town, lining a block with trees, raised beds, and benches. This Georgia ver-sion of a promenade made a perfect place to sit and watch as local musicians walked around the corner from Kinko's to staple band flyers to the kiosks. Chapter Three had closed, but Wuxtry and Ruthless Records continued to function as clubhouses where record clerks and shoppers, guys especially but also a few women, listened to records and argued about music.

I also heard the scene on the radio. If you were not yet a "townie," a term people increasingly used to describe scene participants, shifting the dial to the left to the campus station WUOG 90.5 FM with its clear, strong sig-nal felt like eavesdropping on another world. Student deejays interviewed members of local bands, played local music in regular rotation as well as on a show called *Sound of the City*, and gave away tickets to local shows. At a time when clubs barely advertised and you had to know someone to find out about parties where bands played, WUOG, with its local music programing, was right there on your radio, accessible and free. Before I saw them live or bought their records, I heard Pylon, R.E.M., and Love Tractor on WUOG.

Soon I was dragging my friends to R.E.M.'s free concerts at the univer-sity's Legion Field, an annual tradition between 1982 and 1985. I learned how to pick through racks and piles at thrift stores for treasures like a Peter Pan collared shirt in an overall pepper mill pattern that I still wear today. At night, I went to the 40 Watt and a newer club called the Uptown Lounge to see local bands, dancing madly until I was so happy and dizzy I could hardly stand. Mike Webb, a clerk at Ruthless Records, taught me punk and post-punk music history and took me to see out-of-town bands like the Minute-men, Black Flag, the Replacements, Fetchin Bones, and the Fleshtones with his permanent spot plus one on local guest lists. At shows, at Ruthless and Wuxtry, on the streets downtown, and at art openings at the Lyndon House and the Tate Student Center Art Gallery, I met other people trying to learn to play their instruments, forming bands, and making art. It took a lot of work to transform our suburban and small-town selves into bohemians, but the reward was an expansive sense of agency and possibility that made the world seem bigger than our parents' anxious dreams.[42]

The adults in our lives worried about our futures because they under-stood that even with a college degree, finding a secure, middle-class job was becoming much harder in the late seventies and early eighties. Beginning in 1972, one economic shock followed another as the United States weathered an oil crisis, a deep decline in the stock market, the arrival of something economists had not thought possible — high unemployment and high inflation — another oil crisis, and extremely high interest rates. Then in 1981, the Reagan recession hit. The U.S. economy's poor performance — its worst extended period since the Great Depression — scared our parents. Some young people reacted by pursing a pragmatic major like business or a pre-med or pre-law track. Others did the opposite. If there were not any good jobs, why not pursue your passions and have fun with your friends? A few like me split the difference — choosing the practical major before deciding that a career as an accountant sounded like a death sentence in slow motion. Joining the scene felt like freedom, like escape from the cages of middle-class and southern expectations. It felt like a way to achieve a more meaningful life.

No one was born a bohemian, not me, not locally famous people like Vanessa Briscoe Hay, and not even Michael Stipe. A passionate R.E.M. fan then, I would have been shocked to find television news footage of a teenage Stipe in drag at a screening of *The Rocky Horror Picture Show* in St. Louis. Pushing into the angle of the camera and speaking in an accent I do not recognize but in a deadpan delivery that I do, he tells the reporter, "It's an excellent movie, it really is, and we're all quite normal, really." Even then he is the front man, dressed as Doctor Frank-N-Furter, a transvestite mad scientist played by Tim Curry in the film. But this is a glammier image, a glitzier and more obvious drag, than Stipe ever worked around Athens. He wears pearls, a royal-blue skirt, and a black corset under an unbuttoned jacket with Blue Oyster Cult's question mark–cross symbol pinned to his lapel. Shimmering blue eye shadow sweeps from his lids up to his bushy eyebrows. Dark eyeliner and mascara ring his eyes. Red, painted lips make his familiar, widget-shaped pout.[43]

Like Curry's role in the movie, Stipe's performance is an obvious impersonation, an act that celebrates that it is an act as it puts how we understand manhood and womanhood on display. "Normal" is easy, Stipe suggests, telling the television journalist that he and his friends could just show up at the theater instead in rock radio station KSHE 95 pig t-shirts and jeans. Even then, he knows the telling detail. He is bold and sassy and not at all afraid to be on TV, not the Michael I knew enough to speak to in the 1980s, but a younger and much more extroverted version and just as beautiful. He seems to have been charismatic long before he met Jerry Ayers, but he is not yet a bohemian.[44]

New York photographer Laura Levine made this production still when she visited Athens and made a never-released film called *Just Like a Movie* **with scene participants.** *Seated left to right:* **Cyndy Stipe, Lynda Stipe, Laura Levine, and Michael Stipe.** *Standing left to right:* **Matthew Sweet, Linda Hopper, Bill Berry, and Chris Slay. (Photograph © Laura Levine)**

For most people, the transformation was an alternately awkward and exhilarating process made up of mostly small acts of self-invention. Participants threw away their tie-dyed tees and sundresses, boat shoes and Birkenstocks, and adopted new styles. Some women paired cotton house dresses, long-john pants worn as leggings, and work boots with men's suit jackets. Others went for fitted sixties mini-dresses, paisley anything, or oversized men's shirts. Some guys stuck with jeans and T-shirts, but others wore flapping, French-cuffed shirts with wool pants held up by suspenders. People of both sexes cut and pegged wide-legged pants and turned silk pajama tops and dressing jackets into clothes. Some men and women adopted a style Julie House called "southern gothic" and wore oversized old clothes that hung off their bodies like Spanish moss drooping from the limbs of live oaks. Young androgynous men and women copied Jerry Ayers, who went through a phase of wearing a top hat and tails. As scene participant Velena Vego put it, "The way we dressed was like Halloween every day."[45]

People in Athens were just beginning to use the term "vintage," but these old dresses were so hip guys often wore them too. Drag-themed parties gave guys an easy excuse, and surviving photographs and videos showed Mike Green of the Fans, David Gamble of the Method Actors, Mark Cline of Love Tractor, and Mike Mills and Bill Berry of R.E.M. wearing dresses. Buck claimed that most guys in the scene had at some point worn a dress to a party. "Younger and thinner then," he confessed, "I used to wear my girlfriends' clothes too." Male musicians, including Pete Buck and Michael Stipe, sometimes performed in dresses. At R.E.M. shows, Mike Mills some-times sang a line, "I've got dresses in my closet," a lyric that did not make it into the 1984 recording of the song "Second Guessing."[46]

Used clothing was easy to acquire and cheap. When people moved or their relatives died, they donated old items to thrift stores. In the eighties, you could still find clothes from the forties, and items from the fifties and the sixties were common. At the Potter's House, a quarter and then a dollar and then two dollars bought a brown paper grocery sack stuffed full of items picked out of the infamous pile. Once, someone shopping and smoking at the same time set fire to the giant heap of clothes. People also shopped the regular racks there and at the Salvation Army, as well as yard sales. At the UGA library, bound copies of old issues of fashion magazines provided inspi-ration. Scene people also loved the colorful sketches of twenties and thirties costumes in the 1985 show *Paris: Women in the Follies* at the Georgia Museum of Art.[47]

Locally, used and visibly out-of-style clothing functioned as a badge of bohemianism, a way for people to communicate their alternative iden-tity to others. But wearing secondhand clothing also helped small-town and middle-class suburban kids like me remake ourselves as bohemians. Like childhood dress-up games, school theatricals, and Halloween parties, try-ing on odd garments and putting them together to create different styles enabled you to play with alternate identities. Clothing framed the edge of the self, for the wearer as much as for people you encountered in town, at work, or in class. Qualities like the texture, feel, color, and shape of a garment and the way it enabled or constricted movement, exaggerated or veiled gen-der and sexuality, and conveyed casualness or formality could make you feel bold, brave, and different, ready to try something new.[48]

Beyond the costumes, ephemeral and surprising activities and events popped up and then were gone as if carried along on an underground cur-rent of creativity that sometimes broke through the landscape of ordinary life. In an early example, Jerry Ayers, Kate Pierson, Cindy and Ricky Wil-son, Keith Strickland, and other friends painted their faces white, put on

Victorian-style costumes they made out of used clothes, and to the confusion of everyone else involved, crashed an Athens neighborhood's Mardi Gras parade. Pierson and her friends set up a "living room" with sofas, chairs, lamps, and rugs at the busy intersection of College and Broad and then sat there and watched the traffic. Jerry Ayers sometimes "borrowed" a formal garden on the UGA campus and threw late-night dinner parties complete with candles and china for his friends. After someone checked out a tape of African tribal music from the UGA library, Ricky Wilson played it on his tape recorder in a field. While Wilson, Pierson, and their friends danced, a circle of curious cows bobbed their heads to the beat. Pierson repeated the often-used line to a reporter, "We had to make our own fun."[49]

For a while, as April Chapman remembered, local bohemians developed a passion for clubs. The U-Haul club started because people moved all the time, and after hauling someone's belongings, they would turn the moving truck into a mobile dance party. The sofa club began after a group dragged old couches, left on the curb by students at the end of the term, to an empty lot on Hawthorne Street and arranged them in a circle. Late at night, after the bars closed, they would go to "the club" to build a fire, watch the stars, and tell stories. A new wave of young people moving into the scene in the early eighties encountered these kinds of happenings or heard older scene participants talk about them.[50]

Athens's historic downtown, nearby neighborhoods, and rural outskirts provided the perfect setting for these activities. Despite the growth of suburban shopping centers like Beechwood and the Georgia Square Mall, Athens's working city center, with its old-fashioned restaurants and shops, postwar facades on prewar storefronts, and empty buildings, offered an eclectic mix of architectural styles, businesses, and people well into the 1980s. To kids who moved there from the suburbs and for out-of-town visitors from places like New York, downtown Athens seemed like another time, the past somehow magically surviving into the present. Residents who were not students still came downtown to work, shop, and eat. Women bought wigs at Lees. Salesmen in awkward suits sold furniture and restaurant equipment in high-ceilinged, wooden-floored showrooms. Waitresses with teased hair and cat-eye glasses served grits and eggs at Helen's. Greasy mechanics fixed cars at Snow Tire. In the daytime, men in overalls strolled over from Farmer's Hardware to buy cigs and girlie magazines at Barnett's Newsstand. At night, just outside the same store, male hustlers in tight white jeans with giant combs in their back pockets solicited customers.[51]

As art student Lauren Fancher remembered, a deep love for "the old" shaped the scene, and participants "could take these authentic pieces of old Athens and play with them." Bohemians purchased supplies for their art projects at the hardware store, with its metal bins full of nails and screws, and the stationery shop, where a dark grid of wood shelves displayed old paper stock in every texture and hue. They bought guitar strings and music magazines at Bowden's Music Shop and ate meat-and-threes at the Mayflower. They shopped at Allen's, a men's store owned by an elderly couple where unused shoes and shirts from the 1940s were still for sale on the dusty back shelves. Scene participants transformed previously abandoned upper floors in buildings with ground floor businesses into studios, practice spaces, and "secret coffee shops and clubs" without signs, like the Kaffee Klub and the original 40 Watt. Downtown felt like their playground.[52]

On campus beyond the art school, the dorms sometimes nurtured knots of friends and acquaintances who made their way into the scene. In the late seventies and early eighties, attendance soared at public colleges and universities as young people reacted to economic stagnation and recession by seeking degrees in record numbers. At UGA, new students lived in a crowded mix of new and old facilities with few regulations and often minimal supervision by RAs. For a few years, arty and nerdy kids collected in UGA's Experimental Learning Community in the Mell and Lipscomb dorms, near Legion Field at the bottom of Baxter Street. Art students and Mell-Lipscomb residents Margaret Katz, Debbie McMahon, Keith Bennett, and Neil McArthur entertained themselves by wandering through town, drawing with smashed together bits of old chalk pastels and Conte crayons that formed a grayish color they called grunt. Katz hung a machete on her wall and lounged under it wearing a muumuu and reading Beckett, turning her dorm room into a kind of salon. John Seawright prepared for his future as a writer and the scene's resident intellectual by reading piles of books not assigned by his professors. A guy who was not enrolled at UGA squatted in a fourth-floor study hall, keeping his clothes and records in the corner and sleeping on a sofa.[53]

When Bill Berry moved into Reed Hall in the middle of the 1978–79 academic year, he met a group of residents who would become key figures in the next wave of the scene. Sandi Phipps, future photographer and R.E.M. office manager, and Linda Hopper, future member of Oh-OK, had been friends since high school. Mark Cline and Carol Levy, an art student who would play in a band called Boat Of, became close collaging the dorm's walls with images cut out of porn magazines. Kathleen O'Brien, who would throw that party at the church, started growing pot on her bottom bunk after her roommate moved out. Sometimes, Cline entertained them all by picking out songs like "Rock Lobster" on his guitar, and a group of these Reed Hall friends went together to see the B-52's' Memorial Hall show. Often, they danced, not the usual white kid, prom-date lurch, but a wild bumping and thrashing to an eclectic mix of songs by the Monkees, the Archies, the Beatles, and James Brown. Because Cline had an older brother, Peter, he heard about things happening downtown. At Pylon's show above Chapter Three Records, Cline and the rest of the Reed Hall group met the older art crowd.[54]

While the dorms might work as a start, if you really wanted to be a bohemian, you had to live in an old house. For an inexpensive living space with features like high ceilings, wood mantels, and pocket doors, renters braved peeling plaster, unvented gas heaters, and bad plumbing and wiring. Notoriously cheap art professor Jim Herbert rented rooms in his house on Dearing and in the small buildings out back that everyone called the "slave shacks," in an insensitive reference to their previous history. For many residents, the sense of community and the serious conversations about art made the rationed toilet paper and the timer beside the shower endurable. Waves of bohemians including Julie House, Mark Cline, and Craig Woodall lived in the rambling "Jester House," with its seven bedrooms and three-storied central tower down at the end of Cobb Street near the hospital. On the other end of the street, a changing roster of roommates, including Vic Varney and his Method Actors partner David Gamble, lived in another run-down Victorian that everyone called the Cobb Institute because residents and visitors like John Seawright often sat up arguing about ideas until morning. Musician Tom Smith met Michael Stipe there when the singer brought over the no-wave band DNA's "Little Ants" single. Stipe later played in and created art installations for Smith and Carol Levy's art noise band Boat Of which also included Mike Green, Sandi Phipps, and David Gamble in its changing lineup.[55]

When the Reed Hall crowd left the dorms, they joined other scene participants in colonizing the first few blocks of Barber Street behind the gas station and Bell's grocery on Prince. On these blocks, worn Victorians and bungalows alternated with cheap infill including a coin-operated car wash and a small apartment complex. White women with henna-red hair wearing old church dresses paraded down the sidewalks past African American women wearing purple polyester pantsuits and wigs. White men in round glasses and too-big trousers tripped past African American men in tight tees and flared jeans soaping seventies cars. A small crowd of homeless men whom the new residents nicknamed "the Barber Street Motor Club" spent

**The members of R.E.M. on the patio of the Barber Street house
where some of them lived. *Left to right*: Mike Mills, Bill Berry, Peter
Buck, and Michael Stipe. (Photograph by Sandra-Lee Phipps)**

their nights and days in dead vehicles including a broken school bus left behind the gas station.[56]

At various times, Pylon members Michael Lachowski, Randy Bewley,
and Curtis Crowe, artists Neil McArthur and Sam Seawright, Side Effects
guitarist and singer and Love Tractor drummer Kit Swartz, and Love Tractor guitarist Mark Cline lived at 265 Barber in a Victorian subdivided into
three apartments. Future member of Oh-OK Linda Hopper, Michael Stipe,
off and on again UGA students Leslie Michel, Mark Phredd Rizzo, and Lynn
Friedlander, future members of the Little Tigers Larry Marcus and Paul
Lombard, and R.E.M. manager Jefferson Holt all lived at 169 Barber, another
historic home turned into a triplex. Lauren Hall lived in another subdivided
house next door where Ann Boles and her boyfriend Pete Buck also rented
a place. When Hall got together with Mike Mills, she, Mills, and Bill Berry,
who had stopped living with O'Brien, shared the three-room apartment. As
Barber Street filled with bohemians, people spread out, renting parts of old
houses on nearby streets like Grady Avenue and Boulevard, too.[57]

Proximity spurred creativity. Jacked on cigs and coffee or mellowed by daiquiris and beer, neighbors dressed up and danced or drew and talked about the meaning of life until dawn. Smoking pot, they played around on instruments, picking out tunes, and had sex with little attention to the rules that were supposed to separate committed relationships from friendships and gays from straights. When they got hungry, they shoplifted snacks at Bell's or walked a few blocks to the Taco Stand where people could eat for $2 if they left off the meat. When they wanted something different to wear or were too lazy to wash, they walked the few blocks downtown to the Potter's House and bought another sack of used clothes. When they were bored, they formed new bands. Love Tractor debuted in July 1980 in the center hallway of 265 Barber Street with Cline and Mike Richmond on guitar and Kit Swartz on drums. The Little Tigers, a five-piece group that played ska- and reggae-influenced songs, formed before the end of the year.[58]

The scene was not always fun. Many people were poor, and $20 seemed to many participants like a fortune. Although most of these kids grew up middle-class and were at least part-time college students, many of their parents either could not or would not—because of their behavior or bad grades—support them. Some Barber Street residents remembered digging in the dumpster behind Bell's for expired but still edible food to supplement their groceries. Others bought day-old bread and begged free meals from friends who worked at restaurants. One summer, several women in the area were raped. One resident remembered that the bathroom of her apartment was such a poorly built addition that it was falling off the back of the house, and "you could literally see outside." She had to get up early for work, and in the winter, she would stand in the shower and cry "because [she] couldn't get a hot bath."[59]

Most scene participants had jobs whether or not they were students. Some bohemians like Jerry Ayers, who seemed to have some mysterious source of funds other than wages, worked as little as possible in order to devote their time to their art or music. Yet even when people worked long hours, they earned little. Hourly pay rates remained low because every year a new batch of young people arrived in Athens ready to work. And during and after the Reagan recession, even new college graduates who moved to cities like Atlanta struggled to find good jobs. Low wages, irregular hours, weak unions, a lack of job security, and lax regulation were not features that arrived with the twenty-first-century gig economy or even the transition to a more service-oriented jobs in the 1970s. They were long-established features of the state's economy.[60]

UGA art-school graduate Lauren Fancher could not see the point of trading her friends and her freedom to pursue her art for slightly higher pay in a job she would hate and decided, "I might as well stay in Athens and be creative." Like many bohemians, she held a string of jobs. Fancher worked for "Rick the Printer" Hawkins at the Print Shop, helping typeset a gay paper from Atlanta called the *Outlook*. Looking for employment that drew on her art skills, she worked as a graphic designer at the *Athens Banner-Herald* and a screen printer at several local printing businesses. For a while, she made drawings of clothes for advertisements run by Belk's department store. She also worked as a parking lot attendant at the *Banner-Herald* because she could read while sitting in the booth. On Thursdays, she and other scene participants sold the local progressive weekly the *Athens Observer* on downtown streets. Fancher sometimes also worked at restaurants like the Bluebird and for a while held a computer-processing job on campus that paid $4.64 an hour. Athens, like many college towns, was filled with "over-educated people doing bad jobs." Tired of the poverty, some people left the scene, moving away to take jobs in cities or attend grad school. Others found that their checkered employment histories and in some cases lack of a degree made it hard for them to get good jobs anywhere.[61]

While people could possibly make more money going back to "straight" life, women enduring the sexism within the scene did not have any obviously better options given the rampant discrimination against women in much of America at the time. Early on, most Athens bands—the B-52's, the Tone Tones, and Pylon—included female musicians, but the all-male bands R.E.M., the Side Effects, and Love Tractor recreated that old dynamic of male musicians and female fans. Women showed up for the shows and danced wildly into the wee hours, whether the gig was in Athens or Atlanta or Chapel Hill. They used their cars to haul their friends and lovers' band equipment and wrote bad checks to pay for the gas. When things got romantically serious, they worked the shit jobs that paid the rent on the apartments and bought the beer and groceries while the guys toured. They endured long absences, collect phone calls, road infidelities, and press interviews in which their friends and lovers never mentioned their sacrifices and support. Lauren Hall, Ann Boles, Linda Hopper, and Kathleen O'Brien even earned a local nickname for a while, "the R.E.M. wives." Women were bohemians, too, and yet in gender terms, some of them played the role of the fifties housewives whose dresses they wore.[62]

According to O'Brien, "I was the only one with a reliable car and any kind of credit, so I took it upon myself to start calling clubs trying to get [R.E.M.] opening dates. I thought I wanted to be their manager but Bill was

Vanessa Briscoe Hay of Pylon (*left*) and Linda Hopper of Oh-OK
(*right*) eat at the Taco Stand with photographer Sandra-
Lee Phipps between them. (Photograph © Laura Levine)

like, 'No girlfriend of mine is going to manage this band.'" Still, until they
hired Jefferson Holt as their manager, O'Brien kept doing a lot of the work.
She "had invested so much time and energy," she did not want to give the job
up. As Sandy Phipps, who later lived with Holt and worked in R.E.M.'s office
as a secretary and fan-club manager for years, explained, "I don't think they
wanted a woman doing it. That's kind of their attitude." Later, after R.E.M.
became successful, O'Brien wondered whether band members even remembered her efforts and the aid provided by other early fans, "the total collabo-
rative effort." The partying and the sex might be fun, but many women in the
scene were still playing the secondary role, supporting the creative work of
the men they loved. In this way, bohemianism did not offer much of an alternative to the rest of America.[63]

Go Your Own Way

Only in hindsight did R.E.M. look like the most important Athens band in
the early years of the eighties. Some local bohemians continued to criticize
R.E.M. as too pop. In response, others developed a kind of *anti*-anti-R.E.M.

sentiment and embraced the band, making "fuck art; let's dance" their motto. Still, in Athens, the pop label that few people understood as a compliment lingered. Buck recalled that R.E.M.'s reputation then as a pop band was odd; he observed, "We're not all that poppy. Then when we went out of town everybody thought we were really weird." When *Rolling Stone* named R.E.M. "*the* important Athens band," many locals disagreed. R.E.M. might be popular, but until Lachowski, Bewley, Briscoe Hay, and Crowe broke up their band at the end of 1983, Pylon remained the most important local group.[64]

In this fertile period, the growing Athens underground and its most famous band grew up together. The R.E.M. members matured as song writers, learned to navigate the music business, and released the single "Radio Free Europe"/"Sitting Still," the EP *Chronic Town*, and the album *Murmur*. Unable and unwilling to follow the model for how to be a band created by the B-52's and Pylon, R.E.M. developed an alternative path and their own networks of support. Their way became, in turn, a model for many local bands that followed.

In early 1981, though, all that success was still in the future, and R.E.M.'s prospects looked decidedly mixed. Berry was hedging his bets, drumming for art-school favorites Love Tractor, as well as R.E.M., as he tried to convince the other members of either of his two bands to quit college and focus on music. In the photographs that illustrated Varney's piece in *New York Rocker*, Berry appeared twice, wearing a hat to shade his face with R.E.M. and identified as "Leroy" with Love Tractor. Stipe, too, continued to perform in Boat Of, another art noise band called Tanzplagen that he formed with local musician Will Self and art-school graduate Neil McArthur, and a solo project he called 1066 Gaggle O' Sound.[65]

Financially, R.E.M. was doing better than any other local band. No other group made enough money in Athens to subsidize their out-of-town gigs where audiences were often small and guarantees few. Sometime in 1981, band members quit their day jobs, a concrete enough measure of success, though Buck clerked at Wuxtry regularly over the next few years, taking his pay in records.[66]

Buck, Stipe, Mills, and Berry also rapidly improved their songwriting. In the summer of 1980, band members wrote "Gardening at Night," a new kind of song they liked so much they named their music publishing company Night Garden Music. Looking back, they called it their first "real" composition. Over the next year and a half, the members of R.E.M. wrote enough of these to fill their EP and first two albums.[67]

Michael Stipe, in particular, contributed to this shift in R.E.M.'s style.

Jeremy Ayers, the town's most bohemian resident, became something of a mentor to Stipe and other young musicians like Mark Cline around this time. "He was a huge influence on us, how we dressed, how we looked, how we formed our bands, how we made music," Cline remembered. "We all wanted to be like him." Stipe adopted Ayers's habit of wearing multiple layers of old-fashioned menswear. He also copied Ayers's introverted style, a way of holding back and creating mystery by letting people wonder. Extending this ambiguity to his relationships, Stipe blurred the lines between friends and lovers and did not limit the gender of either. This refusal to explain or clarify not only fit well with Stipe's desire for privacy. It also meant, in a time of strong homophobia, that no one could pin him down as queer or bisexual or gay.[68]

After Stipe took up Ayers's habit of jotting down things he heard people saying as a kind of found poetry, he told a journalist: "I watch people a lot. Three quarters of my lyrics probably come from overheard conversations." Stipe also began to change how he sang. Stretching out words and phrases, he slowed down R.E.M.'s songs. The new lyrics and Stipe's new way of singing produced a sense of narrative based more on the emotional impact of the sound than on the meaning of the words. Ayers also shaped R.E.M.'s music more directly. Just as he had with the B-52's' song "52 Girls," Ayers received a writing credit for his work on the early R.E.M. song "Windout" and on a later song, "Old Man Kensey."[69]

What R.E.M. lacked was a record deal. The Side Effects and Love Tractor—bands so close to R.E.M. that for a while they all shared a Jackson Street practice space and equipment—followed Pylon and the Method Actors and signed with Atlanta independent DB Records. Danny Beard had worked a deal where he could use a big, old-fashioned studio in the Protestant Radio and Television Center on Clifton Road next to Emory University in Atlanta for free. While the bands did not make much money on DB, they got something on vinyl to sell fans and send out to critics and clubs. Beard certainly had opinions. As Vic Varney of the Method Actors recalled, "Beard hated the studio approach. He wanted the band to sound like they were playing live in a really good space." Still, as Kit Swartz remembered, "Beard did not try to put his fingerprints on everything. . . . He would just be there and pay." But Beard did not sign R.E.M. And when Buck, Stipe, Berry, and Mills paid for their own time at Atlanta's Bombay Studio in February 1981, they disliked the results so much that they scrapped plans to turn the tapes into a demo.[70]

In April, the band tried again. Because the established Athens path was not working for them, they looked elsewhere for a place to record. North

Carolina native Jefferson Holt asked his friend Peter Holsapple, then a member of the dB's, a New York band made up of four guys from Winston-Salem, about recording studios. Holsapple knew Mitch Easter, a musician who moved back home to Winston-Salem in the summer of 1980 after a stint in New York City and opened his own place in his parents' garage, calling the studio the Drive-In. Close in age to the R.E.M. guys, he had learned from punk that musicians without a lot of technical skill could make interesting music. According to Holsapple, Easter had a "predilection for trying anything to get an interesting sound" and an "easygoing attitude toward recording." His small, isolated studio had a casual, homey vibe. He let the guys spend the night with him before the session to save the cost of a hotel room. Sometimes, Easter's mother even brought over homemade treats.[71]

On the road across the South, R.E.M. had learned how to be a bar band. In April and May 1981 visits to the Drive-In to make a demo tape and a single, they began learning how to make music in a studio. As Easter remembered, "they pretty much just bashed it out," recording "Radio Free Europe," "Sitting Still," and "White Tornado" like they performed the songs live and then adding a few overdubs. Stipe cut his scratch vocals in the drum booth because "he didn't want anybody to see him sing." Easter understood Stipe's new, undecipherable singing style as part of a "grand tradition of singers who you have no idea what they're saying, and so I thought Michael just sounded cool." He "really was one of those glorious amateurs — he didn't have a long heritage of being in bands, and he was like a classic art student who thought it was his job to invent something. . . . He wanted his own sound."[72]

The Easter-produced Drive-In recordings became R.E.M.'s first real demo, and they mailed cassette copies to record companies and critics including Robert Christgau, who announced in the *Village Voice* that R.E.M.'s tape had "lots of impressive first-time songs on it." Atlanta musician Jonny Hibbert heard the tape and agreed to put out their single as the first release on his new Hib-Tone record label. In May, Hibbert drove up to the Drive-In to mix the record himself. Easter made a mix too, but the aspiring label owner insisted that since he was paying, he got to choose. Hib-Tone released "Radio Free Europe"/"Sitting Still" on July 8, 1981, the same day Pylon released a new DB single, "Crazy"/"M-Train." Some people remembered Buck was so mad about the murky sound that he smashed the record and nailed the pieces to the wall. He was also upset because, as he admitted years letter, he thought "Crazy" was a better song.[73]

As Craig Williams, a WUOG deejay and then the station's program director, remembered, radio staff would move local bands they loved into heavy or medium rotation to bring them to the attention of other college stations with which they shared lists. Pylon's "Crazy," the first song Briscoe Hay ever wrote on her own, captured something of how she felt during a bad break-up the previous winter, and it got a lot of airplay that summer. Still, not even Pylon's single could match the popularity of R.E.M.'s first record. Before Hib-Tone officially released "Radio Free Europe"/"Sitting Still," the disc jockeys at WUOG got hold of a copy. Listeners called in so often to request the songs that station managers put a note on the cart: "No! You can only play this once every three hours."[74]

By the time R.E.M.'s single went on sale, a startling variety of Athens bands were playing Tyrone's and the new 40 Watt, which had reopened in April 1981 in the cave-like, street-level space at 256 W. Clayton with Pylon headlining and its own legitimate beer and wine license. Michael Lachowski told a reporter for the *Atlanta Constitution*, "Music is listened to and done so much around this town that sooner or later, the more enterprising people can't keep their hands off an instrument." Only Pylon remained of their earlier wave, but bands formed in 1980 including the Side Effects, Love Tractor, and the Little Tigers played regularly, and new bands continued to appear.[75]

Sometime in early 1981, Ayers and his friends including Craig Woodall and Dominique Amet formed a new arty, avant-garde group. Limbo District sounded like Tom Waits in his *Swordfishtrombones* era if someone cut a tape of one of his songs into pieces and then randomly spliced together the results. As Stipe, who rarely played it straight in interviews in the early years of his career, described his friend Ayers's band to a reporter, "They're very small. As of yet, they're still scaring away audiences everywhere they play. But they're probably the greatest band to come out of America since the Lovin' Spoonful. They're incredible. 'All Tomorrow's Parties' by the Velvet Underground—they're like that, exactly."[76]

Stipe facilitated the formation of another new Athens band, Oh-OK, in May when he debuted his solo project 1066 Gaggle O' Sound featuring pre-recorded music, films, and the singer playing an old organ at the 40 Watt. As a senior in high school, Stipe's sister Lynda had come to parties with her brother alternately wearing her Burger King and McDonald's uniforms, depending on which fast food outlet she was working at that night. Michael introduced his sister to Linda Hopper, and the three of them quickly became close. The next year, as a freshman at UGA, Lynda borrowed Jimmy Ellison's bass and started trying to write songs. According to Hopper, Stipe suggested that the two young women form a band. According to Lynda Stipe, when

Michael told them he was looking for an act to open for his performance at the 40 Watt, the two women volunteered. The original plan was for Hopper to play guitar, but she was just learning, and they liked their sound without the instrument. Lynda Stipe mostly wrote the songs, but she had trouble playing bass and singing lead, so Hopper became the frontwoman. David Pierce played drums.[77]

The members of Pylon heard Hopper, Stipe, and Pierce perform the only four songs they knew at the 40 Watt and liked them so much they invited Oh-OK to open in New York. At the big-city club, the members of Pylon had to threaten not to play to force employees to give Oh-OK a sound check. Vic Varney described Oh-OK's rapid rise to a reporter for the *Atlanta Journal-Constitution* that summer, with only a little exaggeration: "When I left to go to Europe in April, nobody who's in Oh OK [*sic*] even had an instrument or knew how to play. They went to New York and played at the Peppermint Lounge on their second gig." After New York, the new band played the 40 Watt again and the opening of Leslie Michel's new late-night coffee club the Night Gallery in its upstairs location at 199 Prince Avenue. Danny Beard signed the group to DB, and by the fall Oh-OK had started recording the songs they would release the next May as a seven-inch EP called *Wow Mini Album*.[78]

More than a year after their debut, R.E.M. was still struggling to break into the New York underground scene so crucial in providing new music bands with critical legitimacy. Athens musicians got gigs and drew audiences in the big city by working the connections first established by Jerry Ayers, members of the B-52's and other Athens residents who had moved to the city. "When Athens bands come to New York," Kate Pierson told a critic in 1981, "we go see them play and they visit us. We're willing to help in any way we can." As Michael Stipe told a journalist in January 1982, "the B-52's brought Pylon, Pylon brought the Method Actors, [and] the Method Actors brought Love Tractor." By early 1981, the Side Effects had also played New York City twice, opening for Pylon and then playing at Hurrah. In July, R.E.M. finally debuted in the city, using their own connections to Copeland to land a gig opening for the Gang of Four on back-to-back nights at the Ritz.[79]

Leslie Berman remembered seeing one of these performances with the music critic Tom Carson, then her husband. "Awkwardly trying to fill the huge stage of the Ritz," Buck, Stipe, Berry, and Mills were "strung out along the front perimeter of the stage, where they could neither see nor interact with each other." R.E.M. played so badly that Berman and Carson, who loved the demo tape, "cringed." Christgau was there and formed a lasting impression of the band as loose and amateurish. Critic Michael Azerrad, too, saw this show and thought R.E.M. "sucked." The New York dates kicked off a little Gang of Four–R.E.M. mini-tour down the East Coast that culminated in a rare ticketed and sold-out show at Tyrone's in April. In a scene in which the B-52's and Pylon's first New York shows were legendary moments of critical recognition, R.E.M.'s large number of Athens fans did not completely counter their big-city failure. Later, Buck and Stipe seemed to "forget" their own connections as well as these gigs and a third Ritz date opening for another Copeland act in July. Stipe bragged to a reporter, "We're one of the only ones [among Athens bands] who went to New York on our own."[80]

Buck later described a fall date opening for the Bloods at the Pilgrim Theater on the Lower East Side, as part of the "Music for Millions" series, as the band's first New York City gig. In the issue out then, *New York Rocker* included a review of R.E.M.'s demo tape that helped draw people to the show. "It's always a pleasant surprise to see faith restored in a played-out cornerstone of pop when it's *done right*," Gary Sperrassa wrote. "As with other groups from their area (B-52's, Pylon), R.E.M. attempt a new twist on guitar-laden pop. . . . Vocals are husky and likeable (though strangely unintelligible), guitar lines are well thought-out and avoid cliché whilst harkening to past eras, and the whole tape (dare it be said in these yawnful time?) ROCKS!" An article in a later *New York Rocker* claimed R.E.M. "cleanly blew away Manhattan's own Bloods." According to Buck, an audience full of music critics went "wild" when R.E.M. did not leave the stage after the PA broke but instead "played instrumentals" and took requests. Yet five days later, R.E.M. drew so few people to the hip Mudd Club in Tribeca that the club refused to pay them.[81]

At the end of 1981 and beginning of 1982, reviews of the single and inclusion in year-end lists brought a much-needed boost for a band that wanted to do more than fill clubs in Athens and Atlanta. R.E.M. scored well in *New York Rocker*'s end-of-year readers' poll, winning the number three slot in the "favorite single" category after records by the Go-Go's and the Gang of Four and ranking fourth on the readers' list of "favorite unrecorded (non-album) bands." While R.E.M. did not earn a top-ten slot in the *Village Voice*'s annual poll of music critics, head *Voice* critic Robert Christgau gave the group an honorable mention, and participating critics Ira Kaplan and Tom Carson both ranked "Radio Free Europe" high on their ballots. Carson called it "one of the few great American punk singles." The biggest break of all came in an unlikely place, the *New York Times*, where Robert Palmer, a respected critic with broad and eclectic taste, ranked R.E.M.'s record number ten on a visionary list topped by singles from hip-hop pioneers Grandmaster Flash and the Furious Five and the Funky 4 + 1.[82]

The praise continued in January as Andy Schwartz wrote a piece in *New York Rocker* that began in all-caps: "IT'S HAPPENED again. Another new young American band has emerged out of the provincial blue yonder sweeping through Manhattan's mean streets with a whoosh of fresh air." R.E.M.'s songwriting abandoned "the old verse-chorus-verse formula for winding narratives punctuated by brief, obsessive refrains, creating a sound that blended Pete Buck's ringing Rickenbacker triplets and shimmering chords (no solos!) with the persuasively pumping bass and drums of Mike Mills and Bill Berry and the sometimes-yearning, sometimes-jubilant voice of Michael Stipe." Schwartz understood that the band was "reaching for total feeling rather than specific meaning," and that at their best, the songs conveyed "emotional undercurrents." But Schwartz did not like Stipe's vocal style that "intentionally and effectively prevents me from understanding a good 80% of their lyrics, both live and on record." The critic wanted to know what the band had to say.[83]

R.E.M.'s single did not win over all the critics, any more than their shows won over all the new-music fans in Athens. Buck, Stipe, Mills, and Berry had reached a crossroads. With Palmer's praise and their Copeland connections, they could embrace the widest possible audience and work to get a major-label record deal. Or with Schwartz and Carson and *New York Rocker* on their side, they could keep working to win over the local and New York City gatekeepers that got to decide what music counted as original enough to be considered underground art.

Around the same time the year-end praise for R.E.M.'s single began to appear, back in Athens the scene lost one of its two key venues. Tyrone's caught fire in the early hours of January 8. The fire trucks arrived just before six, and twenty-five firefighters battled for about an hour to control the blaze. Everything was lost, including regulars' long bar tabs and the instruments and other equipment of the two bands who had played the night before, the Little Tigers and Men in Trees. According to the owners, the club "was between insurance companies." A photograph by Sandra-Lee Phipps the morning after showed overturned stools beside a bar under some charred rafters and an open sky. Around noon, while the ruins were "still smoking," Jimmy Ellison of the Side Effects talked to *Red and Black* reporter Chuck Reece about the venue that had nurtured his own and so many other bands. Visibly shaken, his voice "barely above a whisper," Ellison said, "This place was like home to me."[84]

Catapult

Unlike other bands that had a less complicated relationship with the original Athens bohemians, R.E.M. members learned from their mixed reception in Athens that the scene that could be nurturing and inspiring could also be petty and limiting. Assessing their own and others' successes and setbacks, Buck, Stipe, Berry, and Mills, backed by their manager Holt, learned how to trust their own collective judgement. Stipe put it this way: "All of our decisions are made from a gut feeling. Something can look right as rain, but if the gut feeling is wrong, then we won't do it." As Buck often put it, "We just do things to please ourselves." For the R.E.M. guys, the point of underground music was not formal originality or left-wing politics but autonomy, the freedom to make your own decisions about your music. Buck argued, "Punk was never about buying a leather jacket and singing songs about Ronald Reagan. It was about liberating yourself from the strictures of the music industry." Punk meant not having to do what other people told you to do.[85]

New York City seemed to fall for R.E.M. that winter. Jim Fouratt, the promoter who had given Pylon their first New York City gig and had heard R.E.M. when he visited Athens, booked the band to play the opening of Danceteria at its new location. "I wanted them . . . because I thought it was very hip," he recalled. "I knew I would get critics." *New York Rocker* asked, "How come these guys don't have *some* kind of record deal yet?" Behind the scenes, Fouratt was working on solving that problem. Together with New York producer Kurt Munkacsi, then working with other up-and-coming bands like the Waitresses, Fouratt had created a production company with connections to RCA. He arranged for R.E.M. to work with Munkacsi at RCA studios both before and after the Danceteria dates.[86]

In February 1982, Buck, Stipe, Berry, and Mills recorded at the Drive-In, drove north to play Maxwell's in Hoboken, spent two days at RCA Studio C in New York, drove to D.C. to play the 9:30 Club, and then went back north to New York to work at RCA. The completed seven-song demo — "Romance," "Wolves, Lower," "Laughing," "Shaking Through," "Stumble," "Catapult," and "Carnival of Sorts" — hinted at what kind of band R.E.M. might have been in an alternate universe. There, Berry's big, bold drums cracked along at a crisp and steady rhythm. Mills's melodic bass bounced and grooved. And Buck's guitar had a more trebly jangle, less moody than bright. Oddest of all, Stipe's voice — less distinct in its tone, clearer in its enunciation, and often awash in reverb — sang altered melodies that ended repeatedly with rising notes.[87]

The problem with this potential deal was as much timing as style. RCA had a reputation for moving notoriously slowly in signing bands, and Buck, Stipe, Mills, and Berry had grown impatient watching their friends in other bands releasing records. Later, band members would say they always wanted to be on a smaller label. As Berry put it, "We didn't want to get involved with big corporate machines like RCA and CBS." Still without a record contract, the members of R.E.M. once again turned to someone who wanted to launch a new record company, their friend David Healy, to finance the recording of an EP.[88]

In sessions before and after the RCA studio work, R.E.M. continued working at the Drive-In. Back in Athens, scene participants liked the records of local bands — Pylon's *Gyrate*, for example — but they also talked about how the recordings rarely captured the intensity of local shows. At the Drive-In, Buck, Stipe, Mills, and Berry began learning how to make recordings that took advantage of the creative possibilities of the studio rather than simply trying to reproduce an inevitably weaker version of the live sound. Experimentation like changes in tempo and volume began, in turn, to bleed out into their live performances.[89]

The R.E.M. guys also kept driving to New York. That spring, banking on the appeal of "regional rock," some New York clubs began advertising acts by listing their place of origin. This new geographical labeling helped solve New York fans' confusion about the meaning of the vague label "new music" and bands from outside New York who were too new to be punk and yet not quite new wave, as British bands with synthesizers increasingly defined that genre. Understanding musicians as connected to particular places with their own histories and geographies copied practices established through waves of folk revivalism and gave the new music an aura of authenticity. It also enabled New York clubs to break new, out-of-town groups their audiences had not heard of by linking them to more well-known groups from the same places. R.E.M., Pylon, and Love Tractor, always announced as from Athens, played regularly at Fouratt's Danceteria. At one gig, faced with what music journalist Andrew Slater, Buck's old Atlanta friend, described as "a crowd of record executives, rock critics, and fans," Stipe offered this hometown greeting, "Welcome to Tyrone's North." The fact that David Byrne of Talking Heads appeared in the back of the crowd, "smiling and swaying," put an underground seal of approval on the whole evening.[90]

Not long after this April Danceteria show, Berry's Copeland connections finally resulted in an offer. Miles Copeland, head of I.R.S. Records, visited Buck, Stipe, Mills, and Berry's shared room at New York's Iroquois

Hotel, where the guys signed the contract. As an independent record label with important new-music acts on its roster, I.R.S. had credibility in underground circles and a sense of how to break bands to non-mainstream audiences. Yet a distribution deal with major label A&M meant I.R.S. could move more records than most other independents, including the small and underfunded DB. R.E.M. negotiated a deal that kept band payouts low on the front end in return for more control over the recording process. After signing with I.R.S., band members broke their agreement with Healy, killing his Dasht Hopes label. They also used money fronted by I.R.S. to buy the publishing rights for "Radio Free Europe" and "Sitting Still" back from Hibbert.[91]

In August, R.E.M. spent a month in Los Angeles, where I.R.S. executives got to know band members and Holt and worked to break the group on the West Coast. That same month, I.R.S. released five of the songs recorded with Easter as the EP *Chronic Town*. Maybe Buck, Stipe, Mills, and Berry did not have to choose between the music industry mainstream and a tiny and yet rapidly expanding underground. Maybe they could hit the middle, like they did in Athens, and find fans at the intersection of these audiences.[92]

As *Chronic Town* came out that August, Pylon, Love Tractor, the Method Actors, the Side Effects, and Oh-OK had recently or were about to put out recordings. Fearing a backlash, the members of R.E.M. worked to distance themselves from Athens. "To hear them tell it, R.E.M. could have happened anywhere, is happening in cities and towns across the nation, miles from the media centers," *New York Rocker* reported in early 1982. "Athens is accidental, if not incidental." In April, Buck told a critic, "I think the whole Athens thing is blown up. Other than the fact that you are really encouraged to express your art — in poems or painting or music — it's just a dumpy little town. People keep coming up to me and saying, 'God, Athens must be a great place to live.' And I try to tell them it's just a boring place. Frankly, I'm happy to get out of there as much as I do." A reporter for *Rolling Stone* wrote that Stipe had "been up to his adenoids in reviews that threw R.E.M. into the food processor with other notables from the Athens cabal." "We're not a party band from Athens, we don't play New Wave music, and musically, we don't have shit to do with the B-52s or any other band from this town," Stipe complained. "We just happen to live here. It's ridiculous. You'd think anyone with an ear for music, anyone who was really listening, would be able to distinguish between R.E.M. and the B-52s, or R.E.M. and Pylon." Mike Mills told *Musician*, "It's just a mistake to lump all the bands together. . . . We don't sound like anybody else, and if you listen, they don't really sound that much like each other, either."[93]

Ironically, even when the R.E.M. guys were working to distance themselves from Athens, they still followed a path created by Pylon. Pylon's Lachowski told a music critic more than a year earlier, "It's real endearing to people in New York that all this new music could come of the South, but really all the Athens bands have been interesting in and of themselves. We downplay the Athens connection now, primarily because it just makes people ask about the B-52's."[94]

Back home, locals loved the record. At sidewalk cafés, along Barber Street, and at the art school, they argued over the meaning of songs and what they thought were local references. In apartments and dorms, they played the record repeatedly. "If you walked home from school you could hear it coming from ten different houses on one street," a former scene participant remembered. "You could not walk anywhere in Athens without hearing that ep [sic]." *Chronic Town* sold well in Atlanta too. Outside Georgia, some college radio stations placed it in heavy rotation, and some listeners in these places bought the EP. Fans also bought it in New York.[95]

From the record company's perspective, *Chronic Town*, with its mysterious blue gargoyle cover, was neither a hit nor a flop. Like most of the people working at i.r.s., many critics, college deejays, and new-music fans were not sure what to think about a band whose songs they could not understand. Writing ambiguous lyrics and then singing them in a way that made many words impossible to decipher, Stipe challenged one of rock and even punk's essential characteristics, that performing the music was an act of self-expression.

Somehow, *Chronic Town* found its way to two critics who listened like time travelers whose ears could hear not just the EP but the band's future album *Murmur* too. In the *Village Voice*, Billy Altman began "History Lesson" by taking on the intelligibility critique head on: "The next time someone shoves a lyric sheet under your nose and tries to convince you that the song you can't stand is, in actuality, a great work of art once you know the words, I suggest you counter attack with any or all tracks of R.E.M.'s new *Chronic Town* EP." "Rock and roll often has much more to do with things like attitude, mood, and rhythm than such paltry items as metaphor or symbolism." Altman also nailed the key effect of Stipe's ambiguous lyrics. While the lack of transparency put some potential fans off, it simultaneously drew others back for repeated listening. "This record has been spinning merrily on my turntable for over a month now, revealing bits and pieces of its mysterious self with each new listen." Just as pioneering rock critic Greil Marcus had written about a decade earlier, praising music that did not try to offer a political message, "the element of uncertainty" produced "the tension that open[ed] up the senses." Ambiguity made R.E.M. sound "smart."[96]

What the *Village Voice*'s Altman did not like was band members' clothes. Onstage at the Peppermint Lounge on October 8, Buck, Stipe, Mills, and Berry "dressed like a quartet of junior card players dragged away from the pinochle table in the student union ratskeller (i.e., three button-down long-sleeved shirts and one inside-out sweat-shirt)."[97]

In Britain's *New Musical Express*, Richard Grabel described how "Michael Stipe's voice comes close, gets right up next to you, but his mumblings seem to contain secrets. Intimacy and distance. The voice tells of knowledge but doesn't give too much away." "Stipe scrambles language, plays with it like a dyslexic poet, scatters loaded words around like leaves in the wind," Grabel continued. "Pete Buck's chords ring memory bells, push buttons of good feelings. Stipe's voice vibrates with wonder." *Chronic Town*'s songs offered "perfect economy of expression, a perfect puzzle, perfect enchantment." Even Christgau came around, ranking the record third on his 1982 EP list, one step above Oh-OK's *Wow Mini Album*. The record did even better in the "Pazz and Jop" poll Christgau ran every year for the *Village Voice*, placing second on the EP list. *Creem* called it "the sleeper EP of the year."[98]

As some critics understood, *Chronic Town*'s five songs did something quite distinct in underground music in that moment. They made listeners work to make their own meaning, and they suggested that interpretation always hinged on perspective. For nerdy, college-student fans in particular, R.E.M.'s songs translated the new postmodern theory they read in their classes into sonic form.[99]

When R.E.M. played the Pier, a Raleigh, North Carolina club, on October 10, 1982, a local cable channel recorded the show, capturing the band's live sound just after the release of *Chronic Town*. In an opening that owed something to Pylon despite R.E.M.'s denial, Stipe started the first song, "Wolves, Lower," speaking the words "mirror," and "flower" as Berry pounded a four-four beat. As the guitar and bass joined in and the volume built, Stipe mumbled something and gasped out "ehhhhhhh." Then he left the mic to dance, and his body spun and jerked like a spark had started at his head and worked its way rhythmically down to his feet. When he stepped back to the mic, he sang in a low and gravelly voice, "Suspicion yourself / suspicion yourself / don't get caught."[100]

Later in the song, Buck played his guitar close to Stipe, who was holding the mic, and Stipe popped his eyes wide and smirked in what could only be described as a leer. Buck looked down, smiled, and moved away. Stipe and

Buck flirted like a young Mick Jagger and Keith Richards, a once radical and then tired gesture somehow revived by Stipe's androgyny and Buck's drag, his performance of Patti Smith's impersonation of Richards.[101]

Throughout the set, Stipe displayed a charismatic sexual identity as indecipherable as his lyrics. His dancing was fluid and loose, his supple body speeding up and slowing down, in and out of sync with the rhythm, a flowing version of Vanessa Briscoe Hay's snapping twirls. He wore eye makeup and a Greek-letter jersey like a sorority girl under a baggy suit jacket with a scarf hanging out of his pocket. Channeling Briscoe's take on male rock moves, copying a woman copying a man, Stipe mouthed the microphone and made love to the stand, moaning what could be words in an unknown tongue or sounds of pleasure. Buck wore a cut-off black t-shirt, and by a few songs in his dark curly hair hung in his eyes in wet tendrils. When he looked up from his hands at Stipe or Mills or made a little rock star move, he let go of his grimace of concentration and flashed a coy and knowing smile. Mills, on the other hand, expressed little emotion. He wore a white button-up shirt with flapping French cuffs just like Buck often wore in band photos. His short, straight bangs revealed a field of forehead as he played bass like a guitar. He came across like a mash-up of nerdy new waver and earnest folk revivalist, an eighties version of the sixties Pete Seeger.

In performance, the vocal harmonies of Stipe, Mills, and Berry sounded simultaneously sweet, transgressive, and sexy, male voices merging like the singing of a Motown girl group, men playing women and also perhaps playing too close, playing around. Channeled through the women of the B-52's and Pylon, R.E.M.'s gender ambiguity made rock masculinity seem real again. And the contradictions worked in other registers as well. Throughout the set, Berry's melodic bass and Buck's jangling guitar produced a folk sound that in its contrast cut through and redeemed rock-and-roll gestures that over time made intensity and detachment into inauthentic conventions. The band seemed to have absorbed from sixties folk rock not just a sound but even more importantly an affect—the folk music revival's belief that beyond an attachment to place, authenticity lay in getting the feelings right. At the Pier, R.E.M. offered the audience a fusion of folk sincerity and melody and punk-rock simplicity and attitude: four yearning middle-class kids grabbing hold of the region where they had landed by making folk revivalist punk music, the sound not of anger but of longing and desire.[102]

As R.E.M. got ready to record again, I.R.S. had big ideas about how to translate R.E.M.'s live magic into a debut album with broad appeal. In December 1982, the label sent R.E.M. into an Atlanta studio with Stephen

Hague, who had worked with the Human League, to record a song as a trial run. Hague made the band use a click track to set a rigid beat as they played "Catapult" what band members recalled alternately as thirty-five or forty-eight times. Hague then worked by editing together the chorus from one take, a verse from another, and a bridge from a third. For band members, this process killed all the joy of music-making. Nothing about this work was fun. Yet as hard as it was to endure the recording process, for the band the results were worse. Hague smoothed all the grain out of Stipe's voice, pushed all the vocals up in the mix, made the drums louder, erased much of the dissonance, and added synthesizers. According to Mark Cline of Love Tractor, who heard the recording then, it would have been a hit. Band members hated it.[103]

In January 1983 at Reflection Sound Studios in Charlotte, North Carolina, "a big, 70's-style room" with a twenty-four-track board and a mix of new gear and vintage equipment used mostly for recording gospel music, the R.E.M. guys tried again with Easter and his friend, the musician and producer Don Dixon. Unlike in their earlier sessions at the Drive-In, Easter found band members had grown "wary of studio techniques" and "conservative" about everything. The producers' challenge was to "regain their trust in using the studio to enhance the basic live sound."[104]

At Reflection, band members, Easter, and Dixon collaborated and tried out ideas together, adding parts played on studio instruments including piano, vibes, and Hammond organ and creating texture by layering in voices, acoustic guitars, pianos, and percussion. For "Talk About the Passion," they hired a cellist. On "Perfect Circle," they added a simple, "childlike" riff played on both a grand piano and an old, "out-of-tune upright." Berry wanted to be recorded playing in Reflection's little drum booth, a "holdover" from the seventies, and they set him up there. Stipe "still had this thing of loving to be invisible," so Dixon and Easter placed a microphone "on the landing of a staircase positioned just below the control room and above a recreational basement area." Easter and Dixon saved little "found" sounds that they inserted into the mix. According to Easter, "Those guys were art-farts in a way, and they loved that sort of musique concréte stuff that can happen from some random noise." The producers discovered that band members "liked stuff if they could see it from an art angle, but the minute they thought something was hokey or done for commercial appeal they hated it."[105]

Although Buck, Stipe, Mills, and Berry publicly disavowed Athens in this period, the way they worked in the studio made it clear they shared aesthetic ideas with other Athens bohemians. In this way of thinking about formal originality, professionalism and polish—the steady beat of a click track or crisp and upfront vocals or the addition of electronic instruments like synthesizers—came across as inauthentic and fake. The slick (in comparison) production values of the B-52's albums, released on major label Warner Brothers, might have increased record sales, but they also smoothed out and erased the band's punky drag power. For most Athens bands, the problem was coming up with an alternative in the face of limited recording budgets. Pylon's first single conveyed the fresh energy of the band's then-new songs "Cool" and "Dub." Yet on their first album, *Gyrate*, and their second single, "Crazy"/"M-train," the group struggled in the studio to capture the intensity and passion of their live shows. The Side Effects and Love Tractor faced similar challenges. Of these early Athens bands, only R.E.M. learned to use the studio to create a richer, more complex sound. It was probably not a coincidence that they also had more money to spend on recording than other local bands.[106]

After *Chronic Town*'s release, the members of R.E.M. were rarely in Athens long, but the scene there grew steadily. Pylon put out another DB single, "Beep"/"Altitude." The Method Actors and the Side Effects broke up. Oh-OK, described in the *Red and Black* as "a band both loved and hated but never in between," played the 40 Watt's Valentine's Day party, opened for Pylon at 688, and celebrated their first birthday at the i and i. A reporter for the *Red and Black* described Limbo District as "more like a performance art ensemble, or play actors in a strange kind of circus troupe rather than a band." While they had a core group of bohemian fans in town, outside of Athens the band's show could quickly clear out a club. In early 1983, art professor Jim Herbert made an eleven-minute film titled *Carnival*, featuring four Limbo District songs and band members wandering around in the country wearing fantastical Victorianesque costumes and leading a horse. Love Tractor grew popular enough to headline two-night stands at the 40 Watt and released two albums, *Love Tractor* and *Around the Bend*.[107]

In January 1983, the magazine everyone read in checkout lines and doctor's offices introduced mainstream America to this unlikely underground. *People* understood Athens as part of a larger cultural development. Young people were creating new kinds of music in marginal places like "rap" in the outer boroughs of New York and "regional rock," a "flourishing grassroots movement characterized by strange compulsions to *not* move to New York or Los Angeles." In Athens, *People*'s reporter listened as scene participants explained "the atmosphere" was "not New Wave, not punk" but "more bohemian, '50s beatnik."[108]

Love Tractor performs at the original 40 Watt in 1980. *Left to right:*
**Armistead Wellford, Mark Cline, and Mike Richmond. Drummer Kit
Swartz is not pictured because he had not yet joined the band or is
outside the frame. (Photographer unknown, courtesy of Mark Cline)**

When the magazine's photographer visited, the bohemians had not been
too cool to pose. Members of at least twelve Athens bands and a few pioneering photo-bombers dodged the rare car to gather in the middle of Broad
Street, around the base of a monument commemorating a Revolutionary
War hero. In the full-page photograph that illustrated the article, members
of Pylon, Love Tractor, Limbo District, Oh-OK, Art in the Dark, the Little
Tigers, and other bands and then defunct groups like the Side Effects and
the Method Actors proclaimed that the B-52's were just the start. Off playing
gigs in Florida, Alabama, and Rhode Island and recording, the members of
R.E.M. missed the photo shoot.[109]

Southern Rock

In the context of the Athens scene, R.E.M.'s first album, *Murmur*, released in
April 1983, sounded like an answer to inside-the-scene critics. The band that
had started out playing covers and sixties garage rock–sounding originals
had put out an art record.

Athens scene participants heard *Murmur* in a context shaped by their
familiarity with the band's history as well as a local tragedy. On April 14,
a group of Athens bohemians piled in a car and drove to Atlanta to see

Smithereens, a film about pioneering punk musician Richard Hell, who was scheduled to appear at the screening. On the way home, another vehicle hit the car of the Athens kids, causing it to flip and roll into the median. Art student, photographer, and musician Carol Levy and Little Tigers keyboardist Larry Marcus were killed. Levy had met Stipe, her friend, sometimes lover, and artistic and musical collaborator, through the art school, and played with him and others in a series of experimental bands. She had even written Oh-OK's song "Brother." Stipe was away on tour, and when he got the news, he was so "trashed," he later confessed, that he could not cry. The next morning, he decided to quit doing drugs entirely. That summer he wrote about Levy in the R.E.M. song "Camera":

> *Will you be remembered? Will she be remembered?*
> *Alone in a crowd, a bartered lantern borrowed*
> *If I'm to be your camera, then who will be your face?*

People in Athens first listened to *Murmur* during a long, sad spring.[110]

As the album shipped, R.E.M. played a string of arenas in the Northeast and Canada, opening for another band connected to the Copeland brothers, the English Beat. Interviewed by UGA student journalist Jay Watson after the Boston show, Stipe, Buck, and Mills confessed they missed Athens. Stipe pleaded, "Take me home! Take me home!" before listing all the things he longed for: his friends, his bed, Bell's shopping center, the Taco Stand, (restaurant owner) Bob Russo, and Dunkin Donuts, and even, jokingly, his enemies. Buck wanted to reestablish his routine and hang out in the local clubs. Mills mentioned Walter's Barbeque, his stereo, his records, and "being able to sleep all day." Then playing their first tour of large venues, they all agreed they preferred small clubs where, as Mills put it, the band met the crowd "at a close level" and "you live or die by the quality of what you do." And Stipe confessed he had been "half expecting some kind of backlash" against *Murmur*, people saying, "Oh, they sold out: you can hear the words, you can hear everything, they've got the piano, they've got the cello." When he added, "So what? It's what we wanted to do so we did it," he sounded more like he was trying to convince himself than Watson. He admitted he called home sometimes "to make sure everything's okay," the closest he came to mentioning Levy's death the week before.[111]

By late April, reviews of *Murmur* began to appear in Athens papers. In his review for the *Athens Banner Herald/Daily News*, Jimmy Ellison warned listeners that they would not find the sound which attracted "1,200 Athenians to each R.E.M. show" on this "surprisingly bold" record. "Forget it, kids.

This ain't no party." As Chuck Reece, writing for the *Red and Black*, put it, "At the club, you get R.E.M.'s rock chops. On the record, you get something else entirely. It too is mesmerizing enough to be scary."[112]

Instead of a dance party, according to Ellison, the twelve songs on *Murmur* offered slower tempos, up-in-the-mix melodies, and vocals clear enough to convey "varying tones and inflections" drowned out in the band's live shows. The fact that "half the lyrics" were still "indecipherable" was "unimportant." R.E.M. was "not a sing along group." For Reece, Stipe was the key to the band's new "luscious sound." The singer created "fleeting images with his words," "not stories" but "little pictures of characters." On "Perfect Circle," he half pleaded, half commanded, "Pull your dress on and stay real close." On "Catapult," he asked urgently, "Did we miss anything?" For Reece, Stipe's "nicely poetic knack" for writing lines that "spark[ed] a different image in the mind of each listener" created an emotional richness new in R.E.M.'s music. He hoped R.E.M.'s new album might inspire teens to give up on MTV bands. Ellison wanted to resurrect the old days at Tyrone's: "You've done your art guys," he ended his review; "now let's have some fun."[113]

Whether or not they expected a party, listeners everywhere were set up to hear *Murmur* as "southern" music. Outside of Athens, advertisements and music listings often mentioned R.E.M.'s hometown. I.R.S., R.E.M.'s record company, worked to exploit the regional-rock trend by promoting its bands in particular segments of the national market. For R.E.M., this approach meant pushing the band as a southern act.[114]

Even *Murmur*'s cover suggested a deep regional affiliation. On the front, a Carol Levy photograph depicted kudzu swallowing a landscape. On the back, photographs by Sandra-Lee Phipps presented band members and a local railroad trestle. Years later, Buck confessed that band members were looking for something "real Flannery O'Connor" when they chose the cover image. Jay Boberg, president of I.R.S., liked that R.E.M. created such a "unique sleeve": "I thought kudzu was a regional thing that had to do with their roots and where they came from." Even the name of the album suggested a pastoralism—the murmur of bees or a creek—that fit the rural image of the region. When I.R.S. pushed reluctant band members to make a video, they chose the quirky Paradise Garden, the Reverend Howard Finster's open-air art installation near Summerville, Georgia.[115]

Music journalists, too, played up the band's regional identity. Reviewing a May show at the New York club the Ritz and the album in the *Village Voice*, John Piccarella argued for the southern qualities of R.E.M.'s sound by tracing a line of southern musicians. In an early 1983 review of *Chronic Town* in *Creem*, Robert "Robot" Hull, a native of Memphis, had first suggested this genealogy. Instead of playing "minimal dance rhythms" like "Athens' other better-known combos (Pylon, the B-52's, Oh-OK)," Hull argued, R.E.M. sounded "stylistically more akin to such practitioners of the southern pop consciousness as, say, Alex Chilton, or the dB's." Piccarella filled in more details of Hull's southern history. R.E.M.'s "combination of Southern pop-rock and Velvet Underground lyricism," he argued, began with Alex Chilton, "came with him through New York via Chris Stamey [of the dB's]," and ended up in Mitch Easter's Drive-In Studio in North Carolina.[116]

In the early eighties, the South conjured contradictory meanings. For many Americans from elsewhere, the region seemed poor and backward and full of racist whites. As Pete Buck put it, "the [white] Southerner is the terminal outsider. In movies and on TV, the Southerners are always hicks. They're idiots. Everyone tends to look at you as if it's a miracle that you're a normal person from the South." Music historians, on the other hand, understood the region as a reservoir of cultural authenticity, the birthplace of jazz and the blues as well as country music and the still-popular genre of southern rock.[117]

In sonic terms, as journalist Amanda Petrusich has argued, this difficult-to-define musical genre was "a blues-based, r&b-influenced, heavily guitar-driven strain of rock music." Southern rock, in other words, drew on musical forms and styles understood in the 1970s and 1980s as African American. Yet what Petrusich has called its "iconography," its broader cultural symbolism—the Confederate flags, pickup trucks, and celebrations of rebellion, the lyrical evocation of the ideals and excesses of rural, working-class southern life—was often problematically white. After the early seventies success of the interracial Allman Brothers Band, later groups like Lynyrd Skynyrd and the Charlie Daniels Band shaped a genre known as much for its macho bravado, regional boosterism, and sonic self-assertion as for its guitar solos. At the easiest level, like the original rock and roll of the 1950s, southern rock romanticized rebellion against respectability, throwing a big "free bird" in the face of middle-class culture. And the music was popular with young people in places like Japan who knew little about U.S. history. Yet in the post–civil rights movement South, where many whites felt looked down on and criticized by Americans from elsewhere for their racism and backwardness, this romanticizing often worked to excuse and even justify white racism under the guise of southern pride. Growing up in the seventies in Macon, Mills and Berry were surrounded by southern rock even before Berry went to work for Paragon, Capricorn's booking company. In Atlanta, Buck, too, would have found it impossible to avoid this music.[118]

R.E.M. offered an alternative vision of the South. As listeners struggled to both decipher and interpret the songs, it was easy for them to understand what the *Rolling Stone*'s four-star (out of a possible five) review of *Murmur* called "elusiveness" as a regional characteristic, a kind of southern indirection. For an article that followed up on that review, Stipe even acted out this quality. "On the vocals, I go for what I call the acid *e* sound, which is a nasal thing where you take the sound of *e* and make it as terrible as you possibly can. Tammy Wynette and Patsy Cline knew a whole lot about it," Stipe insisted, performing a version of southern indirection that might also be called, in less romantic terms, bullshitting.[119]

Even *Murmur*'s sound evoked southern mystery. The music spoke in metaphors, as one instrument became an odd stand-in for another, a piano for a guitar, for example, or a cello for a voice. And Stipe never sang straight. His words, his sometimes-doubled vocals, the placement of the vocals in the mix, the relatively spare and deliberate use of reverb, and his occasional use of a deeply southern pronunciation all conjured ambiguity. People in Athens who knew Stipe's history might interpret his indirection as related to his not publicly acknowledged bisexuality, what he later called his queerness. Yet even this understanding could be subsumed within a romantic vision of the region as a place where people were not transparent, where they did not say what they meant, where the surface hid the depths.

As early scene participant Sean Bourne put it, "Sure there were Elvis Costello and Talking Heads, but they didn't speak about mystery. The Clash sang about social injustice. The B-52's sang about having a good time. R.E.M.—nobody knew what they were speaking about, but they caught all this 'stuff,' like the kudzu on the cover. . . . Their listeners saw weird, fragmented images of an unfamiliar place. . . . They basically gave people that weren't used to seeing things like that something to research. And people responded to it."[120]

Instead of offering a counter message to southern rock's regional (and often racist) chauvinism, R.E.M. abandoned the idea that musicians should offer any message at all. When journalist Jim Sullivan interviewed band members for an article in *Record* in July 1983, Stipe pushed back against the idea that music should be "a vehicle for your heartfelt passions, political [and] personal." "I'm not willing, and the whole band is not willing, to throw a diatribe at anybody," he insisted. "Nobody cares, or nobody would care, about where I stand politically or socially or what my love life is like." "I'm not some great genius," he continued. "I have no great story to tell. No great anecdotes. None of us do." Sullivan kept pushing, given the great tales the band was actually telling him right then about their life on the road. And both Stipe and Buck replied "screw it," probably a translation of a harsher phrase that *Record* could not print. Stipe and Buck denied that rock-and-roll musicians could or should be understood as spokespeople, political or otherwise, for others. In the interview, they asserted their right not to assert themselves in their songs. They enacted the ambiguity of R.E.M.'s song lyrics. In the post–civil rights movement South and a period of rising conservatism across the nation, not having a message meant not having to take a side. R.E.M. made southern rock that was white rather than white supremacist, music that educated white southern kids could like without rejecting their region or feeling racist.[121]

Back in Athens, where most participants in the scene were born and raised in Georgia or nearby states, some people found R.E.M.'s reinvention in the press as a "southern" band surprising. For them, southern identity was about family history and deep connections to southern places. Even kids who moved to Athens from the Atlanta suburbs often had parents from southern small towns where their grandparents still lived. Berry and Mills, with their Macon childhoods, fit this understanding of southern, but Buck and Stipe, raised in California and on army bases, respectively, did not. Since Buck and Stipe were the R.E.M. members who most often spoke to the press about the band's regional connections, their biographies became an issue for some. One scene participant remembered Berry and Mills as "really Southern," but not Buck and Stipe: "Being *really* Southern myself, I thought it seemed like a real marketing ploy that they were representative of a new South. For Pete Buck to speak for the South was kind of a joke." "I don't think R.E.M. were about the South as much as they were intrigued by it," art student Sean Bourne recalled.[122]

In the *New York Times*, critic Jon Pareles identified "folk-rock" revivalism as part of a new trend in underground music. Athens groups R.E.M. and Love Tractor shared with new British bands like Aztec Camera a sonic palette that included "reverberating electric guitar licks" and "straightforward march rhythms." Since protest, one of folk-rock's main functions, had been taken over by punk-rock and hardcore, what was left was what Pareles called "precocious innocence," the earnest sincerity of the mid-sixties. If the new folk rockers could figure out how to deflect the built-in nostalgia, they could own the emotions. They could mean them again. And this was easier for kids from Athens who many fans and critics understood as stranded in a place outside of modern America anyway, just like these older folk musicians whom folk revivalists and then folk rockers had been inspired by in the sixties. No one expected Athens musicians to know recent music history. Even after the punk pop-art drag of the B-52's and Pylon, no one expected them to do irony. What played for some people as a conscious reworking of a sentimental and long vanished past could be understood, if a listener was inclined, as an authentic expression of the southern present. White southerners—heirs to Faulkner and Flannery whether they'd read them or not—could get away with romanticism. As one scene participant put it, "the South has come out looking better because of R.E.M."[123]

4

Tasty World

Sticks, stones,
hands, bones,
eyes, stars,
heart—
drums and guns,
don't shoot.
It's only a flute.

The Squalls, "Elephant Radio" (1984)

They had the idea first. Before they knew how to play any instruments, Arthur Johnson, Claire Horne, and Laura Carter wanted to be in a band. That winter, sometime in late 1983 or early 1984, they got another friend to shoot "band" photographs of them posing dreamingly around the UGA campus. In some shots, they pile into a dorm bed. In others, they goof off around the grounds. Always, they stare self-consciously at anything but the camera, trying to look like they are not trying to look cool.[1]

They had all moved to town to go to the university. Smart, with a smile like a grow light, Johnson moved to Athens in the fall of 1982, the same year I arrived. Unlike a lot of UGA freshmen, he had already seen some Athens bands perform. Looking for something different to do in high school in Atlanta, he and his best friend had started going to the Silver Screen in the Peachtree Battle Shopping Center to see the weekend midnight movie, *The Rocky Horror Picture Show*. There, they met other teens and young adults defying their parents' ideas about sexuality and gender by dressing up like the film's characters and acting out its scenes. They began to hang out in what some Atlanta people called the freak scene, a world Robert Burke Warren, another participant and also a future Athens musician, has called "the Atlanta New Wave Queer underworld." After a while, Johnson got to know the door-

Before Arthur Johnson, Claire Horne, and Laura Carter formed a band, they posed for "band photos" in their University of Georgia dorm. (Photograph by Todd Skelton, courtesy of Arthur Johnson)

man at Atlanta new-music club 688 well enough that he got in despite being underage. Before he graduated from high school, Johnson saw Pylon at the Piedmont Arts Festival and bought the band's album and a single. He also saw R.E.M. open for Bow Wow Wow at the Biltmore.[2]

A few weeks after he moved to Athens, Johnson and another new UGA student he knew from Atlanta, Craig Williams, were waiting for the night bus behind their dorm, Russell Hall, when they saw Curtis Crowe putting up Pylon flyers. In a gesture that both Johnson and Williams remembered as beautifully generous, Crowe offered to put them on the guest list for his band's upcoming show at the i and i. For the two freshmen, it was the Athens version of the golden ticket, not just a chance to see the most important local band for free but an all-access pass into the innermost circle of the scene. At the i and i, not just Crowe but also Briscoe Hay, Bewley, and Lachowski were friendly and welcoming, willing to fold these new kids right into their crowd. From that fall 1982 gig until Pylon played their farewell show in December 1983, Williams and Johnson were backstage at every local show, like little siblings, or as Williams put it, the band's lucky charms. When Pylon opened for R.E.M. at the Fox Theater in Atlanta in May 1983, Williams and Johnson

Tasty World

returned to their hometown as part of the show, dancing onstage as their Athens friends performed.[3]

Laura Carter arrived in Athens to go to UGA the next fall. Androgynous, so brave she scared people, and wickedly funny, Carter was a year behind Johnson at the Atlanta private school Westminster and a regular, too, at *Rocky Horror* screenings. Craig Williams, by then a WUOG deejay, got Johnson and some other students he knew passes to see Talking Heads in Atlanta that November. Johnson ended up giving another of the recipients, Claire Horne, a student deejay with a dry wit, a ride to the show. Back in Athens, he and Carter started hanging out with Horne and going to clubs. Fairly quickly, they fell in love with a group that had debuted the spring before, the Kilkenny Cats. The way Johnson remembered it, he was more than a fan; he wanted to be in the band. Since the Cats were not recruiting, he, Carter, and Horne decided to form their own group. First, though, they actually had to learn to play. Horne began practicing on bass, Carter on guitar and vocals, and Johnson on drums. They named their group Emotional Female.[4]

A few months later, Carter, Johnson, and Horne debuted at the Uptown Lounge, opening in late May and again in June for a version of the band that inspired them, the Kilkenny Cats playing covers under the name the Hollowmen. For the three young musicians, it was a dream come true, despite the fact the *Red and Black* listed their new band's name as "Emotional Feedback." Their short set contained a few originals, including "Elvis H. Christ" and some sloppy covers, like the Cramps' "New Kind of Kick" and the Stooges' "I Wanna Be Your Dog."

I missed these gigs — I did not see Johnson's band play until about a year later, but he assured me that the trio was terrible. Yet Carter's close friend David Barbe, then a twenty-year-old UGA student with a future in the band Mercyland and the founding of an Athens recording studio ahead of him, remembered this same show differently. "Charismatic . . . an explosive live show," in Barbe's words, the new band's performance made "a truly artistic statement." "Immediately, I realized this was 10,000 times better than the band I played in. And these folks can't even hardly play their instruments yet." Soon after, Barbe quit his "pop" band and began looking for musicians to form a new group. Johnson, Carter, and Horne's raw art gave Barbe the courage to take his own musical ideas seriously.[5]

By mid-July, when the three friends played the Uptown again, they had changed their band's name to the Bar-B-Q Killers, a phrase they heard a television news reporter use to refer to a criminal who murdered people at backyard parties. Sometime that fall, Horne started writing actual guitar parts, and it seemed natural for her to perform them as well. Freed from lead, Carter continued playing guitar on some songs but mostly focused on vocals, developing a dramatic stage persona. Johnson continued on drums, and their friend and fellow UGA student David Judd joined them on bass. As a quartet, they were still sloppy, loose, and loud, but also somehow profound. It was hard not to watch Carter as she stalked the stage screaming about *The Love Boat* and penis envy, baring her breasts or shoving the microphone down her pants like a dildo. A *Red and Black* reporter pushing the band's November 30, 1984, gig captured the appeal: "Still raw as meat, the Killers have the spark and more guts than most of the bands in town. I admire their roughness."[6]

In January 1985, in what was probably their first press interview, Horne and Carter parodied earlier Athens bands and older bohemians as they talked to Jimmy Tremayne, a student reporter for the *Red and Black*. "We don't want to make background music. . . . We've never professed to be musicians or anything," Horne said. "It's amazing that we've even played in clubs before because of a total lack of talent, but I think we really have a good idea of what we want our stuff to sound like." Carter confessed, "I just want to offend as many people as possible and shop at Davidson's [a department store]. New clothes, not used." Tremayne also got into the act, writing up a short history of the origins of the band that made it sound like he was describing R.E.M. From one perspective, the piece read like another interview with members of an Athens band trying to sound eccentric. Yet for scene insiders, the article was less an interview than a piece of performance art, a gutsy crack at Athens's most famous musicians and a funny jab at all the other local groups trying so hard to follow R.E.M.'s model of how to be a band. The members of the Bar-B-Q Killers might still be learning to play their instruments, but they already possessed a keen sense of Athens music history and a refreshing ability not to take themselves or the scene's already mythologized past too seriously.[7]

Like Johnson and Carter, many of the young people who would become local musicians, artists, and bohemians in the mid-eighties arrived in town already knowing something about the local scene. In high school in Columbus, Georgia, Jimmy Tremayne learned about Athens groups because his best friend's older brother went to UGA and worked as a reporter for the *Red and Black*'s entertainment section. "Military brat" Keith Landers learned about the B-52's in high school in New Jersey because he had a friend whose sister was formerly Kate Pierson's roommate. After moving to Athens to go to the university in the fall of 1981, it took him one trip to the 40 Watt to realize that his tight parachute pants were not going to work in bohemian Athens. Later, he played guitar in Fashionbattery and then the band that Johnson had wanted so badly to join, the Kilkenny Cats. Slightly older, Barry Marler, who played in bands in Clemson, South Carolina, when he attended the university there, heard enough about the Athens scene to make the three-hour roundtrip drive to town to check out the place in person. After stumbling into a Limbo District show at a "tiny, dark, sweaty room" he later discovered was the 40 Watt, he decided to move to Athens. In the fall of 1983, he packed up his guitar and other equipment, drove back to Georgia, and got a job at the Grill on College Avenue where many of his coworkers were scene participants. By early 1984, Marler was playing in his own band, Dreams So Real.[8]

Kelly Noonan also moved to Athens, not for college but for the scene. When she was sixteen or seventeen and a classmate of Laura Carter's at Westminster, Noonan heard about a new Athens band called R.E.M. She was "so nervy" that she used a friend's older sister's birth certificate to get a driver's license that said she was twenty-six. With fake ID in hand, she went to an R.E.M. show at 688 and decided Michael Stipe was cute. Soon, she was sneaking out of her house to catch other acts at Atlanta's most important new-music club. That fun ended one night when she saw her father walk in looking for her, and she ducked and crawled into the back where an employee let her out an emergency exit. Because her father threatened to call the police if 688 employees let his underage daughter in again, she started going to another new-music club called the Strand in nearby Marietta. Soon, she was learning to play the bass in a band made up of two guys she met there and her best girlfriend. One night in 1984 when this group, A Few Good Men, played Athens, she met Paul Lombard, formerly a member of the Little Tigers and then playing in a band called Music School. He talked her into moving to Athens.[9]

Like the Bar-B-Q Killers, who traded the moody darkness of the early Kilkenny Cats for humor and a harder-edged sound, bands that emerged in these years as part of a new wave of local music-making worked hard to fill some gaps in the local sonic landscape. The influences might have been different than in the earliest days of the scene—less Patti Smith and the Velvet Underground and more X and the Gun Club—but the guiding principle was the same. Everyone tried hard not to sound like other local groups, yet as more bands formed, this goal became harder to achieve. When the Squalls started in 1981, member Bob Hay counted six bands performing new music regularly around town. A few years later, a new local group Banned 37 took its name from its members' count of the number of new-music bands in Athens.[10]

This same principle of diversity applied across the breadth of the scene as participants brought DIY methods of production to bear on other kinds of creative projects. Artists worked to establish distinct styles of painting or photography, created elaborate installations, and experimented with the blurred boundaries between performance art and theater. Writers tried out new forms and new content in local publications they put out with their friends.

In all these mediums and forms, participants pushed against the styles and aesthetic concerns of the bands, artists, and other bohemians that had come before them. All this experimentation and creativity, in turn, reproduced the central idea of the earlier scene makers. What was important was to be more than a passive consumer of art and music made by people you did not know. What was important was to make your own culture.[11]

Yet these efforts did not map easily onto even the underground music business. In 1982, *College Media Journal* morphed into the *CMJ New Music Report*, a kind of a trade magazine for the students who staffed the FM stations that had begun appearing on college campuses in the 1960s. Influenced by CMJ, college radio deejays around the country and some music critics began to call the new music "college rock." The term referred to the places the music originated and circulated and to the business of selling the music as much as a particular set of sonic qualities. Whether or not music labeled college rock was more melodic or intellectual or lyrically ambiguous than other rock music, as some critics suggested, it was usually made and appreciated by people living in college towns and student-dominated neighborhoods of bigger cities who listened to college radio stations. College rock exuded a kind of underground sensibility, a sense that it was produced not for some expansive and commercialized mainstream who would never be smart enough to understand it but for a more elite and discerning group of people: students. "College" suggested a middle-class background and a certain level of intellectualism. It also meant most participants were white, given the racial composition then of most institutions of higher learning that were not HBCUs — historically black colleges and universities.[12]

Because Athens was a college town, it was easy for critics and fans to fit much of the music made there into this category. Indeed, college rock as a genre rose in importance and audience in parallel with R.E.M., whose recordings did very well on the CMJ charts. Still, outside the studios of WUOG, people in Athens rarely used this term.[13]

In this same period, some critics and fans across the country adopted a label they found more expansive stylistically and geographically: indie or alternative rock. Like college rock, the indie genre label focused as much on how and where the music circulated as on its sound. It also referred to music with an underground sensibility, works produced by musicians un-interested in and often outright hostile to any idea of mainstream popular music and the corporate industry that produced it. "Indie" made room for communities not dominated by college students, like the southern Califor-nia hardcore scene with its louder, faster, and mostly all-male, guitar-driven bands. Unlike college rock, which required that new music appeal to college radio's alternative audiences, indie rock generated a more explicit politics of DIY production, a kind of twentieth-century adaption of an old nineteenth-century ideal that real Americans were people who actually made things.[14]

From one perspective, the definition was simple. Indie music was music people created for themselves and their friends outside the channels of the corporate music industry. But if anyone was going to get paid, the devil was in the details. Someone had to own and operate even the most primitive recording equipment and organize and pay for the pressing of a record. Someone had to store the product, advertise that it existed, and ship it to places people could buy it. And someone had to collect royalties from radio play and other performances. In places like the southern California hardcore scene and the D.C. straight-edge scene, participants defined "indie" as anti-corporate, as music made and distributed by independent record companies like SST and Dischord and other entities outside the corporate music busi-ness. Michael Azerrad has defined indie music this way in *Our Band Could Be Your Life*, his important history of eighties and early nineties American indie music.[15]

In Athens, despite some local musicians' criticism of major labels, indie, short for independent, meant something less material and more conceptual. It had less to do with the technicalities of business ownership and more to do with agency, with who held the power to make decisions about your sound, look, and style. It meant not having to do things you did not want to do just because someone — whether that person worked at your record com-pany or your booking agency or your recording studio, no matter who owned them — told you to do them. "Indie was a bohemia," the critic Robert Christ-gau has argued, an alternative world fueled less by any sixties kind of commitment to social justice or even Reagan-era anticorporate politics than by a preoccupation with and cultivation of individualism. The history of bohemia has been "full of promoters and self-expressers set on turning art into rent," and Azerrad's "indie rock" world was no exception.[16]

As critic Gina Arnold has argued in her account of eighties indie music, *Route 666*, no other band was more important in the creation of this bohemia than R.E.M. For Arnold, the point was the particular kind of individualism the members of R.E.M. projected. The Athens band's "niceness stood in bright relief against the scary world of angst and pain that the rest of rock n' roll celebrated. . . . They were our mirror [the Velvet Underground metaphor was mandatory], put on earth to reflect what we were, in case we didn't know, and what we were, it turned out, was sick of anger and ugliness and anti-everything cant." R.E.M. "made indie rock into a community."[17]

In a piece published in *Record* in 1984, Peter Buck offered his own insider's view of America's alternative music scene. He also expressed many scene members' radical opposition to a greed-is-good ideology increasingly powerful in the Reagan era. Buck criticized the music industry's tendency to conflate sales and importance. Great music was not a record that sold or a song that made a band famous. It was music "done by people who convey[ed] a sense of self, a feeling that they'd continue making music even if they weren't making records" — Muddy Waters and the Velvet Underground and the whole "gamut from Hank Williams to Black Flag." Like other people who made this kind of music, the members of R.E.M. started playing together because they loved it and yet quickly realized that the band could also make money. The challenge, Buck confessed, was figuring out the line "between doing [music] for its own sake and doing it because it's a potentially profitable career."[18]

In Buck's way of thinking, I.R.S., despite being distributed by A&M, was "still an independent label similar to other small labels around the country like SST, Slash, dB [sic], TwinTone, 415, and Ace of Hearts" because R.E.M. retained creative control. Still, when problems did arise, the key was to retain the authority to say "hell, no" when people tried to "tell you about videos, how you dress, what you should say to the press and how you live your personal life." What made a band independent was not being represented by a small record label with little money and spotty distribution. Instead, the members of indie bands made their own decisions based on what they felt about their music and their lives. Independence meant agency.[19]

For Buck, the "belief that to follow their heart [was] more important than to follow trends" linked bands with very different sounds. By helping each other tour, bands like the Minutemen, Hüsker Dü, the dB's, and other groups created a network that helped musicians build audiences in new places. "When we started touring, there was a social network that had been set up by R.E.M.'s people when they started touring in 1982 or 1983 that adopted us," Jonathan Segel, member of the Santa Cruz band Camper Van Beethoven, remembered. "We stayed at people's houses. They just passed us along from place to place." As this web of relationships helped individual bands, it also generated a shared sense of purpose across all the local scenes that made up alternative or indie culture.[20]

Back home, the members of R.E.M. had seen firsthand how a network enabled earlier Athens bands to play New York City, get critical attention there, and sign with DB Records. They had also experienced what it meant to be marginalized in a musical community defined around a set of sonic characteristics that wrote them off as a pop band. From this perspective, Buck could be seen as arguing for a definition of the new-music underground that did not leave R.E.M. in the same position nationally that they experienced locally at the start of their career. But he was also describing the kind of musical community he had experienced at times, both on the road and at home, in the wake of *Chronic Town* and *Murmur*'s success. In this kind of place, people were inspired to create new groups not by a particular sound or style but by a particular way of being a band. They then made the music they wanted to make, that meant the most to them. They followed their hearts. And they supported other bands, not because they played the same kind of music but because they and their fans had the same commitment to what was important, what was real, not stardom but the attempt to make art, not just the money but also, always, the community. In this way, the punk idea "that anybody could do it" did not just produce a new musical genre. It inspired waves of new bands and a cacophony of sounds. It produced scenes. And all this participation, this production as well as consumption of culture, made it possible to imagine a whole new indie nation.

In Athens, new bands emerged, playing all kinds of music from funk and jangle rock to hardcore. And locals also experimented with other art forms, creating installations and eclectic venues, little magazines and experimental theater troupes. The members of the Bar-B-Q Killers might not know how to play their instruments. And they probably did not read Buck's article. But they were part of the scene that served as a microcosm of the new indie world that R.E.M. had done so much to build. They were making their own community out of their own "real" music. They were living Buck's dream.

Uptown

Somehow it became a ritual. They were just friends then, in the fall of 1983, broke students mostly living in the dorms, when they started hanging out weekday afternoons in an East Washington Street dive called the Uptown Lounge, little renovated from its days as the Paris Adult xxx Theater. Along with assorted roommates, lovers, and coworkers, they watched reruns of the old series *Batman* on the bar's TV and drank happy-hour pitchers for around a dollar. Some of them were in bands already. Keith Landers, Harry Joiner, and Sean O'Brien, who was also in the Kilkenny Cats, played in Fashion-battery. David Barbe was playing in a band called the Legion with guys he knew from high school. Bryan Cook had been in Is/Ought Gap which had "officially" broken up although they still played occasional gigs. Some of the Atlanta kids like Carter and Judd knew each other already or had mutual friends. In UGA's dorms, they met other young students who liked the new music and dragged them along.[21]

Many scene participants, especially the guys, loved superheroes. In the late 1970s, *Batman* brought together an earlier generation of artists and musicians who sometimes watched reruns of the series on the television in Michael Lachowski's downtown studio. The old show was perfect—a comic book come to life, an artifact of sixties pop culture, and an ideal embodiment of fantasies of individual power. Pylon covered the theme song, and the record store Wuxtry sold Batman t-shirts alongside band merchandise. Later, R.E.M. covered a song called "Superman" by the Clique, and David Barbe chose a beefy superman look-a-like using his muscles to break his chains as the logo for his recording studio.[22]

In the mid-eighties, the ritual of watching *Batman* nurtured a new set of Athens bands. After the show, people would linger and drink beer and talk about music. If anyone in the group was hiding a superhero identity under their street clothes, it was probably Laura Carter. Barbe remembered her as "zero-percent bullshit" and brilliant. She badgered them all to listen carefully to records she discovered. She also insisted on keeping music and people separate and would talk frankly about local bands with what felt to Barbe like a radical and refreshing honesty.[23]

Over the next two years, members of the *Batman* crowd formed and played in a series of harder-edged Athens bands that produced a new darker aesthetic. Many of these bands practiced at the storage spaces where Pulaski dead-ended into Broad Street on the edge of downtown. A local cover band had figured out musicians could rent a section of what were essentially long garages with electricity, if not heat or air-conditioning. No one seemed to care if they cranked up the volume after hours because nearby businesses shut down around five, and the low-income and mostly African-American residents of an adjacent public housing development were not likely to believe the police would care if they complained. With their location close to campus, the dorms, and downtown, the storage spaces were easy enough to walk to, and friends sometimes stopped by with a six-pack of cheap beer to watch them play. Over the next few years, local bands including Fashionbattery, Is/Ought Gap, the Bar-B-Q Killers, Banned 37, and Mercyland practiced there.[24]

Sometimes, the tired musicians would return to the Uptown in the evenings after rehearsing. Keith Landers' roommate worked there as the bartender and manager, and even after happy hour, the drinks were cheap. Both the i and i club and the Last Resort, the old folk and jazz club that sometimes booked the new bands, had closed, and the 40 Watt Uptown, in the Broad Street location, had become relatively upscale with a bar and $3.00 cover charges that seemed pricey to the budget-conscious students. As they sat around with friends talking about the music they liked, the music they were playing, and what band was performing that night at the 40 Watt, someone inevitably complained about the lack of new music venues. With only one club in town, newer bands were especially frustrated. "Unless a band is a really big draw," Harry Joiner, Fashionbattery's drummer, told the *Red and Black*, "they can only play the 40 Watt about once every five weeks." Even then, newer bands could only headline earlier nights of the week or open for a more established Athens band like Love Tractor or an out-of-town band with a local following, like Nashville's Jason and the Scorchers, on the weekend. As Bryan Cook recalled, "days of the week really mattered" then. Headlining a Thursday, Friday, or Saturday night during the UGA school year paid off in terms of both status and money. Local musicians found the summer of 1983 particularly frustrating because Doug Hoeschst, the owner of the 40 Watt Uptown, had shut the place down after most college students left for the summer, leaving bands with nowhere to play.[25]

The owner of the Uptown, the bar they liked, had bought the shuttered porn theater after he retired from the Gold Kist chicken plant so he and his former buddies from work could hang out and drink, and the place was never that crowded. What if bands brought their own PA and just played there, where they were hanging out anyway? The Uptown manager talked the owner into trying live music by promising him the bar would sell a lot of beer.[26]

In October, the members of Fashionbattery set up right on the floor in front of the wall on one of the long sides of the rectangular room and launched this experiment. Two weeks later, on Halloween, always a major holiday in a scene where people loved to dress up, they played there again. Between Joiner's Atlanta friends, bass player McCall Calhoun's Phi Delta fraternity brothers, and guitarist Landers's coworkers from Dominos, Fashionbattery could fill the bar on weekend nights, and gradually they became a kind of de-facto house band. Soon, other Uptown regulars got dates for their bands too, and the bar began to host live music on more nights. The owner of the 40 Watt Uptown was so mad about the competition that he told Fashionbattery and the other "Uptown bands" that they could not play his club, a threat he followed up on by canceling some groups' upcoming gigs. At the Uptown, the owner liked the beer sales but hated the music, and the growing crowds of young people ran off his drinking buddies. By April 1984, he had sold the place to Kyle Pilgrim, who completed the stage planned before the sale, bought a PA system, and worked hard to wrestle groups away from the 40 Watt. The competition that Pilgrim called "the gig war" was good for local music. The Uptown Lounge had become a real club.[27]

As the scene expanded in 1984 and 1985, what had been one big circle of participants fractured into overlapping crowds organized around bands and venues. The town might be small, but bohemians, as Velena Vego, a member of the band Mystery Date, recalled, "went out every night. Nobody stayed home and watched TV." Rare events like R.E.M.'s "secret" show at Stitchcraft in September 1983 and Pylon's last performance at the Mad Hatter that December brought almost everyone together, but, day to day, musicians, artists, and other bohemians interacted within smaller, overlapping webs of acquaintances, friends, and lovers. One important distinction was old versus new, or when a person first became active in the scene. In this era, people who became bohemians after the release of *Chronic Town* were the young crowd. People who saw Pylon and R.E.M. at Tyrone's were old-timers.[28]

While older bohemians did not always recognize this divide, the new people remembered being a little intimidated by these musicians and artists. They also recalled how some members of earlier Athens bands encouraged them. Pete Buck, in particular, introduced a lot of young fans not yet in bands to "cool music" through his job as a clerk at Wuxtry's Baxter Street branch near UGA's high-rise dorms. Keith Landers remembered meeting all the members of R.E.M. after he showed up at their sound check, probably at the i and i in October 1982, because he was still a few days shy of nineteen then, the legal drinking age. He figured he would avoid being carded by just staying in the club. By the time R.E.M. went on hours later, Linda Hopper and Lynda Stipe were treating him like "backstage guy," and the band invited him up onstage along with their friends to dance during the encore. Younger musicians remembered Hopper, vocalist for Oh-OK, as particularly supportive. Jerry Ayers also continued to inspire many young artists and musicians, just as he had mentored Michael Stipe and Mark Cline when they were learning to be bohemians.[29]

Class also divided scene participants. David Barbe did not hear about R.E.M. until after *Chronic Town* came out. Like Landers, he remembered seeing one of the band's back-to-back gigs at the i and i that October, and "it was mindboggling how great they were." That same fall, Barbe recognized Evan Lieberman, a musician he had played with in Atlanta when they were both in high school, in a photograph of the Little Tigers in the *Red and Black* announcing an upcoming show at the Clayton Street 40 Watt. In "that tiny room" "packed with people," he saw a performance "no less exciting" than the R.E.M. show, and he remembered thinking "these are my people. This is who I need to be hanging out with." Yet as a jeans and t-shirt guy with classes to attend and sweaty summer work filling cracks in parking lots across Atlanta, he was not sure how to get into this "bohemian townie hipster" world. After months of going to shows and hanging out, he became friends with other musicians including the members of Fashionbattery, the Kilkenny Cats, and the future members of the Bar-B-Q Killers whose busy days, too, were filled with jobs and classes. Later he realized "people can only sit around and drink espresso and look cool all day long if they don't have to work." Some bohemians were privileged enough to have parents or other sources of income to cover their tuition and expenses, freeing them to hang out and make art and music without thinking about earning a living.[30]

As the scene exploded, newer scene participants coalesced around the Uptown bands, the more pop Fashionbattery, the gloomy Kilkenny Cats, the harder-edged Bar-B-Q Killers, and later, in 1985, the funky and explosive Time Toy and the fast and melodic Mercyland. By the summer of 1984, the *Red and Black* reported that the once-promising Fashionbattery had "stagnated into a moody, detached dance-pop rut, despite the furious drumming of Harry Joiner." Booked by an agent who did A and R work for RCA, Fashionbattery recorded a four-song demo and played up and down the East Coast that fall. Under pressure from their parents to keep their grades up, band members spent the spring of 1985 going to school Monday through Wednesday and leaving town for Thursday, Friday, and Saturday night gigs at clubs and fraternity parties in the southeast. Then Joiner's dad pressured him to take a job in Europe, and Landers and O'Brien were left stewing in Athens over the summer of 1985 with nothing to do and the band on "temporary leave." By the time Joiner returned, Fashionbattery had fallen apart.[31]

The Kilkenny Cats, in contrast, were thriving. Originally, the four musicians who formed the band—Haynes Collins on bass, Allen Wagner on drums, Tom Cheek on vocals, and Sean O'Brien on guitar—thought of the group as a side project. O'Brien was also in Fashionbattery and the other three members played in Is/Ought Gap with Bryan Cook. Cheek and Cook had met in the fall of 1980 when the two freshmen moved into Myers Hall at UGA, and Cook followed the sound of a Sex Pistols record to Cheek's room. Soon, Cook and Cheek began playing together in their dorm's piano practice space. The next year, Cook moved to a different dorm and bought a bass that he played through a cord plugged into his old stereo while Cheek picked and strummed his guitar. In the fall of 1981, after Haynes Collins, Cheek's friend from his hometown in North Carolina, moved to town, they rented the old Mack and Payne funeral home next to the Morton Theater for $75 a month in order to have a practice space. As Cheek worked to learn guitar, Collins learned bass, and Cook experimented with singing, they followed what by then had become the Athens way and did not let the fact that they could not really play their instruments stop them from forming a band. All they needed was a drummer. After Harry Joiner played with them for what Cook remembered as "a minute," the new group recruited Allen Wagner, who originally came to Athens to attend UGA and play in the university's famous Redcoat Band.

Set to debut at a house party advertised on Michael Lachowski's party line, the four guys decided to name their new band Is/Ought Gap after a philosophical problem. At Leslie Michel's Night Gallery on Prince Avenue, their first real gig, the nervous quartet played beneath an art installation of red sticks hanging from the ceiling, and the small crowd included Vanessa Briscoe Hay. With perfect timing, Is/Ought Gap finally got a gig at Tyrone's but the club burned a few days before the date. By early 1983, the group had worked up to a Thursday night at the 40 Watt and toured some, performing at 688 in Atlanta, clubs in Knoxville, Nashville, and Greenville, the kind of well-paying frat parties at UGA and Georgia Tech that new music bands did not like to admit they played, and one CBGB's gig in New York. Bizarrely, just as the band was winding down, the guys decided to spend the money that they had saved from their shows to record an EP with Vic Varney producing at the twenty-four-track Songbird Studios in Atlanta.[32]

Cook was an odd front guy, a warm bear-hug of a man rather than an angsty art rocker or a brash punk. Onstage, he sometimes wore what looked like an old GI helmet, and his goofy moves and fluid facial expressions made his at times biting insights seem like a form of eccentric comedy. In a song called "Artsy Peace and Love," for example, Cook sang about a trendy party he went to at Jerry Ayers and his boyfriend and bandmate Davey Stevenson's house where people spoke French and Spanish and smoked "hash-laced cigarettes." Cook's lyrics and his jerky stop-and-start style conveyed an experience he shared with other young bohemians, a feeling of being simultaneously "totally welcomed and way out of place and over my head." Like most Athens bands in the wake of R.E.M., Is/Ought Gap expanded their set list by throwing in a few quirky covers among the originals. An anything but glam Cook belting out the New York Dolls' song "Personality Crisis" showcased the singer's sharp, self-deprecating humor.[33]

As the success of the Kilkenny Cats dissolved Is/Ought Gap, Cook stayed busy playing keyboards with the more hippie Club Ga Ga and singing in Pete Buck, Bill Berry, and Mike Mills's cover band the Hindu Love Gods. Is/Ought Gap occasionally reunited for gigs, and the Red and Black reported that the "dead" band sounded better than the functioning version. Cook also created the popular parking lot festival Sonstock, a summer tradition in Athens in the mid-eighties with cups of beer and slices of Sons of Italy pizza for a quarter and free live music.[34]

As the Kilkenny Cats developed a dark and moody Joy Division sound, band members deepened the gloom by decorating the stage with skulls, lighted candles, and flowerpots filled with dead scrub. Six months after their debut, Slash Records expressed interest but did not sign them. Michael Lachowski, on the road on what would be Pylon's last tour, shared their tape with his contacts at other labels and at clubs, and got the young band some out-of-town dates. When Sean O'Brien quit to focus on Fashionbattery, another UGA student, Mark Craig, who knew the Uptown crowd and dated Laura Carter for a while, joined on guitar. That summer, as the Red and Black's entertainment editor Charles Aaron reported, the Kilkenny Cats abandoned their "sluggish, meandering, Doorsy dirges" and the mood Arthur Johnson and his friends had loved. The addition of "a talented, let-it-rip guitar player" had improved the "sleepy, uncertain band" so much the student critic named the group "Athens' most exciting band."[35]

In the fall, Kilkenny Cats took this new sound into Songbird Studios in Atlanta and recorded a demo with Michael Lachowski producing. The tape got a lot of airplay at WUOG. Hoboken, New Jersey–based Coyote Records signed the band and released the recording as a single, "Attractive

Figure"/"Of Talk," at the end of 1984. On the A side, Cheek ran through all of Stipe's early vocal techniques as he varied the volume and tone of his voice and mumbled, hiccupped, and scatted, producing more mood than meaning. Choruses with an aura of languid desire alternated with verses that stopped and started, building to a moment when the bass, guitar, and drums suddenly ceased, and Cheek sexily sucked in a breath. It took a certain kind of courage for Cheek to sing this way and for Craig to write a three-note guitar solo, a classic Pete Buck move. In Athens, copying R.E.M.'s way of being a band was cool, but sounding too much like the indie stars was risky. Working this edge, the Kilkenny Cats drew UGA students who had not heard R.E.M.'s early, live sound. Former Pylon bassist Lachowski's involvement, too, cut the risk that the band would be labeled unoriginal. "Attractive Figure" became a local hit. David Barbe remembered that Craig wrote the song, though the sleeve, in another debt to R.E.M., credited the entire band. Craig also played guitar on the recording. But by the time the single hit the stores, he had quit the band in frustration, angry about too many bus trips from Atlanta, where he was living with his parents as he took a break from college, for Athens practices that did not happen. After rumors of a breakup, guitarist Clifton Hill replaced Craig, and the other members dropped their UGA classes so the band could spend the winter touring the East Coast.[36]

Perhaps the most important of the Uptown groups, the Bar-B-Q Killers stood out in that wave of guitar-driven boy bands. Horne, Carter, Johnson, and Judd readily admitted their lack of experience and did not take themselves too seriously. In a period when R.E.M.'s growing fame brought more attention to Athens bands, the Killers' lack of professionalism came across as refreshing, a return to the musical amateurism so essential in the earliest days of the scene.[37]

With Pylon retired, Carter, Horne, Johnson, and Judd looked elsewhere for inspiration, to out-of-town bands that featured powerful women, including the Cramps and the Fall. Onstage, Laura Carter was sexually suggestive and aggressive, and her boyish looks confused people. Tan and fit from outdoor work on UGA's landscaping crew and David Barbe's parking-lot patching team, she was frequently mistaken for a Latino man. She spoke as well as sang in a low voice. Kelly Noonan, who first met her in middle school, remembered being shocked when the teacher called out her name, and Carter answered "here" in a voice that sounded like a boy. Yet she was not transgender in ways people would later understand that term. She did not refer to herself as "he" or bind her breasts, a fact she made clear many times when she ripped off her shirt onstage. She did not restrict herself or her intimate

Athens bands like the Bar-B-Q Killers played often at a club in Atlanta called the White Dot. *Left to right:* **David Judd, David Barbe, Arthur Johnson, Laura Carter, and Claire Horne. (Photograph by Jason Vise, courtesy of Tony Paris Archives and Arthur Johnson)**

partners to a single gender and had serious relationships with both men and women. In contemporary terms, Carter might have been called nonbinary or queer. Then, she was just Laura Carter, one-of-a-kind, her own category, bold and sexy and out there.[38]

In counterpoint to Carter's intensity, Claire Horne played slashing and original guitar with a quiet tomboy beauty that drew a circle of admiring male musicians, many of whom developed serious crushes. She felt that people were drawn to her guitar playing, a sound that she described as "dark with a snarl to it," because it did not seem like the way a girl would sound. Fans always told Horne she seemed "aloof on stage, but it wasn't intentional." "I had a hard time performing. I had to really concentrate to hit eighty percent of our mark on a given night."[39]

In contrast to both Horne's calm and Carter's thrash, David Judd, a blonde and punk beanpole of a bass player, bounced around with a manic energy. Behind his bandmates, Johnson slammed his sticks into his drums and built the aural framework that held Carter's screaming vocals, Judd's thumping sludge, and Horne's blasted fragments of melody together in an at times exquisite tension.

Sonically, the Bar-B-Q Killers announced that whatever people had meant in the past by an Athens sound, these young musicians were after something wildly different. Rejecting the sublimated desires that haunted both the B-52's' campy party and R.E.M.'s romanticism, they said what they wanted directly. They put it all out there. They screamed. David Barbe, who briefly joined the Bar-B-Q Killers as an additional guitarist, has called them Athens's first hardcore band.[40]

But the Bar-B-Q Killers were also a throwback to the original scene, to the performance art and gender play so essential to the appeal of the early B-52's and Pylon. Their theatrical shows were only amplified by a series of themed performances they did in collaboration with Carter's then-girlfriend Mary Wilson. For an Easter tableaux, Carter took the role of Christ and had her bandmates carry her onto the stage strapped to a cross. In another performance, she and Wilson got married onstage. Carter played with gender and desire in ways that built on the originality of Cindy Wilson, Kate Pierson, and especially Vanessa Briscoe Hay's radical performances. And she not only acted out sexual desires; she also transgressed another taboo. She acted out anger. That emotion was a problem for women everywhere but especially in the South. When Carter ripped up her shirt and showed us her breasts and her farmer's tan as she screamed, she made it clear she was not only queer. She was also a mad white woman. She acted out courage.[41]

Back then, I wanted to be cool so I did not admit that the Bar-B-Q Killers actually scared me a little. I went to their shows, though. I felt like I had to. A few years later, when I signed up for a graduate course in feminist theory, I worried because I had so little background in the subject compared to my classmates. As soon as we dug into the material, I realized all those nights spent at the Uptown had been their own kind of education. Like a punk Judith Butler but more fun, Laura Carter had taught me all I needed to know about performance, gender, and sexuality. Thanks to the Bar-B-Q Killers, I was going to be fine.

Big Time

In the mid-eighties, Athens became a kind of brand in alternative-music circles. Record company executives would listen to tapes mailed from Athens addresses, and club owners around the country were eager to book bands from the town. As Mark Cooper Smith, drummer for the Squalls, put it, "you could call any club on the East Coast and say you were from Athens, and they would say 'come on.'" Athens was so big that bands from other parts of Georgia like the Swimming Pool Q's and Guadalcanal Diary were often advertised as Athens bands when they played outside the state. While some promoters simply did not understand Georgia geography, others hoped the "Athens" label would bring more people out. Guadalcanal Diary played second fiddle to R.E.M. in indie-music circles so often that they named their 1984 DB Records release *Walking in the Shadow of the Big Man*. Yet by the time Guadalcanal Diary signed with major label Elektra in 1985, some members of this group — bassist Rhett Crowe (the sister of Pylon's Curtis Crowe) and guitarist Jeff Walls — had actually moved to Athens.[42]

Alongside the new Uptown bands, older groups like Love Tractor and Oh-OK continued to thrive, releasing records, touring heavily, and drawing larger crowds. R.E.M., by then too big for the local clubs, performed at UGA's Legion Field and the Civic Center or the Fox Theater in Atlanta or booked an occasional secret show under an alternate name. Older bohemians formed new groups like the Squalls, whose lead singer, main songwriter, and guitarist Bob Hay lived with and later married Pylon's Vanessa Briscoe, and Go Van Go, a band that lasted less than a year but included Vic Varney of the Method Actors and the Tone Tones, Dana Downs of the Tone Tones, Juan Molina of the Little Tigers, and Robert Warren. Predicting which band would follow R.E.M. became a popular local pastime, second only to heading out to the clubs.[43]

Many locals bet on Love Tractor. Richmond, Cline, Wellford, and Swartz had finished school. Able at last to tour fulltime, band members had learned to sing and honed a tight, funky groove. Performing in dresses as the cover band Wheel of Cheese, they developed a sexy, easy style that bled over into their Love Tractor gigs. It did not hurt that all four members were cute as hell.[44]

Like R.E.M.'s *Murmur*, Love Tractor's second album, *Around the Bend*, embraced their regional connections. Mark Cline played an occasional banjo part, and Richmond, Cline, Swartz, and Wellford all sang sparse vocals in heavy southern accents, creating a kind of sonic twang. As the *Village Voice's* review of the album put it, Love Tractor "had radically expanded their musical vocabulary while starting to revel in the down-home flavor only hinted at before. . . . There's fluid finger-picking galore, mandolins and sitars evoked not faked, the most noncliched [sic] use of fuzz and wa-wa in years, and even some fairly funky kicks and spins."[45]

In June 1984, MTV's program *The Cutting Edge* broadcast the video Atlanta director Howard Libov made for the Love Tractor single "Spin Your Partner." Launched in August 1981, MTV originally worked like a television version of AOR radio as "veejays" hosted programs filled with visual versions of rock songs. Soon, young adults and teenagers—a key segment of the music-buying public—were regularly watching the all-music channel. Yet MTV's restrictive programming left out emerging musical genres like hip-hop and college rock. To promote the label's acts and other performers not usually seen on MTV, I.R.S. Records decided in 1983 to start producing a program for the network. *The Cutting Edge* introduced viewers to musicians like pre-famous Madonna and bands like R.E.M. For Love Tractor, being on MTV was a big break.

With its cartoon story of a band of rural southern boys making it big, the "Spin Your Partner" video positioned the members of Love Tractor as southern hick bohemians. Black and white photographs, antique tractors and trucks, an old-fashioned telephone, and a rusty-roofed barn with gaps in the wall planks like the missing teeth in an old farmer's mouth established a vaguely anti-modern time period. Front porches and a billboard for a Pentecostal church asking passersby "Have you spoken in tongues?" located this past in the South.

On its surface, for anyone willing to take it straight, the video told the story of a white southern band too good to languish uncelebrated in the sticks. After making a recording on their front porch, they sent the tape off to "Mr. Record Producer," played by ex–Method Actor David Gamble, in the big city. He loved the music, of course, and immediately signed the group. But money raining down profusely from above and stardom did not corrupt them. At the end of the video, band members played a gig at the new Broad Street location of the 40 Watt, bought a nicer old truck, and returned to a larger old house. Like all good Athens bands after the B-52's, they stayed home. Love Tractor's video made loving fun of the band's "partners," critics, and fans with their "wow, they can actually create down there in the South" attitude.[46]

Trying to build on the growing popularity of this song, the band put out two records on DB in 1984, an EP called *'Til the Cows Come Home* featuring new drummer and former UGA student Andrew Carter and a compilation album called *Wheel of Pleasure*. Both releases included a version of the German band Kraftwerk's song "Neon Lights." Its fusion of funk, southern twang, and Krautrock suggested the way Love Tractor's sound continued to push everyone onto the dance floor even as it evolved. More than any other alternative band in town at the time, Love Tractor drew on sounds and rhythms historically associated with African American music. By the end of the summer, Love Tractor had earned a coveted Friday-night spot as part of New York City's New Music Seminar, headlining at the showcase club Irving Plaza.[47]

Interviewed in New York that week, Cline described learning to navigate the industry: "You can be cloistered in your own little world and write your music, but at some point you do have to come outside of it, and if you don't get wise about the business end, you will get screwed." After a series of booking agents, Love Tractor ended up with Bob Singerman, who frequently paired them with other groups he represented, including Hüsker Dü, 10,000 Maniacs, and the Replacements. At a gig at Maxwell's in Hoboken, Cline introduced his former boyfriend Kevin O'Neill to Bob Mould, and the two men, as Cline remembered, became a couple "before the show was over," a relationship that lasted for years. In New York City, after a piece in the *East Village Eye* suggested all the members of the band were gay instead of just Cline, Love Tractor began drawing a large gay male audience. In 1986, the band signed a contract with Big Time, a subsidiary of major label RCA.[48]

The downside to all this traveling was that band members were less a part of the local scene. On rare occasions when the members of Love Tractor were in Athens for more than a quick gig at the 40 Watt and a night or two in their own beds, Cline would go out with his roommate Sam Seawright and find the scene that he had helped build was now full of people and bands he did not know. When MTV held a contest in which the prize was a weekend in Athens with Mark Cline, the guitar player showed the winner and her friend all the local sights, including Michael Stipe's house. Stipe was so angry at Cline that the old friends stopped speaking for a while. Only later did Cline understand that while he had been away, R.E.M. had become so famous that overly zealous fans had started stalking the singer.[49]

Like Love Tractor, the Squalls were regular headliners at downtown clubs in the mid-eighties. A hippie-flavored fusion of Pylon and the Side Effects, the band emerged out of late-night jam sessions at Al Walsh's house that participants called "squalls." One of the regulars, Bob Hay, had followed his friend, fellow musician, and Grateful Dead fan Ken Starratt from Maine to Athens in 1977 after college in Michigan and a stint in a commune. He used his tax refund to buy a decent guitar and amp at Chick Piano in downtown Athens and then convinced Walsh, also a guitar player, to purchase a bass. Starratt played guitar too, and Mig Little, his girlfriend, played drums, while Diana Torrell, Walsh's girlfriend, added keyboards and backing vocals. As a band began to emerge out of the fun, the name stuck. After a few late-

The Squalls perform in costume at a 1982 Halloween gig at the 40 Watt. *Left to right*: Al Walsh, Diana Torrell, Bob Hay, and Ken Starratt. (Photographer unknown, courtesy of Bob Hay)

night, casual performances at the Bluebird, the restaurant that replaced the El Dorado, the Squalls played what members called their first gig, a December 1981 date at the Clayton 40 Watt.[50]

The Squalls really came together that next fall when Mark Cooper Smith, Walsh's former roommate at West Georgia College and a drummer, moved to Athens to get an MA in anthropology at UGA. As soon as Smith arrived, he joined the jams at Walsh's, and Mig Little moved over to percussion. These changes, plus twice-a-week practices, tightened up the Squalls' sound. Because band members were older than most local bohemians and had full-time commitments — Cooper was a graduate student, Hay was a manager at Kinko's, and Torrell clerked at Davidson's department store — the Squalls mostly played weekends. In the *Red and Black*, Jimmy Ellison described the Squalls' "danceable pop" as a fusion of "brilliant harmonies, steady drum beats, and psychedelic guitars." Hay said the band sounded like "birds flying above an avalanche." In late 1982, members of the Squalls posed with other local musicians for the group portrait that appeared in *People* magazine's January article about the Athens scene. In April 1983, Little was in the car with Larry Marcus of the Little Tigers and Carol Levy of Boat Of when these two Athens musicians died. She moved away afterwards, and the Squalls became a five-piece. Later, two former members of the Little Tigers joined the group, first Paul Hammond on sax and then Juan Molina on bass.[51]

In the spring of 1984, the Squalls went on a little East Coast tour, packed into Starratt's old red and white VW van and smoking pot the whole way. They played the Milestone in Charlotte, North Carolina, opening for Oh-OK before a crowd of teens who filled the club after word got out that the owner had stopped carding, Cat's Cradle in Carrboro, right next to Chapel Hill, where the three people who turned up danced to every song in the set, and D.C.'s 9:30 Club. In New York for their big-city debut, they stayed with Diana's sister Tekla Torrell, who had lived in Athens in the late seventies and was friends with the members of the B-52's, in her second-floor walk-up with its shared bathroom. To use the toilet, Smith remembered, you had leave the apartment and remember to carry the seat with you. Manhattan was run-down and crime-ridden then, but to the members of the Squalls the city felt like the center of the universe. They played CBGB's—in Hay's words "the worst dive on earth"—the Peppermint Lounge, and Maxwell's in Hoboken, where they drew a crowd of about 100 people that reminded them of home. Despite nursing a hangover, *Village Voice* critic Van Gosse had a ball. The "yearning hominess" of the vocals, "the lazy, jerky interplay of sweet, whiny guitars," and the "rolling excited builds that surprise them as much as the audience" reminded him of the "rangy, rambling eclecticism of the best San Francisco groups of old."[52]

Back in Athens, Jimmy Tremayne, who wrote the *Red and Black*'s "After Hours" column in the spring and fall of 1984, called the Squalls "our favorite band right now," and plugged them every time they played: "The Squalls are great whether you're a dickhead or a waver or whatever." The band recorded an EP at local musician Jim Hawkins's new recording studio on Boulevard. After putting it out on their own label Mbrella in November, they mailed it to college radio stations and clubs up and down the East Coast. The production was professional enough that a new Athens band seeking a record deal with Mbrella sent them a demo tape. The next year, "Na Na Na Na," a song off the album that sounded like a message to an ex-lover but instead expressed Hay's anger at owners of the El Dorado for closing the restaurant where he worked, went to number two on the college rock chart.[53]

Locally, the Squalls made good money, packing the Uptown, playing an occasional fraternity party, and helping yet another iteration of the 40 Watt, back in the old spot on Clayton Street, survive its lean start. Fans loved the way Hay's quirky, poetic lyrics, delivered in his deadpan style and layered with Torrell's backup vocals, rode the hippie groove laid down by Smith, Walsh, and Starratt. Like R.E.M. at Tyrone's, the Squalls' shows at the 40 Watt Uptown drew a large and eclectic audience. Scene participants danced until they were dizzy right alongside a few Greeks and older back-to-the-land types. A sorority girl, a scholarship student, and a wannabe bohemian, a mixed crowd all by myself, I went often. And sometimes something profound happened. Heartbeats, drum beats, bass notes, and breaths aligned. The usual me/you grammar dissolved. Audience members and musicians moved together, a momentary, collective manifestation of the participatory culture at the heart of the scene.[54]

By 1984, Athens had both a reputation in the larger world as a new-music center and a growing infrastructure of clubs, studios, and fans. For the first time, fully formed bands started moving to town. Mystery Date, an Atlanta quartet made up of four women that played in Athens often, arrived in mid-1984. The next year, members of the San Antonio band the Butthole Surfers rented a house outside Athens in the tiny town of Winterville and began playing local clubs and dreaming up schemes for interacting with members of the band they were obsessed with, R.E.M. That same year, a North Carolina group called the Flat Duo Jets arrived from Carrboro. While it was cool to come for college or to live in Athens because you grew up in the area, moving to town to try to join the scene remained suspect. Some local bohemians never accepted these bands or musicians as part of the scene.[55]

Live, Mystery Date had an Athens-style amateurism, the kind of danceable beat local fans loved, and startlingly beautiful members with real bohemian style: guitarist Vanessa Vego, her sister the singer Velena Vego, bassist Robin Edwards, and a string of drummers that never quite stuck. Vanessa Vego had real stage presence, a petite, feminine take on "Jimi Hendrix cool and Johnny Thunders abandon." Edwards, in contrast, radiated a more quiet aura that made it hard to look away. When the band rented a studio space in Athens, she commuted from Atlanta for a while before moving to town where she became one of a handful of African Americans active in the scene. Because Vanessa Vego dated Mike Richmond of Love Tractor and Velena Vego dated R.E.M. manager Jefferson Holt, Mystery Date had the right connections to manage the transition.[56]

Other transplants struggled. The Uptown crowd, with their harder, darker aesthetic, loved the Butthole Surfers, but the band's harassment of R.E.M. angered many bohemians. The revivalist Flat Duo Jets drew an eclectic mix of people, from the art-school crowd to frat guys, but all my friends

**Robin Edwards, the bass player for the band Mystery Date,
was one of a handful of African American musicians active
in the Athens scene. Other members of the band were Velena
and Vanessa Vego and over ten different drummers, including
Helen, pictured here, whose last name no one can remember.
(Photograph by Bill Howard, courtesy of Robin Edwards)**

thought it was a problem that they tried to claim Athens. Both the Butthole Surfers and Flat Duo Jets moved away after less than a year.[57]

Like Love Tractor, Oh-OK seemed destined for indie stardom. Critical reception of the band's DB release *Wow Mini Album* had helped make arty pop cool in Athens, opening up space for bands like the Squalls and Mystery Date. *Village Voice* critic Robert Christgau, who caught an early Oh-OK gig, became a devoted fan. He described the band's music as "another Athenian alchemical reworking of the tiny, hidden, formulas of pop, with no concession to kitsch either," "eerie, unsettling even in its pretty, furious quietness, just melody and pound." For Christgau, Oh-OK took "the radical deconstruction of rock 'n' roll that the B-52's initiated to its farthest extreme by liquidating all chords — no guitars, no keys."[58]

More than any other Athens band, Oh-OK communicated the childlike sense of wonder and play so essential to the Athens scene. Like Vanessa Briscoe Hay of Pylon, Linda Hopper and Lynda Stipe did not have the kind of androgynous, stick-straight bodies and serious pale faces of many new- and no-wave musicians at the time. Their torsos curved, their hair curled, and their lips smiled. They wore forties and fifties dresses and ribbons in their hair, and when they performed they bopped and shook like the dancers in *A Charlie Brown Christmas*. Hopper's high-pitched, matter-of-fact vocals provided a confident counterpoint to Stipe's bass, offering up at times a sweet and awkward dissonance that mimicked a kid singing along to a favorite tune. Stipe's hooky, bouncy bass lines, in turn, made it impossible to listen to this music without wanting to tap or spin or leap or sway like a toddler getting used to her feet.[59]

In "Brother," a song written by Carol Levy, Hopper sang a verse about a sibling "too young to go to the discotheque": "My little brother / he's for himself / he's for nobody else / once somebody in a red mini-skirt / tried for it." Then the chorus rang out, "He is for an expanding whole." The opening of the song "Person" sounded like the manifesto of a kid on the cusp of becoming a teenager, both narcissistic and vulnerable: "I-I-I-I-I-I-I-I-I am a person. / I speak to you. / I am a person, I am a person and that is enough."[60]

Oh-OK took up the refusal of maturity inherent in punk amateurism and anger and turned it toward innocence and pleasure. Child's play meant the valuing of passion and self-expression over craft and money. It meant a primal sound, a juvenile visual and narrative style, and a mood that oscillated between innocence and knowingness, wonder and terror. Together, all these evocations of childhood provided a route back into emotional expressiveness without borrowing what most white musicians understood then as "black" gestures and styles, sexual and other physical pleasures communicated through funky, syncopated beats, soaring melodies and vocals, and evocative lyrics.[61]

At the end of 1982, mistrust between former lovers Lynda Stipe and David Pierce spilled over into the band, and Pierce left. Bill Berry sat in on drums for a gig or two, until drummer David McNair joined. Instead of building on a successful start, Oh-OK spent 1983 struggling to maintain a steady lineup. After two guitarists came and went, Athens newcomer Matthew Sweet joined.[62]

Members of Athens band Oh-OK dress up for New York photographer Laura Levine. *Left to right:* **Lynda Stipe, Matthew Sweet, Linda Hopper, and David McNair. (Photograph © Laura Levine)**

A fan of the B-52's in high school, Matthew Sweet read about the Athens scene in *New York Rocker* and listened to recordings of Athens bands. When R.E.M. played his hometown of Lincoln, Nebraska, Sweet slipped Michael Stipe a tape he made in his bedroom of songs he had written. According to Sweet, Stipe urged him to come to Athens, and the eighteen-year-old decided to attend the University of Georgia. Sweet told the *Washington Post* a year later, "When I told my parents I was going to Georgia, they thought I was crazy," but they relented enough to pay for it. Soon after he arrived, Sweet began collaborating with Michael Stipe in a duo they called the Community Trolls. He also joined Lynda Stipe's band.[63]

Sweet brought to Oh-OK not just his talent as a musician and songwriter but also funds to help finance a second record. Some people remembered his parents gave him money. Others recalled that after Sweet moved to Athens, he signed a writing deal with a major label and had money to burn on both studio time and drugs. In August, Oh-OK followed R.E.M.'s example and worked with Mitch Easter at his Drive-In Studio to record *Furthermore What*.[64]

At the end of 1983, just before DB Records released Oh-OK's new EP,

Sweet quit. In an example of the incestuous nature of local music-making, not long after Sweet joined Oh-OK, he also started playing music with Oh-OK's ex-drummer David Pierce. Pierce had learned to play drums in high school band. Sweet was a prolific composer and a skilled musician who could play keyboards, bass, guitar, and a hybrid instrument with two high-end bass strings and two low-end guitar strings that he called a bagbone. Pierce's "disco plus marching band" style put a fun groove under Sweet's jangle-pop sound. They called their new group Buzz of Delight, a phrase Michael Stipe coined at a party at Linda Hopper's place. In late 1983, using $1,200 borrowed from Sweet's parents, the duo also followed R.E.M.'s example and traveled to North Carolina to record with Don Dixon at Reflection Studios. They knew Danny Beard through Oh-OK, and DB released a Buzz of Delight single "Christmas" in late 1983 and an EP called *Sound Castles* about a month and a half later and in direct competition with Oh-OK's new disc. Sweet told *Red and Black* that he and Pierce had quit Oh-OK because touring "was killing all our inspiration and making us unhappy." Yet Pierce had left Oh-OK long before Sweet joined, and the band had not traveled that much during Sweet's half-a-year tenure.[65]

After living in Athens about a year, Sweet confessed to the *Washington Post* reporter writing about the scene, "I calculated it. I'm trying to find a way to make my music." When Buzz of Delight played in New York that winter, major-label reps turned out to talk to Sweet. A few months later, he signed a solo contract with Columbia, and moved to New York. In less than two years, Sweet had gone from unknown high school grad to Athens newcomer to major-label musician. Pierce, abandoned in the process, has said that he never had hard feelings, though people remembered him as mad at the time. Years later, some people still refused to talk about Sweet or remembered him as obscenely ambitious. According to Rodger Brown, who lived in Athens and wrote a book about the early days of the scene, Sweet actually told people that he "came to town to climb the ladder." Yet others remember Sweet as hyper-talented and kind and no more ambitious than some other local musicians. What Sweet did was expose the contradictions inherent in the R.E.M. model and just how difficult it was to walk that line Pete Buck had talked about between meaningful music and money.[66]

Whether or not Sweet abandoned Pierce, he certainly left Oh-OK in a difficult situation. With a new record to promote and F.B.I., the agency that booked R.E.M., setting up dates, Linda Hopper and Lynda Stipe scrambled to fill out their band's lineup. Bryan Cook, who got to know Lynda Stipe in UGA classes as well as working at Sons of Italy, was willing, but he played keyboards and was barely competent on guitar. When in doubt, Pete Buck told him, trying to be reassuring, just play a D chord. Cook limped along that winter and spring of 1984 to help his friends, and in May, Lynn Blakey, who had played in Mitch Easter's band Let's Active and also sang, became Oh-OK's guitarist.[67]

Christgau reviewed Oh-OK's EP *Furthermore What* in the *Village Voice* and gave it an A-. "A slight letdown," he wrote, "threatening to cross the line from unflappably fey to oneirically arty." The songs conjured "half-remembered melodies in much the same way the lyrical catchphrases do, and Georgia boys" (he was not quite right on this point) contributed "Georgia guitar and Georgia drums." Overall, he argued, "it's as charming and sexy as it intends, which is plenty." *Furthermore What* did well on the independent charts, and articles about the band appeared in *Mademoiselle* and *Creem* that summer. Fronted by three powerful women, Oh-OK seemed to be back stronger than ever. Maybe Love Tractor would not be the next band out of Athens to break.[68]

A Party on Every Page

By creating their own way of being a band and building their own networks, the R.E.M. guys made the Athens underground that had not originally accepted their music into a powerful model for other outposts of the bohemian diaspora. Other Athens bands followed them and continued to spread news of Athens everywhere they played.

While R.E.M. was on the road, Athens grew and changed. Some scene veterans moved away and beloved local businesses closed. Musician and journalist Jimmy Ellison, the scene's irrepressible clown and booster, developed a malignant brain tumor and died. New places opened. When the poet and activist Allen Ginsberg visited UGA in May 1984, he followed his lackluster official reading at the college with a wild after-hours performance with musical accompaniment in a room in the old Stitchcraft factory. The success of this event inspired its organizers Chris DeBarr and Paul Thomas to transform that space in the old Stitchcraft factory into the alternative venue Lunch Paper. Visual art also flourished in places like the art gallery in UGA's new Tate Student Center. At times in the mid-eighties, locals who could keep the confusing venue names straight could hear new music regularly at four locations—the 40 Watt Uptown, the Uptown, the Old Forty Watt, and Lunch Paper. A new community access television program, Chip Shirley's *Partyline* on Observer TV, nurtured local comedy and opened up another medium for sharing Athens music, theater, and filmmaking. Watching *Partyline* was like peeking through the window at meetings of a creative and not entirely sober club. And at the center of it all, a new publication called *Tasty World Magazine* supported all this home-grown culture by keeping locals and interested people elsewhere informed about what was going on in Athens and nearby Atlanta.[69]

Like many of the bands it covered, *Tasty World* made a bold and sloppy debut. The execution of that first issue—launched locally in July 1984 with a Buzz of Delight show at Lunch Paper—might have been a little ragged. Typos sprouted like mold in the leaky bathrooms jammed on the cheap onto the back porches of subdivided Victorians. Page numbers were added by hand. Band-poster, copy-shop-style graphics featured cut-up images xeroxed from old books and magazines. Yet the first issue of *Tasty World* had a certain spark. Images of Oh-OK and the Replacements—both the local group and the out-of-town band were enjoying underground buzz at that moment—appeared on the cover. The record reviews covered a broad range of musical genres, including funk and rap and an odd selection of oldies as well as the expected alternative bands. D. Loring Aiken's column "Another Life to Live," with its title that punned on a long-running soap opera while also suggesting the self-transformation at the heart of bohemian culture, circulated local music news. Below the headline "People Talk About People," Aiken did just that, mixing gossip and reporting in just the right proportions to make newcomers believe they were getting the inside scoop while also drawing the attention of old-timers interested in reading about themselves. In the context of the Athens scene, the rawness—the amateur production values, cheap paper, and tabloid format—made the magazine feel authentic.[70]

Like other Athens origins stories—the B-52's at that Valentine's Day party and R.E.M. at the church—events around the launching of *Tasty World* quickly turned into myth. Because the Replacements were on the cover, someone showed the first issue to the band's front man, Paul Westerberg. He had met Lynn Blakey the previous fall, when the Replacements shared a bill at a San Francisco club with Let's Active. In the months since, the two guitarists had been writing each other and occasionally talking on the phone as Blakey moved to Athens to join Oh-OK. When Westerberg sang about the "pretty girl" "playing make-up, wearing guitar" in the Replacements song "Left of the Dial," he was describing Blakey. When he sang "heard about your band in some local page" and mentioned "the sweet Georgia breezes safe, cool, and warm," he was referring to Oh-OK, *Tasty World*, and Athens. Since he and Blakey were apart, Westerberg would just have to listen for Oh-OK on college radio wherever he was traveling, on one of those stations "left of the dial." The local publication had barely begun before it was immortalized in a song that became a college-rock anthem.[71]

Tasty World was not the scene's first publication. A few years earlier, Rodger Brown had published a few issues of a political and literary magazine called *Line of Sight* and Rick Hawkins put out an issue or two of a publication he called *Hot Java*. Hawkins's business the Print Shop simultaneously housed printing presses, a bike and Volkswagen repair shop, and an informal salon space complete with one of the town's only espresso machines. For a while, a family of illegal immigrants stayed there. At another point, some of the members of Limbo District moved in and the band rehearsed in the coffee room. Michael Stipe later said the lyrics of the R.E.M. song "We Walk" described the Print Shop. To get to the room where people sipped espresso, talked, and occasionally ate mushrooms, visitors — "customers" was not quite the right word as paying meant maybe putting some money in a jar — had to go upstairs and walk through the bathroom. It was not uncommon to find someone there soaking in the old tub, an image that reminded Stipe of Jacques-Louise David's painting of the bathtub murder of French Revolutionary leader Jean-Paul Marat. *Hot Java* grew out of this hippie-boho salon. Hand-set, printed on old equipment, and hand-distributed, Rick the Printer's short-lived publication with its smeared coffee ring logo gave locals a little taste of what it would mean to have their own rag. The Atlanta magazine *Beat Atlanta*, which in its twelve issues published Georgia alternative-music news and even an A-to-Z "Atlanta and Athens Band Guide" was also a model. But in the summer of 1984, Hawkins was deep into another project, the opening of a music venue confusingly called the Old 40 Watt in the club's former location on Clayton Street.[72]

David Pierce had Hawkins's *Hot Java* and the by-then-defunct *New York Rocker* in mind when he launched *Tasty World* with a volunteer staff and one paid employee, scene veteran Kathleen O'Brien, who got a commission on the advertisements she sold. Pierce was older than most bohemians. As an Air Force veteran, he had VA benefits that paid for his classes, and he tried out a lot of majors. During a stint in the journalism school, Pierce served as the editor of a student quarterly. Later, he switched to the art school to study graphic design and photography. Listening to scene participants complain that they had to read New York and British publications to find news about local bands, Pierce decided Athens needed its own music magazine.

In the late spring and early summer of 1984, Pierce created a mock-up of what the magazine might look like and went to see Chuck Searcy and Pete McCommons, the publishers of the weekly paper the *Athens Observer*. They liked the pitch, but they were stretched too thin running their new venture Observer Television, in addition to their weekly paper, to take on another publication. Instead, they invested in *Tasty World* by securing Pierce a two-room office on a run-down and mostly abandoned upper floor of the Georgia Hotel, right across the street from *Observer* headquarters. They also provided chairs, phones, and tables that *Observer* employees carried across the street to furnish the space. Eventually, Searcy, McCommons, and Pierce formed a company called the Capram Corporation to print and distribute the magazine.[73]

Pierce served as *Tasty World*'s editor, managing a large staff of volunteers who came and went as many people's willingness to work for free evaporated over time. No one seemed to do much copyediting, and production, overseen by Mike Dellinger, was barely automated. To typeset each issue, volunteers had to enter computer codes as well as every word of text into the *Observer*'s two-hundred-pound Osborne computer with its two four-inch screens and seven-inch disk drive. Pitched as a monthly, the magazine rarely stayed on schedule. Distribution occurred mainly through independent record stores, which got the magazine from record distributors that carried independent record labels. Ads, store sales, and subscriptions covered the cost of production.[74]

Tasty World boldly stated its ambitions right on the cover. The new publication would cover "the music of the South," a region the masthead described more realistically as the southeast and which in practice mostly meant Athens and Atlanta until the last few issues. Articles and reviews of performances also covered out-of-town musicians like Mitch Easter and Alex Chilton when they performed in Athens. The writing mostly avoided the Christgau school of serious music criticism and took a zine approach, fans writing about music they loved. Local characters like record collectors Kurt Wood and William Orten Carlton, better known as Ort, and artist and former Pylon bassist Michael Lachowski wrote record review columns. As he did as a clerk at Wax 'n' Facts, Lachowski continued to push local bohemians to listen to funk, hip-hop, and other music being made by African Americans. Dan Matthews, who wrote for the *Red and Black* as a student, served for a while as managing editor. David T. Lindsay, who wrote for Atlanta independent paper *Creative Loafing*, contributed articles about bands. After the first issue, *Tasty World* added regular columns on exhibitions and experi-

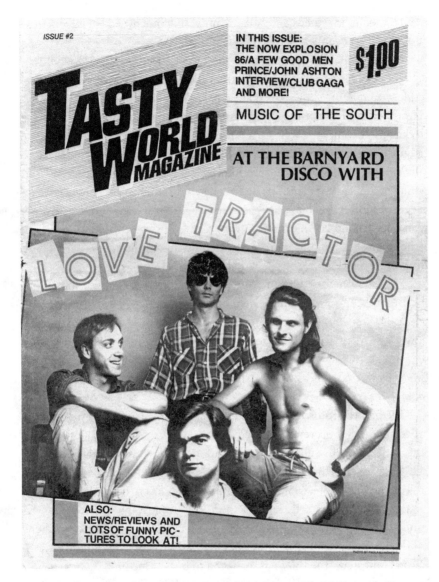

ISSUE #2

IN THIS ISSUE:
THE NOW EXPLOSION
86/A FEW GOOD MEN
PRINCE/JOHN ASHTON
INTERVIEW/CLUB GAGA
AND MORE!

$1.00

TASTY WORLD MAGAZINE

MUSIC OF THE SOUTH

AT THE BARNYARD
DISCO WITH

LOVE TRACTOR

ALSO:
NEWS/REVIEWS AND
LOTS OF FUNNY PIC-
TURES TO LOOK AT!

Between July 1984 and January 1986, editor David Pierce and a
mostly volunteer staff put out ten issues of *Tasty World* magazine,
the scene's first regular publication. (Author's possession)

mental theater in Athens and Atlanta, providing much-needed information about local art events.

It was probably inevitable that the hip upstart *Tasty World* would attack the student newspaper, the *Red and Black*. In the "After Hours" critical guide to upcoming shows, the college paper's entertainment editor Charles Aaron had been slamming local bands all summer. In June, he fired off a backhanded compliment at Love Tractor. Band members might seem like "a bunch of pretentious poseurs who play instrumentals," but compared to "the derivative refuse floating around the area," they were actually "a fascinating bunch of musicians." In August, he committed an act of outright sacrilege, describing Pylon's songs as "rather self-consciously obtuse art-funk workouts" rendered tolerable only by Curtis Crowe's drumming, which "whomped such a monster groove behind them" that listeners could ignore the pretense and dance.[75]

He also went after Oh-OK. Sure, he admitted, the band was fun, but to think that the music was "innovative, refreshing, or God help us, important" was "a little much." In July, he offered a more than a little sexist "musical rundown" on "Athens' cute little pop ingénues" who needed to give their "self-serving cutesiness" a rest. "When these two women jam their fingers in their ears and start singing with unabashedly poor results," he confessed, "I start looking for the exits."[76]

The band Aaron really went after, though, was Pierce and Sweet's Buzz of Delight. In a short review of the EP *Sound Castles*, Aaron announced that "this self-conscious silliness," was "about as dazzling as underarm deodorant." Denouncing their "'dance-pop'" as "a recycling of 'new music' cliché after cliché," he wrote, "Somewhere the plug just has to be pulled on all this gimmicky, contrived 'artistic expression.'" By August, he was accusing the band of exploiting the local scene. "Regurgitating innovation from Athens bands too numerous to name and doing it all with a self-important smirk," Aaron confessed, "the Buzz has managed to bother me more than even the heavy-metal lunkheads." This music, he argued, was why "trendy" had "become such a repulsive word."[77]

Ironically, it was Aaron's offhand comment about Fashionbattery that provoked a response that dragged *Tasty World* into a fight. Aaron had often written positively about the band, but before their end-of-summer Uptown date he declared, "These guys take themselves way too seriously, a problem that may take a while to remedy. Anybody got a pie?" One evening after this *Red and Black* hit the stands, a member of Fashionbattery asked Aaron to step outside the 40 Watt for a "chat." Waiting in front of the club, the other two members of the band hit the critic with pies made out of Comet, molasses, and barbecue sauce. According to Pierce, who wrote about the incident in *Tasty World*, witnesses "doubled over in laughter or cheered with delight" at the "dripping" "Omnipotent After-Hours God," as Aaron, in a Lester Bangs–style self-mockery, had called himself. The issue even included a small photograph by Fashionbattery's Joiner of Aaron's head and face covered with goo. *Tasty World*'s caption announced, in a journalistic version of the kind of cute smirk Aaron hated, "An Athens Music Critic Gets His Just Desserts." Aaron won this fight, though it took a few years. Fashionbattery broke up without putting out a record, and Pierce ended up something of a scene outcast in many circles. After graduating from UGA, Aaron worked his way up from freelance music writer to a staff member and then editor of the national music magazine *Spin*.[78]

While the attack on Aaron certainly qualified as local news, Pierce used the occasion to call the *Red and Black*, *Tasty World*'s closest local competitor, "an anti-music publication." If Pierce read the UGA student paper during his years as a student, then his memory was faulty. Student journalists wrote frequently about Athens music, including early and insightful articles about Pylon and R.E.M. in particular. Aaron simply carried on this coverage, building on the work of *Red and Black* music critics like Jay Watson, J. Eddy Ellison, Chuck Reece, Aaron's colleague and roommate Jimmy Tremayne, and Raymond Valley, also Aaron's friend. These student journalists took local music seriously enough to listen to bands repeatedly and think deeply about changes in their sounds. Music criticism required analysis and judgment. It was, in a sense, a more serious and collective kind of fandom. The point was to make the music better by offering feedback on what did and did not work, calling out lackluster shows or copy-cat sounds. Pierce accused Aaron of hating local music, but he loved it enough to go out most nights of the week and listen to multiple bands. What the critic actually disliked was Pierce's group Buzz of Delight.[79]

What seemed like a minor melodrama was in the context of Athens a major public violation of the norms of the scene. Sure, Athens musicians could be petty. Several people remembered that Michael Stipe once promised comp tickets to see R.E.M. at the Fox to Atlanta critic and *Tasty World* contributor David Lindsay, who had in the early days ignored R.E.M. When Lindsay picked up his envelope at "Will Call," the only thing in it was a snarky note from Stipe. Still, this attack was relatively private. The B-52's had modeled a generous way of being a band that members held onto as they became famous. Pylon planted that humble and supportive model deep in the local scene. Some participants felt like Vic Varney violated the rules and stopped supporting the Method Actors as a result. Love Tractor and especially R.E.M. took this model on the road, helping establish a national network of alternative bands whose members saw each other as friends and fellow fans rather than as rivals. The Athens scene nurtured an inclusive culture that cast everyone as a participant. And doing things, participating, was hard. People had to support each other. The fanzine approach, with its blurring of the line between writers and readers, fit the music, with its erasing of the line between musicians and fans. In both cases, the cultivation of an intimacy between cultural producers and cultural consumers suggested that everyone that supported the underground could join the club.[80]

The key of course was defining "support." Aaron did not see exaggerated praise of every group of local musicians who climbed up on a stage as good for the collective endeavor of music-making in the town. Pierce understood support more broadly, as praise but also as action, as going to see bands and helping other people bring their creative visions to life. Yet in seeing *Red and Black* writers as rivals rather than fellow scene members, Pierce failed to embody the Athens ethos even as he actively benefited from it. Because what made *Tasty World* worth reading was the hard work of volunteers who covered the scene for free.

At their best, *Tasty World* writers, often uncredited or using pseudonyms, covered special events and irregular venues in a way that made readers feel like they were there. Sometimes a column offered just the right detail. Bryan Cook, vocalist for the Hindu Love Gods, was essentially replacing Michael Stipe in R.E.M.'s version of the local ritual in which established bands adopted alternate names to play gigs in which they only performed covers. In an article about a special triple bill featuring Hindu Love Gods, Kilkenny Cats, and Barry Marler's new band Dreams So Real in the Georgia Hotel's basement, *Tasty World* reported that Cook walked up to the mic, grabbed it, and belched, making it clear that he would be Michael's alterego, a kind of anti-Stipe. Another *Tasty World* piece described Bob Hay singing favorites like "Elephant Radio" wearing his sunglasses when the Squalls performed at the new club called the Old 40 Watt. The karma of the Clayton Street location, the magazine suggested, was so bright that Hay needed shades to see. At other times, *Tasty World* reported events that would never have been covered elsewhere, like people chasing each other with water guns and playing in the street at the party and band poster exhibition that marked the closing of Wax 'n' Facts, the downtown Athens branch of Danny Beard's record store.[81]

Over ten irregular issues between July 1984 and January 1986, *Tasty World*'s underground aura put off casual readers while rewarding bohemians and people trying to join the scene, as well as out-of-town Athens music fans. Persistent boosters rather than critics, *Tasty World* writers repeatedly urged readers to give new bands and venues a try. Thomas and DeBarr's Lunch Paper depended on this kind of coverage to draw people to what was then an odd space in a closed factory that offered an eclectic calendar: a "garage punk" fashion show, poetry readings, and plays, as well as music. "The fresh air is free," a *Tasty World* staffer wrote, and flowing right behind the complex, "the river comes in handy if you're prone to bouts of persperation [sic] while dancing." Athens had been missing this kind of place since the Night Gallery, a coffee shop in the building at 199 Prince Avenue, had closed. DeBarr even wrote for *Tasty World*. Who would not want to go?[82]

Most bohemians including the *Tasty World* staff did, when the Replacements played at Lunch Paper in September 1984, a gig set up by Charles Aaron. Earlier that year, he had bought the Minneapolis band's first album *Sorry Ma, Forgot to Take Out the Trash*, released in the summer of 1981, at a store on Jackson Street (probably Go Clothing) that sold used clothes and other old stuff in addition to used records. More than anything, Aaron and his friends wanted to see the Replacements live, but the band had never played Athens. So Aaron called the group up and told them he would pay them $200 if they came to town and performed. He figured if he charged a $2 cover, he would be able to make the guarantee.[83]

At Stitchcraft, DeBarr and a volunteer crew strung extensions cords together and ran electricity for the band's equipment from a nearby building. Local groups Tragic Dancer — Arthur Johnson was the bass player — and the Primates — "Athens's favorite redneck band" — opened. The Minneapolis band played a preview of their soon-to-be-released Twin/Tone album *Let It Be* for a crowd so large that some people had to stand outside and listen through the windows. Charles Aaron was so inspired he pounded out a Lester Bangs–like spew of words for the *Red and Black*. The Replacements' cover of the Edison Lighthouse song "Rosemary" transformed him as completely as a conversion: "the simple, dumb-as-dirt melody" "destroyed my quavering little manure pile of faith and helped me begin to build a new hope and will." Others felt the magic, but kept down the word count. *Tasty World* staffer D. Loring Aiken called the evening "a night of sheer and unadulterated good times."[84]

By the time the fourth issue of *Tasty World* appeared on local newsstands in February 1985, Lunch Paper was in limbo, shut down by the city not for noise complaints but because the plumbing and wiring failed to meet city code. The magazine fared better, hanging onto its early spunk as volunteers learned the magazine equivalent of basic musicianship—tasks like copy-editing, selling ads, and actually getting the page numbers to print. Staffer D. Loring Aiken expanded her insider coverage of local band news and other happenings to include reports on the alternative scenes emerging across the Southeast. Staffers drew on interviews to write more in-depth articles about local bands, out-of-town groups like Charlotte's Fetchin Bones, and artists like Howard Finster.[85]

Sometimes, the casual intimacy between staffers and local musicians produced revealing exchanges. In an article about the Bar-B-Q Killers, Laura Carter started out working her stage persona. Members of her band, she bragged, were "better in bed" than they were at playing their instruments. But she also demonstrated how seriously she took her music. Knowingly or not, she cited Michael Stipe's own early vocal influences—Patti Smith and Lux Interior of the Cramps—as the singers who had most influenced her own craft. She only yelled insults at the audience between songs, she con-fessed, because someone had to wake them up: "What are we supposed to do, just let 'em act like vegetables?" And she seemed genuinely perplexed that people were taking her literally. Sounding like a hipster Holden Caul-field, she asserted, "I mean, I'm facetious as hell. I'm kinduva jokester at heart."[86]

David Pierce's interview with Michael Stipe while the singer was wash-ing his clothes at the Snow White Laundry also adopted this person-behind-the-performance approach. When Pierce asked his old art-school friend about making art on the road, the singer replied that he took photographs and that his music, too, was art. All forms of creativity, Stipe insisted, were related in creating a kind of release. He did all the visual design for R.E.M. as well, because no one else in the band wanted "to fuck around with it." It was an R.E.M. inside joke that Stipe functioned as their token art student. The next full page of the magazine reprinted Stipe's tour diary, stream of con-sciousness notes on dreams, meals full of fish and pumpkin, Tokyo sights, concert venues, beautiful women, and interesting clothes from R.E.M.'s re-cent travels to Hawaii and Japan.[87]

Tasty World coverage of visual and performance art provided much needed support for local creative work that was not music. Dori Cosgrove's "Art" and Neil Bogan's "Stage" columns covered activities in Athens and Atlanta. Sometimes, music and art mixed in the local clubs. Early on, Watt King's light shows and Michael Lachowski's sculptures had turned some

Pylon shows into art installations. From 1979 to 1983, King and Michael Paxton's Rat and Duck Playhouse produced original plays and performance-art pieces featuring John Seawright, Neil Bogan, and Jean Shipp at its Foundry Street, Prince Avenue, and final Stitchcraft locations. After Pylon broke up, Michael Lachowski continued to work across creative mediums by exhibiting his drawings and paintings, including "oversized portraits of everyday objects like an electric toothbrush, a girdle, [and] a mechanical pencil," at the Uptown Lounge. Nacoochee Scrap Theatre also performed their indoor circus act in local clubs. Meridian, a theater troupe formed in 1984 by Neil Bogan and two other artists, put on Sam Shepard and Patti Smith's play *Cowboy Mouth* at the Uptown and UGA's Memorial Hall and other works at 688 in Atlanta. Outside of the galleries in the Jackson Street art building, most art exhibitions took place in ad hoc spaces like the walls of scene-oriented businesses or artists' studios. Lunch Paper featured visual and performance art and experimental theater regularly. Yet when these scattered art events occurred, people had a hard time finding out about them unless they had a friend involved or saw a flyer. By letting people know about exhibitions and performances, *Tasty World* expanded the audience for local art across the scene.[88]

In particular, the publication's coverage helped make UGA's Tate Student Center art gallery, with its easy sign-up process, an important art venue for local bohemians. Cosgrove's *Tasty World* reporting provided rare, in-depth coverage of exhibitions there, like Michael Stipe and his friends Chris Slay and Dru Wilbur's show the *R. Door Photographic Exhibit* and another local group show that included Jill Schultz's pastels. In late February and early March, Cosgrove covered local artist Patrik Keim's series of controversial installations that almost shut down the gallery.[89]

Keim, who moved to Athens in 1980 or 1981, was a student in the university's MFA program when he showed his work at the Tate Gallery. Although the cast of students was different, in almost every other way the art school remained the open space of creativity it had been in the late seventies and early eighties. Hippies and bohemians still treated the Jackson Street building like a clubhouse, and some students had even started skateboarding in the halls. But no one was more at home in the Jackson Street art building than Keim. Sometime during his time as an MFA student, he simply moved his bedding and other belongings onto the no longer used catwalk and projection room of one of the old "art in the dark" classrooms. He slept there, worked in the studios at all hours, took his meals at the dining hall, and showered at the campus gym.[90]

Art student Patrik Keim created performance pieces and installations in galleries and public spaces at the University of Georgia, becoming one of the scene's most respected artists. Here, Keim talks to Paul Thomas in his downtown vintage and junk store, the Swap Meet. (Photograph by John Lee Matney)

With his grass green hair, red jumpsuit, and then-rare tattoos, Keim was easy to find. He had the kind of laugh that made people wonder whether he found them funny or absurd. Like Michael Lachowski, he radiated a creative aura. Everyone, including the professors who actually followed contemporary art, knew he was talented. Inspired by German artists including Joseph Beuys and Kurt Schwitters, around 1983 Keim began working to create "Gesamtkunstwerke," or "total works of art," around the art building. In a 1984 piece called *Sucking the Heads of Above Average Crawfish*, Keim hung a naked Ken doll from a standard school desk. In the poem glued to the desktop, a young boy described being forced in school to change the way he drew pictures and an afterword informed readers that the boy had committed suicide. For an exhibition called *Asylum, Asylum, Precarious Yet E Pluribus Unum: Body and Blood*, he filled the glass cases in the front of the art school with nail clippings, hair, and other body samples and posed nearly naked in one of the galleries. Another time, he filled a gallery with industrial garbage and sat in the center punching a time clock. Sometimes, when he needed money, Keim would set up wire stands on the benches in the art building and sell sunglasses for a dollar along with his collages.[91]

Because of Cosgrove's reporting, detailed descriptions survive of Keim's installations at the Tate Gallery in February 1985. For *Utopia, Termite Season*, an installation Keim called a "room of adventure," the artist lined the entire Tate Gallery with paper, threaded strings between the walls, and dangled sheets of newspaper and a large venetian blind from the ceiling. At the back of the gallery, spotlights illuminated a poem pasted on the back wall and a pile of burnt matches. At the front, a projector played a film-loop of Keim "in action." Keim described *Utopia* as "the ideal environment that still has termites chewing at the core." Not surprisingly, the fire marshal shut the exhibition down after allowing a security guard to take a few people at a time through the work at the opening. People stood in line to see the installation that night, and then it was gone, utopia opening and then closing on the same day.

With most of his two weeks left, Keim created a second installation called *Translucent Ltd.* that featured "folding chairs arranged in a crucifix, more burned matches, a basket on the ground, crustaceans in ketchup, and a cow's tongue atop a pile of broken glass." After a few days, the tongue began to stink and Tate Center employees removed it without consulting Keim. In response, he dismantled the exhibit and created yet another installation *Witticisms and 48 Hours of Bliss* for the last days of his allotted time. For this piece, he stapled to the walls friends and critics' comments on the first two pieces and placed a record player topped with a photo of himself grinning and a celebratory flower arrangement at the center of the gallery. A note on the record player warned, "play at your own risk." If a viewer rose to the challenge, Ray Conniff's *Greatest Hits* filled the space. Mad at the time, Keim later showed up at the University Union's banquet to accept the "fire extinguisher award."[92]

Over the next few years, Keim became more openly gay. He moved to New Haven, Connecticut, and then Amsterdam, but always ended up back in Athens. I saw a lot of his art, installations and wall-hung work about torture, suicide, murder, and war that fit with the darker aesthetic of many Uptown bands. None of these pieces prepared me for *Man Student*, a performance piece he staged on the UGA campus near the art building. Chained and nearly naked with his head shaved, Keim stood mutely in punishment for some unnamed crime as students and faculty members streamed by between classes. Everything about him—posture, gestures, face—radiated pain. Most people refused to really look at him. I knew him a bit so I stopped. He stared back, opening and closing his mouth soundlessly like a fish out of water. My eyes watered. To leave seemed insulting, but I could not bear to stay. He did not make it easy. As I turned to go, he reached out, beckoning after me with his chained hands.[93]

Of course, the myth of Athens bohemia as a kind of utopian community, a place where people were friends rather than rivals, was not really true. Bands competed with each other for the choicest local gigs, for an audience when they played different clubs on the same nights, and for record deals with DB and new Atlanta independent Twilight and out-of-town indies like Coyote and Twin/Tone. Artists competed for exhibition space in the art building and at the Tate Gallery and inclusion in the annual Lyndon House juried art show, as well as for the few patrons with enough money to buy even inexpensive pieces. Some bohemians thought Vic Varney, Barry Marler, and Matthew Sweet were too ambitious, more interested in fame and money than art. A few locals like Jerry Ayers lived that kind of purity. Most never had a chance to see whether they would "sell out." Sexual jealousies, too, divided people. Bad breakups, casual hookups, and infidelities piled up in such a small town, and some grudges stuck. Every band could not be the next R.E.M. Everyone could not be the person everyone else wanted to fuck. The miracle in hindsight was that people helped each other as much as they did, that genuine kindness was valued and even celebrated. It was a local badge of honor to share a practice space or equipment, fill in when a band with scheduled gigs lost a member, or to help launch a new band with a coveted opening slot.

Oh-OK did not make it. The new lineup of Blakey, Hopper, Stipe, and McNair toured in support of the record and worked up some new covers, like R.E.M.'s "Body Count" and AC/DC's "You Shook Me All Night Long." The *Red and Black* called it the "best" incarnation of the band yet. But somehow the new lineup did not hold together. In October 1984, when Oh-OK played a farewell show at the 40 Watt Uptown, Lynda Stipe stayed away. Matthew Sweet, of all people, replaced her on bass, and Pete Buck sat in on guitar on a few songs. Buzz of Delight opened, and Hopper and Blakey spent the whole opening set bouncing up and down on the side of the stage. Hopper seemed to have put the difficulties with Sweet and Pierce behind her. Michael Stipe, long supportive of his sister's group, spent the evening at the Uptown sitting in on vocals with the Kilkenny Cats cover band, the Hollowmen.[94]

Bands with women in them did not fare as well in this period. R.E.M.-influenced boy bands were on the rise. The shift from parties to clubs where musicians had to deal with sexist club owners, bookers, and sound men did not help. Right up until the end of Oh-OK, sound men tried to explain to Lynda Stipe how to play her bass. During an out-of-town show, a guy from the audience unplugged her instrument in the middle of a song. The great new indie underground Pete Buck celebrated had less room for women as artists than the early Athens scene.[95]

Somehow, the Bar-B-Q Killers always functioned as the exception. Superhero Laura Carter, braver than all the guys, took risks on stage that made her male counterparts look like they were performing in a bad school play. Claire Horne, a true heir to local guitar legends Ricky Wilson and Randy Bewley, perfected her own original style. Older bohemians found the Bar-B-Q Killers hard to listen to, but in the late 1970s hippies and folkies did not know what to make of the B-52's either. The young band seemed incapable of taking themselves too seriously, a rapidly spreading affliction in the growing scene. Chip Shirley's local television variety show *Partyline* aired Sunday mornings in 1984 and 1985 after the clubs shut down Saturdays at midnight to comply with alcohol regulations. Instead of actually performing, the Bar-B-Q Killers lip-synced and played a tennis racket, a vacuum, and a mop to the Rolling Stones' song "When the Whip Comes Down." Horne even wore yellow dish gloves. Though everyone on the set seemed to be having a ball, the gesture offered a sly critique of the R.E.M. model and Stipe's by then well-known refusal to lip-sync in videos. For insiders, Carter's Butthole Surfers t-shirt brought that jab home. Local musicians could now rebel against R.E.M. and the whole eccentric and romantic image of the Athens scene.[96]

Local Color

If you need inspiration
Philomath is where I go.

R.E.M., "Can't Get There from Here" (1985)

On Saturdays, students enrolled in Aspects of Folk Culture piled into a van at the art building on Jackson Street and got out hours later in tiny Georgia towns like Penneville or Trion or Rabbittown. The unusual course grew out of a radical and yet simple idea. A rich, mostly rural vernacular culture still survived in pockets across the Deep South. Art professors Art Rosenbaum, a painter, serious folk-revivalist musician and scholar, and a founder of the Athens Folk Music and Dance Society, and Andy Nasisse, a ceramics artist and an important folk-art collector, wanted their students to stop looking at the New York art world for direction and "value what they had right here." During traditional class meetings, the professors used slides and recordings they had made in their own visits with artists, artisans, and musicians who drew on skills, techniques, beliefs, and forms passed down in families and communities. But on the weekends, Nasisse and Rosenbaum made it clear they were not art historians but artists. They took their students into the field to talk to the people that made the work.[1]

Most of these "folk" artists lived in what seemed to many of the students like a radically different world. In unincorporated settlements or down gravel or blacktop roads, ancient cabins and early twentieth-century farmhouses shared space with trailers, tractors, and outbuildings. I learned about what my grandfather called "home places" on summer visits to my Mississippi relatives. Georgia students from small towns and other suburban kids with rural grandparents had probably seen them too. Because people in the country often kept things that might prove useful later, you could read the history of a spread just by looking at what was rusting in the yard. Occasionally the van pulled up at a home that met a middle-class definition of neat, but even small lots in towns were often filled with old stuff. Nasisse and Rosenbaum's "fieldwork" forced the students to confront class difference as well as their narrow understanding of the meaning of art.[2]

When the course stopped at the Meaders's pottery business and home in Mossy Creek one Saturday morning, Jennifer Hartley and her friend went into the woods to pee. Looking for privacy, they stumbled upon the place the family dumped trash that would not burn. The two art students picked two face jugs with their chins popped off out of a weedy pile. Many of the artists that class members met each week sold their work, but Hartley, paying her own way through school, could not afford to buy. Back in Lanier Meaders's shop with the homemade wheel and the shelves sagging with jugs, pitchers, and mugs, she cradled her treasure in her lap as the potter talked to the students. One of the professors, Art Rosenbaum, remembered being upset. He thought the young people knew better than to handle the work like that. As Rosenbaum began to apologize, Hartley explained they found the jugs in the woods. Meaders told the students they could have these seconds for five dollars apiece.[3]

During most class visits, an artist like Meaders or a musician like W. Guy Bruce would say a few words and then play something or show some pieces. At places where the grounds themselves doubled as art installations, like Finster's Paradise Garden and R. A. Miller's whirligig farm, everyone wandered around looking at stuff the artists had collected and made. Hartley remembered hating the way some of her classmates "looked down" on the artists and musicians and their family members. In contrast, Rosenbaum and Nasisse modeled a "beautiful" respect.[4]

Outside of class, students talked about the artists and musicians they met and went back to see them with their friends in tow. Then those friends told others. Fascination with "outsider" or "self-taught" artists and "traditional" or "roots" musicians rippled outward from the course. Most people I knew had visited folk artists. Bohemians who could not afford Finster's paintings nailed the cutout tin figures Miller called "Blow Oscars" to their walls and hung his whirligigs from their porch ceilings where they could spin. I still have the Miller red devil I bought from the artist, but Hartley sold her beloved Meaders jug on eBay in the aughts for enough money to buy two tickets to Paris.

Visiting folk artists became a bohemian rite of passage in Athens. Our town might be far from world-class museums and galleries, but cultural riches filled the countryside if you knew where to look. For UGA students

**New York photographer Laura Levine took photographs of R.E.M.
at folk artist R. A. Miller's whirligig farm in Rabbittown, Georgia.
(Photograph © Laura Levine)**

like me from the metastasizing Atlanta suburbs, folk artists suggested a rootedness in place and connection to older ways of living that seemed radical and interesting. For students from small, Georgia towns, folk artists provided a way to link childhood experiences with current interests in art and
music and alternative ways of seeing the world. The fact that most Americans
not only ignored folk artists and musicians but did not believe rural southern
art really existed only made us feel more connected to these outsiders. Like
the music being made across the new outposts of indie America, their work
seemed like our secret.[5]

    Chuck Reece, a scene participant from Ellijay, a small town in northern
Georgia, explained the appeal. Before he saw R.E.M.'s video shot at Paradise Garden, Reece could find "absolutely no point of intersection between
the small town religious culture I grew up in and the kind of weird music
I was hearing and weird art I was seeing when I got to Athens." Meeting
Finster at Paradise Garden changed him. "Howard was like any old hellfire
and brimstone Baptist preacher I grew up being yelled at by." Reece realized, "There was something in the weird circle of southern culture, a way
that people like him and people like [Michael] Stipe could be after the same

thing." Discovering this "common ground," Reece remembered, "fundamentally changed my conception of the region I grew up in and its culture." Maybe the South meant more than white supremacy, slavery and the Civil War, lynching and segregationists. Maybe the place had nurtured something admirable, too, forms of religious practice and art and music-making, faith and beauty. As Reece put it, "now we can be proud of something cool we've done instead of all the stupid shit we used to do."[6]

Growing up after the mass activism but before the television series *Eyes on the Prize*, a generation of southerners moved through school in an integrating region without an integrated history. In our classrooms, we rarely heard the stories of southern activists who had created the civil rights movement. And while too many of our textbooks still presented Lost Cause fantasies as southern history, popular culture offered two possible takes on our region, an image of stupid, backward barbarism, and southern rock's rebuttal, a romanticized and too often racist regional pride. For Athens scene participants, black and white folk artists and musicians suggested alternative ways to think about the region. Figures like Reverend John D. Ruth, Doc Barnes, and Dilmus Hall made punk practices like DIY production, the recycling of old materials, and existence on the margins seem like southern "traditions." When Athens bohemians visited folk artists, they took home an understanding of a quirky and creative South with its own homegrown forms of cultural expression. They also acquired an alternative, eccentric persona, a usable southerner. They learned to play the folk.

In these exchanges, Athens bohemians traveled in the well-worn paths of earlier waves of folk revivalism, whether or not they knew about this history. In the late fifties and sixties, in particular, increasing numbers of mostly white college students had fallen in love with songs and styles of playing that originated in rural working-class communities. As these young people with little to no connection to "the folk" learned the older ways of playing and singing, they worried about the authenticity of their music making. How could white college students play "real" white working-class or black music? In the early sixties, revivalists like a young Bob Dylan solved this problem by inventing autobiographies that linked them to the people who had originally created the music. Others like Mike Seeger tried a different approach, carefully studying "traditionalist" musicians in order to reproduce their sound. Still other revivalists like Joan Baez developed a new understanding of authenticity that depended not on biography but affect. In this way of thinking, "real" folk music enabled listeners to feel the emotions of the original performers of the music and their audiences. The right expression of feelings rendered performances authentic, even if the musicians had no personal connection to the communities where the music originated.[7]

When the folk music revival faded in the late sixties and early seventies, interest in the form remained strong in some southern college towns with ties to the countryside. Lefty and hippie back-to-the-landers settled around places like Athens and Chapel Hill and created their own rural communities that came together to listen to and perform traditional music. Long before punk hit the Deep South, local revivalists and hippies modeled DIY culture. Kate Pierson of the B-52's, a folksinger before she moved to a farm outside Athens, connected local revivalists and early bohemians like Jeremy Ayers.[8]

Interacting over the years, folk revivalists and traditionalists blurred the old, easy distinctions. Members of the Athens Folk Music and Dance Society like Art Rosenbaum brought these communities together for concerts, dances, and weekly song swaps. Once a year, the active group hosted the North Georgia Folk Festival, an annual event that provided a venue for musicians who had grown up playing old-time music with family and community members. At Sandy Creek Park in Athens, musicians like local resident Doc Barnes and Granny Maude Thacker of Pickens County performed and folk artists like Howard Finster displayed and sold their wares. Back-to-the-landers, old hippies, college students, revivalists, and rural artists and musicians and their families mingled together among the booths and sat beside each other on lawn chairs and blankets as they watched the performances. Out in the country, these different kinds of people were neighbors. Off-the-grid, hippie junk dealer and political ephemera collector John Gingrich, for example, had almost as much in common with Finster as he did with Rosenbaum. By the early 1980s, some revivalists and traditionalists had developed years-long relationships.

By the mid-eighties, the folk aesthetic that Rosenbaum called "local creativity" had become a profound influence in the Athens scene. Love Tractor had pioneered a new country-folk sound on their 1983 album *Around the Bend*. The next year, R.E.M. put a Finster painting on the cover of *Reckoning*, made a film with Jim Herbert at R. A. Miller's whirligig farm, and began the songs about eccentric outsiders that would fill their third album. Asked by an interviewer to pin down the band's style, Stipe called it "folk music." Love Tractor, R.E.M., and newer groups like Billy James and the El May Dukes adopted sonic gestures associated with traditional southern music — lyrics sung in drawling and twangy voices, guitar parts mimicking banjos and fiddles, actual banjos, and songs that told stories. Artist Joni Mabe, who took the folk-culture class twice, fused Finster's folk aesthetic with elements of fan culture and pop art to make elaborate Elvis installations. Jennifer Hartley's figurative paintings, with their expressive lines, bold colors, and strong storytelling, experimented with venerable traditions much like the more detailed faces Lanier Meaders cut and smoothed into his later jugs. Artists like John Hawkins, Jill Schultz, and later Lillian Heard and Jill Carnes bucked art-world trends and painted figurative romances or self-consciously primitive characters. John Seawright wrote poetry that drew its power from folk rhythms and vernacular phrasings. Encountering the "folk" changed how many scene participants thought about form and beauty and genre.[9]

Beyond art and music-making, going to folk artists and musicians' houses and studios also exposed Athens people to alternative ways of living. While country people used old things because they could not afford new, local bohemians developed an aesthetic appreciation for handmade, outdated, and worn items. Rusting gliders, tin signs, old tools, and broken toys began to appear on sagging porches. "Crazy" quilts made out of scraps of old clothes covered futons on the kinds of iron bed frames that appeared in Walker Evans's Depression-era photographs. Hoosier cabinets with metal countertops and built-in flour drawers added storage space to jerry-rigged kitchens in subdivided Victorians. Country junk shops and flea markets overflowed with these cast-off materials of rural life. All you needed was a car, some gas, a little cash, and the time to drive around and look.

As always, Jerry Ayers with his romantic "folk" style, his bohemian-as-hobo look, got there first. Soon, Michael Stipe, Armistead Wellford and Mark Cline of Love Tractor, Stipe's friend Chris Slay, John Seawright, and others started copying Ayers's clothes. Old-fashioned work pants like farmers wore held up with suspenders, wife-beaters or the tops of union suits peeking out from under dark woolen suit jackets, clunky brogans or work boots, and worn fedoras or railroad caps became a local uniform. Women like Ayers's close friend April Chapman created their own version—long, just-out-of-bed hair, flowing skirts or cinched-waist dresses worn with work boots, men's jackets, layered scarves, and vintage hats. Men and women alike turned antique pajamas and underwear into clothes, wearing old-fashioned gowns, robes, slips, bloomers, camisoles, union suits, and long johns to work and to the clubs.[10]

The folk influence emerged in more subtle ways, too. Eighties alternative culture's romantic sense of place owed a great debt to earlier waves of revivalism. Even harder-edged bands that played music that sounded nothing like "folk" embraced and made more militant the localism and DIY ethic of revivalists. In Athens, bands like the Squalls and Time Toy recorded and released their own records. David Barbe of Mercyland founded a local record label. And Bryan Cook of Time Toy and Dru Wilbur of Eat America organized a four-band-plus-fans bus tour of Florida. Rooting themselves in local networks and a focus on getting the feelings right, a newer wave of Athens bands and their fans acted like folk revivalists. Folk did not have to mean your look or your genre. Instead, it could mean your attitude.

In Athens and other new bohemias, an investment in the eccentric particulars of local places worked as a counter to Reagan's nostalgic evocations of midcentury middle America. Indie folk practices connected scene participants to the leftist politics of earlier waves of revivalists. They also coincided with a national folk-art revival. UGA art professor Judy McWillie conducted pioneering research on outsider artists like Lonnie Holley. Andy Nasisse assembled an important folk-art collection. And dealers like Atlanta-based Bill Arnett hunted for southern artists who were not formally trained and bought up their work. Some of these artists, in turn, began to attract national attention. Finster won a National Endowment for the Arts award for his sculpture, and Mississippi blues musician and artist Son Thomas exhibited his work at the Corcoran Gallery of Art in D.C. The search for "undiscovered" folk artists in the eighties replicated efforts to find old blues and hillbilly performers in the sixties and seventies.[11]

Underground music critics, fans, and independent record companies searching for interesting music from out-of-the-way places—what the critic Tom Carson called "regional rock"—took off on a similar quest. To New Yorkers in particular, Athens bohemians seemed quirky and fresh. They spoke with slow and exotic accents and wore colorful used clothes rather than black and other bruise-toned attire. They did not spit or throw things. Unafraid of being labeled as hippies or disco fans, they danced exuberantly. For many New York music critics, the rural South might as well have been another planet, a place they imagined but had rarely visited, antimodern and full of poor blacks and racist whites. Journalist Anthony DeCurtis made the comparison explicit, drawing on his experience working in Atlanta and then in New York. Critics looked for Athens bands, he told me, like art collectors scoured the southern countryside for outsider artists. Scene participants had learned from folk artists how to be the kind of eccentric southerners that appealed to these critics and fans. By the mid-eighties, indie revivalism helped position Athens bohemians as contemporary examples of "the folk."[12]

For New Yorkers anyway, Athens also had a more nostalgic appeal. According to DeCurtis, the scene in the small southern town reminded older critics and fans of moments from New York's own past, those early days of the Warhol Factory or the Mercer Arts Center when in the city, too, anything had seemed possible. Though DeCurtis did not know the history of how Ricky Wilson, Keith Strickland, and Jeremy Ayers had all been shaped by the Factory, this fantasy had firm basis in fact. In the early to mid-eighties, Ayers learned from southern folk artists like a decade earlier he had learned from New York drag queens. Gorgeous, creative, and queer and also downhome, white, and southern, Ayers contained all the contradictions that made the Athens scene.

Indie Folk

You had to be sharp to catch the collective sense of humor of Pete Buck, Michael Stipe, Mike Mills, and Bill Berry. When Athens bohemians called R.E.M. a cover band, the guys started performing songs by the original art rockers, the Velvet Underground. When music critics said the group sounded like the Byrds, they covered "Eight Miles High." Because people thought a group from Georgia must sound "southern," band members put a photograph of kudzu on the cover of their first album. After fans and critics complained about not being able to understand Stipe's lyrics, band members named that record *Murmur*, a synonym for mumble. A year later, they followed the kudzu with a snake and named their second album *Reckoning*, a reference to the southern saying "I reckon" and their sense that given *Murmur*'s critical success they were due a day of judgment.[13]

By the time Michael Stipe asked Howard Finster to paint the cover, all the members of the band knew this "man of visions." Stipe, whose grandfather had been a preacher, felt a deep connection to the former Baptist minister, then in his late sixties. The singer met Finster first, before the other guys in the band, when Andy Nasisse arranged for the folk artist to play his banjo and show slides of his work at the botanical gardens in Athens. Stipe, still an art student then, went with an art professor to the event to see why Nasisse had been making such a fuss about the man. Later, Stipe began driving around rural Georgia with friends Chris Slay, who had taken the folk course, and Jeff Gilley, who grew up near the small town where Finster lived and was thanked on the back of *Reckoning*, to visit self-taught artists. A frequent guest at Paradise Garden, Stipe often watched Finster paint, and the two men talked and sometimes made music together. According to Art Rosenbaum, Finster was "a singer, a rough-and-ready banjo-picker, a songsmith, and a poet — actually one of the finer American vernacular voices." At least once, Stipe spent the night in the garden. He helped the artist put the steeple on his church and gave him vitamins. Stipe and his bandmates even found someone to weld Finster's broken water pump.[14]

When I.R.S. pressured R.E.M. to make a video for the *Murmur* version of "Radio Free Europe," Stipe suggested Paradise Garden. Finster, "commissioned by God," had started building his rambling, multi-acre art installation in Pennville—an unincorporated settlement near the town of Summerville and about three hours from Athens—in 1970. By the eighties, the church Finster constructed in stages had grown into a tower made up of four circular, leaning stories and a steeple perched crookedly on top of a small, tin-roofed wooden building it seemed determined to crush. Nearby, another tower emerged out of a tangle of old bicycle parts and hubcaps and Finster's own sculptures studded with spark plugs, old photographs in frames, doll parts, broken tools, and clocks. In the middle of a small pond, a mountain of cement serpents stood guard. To explore the place, you followed walkways inlaid with fragments of mirrors, glass beads, pennies, and broken pottery past painted messages to get right with God and images of angels, celebrities, and presidents. At Paradise Garden, Finster covered everything with his sacred art, even his Cadillac.

When Stipe asked Finster to make a painting for the band's second album, the singer gave the older artist a winding outline of a snake. Finster added washes of color and painted the background black. Then he filled every inch of this dark ground with imagery, including faces, a sea of eyeballs, and a tiny landscape. Stipe would complain repeatedly over the years about how I.R.S.'s bad reproduction of Finster's piece erased the original work's intricate detail. Yet even in its reduced state, the cover of *Reckoning* suggested a raw and biblical strangeness.[15]

With its stripped-down recording style, country and folk gestures, and a directness that even included some decipherable lyrics, *Reckoning* also sounded different. Mitch Easter, coproducing along with Don Dixon as he had on *Murmur*, nicknamed it *Led Zeppelin II* in frustration over the fact that band members would not let him layer in sounds as he had on their earlier recordings. The tracks on *Reckoning*, he complained, were "like field recordings compared to most pop records." As a "little inside joke," band members even slowed down their usual "punked-out version" of "Don't Go Back to Rockville" and upped the southern twang in their vocals, transforming a song about a woman Mike Mills liked who was leaving Athens to spend the summer in her hometown in Maryland into a country ballad.[16]

The way the R.E.M. guys described their new album, they were simply getting back to their roots. Mike Mills and Bill Berry grew up with country music, and Stipe heard the genre on the radio when he was a kid and his dad was stationed in Texas. As an independent record store clerk and record collector, Pete Buck had listened to old forties and fifties country stars like Hank Williams. He learned to play guitar, he told journalist Anthony DeCurtis, by playing along with these records. More recently, Stipe had developed an interest in country singers like Patsy Cline. Classic, midcentury country music had deep roots in the South, in Appalachian ballad singing, the string-band tradition, and what the industry sold in the twenties and thirties as "hillbilly" music, the working-class, white counterpart to "race" music. For a while in the forties and early fifties, before the word became tainted as "communist" during the McCarthy era, the industry even used the label "folk" to categorize the music later called country. Capacious enough to be both commercially recorded and the white side of American folk music, both pop and art, country with its strong ties to the South proved a fitting model for R.E.M.'s desire to be both underground and popular.[17]

Back home, R.E.M.'s folk turn deepened the divide between the "artsy" older bands and the new, harder-edged Uptown groups like the Bar-B-Q Killers. This local split, in turn, mirrored growing national divisions between new-music groups, whether they considered themselves indie or alternative or college rock. As Minor Threat from D.C. and Black Flag from southern California helped launch a hardcore subculture, R.E.M. joined other indie musicians like the Los Angeles band X in a simultaneous roots revival.[18]

In some ways, this mining of old forms replayed punk's own search for inspiration in the rock past. When new-music groups like the Cramps incorporated elements of rockabilly in their music, underground critics and fans could interpret these sonic gestures as punk moves, alternate routes back to the purity and rawness of early rock and roll. When members of X and other L.A. bands like the Blasters began listening to and collecting records by classic country singers like Hank Williams, Lefty Frizzell, and Patsy Cline in the early 1980s, they, too, resurrected the past. Because these recordings predated the emergence of rock, when groups started including loud and quick covers of songs by these and other country musicians in their sets, they broke away from punk's focus on rock's origins. X's album *Under the Big Black Sun*, released in July 1982, translated this trend into vinyl, with songs that laid classic country gestures on top of a fast and raw foundation. When I.R.S. brought the members of R.E.M. to California to spend the month between mid-August and mid-September 1982, they would have heard this kind of country-punk fusion frequently in L.A. clubs. Over the next few years, in addition to R.E.M., bands like Rank and File, the Violent Femmes, the Meat Puppets, Jason and the Scorchers, Lone Justice, the Mekons, and Fetchin Bones also began to mine country and hillbilly material. In Athens, you could hear this music on WUOG and see these bands perform at the clubs and at University Union concerts, like the X show at the Tate Student Center in November 1983.[19]

From the perspective of the now-national underground, R.E.M.'s turn toward a more country sound fit into an indie trend that some critics called "cowpunk" but that was better understood as a broader interest in multiple forms of roots and folk music. "It's kinda stylish right now to be into rural cultures," one of the members of Jason and the Scorchers told the *Village Voice* in 1984. As both revivalism and hardcore surged and at times overlapped that year, indie bands produced a slate of celebrated albums, including the Replacements' *Let It Be*, Hüsker Dü's *Zen Arcade*, the Minutemen's *Double Nickels on the Dime*, and R.E.M.'s *Reckoning*, and even, though there was more critical disagreement here, the Meat Puppets' *Meat Puppets II* and the Violent Femmes' *Hallowed Ground*. Music critics Gina Arnold and Michael Azerrad have both named 1984 as the high point of eighties indie music.[20]

"Little America," the name of R.E.M.'s seven-month world tour launched that April with the release of *Reckoning*, might have been another of R.E.M.'s jokes. The album also included a song by that name, another nonlinear, stream of consciousness tale. "I can't see myself at thirty," Stipe sang, before throwing in flies, a horse, an empty wagon, and a museum. References to endless touring appeared — "another Greenville, another Magic Mart" — and to R.E.M.'s manager — "Jefferson, I think we're lost." Maybe Stipe meant this disorientation as a metaphor, a lament for a homogenizing and increasingly conservative nation, but the sound of the song cut against this interpretation. Berry's agile drumming framed Pete Buck's ringing guitar notes as an irrepressible march forward. Driving across the country, the members of R.E.M. might not always know where they were, but they knew where they were going: the new bohemias created by indie musicians and fans. Yet the 1984 presidential campaign made the marginality of this world, the expanding network of alternative scenes linked by bands like R.E.M., glaringly apparent. A very different country completely surrounded these tiny bits of indie territory. As R.E.M.'s Little America tour ended that fall, Ronald Reagan won every state except Minnesota, the home of his opponent, Walter Mondale.[21]

The new bohemians might not like Reagan's morning in America, but few of them got up early enough to see it anyway. Like left-leaning intellectuals during the Cold War, eighties indie rebels had grown up on the soured dreams of the generation before them. From their perspective, the sixties and seventies social and political movements had not stopped a growing conservativism from taking over the nation. The cold war, conservative Christianity, racism, homophobia, and corporate greed were back, if they had ever really been gone. The whole system seemed fucked. Somehow, the hippies even let big business take over their music. If young people wanted to live in a different world, indie kids reasoned, they would have to build their vision themselves, locally, at the margins, like Finster.

Promoting *Reckoning* and recording R.E.M.'s third album *Fables of the Reconstruction*, Stipe in particular seemed to fall in love with this rural, eccentric South. Stipe told *Melody Maker* that spring, "There's a very wonderful old tradition of storytelling. I think it comes with every culture, but in the South it's kind of been built up into a wonderful thing. In a way I think I am carrying on that tradition." He liked "that kind of homespun feeling," the sentiment produced by his favorite stories: Uncle Remus tales, Aesop's fables, and *The Wind in the Willows*. He even listened to old music "recorded in Tennessee, in the mountains, Appalachian folk songs, field recordings, someone with their tape recorder recording an old man with a fiddle, with a woman in the background with her hand on the stove." "That sort of image," Stipe told a journalist, "really infected the way I wanted [the next album] to sound."[22]

In June, R.E.M. gave a live acoustic performance at I.R.S.'s Hollywood office that the label taped for broadcast in July on its MTV show *The Cutting Edge*. Surprisingly, the band played few songs from the new album. The video of "Time After Time (Annelise)" began with shots of Stipe's beat-up, doodled-on Converse All Stars and the sound of the band trying to work out a stripped-down arrangement. The country mood of "Don't Go Back to Rockville" seemed to seep into everything else they played that day, including covers like the Velvet Underground's "Femme Fatale." At a time when the only men with long hair were old hippies and Finster's painted angels, Stipe's striking curls spilled out from under his railroad cap like a halo of golden springs. As he sat cross-legged on the riser of a makeshift stage, he pushed his voice through his nose and sang with a deep Georgia twang. Bill Berry patted a pair of bongos and tapped a tambourine. Mike Mills and Peter Buck fingered and strummed twin acoustic guitars.[23]

Some of the songs R.E.M. played that day would end up on their next album. "Driver 8" sounded like a railroad trip through the rural South. Rolling guitars and clacking percussion framed Stipe's lyrics about bells and the "Southern Crescent," the name of the train running the Amtrak route from New York to Atlanta and on to New Orleans. "We can reach our destination," Stipe repeated, "but it's still a ways away." A song they said they had written that day, "Wendell Gee," told a tale about an eccentric loner, "reared to give respect":

> He had a dream one night
> That the tree had lost its middle
> So he built a trunk of chicken wire
> To try to hold it up
> But the wire, the wire turned to lizard skin
> And then he crawled inside.

Outside of Athens, the road heading toward Miller's Whirligig Farm passed a business called "Wendell Gee's Autos." Immersed in his own vision and trying to build a world while whistling, the narrator of the song sounded just like a folk artist. When the band recorded the song a year later, Buck deepened the folk aesthetic by adding a banjo solo.[24]

On tour from April to December in the United States, Canada, Europe, and Japan, the members of R.E.M. wrote, performed, and polished the songs that would appear on their next album. The lyrics of many, like "Wendell Gee," described marginal and sometimes magical but always enigmatic men, loners and visionaries. "The new material," Buck told a journalist that year, "a lot of it seems to be about people that we know, or that we met, or other experiences that really happened." In concert, Stipe sometimes dedicated the song "Maps and Legends" to Howard Finster, and the lyrics suggested a Finster-like character:

> Called the fool and the company
> On his own where he'd rather be.
> Where he ought to be and sees what
> you can't see can't you see that?

"Paint me the places you've seen," Stipe sang. "Maybe he's caught in the legend / Maybe he's caught in the mood," the chorus repeated and rhymed. "Maybe these maps and legends / Have been misunderstood."[25]

Jerry Ayers helped write "Old Man Kensey," another 1984 song that made it onto the next album. A schemer who lived near Finster and sometimes worked for him, Kensey once kidnapped dogs, held them for ransom, and then used the money to get drunk. The song "Life and How to Live It" played on the title of a vanity-press book *Life: How to Live* written by Brivs Mekis, an Athens eccentric and neighbor of Ayers's who probably suffered from schizophrenia. After he died, people discovered that he had divided his house in two and alternately lived in each of his separate, furnished apartments. Splitting their time between life on the road and rare weeks in their own apartments in town, band members understood what it meant to live a compartmentalized life. Another new song, "Feeling Gravity's Pull," conveyed the feel of visiting folk artists and musicians: "time and distance are out of place here." "Can't Get There from Here" explored this topic too. "If you're needing inspiration," Stipe sang clearly, Philomath, a town less than an hour from Athens and near where the Reverend John D. Ruth had constructed his sprawling "Bible Garden," "is where I go." "Lawyer Jeff he knows the low down," or the dirt, Stipe sang, piling on the rural sayings and describing Jeff Gilley, his companion on these rural adventures. "He's mighty bad to visit home." "The clay that holds the teeth in" sounded like a folk sculpture or a face jug. As Stipe told a filmmaker in 1985, the year R.E.M. recorded this song, "people from Athens kept going out there," to Philomath, "and meeting all these interesting people." In the mid-eighties, Stipe learned from folk artists how to spin his own tales.[26]

Over the years, R.E.M. members have described recording their third album in March 1985 in a studio outside London with Joe Boyd, a producer who had worked with Nick Drake and Richard Thompson, as the closest they came in the first half of their career to breaking up. Homesick, uncertain of their future, and definitely not having fun, they produced their most "southern" album. Stipe's dad suggested they call the new album "reconstruction," another word with multiple meanings and southern roots that could, depending on a listener's inclinations, suggest rebuilding and repair, an era of white southern humiliation, or the first flowering of African American citizenship. Reconstruction also evoked the work of folk artists like Finster and Ruth who used trash and other recycled materials to translate their scared visions into earthly forms. In the end, band members decided three single-word titles in a row were too many. Unable to choose between *Fables of the Reconstruction* and *Reconstruction of the Fables*, they used both.[27]

In April 1985, R.E.M. played another free, University Union–sponsored concert on Legion Field, this time with another self-consciously southern musician, Alex Chilton, opening. Posters for the show featured a folky silhouette of a yokel in high-water pants, an old hand pump, and what looked like a wife and kids sitting in an ancient jalopy. *Tasty World* put the Memphis native on the cover of its issue that month and described him as the key link between an earlier era of serious white southern pop music and its current iteration in bands like the dB's, the Bongos, Chris Stamey, Let's Active, and, of course, R.E.M. The magazine even quoted Chilton on his home region: "The South sucks. All those clichés about our racism and sleaziness are true."[28]

For Chilton, it must have seemed like a great idea, opening for R.E.M. at home on a glorious spring evening. The thirty-five-year-old musician had been in Athens before, and the R.E.M. guys loved him. In addition to his work on the classic Big Star albums, he demonstrated how a white southerner could draw upon and be influenced by the tangled history of white and black music making in the region without coming across, as the members of southern rock bands often did, like apologists for white southern racism. That night, Chilton had to go on early, around 7 P.M. As he played songs from his already-long career—some Big Star favorites and the Boxtops' hit "The Letter"—he faced a rapidly growing crowd. But audience members milled about, talking to each other and drinking, seemingly more interested in each other than his set.[29]

When the hometown favorites strolled out onto the stage and Pete Buck hit the first three notes of "Feeling Gravity's Pull" on his black Rickenbacker, it felt like every single member in the record-breaking crowd of between 10,000 and 12,000 roared. Apparently, the University Union's attempt to limit out-of-town fans by waiting to announce the show until after the *Rolling Stone* and MTV's concert calendars for the period were set had little effect on attendance. The Union's effort to control the alcohol by keeping people from rolling kegs right onto the field did not prove very successful either.[30]

Somehow, none of it—the crush of people, the partying, and the fact that Stipe spent most of the evening singing with his back to the audience—mattered. I remember feeling drunk on the luck part of life, the web of decisions and chance that put me in Athens at that moment. Over about an hour and a half, the band nailed older songs like "South Central Rain" and "Rockville" and introduced many of us to newer tracks like "Driver 8" and "Auctioneer." Locally, people talked about the show as the unofficial kickoff of R.E.M.'s new tour. What it felt like, hearing the music while standing under the stars with all those other fans, was the band's great big, hometown thank you. Then, as suddenly as the magic had started, the concert was over. Responding to what they later reported as about forty noise complaints, the university police shut down the show fifteen minutes before the noise ordinance deadline, killing the collective buzz and bringing us all back down to earth.[31]

On a short Preconstruction tour before the new album's release in June and a longer Reconstruction tour afterward, R.E.M. shared their "folk" vision with fans in North America and Europe. Stipe as usual handled the band's design duties, creating posters, t-shirts, and other promotional materials with an odd and folky aesthetic. Out on tour, R.E.M. often opened shows with a recording of a train. Between songs, Stipe told stories, fantastical little tales about drunks, dreamers, and preachers. Often, he wore the full "boho as hobo" look, shoes and pants with holes, layers of ragged shirts, and paper hats that looked like he made them himself. Their new songs might not sound like a traditional idea of folk music, but Buck, Stipe, Mills, and Berry positioned themselves as folk artists, making a new "old" world by pursuing their own eccentric visions.[32]

When *New York Times* critic Jon Pareles reviewed the new album in August, Peter Buck told him the songs suggested "home seen from a faraway perspective." To Stipe's folk vision, Buck added a related romanticism, a sense of the small-town South as a kind of time travel. "When you go to a big city," Buck argued, "everybody's got to be real modern and hip and cool." "In Athens you get a real different sense of the way the world was twenty years ago. Everyone sits around their porches and talks and drinks lemonade; it's kind of like Mayberry." Out on tour, band members sometimes left the stage to the whistled theme song from the *Andy Griffith Show*.[33]

The fact that the members of R.E.M. were engaged in mythmaking ought to have been clear to everyone. At the very least, no one in the Athens scene was drinking lemonade, unless it was spiked.

Alt White

Back home, R.E.M.'s influence was everywhere in the mid-1980s. You could hear it in the vocals buried in the mix, the jangling guitars that did not really solo, the melodic basses, and the driving drums. You could see it in the return of the all-male lineups and the classic quartets with their guitar, bass, and drums instrumentation. Even bands that created radically different sounds adopted asymmetrical song structures, eccentric titles, and impossible to understand lyrics. They also copied the ways Peter Buck, Michael Stipe, Mike Mills, and Bill Berry went about being a band: knotting together friendship and business, sharing songwriting credits, quietly hiring managers and lawyers and booking agents, and downplaying ambition. The difficulties other local bands had just staying together made it clear how hard it was to stay on top of the little that was in a group's control, let alone think about the art and the business of music-making. R.E.M. made it all look easy.

But even R.E.M. had difficulty navigating the politics of race and region. Being known as "southern" grounded the band within the region's rich history of music-making, but it also risked linking white band members to the region's long history of white supremacy. The modern popular-music industry emerged during a period when white Americans and especially southern whites were actively expanding segregation. Over the years, music-business people, folklorists, critics, musicians, and collectors had all played distinct but intersecting roles in fusing race and genre. In the 1980s, most people who listened to popular and even underground music still divided genres, styles, and even sonic gestures like a horn solo into racial categories.[34]

While older bands like the B-52's and Pylon and newer groups like Time Toy drew on sounds people thought of then as "black," R.E.M. in this period, with a few notable exceptions, sounded "white." Reviewing *Reckoning* for the *Washington Post*, a critic wondered whether the "few seconds of inept funk" that formed a bridge between the echoing ending of "Camera" and the rolling country-western sound of "Rockville" might be "a satiric comment on rock bands who insist on copping fashionable black rhythms." "Can't Get There from Here," written in the late summer or fall of 1984, extended this experimentation with sounds band members understood as black. "It's just a kind of self-parody," Peter Buck told a journalist the next year when the band recorded the song for their third album. "Y'know, white boys doing a soul-type song. And if you've got a soul song, whaddya do? You put horns on it." Michael Stipe even resurrected his old rockabilly voice.[35]

In mostly avoiding sonic references that might be construed as "black," R.E.M. followed a practice established by some white punk musicians. Jon Holmstrom, cofounder and editor of *Punk* magazine, bluntly explained a popular punk attitude: "The 'white nigger' was Norman Mailer's fifties lesson in how to be cool. We were rejecting the fifties and sixties instructions on how to be hip." "If you're white, you're like us," he argued. "Don't try to be black. What I thought was stupid was white people trying to act black." Pete Buck took this kind of "anti-racist" approach when he told a journalist that copying "some black music styles" felt like "stealing."[36]

Critic Lester Bangs described this strand of musical history in a bombshell of an essay he published in the *Village Voice* in December 1979 that Buck probably read, "The White Noise Supremacists":

There's an evolution of sound, rhythm, and stance running from the Velvets through the Stooges to the Ramones and their children that takes us farther and farther from the black-stud postures of Mick

Jagger that Lou Reed and Iggy partake in but Joey Ramone certainly doesn't. I respect Joey for that, for having the courage to be himself . . . a white American kid from Forest Hills, and as such his cultural inputs have been white, from "The Jetsons" through Alice Cooper.

The problem, Bangs argued, was that this whiteness stood in contrast to "the fact that most of the greatest, deepest music America has produced has been, when not entirely black, the product of miscegenation." Being your "white" self could mean giving up a lot of musical terrain.[37]

According to Bangs, some white punks even thought they had invented a new kind of cool. Adopting a stance of opposition toward everyone in contrast to those wimpy hippies, they put "love" aside, faced the issue of race head on, and said "nigger." Bangs confessed that he had written stupid things in this vein in *Creem*. "Everybody has been walking around for the last year or so acting like faggots ruled the world," he argued in piece he published there about David Bowie's soul phase, "when in actuality it's the *niggers* who control and direct everything just as it always has been and properly should be." The critic also admitted he had said stupider things at parties. Though he did not mention this in his *Voice* piece, he had for a while worn a black t-shirt with white letters that spelled out "LAST OF THE WHITE NIGGERS." All too readily, he now realized, his and other white punks' "casual, even ironic embrace of the totems of bigotry" crossed "over into the real poison." The comedian "Lenny Bruce was wrong." People "shouldn't sling" those "lethal" words around "for effect." Saying this "shit," you risked "misinterpretation by some other bigoted asshole; your irony might just be his cup of hate."[38]

Even at their snarkiest, none of the members of R.E.M. were these kinds of punks. You had to be an idiot to be a white southerner and say anything like James Chance, a white, New York no-wave musician who called black music "just a bunch of nigger bullshit." Not even southern rockers who waved the Confederate flag and wrote songs that made excuses for white southern racism went this far. Mostly, the members of R.E.M. followed the Ramones and just tried to be their own white selves, and many other Athens bands took up this model, too.[39]

Scene participants then did not talk much about race as a category. They might not know a lot about the civil rights movement, but growing up in the seventies, they had been part of the first generation of Deep South students to attend fully integrated schools. Curtis Crowe of Pylon, his sister Rhett Crowe, and her bandmate in Guadalcanal Diary and future husband Jeff Walls were from Marietta, a town just outside Atlanta, and they attended the formerly all-white Marietta High after the closing of the formerly all-black Lemon Street High and the integration of the school system. Lynda Stipe, whose parents moved from outside St. Louis to the country outside Athens after her dad left the military, remembered attending a racially divided and tense Cedar Shoals High School on the east side of Athens. Bill Berry told a journalist that his family moved to Macon on the very day the schools there integrated. He also remembered being beaten up by some African American guys because he had expressed an interest in dating an African American girl. A filmmaker who visited Athens around 1985 who had grown up in Seattle remembered being shocked when, one night over beers, everyone started reminiscing about when their schools desegregated.[40]

Atlanta's large private schools also enrolled more African Americans in this period. Laura Carter, Kelly Noonan, and Arthur Johnson went to Westminster, an independent school which admitted its first African American students in 1967. On the south side of town, Woodward Academy, my own alma mater, had more African American students than other Atlanta private schools in the mid-1970s and early 1980s because of its location near middle-class black neighborhoods. While neither of my parents, Deep South natives, earned a college degree, my African American classmates were the children of Spelman and Morehouse professors and administrators and doctors.[41]

These kinds of experiences shaped the kids who created the scene. We understood racism as something ugly and blatant—southern whites talking opening about their racial superiority and actively fighting integration. What most of us who were white and had gone to integrated schools did not understand was that racism could also be something more subtle.

For most scene participants, the answer to their region's history of violence and discrimination was not to talk but to act. We had experienced enough talking, another white southern tradition we were ready to abandon. But acting did not mean political organizing. It meant creating a different way to live. Sometimes this alternative consisted of a kind of "colorblindness," a "let's live together and ignore race" attitude that seemed to some young people like an attractive alternative to the tension and conflicts they had experienced in their schools. In contrast to white southerners who openly supported white supremacy and fought against the civil rights movement, "colorblind" whites understood their own position as an intervention in their region's long and bloody history. Some blacks and Latinos also adopted this strategy as a way to take advantage of the opportunities won as a result of all those civil rights battles.

Today we understand colorblindness as a more subtle but still damaging form of racism, an ideology that does nothing to combat white privilege and microaggressions and the way whiteness too often stands invisibly as the norm. Then, not talking about race but simply trying to live in an integrated world seemed like a viable and even radical alternative, embraced by a diverse coalition of people who thought of themselves as antiracist. Within the national networks and local scenes that formed the world of indie culture, this approach allowed white participants to be proud of their racial liberalism without having to think very much about why so few people of color were drawn to their "alternative."

In a scene where most participants were current or former college students, it did not help that UGA remained a very white institution long after it integrated in 1961. The university's own official statistics, published every year as the UGA *Fact Book*, provide the abysmal numbers, and the names used for the categories suggested a university that had not thought very hard about how to welcome and nurture nonwhite students. In 1985, for example, only 1,262 "American Negro" students attended UGA, about 5 percent of the student population, alongside 110 "Oriental American" students, 140 "Spanish American" students, and 22,172 "Caucasian" students. The number of students of color fluctuated a little each year but overall stayed so small that the student body remained about 90 percent white. In the art school then, a place that connected many students to the scene, art professors remembered only a handful of students of color majoring in art. To a large degree, the whiteness of the scene reflected the whiteness of the university.[42]

The scene also had little to offer local African Americans, who made up over 30 percent of the population of Athens across the 1980s. Many Athens blacks were working-class, and a bohemian penchant for elected poverty and denial of any desire to make money would not have been attractive to them any more than these characteristics appealed to most working-class whites. Also, people with creative ambitions could easily move to Atlanta, with its large black middle class and strong tradition of black intellectual life and black arts connected both to Atlanta's historically black colleges like Spelman and Morehouse and to community organizations. Atlanta's own indie scene in this period, coalescing around venues like 688 and the Celebrity Club, seemed able to attract more African American participants, including RuPaul, before he moved to New York City, than the Athens scene.[43]

These years when a folk aesthetic strongly shaped the scene presented another problem. Working-class blacks as well as whites who could not always afford new items and had to make do with used goods were not as in-clined as mostly middle-class scene participants to find the vernacular aes-thetics of low-income rural southerners exotic or interesting. African Ameri-cans, in particular, had a complicated relationship to the rural South where traces of the landscape of slavery still survived. As a result, while there were both white and black folk artists and musicians in the area, folk revivalists, like Athens bohemians, tended to be white.

Another reason the scene was so segregated was that Athens's own long history of African American music-making offered local blacks an alter-native to the scene's alternative culture. In the late 1970s and 1980s, Afri-can American night clubs featured jukeboxes, deejays, and also live music. A little ways outside of town on Jefferson Avenue, soul bands played at a place called the Hawaiian Ha-Le. Along Washington and Hull Streets in the historically black commercial district called the Hot Corner, the old black vaudeville theater the Morton remained closed because the space did not meet code, but the Manhattan Café drew crowds that spilled out onto the sidewalk at night like the bohemians around the corner at the Clayton Street 40 Watt. A few blocks west of downtown on Broad Street, African Ameri-cans danced and listened to music at Gresham's Disco Lounge.[44]

In black-owned businesses that hosted live music and catered to black audiences, musicians perpetuated a culture of professionalism with a long history in African American communities where playing music had been one of the few attractive jobs. The amateurism of the Athens scene bands made no sense within the context of this cultivation of craft. Sometimes scene participants went to these African American venues to hear musicians perform in the local version of the bohemian tradition of "slumming," but few local African Americans went to the shows at the Uptown or the 40 Watt. Why, they probably wondered, would anyone pay to see someone who could barely play?[45]

After R.E.M.'s new folk vision and indie fans' investment in place linked the band even more strongly to the South, band members occasionally got defensive about the way people from other parts of the country looked down on the region. In these moments, their whiteness did not look so innocent. In July 1985, Mike Mills published "Our Town," a piece about the Athens music scene, in the third issue of a new national music magazine. *Spin*, founded by Bob Guccione Jr. and funded by his father's *Penthouse* fortune, aspired to be a new generation's *Rolling Stone*, with edgy coverage of music, including col-lege rock and hip-hop, and news that appealed to younger music fans. While "the buzz," according to the magazine's editors, suggested Athens might be the "hippest" place for music in America, Mills argued against this hyperbolic claim. People like him who had been there "four or five years" rejected the very idea of "a scene." Athens was just a small place, a great college town, sure, but hardly unique, not "the bizarre happening people peg it as."[46]

If Mills wanted to push back against the cool-town image and stop people from moving to Athens for the scene, much of what he wrote contradicted that argument. Naming and ranking his favorite up-and-coming local bands — the Kilkenny Cats, the Squalls, Dreams So Real, Banned 37, Fashion Battery, the "sloppy" Bar-B-Q Killers, and jazz fusion group the Land Sharks — he revealed a rich musical landscape even as he made locals jockeying to be the "next" R.E.M. mad. He covered the clubs, the record stores, the radio station, the local rag *Tasty World*, and the partying. And he introduced *Spin* readers to Howard Finster, who claimed to be "a traveler in space," "put here to bring the word of God to people through folk art." He even had a kind word for UGA's Greeks, whom he credited for sometimes supporting local music.[47]

The accompanying photographs also deepened the Athens allure. A large color image caught Jerry Ayers and Mark Cline wearing Western vests and string ties, Vanessa Briscoe in heels and a man's suit, and a visiting Fred Schneider sporting a sweater vest and bow tie on a Sunday stroll near Prince Avenue. A black-and-white photograph shot with a flash at night revealed Stipe lounging in a porch swing and holding a whirligig. Other images presented the ruins of the burned Tyrone's and band pictures of R.E.M., Dreams So Real, and the Squalls.

Then, midway through an article that seemed, for all Mills's denials, like another indie celebration of Athens, Mills swerved into entirely new territory. Most college students, he argued, cared about two things, "getting a degree and getting a good job," and it was not for him to say that they were wrong. The growing conservatism of college students made "youth culture" in the eighties radically different from the sixties. The "political activism" of that decade had turned to "cynicism" "pretty quickly." The current situation was "not so much apathy" as a sense that "nobody's gonna change the world, and everybody might as well realize that," including rock musicians. "Kids in Athens or *anywhere*" did not want "anything," especially not a new Dylan, "an icon to lead them into a new age."

Maybe, Mills conceded, he and his bandmates had a "small town mentality," but that made their music more "real," "more connected to everyday life," a vehicle for creating and sharing feelings rather than preaching ideologies. And this line of thinking brought him back to the South:

It's not isolated here—you can't act like this is Antarctica. But that's the way people think—that you're down here in the pine forests "hangin' niggers from trees." The South is a weird place. If you go out in the woods you're gonna end up with a lot of inbreeding and the kind of people who are behaving really strangely. But would you want to live in the suburbs of Boston, or Long Island, or the South Side of Chicago? Take your pick. People are deadly anywhere you go. Human nature is a sorry thing. All you can do is try to improve it. . . . You get out in the woods anywhere—not just Georgia, not just the South—and they're gonna be some weird people doing weird things.[48]

In criticizing how outsiders viewed the South through a fantasy of gothic horror that stretched from Erskine Caldwell's novels to more recent popular movies like *Deliverance*, Mills revealed his own knee-jerk sense that southerners—and, by extension, Athens scene participants—were white. Arguing against the way outsiders often caricatured southern whites, he indulged in stereotypes of his own.

Across the country, alternative cultures in the eighties remained pretty segregated. In the late 1970s, black punk band Bad Brains, named after a Ramones song, helped create the hardcore scene in Washington, D.C., but most of the musicians in the bands that formed after them there were white. A downtown–outer borough exchange in New York in the early 1980s brought pioneering hip-hop stars and graffiti artists like FAB 5 FREDDY to downtown centers like the Mudd Club, but this Big Apple version of the "beloved community" did not last. There and in other undergrounds, white record store nerds especially—clerks, collectors, and critics—listened to rap and followed that other alternative culture growing up around it, the hip-hop scene. In Athens, Michael Lachowski promoted funk, soul, and hip-hop discs and tapes as a clerk at the Athens branch of Wax 'n' Facts, wrote reviews of these recordings for *Tasty World*, and played these genres when he worked as a deejay at the 40 Watt. White *Village Voice* critic Robert Christgau did similar work on a more national level in supporting black musicians performing a wide range of genres in his record reviews and annual polls. Still, pick whichever overlapping but not synonymous genre term you preferred for the new music and the network of scenes associated with the sounds—indie or alternative or college radio—and despite the participation of some Latino/as, African Americans, and Asian Americans, most musicians and fans were white.[49]

In Athens, a smallish knot of scene regulars included a few African Americans. Robin Edwards, the bass player for Mystery Date, moved to Athens after commuting from Atlanta for years after the other members of the band relocated. "I remember Robin being skittish when we were in smaller Southern towns, and that was super-sad to me," her bandmate Velena Vego remembered. Edwards felt more comfortable in Athens because "no one had any prejudice — they thought she [a black female band member] was the coolest thing on earth." Looking back, Edwards contrasted the acceptance she felt in the scene with the racism she experienced in Athens more generally. Frank Mason worked off and on at the clubs, especially the 40 Watt. In the fall of 1988, J. R. "Superstar" Greene, a local deejay, became the manager and part-owner of a venue called the Rockfish Palace that opened the year before. Calvin Orlando Smith hung out at the clubs and danced like crazy, especially on nights when deejays like Michael Lachowski took over, and later became a deejay himself and then an actor. In the early nineties, Brian Harris appeared in an R.E.M. video and then formed a band called Asa Nisi Masa in which he played a custom-made, eight-string bass. Latino Juan Molina of the Little Tigers, Go Van Go, Time Toy, and the Squalls was a scene fixture for years. Asian American Lesley Ganchow grew up in Athens, where her dad was a history professor, hung out in the scene, and turned out regularly for shows by bands like the Bar-B-Q Killers. Surely, there were others I am missing, but the fact that I can make a list with any degree of completeness confirms the point. However much the Athens scene offered an alternative to "mainstream" culture, it was still a mostly white alternative. Launched in a conservative region in a conservative moment, the decade or so lull between the black power, radical feminism, and gay liberation of the seventies and the confrontational AIDS activism and the fierce college-based identity politics of the late eighties, the Athens scene featured what scholar Wini Brienes calls a "prefigurative politics" approach.[50] Scene participants attempted, in a way that was more attractive to whites than to people of color, to live in a world in which racial divisions did not matter.

Only a white musician like Stipe could claim to love *Uncle Remus* tales. Only a white musician like Buck could wax nostalgic about Mayberry, a fictional North Carolina town where no black person spoke until the *Andy Griffith Show*'s seventh season, and brag that Athens had the same kind of old-fashioned community. Only a white musician like Mills could be so flippant about the history of southern lynching and suggest that as weird as the South was, people behaved badly in the historically black area of the South Side of Chicago, too. Mills here took a step beyond Stipe's white romanticism and

Buck's white nostalgia. Consciously or not, his argument that crazy, violent people lived everywhere deflected and excused a long history of white southern racism. He offered a pessimistic view of human nature in line with the New Right's expanding attack on liberal optimism.

I am picking on the members of R.E.M. here not because they were unique but because they were by the mid-eighties already a kind of underground famous — and outside of what then passed as run-of-the-mill sexism in what was decidedly *not* a "#MeToo" moment, pretty damn decent guys. In so many ways, the Athens scene was liberating and generative. But again and again I come back to this question. If the scene was really "alternative," why did its expansive sense that anything was possible mostly just work for white people? And the answer is not pretty. The culture that so many of us loved was not enough of an alternative to the long history of American white supremacy.[51]

Inside Out

In the mid-eighties, would-be filmmakers Bill Cody and Tony Gayton were barely making a living in Los Angeles trying to break into the movie business, and they found just about everything about Hollywood strange. Then they saw *Vernon, Florida*, Errol Morris's 1981 documentary about eccentric people in a tiny Florida town, a place that seemed weird in a much more interesting way. Because they both loved R.E.M., Cody and Gayton decided to try to make their film, "*Vernon, Florida* but with music." Then they could hang out in a place about as far from southern California and yet still in the United States as they could imagine: Athens, Georgia. Cody went up to his hometown of Seattle to see an R.E.M. show there, probably the band's July 1985 performance at the Paramount, and pushed his way into a meeting afterward. Although band members offered no firm commitment, they seemed amenable to participating in the project.[52]

When Cody and Gayton made their first trip to Athens, sometime in the summer or fall of 1985, the whole idea suddenly seemed more complicated. The filmmakers who created the documentary that showed kids who watched MTV what a scene could be almost quit before they got started. Only the members of Love Tractor, out of college and working to push their career up another level, seemed open to working with film people from Los Angeles, the very center of the mainstream culture Athens bohemians hated. As Cody remembered, Athens felt so "shut down" that he and Gayton had already decided to "bag it" when they finally got a meeting at the R.E.M. office with no assurance of who exactly would attend.[53]

Partying so much the night before that he mistakenly slept in his contacts and could not wear them the next day, Cody showed up for the appointment practically blind. The future producer had met so many Michaels in Athens that he actually did not know he was talking to Stipe until far into the conversation, a mistake that meant he did not turn the singer off by acting starstruck. Stipe immediately understood how Cody and Gayton planned to use *Vernon, Florida* as a model and suggested hiring Jim Herbert to shoot the movie. Someone gave the filmmakers directions, and they drove to the painting and film teacher's house. Word about these two meetings seemed to get around town almost instantly, in that mysterious way that everyone seemed to know everything all the time even though many people did not even have landlines. Suddenly, the whole scene opened to the out-of-towners.[54]

It was probably their next trip to Athens when somebody told the filmmakers that they had to meet Jerry Ayers. Everyone they met seemed to talk about him — how he had written a song for the B-52's and then written a song for R.E.M. and played in Limbo District, which had by then broken up. Herbert showed them a clip of his film *Carnival* which featured the band, and Cody and Gayton loved it so much that they used some of the footage in their documentary. About three weeks earlier, Ricky Wilson, the guitar player for the B-52's, had died suddenly of what people later learned was AIDS, and the surviving members of the band came to town for a memorial. Someone took Cody and Gayton to another house, and then Ayers showed up with Kate Pierson and Keith Strickland in tow. Soon, the town's most influential bohemian was acting as an advisor to the film. Ayers suggested Gayton include folk artists Howard Finster, the Reverend John D. Ruth, and Doc and Lucy Barnes in the documentary, though Doc had a heart attack before they could film him. At some point during the few months when the filmmakers traveled back and forth to Athens to make the film, Ayers wrote Tony Gayton a letter listing all the things they should include in the movie. Ayers was so integral to the process of making the documentary that the filmmakers listed him in the credits as a consultant. Making the shift in his name "official," he asked Cody and Gayton to call him Jeremy rather than Jerry.[55]

Because film was so expensive and they had so little money, Cody and Gayton worked by going to talk to people and see bands who might appear in the film first, taking along audio tape rather than film and a camera operator.

They then prerecorded people telling their stories. Back in Los Angeles, the filmmakers pieced together the film before they had even shot it. Then they returned to Athens for short periods of what Gayton called "kamikaze film-making." They used a tiny crew, including locals like UGA film student Lisa Mae Wells, credited as an associate producer, two women who worked in the R.E.M. office — Liz Hammond, credited as a researcher, and Sandra-Lee Phipps, credited as a still photographer — and Jim Hawkins, owner of a local recording studio, credited for the sound. With Herbert mostly behind the camera, Cody and Gayton retraced their steps and shot interviews and live performance footage with their precious supply of film stock. Their method cut costs by reducing the chance that film would be shot and developed and then not included in the finished documentary. People offered more or less detail or told things in a different order than they had in their original interviews, but generally the filmmakers got something good enough to use.[56]

Yet in one key interview, the shift from talking to actually filming proved to be a disaster. Ayers spent a lot of time with the filmmakers, but when it came time to get him on camera, he seemed to clam up. Somehow, the footage Herbert shot failed to capture Ayers's striking beauty and his shy, elusive charm. Because Michael Stipe agreed to help "draw Jerry out," the filmmakers made a second attempt at Ayers's house and garden on Meigs Street. Once again, the interview failed, but at least this visit produced some usable footage, a short scene of Ayers, Armistead Wellford of Love Tractor, a woman I have not been able to identify, and Michael Stipe making music in the grass. Another brief shot caught Ayers as he strolled through his bamboo patch grinning, all the filmmakers would get of "gorgeous Jerry." Once again, the man who did more than any other single person to shape the scene remained in the shadows.[57]

You had to know the backstory to identify Ayers, sitting at the table and occasionally visible, not talking but sometimes laughing, in another key scene in the film, an interview with Kate Pierson and Keith Strickland at the Bluebird Café. Though the filmmakers had met Pierson with Ayers early in the filmmaking, the members of Athens first new music band had not agreed then to participate in the documentary. Cody had tried and failed to get hold of them or their manager. Then right at the end of filming, he got a call from Pierson, who then came to Athens with Strickland. Cody had to hold and pay his crew for an extra two days to shoot them, but the resulting interview did the crucial work of setting up the origins of the scene.[58]

Bizarrely, given how much the members of R.E.M. shaped the final film, they, too, were originally reluctant participants. But as Stipe worked with the film crew, he ended up appearing in the footage often, talking, dancing, and hanging out with folk artists. While the inclusion of Pierson and Strickland was important, the band did not play for the filmmakers, who instead used old footage of the B-52's shot by others. In the end, the R.E.M. guys did agree to perform, giving the filmmakers a new song called "Swan, Swan H" and a cover of "All I Have to Do Is Dream," a 1958 Everly Brothers hit.[59]

The biggest challenge the filmmakers faced besides raising the money was choosing which local bands to include in the film. R.E.M., Love Tractor, Pylon and the early B-52's were a given. Beyond that, in a scene with any-where from thirty-five to fifty bands, depending on how you thought about genre and what being an Athens group meant, some musicians would have to be left out. An editor Gayton wanted to work with liked Dreams So Real. Based on the success of the 1985 single "Everywhere Girl" on Hoboken's Coyote Records, some people in town thought the band would be the next in town to make it big. Other locals suggested that prize would go to the Kil-kenny Cats. Cody liked the Squalls, especially their song "Na, Na, Na, Na," and the fact that members of the band, including one who earned his living growing pot, were all older. Front man Bryan Cook, who stood out around town then for wearing a suit coat inside out, remembered that a chance fill-in gig on a Tuesday night landed his band in the documentary. The film-makers just happened to catch Nine Hefty Worms, the cover band version of Time Toy, and loved that the four musicians poured their hearts into making music for about twelve of their friends.[60]

According to Cody, Athens bohemians he got to know complained most about the inclusion of the Bar-B-Q Killers. Davie Giles, then the manager of Ruthless Records, took Cody and Gayton to see the band on a night when Laura Carter arrived on stage strapped to a cross and screaming "fuck Jesus." Given Carter's charisma and the filmmakers' realization that they needed more women in the film, the band made the cut. Because they already had so many male musicians, the filmmakers left out Mercyland, David Barbe's new trio that had debuted at the Uptown Lounge that October. Yet they also left out the new band Billy James, which featured Kelly Noonan on bass and vocals, and Mystery Date, a quartet made up of four women that had re-leased a single on Twilight Records.[61]

People I knew believed the Bar-B-Q Killers belonged and objected in-stead to the Flat Duo Jets. Dexter Romweber and Chris "Crow" Smith had moved to Athens from Carrboro, North Carolina, a former mill town next to Chapel Hill, only a few months before the filming, following Romweber's then-girlfriend who had rented a run-down antebellum house in the country outside Athens. Across the eighties, indie musicians and fans from central North Carolina and Athens had developed strong ties. R.E.M.'s manager Jefferson Holt had moved to Athens from Chapel Hill. Many Athens bands used Mitch Easter's studio in Winston-Salem, and his band Let's Active, in which Dexter's sister Sarah Romweber originally played drums, was really popular in town. The members of the dB's, including Chris Stamey and Peter Holsapple, had all moved to New York City from Winston-Salem, and they played Athens regularly. Fetchin Bones, a newer, folksy band from Charlotte, had started packing the Broad Street 40 Watt. Athens musicians like Pete Buck were friends with many of these North Carolina musicians.

Ayers even proposed that the filmmakers shoot the members of the Flat Duo Jets playing on the columned porch of an antebellum house at the west end of downtown, the home of the local chapter of the fraternity SAE. Despite weather so cold on January 27, 1986, that they could see Romweber's breath as he sang in front of a small crowd of freezing Greeks, the filmmakers did exactly as Ayers advised. In the finished film, the scene plays like a re-enactment of a fifties frat party, the kind of event where black R & B groups entertained rich white kids—except that in this version, the musicians, too, were white.[62]

Cody and Gayton came to Athens looking for a small town filled with weird southern folk, and Athens bohemians helped them find it. From this perspective, indie music made by untrained locals and circulated outside of the contours of the corporate music business looked like outsider art. *Athens, GA: Inside/Out* presented the scene as a folky southern bohemia.

Borrowing its collage structure from Morris's *Vernon, Florida*, the documentary created visual rhythms by cutting between scenes of different lengths. Almost everyone speaks in a deeply southern accent. In an opening montage, images like shots of houses with screen porches fix the location as a small southern town. William Orten Carlton, known to everyone as Ort, stands in a bare room under a naked light bulb and describes "the Zen of Athens." Stipe's friend Chris Slay recites his folk-flavored poetry. Footage of the members of R.E.M. wearing old-fashioned clothes and performing a new song called "Swan Swan H" conjure another century. Berry sits on the back of a wooden chair with his cowboy boots in the seat while he taps a high, single snare drum with brushes. Mills and Buck play acoustic guitars. Stipe repeats the line "we're all free now," mentions "Johnny Reb" and "marching feet," and lists gruesome souvenirs of the Civil War like "bone chains and toothpicks." The location of the performance, a once-elegant nineteenth-century chapel then being restored on the campus of a former Athens girls school called the Lucy Cobb Institute, deepens the archaic mood.[63]

In this scene and in later shots of R.E.M. doing "All I Have to Do Is Dream," Stipe mostly closes his eyes as he sings and shakes his head like a blind man feeling the music. Sometimes, he does a little marching dance, waving an old wooden spindle from one of the building's railings out in front of him horizontally. In other scenes, the singer claps the film slate and announces that "this is how Popeye exercises," before launching into another eccentric jig, a kind of tap dance simulation complete with the sound of his shoes clacking on the wooden floorboards. He also tells a weird story about how Mike Mills can smell ants. In *Athens, GA: Inside/Out*, Stipe did not just take the filmmakers to meet with folk artists. He adopted his own odd, "only the blind can see" persona. He played the folk.[64]

Maybe the *Vernon, Florida* model explains why the completed documentary includes so many eccentric male characters. Folk artists Howard Finster and Reverend Ruth are presented as if they actually live in Athens. Not just Stipe but many of the guys in the film including recent college graduates also put on crazy "folk" personas. Ort, a generation or so older than most scene participants, describes how he recently had to move away from town and is only back for a visit because he felt like "every day I was getting up to get inked into my own panels." His voice weary with the burden of celebrity, he talks about his life as if he is actually world famous instead of just an odd local character. Pete Buck wanders around a street named the Plaza near his house carrying a can of Bud and wearing an old robe and pajamas and then returns home to sits on the wide porch of his yellow Victorian. Local writer John Seawright looks and sounds like a Depression-era preacher as he reads his vernacular poetry at the 40 Watt. Providing his own salty take on the kind of double entendre made popular by black blues singers half a century before, he drawls,

> A man needs a saw so he can cut around.
> The way he needs a pony so he can ride to town.
> But I broke my saw. I broke my saw.
> And nothing like that to shut your circuits down.

Melanie Haner, who moved to Athens and became a part of the scene in 1985 around the time the filmmakers started visiting, remembers people creating and living "these crazy personas." *Inside/Out* seemed to both capture and deepen this trend.[65]

In contrast, most African Americans in *Inside/Out* are unnamed figures in the background like the black extras in *Andy Griffith*'s Mayberry. Stipe tags along as the filmmakers visit Reverend Ruth, an African American who actually gets to speak, near Philomath. Ruth and his wife play what Stipe calls a "Kmart organ" and sing, and then the preacher talks about how he always had a feeling "to take nothing and make something." Despite having a stroke, he is still "carrying on" his work on his multi-acre installation, the Bible Garden, "for white churches, yellow churches, brown churches, for everybody." Walter Rittenbury, who owns Walter's BBQ, and an unnamed African American man who appears to be an employee also speak on screen. Rittenbury describes how the R.E.M. guys always come to his place when they are in town and tell everyone they miss his food when they are away. He also shares how another band—"they try to pattern themselves on R.E.M."— eats at his place often, and he struggles to remember the name of this group before coming up with the not-quite-right "Asshole Surfers."[66]

Only one woman gets the kind of solo screen time lavished on all the odd men. Old footage of Pylon playing in what looks like the old Rat and Duck theater space at Stitchcraft alternates with Michel Lachowski and Vanessa Briscoe Hay talking separately about their former band. Speaking in a soft and drawling southern voice, Hay confesses that when she hears Pylon songs, "I don't really recognize my own voice on the tape or the record as my voice that I hear when I'm speaking. It just makes me feel funny." Instead of making music, she works now at "a Xerox shop. I make copies." She had "a real good time" in Pylon, she insists, but does not miss playing because she "never planned on being a musician." "I don't have any plans," she confesses, shaking her head and then smiling and laughing. "I don't. I never made any plans. I never planned to be in a band. I never planned anything."[67]

Near the end of *Inside/Out*, another short clip from the interview with Kate Pierson and Keith Strickland appears in a collage of very quick scenes setting up a kind of closing rhythm, like drum fills that sometimes signal the end of a song. Pierson asks Strickland, Ayers just off-screen, and by extension everyone viewing the film, "Why *did* we move to New York?" Then members of the Kilkenny Cats insist that if they make it, they will stay in Athens, and John Seawright says, "As soon as I find a better place to go, I'll go there." After a few more clips, R.E.M. performs "Dream." As the song ends, Stipe and Mills send their slightly off and yet harmonizing voices high. The shot holds a beat or two afterwards, capturing the way sound reverberates in the tall space of the chapel. Then the film fades to Stipe alone again in the old theater as he walks up to a fake door painted into the faded background and gives it a loud kick.

I had no plans to be an unpaid extra when a friend invited me along to the Uptown Lounge on February 4, 1986, a date I only know because it is listed on the *Athens, GA: Inside/Out* soundtrack album. The film crew was shooting performances by the Kilkenny Cats, the Bar-B-Q Killers, and Time Toy at the Uptown Lounge, and they needed people to be the audience. If you watch the film carefully with your finger near the pause button, you can see me dancing as the Cats play "Nightfall," a striped scarf I still own whipping around my flying hair. All these years later, I still remember the weird combination of exhilaration and awkwardness. The filmmakers told us to just do what we would do at the club on a regular night there, but somehow that was actually difficult. What exactly do you do when your task is to act like yourself?[68]

On a much grander scale, this was the dilemma Stipe, Briscoe Hay, Ort, and Ayers faced in making *Athens, GA: Inside/Out* and, as the myth of the Athens scene grew, sometimes even in life. Stipe did his eccentric folk act. Briscoe Hay described the distance between her current life and the person she had been performing in Pylon. And Ort both presented himself as a local character and confessed he had moved away to get a break from playing that role. Only Ayers, the former Warhol superstar Silva Thin then changing his name again, proved unable to "act" like himself. Instead of playing the visionary, Ayers largely provided the vision. Gayton and Cody's documentary made Jeremy's Athens into the most visible image of the scene.

Inside/Out had its "southern" debut November 30, 1986, at an invitation-only event at Atlanta's Buckhead Cinema and Drafthouse, for critics and for people featured in film. That same night, MTV's show *The Cutting Edge* ran the documentary. In 1987, the film began a limited theatrical run alongside Hollywood films like *Wall Street*, playing in a few cities like New York and Los Angeles and in college towns. In early 1987, I.R.S. Records put out an accompanying soundtrack. Music critics and college deejays paid attention, and R.E.M.'s contributions as well as a few other songs on the compilation received college station airplay. The Squalls song "Na Na Na Na," released as a single backed with the Flat Duo Jets song "Crazy, Hazy Kisses," eventually hit number two on the college charts. MTV promoted an "Athens weekend," broadcasting the film again and playing videos by Athens bands. Over the next few years, *Inside/Out* popped up on MTV occasionally and in screenings at college theaters. Some bands in the film played an *Inside/Out* showcase in Nashville and others hit the road on a month-long national *Inside/ Out* bus tour.[69]

The movie *Inside/Out* gave people who had not been to Athens a picture of something many of them had a hard time imagining: a southern, small-town bohemia. Mark Cooper Smith of the Squalls called the release of the film "the demarcation line." Capturing what many of us thought at the time, he told me, "The movie changed everything." In its wake, the scene exploded, growing in both self-consciousness and size.[70]

Better than TV

David Barbe was too busy to worry about the fact that his band Mercyland did not make it into the Athens documentary. Finished with his UGA degree, he turned his summer work filling cracks in parking lots into a full-time job and spent his nights practicing and performing and going to clubs to hear his friends' bands. Athens still did not have an independent record label, though Atlanta-based DB and Twilight signed a lot of Athens acts. Sometime before the summer of 1986, Barbe decided to fill this gap by founding DRG Records. The initials stood for "Dominant Rock Gods," the kind of joke that worked both as an admission and a denial of ambition.[71]

DRG quickly released its first recording, a cassette called *Proud of Me Gluttony* with fourteen songs by seven previously unrecorded local bands. *Red and Black* writers liked the tape so much they reviewed it twice. The compilation opened with three Mercyland songs: local favorite "Fall of the City," "Western Guns," and "Vomit Clown," a song with the line "puking up burritos on the side of the road" that should have been a teen anthem. Raymond Valley, then entertainment editor of the UGA paper, wrote that Barbe sang like he had "a cold. Right through the nose." Mercyland made "kickin' rock 'n' roll that sounded hardcorish but not noisy," music with a "melody" that listeners could "hum." The other reviewer called Barbe simply "the best pop songwriter in Athens." The compilation also included *Inside/Out* veterans Time Toy and the Bar-B-Q Killers. The oldest of the harder edged bands, the Bar-B-Q Killers played "gothic show punk." "Mark E. Smith," a song named after the singer for the Fall, was a "sheet of white noise" that actually hurt. "Chester Drawers," a cut so good, one reviewer claimed, that it could be mistaken for an actual Fall song, sounded like it was "falling off a cliff." Other bands on the compilation—Eat America, the La Di Das, and the scene's most hardcore band, Porn Orchard—had started playing the year before. Originally a cover band, the Primates had recently started writing their own

**David Barbe's band Mercyland debuted in 1985 and quickly
became one of the most popular of the new harder-edged
Athens bands. Here, Barbe sings and plays bass while
Andrew Donaldson plays guitar and Harry Joiner drums at
a New York City gig in 1987, probably at the Lismar Lounge.
(Photograph by Spyder Lynch, courtesy of David Barbe)**

"hardcore/country" originals, songs for "Southerners" who liked "the Ramones better than George Jones" but appreciated both. For younger scene
participants and especially fans of that harder-edged, second big wave of
music-making that started with the Kilkenny Cats and the Bar-B-Q Killers,
Proud of Me Gluttony became the soundtrack of the summer.[72]

It's hard to describe how radical and transformative it felt then to fill
our lives with our friends' music. The cassette I bought for $4 at Ruthless
Records on College Avenue may not have looked like much, a copy art cover
surrounding a little plastic box, but it seemed to me like a sacred object. I had
seen most of these bands perform live. I loved Time Toy and Mercyland and
was just discovering the Bar-B-Q Killers and the La Di Das. I knew some of
these people and had been on a few guest lists. That tape seemed like tan-
gible proof we were part of something bigger than any one person or band
or show.

The scene younger participants like me were creating felt mostly left
out of *Athens, GA: Inside/Out*, with its parade of odd and eccentric men. In
late 1986, around the time the documentary debuted, our version of Athens

hit the road with much less fanfare when the members of four bands and assorted partners and friends filled a chartered bus and rambled across Florida playing scattered gigs. Outside the easy everydayness of home, we gained a sense of how other people saw us. And we gave people who came to the shows a glimpse of not just our music but the networks of friendship and community out of which it grew.

Though both Mercyland and DRG were involved, the "Better Than TV" tour was not originally David Barbe's idea. As much as Barbe worked to make it a success, Bryan Cook, the singer in Time Toy, and Dru Wilbur, the singer for Eat America, came up with the scheme for a multi-band Florida tour. It all started when Wilbur got Eat America a date at a Tallahassee club and talked to Cook about bringing Time Toy along to open. Soon the two musicians were talking about bringing more bands. As Cook recalled, "We figured out a bus would be real fun." By the time they got it all organized, Tallahassee was out, replaced by gigs in Tampa, Orlando, Gainesville, and Jacksonville. Barbe got involved because they invited Mercyland. They also asked the Bar-B-Q Killers. To raise money to cover expenses, they decided to sell tickets to friends who wanted to come along. I had a friend who was dating a drummer in one of the bands at the time, and he offered me a ticket. I think I was supposed to pay $20, but I don't remember anyone ever collecting the cash.[73]

Because Barbe was already involved in the Florida tour as a musician, it seemed like a good idea for DRG to put out a record with one song by each band that the musicians could sell on the tour. Barbe sometimes worked for John Keane then and he got the town's best engineer to record the tracks at his studio in Cobbham. Because the budget was so tight, band members did the rest of the work themselves. They bought plain, white album covers because they were cheaper. Ted Hafer, a member of Porn Orchard, made stickers out of an old photograph of a horse with the name of the album *Some* in blue at his job at a local printing place, and they stuck those on one side of the cover to make the front. Wilbur carved an abstract design into a piece of linoleum, and they hand-printed that as well as the names of the bands on the back and then hung the covers on a line to dry. Laura Carter of the Bar-B-Q Killers did the inner sleeve, writing something about each band — two to a side — in what Cook called "grungy" letters. At the end of one side, she wrote "Stomp or Die" but because she had not used exactly the right size paper, part of the "e" got cut off in the copying. Yelling "stomp or Dif" became a favorite inside joke for participating bands.[74]

For the send-off, all four bands played a show at the Georgia Theater, at

In the fall of 1986, David Barbe's DRG Records put out a
compilation EP called *Some*, which featured one song by the
four bands—Mercyland, Bar-B-Q Killers, Eat America, and Time
Toy—on the Better than TV Tour. Band members used ink and
a wood block to hand stamp the covers before drying them
on a clothes line at the Eat America house on Reese Street.
(Photograph by David Barbe)

the time still mostly a venue for second-run movies. The $5 cover was high then in Athens, and most of the people who came including me had at least one friend in one of the bands and ended up on the guest list. This dilemma—incredibly intense and at times brilliant shows and very small *paying* audiences—would prove to be a trend. After the show, the not-exactly-sober band members struggled to stow the equipment the bands would share in the luggage holds. By the time we were piling onto the bus and shoving our bags in the overhead racks, it was 3:00 A.M. As most of us passed out in our seats, our driver, a fifty-something-year-old man with a midcentury haircut and clothes we would have worn ironically, climbed on board. With a lit cigarette almost always in his steering hand, Arthur Neighbor managed to drive through the rest of the night and well into the morning. The sign on the front of the bus that listed our destination said it all: "Special."[75]

The first show took place the next night in Tampa in a part of town called Ybor City at a beautiful old theater called the Ritz. By turns fierce and funny, sloppy and tight, the bands gave the kinds of heartfelt if not always polished performances all of us along for the ride loved. But the organizers of the trip had made a deal for the door, and in a venue that held up to 2000, according to David Barbe, only eighty-three people paid. Someone—I am not giving him a name—had gotten on the bus in Athens with multiple sheets of blotter acid and a plan to sell hits for cheap in order to pay for his own food and beer. On the original itinerary, the bands had a gig at Faith in Physics in Orlando the next night, but the club cancelled. After staying in a hotel in Tampa, we spent a free day tripping at the beach and the Dalí Museum. Then our chimney of a driver drove us to Gainesville, the location of the tour's second date.[76]

One of the people on the bus was a UGA film student named Erica McCarthy. While she shot footage, she got other people on the bus to work sound. Back home, she edited images and sound recordings and the tracks on the *Some* EP into a documentary she called *Some: The 1986 Better Than TV Tour*. Unlike *Athens, GA: Inside/Out*, *Some: The 1986 Better Than TV Tour* was an inside job, a DIY movie about the next wave of Athens musicians and fans.

In McCarthy's documentary, we are on the way to that Florida college town when art student Jennifer Hartley starts questioning Bryan Cook. Holding out the microphone, Hartley askes Bryan Cook in her melodic drawl, "I was just wondering . . . whaaaat are *we* doing *here*?" In reply, Cook offers a brief account of the history of the tour. Hartley nods but asks a follow-up question: "Did you ever think this would really come together?" Cook smiles ruefully and answers, "It still isn't come together. We need, like, some enormous person to give us money for free." Later, that would kind of happen, but the road to that eventual salvation was twisting and long. In the film, Hartley waits patiently, and Cook grasps about for a more practical solution. "Tomorrow in Gainesville, we need everybody to go out and wear the t-shirts and prostitute yourself if you have to." Maybe the acid would help? Not to end on a downer, he stresses that he is "really glad people came" and that "people are getting to know each other and it's not as fucked up as it could have been." When the colors stopped dancing and the beer buzz faded, most of us got to drift off to sleep with the music still singing in our heads and the taste of a lover's mouth on our tongues. It must have been hell to be the head merry prankster and have to worry about how we were going to pay for that bus.[77]

In Gainesville, an incredibly generous or maybe insane guy invited all forty of us to stay in his house, an old Victorian full of nooks and crannies where people could squeeze a sleeping bag. I don't think anyone stooped to sex, but we did hang flyers all around town and talk up the show—four bands for four bucks at the American Legion Hall. Enough people showed up to feel like a crowd, and the tour made almost $400. Dru Wilbur stole an American flag off a pole outside a church that afternoon and performed with it wrapped around his ass like a diaper. Laura Carter sang with tampons stuck in her ears. That night all four bands played their best shows of the trip. The next morning, some of these badass rockers including Claire Horne of the Bar-B-Q Killers got up early enough to sweep, clean the kitchen, and take out the trash before packing up. Then the bus headed to Jacksonville Beach for a last gig at the club Einstein a Go Go and an overnight drive back to Athens.[78]

I must have been asleep on the way home when band members learned they were more than $1,900 in the hock. Yelling at the bus company from a rest-stop pay phone did not resolve the problem, and the company said no one would be allowed off the bus in Athens until someone paid. David Judd, bassist for the Bar-B-Q Killers, eventually agreed to charge the bill to his mother's American Express card. Back in Athens, we limped dirty and exhausted into the late morning. I only had an hour before I had to show up at Rocky's Pizza for my shift.[79]

Once everyone had caught up on their sleep, reality hit. Judd's mom must somehow be paid back, and the amount of money seemed staggering. Each band agreed to play a benefit at the 40 Watt, but none of these shows during winter break earned much money. A few weeks before the tour, Hartley had opened a little art gallery and coffee shop with a partner, and she agreed to host a benefit exhibition and sale. Tour organizers asked all the band members to make two pieces of art with the only requirement that each had to sell for $10 or less. Michael Stipe donated two blue pastel drawings made on U.S. Department of Wildlife Resources ecosystem diagrams. Art sales brought in another $300.[80]

Then the tour found a savior. Lynda Stipe, then dating Dru Wilbur, asked her brother Michael Stipe to perform at yet another benefit at the 40 Watt on Martin Luther King Day. As the *Red and Black* reported, "rumors around town had it that R.E.M. was going to play, cover would be $2, and the Bud goosenecks were going for 50 cents apiece." Despite the fact that this gossip was not true, it worked. The 40 Watt sold out. Michael did two or three songs with his sister Lynda instead of his bandmates, and the show ended with all the Florida tour musicians on stage together performing a cover of the Stooges' song "Loose." Cook and Wilbur paid off the tour's debt with sixty dollars to spare, a "profit" they split.[81]

It took Erica McCarthy a while to edit her footage down into something organized enough to call a film. In a typical scene, Todd Skelton, Claire Horne's boyfriend, runs into Deonna Mann on the street in Gainesville and tries to talk her into hanging out. Never one to say no to a party, Mann pushes back against Skelton's pleading: "I know, but I'm spent." Her drawl is so thick and drawn out that it makes her five words sound like a song. Throughout the film, McCarthy uses footage of each of the four bands performing but also includes intimate, offstage moments. In one shot, David Barbe and Arthur Johnson sit in the open luggage bins of the bus, scatting, howling, and making animal noises while strumming away on unplugged electric guitars. In another, Jennifer Hartley looks like a Renaissance Mary wearing a gilded halo as warm light streams through her curly blond hair. For a few perfect seconds, Johnson plays air guitar as the neon lights of a parking lot carnival make circles and swirls behind him. Near the end, Gene Lyon, the drummer for Eat America, expresses what all of us who did not have to worry about the money are feeling: "I want to do this again." More than thirty years later, Johnson can still identify every one of the almost forty people on the trip. In contrast to *Inside/Out*, McCarthy's *Better Than TV Tour* depicts the scene not as folk art but as a bohemian version of family.[82]

Grit

The way Jennifer Hartley remembered it, she had the name before she had the place. Sometime around the fall of 1985, she began telling her friends,

"I'm gonna open a coffeehouse–art gallery and it's gonna to be called the Grit." She liked the sound of the word as well as its meanings: "Southern, like grits," and "humble, like a single molecule or a speck of something." She did not mention courage and perseverance, but those qualities ended up being important, too. When she transformed her idea into a business in October 1986, about a month before she took off on the Better Than TV tour, Hartley and her partners gave Athens a new kind of venue. They drew upon the look and feel of the scene's folk aesthetic to create a gallery rather than a club, a place that existed to show visual art, even if over the years it increasingly hosted musical performances as well, a space where artists were the stars.[83]

The idea came together after Hartley returned from Italy. Working her way through school, she sat out a quarter or two, but in her fifth year she managed to scrape together the money to spend the summer of 1985 at the UGA art school's study abroad program. In Cortona, she fell in love with Italian coffeehouse culture.[84]

That fall, as Hartley finished a degree in painting from UGA and the next spring and summer after she graduated, she worked at Sparky's, a seafood restaurant in the Athens flea market, and Gus Garcia's, a Mexican cantina next to the Broad Street version of the 40 Watt. Waitressing left Hartley time to paint in the studio she rented with fellow artists Terry Boling and Beth Ensign on the second floor space of a building at 199 Prince Avenue, the former location of the Rat and Duck Playhouse. She could also plan her work schedule around which bands were coming to town, and as a Gus's employee, she got into the 40 Watt free. Club nights meant "dancing, flirting, drinking, and smoking," and she remembers being as interested in talking to the boys as listening to the bands. A lack of open container laws then made it easy for people to drink outside, and in hot weather a lot of socializing happened on downtown sidewalks in front of the clubs. Friends with the "Lindas," she missed Oh-OK but found new bands to follow like her pal Bryan Cook's group Time Toy, a new group called the La Di Das that included Vic Chesnutt, and out-of-towners like Jason and the Nashville Scorchers and Hüsker Dü. One perfect night, Hartley saw the Replacements play at the Broad Street 40 Watt.[85]

At Sparky's, Hartley watched two coworkers leave to open a tiny, Tex-Mex "shack" downtown called the Mean Bean. Around the same time, scene participant Joey Tatum opened a dessert café called True Confections in a little, below-street-level spot right on College Avenue. Instead of experience and capital, these would-be entrepreneurs had creative ideas, a willingness to work hard — they did that anyway for businesses they did not own — and the scene's "anything was possible" attitude. If anyone could start a band, why not a local business, too?[86]

In early 1986, Hartley began to think her dream of opening a real coffee-house might solve another local problem, too: the lack of places where artists who were no longer college students could show their work. A commercial gallery or two came and went in town, and the Lyndon House had its annual juried art exhibition. More recently, Tatum allowed local artists like Brant Slay to hang their work on the walls of his short-lived place. In April, four art-school graduates—Charles Ratcliff, Marie Cochran, Lauren Fancher, and Beth Arnold—organized the Corner Art Show, a five-day exhibition of multiple local artists in the former Fuse Box arcade space on the corner of Broad Street and College Avenue. Still, in a town full of artists, these options were hardly enough to meet local demand. What if selling coffee and tea, snacks and desserts, and beer and wine—with the exception of liquor and cigarettes, the array of items on sale in a coffee bar in Italy—financed the gallery? With her friend Peggy Cozart, Hartley created a business plan for a gallery–coffee shop hybrid, a venue that could host experimental work including performance pieces because it did not have to sell art to stay in business. Once they had the plan, they started looking for a space.[87]

Sometime in March 1986, they solved this last problem after Hartley and her friend Melanie Haner met for lunch at the Gyro Wrap. At the time, Haner was working fulltime at the local pizza place Sons of Italy and taking home about $100 a week. Unlike many scene participants who attended UGA, she had studied English at the University of Virginia and discovered Athens music when she saw Guadalcanal Diary and Love Tractor play fraternity parties there. After she graduated, Haner moved to Atlanta for a job that she quickly realized she hated. One weekend, she had a chance to visit an old friend who lived in Athens in a house on a Prince Avenue corner that everyone called the Pink Pleasure Palace. Go Clothing, a local vintage store, had moved to a new location on Clayton, and she went that night to the opening party before spending the rest of the evening going back and forth between a Fetchin Bones show at the Broad Street 40 Watt and Gus Garcia's. A man she later learned was Paul Wade wandered around downtown in a flowing robe passing out handfuls of poems. The members of Fetchin Bones showed up at the after-party at her friend's house, and photographer Todd Eberle, then living in town, came over to take pictures of them.[88]

Athens, Haner suddenly realized, was nothing like preppy Charlottes-ville, the southern college town where she had lived as a student. After that first visit, she began driving over from Atlanta on the weekends. A month or so into this commute, she just quit her job and moved. At first, she stayed with friends. Then Cook, her coworker at Sons, got a new place, and she became his roommate. Through Cook, she got to know scene people like John Seawright and Chris Slay. Through Jennifer's brother David Hartley who also worked at Sons, she met her future business partner.[89]

That spring day in 1986, Hartley and Haner started talking about their "dream jobs" as they lingered over after-lunch coffees. Hartley suggested they wander down to the Station, a long brick building where Hull Street bent to the right and turned into Hoyt. The south end of the former Southern Railroad depot housed a popular saloon with a big, outdoor deck called T. K. Harty's, but much of rest of the long brick building stood empty. By chance, the man who owned the place happened to be there, and he offered them the storefront with the big, rolling metal door at the north end. The space was in bad shape—not much more than a brick shell with a wooden loft in the back—but the owner told them they could have it rent-free for the first six months and then pay $300 a month after that.[90]

With some help from Cozart, who had moved away from Athens in the many months it had taken to find a space, Haner and Hartley went to work raising money and renovating. Most of the funding came from Hartley's mom, who took out a home equity line to loan her daughter $5,000. Cozart's dad built the stairs that turned the loft into a cozy spot to sip coffee or tea and read or play board games. Hartley and Haner sealed the exposed brick walls and created a space for a makeshift kitchen by tacking linoleum to the underside of the loft to prevent things from falling in the food. They scoured thrift, junk, and discount stores for equipment and furniture, purchased a coffee grinder and an espresso machine at a department store, and built their own food-prep table. Work sessions turned into dance parties as friends climbed scaffolding to paint and hang homemade track lighting as a boom box played KC and the Sunshine Band. Haner remembered, "We cobbled the place together."[91]

"Not really thinking restaurant," Hartley, a vegetarian, created the small menu by simply listing all the things she knew how to cook: beans and rice, bagels with toppings, and soup. In its original phase, the Grit served the kind of simple food you might make for yourself at home if you wanted to eat something healthy and actually went to the store. Rosa's bagel—sliced tomato, white cheddar, and a smear of homemade Italian dressing, all melted together in the toaster oven—developed a bit of a cult following. In the spring of 1987, I stopped in on rare days off from my catering and waitressing jobs to eat a Rosa, linger over a pot of Earl Grey tea, and read.[92]

Looking back, Hartley called the original Grit "a glorified Kool-Aid stand." That description captured the DIY aspect, but not the aesthetic or the feel. In its Hoyt Street location, the coffee shop–gallery hybrid looked like the apartments of local artists and other bohemians with a talent for thrifting. Even when it was new, the place felt lived-in and eccentric. Because it was not a bar, people could read a book, write, or draw there, and they could really talk. The long, late-night hours encouraged people to just settle in and stay. Most people went to the Grit after the bands played and the bars closed.

Something about the atmosphere attracted a small core of regulars who treated the place like their private clubhouse. Vic Chesnutt, a musician who had moved town in 1985 and was then playing in the La Di Das, would drive up in his van, let his lift down on the wooden planks of an elevated walkway that ran down the side of the former railroad depot, drag himself into his wheelchair, and roll right in before the Grit even opened. Haner or Hartley would still be doing prep work, so Chesnutt would pull up to the espresso machine in the little kitchen space, line up some small cups, make four or five shots, and drink them all. John Seawright, another regular, would sometimes sit at a table and write, but more often he would "float from table to table," creating "fabulous conversations" with whoever happened to be present. Whenever someone had a question about something and Seawright was not around, Hartley saved it for the man she later called "our Google." Jeremy Ayers and local artist Terry Boling also came by daily. On a rare night when an art opening drew a crowd and the Grit sold as much as $200 worth of coffee, snacks, and $1 longneck Buds, loyal customers like the lawyer Jeff Gilley would head back to the sink and wash dishes.

In an era before Starbucks was a nationwide chain, coffee snobs had a hard time finding a passable cup, not just in the small-town South but in most of America outside a handful of cities. As rare as real coffee was, spaces where you could buy something small and sit and read or work for hours were even harder to find. Before the Grit opened, people would hang out at True Confections downtown or at a little dessert café called the Flamingo Room beside the dorms at the top of Baxter Street. When Lynda Stipe worked there, Sam Seawright, Brant Slay, and Michael Stipe would sit for hours, getting "jacked up on free coffee," as Seawright recalled, and doodling on napkins. But the Flamingo Room was a long walk from downtown and the art building, and True Confections was small and closed after about a year.[93]

When the Grit opened, Hartley was sharing an apartment in the yellow Victorian at the corner of Virginia Avenue and Boulevard with Lynda

The Grit, a combination art gallery/coffee shop opened by
Jennifer Hartley and Melanie Haner, gave Athens bohemians
a place to hang out that was not a music club. Here, Grit
regulars and brothers John Seawright, a poet (*right*),
and Sam Seawright, a painter, hang out outside the Grit.
(Photographer unknown, courtesy of Sam Seawright)

Stipe, and her sister Cyndy Stipe lived in the house's other apartment. Both
the Stipe sisters had helped Hartley and Haner get ready to open, and along
with their brother Michael when he was not away touring, they stopped by
often. One afternoon toward the end of that first fall or winter when Haner
was working at the Grit alone, Stipe came in carrying a boom box, bought a
coffee, and climbed up the stairs to the loft. While Haner cooked, Stipe repeatedly hit play and stop and rewind, repeating little snatches of an instrumental. Somehow, in the safe space of the Grit, he managed to break through
a period of writer's block he had suffered off and on in 1986 as he struggled to
develop a new, less folky and more political style. In part, the lyrics to "Welcome to the Occupation" revisited an issue he had also written about in other
recent songs, American intervention in Central America. But the song also
voiced an indignation at people's ignorance. "Listen to me," Stipe repeated
over and over at the end of the song. The line "sugar cane and coffee cup"
memorialized the place where the words finally flowed.[94]

Jeremy Ayers became the Grit's first employee when Haner and Hartley
realized they would not be able to do all the work themselves. As a young art

student, Hartley remembered seeing Ayers around town and thinking he was incredibly beautiful. Chance encounters left her feeling "starstruck." The first time she got up the courage to talk to him, she was at a house party on Barber Street. Somehow, she, Ayers, and another person she did not know yet, the artist and musician Jill Carnes, started playing a Scrabble game Carnes had brought to the party. By the time Ayers started working at the Grit, he and Hartley were close. Hartley remembered Ayers as a powerful model of how to live a good life because he "never got bored" and "never lived in the past." He was "always ready for the next thing."

From the start, the Grit's owners, employees, and customers had trouble with the Greeks who filled T. K. Harty's and a new place in the depot called the Flying Buffalo. Drunk college kids often yelled at the scene folks and called them "Gritters." More than once, people smashed the gallery's outdoor tables. Late one night after Ayers started working at the Grit, he and Hartley found themselves with no customers and climbed up into the loft to talk. Suddenly, a line of frat boys started filing in the door, and Ayers and Hartley were worried. Soon the men started chanting "performance art at the Grit," and the two friends broke out laughing and then applauded. The Grit had actually inspired these traditional college guys to make art![95]

Because it was a gallery, events at the venue were organized around art rather than music. Sam Seawright, who had moved back to Athens in 1985 after getting his MFA at the University of Texas, was one of the area's most successful local artists. His paintings appeared every year in the annual juried exhibition at the Lyndon House Art Center, including in 1986 when Judy Chicago served as curator. Often, one of his pieces won one of the coveted, cash-prize merit awards. According to Seawright, the Grit elevated the status of artists in the scene. "When you are in a community and have a show, it makes what you do known to others. They see your work," he recalled. It was "nice to have a venue for artists," a place where "all the social aspects of the art scene" could occur. The Grit enabled scene participants to spend time with work in a casual and intimate setting, to become fans of local art just like we had become fans of local music.

In the years when the Grit was primarily a gallery, many locally and regionally celebrated artists had exhibitions there, including romantic figurative painters Jill Schultz and Lillian Heard and Patrik Keim. Sandi Phipps, then supporting herself by working in R.E.M.'s office, had her first show at the gallery, and credited the Grit with helping her start a career as a photographer. Lynda Stipe wrapped the place in scarves in a thrift store version of Christo and Jeanne-Claude's work. Jeremy Ayers, who worked in mul-

Flyers were a major art form in the Athens scene. This example by Sam Seawright announces "Seawright State Park," his exhibition of landscape paintings at the Grit. (Courtesy of Sam Seawright)

tiple mediums but rarely exhibited his pieces, felt comfortable enough at the Grit to display a set of small, representational drawings done in charcoal on sheets of white cotton paper. Sam Seawright mounted "Seawright State Park" an exhibition of the landscapes he had started making in Austin and another exhibition of sculptures he made out of chicken wire covered with papier mache.[96]

Even the UGA art professor Andy Nasisse, a nationally known ceramics artist, put on a show at the small gallery by attaching his ceramic pieces to the walls. Even though he did not get "credit" as an academic for this kind of exhibition, he wanted his friends in town to be able see his work. As Hartley remembered, Nasisse had a refreshing "lack of preciousness" in relation to his art and was not worried that the Grit was too poor to have insurance. If something got chipped or broken, he told the Grit's owners, he would just fix it.[97]

For his Grit exhibition, Nasisse created a central piece as a kind of "tribute" to his own undergraduate painting teacher Orlin Helgoe at what was then called Southern Colorado State College. As a young man, Helgoe had shot and killed a deer, and the experience proved so disturbing that he made paintings and drawings about the incident until he committed suicide in the 1970s. On the day of the opening, Nasisse and a few of his friends constructed a twelve-foot-tall structure that "looked like a giant bush" out of bales, loose straw, and dry branches on the Grit's brick patio. The artist called the piece *The Deer Who Killed the Man*.[98]

On the night of the opening, Nasisse poured two bottles of lighter fluid on the straw. Ayers, wearing a top hat, used a long torch to light the pile as others stood by with fire extinguishers. As the flames rose twenty feet into the air, about three hundred dollars' worth of fireworks hidden inside the pile went off in all directions: bottle rockets, whistling things, Roman candles, and firecrackers. Terrified, Nasisse worried for long seconds that a spectator might get burned. Then the huge flame fell away and revealed a giant white ceramic hand with a deer head in its palm and a glaze that looked like dripping blood. People gasped. Grit regulars clapped and cheered. College students headed to the bars at the other end of the depot walked away wondering what strange ritual they had witnessed on their way to get a beer.[99]

Too hot in the summer and too cold in the winter, the Grit's space was hip but it was not comfortable. It must have been really hot in July 1987 when the artist and musician Robert Longo came to town to shoot a video for the R.E.M. song "The One I Love," scheduled to be released as a single from R.E.M.'s new album *Document*, due in stores that September. In the completed piece, R.E.M. members and other scene participants including Lynda Stipe, Pete Buck's new wife Barrie Greene Buck, who co-owned the 40 Watt, Mystery Date bassist Robin Edwards, and UGA art student Caroline Wallner appeared in various Athens locations including an overhead shot of a crowd dancing at the Grit, filmed from up in the gallery's loft. By the end of the year, "The One I Love" had become R.E.M.'s first mainstream hit.[100]

Because everyone in town seemed to play and Hartley and Haner needed to make more money, the Grit gradually began hosting more musical performances. The Athens Folk Music and Dance Society started holding song swaps there on Sundays. Participants would sit in a circle and take turns contributing a song. Art Rosenbaum would pick his banjo. Then Moira Nelligan might join in on fiddle. Other regulars like Joe Willey added guitar or another banjo or a harmonica. Some people might stomp or clap a rhythm. Everyone would sing. The point was to make old-time music together, to keep traditional songs alive. People were not supposed to bring in new songs. One night Chesnutt rolled in wearing a straw cowboy hat and carrying his beat up guitar and joined right in. Since he was always at the Grit drinking coffee, he became a regular. Occasionally, he even performed one of his own compositions in violation of the rules, but no one told him he couldn't, because his songs were so good. At the Grit, Chesnutt and other scene musicians had a chance to meet local folk revivalists and learn old-time story-telling songs and traditional styles of playing.[101]

Later, Chesnutt started playing solo at the Grit on Friday afternoons, and references to the Grit popped up in some of the songs he wrote around this time, like "Where Were You." Sometimes out-of-town bands like Shiva Gondi from Hamilton, Ontario, and Downy Mildew from Los Angeles, in town to visit friends or record, played impromptu shows for small and happy crowds. The place had awful acoustics for electrified music, yet a band called Five Eight, whose members met at what was then SUNY Binghamton, moved to town and talked their way into playing every Friday night for free until Haner asked them to stop. Crack, another loud band whose members included Joey Tatum and Deonna Mann, performed standing on scaffolding inside the gallery at what was probably the original Grit's most profitable night.[102]

By every measure except financially, the Grit was a success. Hartley and Haner had created a place that drew all their friends, local artists and musicians, and other bohemians. Yet their customers had so little money that the place barely cleared anything after expenses. To pay their own bills, Hartley and Haner took turns cleaning the Carafe and Draft, the cheap pitchers and dollar movie place housed in the old Georgia Theater, three times a week for $30 per job. Haner recalled, "We were so broke. I was so nervous because I was the one managing the books and paying the bills. . . . It was so incredibly stressful for me." By her own admission not a "social person," Haner also struggled with that aspect of running the Grit. "It was like we were hosting a party for our friends every night." Hartley, on the other hand, was a "social magnet," and people thought of the gallery as her place. In February 1988, Haner simply walked away, and Hartley ran the business for about another year and a half with employees like Ayers and Hartley's future husband John Rogers, who started out trading electrical and maintenance work for food.

Sometime in 1989, Hartley sold the business. Jessica Greene, Barrie Buck's sister, and a series of partners bought a secondhand home range and expanded the menu. Ted Hafer, singer and bass player in Porn Orchard and Greene's future husband, helped develop a real menu. In May 1990, after Michael Stipe bought and renovated the Prince Avenue building that had formerly housed Hartley's art studio, the Grit moved there and became a real restaurant, a bohemian version of the old-South-meets-hippie vegetarian places the El Dorado and its successor Bluebird. The "folk food" was great and the owners accommodated their employees' touring schedules, but the original venue with its clubhouse-for-artists feel was gone. A few years later, the by-then abandoned depot burned to the ground.[103]

In the first few years of the scene, the fact that Athens was a *southern* small town seemed like a bigger deal to outsiders — New Yorker music critics and the British music magazines especially — than it did to many people who actually lived there. Most scene participants came from Georgia or nearby states, and regional identity seemed to them like a given, not something to be noticed or questioned. But the very existence of the Athens scene began to transform how many people in it understood what it meant to be from the South.

As members of both the first and second waves of Athens bands toured the United States and Canada, and, more rarely, Europe, they had a chance to talk to fans and musicians elsewhere and think about what made their home different from other places. They also learned a lot about how people from elsewhere thought about their region. Back home, people began to think more self-consciously about how the South shaped their music and their art. They began to pay attention to rural vernacular culture, an alternative South with its own signs and symbols and sounds and artifacts. It took about a decade, but scene participants gradually developed their own bohemian version of southern pride. *Athens, GA: Inside/Out* presented Jeremy Ayers's alternative South. On the Better Than TV tour and at the Grit, younger scene participants created others. But Athens bohemians never quite solved a related problem, how to create an alternative culture that more than a handful of people of color might actually want to join.

6

New Town

Have I learned anything from all of these lectures?
I think it's my attention span clipped by TV at an early age
Who heard of radio [at] five years old?
I used to watch Speed Racer with that hyper attitude
that carried me here to this a fluorescent enlightenment.

I'm not a victim
I know the system
I am intelligent
I'm not a victim
I am an atheist.

The idea of divine order is essentially crazy
the laws of action and reaction are the closet things to truth in the universe.
So don't try to spray me with your archaic rites of soul.
Your vision is a biological one
I can dodge the thunderbolts,
and scratch out an existence on this glorious but simple plane.

Vic Chesnutt, "Speed Racer" (1990)[1]

The first time I saw Vic Chesnutt, he was sitting in his wheelchair behind a piece of poster board attached to a card table on the sidewalk near the University of Georgia's arch, where the old part of campus met downtown. Chesnutt, I learned later, could be a bit of a drawling Laura Carter when the mood struck him, a provocateur, just the kind of unlikely word he loved to work into his song lyrics. That day, behind a hard-to-read, hand-scrawled sign that announced "No God," he accosted passersby with pamphlets about unbelief just like Jehovah's Witnesses handed out the *Watchtower*. You had to be willing to risk eye contact and having to take his literature or listen to his pitch to get close enough to see that he was actually not another evangelizing Christian. In those days of a rising religious Right, my best friend Jessica Hunt and I joked in private that we were the only two atheists in Bible Belt Georgia. Dissent then meant disagreements between evangelicals, mainline Protestants, and Catholics. Skeptics were people inching their way toward agnosticism.[2]

Out on that sidewalk, Chesnutt took a common act—proselytizing on the street of a southern town—and turned it toward radical ends. Later, I learned he could do the same thing with storytelling and the colloquial phrases of southern English. Sometimes he was direct, like when he kicked off his first album, *Little*, singing, "I can't believe you own this attitude" or advised, in a song from his second album, *West of Rome*, "When the bug hits, that's the time to scratch it." Other times, he wrote in layers, and you had to pay attention to catch the play of meaning, like the song "Soft Picasso" in which he turns that artist's style into a metaphor for modern relationships. Only a lover of both language and self-deprecation would write "I do temper tantrums as sissy anthems" and rhyme a word like "histrionic" with "tonic." Only a writer with a sly sense of humor would use a song about Pinocchio and his maker Geppetto (which Chesnutt spelled "Giupetto") to sidle up to his own feelings about being the adopted atheist son of evangelicals:

He took a week
to learn how to speak
but the language hurts
the consonants tweak
mute malaise
heavy haze,
the reparations only partly pays.

but your sorrow is so silly,
what was there to keep him in Italy?

Chesnutt had to be brave as hell to be an atheist in a wheelchair in a time and place where about the only comfort on offer took the form of mumbled references to God's plans.[3]

Chesnutt was the rare Athens musician not a member of R.E.M. who could still draw people from all parts of the late eighties scene out to see a performance. At a seven-month series of shows at the 40 Watt in 1988—as a poster announced, "every Tuesday until hell freezes over"—and at multiple gigs at the Downstairs in 1989 and 1990, he could be brilliant. On nights when

Vic Chesnutt attends a party at a house on Hill Street.
(Photograph by David Barbe)

he did not drink or smoke too much or feel the deadness of depression, he might turn unexpected words and simple chords into songs that made you want to cry. At other shows, usually the ones to which you dragged a friend not yet converted to the cult of Vic, he would purposefully torture his audience until the room cleared and your companion doubted your sanity. Chesnutt, like much that was magical about Athens in those days, was an insiders' pleasure. You had to go back and risk the awkward, the boring, and the just plain bad to catch those moments of transcendence.[4]

After *Athens, GA: Inside/Out* and MTV Athens weekends and R.E.M.'s appearance on the cover of the *Rolling Stone* as "America's Best Rock & Roll Band," after major label Electra signed Guadalcanal Diary and Arista signed Dreams So Real and independents from across the country signed Love Tractor, the Kilkenny Cats, the Bar-B-Q Killers, Mercyland, and new bands Hetch Hetchy and the Chickasaw Mudd Puppies and even Vic Chesnutt— Athens was hardly a secret. Alternative-music fans graduating from high school convinced their gullible parents they wanted to study at the University of Georgia. Individual musicians rode the Greyhound with their suitcases and guitars or pulled into town in old cars full of records, instruments, and amps. Entire bands appeared, like Five Eight from upstate New York, whose members saw the Athens documentary in New York City and thought, as vocalist and guitarist Mike Mantione later recalled, "wow—we have to go to Athens." And tourists came looking for the scene from as far away as California and Colorado, Europe and Japan. Three people who visited Athens in 1989 from Newcastle upon Tyne reported that kids from "the frozen unemployed Northeast of England" knew about the town, though the ferociousness of its humid summer heat surprised them. "Four venues and four bands later, past last orders and still 3 am disco to go," one of them wrote, explaining her new Athens friends' attitude, "why hell y'all cos its 90 deg. doesn't mean you can't dance until the music runs out." Even British postpunk musician Nikki Sudden visited in the spring of 1990 and liked the town so much he stayed at Pete Buck's place on Cobb Street for several months and made some recordings around the corner at John Keane's studio. The way Buck put it, Sudden had "never been south of New York, so we took him down South and blew his mind." As a journalist put it, Athens was "the most famous city of its size in the world."[5]

With a constant churn of new people moving to town and new bands forming, the scene in the late eighties continued to expand and fragment. Unlike in the Pylon Park days or the months when the 40 Watt was the only new-music club in town, overlapping networks of friends and lovers collected around all the varied places people hung out and lived, like the 40 Watt and the Grit, the Porn Orchard house on Finley Street, Pete Buck's grand Victorian with the backyard pool on Cobb, and Michael Stipe's house behind a wall of bamboo on Grady. Though Ort tried, it had become impossible for one person to know everyone and everything connected with the scene.[6]

All that music- and art-making grew out of a perfect mix of confidence and naivete, intelligence and ignorance. If you really did not have to know how to play an instrument to form a band, scene participants started thinking in the late 1980s, then maybe passion, vision, and a willingness to work trumped professionalism, expertise, and even experience in other arenas of life too. I wanted to play the cello, so I bought one for $50 at a junk store, called the music school at UGA, and got the name of a PhD student who would teach me for cheap. Quinton Phillips found a Super 8 camera and started making experimental films and then projecting them at places like the Grit and the Downstairs. Chris DeBarr, who had formerly run Lunch Paper at Stitchcraft and had by then become the head cook at the Downstairs, wrote plays and put them on there and up and down the aisles of the twenty-four-hour Kroger. Local writers Mona Hawkins and Mary Beth Mills started a literary magazine called *Lift Archaic*, and Cathy Hestor created one called *Blue Plate Special* to circulate their own writing and the work of their friends. Pat Cardiff sold boomerangs he carved himself and gave people free throwing lessons. If you wanted, he would shape a design guaranteed to fly out of whatever you chose, like the knife and fork he made for the Downstairs and the jumping horse he made for me.[7]

Another "new" activity, at least for most bohemians, was local politics. With *Tasty World* long gone, the *Red and Black* becoming more "preprofessional," and the local Athens papers subject to space restrictions, 40 Watt co-owner Jared Bailey believed the town needed a new publication to circulate club listings and cover the local music news. The first issue of a new, free publication, *Flagpole*, the "colorbearer of Athens alternative music," arrived on October 1, 1987, with lots of ads and club listings but little content. One exception was Bryan Cook's attempt at an editorial. "Ok, I can write anything I want so here goes," Cook began. "Anybody who lives in Athens and is not registered to vote should register now! The only way to change the archaic rules the Prince Avenue Baptist Church pushes on the city is to elect some councilmembers who are not intimidated by the 'so-called' Christian wishes." Over the first few years, a mostly volunteer crew of two-fingered typists working on an original Macintosh, with production by the folks at

Rick the Printer's coffee and print shop Java, turned a booklet of ads and club calendars into a real alternative paper. As Bailey admitted in an interview in 1990, "I wanted *Flagpole* to be a little more liberal and no-holds-barred." This coverage turned away some readers. A UGA student told the *Red and Black*, "The *Flagpole* pisses me off because it's too political." For other readers, the paper had the opposite effect. *Flagpole* pushed many scene participants to pay attention to local politics.[8]

In the second half of eighties, the place-based structure of alternative culture played a key role in propelling this new political engagement. From Lawrence, Kansas, and Hoboken, New Jersey, to Athens, new-music scenes were deeply rooted in particular places, and development threatened the historical buildings where scene participants lived and worked, practiced, painted, and went to shows. R.E.M. members have earned well-deserved credit for reversing their own earlier refusal to mix music and politics. "Think globally, act locally," an environmentalist slogan printed, along with the addresses of Greenpeace, Amnesty International, and Bread for the World, in the tour book R.E.M. sold on its 1985 Reconstruction tour, made sense to people concerned about losing the cityscapes they loved.[9]

In Athens, growing activism around the effort to save the old parts of the town had gradually turned many scene participants, including the members of R.E.M., into registered voters concerned about historic preservation, environmentalism, and homelessness. By the end of the decade, voting had become almost as important a form of participation as playing in and going to hear bands. Over time, these new voters changed the town, shifting the area left as most of the rest of Georgia moved right.[10]

This growing political energy coincided with unprecedented levels of success for the scene's bands. Early in 1988, R.E.M. left I.R.S. for a deal worth a reported $6–12 million with the major label Warner Brothers. *Green*, the band's first album on their new label, dropped on the day of the 1988 presidential election. A few months later, the single "Stand" reached number six on the *Billboard* Hot 100 chart, outperforming "The One I Love," a single off their previous album *Document* which had peaked at nine. Other local bands seemed poised to follow in R.E.M.'s footsteps. Dreams So Real released *Rough Night in Jericho* on Arista in 1988, and both the album and the single of the same name did well on *Billboard*'s new modern rock charts. And in the summer of 1989, the B-52's, the band that started it all, roared back with *Cosmic Thing*, their most successful album yet and their first recordings since Ricky Wilson died of AIDS in 1985. Two of their singles, "Deadbeat Club" and the number-three hit "Love Shack," even looked back at their days in the Georgia college town a decade before. Athens musicians also caught the interest of independent, Santa Monica–based Texas Hotel Records. The label put out a series of EPs and albums by local bands including the Kilkenny Cats' *Hammer*, Hetch Hetchy's *Make Djibouti*, the Chickasaw Mudd Puppies' *White Dirt*, and Vic Chesnutt's *Little*.[11]

To quote Chesnutt, "those were the days" when we felt "so cosmopolitan." Athens then seemed liked the center of the world. I was twenty-three in October 1987 when we opened the Downstairs, and a few months later, I began playing cello in the band Cordy Lon. My historian self has interviewed everyone who will talk to me, reread all the *Flagpoles*, cross-checked people, issues, and events in the *Red and Black* and the *Athens Banner Herald/Daily News*, and listened to all the old recordings I can locate. But that self has to contend here with a younger, more bohemian self who actively participated in this history. To be in the scene then was to soak up the expansive, heady feeling that we could do almost anything — we were *making* history. That experience profoundly shaped the historian I eventually became. Not all of our dreams were about music.

I Am an Atheist

The way Todd McBride told it, he met Chesnutt at a branch of a chain record store in a strip mall in Griffin when both of them were still in high school. "I'm working at Turtles and I keep seeing this character walking in pretty much every weekend" wearing "a Gilligan hat, a Columbo raincoat, highwater jeans, and Donald Duck sunglasses," McBride recalled. "He never really said anything, but he always bought cool records." A future member of Athens bands the La Di Das and the Dashboard Saviors, the teenage McBride already wrote songs and played a little guitar. One day in Chesnutt's parents' basement, McBride amazed his friend by pulling out his notebook and singing some songs he had written.[12]

Chesnutt, too, was already a songwriter — family members recalled that he wrote his first song "God" when he was around five. Adopted as a baby, he grew up in Zebulon, a tiny, mid-Georgia town in Pike County. His parents commuted to Atlanta, about 100 miles roundtrip, where his dad hauled bags for Eastern Airlines and his mom worked for the Atlanta office of the Immigration and Nationalization Service. As a result, Chesnutt and his younger sister spent a lot of time with their grandparents, especially his dad's mother, Granny, who lived with the family in their modest ranch house off a dirt road and beside a pond. On weekends, his mother's parents Clara and Homer

"Sleepy" Carter performed country music at fairs and gatherings across Georgia, and they often took Vic and Lorinda along with them. Grandfather Carter also taught his young grandson to play the guitar. Chesnutt understood writing songs was just something people did—his grandfather wrote music and his grandmother and mother wrote lyrics. Yet until he met McBride, he did not know any other teenage songwriters in Pike County. When McBride stopped playing that day in the basement, Chesnutt told his new friend, "OK, we're starting a band dammit." They named their group the Screaming Id.[13]

After graduating from high school in 1982, Chesnutt decided to stay home and attend nearby Gordon Junior College. He and McBride met some other guys trying not to be rednecks. "Man, I thought those guys were so sophisticated," Chesnutt told a writer for *Rolling Stone*. "And I felt like such a hick. The only thing I knew about culture was what I'd seen on PBS and heard on Leonard Cohen records." Together, these friends formed a band they eventually called the La Di Das.[14]

Less than a year after his high school graduation, Chesnutt got "drunk as a coot," drove his 1968 Buick LeSabre into a ditch, "flipped the car over," and broke his neck, partially severing his spinal cord. It was about 2 A.M. on Easter Sunday. His friends thought he had tried to commit suicide. And for the first two months after the accident, he looked like he might have succeeded. Doctors did not think he would survive. More than once he technically died and was revived. Altogether, he spent about fifteen months in the hospital.

A former star student at Pike County High with evangelical parents was not supposed to kill himself. Unwilling to admit what he had done, he refused to talk to anyone from Pike County. Unable to play his guitar, he spent a lot of time alone listening to music. He also discovered books. "I didn't read until I broke my neck." Only then, in his words, did he realize, "oh, this is what words do. Oh, they're powerful."[15]

About a year after he got out of the hospital, Chesnutt learned to play the guitar again by gluing a pick to a leather, fingerless glove and wearing it on his right hand for strumming and then using his left, less-paralyzed hand to makes simple chords like G, F, and C. As he described his physical health years later, "I have feeling all over my body and can move my legs a little but my fingers don't move too good at all." Because in Chesnutt's words, only "one half my diaphragm kind of works," singing was also difficult. Playing music was "hard work."[16]

When Chesnutt reconnected with his Pike County friends after he got out of the hospital in July 1984, they decided they were going to be an Athens band. They had heard of R.E.M., of course, then playing across the country and overseas on their Little America tour. But the real attraction was proximity. From what they read, this college town only two hours away was full of Georgia kids who had also grown up preferring the new music to southern rock and were now creating their own bands. Where else would they go?[17]

Chesnutt described their early days in town in 1985: "Athens was a different world. . . . We saw bands every night. When I discovered punk rock was when I moved to Athens." He also studied English at UGA and wrote poems and turned them into flyers that he copied and pasted up around town. Kinkos manager Vanessa Briscoe Hay "always liked them, so I got encouragement from day one. That was huge for me." But all the music was seductive, and after the La Di Das started playing gigs, Chesnutt quit school.[18]

Chesnutt's poetry made clear his commitment to the craft of writing. In high school, he remembered, his lyrics had "sucked." After his accident, he read and learned. A key turning point came when he shoplifted an anthology of modern poetry and discovered the work of British poet Stevie Smith. Her fusion of what he called "hilarity and deathly seriousness" showed him a way to write about his own life. In later years, he also acknowledged a debt to another southerner interested in religion and death, Flannery O'Connor. At times, he told people he was working on a novel or writing short stories.[19]

Not just his lyrics but Vic Chesnutt's overall approach to songwriting changed as he became a part of the scene. In the working-class, country-music world of his grandparents, songwriting was something people did, "like whittling." A few people even made money from it. He recalled, "As I got older, I discovered rock 'n' roll, and I discovered bohemian type people. . . . And then it wasn't about making money anymore. It was more like I wasn't going to sell the little icon I was whittling. It was something for me." Instead of trying to create something that would please an audience, he began to write songs to explore his own ideas about form. He began to think about his music as art.[20]

In Athens, it was cool to study seemingly eccentric and esoteric subjects on your own. One day, Todd McBride told Chesnutt that he had dreamed he was dancing with Isadora Duncan, an avant-garde dancer from the early twentieth century, and the musician turned his friend's dream into what he called his first real song. "I wanted to have these deceptively sad-sounding songs that had humor in them. . . . Here was Isadora Duncan, who was a great artist. She said, 'I'm not a dancer, I'm a poet.' She was a great thinker and innovator of the new collective communist worldview in that she was an atheist." Yet one day a silk scarf she was wearing became entangled in the wheel and axle of an open car in which she was riding. Pulled from the vehicle, she died from the force of the fall, probably as a result of a broken neck. Their shared injury intrigued the young musician. In Chesnutt's words, "her fashion killed her."[21]

"That was the beginning. I realized that you could sing anything and that words that aren't often sung are amazing to sing." Over the next year or so, he decided that every word was important and needed to be in a song. To join his carefully crafted lyrics to his melodies, which he found easy to write, Chesnutt drew out or smashed together syllables, creating wildly eccentric phrasings. "I'm not going to change the words if the syllables aren't the perfect meter. I can shove them in, no problem." At the same time, he worked to cultivate mystery. He held back. Like Athens's most famous lyricist, Michael Stipe, Chesnutt wanted listeners to collaborate with him in creating meaning.[22]

For a couple of years, Chesnutt lived in a house on Newton Bridge Road about five to six miles out in the country with Andrew Donaldson, who grew up in New Jersey before moving to Athens to go to UGA, and Seattle transplants Matt Hansen and John Rogers. They paid $375 a month for four bedrooms, lots of land, and a pecan grove. The La Di Das started practicing there, Todd Butler and Chesnutt and their middle Georgia friends Rick Steele and Terry Sphinx. Donaldson played drums with them for about three practices before another of their friends from back home took over. One day, not long after they moved in, Chesnutt and Donaldson were sitting on the front porch when a woman showed up. She could not call because they did not have a phone, but she lived at Rick the Printer's communal house on Meigs Street where alcohol was banned as "bad energy," she told them, and so she had just walked all the way out there with her bottle of tequila. Vic and Andrew looked at each other and then at her and said, "Welcome to the Bad Energy Ranch." The name stuck. When Hansen and Rogers moved out, Beverly Babb and Deonna Mann moved in, and together the four friends turned the Bad Energy Ranch into a kind of studio.[23]

As Mann recalled, they were in their twenties and just discovering the possibilities of the creative life: "We were in a specific place where we could do whatever we wanted to do." Chesnutt was writing songs and performing in the La Di Das. Donaldson played guitar in a local band called Terrakota Swayed. Curtiss Pernice and Ted Hafer, members of the band Porn Orchard who also made films and videos, started hanging out with cameras in tow. Laura Carter and David Barbe stopped by often to party and jam. In the fall of 1986, just before the Better Than TV tour, Barbe had offered Donaldson a dream chance to try out to for Mercyland, who was losing guitarist Mark Craig to graduate school. Donaldson loved the band—no one else in town then had that kind of punk pop, Buzzcocks meets the Jam sound—but he was self-taught and learning ten songs quickly from the tape Barbe gave him was going to be hard. Chesnutt offered to help. He had such a terrific ear that as they went through the tape together, he simply called out the chords. Donaldson wrote them down and memorized them. At the audition, he nailed the first song so perfectly that his soon-to-be bandmates Barbe and Harry Joiner applauded.[24]

With aid from Chesnutt, Donaldson, Babb and other friends, Mann produced her first real work of art at the ranch, her version of the folk-art gardens created by outsider artists across the South. A long pathway started beside the barn and wound its wheelchair-accessible way past a Bradford pear and native plum trees, through an archway woven through a hedge, and into a field of what Mann called "sculptures that made noise"—trees hung with records, pipes, pieces of glass, and other found objects that turned into chimes. In one area, Mann used old mirrors, scavenged crystals, and broken glass, including pieces salvaged from the Uptown's smashed front door, to construct a waterfall. In another, she built sculptures out of mannequin parts like a leg coming out of an old toilet. Mann, who grew up without her mother in a working-class family that moved around a lot, had not understood that life as an artist was possible until she moved to Athens and met people like Chesnutt. As she recalled, the Bad Energy Ranch was a "very beautiful time, an incredibly creative time," when they all realized "you could imagine things and get friends to help pull them off in the world." Chesnutt was inspired to draw and occasionally paint. Mann began to make performance art that included music and later joined the band Crack. Babb, too, became an artist and a musician. The Newton Bridge Road house functioned as a kind of boot camp for bohemians.[25]

In this period, Chesnutt experimented with drugs as well as art. He told a writer for *Flagpole* in 1991, "As a teenager and all through my twenties, I took ungodly amounts of acid. I would never have written the songs that I had written if it wasn't for this kind of kicking open the doors of perception kind of shit. . . . I took it every day for a year in like 1985." "I can see it all over everything I write[,] the influence of LSD." He also smoked weed and did ecstasy. When Mercyland played New York City, Chesnutt tagged along, and he and Donaldson attempted to snort heroin but the white powder they bought turned out to be fake.[26]

Like other scene participants from small towns in Georgia, Chesnutt struggled to reconcile what he loved and hated about his past with his new life in the scene. Zebulon and the country surrounding it had shaped his "whole personality." "I was a little different from the people in my hometown, so I always felt like an outsider a little bit," he recalled, "and also there was a big conflict between my redneck heritage and my bohemian aspirations." "That shaped the way I am a lot. Just growing up in the South, a lot of my songs are filled with this kind of stuff. I love Pike County. I love Middle Georgia. It was beautiful, and it was a great life for a kid. I hunted and fished and was a racist until I got to be a certain age, and I realized that that wasn't how it was." He thought Pike County High School, racially integrated by the time he attended, was "stupid." "The stoner crowd was rednecks, and I fucking hated them. They were dumbasses, and they were racists. They were sick." Late one night, he and a friend took sledgehammers to the segregated bathrooms complete with racial signs still in use behind a little country store outside Zebulon.[27]

Around 1987, after he quit UGA, Chesnutt recalled, "I fell apart in a way—I went down the drain for a while until I popped up on the other side." Homeless, Chesnutt simply parked his van at a local grocery store at the corner of Prince and Barber that everyone called "Ghetto Bell's" to distinguish the place from the Five Points branch where well-off whites and sorority girls picked up groceries. "It was nasty, but it was cheap, and I always shopped there," Chesnutt recalled. "I even lived in the parking lot for three months around 1987 because I didn't have a house. I lived in my van, and Ghetto Bell's was like my home. I used the pay phone as my office. I told people the number, and they would call me there." When not at Bell's, he would leave his van with the wheelchair lift out parked on College Avenue beside the big planters. Chesnutt's "place" became a kind of hangout spot, and musicians like Curtiss Pernice and David Barbe stopped by often to talk. Barbe even convinced Chesnutt to drive Mercyland in his van on a three week summer circuit after the vehicle they had planned to use broke down. At one stop at East Carolina University in Greenville, North Carolina, Chesnutt opened for Mercyland, performing the songs that would appear on his first album. Barbe, who later played in Bob Mould's band Sugar, cofounded and ran a music studio, and produced bands including the Drive-By Truckers, remembered Chesnutt as "ahead of everyone creatively," "a genius."[28]

Sometime in 1987, Chesnutt began playing informal Friday afternoon solo shows at the Grit. At one of those shows, someone recorded a take of "Mr. Riley," and in 1988 the local zine *Samizdat* released it on a compilation

Vic Chesnutt (*left*) and David Barbe eat pickled pig's feet inside the singer songwriter's van somewhere between Greenville and Nags Head, North Carolina, during Mercyland's July 1987 tour. For Chesnutt, this vehicle served a variety of purposes: a secure place to sleep and hang out with friends when he was between apartments, a machine that greatly improved his mobility, and a much-appreciated means of transportation when he or other Athens musicians toured. It was also a place where he felt great despair. (Photograph by Andrew Donaldson, courtesy of David Barbe)

called NINETOGETOUT. Vic did not manage that day to hold a steady tempo with his guitar but his warbling, drawling voice was strong as he sang, "Have you heard the news / about Joan, Joan, our ex-paper girl / they found her swinging from the tree / and idle / just a, just a week ago / she was beautiful / but now now now she's rather vile." The La Di Das had contributed two songs including Chesnutt's "Bakersfield" to the 1986 DRG compilation tape, but this recording of "Mr. Riley" captured Chesnutt's new solo sound.[29]

In this period, Chesnutt began to write songs about people he knew in Athens. As Sam Seawright recalled, hearing him perform was "like reading the newspaper." People went to hear him to find out "what was going on with our friends." Despite Chesnutt's disclaimer in his first album's liner notes that "this song is about almond oil and womanizers[,] not about anyone in particular," everyone at the time thought "Soft Picasso" described a "modern love affair" between Donaldson and Babb, and the common scene practice of sleeping with partners of all genders. According to Seawright, Chesnutt was the scene's "town crier."[30]

Members of the La Di Das disagreed about how much they needed to practice and eventually broke up in 1988, although they played some reunion shows in 1989. As Chesnutt remembered, "I decided that the best way for music to be performed is like a solo guy with an acoustic guitar. What we were doing was too polished. It needed to be stripped down. . . . It was little, as opposed to all the rest of the bands. They were big, you know, loud and rocking." Chesnutt had figured out how to fuse punk attitude with the folk ideas about authenticity he learned at the folk-music song swaps at the Grit. "It was very important that I erase the stage," he said looking back at this period. "I was a little guy with my little songs and my little voice and my little guitar." He wanted to appear "onstage just like I was off stage. That was my purist vision. I wanted to be so small onstage that it was a cool thing—there was no kind of image up there, just me and my songs." Rejecting all the trappings of stardom, he did not even want to be paid. "I like playing benefits," he said in an interview. "A lot of times I just don't feel like I deserve the money. It's good that it goes to something else, because if it goes to me, I'll probably just set fire to it." Playing solo also meant he did not have to get along with his bandmates or play things they had written. He could focus on his own songs.[31]

Chesnutt described his concert at the Unitarian Church on Prince Avenue that June as his "coming out party as a solo artist." Joe and Helli Willey, members of the Athens Folk Music and Dance Society, had met Chesnutt at the Grit song swaps. Believing folk music people they knew who would never attend a late-night club would love Chesnutt's music, they used their connections to secure the venue and borrowed the folk society's PA. Because the concert was at a church, Chesnutt's evangelical family—parents, younger sister, and Granny—who would not have gone to a bar got the chance to hear him perform. That night, on the small raised platform where the minister would have stood, Chesnutt sat alone in his wheelchair with a harmonica on a holder around his neck and his guitar in his lap. To his left stood a folding metal easel on which he propped drawings he had made on poster board, one for each song. As Chesnutt remembered, "the first song I did was 'Speed Racer.' When I hit the chorus, 'I am an atheist!' my parents started blubbering [and] crying." Chesnutt had been an atheist since he was a teen, but somehow his parents always hoped he would change. This public confession "broke their hearts." When he talked to his family after the show, he recalled, "My granny leaned over to me and she said, 'Vic, there's things that everybody does it, but you don't have to sing about it.'"[32]

By the time of this church concert, Chesnutt had traded his solo afternoon shows at the Grit for what people later called his "Tuesday residency" at the 40 Watt, by that point back open in the smaller space on Clayton. Some weeks he played his own songs brilliantly, and other weeks he could hardly sit up and remember what to play. One magical spring Tuesday, he played an entire set of carols, like a summer camp Christmas in July celebration. As Michael Stipe told a journalist, "I'd seen Vic playing around town for a long time, and I thought he was incredible." "Here's this guy who plays all these amazing little songs on a guitar that's a real piece of shit," Stipe explained. "I thought it would be a shame if we didn't go ahead and get some documentation of it. He had reached the point in his live performance where I just knew that he was fixing to change, fixing to move on from what he was doing. So I thought it was really important for us to get down on tape what he'd been doing up to that point." Chesnutt put it this way: "Michael once told me he wanted to record me before I died. Of course I thought it was a great idea."[33]

Stipe had reasons to be worried about Chesnutt's future. When Athens musician Kathy Kirbo's band Greenhouse opened for the La Di Das at the 40 Watt, probably in early 1987, she did not yet know Chesnutt. When she noticed a really drunk guy heave himself out of a wheelchair and start crawling around on stage and yelling, she asked people working at the club to help him. They told her "that's just Vic" and ignored him. When Chesnutt said he burned his share of the door when he played paying gigs, he probably meant he smoked or drank up his money. At times, he did a lot of drugs. According to John Keane, who engineered several of his albums, for a while "he was shooting speed and cocaine and doing all this crazy intravenous stuff." In a 1999 interview in *Flagpole*, the singer-songwriter confessed that he did a lot of heroin in this period. For Chesnutt, who waged a lifelong battle with depression, the years in the late 1980s when he lost his grandparents and father to cancer and other illnesses were particularly difficult. Even the Ghetto Bell's went out of business. "They said they were closing it down because too many people were shoplifting there," Chesnutt remembered. "And I felt bad, because I shoplifted like crazy."[34]

Years later, he told a journalist, smiling at his own pun, "I've always doubted myself, doubted my beliefs, second-guessed my decisions — and it paralyzes me." "I chase depression," he confessed to another journalist. "I'm not one to fight it. I tend to wallow in it."[35]

Michael Stipe had offered to pay for Chesnutt to record his songs, but the singer-songwriter worried that R.E.M.'s front man did not really mean it, as months went by without a studio date. One Tuesday night in October 1988, Stipe stuck around to talk to a "kinda drunk" Chesnutt after his regular 40 Watt gig and asked him to come to John Keane's studio the next day. In a marathon session, Chesnutt put down twenty-one songs in around nine hours. According to Stipe, "when I got him in the studio, he was in a renaissance in terms of his performance and songwriting." Chesnutt described the process in the liner notes: "This record was recorded a day with Michael much on the phone, me feeling rather rough from the long night before, Brenda propped on the couch worried and Rocky's pizza with sundried 'matoes, onions, and extra cheese." According to Stipe, "When I told the guy to sit down and play, he literally sat down and started playing and didn't stop until the pizza came, and then when we finished eating, he played again until one or two in the morning." Though Texas Hotel Records would not release *Little* until June 1990, over twenty months after Chesnutt recorded the material, Stipe got what he wanted. *Little* captured the way Chesnutt sounded playing solo on his best late-eighties nights in Athens.[36]

Mostly, the songs are just Chesnutt and his "little" guitar and his "little" lyrics. The album opens with "Isadora Duncan" and dreams of dancing. Solo guitar starts out alone and perfect, two notes, a sort-of slide, and then another note, a slight pause, and then guitar and harmonica together before Chesnutt's vocals and later, keyboards swell the sparse sound. In the lyrics, a narrator describes his interactions with Duncan and sets up implicit parallels between her world and her rebel spirit and Athens and the attitudes of local bohemians: "She sang 'my smile is more than pearly white / my dreams are more than you. / My yellow eyes are more than mirrors/ and my scarf is more than costume.'" Then Duncan screams what her death makes clear: "There is no shelter in the arts."[37]

On almost every one of the album's ten tracks, the melodies provide a spare and haunting framework for Chesnutt's voice, confoundingly scratchy and southern and old-sounding like a Lomax Library of Congress recording and yet singing of moral ambiguities and modern dilemmas very much of the present. The kind of torque that saturates *Little*—the tension between an old sound and a new story, a joyful melody or a happy voice and a dark or difficult subject, the sadness in the beautiful and the humor in the sadness— would characterize much of Chesnutt's future music. On "Speed Racer," Chesnutt fills out his joyous atheist manifesto based on the philosophy of "Kirkegard" [*sic*] with the sounds of a poor country church, Michael Stipe's keyboards mimicking the sound of a cheap organ and Lynda Stipe's backing vocals creating what Chesnutt calls "angel voices." Always, he seems determined to sing words and make rhymes not previously heard in pop songs. On "Giupetto," he croons, "The candle wicks are asterisks. You carved him yourself out of sticks."[38]

"Soft Picasso" does all of these things and also constructs a perfect little picture of life in bohemian Athens. In this tale about a "modern love affair," Chesnutt's dragged-out, southern pronunciations only heighten the dissonance between the sound of the strummed melody and its subject matter. "The modern girl was elated / with what the revolution gave her / since she was liberated / she could have everything that striked her fancy / And she fancied quite a bit / If it felt good she did it" and "her taste wasn't limited to just modern guys / Since another modern girl showed her / that modern girls know how to hold her." "The modern man" on the other hand, "wasn't so lucky / being shook from his usual role as a heart-breaker / He was completely battered and bewildered" and "discovered a new emotion." At the end, Chesnutt sings of the consequences and turns the style of a famous artist into a perfect metaphor: "So view the modern man / looking like a soft Picasso / He's there with his head in his hand / Repeating to himself an epigram / 'Live by the scam, die by the scam.'"

If *Little* has a muse, it's Stevie Smith, and Chesnutt fittingly ends the album with a song he made out of her poem "Not Waving but Drowning." "Stevie Smith" is the only song on the album not recorded in the one-day session Michael Stipe paid for at John Keane's Athens studio. It sounds like a tape of a practice session because it is—the expected session never happened. Primitive production values and folky contributions from Chesnutt's song swap pals create a contrast with Smith's dry, modernist tone. A recording of Smith speaking serves as an introduction, and includes a line Chesnutt would steal in interviews, "I rather like the idea of death." Then Joe Willey starts the song on banjo, and Chesnutt joins in on guitar. Helli Willey and Moira Nelligan sing together and create the kind of high, Appalachian harmonies that amp up the emotional impact no matter the content of the lyrics. Chesnutt reserves for himself the lines in the poem that work as a kind of refrain: "I was much too far out all my life / And not waving but drowning." Later, Nelligan fills a break with a tentative, slightly off, and achingly beautiful fiddle solo that Chesnutt describes in the liner notes as a first take. Throughout, sharp pops punctuate the music as Helli cracks pecans. Many of Chesnutt's best songs use the earnest sincerity of old-time southern ballad and hymn styles to squeeze meaning and feeling out of modern tales of depression, ambivalence, and woe. On this track, listeners actually get to hear a vital source of Chesnutt's art, his interactions with local folk revivalists.

Not long after Chesnutt made his *Little* recordings with Stipe and Keane, he talked in a remarkably unguarded way about his ambitions for his music with his future bandmate Jimmy Davidson, then documenting Athens bands for a UGA thesis: "I try to be just as sincere as possible. . . . I'm trying to write a song that'll change everybody's life, including my own. . . . I'm just out to do that scary art thing, you know. I want to give everybody the 'art feeling.'" Making music helped him live. Chesnutt confessed to Davidson that what he really wanted was to release a record. He also longed to perform outside Athens, in Atlanta or farther afield, in New York City or even Spain. What he did not say then was that he wanted the record to come out quickly so he could give it to his dad, then dying of cancer.[39]

In his early years in Athens, Vic Chesnutt blossomed into the quintessential bohemian, a perfect embodiment of the late-eighties scene. He read books of modernist poetry and philosophy. He helped his friends make art and music. And he sang folk ballads with local revivalists. Absorbing all these influences and mixing them with memories of his country music childhood, he wrote songs that constructed little vignettes about his past or people he read about or knew and their moments of ugliness and beauty. He brought a new emphasis on storytelling into the Athens scene. And he did all this from the battered wheelchair his friends called "the hot seat," in clubs and cafés and houses and radio stations that lacked ramps he could roll up or down and doors he could open and bathrooms he could use.

Critical success would happen in the future, in more of a slow build than a spurt and in spite of bouts of self-destructiveness, deep depression, and chronic health problems. To explain why the record-buying public never really fell for Vic Chesnutt, D.C.-based indie music hero Ian MacKaye suggested that maybe America was "not ready for a superstar in a wheelchair." In this respect, the Athens scene really did offer an alternative. There, in the place where he grew into one of the country's best songwriters, the man in the hot seat became a star.[40]

Underground

In the late eighties in Athens, Chesnutt was not the only person thinking small. In part, locals responded to R.E.M.'s big. Older bands like Love Tractor had long felt the burden of R.E.M.'s success. As Mark Cline and Armistead Wellford told me, they could not mention their friends without journalists turning the story into another piece about R.E.M. As R.E.M.'s albums *Document* and then *Green* generated hit singles and moved up the charts, these pressures spread throughout the scene. "Little" became a way to separate from R.E.M.'s growing fame and what some bohemians experienced as the commercialization of the scene.[41]

Focusing on scale also helped scene participants reconcile a central contradiction, the role of ambition, a decidedly "mainstream" desire, in an alternative culture committed to critiquing American society and its focus on getting ahead. DIY and a dedication to independence had helped deflect this issue—people making their music (or other art) themselves in their own way, without the help of corporate America. But what did this kind of fierce individualism mean in a world where indie stars like the Replacements, Hüsker Dü, and even R.E.M. signed with Warner Brothers or one of its subsidiaries? And how was this focus on independence a critique in anything more meaningful than a stylistic sense as something we would only much later learn to call neoliberalism took hold, a political and economic restructuring that used the idea of independence to justify an unfettered global capitalism? The freedom to do whatever you wanted meant you could make your music your way. It also meant you could buy a historic house, kick out your bohemian renters, and raze it to the ground. In place-based scenes like Athens, it made sense that thinking about smallness and intimacy—the local—might be an answer. For Athens bohemians, children of a suburbanizing world in which ranch houses and strip malls appeared even in rural Georgia, this attention to the historic landscape of Athens as a place felt like our own transgressive invention. Looking back, we took more from folk revivalists and back-to-the-landers than we were ready to admit, with one significant difference: a focus on making our own culture.

The Downstairs, the café, coffee shop, and music club I cofounded and ran from 1987 to 1991, was a "little" place. Every week the ragged packages piled up on the counter there—TDK, Maxwell, or no-label cassettes wrapped in recycled bubble wrap and homemade press releases crammed into used envelopes or packets made out of repurposed posters or cut-apart brown paper sacks. Occasionally, a new mailer arrived, suggesting a band backed by a well-funded independent record company or what we called a "trust fund," shorthand for someone with money they did not seem to have to earn. Local groups dropped these kits by during opening hours. The mailman stomped down the iron stairs with the rest.

On Sundays, when the place was closed, my bandmate, business partner, boyfriend, and roommate David Levitt sat in the L of the rattan and wood

David Levitt, co-owner of the Downstairs as well as a songwriter, guitar and bass player, and painter, leans on the wicker bar at the underground café/gallery/club. The café's business license is visible over his right shoulder. (Photograph by author)

bar, originally built for some midcentury husband's basement lair, near what passed for our "boom box," a cassette player with aspirations. One by one, he popped the tapes in the deck and punched play. Strands of dirty blonde hair fell out of a fisherman's cap into his eyes as he bent close to the speakers. Usually he let the music go for a minute or two before he hit stop and fast forward or flipped the cassette to listen to another song. More often than not, he then ejected the tape and put it aside to reuse before recycling the accompanying materials. Sometimes, though, he lingered, and the same sly smile he got when he discovered a piece of McCoy pottery at the Potter's House would ripple across his face.

When he wasn't working, David wrote songs and played guitar and bass in our band Cordy Lon. The name—his grandfather's nickname plus a nonsense syllable—did not mean anything. For David, the first person I knew who talked about postmodernism and had read Derrida and Foucault, using nonreferential language was the point. In the music he wrote, he loved the surprise of dissonance wrenched into place by a song's structure and lyrics built from the sound of words that gestured at stories without easily giving up meaning. Mostly we were a trio—Robbie Zimmerman on drums, me on

David Levitt, Robbie Zimmerman, and I played in the Athens band Cordy Lon, seen here in one of the band's promo shots. (Photographer unknown, author's possession)

cello, and David switching between acoustic and electric guitar and a Paul McCartney–style bass. We played the clubs in Athens and Atlanta and at indie venues all over the southeast and put out a tape called *Misanthropic* that sold well enough locally that we had to make another batch. *Flagpole* pushed our shows, and the *Red and Black* praised our "interesting, intricate songs" and called us "a butt-kicking, sort of acoustic, sort of melodic, sort of wonderful progressive folk/pop band," "doing our groovy cello, drums, and guitar thing." Years later, *Flagpole* journalist and music writer Gordon Lamb wrote, "Cordy Lon was the bridge between Athens's folk-rock scene, its jangle-rock scene, and its dark-art/post-new-wave scene. In short, perfect. Sure, I'm gushing, but I seriously cannot convey how much this band meant to me circa 1989–1991."[42]

But David did not impose his own taste on the task of booking the Downstairs. Because he wanted to listen without bias and give every musician a chance, he only read the press materials after he had heard the music. He did not need to know anyone in the band or, if they had one, the name of their manager or their label. He did not need to be familiar with whatever local scene the musicians called home. Despite more famous participants' frequent claims of supportiveness, he also understood that the local scene could be cliquish and closed off. Atlanta bands and groups that formed elsewhere and then moved to town had an especially hard time. If David liked the sound, if the singing or the lyrics or the rhythm or the tone or the mood made him feel something, he would call the number on the xeroxed press kit or even the tape label itself and try to work out a date that fit the group's touring schedule. Local bands did not even have to pass this test. If a band member or two stopped by after dropping off the tape and caught David in the after-lunch lull, he would usually give them what we thought of as the Tuesday night tryout. In this work, he nurtured the ecumenicalism of a scene in which participants created bands as different as the Bar-B-Q Killers, Billy James, Mercyland, and the La Di Das.

By the time David and I opened the Downstairs in October of 1987, we had known each other for just over a year. We met cutting vegetables for party trays at a classic Athens part-time job, Lee Epting Catering. On our first date, we tried to go see the Flat Duo Jets, but they had moved back to North Carolina and had to cancel because their truck broke down. Instead, we borrowed a friend's VHS player and watched *Manhattan*. Then, David was the intellectual, a graduate student at UGA studying critical theory, and I was the bohemian, making rugs and purses out of old clothes and going to see friends' bands at the Uptown while working multiple jobs to fund a trip to Europe. After a rough start, we fell in love talking and drawing late into the night after I finished my shifts at my other job at Rocky's Pizza. At some point, I shared my café dream. It was hard to get a meaningful job in Athens making any money, we thought, so why not open a business and work for ourselves?[43]

While the Grit inspired us, we could see that Jennifer Hartley and Melanie Haner were struggling to stay open. Several abandoned blocks from downtown, the gallery–coffee shop's location at the old depot made it hard to walk there and not really safe to go alone at night. And the Grit's vibe, not just the way it looked but its circle of dedicated regulars, made the place feel like an insiders' clubhouse. For many of us, this aura was part of the attraction, but a lot of people were put off by this atmosphere. As Don Chambers, an artist and musician who moved to town in 1988 to work on an MFA recalled, the Grit was "really intimidating." David thought he could draw on his hobby of hitting a circuit of thrift and junk shops multiple times a week to look for cool stuff. We hoped a Grit-like hybrid, a café, vintage store, and gallery, might draw more customers if we could find a downtown location and serve more food.[44]

I was backpacking in Europe when David discovered a space below street level in an old commercial building a local developer was renovating on Clayton Street downtown. He told me about it when I called him from a pay phone on a beach in Crete. Midcentury construction had extended the first floor of the building out over the space where stairs at both ends led down to two small downstairs storefronts, each with two windows and a door. For the developer, who had based his calculations on renting the street-level storefronts and the apartments, then a rarity downtown, that he was building into the upper floors, the basement space was a bonus. He agreed to let us have the space for $750 a month. We only learned later that he figured we would pay to build and plumb a little kitchen and an accessible bathroom. Then when we failed, the space would be up to code and he could open a bar.

Over a frantic month, the two of us and another short-lived partner, Dean Orlosky, scoured secondhand shops from Athens to Atlanta looking for old dinette tables and chairs, odd pieces of old diner china, and Fiestaware. We found that rattan bar, an old Victorian style sofa and easy chair, vintage lamps that David could rewire, and a cabinet-style record player which would drop and play records from a stack balanced on a spindle. At Kmart, we bought a two-burner electric eye, what passed for our stove. At Macy's, we purchased an espresso and cappuccino machine and home-grade convection oven, the size of a large microwave, for baking. At the Potter's House, we got a used refrigerator and two microwaves. A hired carpenter built a wall with a row of glass bricks across the top to separate the kitchen from the dining area and put in an accessible restroom. Then we painted the entire place ourselves, white walls and trim in colors we all loved: a mustardy yellow, teal, and maroon. We had cobbled together around $10,000 in funding, most of it from David, who had inherited some money when his grandmother died, plus Dean's small savings and about $2,000 I borrowed from my dad. A frighteningly large chunk of our stake went to the plumber.[45]

About a week before our scheduled opening, the plumbing inspector told David he did not like "hippies." He also said our business would need a second accessible restroom. With no money to rebuild the nonaccessible toilet the landlord had put in, we were about to fail before we even opened. As a last-ditch effort, I practiced my drawl, curled my hair, put on a Gunne Sax dress my mom bought me in high school, and went to his office. After I listened to him make sexist jokes that I worked hard to forget and cannot now recall, I smiled at him, batted my eyes, and asked him to give us a variance. In only one of the many ironies here, our landlord was not required to make the entryway to the Downstairs—two curving and steep sets of iron stairs—accessible. Employees and friends always had to carry Vic Chesnutt and his wheelchair into the space.

We had no idea what we were doing. I had grown up baking and followed family recipes for brownies, pies, and pound cakes. Other recipes like Indonesian rice salad we stole from the original *Moosewood Cookbook*. The heart of the menu was a vegetarian version of that southern staple, the meat and three: squash, green bean, and spinach casseroles, cups of homemade soups, salads, and beans and rice or mac and cheese instead of the meat, with a homemade muffin or biscuit on the side. We called the fusion of southern and hippie cooking "white-trash vegetarian," even though we served a few meat dishes and what we thought of as an incredibly sophisticated baked brie as well. It seemed like a miracle that first night we opened when people we did not know actually showed up, ordered, ate, and paid.[46]

The high of translating our ideas into a living place that other people could experience and even grow to love kept David and me going that hellish first year. Dean walked away a couple of months in, overwhelmed by long shifts, low pay, and the toil trying to make the business profitable placed on our friendships. Running the café side of the business was like throwing a dinner party every night and not ever knowing how many people were coming. The vintage store did not require as much day-to-day work, but sales were wildly unpredictable, so we closed it. I did most of the baking, in the mornings before the lunch rush and in the afternoons when a small but steady stream of regulars sipped cups of coffee with free refills and ate chocolate–peanut butter or caramel brownies. Both of us cooked, waited on tables, made plates, and washed dishes. Once a week, someone had to drive to the Atlanta Farmers Market for supplies. Because I kept the books, I understood our cash flow. Being around food all the time and worrying about the money made it hard to eat, and I got really skinny. The band languished. We practiced and played some gigs, but David had little time to write new songs or book dates outside Athens.

Early on, a dedicated knot of regular customers saved us. Friends and former classmates and coworkers and roommates like Jessica Hunt came in and spent their hard-earned cash. But most of our customers were, at least in the beginning, strangers. Mamie Fike, Daryl Black, Brad Jacobson, Rick Naylor, and Trey Ledford, members of a new Athens band called Long Low Rumble, and their friends, like the art student and future art director Chris Bilheimer and the UGA student and writer Darin Beasley, somehow discovered us right after we opened. Ort, who carried around a notebook full of lists of things like weird beers and possible band names, christened Long Low Rumble and then followed them down the stairs to our door. Cathy Edmonds, the first person I knew with a Vespa and a standout thrift-store dresser in a place where the competition was fierce, came in for lunch or tea and dessert multiple times a week. Deb Bernstein introduced her fellow activists to our place by holding meetings over meals there. Debbie Norton brought in her friends in the local lesbian community. Some customers spent so much time there, sitting on the sofa talking or reading, that occasionally they forgot to pay, and we just saved the receipt for the next time. The parents of regulars called often, trying to track their kids in those pre-cell-phone days. Given how grateful we were for every single customer then, I am embarrassed today that I can remember many people's faces and orders but not their names.

No one made more of a mark on the place than Jim Stacy, now a well-inked chef, restaurant owner, comedian, musician, and artist. When he followed Trey Ledford, who he knew from the dorm, to our place, Jim was a clean-cut UGA undergraduate art student and folk music fan with shortish red curls and bare skin. I'm not sure if he was an employee yet when he designed and drew our logo, our menu, and the cartoon featuring our mascots "my brother Pete and dog" drinking coffee that became our ad—maybe we just paid him in food. Jim could cook and talk "a blue streak" at the same time, and we shared a fondness for sayings we got from our grandparents, like "serious as a heart attack." He had an uncanny ability to make all kinds of customers, from young artists and musicians like Deonna Mann just working their way into the scene to his friends in the Athens Folk Music and Dance Society, feel at home in our place. A one-man design department, he painted the signs that we hung up on the railing at street level and drew the cartoons of Pete and dog's adventures for ads in the *Flagpole* and our t-shirts. He could also handle most anything that happened in the course of a shift, even if his go-to problem-solving tool, duct tape, sometimes caused more problems than it solved.[47]

Working at the Downstairs changed Jim. He grew his hair long, formed his own band, the La Brea Stompers, got the first of many tattoos (a very transgressive act for middle-class kids then), and stopped going to his classes and dropped out of UGA. As later employees started following Jim's lead, David and I wondered if we should stop hiring anyone who was still in school.[48]

Now an important New Orleans chef, Chris DeBarr had already graduated with a degree in English and run Lunch Paper. When we met him, he

Jim Stacy, one of the first employees at the Downstairs and later the manager, drew a logo and a series of comics that appeared in ads and on t-shirts to advertise the café, music club, and art gallery.
(Author's possession)

was cooking at the downtown seafood place Sparky's and writing plays and poetry. Sick to death of making hushpuppies, Chris proposed a deal where he would "guest cook" for us on his days off for whatever we could pay him if we let him experiment. In a month, he spiced up our menu with new dishes like curried lentils and fish specials, taught us how to order from food wholesalers like a "real" restaurant, and educated us all on left political issues like solidarity with Central Americans fighting for democracy. I knew how to bake, but Chris taught me how to really cook. He also encouraged David and me to pay for health insurance plans for our full-time employees. Smart, wickedly funny, and never far from his well-thumbed copy of *Diet for a Small Planet*, Chris was too good for our tiny kitchen.

Early on, I had to fire someone we all liked for stealing, a hard thing to do when you are twenty-three, but mostly we had an amazing staff of about twelve employees at its peak. While we paid above minimum wage plus a split of the tips, the main attraction was being part of a creative community, having a chance to experiment with new dishes or to show your art or read your prose or poetry or perform your music. Julie Daniels, the artist Jill Carnes's sister, had learned to do food-service work in the Army and brought her incredible work ethic. UGA English graduate Donna Ashley had managed the east side Taco Stand and possessed a kind of quiet efficiency that made the baking and cooking fly. Dori Cosgrove, a UGA graduate who had written for *Tasty World* and played in the local band Magister Ludi, waited tables, sold beer, and did anything else required. All of these people were creative, smart as hell, and great talkers. When I went back to UGA part-time to work on an MA in history in the fall of 1988, I volunteered to wash dishes so I could think while I worked. If I came up with something I wanted to use in a paper, I wrote a note directly on the wall with a pencil I kept on a string over the sink. Often, I polished my arguments by running them past my co-workers.[49]

From the start, we turned over our wall space to local artists and opened new art shows about every three weeks. Deonna Mann had her first exhibition at the Downstairs, paintings on long pieces of newsprint that she called "Strange Fruit" in homage to Billie Holiday, whose records played frequently on our old cabinet stereo. Her other projects at our place included an installation that covered the walls with fabric and found objects, an adult puppet show, and performance-art pieces like the time she gave live beauty makeovers. Jennifer Hartley and Jill Carnes also exhibited their work.[50]

More than a few people fell in love. Donna Ashley and her future husband Arthur Johnson, drummer for the Bar-B-Q Killers, had their first date at the Downstairs, a fruit and cheese plate shared at the two-top in the alcove between the kitchen wall and the window. Craig Williams, a deejay and later program director for WUOG and Johnson's close friend, also took the woman who would become his wife to the Downstairs the first time they went out. David and I decided to get married and planned the ceremony for early January when business was slow enough that we could close and invite everyone to the party. Chris's girlfriend Poppy Z. Brite, later a well-known horror writer, caught the bouquet.[51]

Because everyone who worked at the Downstairs performed in some way, it was a natural thing to start hosting events. At first, as David told the *Red and Black*, he booked "the kind of acts not comfortable with the club scene." The New Iberian Gospel Contingency, a group formed by Vic Chesnutt, Deonna Mann, Gene Wilson, and others to perform gospel songs while wearing choir robes, played regularly, as well as bands created by local folk revivalists like Put the Strange Damsel to Work and Gan Ainm. Chris DeBarr organized performances, including productions by his own and Darin Beasley's theater troupes, a series called "Poets' Mudwrestling," and a political speakers forum. After the Folk Society moved their monthly song swaps from the Grit to the Downstairs, the folky crowd fell for our Monday night drink special, $1 Mickey's Big Mouths.[52]

At risk of romanticizing, I checked my memory against the archives. An article headlined "The Downstairs Captures the Essence of Athens with Food and Art" in the *Red and Black* described "the cozy little restaurant in underground Athens you've always heard about but were afraid to ask. If you've been there, you love it." With "great homemade food," the Downstairs offered an "underground feel" at a price that "fits the college budget." "Eating at Downstairs" meant "melting into a chair, relaxing and soaking in 1920's jazz" and reading Athens literary magazine *Lift Archaic* while you waited for your order to arrive on "antique plates." "The first bite of mousakka melted in the mouth." Another piece in the *Red and Black* described the Downstairs as "unique" in terms of both "the decor" — "Grandma's house," a combination of "simple tables, University surplus chairs and antediluvian furnishings" — and "the way it's managed." Jim Stacy said that working at the café and club was not just a job but a way to be a part of an artistic community. "Each employee has his creative interests reflected in the restaurant." Often, student journalists used our anniversaries as an occasion to write about a place they seemed to love. "There's a little hole in the wall in Athens that's cozy, homey, entertaining and it even has a great menu. In case you haven't figured it out by now, it's that infamous downtown café/nightclub The Downstairs."

If something can become legendary in just three years, this place has certainly done so," one wrote in 1990. "Frequented by students studying in the daytime and at night . . . the site of a variety of entertaining performances," "this little room underground is one of the most versatile places around."[53]

By 1989, what a *Flagpole* writer described as our "subterranean chow-and-culture mecca" with "more food per square inch" than anywhere else in town had evolved to occupy an essential niche in the local music scene. About ninety new-music bands claimed the town as their home then, and many out-of-town acts with records out on independent labels and significant college-radio airplay also wanted to play. The Uptown dominated the local club ecology in that era, mostly because it was the biggest venue with an official capacity of 225 but some nights that tripled that. Then in the Clayton Street location that housed the third and fifth versions of this club, the 40 Watt was about a quarter the size of the Uptown. Newcomer the Rockfish Palace, which opened on East Hancock in the old warehouse district in the late spring of 1987 and booked blues, reggae, and other genres, as well as alternative music, had a capacity somewhere between that of the Uptown and the 40 Watt. Competition for local gigs, especially at the Uptown and the 40 Watt, grew fierce.[54]

With an official capacity of about fifty and regular attendance of twice that, the Downstairs took on the role that the original 40 Watt with its motto "anyone can play here once" held in relation to Tyrone's O.C. and the Uptown in its early days held in relation to the Broad Street 40 Watt. It became the place where new bands could play, the point of entry into the scene. Groups like Five Eight, the La Brea Stompers, Magister Ludi, 28 Days, Cursing Alice, and Bill Mallonee's band Vigilantes of Love all got their first paying gigs or developed their early audiences there. The Downstairs also introduced Athens people to an overlapping collection of acts that formed in Atlanta's Cabbagetown neighborhood including An Evening with the Garbagemen (later the Jody Grind), the Opal Foxx Quartet, and the performance artist and poet Deacon Lunchbox.[55]

For a while, the Downstairs worked in part as a kind of farm team for the 40 Watt. Jared Bailey, who booked as well as co-owned the 40 Watt in addition to owning the *Flagpole*, sent many bands to the Downstairs to play and then called David to see how they did before he gave them a gig. And despite our size, bands often came back for more gigs even after they could play other places, because they made money. Cover charges were low—$2 to $3 and on special occasions $4 or even $5—but we did not take a percentage or subtract anything except $10 to pay Ort or someone else to work the door and beers for band members at cost. Bands that regularly drew forty people could walk away with over $100 if they kept their bar tab in check. Many musicians complained that other local club owners miscounted the door and miscalculated percentages and deductions, shorting bands at pay out. Whether or not those rumors were true, only groups that filled the Uptown or sold out two-night stands at the Clayton Street 40 Watt or played occasional UGA frat parties were making any real money then in Athens.[56]

Sometimes, the tiny space of the Downstairs was perfect. On his good nights, Vic Chesnutt filled the air with his wonder words, melodies, and phrasings. A Greenpeace benefit David and Jim organized featuring Debbie Norton, An Evening with the Garbagemen and poet Deacon Lunchbox, Cordy Lon, and the La Brea Stompers raised over $600 for the organization, a fortune to us in those days. And one June Monday after the students had left town miraculously broke all our records after local music journalist Dan Matthews spilled the news that Severe Driving Problems was actually an alias for Widespread Panic. The jam band had booked our place to play an intimate show for their friends, but that night we sold every beer in the cooler and then all the hot bottles as well, about a thousand dollars' worth of food and mostly drink. Panic's show gave our lean operation the kind of cushion that enabled us to survive the always-slow time of summer. But even on ordinary days, our customers ate good food, drank espresso or beer or bad wine, listened to old records, and met other creative people. They wrote poems and plays, organized to save the historic structures of our town or to protest U.S. militarism, listened to local music, and looked at local art.[57]

In the early days of the Athens scene, the magic happened in people's apartments in old Victorians and at the art school and at record stores. Later, clubs like the 40 Watt and the Uptown became places where musicians and other kinds of creative people and fans met each other. As R.E.M.'s growing fame meant larger crowds at places like the 40 Watt, the scene began to lose the kind of social relations where most people knew each other and the intimate, creative atmosphere that had characterized places like Pylon Park, the open studios of the art school, and Stitchcraft. In the late eighties, the Grit and the Downstairs helped renew the original scene's essential "anything was possible" vibe by adding new kinds of spaces to the mix, communal dens in which people who wanted to could find and join the scene and experience its creative community as a lived reality.

Field Recordings

In the late eighties in Athens, bands shared a place more than a sound. As a result, people always argued about which groups really counted as Athens bands. In retrospect, these distinctions seem arbitrary. Only a few Athens musicians—including Keith Strickland and Cindy and Ricky Wilson of the B-52's, Lynda Stipe of Oh-OK and Hetch Hetchy, and Rob Veal, a later member of the La Di Das and then the Dashboard Saviors—had gone to high school in town. Everyone else had moved to the place. Matthew Sweet was probably not the first person to enroll at the University of Georgia in order to join the scene. The major difference between college-student musicians and fans and musicians and fans who moved to town and did not go to UGA was class. Middle-class kids usually had parents who could be persuaded to help pay for college. Working-class kids did not have this kind of financial support and usually did not attend UGA. By definition, scenes were places that drew people in. Yet allegiance to a romantic myth of Athens as isolated and outside of national trends—a folk idea of a scene if not a folk sound— privileged middle-class participants who came for school and had an easier time denying their ambitions.[58]

Some bands, like Dreams So Real and the Kilkenny Cats, reacted to R.E.M.'s "big" success by trying to create their own large, radio-friendly sounds. Others continued the harder, faster, and louder aesthetic that began with the early Uptown bands, and the Skin Pops, the Jack O' Nuts—the band Laura Carter joined after the Bar-B-Q Killers broke up—Deonna Mann's Crack, and Beverly Babb's Ray Ugly joined Mercyland and Porn Orchard. At the same time, a wave of bands also began to move in the opposite direction, creating softer, slower, and more eccentric music. These musicians used vocal techniques and dissonance borrowed from performance artists and instruments rarely heard in rock, like violins, cellos, acoustic basses, and stomp boards. For inspiration and songs to cover, they mined old genres like cabaret, big band, classic country, and country blues. Out-of-town bands as different as Fetchin Bones, Hugo Largo, Tiny Lights, Poi Dog Pondering, and the Beggar Weeds and locals like the Chickasaw Mudd Puppies, Long Low Rumble, and Cordy Lon were making this kind of music before the Downstairs became a venue. But David's eclectic booking practices and the hip and intimate feel of the space—"like seeing a band in your living room"—did a lot to nurture new kinds of music in Athens.[59]

What mattered more than your sound was who you knew. Off the road for long stretches from November 1987 through the spring of 1991, with the exception of the eight-month *Green* tour in 1989, the R.E.M. guys became a part of the local scene again and helped nurture another wave of Athens music-making. Peter Buck, Mike Mills, and Bill Berry hung out at the Georgia Bar, the Uptown, and the 40 Watt, then owned by Barrie Buck, Pete's wife. Michael Stipe hit the clubs but also spent time at the Grit and the Downstairs and turned up unexpectedly at parties like the annual Christmas bash David and I threw at our house on Cobb Street. In early 1988, Mike Mills and Peter Buck got to share their take on Athens music history when they guest-deejayed an episode of Jennifer Fox's local music show on WUOG, *Sound of the City*, leading off with Porn Orchard's song about Athens, "Our Band," and finishing seventeen songs later with their own "Perfect Circle."[60]

When R.E.M. members were in town, they often got on stage with their friends in local or out-of-town bands for a song or two. Sometimes, the whole band appeared unannounced. In May 1988, R.E.M. opened for Vic Chesnutt at a benefit for the Grit at the 40 Watt, an event held to help Jennifer Hartley stay in business. Two months later, they appeared at the 40 Watt again, opening for the Primates, in a performance shot by Jim McKay, then a local filmmaker and *Flagpole* writer and later a successful film and television director. R.E.M. members also worked as producers for local bands like the Kilkenny Cats and the La Di Das and out-of-town groups recording at local studios, including John Keane's place and Robbie Collins's Underground Sound. The R.E.M. guys even helped resurrect one of the scene's greatest bands. A reformed Pylon played at the 40 Watt in the summer of 1988 and then headlined a University Union–sponsored concert on Legion Field in the fall before hitting the road the next year, including a series of dates opening for their friends and former rivals on the home stretch of the *Green* tour.[61]

Three years earlier, future scene participant Curtiss Pernice did not know anything about Athens. Twenty years old that summer, he worked at a video arcade in Potsdam, New York, a slightly bigger place down the road from his tiny hometown of Norfolk. He had been a deejay for a while, and he and some of his friends had become fans of Black Flag and other West Coast hardcore. To ease the hurt of a bad breakup, one of those friends had moved to Athens, where his sister was a UGA graduate student. After a few months, Ted Hafer came home for a wedding and told Curtiss all about the music in the small college town. He also said there was a room opening up in the house where he lived for $75 a month. Barely missing a beat, Curtiss said he would take it—he just had to figure out how to get there. Soon another friend suggested a possible solution. Maybe Curtiss could catch a ride with his grandfather who drove his Winnebago to Florida every November to escape the snow? Somehow, the eighty-one-year-old man agreed to take a young guy he had never met down the East Coast. Because Georgia was next to Florida, Curtiss had imagined the old man would simply drive right through Athens. Yet when they got to Florence, South Carolina, the old man pulled the camper off the interstate and left his dazed passenger along with a suitcase, amp, and guitar in the parking lot of a convenience store. Curtiss used the pay phone to call a cab to take him to the Florence bus station. More than thirty years later, he still remembered how strange it was to see the big wooden train trestles as he rolled into Athens on the Greyhound.[62]

His new home turned out to be Curtiss's idea of heaven. Hafer lived at 255 Elizabeth Street with Larry Tenner and Sam Mixon, and the communal house functioned like a round-the-clock practice space. Whenever the roommates and their friends were not working or at the clubs, they hung out and jammed on instruments they left set up in the living room, and Curtiss joined right in. A few days after arriving, he saw the Bar-B-Q Killers. If his new friends had not already told him about Laura Carter, he would have mistaken her for a man as she stomped across the stage and screamed at the audience. As impressive, Claire Horne, only about twenty, had already invented her own way of playing guitar. For the first two months, Curtiss went out to hear bands five or six nights a week. He could hardly believe a place like this existed. Instead of the hardcore scene he had expected, he found something better, the Bar-B-Q Killers and Mercyland and Time Toy and other bands creating their own hard and fast and yet also weird and arty music rather than just sounding like Black Flag clones.[63]

Porn Orchard started when someone from the 40 Watt called the Elizabeth Street house one afternoon in December looking for an act to open that very night. The way Sam Mixon put it, "the first four guys who walked in the door got the job." Curtiss played guitar, Ted sang, Sam played drums, and Ron Hargrove played bass. They were terrible. Before their second gig at the 40 Watt in March opening for Dreams So Real, they got serious and wrote eight or ten of their own songs. They developed an incredible work ethic — practicing for hours five times a week. Soon, Porn Orchard was playing regularly with the Bar-B-Q Killers and Mercyland and then headlining their own dates. According to Mixon, they were the first band in town whose fans formed a mosh pit.[64]

In the spring of 1986, the Porn Orchard guys recorded some songs at their house on Elizabeth Street using two four-track tape players and then got their tracks on WUOG and David Barbe's *Proud of Me Gluttony* compilation. "Our Band" opened with Ted screaming "Our band is great in bed,"

**The trio Porn Orchard, made up of Curtiss Pernice (guitar),
Sam Mixon (drums), and Ted Hafer (vocals and bass),
was the most hardcore band in Athens in the late 1980s.
(Photograph by Larry Tenner, courtesy of Curtiss Pernice)**

before name-dropping everyone in town and making fun of Mystery Date and the Kilkenny Cats. As Mixon remembered, "our volume alone turned heads as did our aggressive sound and controversial posters that featured everything from a mass-murder scene in McDonalds to satirical attacks on anything considered holy."[65]

In my memory, half the women in town had crushes on Curtiss who, unlike most hardcore guys, wore his blond hair in long, straight locks. According to Curtiss, "I was an annoying little shit with a one track mind, but I had just moved from a provincial outpost in upstate New York so I had my excuse." Like most musicians in town, all the guys in Porn Orchard had day jobs, Sam and Ron at the Grill, the retro diner downtown, and Ted at Copy Cat Copies, which explained why Porn Orchard stickers covered the town. Often Curtiss worked more than one place, but his long-term job was baking the bread for Schlotzsky's, a sandwich shop on College Avenue. He loved that he could hire friends like Deonna Mann and set his own hours, either staying up after the clubs closed or coming in early in the morning, as long as the bread was ready when the staff arrived to begin prepping lunch. Most nights, he talked to the homeless people who slept in College Square, and sometimes he made them free sandwiches. He and Ted discovered the

UGA library and figured out how to check out equipment and make films and videos. They also created a press kit for a band they called Strike Out and got the fake act written up in the Boston-based zine *Forced Exposure*.[66]

By the summer of 1987, Porn Orchard was selling their own cassette *Hit the Right People Hard* in town and at independent record stores in other places whose addresses Curtiss found in the San Francisco punk and hardcore zine *Maximum Rocknroll*. This same publication printed lists of clubs with addresses and phone numbers, and Curtiss used this information to book their first "real" tour, three and a half weeks on the road. Without air-conditioning, they drove up and down the East Coast that August, living on $1.75 per member per day. Being cheap paid off—they arrived home with $200, a band fund Curtiss kept in an old tube sock. At some point, they moved into a house two blocks from downtown on Finley Street with six bedrooms they paid $120 each for, plus a common room for band practice. In order to record at home, band members spent an entire day hitting chords on a guitar and listening for rattling and then using duct tape to seal anything that moved. Then they made another demo and sent it to independent record companies and college radio stations around the country whose addresses they found in the *College Music Journal*.[67]

After Ron left, Ted took over bass, too, and Porn Orchard became a trio. They put out a single and an EP themselves, and then C/Z Records out of Seattle signed them. Almost six years after they started, they released their first album, *Urges and Angers*, on both CD and vinyl. Somehow, though they got to tour more and their record appeared in stores where they played, it wasn't enough. None of them had any money. They were still living on Finley Street and working day jobs. By the time they started to win a national audience, they were just sick of it. They broke up before C/Z released their second album.[68]

Michael Stipe knew everybody he wanted to know. In the late eighties, he was not just the front man for one of the most critically acclaimed bands in America. He was also an active Athens artist and collaborator, and he seemed to pop up everywhere arty and folky bands were playing including at least one Cordy Lon show.

Stipe had a fascination with documentary, going back to his own days as an art student. Combining this interest with a love for folk art, Stipe created a kind of Depression-era documentary aesthetic for R.E.M.'s 1987 album *Document* and the associated *Work* tour. In 1988, after codirecting and directing several R.E.M. videos and working on the R.E.M. compilation project *Succumbs*, the singer formed his own independent company, C-00 Film Corporation, with his friend Jim McKay, who had fallen for R.E.M. when he was a college student in Boston and then moved to Athens after he graduated. Around this time, Stipe began a project he called "field recordings," an effort to document local musicians he liked at John Keane's studio and put out some of the work on a compilation. Sessions with Hetch Hetchy and Chickasaw Mudd Puppies and Vic Chesnutt's day in the studio in October 1988 were all part of this work, as well as some Stipe solo recordings. For a while, reports circulated that Stipe would also release a solo record as part of this project. Stipe described his interest as an "almost desperate need or desire to document or capture a piece of time or history, to get it down in some way." Through his friendship with Michael Meister, one of the owners of the Santa Monica–based independent label Texas Hotel Records got involved. In 1988, they released the Hetch Hetchy material as an EP called *Make Djibouti*. But for some reason, the label sat on Vic Chesnutt's recordings until June 1990.[69]

While Stipe helped Chesnutt and Hetch Hetchy, he seemed particularly committed to the Chickasaw Mudd Puppies, a group that embodied local bohemians' love affair with rural southern "folk." Growing up in rural Wilkes County, Georgia, guitarist Ben Reynolds told a music journalist, "I just listened to country and rock 'n' roll—Lynyrd Skynyrd and Ted Nugent. That's what white kids were supposed to listen to, you know. But then I discovered Howlin' Wolf and I became obsessed." He moved to Athens in 1981 to go to art school, where he met his future bandmate Brant Slay, a sculpture major whose brother Chris Slay was friends with Michael Stipe. Reynolds studied photography. Just before he finished his degree, he got a grant to make photographs of fortune tellers. He dropped out of school to complete the project, worked at the Bluebird Café, and borrowed a guitar from his brother. Only then did he try to learn to play the music he loved in high school. He and Slay, also from rural Georgia, started inviting friends like Jim McKay and Sam Seawright to Slay's house once a week or so to drink and play the blues and other rural southern styles of acoustic music. When Michael Stipe was home, he would show up. At some point, he gave Slay a bag of old harmonicas, and the art student learned to play them. McKay made old bones, tin cans, and logs with nails into percussion instruments and also learned to play bass. Often the friends stayed up all night, singing old songs and new ones they made up, "white trash blues." They called it "juking." Sometimes their friend Jeremy Ayers joined in, and he helped write the song "Frogmore." "It was a lot of fun," Reynolds told a music journalist, "but I personally didn't like the idea of getting up on a stage in front of a lot of people. Michael's the one who convinced us to do that."[70]

Reynolds, Slay, and McKay, with prodding from Stipe, performed at the Grit and played a few gigs at clubs, including opening for the La Di Das. In a February 1988 *Flagpole* interview, Slay talked about how he spent the day of a show setting up the stage, hanging quilts on a line for a backdrop, placing objects like rusty old farm tools on the floor, and hanging sculptures he made from found objects from the ceiling. "I hate the idea of sitting up on top of a stage, being on a pedestal," he said, sounding like Vic Chesnutt; "that's just really weird and kinda scary to me." Yet instead of focusing on the words like Vic, he used what he had learned in art school and concentrated on the visual experience. "It kinda draws them into the music, the bones, there's a lot of bones." Slay usually sang lead and played percussion when he was not playing the harmonica. During shows, he sat in an old wooden rocking chair on top of a "stomp board," a wooden platform created by nailing a piece of plywood to a frame made out of two-by-fours and placing a mic under it, and he used his feet, clad in old leather work boots patched together with duct tape, and the bells he wore around one ankle to keep the beat. Jim McKay pounded on odd things and played some bass. Reynolds played guitar and sang. It did not hurt that all the guys were beautiful with their long hair hanging in their eyes and their ragged, neo-hillbilly clothes. Sometimes Reynolds wore a floppy felt hat with Pippi Longstocking braids peeking out of each side.[71]

From the start, band members as well as critics had a hard time categorizing the Mudd Puppies' music. Reynolds always acknowledged he loved the blues, but he worried that if people came out expecting a blues band, "they might be offended" or "a little bit freaked out or disappointed." Slay put it this way, "It's not blues. . . . We take our influences and inspiration and turn 'em out probably a little bit more stepped up, more rock and roll." Later, he called their style "musical gumbo" or "swamp stomp." Talking about how they came to be in a band, they sounded just like the members of that first wave of Athens musicians. As Reynolds put it, "We both started out as visual artists. We consider music, the way we're trying to approach it, as a means of expression." He also waved the banner of amateurism: "We still have a hard time considering ourselves a band." Interviewed for Jimmy Davidson's project the next fall, he explained: "I had no intention of being a guitar player and Brant had no intention of doing, uh, whatever he's doing. We were just killing time and then we were playing at parties and then we played a coffeehouse and it just snowballed."[72]

In June, the *Flagpole* reported that Texas Hotel was signing the Chicka-saw Mudd Puppies and that Jim McKay, running C-oo with Stipe, would quit the increasingly busy band. As a duo, Slay and Reynolds performed at the annual North Georgia Folk Festival that October, sharing the day-long bill with Vic Chesnutt as well as traditional folk musicians like W. Guy Bruce, Howard Finster, and Son House. Jim McKay, Jeremy Ayers, and Mamie Fike were on hand to help them record with Michael Stipe at John Keane's in late January 1989. *Flagpole* announced the record would be out in March.[73]

On the road, Michael Stipe's endorsement helped draw fans and criti-cal attention, but Texas Hotel did not offer the band a contract. Right be-fore the South by Southwest Music Festival in March, the independent label finally sent the paperwork. Not thrilled with the terms and with legal advice from their friend the local lawyer Jeff Gilley, Slay and Reynolds decided to take their chances. In Austin, representatives from record labels threw their business cards onstage as the Mudd Puppies played their showcase and fol-lowed them around afterwards. After Polygram signed them, the major label worked out a deal with Texas Hotel to release the EP *White Dirt* in 1990. Jeremy Ayers provided a drawing, and Jim McKay, thanked as "Bones" on the cover, directed the video for the single, "McIntosh."[74]

As they got ready to make their first album, Polygram asked them to imagine their dream production team. After failing to get Tom Waits, Rey-nolds, who loved Chess Records, thought of Willie Dixon, who somehow miraculously agreed. At recording sessions at Dixon's home in California, the legendary songwriter who helped shape the postwar sound of the blues even wrote a song for the duo called "Oh, Yeah." In a promotional video, Michael Stipe, coproducer on *8 Track Stomp* along with Dixon, described Slay and Reynolds as "untrained" in the way people talked then about folk and "outsider" artists. Speaking on the same video, Dixon seemed to choose his words carefully: "I like the song writing real well because it's definitely different from what's out there now, and it's definitely different from what's been out there in a long time." "If you hear a little," he insisted, "you can bet you'll want to hear some more." Unfortunately for the band, the U.S.-led coalition began bombing Kuwait, the start of the Gulf War, on the night of the New York City listening party for the new album. Despite another suc-cessful South by Southwest appearance that spring, opening for the Violent Femmes on their 1991 U.S. tour, and two dates opening for R.E.M. playing under the alias Bingo Hand Job at a club in London—all gigs packed with journalists—the Chickasaw Mudd Puppies never managed to turn their critical success into a larger audience.[75]

Formally, Slay and Reynolds simply did with old rural blues and other southern country genres understood as folk music what the members of the B-52's had done with mid-twentieth-century popular culture, a punk repurposing that blurred the line between reenactment and pop art. In a mostly white indie America not given to addressing race directly, rural southern identity worked as a stand-in for "blackness," enabling white musicians to play with "black" musical styles without being accused of stealing black music. The B-52's got away with it because they split their funky, jazzy scatting and occasional James Brown rhythms between two beautiful white women and three gay white men. But straight white boys had been playing the blues since at least the 1960s and dressing up and acting like black men on stage since the early nineteenth century. However much they knew about this history and no matter their intentions, Brant and Ben could not escape these old patterns of what the scholar Eric Lott has called "love and theft."[76]

If you wanted to offer the worst possible interpretation of the Chickasaw Mudd Puppies, you could call their performances a form of blackface, with their good looks, more hippy Jethro than Robert Johnson, distracting from the fact that this was simply a speeded-up, rawer and more bohemian version of the kind of thing John Hammond Jr. was doing in the sixties. If you wanted to make the most generous possible assessment—and many fans and critics did—the Mudd Puppies attempted to imagine and act out not just the music but a mostly forgotten and partially but not wholly imagined past in which black and white rural southerners traded licks and styles and made art together despite poverty and white supremacy. A critic for the New York Times called their shows "a theatrical simulation of an American tradition that no longer exists."[77]

Yet white-boy blues acts were possible in these years. The Black Crowes, a Marietta band that once played the Downstairs under their original name Mr. Crowe's Garden, became a mainstream kind of famous reviving seventies-era blues rock. But then they could claim white sources, an earlier generation of white male musicians who had copied black bluesmen. In indie America, playing with "black" sounds was always risky, even when you knew the right people.[78]

Firehouse

In the fall of 1986, Raymond Valley, UGA English major, music fan, participant in the Better Than TV tour, and the entertainment editor of the Red and Black, described the Athens scene as "tucked into itself, oblivious to the outside world." Even during the sixties and seventies explosion of grassroots political activism, Athens did not develop a robust organizing tradition. In 1961, when white students and locals threw bricks and bottles at the dorm where Charlayne Hunter and Hamilton Holmes, the first two African Americans admitted to UGA, lived, police quelled the riot, and the university remained open. As other Georgia cities like Albany, Savannah, and Atlanta became organizing centers, Athens remained relatively quiet with the exception of a series of protests, pickets, and "lie-ins" at the Varsity and other segregated restaurants in 1963 and 1964. A decade after the *Brown* decision, the Athens–Clarke County school district allowed seven African American students to enroll in white schools, the beginning of a slow process of school integration that lasted until 1970. While campus activism increased in the late 1960s, Athens did not develop into a center of New Left politics like other college towns including Madison, Berkeley, Ann Arbor, and even Chapel Hill.[79]

That relative quiet ended in 1970. Months of protests started in late April when African American high school students grew upset about the loss of black history and community after the school board announced the merger of the one surviving black school, Burney Harris High, with the historically white Athens High, where 120 African Americans attended classes with about 1,450 whites. A march that coincided with a string of broken windows at downtown businesses and a series of suspicious fires gave officials an excuse to call in the National Guard. Student protestor Nathaniel Fox organized a local chapter of the Southern Christian Leadership Conference, and national civil rights leaders like Hosea Williams came to town. The mayor refused to issue the protestors march permits, and hundreds were arrested. African Americans' demands expanded into a sweeping indictment of the "Athens white power structure." In May, as these antiracist protests continued, over 3,000 mostly white UGA students marched through town to express their opposition to the Vietnam War. Some of these politicized students began participating in meetings and marches to support local blacks. The protests forced Athens city officials to begin to address entrenched white racism, but the economic recessions of the seventies and early eighties that hit the local African American community hard threatened to undo any progress. In 1980 an African American minister sounded like the protestors a decade earlier when he told a reporter for the liberal Athens weekly paper, "This is a backward city. The power structure in this city is all white."[80]

When Reagan assumed office, most local Athens activists were middle-aged folks politicized by their participation in earlier civil rights and antiwar protests, plus a few younger activists inspired by their example. Michael

Thurmond, who grew up in Athens and graduated in 1971 from Clarke Central High, the school created out of the Burney Harris–Athens High merger, moved back to town in the late 1970s to practice law and continue his earlier activism. In 1986, he became the first African American to represent the area in the Georgia General Assembly since Reconstruction. Ed Tant, who had been writing a political column for local papers since 1974, continued his work as a journalist and as a founder and organizer of the Athens Human Rights Festival, an annual event started in 1979 to mark the deaths of the Kent State activists. After working for the Red Cross in Vietnam during the war and holding other state government and nonprofit jobs in the area of human and social services, Gwen O'Looney moved to Athens in 1980 to serve as director of Neighbors as Helpers, an organization that advocated for the residents of Athens' public housing developments. Later, she helped found Community Connection and secured the grants that established Project Safe and the Athens Area Homeless Shelter. In 1984 O'Looney ran for the chance to represent the Fifth Ward on the Athens City Council. She based her campaign on her liberal social service record and her strong support for historic preservation and won.

In the larger Athens community, Reagan's election sparked a renewal of local activism. Civil rights activists, former antiwar activists, and environmentalists came together in the Northeast Georgia Peace Delegation, formed as part of a nuclear freeze movement that tried to persuade the United States and the Soviet Union to stop building more nuclear weapons. In the spring of 1983, locals packed City Hall to debate whether the city council should vote to support the freeze as activists across the nation prepared for a rally in Washington. Opponents of the movement, including then UGA student and future Christian Coalition leader Ralph Reed, faced off against supporters, including many UGA professors. In the end, a relatively conservative city council adopted a compromise resolution in support of vague actions to promote peace rather than the freeze movement. Despite this setback, local environmentalists grew more active, supported by UGA students and some faculty, including the staff of the pioneering Odum Institute of Ecology. The town's relative proximity to the Department of Energy's nuclear facilities at the Savannah River Plant, where a whistleblower was fired in 1985, helped create new alliances between environmentalists and other voters opposed to Reagan's militarism.

When the Human Rights Festival moved downtown to College Square and began booking local bands, the two-day spring event created new connections between scene participants and left activism. On Friday, hippie carpenters like Ken Starratt of the Squalls would build a temporary stage where College Avenue dead-ended into Broad Street across from UGA. Saturday morning, activists lined the closed street with tables and signs and set up stacks of pins and pamphlets. Beginning around lunchtime Saturday and continuing through Sunday, scene participants and music fans would mingle with both original and second wave hippies and an older generation of activists. An art auction would sell work by local artists to support that year's cause. Alternative bands, folk musicians, and jam bands would perform. As these musicians set up and hauled away their equipment, speakers representing progressive and environmental organizations provided a crash course in left and progressive politics for bohemians, music lovers, and young hippies alike.[81]

Among issues increasingly becoming a focus of local politics, only historic preservation did not share these common New Left roots. As development projects threatened historic houses and entire neighborhoods in the sixties, concerned residents founded the Athens-Clarke Heritage Foundation (ACHF) to preserve historically and architecturally significant local structures. In many areas of the South, whites with ties to old elite families led preservation efforts. While many local preservationists were not Athens natives and did not have personal family ties to the wealthy whites who built most of the structures they were working to save, they still shared a fairly narrow definition of "heritage." ACHF was not created until after "Project 50," the first of two major urban renewal programs in town, was completed, destroying a mixed income African American neighborhood called by planners "a slum" in order to make way for UGA's new high rise dorms Creswell, Russell, and Brumby, my own first-year residence hall. Many white locals considered this progress. Instead, it was the second renewal plan called Project 51, the scheduled destruction of a part of town that included the antebellum Lickskillet neighborhood, that spurred local preservationists to organize to save one of the oldest surviving Athens houses, the Church-Waddell-Brumby House.

Preservation work continued in the 1970s as activists fought businesses and churches who wanted to tear down antebellum and Victorian homes and other historic structures. Leading Athens preservationist and UGA history professor Phinizy Spalding did have family ties to elite antebellum Athens families, and he worked to save the buildings of the Lucy Cobb Institute including the chapel named after one of his relatives where R.E.M. filmed their scenes for *Athens, GA: Inside/Out*. Yet he and his wife Margie Spalding also fought to save Cobbham, a close-in neighborhood of antebellum and

Victorian houses and newer bungalows west of downtown where they had bought and restored a home, from the combined onslaught of Athens Regional Hospital, now Piedmont Athens Regional, at one end and Prince Avenue Baptist Church at the other. Despite getting the neighborhood listed on the National Register of Historic Places in 1977, the fight continued. The next year, a flyer urged locals to turn out for a picket of the Prince Avenue Baptist Church one April Sunday. "Do you want your children to grow up next door to a parking lot?," the caption under a photograph of a partially demolished Victorian asked.[82]

Most bohemians knew little about this local history until the late 1980s. Having grown up with the self-righteousness of the sixties generation, early scene participants like 40 Watt founder and Pylon drummer Curtis Crowe expressed disillusionment with politics. Members of R.E.M. actively criticized the practice of mixing music and activism. As Mike Mills wrote in *Spin* in 1985, "if you want to think about youth culture as one spearhead that's gonna make a difference in the world, it's not gonna happen." "Any rock star who thinks he's gonna make a big difference is deluded." Yet that same year, R.E.M. took Greenpeace representatives along on their *Reconstruction* tour to educate fans and performed benefits for hunger relief and LEAF, the Legal Environmental Assistance Foundation of Georgia. Touring overseas where fans and journalists often critiqued President Reagan and his policies pushed Buck, Stipe, Berry and Mills to think more about U.S. policies. Stipe has also credited Natalie Merchant of 10,000 Maniacs with awakening his interest in politics and inspiring him to write his first political songs. In 1986, band members publicly supported Wyche Fowler, a Georgia Democrat who ran for the U.S. Senate as an environmentalist and won. Over the following years, the members of R.E.M. played benefits and provided other support for organizations working on the environment, poverty, and other issues.[83]

In the mid-eighties, Chris DeBarr had been the rare scene participant who was also a well-informed political radical. By the end of the decade, DeBarr, the first foodie I ever knew as well as a committed left activist, began to look like a trendsetter rather than a time traveler from another era. Under assault on multiple fronts, a bohemian brand of political apathy cracked wide open. Grassroots politics, just like DIY bands and installation art and hip businesses, might just be an option for alternative kids, too. In Athens, an indie Left emerged and grew and formed alliances with older New Left and civil rights activists and preservationists. And these developments occurred across the bohemian diaspora.

Benefit concerts and art auctions worked like a gateway drug, an easy path for combining what we were doing anyway—listening to and performing music and making art—with learning about and supporting worthwhile causes. By the late 1980s, bands played benefits frequently for national as well as local nonprofit organizations working on issues from AIDS and domestic violence to homelessness and the environment. Less frequent but not uncommon were benefits that functioned like Kickstarter or GoFundMe, including the art sales and performances that bailed out the Better Than TV tour and the Grit. Michael Stipe helped Michael Collins, one of the main people running the Human Rights Festival, organize the September 1989 Athens Music Festival to benefit an Athens resident without health insurance who had suffered a violent knife attack. The Chickasaw Mudd Puppies, Vic Chesnutt, Mercyland, and other local bands performed in a packed one-day schedule headlined by Stipe and his friends from Atlanta, the Indigo Girls and then Love Tractor. No cause went without a show. In March 1988, Cordy Lon joined Long Low Rumble and the Mudd Puppies onstage at the Rockfish for an evening billed as a "Benefit for Mamie's Violin" after our friend Quinton Phillips accidently stepped on the instrument at a practice. Benefits were a relatively easy type of participation, a way for artists and musicians to contribute to their community and also perhaps gain an audience for the work beyond their usual circle of friends.[84]

Even the band that started the scene, the B-52's, played a benefit on their *Cosmic Thing* comeback tour, a University Union–sponsored, Legion Field concert that raised funds for the Athens Community Council on Aging. Yet many scene participants skipped the show, uninterested in the music or unwilling or unable to pay the high ticket prices, $5 for students and $10 for nonstudents, or not on the guest list for the 40 Watt invitation-only after-party. At the Downstairs, we celebrated our second birthday that same night with a packed crowd of regulars, $1 Rolling Rocks, and music by Irish music band Gan Ainm and an opening band from Nashville. No one we knew went to see the B-52's.[85]

In Athens then, the Christian Right was not an abstraction. It took concrete form in decisions about alcohol and club hours made by Christian politicians at the local and state level and in the expansion of conservative Christian churches. In 1986 scene participants joined preservationists in fighting Prince Avenue Baptist Church's plan to put up an enormous broadcasting tower in Cobbham, where many scene participants rented and, increasingly, owned houses. I remember attending city council meetings where R.E.M.'s lawyer Bertis Downs and Michael Stipe spoke in opposition. For many of us, this effort was our first foray into local politics. The church lost. Two years later, Mayor Dwane Chambers, a Prince Avenue Baptist Church deacon and the owner of a Christian bookstore as well as a dry-cleaners, and his city council allies passed a law banning open containers of alcohol in the central business district with loopholes that meant on game days, UGA football fans would be exempt. As plans for a downtown civic center progressed, scene participants upset about the potential loss of Athens Firehall No. 1 built in 1912 and much of the old warehouse district down to the Oconee River fought back against the same conservative officials. After Michael Stipe learned that the city did not have the funds to pay for a study of the proposed civic center's impact on historic downtown, he talked to R.E.M.'s lawyer Bertis Downs, who figured out how R.E.M. Ltd. could donate the needed funding. The band's $5,000 grant paid for the report and also supported a local design symposium organized by the National Trust for Historic Preservation.[86]

As the conflict between the local Christian Right and liberals and leftists increased, *Flagpole* volunteers like David Levitt and Jim McKay kept readers informed about the issues. In one article, McKay praised Lester Bangs's article "The White Noise Supremacists," pushed a new compilation album of South African music, and signed off by urging readers to "boycott grapes. Give a dollar. Don't worship." If hip Jim McKay, Michael Stipe's friend and collaborator and sometime member of the Mudd Puppies, could talk about politics even in his music reviews, the scene had come a long way from the *Tasty World* days. Athens bohemians could now be activists.[87]

Some of the credit for this change belongs to Dennis Greenia, who had worked on the *Flagpole* from his position at Java Print Shop and then took on a bigger role beginning in January 1989. That year the paper became a weekly with its own office and telephone number and actual paid staff members. Dennis, a former hippie with experience in left-wing activism as well as printing and journalism, had become disillusioned with national politics after the election of Reagan. The only place to make change, he told me and anyone else who would listen, was at the local level. Under his leadership, *Flagpole*'s announcements about voter registration procedures, locations, and deadlines grew larger. Coverage of political issues expanded. And owner and editor Jared "Mr. Pole" Bailey wrote more frequent editorials. Scene members and their allies won a battle known as the "dance hall hours fight" allowing clubs to stay open after local laws forced them to stop serving alcohol. Bailey summed up *Flagpole*'s mission in an April 1989 editorial: "The rag runs an ad just trying to let all of you out there know that it is VERY SIMPLE to register to vote. We also shoot off at the mouth all the time to try to goad you to participate in the democratic process so you can be counted as a viable segment of the population — right alongside members of the Prince Avenue Baptist Church and the rest of the 'real' citizens of Athens." After praising readers for using their "political muscle" to protect their right to dance, he asked them to go one step further and "take a more active role in our community."[88]

By the end of 1990, the indie Left had become an influential local political bloc, but the year began with a string of losses. It was still winter when developers tore down all but the steeple of St. Mary's Church on Oconee Street, a historic chapel built for mill workers in 1871 that had more recently been the site of R.E.M.'s debut performance. Scene participants turned out for hearings on the creation of the Hull Street Historic District to protect the remaining houses in the city's oldest surviving neighborhood from the Christian College of Georgia, a small Disciples of Christ school then selling off parcels of its campus to fund classes for a tiny number of students. At one of these events, a gray-haired grandmotherly woman spoke to me with tears in her eyes. Taking in my vintage hat, belted fifties dress, and steel-toe work boots, she said, "I don't know where you people are from, but thank God you're here." After months of debate, Mayor Chambers broke the council's tie vote to deny the Hull Street designation. As preservationists scrambled to find someone to buy the 150-year-old Greek Revival Hull-Snelling house, the college brought in a bulldozer one morning at daybreak and began ripping down the structure and most of the surrounding trees, including a more-than-a-century-old magnolia. The Holiday Inn had agreed to purchase the empty land in order to build an overflow parking lot. It looked like Firehall No. 1 and the old warehouses that housed the Athens Flea Market and other businesses would be next.[89]

That summer, the indie Left, preservationists, and other liberals and leftists saw the vote on whether or not to unify the city and county governments as a way to throw out the despised mayor and his city council allies. Social worker and nonprofit administrator O'Looney, a liberal member of the city council representing many of the city's historic districts, ran against four conservative white businessmen to head up the new unified government. Scene participants rallied behind her. Kathy Kirbo, guitarist for Greenhouse and also *Flagpole* and 40 Watt owner Jared Bailey's partner, put her music on hold to run O'Looney's campaign. For the first time in my life, I knocked on doors and made phone calls for a candidate. Pete Buck, Michael Stipe, Bill Berry, and Mike Mills, plus R.E.M. manager Jefferson Holt and lawyer Bertis Downs, each gave O'Looney $1,000. The Chickasaw Mudd Puppies played a benefit complete with a buffet dinner at the Grit. *Flagpole* delivered in-depth political coverage in the two months before the election, including a twenty-five-page spread in its October 31, 1990, issue in which candidates for all open positions answered a series of thoughtful questions. The local political establishment had no idea what hit them. How could these scruffy kids actually raise money and vote? After O'Looney topped the field, earning a slot in a run-off against E. H. Culpepper, the third-place finisher George Bullock described her support as "the woman, minority, preservationist and hippie vote." O'Looney embraced the label, and I bought a t-shirt with this slogan at her headquarters, her Cobb Street house two doors down from mine.[90]

In late November, local scene participant Monty Greene urged all *Flagpole* readers to participate in the process:

> Get back out there and vote in the run-off. If Gwen loses because
> of complacency, we all lose. The same people who don't go and vote
> will be the ones who bitch when the conservative, Baptist, intolerant,
> backward, establishment politicians continue to run their lives. What
> looks like left wing rhetorical garbage on a flagpole [*sic*] editorial
> page, translates to expensive tickets for open containers, early closing
> hours for clubs, strip malls and parking lots instead of carefully
> managed growth, overpriced civic centers that look like cement
> blocks and a dual set of standards for the underground, hippie music
> crowd and Baptist, football, police establishment crowd. You take
> your pick, throw down your vote or shut your mouth.

We all knew that we had helped put Athens on the cultural map, made it famous for something besides football and UGA. When O'Looney won the run-off, we finally had some political power to go with this cultural power. With our allies, the indie Left had figured out how to beat the Christians and the developers and the rednecks. In the thirteen years since the B-52's played a Valentine's Day party at a house on Milledge and showed UGA students and other residents that they could make their own music, everything about the town — the culture, the landscape, and now the politics — had changed. Athens was ours.[91]

There's an intimacy to wholeheartedly loving a place, a physical experience, a fusion. In downtown Athens then, I knew every cracked sidewalk and narrow back alley and flaking brick facade. Losing any part of this landscape, any one of the old buildings still standing, felt like losing a family member.

Late at night, after working until closing at the Downstairs or seeing a band there or at another club, I would head home on my old three-speed bike, cutting diagonally through bank and church parking lots and jumping the seams in the pavement that mapped old boundaries and the foundations of buildings already gone. The wind would cool the sweat of dancing or mopping. The chrome fenders would rattle. The basket would squeak. And jarred by the motion, the rusty bell would let out a series of little dings. Even my bike made music then, a love song of course, the story of a young woman and the place where she learned to make history.

CONCLUSION

Hunting Divine

He is for an expanding whole.

Oh-OK, "Brother" (1982)

In the summer of 1991, I left Athens to begin a PhD program in history at Rutgers University in New Jersey. About 100 alternative bands already worked out of Athens then, and new participants were always arriving. That year, Jeff Mangum and other members of a loose collective of musicians that called themselves the Elephant Six Recording Company began moving to town from Ruston, Louisiana. Once in Athens, these and other newcomers mixed with each other and with veteran participants like David Barbe.[1]

I first met David in 1985 when he was playing bass and singing as the front man of Mercyland, his band that made Buzzcocks-inspired punk almost a decade before Green Day released *Dookie*. When I interviewed him about a quarter of a century later, he still lived in Athens, where he performed and recorded his own music, including a 2017 solo album *10th of Seas* released on the local label Orange Twin Records. He also owned and ran an important Athens recording studio, Chase Park Transduction, and had produced important local acts like the Drive-By Truckers. More recently, he had taken the job of directing UGA's music business program, founded in 2006 as the university moved to formalize its role in nurturing the scene.

Barbe estimated that around 600 bands lived and worked in Athens in the 2010s. Although no other local musicians had rivaled R.E.M.'s fame, Vic Chesnutt, Neutral Milk Hotel, Widespread Panic, and the Drive-By Truckers had all achieved some measure of national success — critical acclaim, sales, or even both. Four decades after the B-52's debuted, Athens musicians played hip-hop and alt country as well as all varieties of alternative rock. Audiences were more racially integrated, too. In Barbe's opinion — and it was his business to know — the scene had never been better. Older musicians like Don Chambers, Kelly Noonan, Bob Hay, and Barbe himself still per-formed. Vanessa Briscoe Hay had created a band called the Pylon Reenact-ment Society to perform her former band's songs. And participants in the nineties wave of music-making, like the second Laura Carter and Andrew Rieger of Elf Power, had stayed in town where even younger musicians who moved to Athens to go to UGA or for the fabled scene joined them. Old net-works of bands and friends came apart as people moved away or got busy with careers and kids, but new ones always formed, enriched by the history of all that had come before.[2]

An Athens resident for more than three decades, Barbe criticized the nostalgia of participants who had a tendency to see the "real scene" as their circle of friends and the bands they created and loved and to think that everything ended when they left town. These veterans, he insisted, just did not know how to navigate the changing creative landscape of the place they left behind.

Jeremy Ayers, the town's most influential bohemian, agreed. Right up until the moment he died of complications related to a seizure in 2016, Jeremy refused to talk about the past. Instead, he continued to mentor younger artists and musicians and connect them with his older friends like Jennifer Hartley and Jill Carnes.[3]

As the scene grew, major political transitions occurred in the town and the nation. In January 1991, Gwen O'Looney, a former social worker and pro-gressive member of the city council, took the oath of office as the new CEO of the unified government of Athens-Clarke County. At last, local bohemians lived under a government that saw as the scene as an asset rather than a prob-lem. The progressive coalition's victory in Athens grew out of local issues, but it also connected with battles against the new right being waged in other places across the country. Global political relationships shifted that year too as America's longtime foe the Soviet Union broke apart, ending the Cold War that had dominated U.S. relations with other nations since the end of World War II. A year later, Americans elected Democrat Bill Clinton presi-dent. For most of us, our adult lives had been spent in what felt like political exile. Over the span of a few years, that Athens sense that anything was pos-sible expanded to include local and even national politics, too.

In 1991, R.E.M. almost had it all. Long the most important college-rock act in the country, our scene's most famous band had earned critical praise and a growing national fan base, made hit records, and won a fat, major-label deal. Only one thing eluded them at that moment: a global mass audi-ence. After releasing *Out of Time* in March, Buck, Stipe, Mills, and Berry announced that they were tired of the road and would stay home that year instead of touring, a move so counter to music industry norms that it seemed designed to halt their ascent and preserve whatever connection to the underground they still retained. In May, the members of R.E.M. were sitting in a packed city hall auditorium with many other scene participants for yet another meeting about the fate of a historic, downtown Athens firehouse. Halfway through the event, Katherine Downs, the wife of their lawyer, Bertis Downs, came in to tell them that *Billboard* had called. The band's second album for Warner Brothers had become the number one album in America.[4]

Over the next year, *Out of Time* went platinum, earned seven Grammy nominations and three wins, and spawned multiple hits. In partnership with Rock the Vote, band members had even figured out how to use the dreaded long-box CD packaging that as environmentalists they hated. Record buyers could cut out, sign, and mail the postcard printed on the back of the box to urge their senators to make voter registration easier by supporting the Motor Voter Act. Three weeks after the album's release, Rock the Vote reported that its office had received thousands of postcards. An official for the organization dumped a cart full of them onto the floor of a Senate hearing. Michael Stipe also made a PSA for Rock the Vote urging young people to call the president: "It's your turn to make history." And R.E.M. did. Always an outsider to the band's early cult following, *Village Voice* music critic Robert Christgau fell hard for *Out of Time*. The album, he wrote, was filled with beauty, like "*Murmur* without walls . . . one of those alternative worlds that music is supposed to create for us."[5]

In the summer of 1991, the single "Losing My Religion" seemed to take over the world. A critically acclaimed video fused surreal fragments including footage of band members in retro-looking clothes, splinters of an Icarus story, and images that looked like reenactments of grand master paintings. On heavy rotation at MTV and elsewhere, it drove the single to what would be R.E.M.'s career high in the United States, number four on the *Billboard* Hot 100. Michael Stipe had used the old southern phrase that gave the song its title to suggest the depths of his narrator's feelings, a colloquial way of saying love makes you crazy. People around the world heard it as an affirmation of human survival. During a coup attempt against Mikhail Gorbachev that August, you could hear "Losing My Religion" all over Moscow, soaring through the open windows of apartments and the doors of stores and telling everyone that life continued even as the things you thought were permanent slipped away.[6]

Out of Time sounded like R.E.M.'s big-budget version of Vic Chesnutt's idea of little. Buck's mandolin part on "Losing My Religion" set the tone for the rest of the album. Acoustic instruments created a lush and romantic sound, that ever-present mandolin plus acoustic guitar, double bass, cello, violin, viola, harpsichord, saxophone, clarinet, and even flugelhorn. In the poetic "Half a World Away," the melancholic "Country Feedback," and the sunny "Shiny, Happy People," rock anthems from 1988's *Green* turned soft and melodic. And though the attempt fell flat, R.E.M.'s collaboration with rapper KRS-One seems at least to acknowledge the problematic whiteness of much alternative rock.[7]

In contrast to grunge, a Seattle scene journalists were calling the new Athens, and Nirvana's 1991 release *Nevermind*, R.E.M. had staked out a distinct sonic territory, a slower and quieter clutch of retro gestures and an anything but angry tone. As always, scene participants disagreed in their reactions to R.E.M.'s sound. Depending on your perspective, *Out of Time* had either failed or succeeded brilliantly. Band members had either sold out, or they had taken Athens and the alternative genre local musicians had helped create right into the center of American culture. *Out of Time* and the following year's *Automatic for the People* showed just how much the local scene nourished Buck, Stipe, Berry and Mills, and it wasn't just the soul food at Weaver D.'s. As Stipe in particular acknowledged in interviews, Athens people challenged and inspired him.[8]

Many locals thought R.E.M. had long stopped being an alternative act, but the massive success of *Out of Time* was an altogether different beast, and the band's new fame made the town into a kind of global stage. Because band members had decided not to tour behind the new album, journalists traveled to Athens to interview them and often included details about the place and other local musicians. Occasionally, Buck and sometimes Stipe and Mills popped up on local stages to play a song or two with friends or turned up at bars or other happenings. Sometimes the whole band played under an alias.[9]

Local venues also grew. Kyle Pilgrim had already taken over the Georgia Theater and turned it into a music club and then shut down the Uptown Lounge. After Pete Buck bought the old Potter's House Thrift Store building downtown, his wife Barrie Buck, by then the sole owner of the 40 Watt, moved Athens's oldest club into that large space. Local recording studios also expanded as Mills, Stipe, and Buck recorded demos and produced local and out of town bands. John Keane's Cobbham studio stayed booked, so Stipe took Vic Chesnutt instead to Scott Stuckey's place in a house on Boulevard to record a new batch of songs that June. Everything R.E.M. touched then got press attention, and they generously carried the town along with them as their fame soared. The band labeled a few years before "the voice of the New South" became an international symbol of an alternative American culture.[10]

Participation in the scene changed Robbie Ethridge's life as much as it did the members of R.E.M. Not a typical Athens bohemian, she grew up in Georgia in a working-class family in which no one went to college. In high school, she worked in a hospital kitchen and became close to two classmates who would go on to college. One of them went to the University of Georgia. Hearing them talk and then visiting her friend at UGA, she fell in love with the whole idea of college, and after working for a year at Red Lobster, she enrolled. College was affordable because her dad had died when she was a baby, and she got a couple hundred dollars a month from Social Security until she reached her twenty-second birthday. She also got a federal Basic Education Opportunity Grant (BEOG, later renamed the Pell Grant) that helped pay for her tuition and books. At UGA, she worked at KFC, then in the campus cafeteria, and later in the archeology lab. Her mother earned minimum wage, but she gave her $5 when she could.[11]

The scene was just getting started when Robbie graduated Phi Beta Kappa in 1978 with a major in anthropology. Over the next two years, she traveled around the country as an "archeology bum," working on digs, but she kept an apartment in Athens. When she was in town, a friend would call her up late at night to see if she wanted to hit Tyrone's or the 40 Watt. She saw most of the bands of that era: Pylon and R.E.M., the Side Effects and Oh-OK. She loved the dancing. To her, all the music just seemed to come out of nowhere, creating a welcome alternative to the hippies. After scene participants Carol Levy and Larry Marcus died in that car crash in 1983, she felt like the atmosphere got a little darker. When her mom died, too, about a year later, she felt she needed to get away. In love with the idea of bohemian Paris in the 1920s, she and Bill Georgia, a friend from the scene, moved to France. He left after six months, but she stayed a little over a year, working under the table for a publishing company run by expatriate Israelis.[12]

When she moved back to Athens, Robbie found that what she had been looking for in Paris existed right there at home. Trying to explain what was happening, a friend told her, "We are all young, beautiful, smart, and talented." Robbie discovered that "everything was art, and everything was exciting." "All those crazy, nutty wonderful artist types" filled the town, and she was there, "on the edge, soaking it all in." She had long been friends with art student Tina Whatley, but after Paris she met a whole new group of people, Vic Chesnutt and the Downstairs crowd. For a while, Robbie dated Watt

King, a visual artist who was also a founder of and key participant in the Rat and Duck Playhouse. When Robbie rented an apartment in a big house on Grady with Tina and another artist friend, Dundy Dunderville, Watt suggested the place was perfect for an art exhibition. A few days before the three moved in, Watt and Robbie told everyone they knew to bring their work by the house on Saturday morning. And everyone did, including important local artists like Sam Seawright and Jennifer Hartley. Then Robbie and Watt spent a few hours hanging the work. That night, they threw a huge party so everyone could see the show.[13]

During these years, Robbie began working as an office manager at a local research firm called Southeastern Archeology. Her coworkers Jean Spencer and Melissa Selby wanted to form a band. While Jean and Melissa had dabbled on guitar, none of them really played. When another friend, Gwyneth Duncan, was able to borrow a kit, she became their drummer. That left the bass for Robbie. It was a classic Athens story. "We are living proof anybody can be in a band." An all-girl group, they decided to call themselves 28 Days. Later, after Duncan quit, Mark Cooper Smith took over as their drummer because they knew him from UGA's anthropology department.[14]

Of course, the inevitable happened. After only a few practices, someone asked them to play a party, and even though they could not really play their instruments, they agreed. Everyone in town was so supportive. When they finally performed at a club in 1988, they got a great slot opening for the Indigo Girls. They loved playing the Downstairs, because they "made tons of money" and could pack the place. Robbie's best friend Tina would come, and together they would carry Vic and his wheelchair down the steep stairs. 28 Days developed a local following, and the songs they recorded got some airplay on WUOG. But band members all had day jobs they liked and did not want to travel. None of them were "ambitious enough to really do the hard work of making it."[15]

Then Melissa Selby moved, and the band split up, and Robbie decided she needed to do something with her life. If she could learn to play a bass onstage while in a band, surely she could do other things, too. She had already earned an MA in historical anthropology at UGA. How hard could a PhD program be? Robbie even found a new local band — Mrs. Atkins — to play in while completing her degree. In 1997, she finally left Athens for good to move to Oxford for a job as an assistant professor of anthropology at the University of Mississippi. Now an internationally recognized expert on the history of indigenous people in North America, Robbie Ethridge still thinks about her scholarship as her creative work, her chosen artistic medium.[16]

Working on my UGA history M.A. thesis at home on Cobb Street in the spring of 1991. Participating in the scene made me feel like I was making history as well as studying it. (Author's possession)

Like Robbie, what I did in the scene—creating and running a business and playing in a local band—gave me the confidence to think that I could be a scholar. In 1991 David and I sold the Downstairs to our cook Chris DeBarr and Andrew Cayce, Robbie's bandmate in Mrs. Atkins. Cordy Lon played a last gig, a benefit for a local environmental organization on the banks of the Broad River. In mid-August, friends threw us a hell of a going away party, and Vic rolled around our Cobb Street yard drinking shots of vodka followed by shots of Cointreau and telling everyone he had invented a new drink called an electric screwdriver. Hungover, David and I filled a Ryder truck with antique furniture, crates of books and records, vintage clothes, musical instruments, our own and our friends' art, and other mementos of our life in Athens. The next morning we put our three sedated cats in carriers in the cab, attached our car to a tow dolly, and set out on the thirteen-hour drive to New Jersey. I cried until well after we passed the Gaffney Peach. In the years ahead, I learned a lot about the snobbery of Americans with elite educations. They did not think southerners could create anything but folk music either, so I just kept studying.[17]

Starting graduate school, I completely missed the publication of Rodger Brown's book about the first five years of the Athens scene, *Party Out of*

Bounds. In the late eighties, an editor at Penguin heard someone who was friends with members of the B-52's telling stories about Athens at a party and thought that a book about the town would sell. The editor asked music journalist Karen Moline for suggestions. Moline called Vanessa Briscoe Hay, who knew Brown from when he had worked for her at Kinko's. By then, Brown had moved to Atlanta, where he wrote for the alternative weekly *Creative Loafing*. He was an odd choice. By his own admission, he was not interested in music, but he knew the right people, including his sometime roommate and close friend John Seawright and Sandi Phipps, a former girlfriend of R.E.M. manager Jefferson Holt and the band's longtime office manager who Brown dated and lived with for a few years. He told himself, "You're cutting your own throat to do this," but he took the $12,000 contract anyway because he wanted to write.[18]

Brown says he approached his manuscript as a mashup of his two favorite books, *Absalom, Absalom!* and *Let Us Now Praise Famous Men*. Trying to recreate the feel of the place, he used "poetic license" to set up the atmosphere and build a "fast-paced" narrative. While the arrival of Matthew Sweet in town and the breakup of Pylon both actually happened in 1983, for him they also worked as "narrative devices" to mark the end of his story. Athens music was the "obligatory stuff" he had to include to "conjure up my dreamscape — exploration and adventure." He wanted to tell a story of southern kids learning to live decadent, bohemian lives.[19]

Changing editors delayed publication for a couple of years, and Brown believed this timing accounted for his low sales, that the Athens moment had passed. Within the scene, the book's reception was mixed, much like that of the documentary *Athens, GA: Inside/Out*. Some people were mad about the way they were included, and others were angry that they were left out. It did not help that journalists following R.E.M. around in the wake of *Out of Time* did not mention the book, and the major music magazines declined to publish an excerpt. Brown went to graduate school at Emory, earned a PhD in American Studies, and continued to work as a writer. A few years later, an out-of-print *Party Out of Bounds* began picking up readers, music fans eager to understand an earlier Athens. Brown has now republished it twice.[20]

L ike Rodger Brown, Vic Chesnutt seemed poised on the cusp of greater fame, and yet he struggled. Trying to stay off drugs and recover from his father's death, the singer-songwriter had moved to Venice Beach for a few months in 1990. His successful shows at McCabe's Guitar Shop in Santa Monica inspired Texas Hotel to stop sitting on his

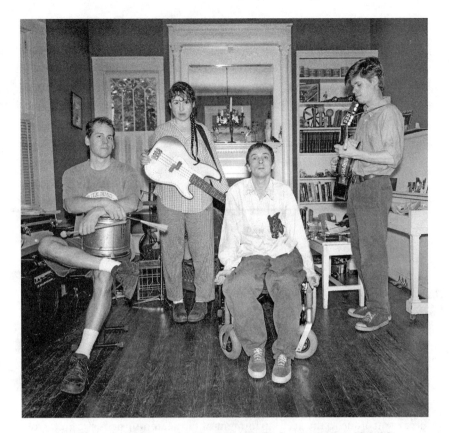

Vic Chesnutt poses in his first Franklin Street home with his wife and bass player, Tina Whatley Chesnutt, drummer Jimmy Davidson, guitarist Alex McManus, and the piano on which he wrote many of his songs. (Photograph by Carl Martin)

1988 recordings, and the label finally released *Little*. An Athens friend, Tina Whatley, who had played banjo in the Athens alt-country group the El Caminos, went to California to visit him. Driving back across the country together in June so Vic could play the 40 Watt club's anniversary party, the pair shocked all their friends by getting married at a Texas truck stop.

That fall, Vic toured relentlessly, often working as a solo opening act for Bob Mould. Mostly he performed newer tunes that would wind up on his second album, *West of Rome*, songs about California and women betraying him and drinking and as always dying. The recordings have a brighter, fuller sound than the cuts on his first album, with guitar and drums and bass and sometimes keyboards and even violin and cello parts. But the message remains bleak. On "Lucinda Williams," he warbles, "Oh, convenient lies, rubber knives / I'm a dastardly villain, doing belly dives / I before E except after me / I'm dowsing my vitals at break-neck speed." On "Stupid Preoccupations," he crows, "I am sick of you / Expecting me to do / All these puny ingratiations / You know I am a terrible patient / I am barely alive / Ever since my daddy died." On "Sponge," Vic croons,

> Pleasure is melting like chocolate
> my blue ribbon gumption is gone
> all my gravy has soaked into something . . .
>
> Throughout this entire ugly outing
> I've been mumbling the convex of what I should be shouting
> But I'll soon be silent you'll soon hear nothing
> 'cause the world, world it is a sponge.

Life takes everything you've got, Vic sings, sucks it all up and leaves you dry. All that is left is the act of expression.[21]

In "Florida," a song about a person Vic knew who killed himself with a nail gun, the darkness thickens. "A man must take his life in his own hands / Hit those nails on the head," he sings. "And I respect a man who goes to where he wants to be / Even if he wants to be dead. / Florida, Florida . . . there's no more perfect place to retire from life."[22]

On the road alone, it must have been hard, singing his guts out night after night alone to the accompaniment of his beaten-up acoustic guitar, reliving old despair in front of Bob Mould's fans. Vic's romanticism about art did not help. John Chelew, the booker at McCabe's, remembered the way the musician sometimes sabotaged his own performances. "He would be doing something beautiful and then just purposefully stop. And he would consider that to be an artistic moment. That served him well at first, and then it started to get in his way."[23]

In mid-November, as the Athens musician chased Mould's bus to the next gig, his battered van broke down outside of Albany, New York. A weary Vic tried to hang himself from the wheelchair lift inside the vehicle. A law enforcement officer spotted the van beside the road and stopped to investigate. Knocking on the window, the policeman told Vic he could not kill himself there. Then the cop loaded the musician and his wheelchair into the police car, drove into the city, and left Vic at the Albany Mission, a homeless shelter run by the Salvation Army in a historic building next to the train station. The sign on the front said it all: "The wages of sin are death." For three or four days, Vic lived at the mission without calling his wife Tina or Bob

In the mid-nineties, Vic Chesnutt seemed to be on the cusp of greater fame. (Photograph by Carl Martin)

Mould. Somehow, in the company of homeless men, he found a renewed will to live.[24]

The Athens scene worked pretty well for Vic Chesnutt, until it didn't. There would be other suicide attempts and lesser acts of sabotage, including an overdose in 1994 when he was performing in Europe. In March 1997, in the midst of his nationwide tour in support of his major-label debut on Capitol, the aptly titled *About to Choke*, he drove off in the van stranding Tina and his then drummer Jimmy Davidson in Minneapolis without their wallets and luggage. Tina had to call a friend collect and ask him to wire money. Only later did she and Jimmy find out that Vic had driven to St. Louis. It was either there or in a similar episode in Jacksonville, Florida, the town in which Vic's birth parents gave him up for adoption, that the musician spent three days sitting in his wheelchair at the side of the pool with rocks in his pockets thinking about rolling himself in.

In December 2009, after putting out the brilliant album *At the Cut* and again reaching the cusp of some kind of greater fame, Vic fell into another deep depression. He and Tina had separated by then, but he actually reached out for help and finally agreed to check himself into a facility. Because he had no medical insurance, a friend who wanted to remain anonymous arranged to pay a deposit to secure him a space. Still, delays continued because the facility did not have a vehicle equipped to handle a person in a wheelchair. While he waited, he swallowed too many drugs and went into a coma. Once again, his atheist life fell into a biblical pattern. He died on Christmas Day.[25]

N either Vic nor the scene he loved was easy. Yet somehow, looking back, many former participants and journalists try to jam the messiness into a story with a neat rise and fall arc. The effort usually reveals more about what people choose to remember and forget about their younger selves than it does about Athens.

Most visibly, the scene changed the way the town looked. Gradually, musicians, artists, professors, and others renovated the historic houses and commercial buildings we were able to save. Scene participants scraped together down payments and bought old homes near downtown, including Michael Stipe on Grady, Pete Buck on Hill, Tom Cheek on Boulevard, Jeremy Ayers on Meigs, Jennifer Hartley on Cleveland, and David and me on Cobb.

But the historic preservation movement and the growth of Atlanta played a much more powerful role than bohemians in Athens's slow process of gentrification. The completion of state highway 316 made Athens with its "real" town center attractive as a bedroom community for people who worked on the east side of the metropolitan area and were tired of the suburban nowhere-land of Lawrenceville or Snellville. People who bought "in town" tended to renovate once subdivided, older houses back to their original status as single-family homes. The number of apartments in old neighborhoods began to decrease and rents for homes and practices spaces and studios in and near downtown increased. Scene folks and more conventional middle-class Athens residents responded by pushing into historic working-class neighborhoods, first in the area around Nantahala Avenue and on Pulaski Street and Cleveland Avenue where they rented small bungalows and wood-frame cottages and later on the other side of the Oconee from downtown, in the old mill workers' and managers' houses around the long shuttered Chicopee Mill, which had become a university facility. By the aughts, this process continued in other areas, in the seventies-era houses of Athens east side "suburbs" and in the African American neighborhood that had hung on to a slice of historic housing stock along Reese and West Broad Streets and West Hancock Avenue. Neighborhoods near the university had felt these pressures for years, but most close-in, working-class neighborhoods around downtown did not survive the one-two punch of increasing numbers of UGA students and non-enrolled scene participants seeking housing. In their own search for affordable places to live, bohemians were part of a process that pushed lower income whites and African Americans out of historic neighborhoods where deep and long-standing community ties had flourished for generations. Yet as prices rose close to downtown, bohemians also became victims of gentrification. Despite these changes, the cost of living stayed relatively inexpensive because scene participants continued to find low rents on the east side and in small towns outside of Athens and food remained cheap.

The University of Georgia also changed. When the scene began, UGA was a middle-of-the-road public university managed by good old boys and dominated by football coach Vince Dooley. In the eighties, a former professor Jan Kemp sued the school, claiming that she had been fired because she refused to pass football players who were failing her remedial English class. When she won her case, the president of the university resigned, but Dooley kept his job. Still, the new president invested in faculty research and new facilities and began the transformation of UGA into a more serious academic institution. Even more important, the lottery-funded Hope Scholarship launched in 1993 made Georgia public colleges free for the state's high school students who graduated with high grades. More of them stayed in state, and UGA admissions became much more selective.

In the late seventies and eighties, kids that felt like outcasts or weirdos in their small towns or suburbs had flocked to Athens, drawn to the art school at first and later also to the scene. Across the university, a lack of oversight meant students who wanted to could often use university facilities and resources for their own purposes. In the new century, officials noticed when people squatted in dorm lounges or crashed the art studios, and many rebellious Georgia teenagers could no longer get into the school. Like most public universities, UGA began operating in a paradigm of scarcity that together with rising tuition costs transformed how both students and employees thought about its resources. Bohemians did little to cause and mostly did not benefit from these changes in Georgia's flagship university.

Like UGA, the broader culture of Athens also changed in these years, and here local bohemians did play a role as they helped make this little piece of the South more liberal—less white supremacist, much more tolerant of gay people, and more generous in the provision of social services. As members of the first generation of southerners to spend significant time in integrated schools, scene participants resisted the Reagan-era backlash against the civil rights movement. Scene participants like David and me turned out for protests, including a 1987 civil rights march in Forsyth County, Georgia. More subtle but also important, white bohemians rejected on a daily basis the casual racism of white coworkers, relatives, and neighbors. Like Vic, many of us realized that not being a redneck and not being a racist went hand in hand. Racism, a central characteristic of the southern culture we were rejecting, was not "cool." None of this was news to southern blacks, but the scene did push white kids to question a kind of taken-for-granted white supremacy. And while some scene people did practice a kind of "folk" primitivism, for better or worse they ladled this romance and its denial of equality out on rural white and black working-class people alike.[26]

Fittingly, in a scene that started with a drag act, scene participants also made Athens an oasis for what were not yet named LBGQTA+ rights. Jerry Ayers and his friends Ricky Wilson, Keith Strickland, and later Fred Schneider had lived their gender and sexuality out and proud in forms then unheard-of in small-town America. If you wanted to be an Athens bohemian, you had to lose or at least hide the homophobia you learned growing up. Making assumptions about people's sexual preferences was taboo, and men and women flirted and had sex with men and women. Every place I've ever lived since has seemed flawed, or, to use a word we did not have then, heteronormative, in comparison. Being a bohemian meant experimenting to learn where you fit on the queer continuum. Few of us believed anyone was entirely straight.

And while the politics of benefits in the wake of the 1985 "Live Aid" concert are easy to critique, Athens musicians and fans supported a lot of local nonprofits and people as well as state and national organizations. Many of these local groups worked to hold the Athens and Georgia governments accountable for protecting the local environment and providing local services. Other area nonprofits worked directly with affected people to help care for the homeless, victims of domestic abuse, and people with AIDS. As scene participants got older, some of them went to work for these organizations or for local government agencies or institutions that served the public like the regional library. This work and scene participants' support for liberal politicians made Athens–Clarke County a more humane place than it would have been in an era of growing conservatism when state and local governments were cutting funding directed to these issues.

Together, Athens and the other scattered sites of indie America played a mostly unacknowledged role in creating a new kind of place-based and yet cosmopolitan and forward-looking American culture and a renewed interest in the local. Anti-corporate, anti-suburban, and environmentalist, scene participants in Athens and other centers of alternative culture were obsessed with creating new music and art within the historic landscapes and structures of particular places. When national chains like Starbucks and the Gap began expanding into historic downtowns, indie folks resisted what they saw as an invasion and refused to patronize these businesses. In Athens, we were all proud when a Wendy's that opened at the corner of College and Broad did not last long. A lot of people who grew up to be foodies in the aughts came of age falling in love with the collections of "local" music that made up college and indie rock and hip-hop. A love for local bands prepared people to love local food and businesses too.

Just as important as this investment in the local was the way participation in the scene opened people up to the world. The experience of creating and expanding alternative culture in Athens knocked participants off the life course they had been on and made them question everything they thought they knew about the contours of a good life and the meaning of success. Even as the cast of characters and the bands and the businesses changed, alternative culture continued to have this effect, transforming new waves of young people swept into its orbit.

A narrow focus on the bands that "made it" ignores the ways the alternative culture we all helped create launched practices and vocations unrelated to music too. A partial list of former participants includes artists, artisans, art directors, chefs, writers, journalists, music critics, editors, filmmakers, casting directors, graphic designers, fundraisers, nonprofit directors, and academics. Yet there was a flip side to these achievements. No one talks about it much, but some scene participants also experienced profound downward class mobility. People that continued to make music their priority while they worked "day jobs" without benefits suffered. At least one long-time scene participant went to jail for his local business, selling drugs to his more famous friends. A not insignificant number of people had college degrees but earned working-class salaries. One woman I interviewed was missing many of her teeth.

But the most profound change that occurred in Athens was so obvious that no one commented on it even as it transformed our daily lives and art and music-making. And while it is hard to date with any precision, our collective success actually had its own effect. Over the years, bohemian Athens developed its own myths and rituals and traditions. It became less a young and creative punk and more an arty old aunt or uncle, a part of the cultural landscape rather than a challenge to it. Forty years after the B-52's debuted, no one could argue that Athens remained an *unlikely* bohemia.

In the process, DIY changed from a method, a way of inventing our own art, music, and meaning, into a culture, a set of established models, formats, rituals, and meanings. The biggest casualty was our vaunted amateurism. Before the scene existed or when it was small and not very visible, young people moved to Athens mostly to go to college. After the scene matured, some kids chose UGA because of the scene or they skipped the university altogether and just moved to town to be a part of the area's alternative culture. Many later bohemians already knew how to play their instruments. But more than that, no one remained an amateur in the broader sense of the term. Established participants modeled how to start a band and book gigs and record and look for a label. They also demonstrated how to make and exhibit art or start a publication or furnish an apartment or any of the other countless scene versions of the things people do in the course of their everyday lives. Rather than inventing small-town, southern bohemia, later participants increasingly inhabited it. And while this division was never complete — later participants changed older practices and forms and invented new ones — what had been unlikely was now expected. Bohemian Athens would never completely surprise either participants or outside observers again.

Like America, the Athens scene was a collective creation. All of us built this astonishingly generative place, but only some of us profited. It should not be surprising that alternative culture did not kill capitalism.

Despite that fact, Athens as site of alternative culture has much to tell us as our national crisis over this collective making and individual taking grows acute. If we are going to turn this America around, we need some of that Athens "anything is possible" magic, that combination of intelligence and creativity and a love for bodily pleasure not yet disillusioned enough to be cynical. Like the young people who created the Athens scene all those decades ago, we need to stop thinking we will inherit a future and start building it ourselves. We need to believe that an unlikely cast of characters in an unlikely place can make a surprising and beautiful new world.

Acknowledgments

For helping me recover the history recounted here, I am grateful to each and every one of the Athens scene participants who agreed to speak with me either on the phone or in person or who talked with Chris Starrs, a good friend as well as a freelance journalist who completed an early round of interviews for me. I knew some of these people before I interviewed them. Others I admired and wanted to know. In writing this book, I struggled at times over whether to use first or last names in reference to scene participants. Mostly, I defaulted to last names, even with people I knew. At times, especially in the last chapter and the conclusion, which cover people and events I knew about and often participated in, this practice simply felt absurd. In those cases, I have used first names. Among those people, I especially want to thank David Levitt for living this history with me.

About midway through the process of researching this book, Christian Lopez invited me to be a part of the University of Georgia–based Athens Music Project, and our collaboration has greatly enriched this work. I am grateful to him for everything from tracking down former participants and organizing interviews to sharing with me his vast knowledge of oral history as both a form and a practice. Through Christian, I got to work with Athens musician and sound engineer Curtiss Pernice. I also learned a great deal from interviews Curtiss conducted with Athens scene participants for the Athens Music Project. Special thanks to Robbie Ethridge, Jennifer Hartley, Vanessa Briscoe Hay, Michael Lachowski, Bertis Downs, Keith Bennett, Arthur Johnson, David Barbe, Mark Cline, Sam Seawright, and Curtiss Pernice for providing essential information or for helping me track down other participants or locating and enabling me to use rare photographs. I also benefited from thoughtful conservations with Roger Brown, who wrote the first book about the Athens scene, and music journalist Anthony DeCurtis, who wrote some key pieces about the early years. I am indebted to former UGA art professor Robert Croker for inviting former art students, colleagues, and friends to a viewing of his old sketchbooks at the Georgia Museum of Art, which helped jog memories and connected me to some of the earliest scene participants. I also want to thank Joe Crespino and Becky Herring of the Emory University history department for arranging for me to use a room there for an interview and Rachel Seidman and Sara Wood at the Southern Oral History Program at the University of North Carolina at Chapel Hill for setting me up in their space with their equipment for another interview.

At the University of Virginia, I am grateful to my amazing colleagues in UVA's American Studies Program for building the kind of intellectual community that nurtures both our research and our students. Former history department graduate students Scott Matthews, Emily Senefeld, and Megan Stubbendeck did early and important research for this project. More recent former graduate students Cecilia Marquez, Jon Cohen, and Joey Thompson inspired and challenged me over our long conversations about music, history, race, and the South. All of these young scholars, and also current graduate students Gillet Rosenblith, Monica Blair, Allison Kelley, and Connor Kenaston, have taught me as much as I have taught them, maybe more, and I am grateful for our work together.

Early on, music professors Richard Will and Bonnie Gordon invited me to present my thoughts about the Athens scene to the UVA music department and helped me get started. A few years later, I got very helpful feedback from the UVA American Studies Program's New Americanists workshop. Over the years, I greatly benefited from a brilliant circle of UVA scholars working on the history of popular music: Claudrena Harold, Jack Hamilton, and Karl Hagstrom Miller. For reading some or all of the manuscript and offering thoughtful comments and corrections, I am deeply grateful to these friends and colleagues and to Bill Wylie, Bryant Simon, Joey Thompson, Jon Cohen, Liza Pittard, Lisa Goff, and Christian Lopez. I want to thank department and program heads Paul Halliday and Karen Parshall in history; Anna Brickhouse and Sylvia Chong in American Studies; administrative staff members in history and American studies Kathleen Miller, Barbara Moriarty, and Carol Westin; and Ian Baucom, the Buckner W. Clay Dean of the College and Graduate School of Arts and Sciences, for supporting this research.

I am grateful to the amazing audiences at the 2016, 2018, and 2019 versions of PopCon, the annual pop music conference held every spring at

MoPOP in Seattle, for their feedback and encouragement and for the chance to share my work with brilliant music critics and journalists like Ann Powers, Elijah Wald, Holly George-Warren, and Robert Christgau. I also want to thank commentators and audience members at the many conferences and universities where I have presented this research, including the University of Georgia; the University of Michigan; the University of Mississippi; Montana State University; Keio University in Tokyo, Japan; and the University of Leipzig, the University of Münster, and New York University–Berlin in Germany. I thank Lindsey Freeman, Shawn Chandler Bingham, Ted Ownby, and Allen Tullos for including pieces of this work in their edited collections and in *Southern Spaces*.

At the University of North Carolina Press, my editor, Mark Simpson-Vos, has read every word of this manuscript more than once and urged me at every step to think about pacing and narrative, flow and audience. I am not always easy to "edit," but Mark just keeps quietly pushing, and most of the time I have to concede that he is right. For his belief in this book and the gift of so much of his precious time, I am deeply grateful. I also want to thank Jessica Newman and Jay Mazzocchi for their help with copyediting, permissions, and dealing with all the work that flows from including so many photographs. I also want to thank my brilliant anonymous readers for their very useful suggestions regarding revisions.

I am deeply thankful for dear Charlotttesville friends and colleagues Cori Field, Lisa Goff, Anna Brickhouse, Sandhya Shukla, Tom Klubock, Claudrena Harold, Sarah Milov, John Pepper, Bruce Holsinger, Mandy Hoy, Sarah Betzer, Sheila Crane, Carmen Higginbotham, Jennifer Greeson, Kevin Everson, Matt Hedstrom, Lisa Woolfork, Philippe Sommer, Brian Balogh, Amy and Paul Halliday, Trina Player, Tim and Virginia Michel, and Karl and Amy Hagstrom Miller. For more help than any neighbor has a right to ask for, I thank Ann Hill Williams. Outside of Charlottesville, for community, both intellectual and otherwise, and often lodging and meals to boot, I need to thank Franny Nudelman, David Holton, Leo Holton, Margaret Hall, Jack Murray, Chris Starrs, Gina Coleman Drosos, Emmet and Edith Gowin, Carol LeWitt, Heather Thompson, Sara Blair, Ted Ownby, Bill Ferris, Marcie Cohen Ferris, John Gennari, Eric Lott, Cindy Katz, Kamalini Ramdas, Sanjay Jain, Dave Woody, and Sonya Glasserkey. Finally, I am eternally grateful for my soulmate, Jessica Hunt; my one and only O.F.F., Liz Witner; and my favorite historian and editor, Bryant Simon.

For love and support, I want to thank my siblings, Tres Hale and Joanna Hale Prior; my brothers-in-law, Jim Fisher and Mark Prior; my nieces and nephews, Ashton Sims and Hale, Noah, and Sam Prior; my mom, Joan Berry Hale; and the person I have missed every single day since he died, my dad, Lester Hale. Watching my amazing daughters, Sarah Ellen Hale and Emma Chandler Hale, grow up to become young women of fierce and passionate intelligence, deep kindness, and moral and ethical courage has been the greatest joy of my life. I hope they find their own versions of Athens! Bill Wylie came into all our lives at an unexpected moment, and the importance to me of the family the four of us have made together cannot be expressed in words. During the years I have been writing this book, Bill served as my sounding board and first and last reader. He also scanned and adjusted old photographs. But most of all, in both the way he makes his own work and the way he lives, he reminded me to think about my writing as art. This book is for him, for the music we have made together, for teaching me what beauty can do in the world, and for love without measure.

Notes

INTERVIEWS

(Note: asterisk indicates more than one interview)

Charles Aaron
Terry Allen
Jared Bailey
David Barbe
Keith Bennett*
T. Patton Biddle
Sean Bourne
Roger Brown
Bryan Burke
Paul Butchart
William Orten Carlton
Don Chambers
April Chapman
Mark Cline*
Bill Cody
Bryan Cook
Robert Croker*
Bill David
Anthony DeCurtis
Andrew Donaldson
Blair Dorminey
Bertis Downs*
Dana Downs
Robbie Ethridge
Lauren Fancher
Peter Fancher

Betty Alice Fowler
Jennifer Hartley
Bob Hay*
Vanessa Briscoe Hay*
Claire Horne
Julie House
Arthur Johnson*
Manfred Jones
John Keane
Watt King
Kathy Kirbo
Andrew Krieger
Michael Lachowski*
Keith Landers*
Nancy Lukasiewicz
Deonna Mann
Barry Marler
Dan Matthews
Pete McCommons
Maureen McLaughlin
Judy McWillie*
Mamie Fike Mills
Annelies Mondi
Jeff Montgomery
Heli Montgomery Dunn
Andy Nasisse

Kelly Noonan
Gwen O'Looney
Richard Olsen
Bill Paul
Michael Paxton
Curtiss Pernice*
David Pierce
Kyle Pilgrim
Chris Rasmussen
Chuck Reece
Ben Reynolds*
Melanie Haner Reynolds
Art Rosenbaum*
Sam Seawright*
Mark Cooper Smith

Sally Speed
Karen Stinnett
Lynda Stipe
Kit Swartz*
Ed Tant
Larry Tenner
Jeff Walls
Armistead Wellford
Joe Willey
Craig Williams
Cindy Wilson
Vic Varney
Rob Veal
Velena Vego

INTRODUCTION

1. Bernard Gendron, *Between Montmartre and the Mudd Club: Popular Music and the Avant-garde* (Chicago: University of Chicago Press, 2002); and Tricia Henry, "Punk and Avant-Garde Art," *Journal of Popular Culture 17, no. 4* (Spring 1984): 30. Another, early node of DIY culture in an unlikely place was the scene which formed in Akron and Cleveland, Ohio, two adjacent and then-deindustrializing cities, after the formation of Devo in 1973. See Calvin C. Rydbom, *The Akron Sound: The Heyday of the Midwest Punk Capital* (Charleston: History Press, 2018). On the relationship between the Akron scene and Kent State University, see Tim Sommer, "How the Kent State Massacre Helped Give Birth to Punk Rock," *Washington Post*, May 3, 2018, online at https://www.washingtonpost.com/outlook/how-the-kent-state-massacre-changed-music/2018/05/03/b45ca462-4cb6-11e8-b725-92c89fe3ca4c_story.html?utm_term=.c039d9bcc69d. See also the publication *D.I.Y: The Do-It-Yourself New Music Magazine*, published in Manhattan Beach, California, in 1980 and 1981. Issues included lists of clubs that would book punk and other kinds of new music, independent record stores, and college radio stations, as well as coverage of scenes in Cleveland, New York, Los Angeles, and a few other cities.

2. Contrast Coran Capshaw, the manager of Charlottesville's most famous musical group, the Dave Matthews Band, with Bertis Downs, R.E.M.'s lawyer and manager, who still runs the business end of that former band. Capshaw is an entrepreneur who runs multiple companies and a real-estate empire in the college town where I live now, while Downs spends most of his time as a local and national advocate for public schools.

3. Population figures are from the 1980 U.S. Census, publication PC80-1-A12 Ga., *Characteristics of the Population: Number of Inhabitants: Georgia*. In a 1990 referendum, residents voted to unify the city and county governments. The Athens–Clarke County unified government took over in early 1991.

4. The University of Georgia was incorporated by an act of the Georgia General Assembly on January 27, 1785, after the same body set aside 40,000 acres as an endowment for a college or seminary the previous year. See the official history of the University of Georgia, online at https://www.uga.edu/history.php.

5. Bill King, "Athens: A City Attuned to a New Wave-length," *Atlanta Journal-*

Constitution, August 30, 1981, 1F, 6F; and Art Harris, "O Little Town of Rock 'n' Roll," *Washington Post*, August 29, 1984, B1, B8.

6. King, "Athens: A City Attuned to a New Wave-length," 6F; and Harris, "O Little Town of Rock 'n' Roll."

7. King, "Athens: A City attuned to a New Wave-length," 1F, 6F; Harris, "O Little Town of Rock 'n' Roll"; Andrew Slater, "Athens Band a Hit in New York," *Atlanta Journal-Constitution*, May 2, 1982, 1G, 7G; and Vic Varney interview. For an academic article on Athens, see Arthur Jipson, "Why Athens? Investigations into the Site of an American Music Revolution," *Popular Music and Society*, September 2017, 19–29.

8. Vic Varney interview.

9. We also like our identities set rather than fluid. In the United States, contemporary culture mostly follows the mantra that if a person is not born an identity, they should not perform that identity. In our quest to create a more inclusive and tolerant world in which everyone's particular voice is heard — a project that I am politically sympathetic to — we sometimes forget that fluidity and performance are not just tools for making fun of or denigrating categories of people. They are also tools for empowering individuals to escape conventional categories and indeed key sites for constructing new possibilities of identity. From a different perspective and with a more theoretical lens, José Esteban Muñoz explores these issues in his books *Disidentifications: Queers of Color and the Performance of Politics* (Minneapolis: University of Minnesota Press, 1999) and *Cruising Utopia: The Then and There of Queer Futurity* (New York: New York University Press, 2009). For the history of gays and lesbians in the U.S. South, see John Howard, ed., *Carryin' On in the Lesbian and Gay South* (New York: New York University Press, 1997); and Howard, *Men Like That: A Southern Queer History* (Chicago: University of Chicago Press, 1999). See also Mary L. Gray, Colin Johnson, and Brian J. Gilley, *Queering the Countryside: New Frontiers in Rural Queer Studies* (New York: New York University Press, 2016).

10. Vic Varney, "'Nineteen Hours from New York': Small Town Makes Good," *New York Rocker*, March 1981, 20; Vic Varney interview; Mark Cline interviews; Sam Seawright interviews; Keith Bennett interviews; Robert Croker interviews; and Bill Paul interview. Out of sensitivity to participants in this community, some of whom remain very private and some of whom have died, and because I was unable to research this group's history thoroughly (a project worthy of its own book), I am making a conscious choice not to provide the names of participants that I did learn.

11. For the best explanation of this period of U.S. history and "neoliberalism," the political and economic order that in the United States began to replace the New Deal order in the early 1970s, see Bryant Simon, *Hamlet Fire: A Tragic Story of Cheap Food, Cheap Government, and Cheap Lives* (New York: New Press, 2017). Simon mostly avoids the term "neoliberalism" and offers a persuasive and accessible explanation of the shift from a New Deal order of "more" to a neoliberal order of "cheap": cheap wages, cheap government, cheap goods, and cheap and expendable places. The figures are from p. 43 of the 1991 *UGA Fact Book*, published by the University of Georgia and available online as a PDF at https://oir.uga.edu/factbook/pastfactbooks/.

12. Marilynne Robinson, "Save Our Public Universities," *Harper's Magazine*, March 2016, online at https://harpers.org/archive/2016/03/save-our-public-universities/.

13. Gina Arnold, *Route 666: On the Road to Nirvana* (New York: St. Martin's Press, 1993); Barry Shank, *Dissonant Identities: The Rock 'n' Roll Scene in Austin, Texas* (Middletown: Wesleyan University Press, 1994); Ann Powers, *Weird Like Us: My Bohemian America*

(New York: Simon & Schuster, 2000); and Michael Azerrad, *This Band Could Be Your Life: Scenes from the American Indie Underground, 1981–1991* (New York: Little, Brown, 2001). See also the terrific Mary Montgomery Wolf, "'We Accept You, One of Us?': Punk Rock, Community, and Individualism in an Uncertain Era, 1974–1985" (PhD diss., University of North Carolina at Chapel Hill, 2007).

14. Academic books that examine aspects of indie/alternative music include Holly Kruse, *Site and Sound: Understanding Independent Music Scenes* (New York: Peter Lang, 2003); Andy Bennett and Richard Peterson, eds., *Music Scenes: Local, Translocal, and Virtual* (Nashville: Vanderbilt University Press, 2004); Wendy Fonarow, *Empires of Dirt: The Aesthetics and Rituals of British Indie Music* (Middletown: Wesleyan University Press, 2006); Matthew Bannister, *White Boys, White Noise: Masculinities and 1980s Indie Guitar Rock* (Burlington, Vt.: Ashgate, 2006); Gaye Theresa Johnson, *Spaces of Conflict, Spaces of Solidarity: Music, Race, and Spatial Entitlement in Los Angeles* (Berkeley: University of California Press, 2013); and Dewar MacLeod, *Kids of the Black Hole: Punk Rock in Postsuburban California* (Norman: University of Oklahoma Press, 2011). On the continuity of anti-corporate rhetoric, see Fred Turner, *From Counterculture to Cyberculture: Stewart Brand, the Whole Earth Network, and the Rise of Digital Utopianism* (Chicago: University of Chicago Press, 2006). For an argument that is too dismissive of the transgressive potential of oppositional cultures, see Thomas Frank, *The Conquest of Cool: Business Culture, Counterculture, and the Rise of Hip Consumerism* (Chicago: University of Chicago, 1997). Popular accounts of punk and postpunk music that I have found helpful include Greil Marcus, *Lipstick Traces: A Secret History of the Twentieth Century* (Cambridge: Harvard University Press, 1989); Clinton Heylin, *From the Velvets to the Voidoids: A Pre-Punk History for a Post-Punk World* (New York: Penguin, 1993); Heylin, *Babylon's Burning: From Punk to Grunge* (New York: Conongate, 2007); Simon Reynolds, *Rip It Up and Start Again: Postpunk, 1878–1984* (London: Faber and Faber, 2005); Reynolds, *Totally Wired: Postpunk Interviews and Overviews* (New York: Soft Skull Press, 2009); and Legs McNeil and Gillian McCain, *Please Kill Me: The Uncensored Oral History of Punk* (New York: Grove, 1996).

15. On the history and theory of bohemia, or what oppositional culture can do, see Theodore Roszak, *The Making of a Counterculture* (1969; repr., Berkeley: University of California Press, 1995); Dick Hebdige, *Subculture: The Meaning of Style* (1979; repr., New York: Routledge, 1988); Jerrold Seigel, *Bohemian Paris: Culture, Politics, and the Boundaries of Bourgeois Life, 1830–1930* (New York: Viking Penguin, 1986), quote, 394–95; and Stuart Hall, *Cultural Studies 1983: A Theoretical History* (Durham: Duke University Press, 2016). Books like Simon Frith's *Performing Rites: On the Value of Popular Music* (Cambridge: Harvard University Press, 1996); Christopher Small, *Musicking: The Meanings of Performing and Listening* (Middletown: Wesleyan University Press, 1998); Josh Kun, *Audiotopia: Music, Race, and America* (Berkeley: University of California Press, 2005); Carl Wilson, *Let's Talk About Love: Why Other People Have Such Bad Taste* (New York: Bloomsbury, 2014); David Byrne, *How Music Works* (San Francisco: McSweeney's, 2012); and Barry Shank, *The Political Force of Musical Beauty* (Durham: Duke University Press, 2014) have expanded and sharpened my thinking about music, a process that began decades earlier in conversations with people in the Athens scene like David Levitt and Mike Webb. On the relationship of avant-garde art and popular music, see Gendron, *Between Montmartre*.

16. See Jody Rosen, "Pop Art," *New York Times Magazine*, February 3, 2019, 9–11, for an example of incisive thinking about the nature of "creative" freedom in contemporary

America: "creative . . . dresses up a ruptured social compact, the raw deal of the gig economy as bohemian freedom" (10).

17. C. Carr, "Bohemian Diaspora," *Village Voice*, February 4, 1992, 27.

18. Cordy Lon, "Hunting Divine," *Misanthropic* (self-produced tape, 1990), author's possession; and Ernst Bloch, *The Principle of Hope: Volume One* (1954; repr., Cambridge: MIT Press, 1995), 198.

19. Or as cultural studies scholar Simon Frith put it, "The issue is not how to live outside capitalism, but how to live within it." Simon Frith, *Sound Effects: Youth, Leisure, and the Politics of Rock* (New York: Pantheon, 1981), 272.

CHAPTER 1

1. This description of Jerry/Jeremy Ayers draws on my own observations—I knew Ayers for years—as well as many interviews with people who knew him, including Mark Cline, Sam Seawright, Annelies Mondi, Julie House, Lynda Stipe, April Chapman, and Jennifer Hartley.

2. Rodger Brown, *Party Out of Bounds: The B-52's, R.E.M., and the Kids Who Rocked Athens, Georgia* (New York: Plume, 1991), 24, 60, 126–27, 157; Steve Dollar, "Brown Goes 'Out of Bounds' with Look at Athens Rock Scene," *Atlanta Journal*, August 18, 1991; Denise Sullivan, *R.E.M.: Talk About the Passion, An Oral History* (New York: Da Capo Press, 1998), 17; B-52's, "Rock Lobster"/"52 girls," DB Records, 1978; and *The B-52's*, Warner Brothers, 1979.

3. Tim Jonze, "R.E.M.'s Michael Stipe on his 37,000 photos—of Stars, Lovers, and Kurt Cobain's Hands," *The Guardian*, April 24, 2019, https://www.theguardian.com/artand design/2019/apr/24/rem-michael-stipe-7000-photos-stars-lovers-kurt-cobains-hands; Brown, *Party Out of Bounds*, 126–7; Sullivan, *R.E.M.: Talk About the Passion*, 17; and R.E.M., *Fables of the Reconstruction/ Reconstruction of the Fables*, I.R.S. Records, 1985. Richard Smith calls this "is he or isn't he?" and "is he a she?" act "ambisexuality," links it to minstrelsy, and says gay people see musicians who work this ambiguity as "gay cowards or straight thieves. . . . Come out or fuck off." See Richard Smith, "Ambisexuality," *Melody Maker*, December 12, 1992. Still, in the seventies and eighties, drag provided a rare means of publicly exploring gay, bisexual, and transgendered identities. The male members of the B-52's were out as gay to their friends and to many Athens locals, and their sexuality was certainly present in their performances in a way anyone looking could see. Still, fewer people then talked explicitly with reporters or other people they did not know well about their sexuality. In the late 1970s and especially in the 1980s, as the AIDS epidemic spread, many LGBTQA+ people lived neither in nor out of the closet but made different choices about how much they wanted to reveal about their sexual identity in different contexts. Also, as this book will describe across multiple chapters, in the Athens scene, many people had sex across all the categories, experimenting with gender and sexual fluidity in ways that parallel how teens and young adults today think about a range of identifications and sexual and gender identities. For many on the local scene, "gay" seemed as limiting as "straight," and many people sampled it all, sleeping with friends and acquaintances of both sexes. While pro-pleasure and certainly transgressive in the context of middle-class conservatism about sex, this kind of thinking sometimes sidestepped rather than addressed issues like sexism and homophobia. See Michael Stipe's thoughtful discussions of his own "queerness" and his fears of AIDS in Christopher Bollen, "Michael Stipe,"

Interview, May 4, 2011, http://www.interviewmagazine.com/music/michael-stipe/. See also Joanne Meyerowitz, *How Sex Changed: A History of Transsexuality in the United States* (Cambridge: Harvard University Press, 2004).

4. On the Athens/New York connection, see Brown, *Party Out of Bounds*; Maureen McLaughlin's "The Athens, GA/ NYC Axis: This is Where It All Began," *Daiquiris on Call: Where Sweet Tea Meets Coffee Regular*, blog, Jan. 27, 2013, http://maureenmc2000.tumblr.com/post/41663852236/the-athens-ga-nyc-axis-this-is-where-it-all; John Martin Taylor, "The B-52's and Me," *Hoppin' John's*, February 16, 2008, http://hoppinjohns.net/?p=263; Lachowski interview; Rosenbaum interview; and Croker materials, Art Rocks Athens Collection.

5. Andy Warhol, *Silva Thin* (circa 1970), unique polaroid print mounted on board, for sale at Christies June 16–25, 2015, as part of a lot called "Andy's Randy Summer," https://onlineonly.christies.com/s/andy-warhol-christies-andys-randy-summer/silva-thin-40/17910#. For other evidence of Ayers and his connection to the factory, see Silva Thin in Jackie Curtis, *Vain Victory*, clip of 1972 performance online at https://www.youtube.com/watch?v=a-9SilkF4ZI (Ayers appears at around 1:40); and Silva Thin, "Theater: Interview with the Cockettes," *Interview* (February 1972), 48–49. On gender fuck, see Laud Humphreys, *Out of the Closets: Sociology of Homosexual Liberation* (Englewood Cliffs: Prentice-Hall, 1972), 164. On the new "macho" transvestitism and drag as a satire of female impersonation (men in dresses, makeup, heels, and beards), see Tom Burke, "Gays in Arms: The Violet Millennium," *Rolling Stone*, August 30, 1973.

6. On drag, see José Esteban Muñoz, *Disidentifications: Queers of Color and the Performance of Politics* (Minneapolis: University of Minnesota Press, 1999); and Muñoz, *Cruising Utopia: The Then and There of Queer Futurity* (New York: New York University Press, 2009); Marjorie Garber, *Vested Interests: Cross-Dressing and Cultural Anxiety* (New York: Routledge, 1997); and Judith Butler, *Gender Trouble: Feminism and the Subversion of Identity* (New York: Routledge, 1990). Butler argues that drag performance was the norm in the regular world, outside the drag show. On the long history of people playing with mass culture to create transgressive new meanings and identities with which to oppose mass culture, see Stuart Hall, "Notes on Deconstructing the Popular," *People's History and Socialist Theory*, ed. Raphael Samuel (London: Routledge and Kegan Paul, 1981), 227–40; and Hall, *Cultural Studies 1983: A Theoretical History* (Durham: Duke University Press, 2016); Dick Hebdige, *Subculture: The Meaning of Style* (1979; repr., New York: Routledge, 1988); and Simon Frith, *Sound Effects: Youth, Leisure, and the Politics of Rock 'n' Roll* (New York: Pantheon, 1981). On what gets to count as real, see Walter Benjamin, "The Work of Art in the Age of Mechanical Reproduction" (1936), reprinted in *Illuminations* (New York: Schocken, 1968); and Miles Orvell, *The Real Thing: Imitation and Authenticity in American Culture, 1880–1940* (Chapel Hill: University of North Carolina Press, 1989).

7. Thomas Crow, *The Long March of Pop: Art, Music, and Design, 1930–1995* (New Haven: Yale University Press, 2015); Hal Foster, *The First Pop Age: Painting and Subjectivity in the Art of Hamilton, Lichtenstein, Warhol, Richter, and Ruscha* (Princeton: Princeton University Press, 2014); Bernard Gendron, *Between Montmartre and the Mudd Club: Popular Music and the Avant-Garde* (Chicago: University of Chicago Press, 2002); and Tricia Henry, "Punk and Avant-Garde Art," *Journal of Popular Culture* 17, no. 4 (Spring 1984): 30.

8. Candy Darling came out years later as transgendered. Ellen Willis, "Velvet Underground," 71–83; and Robert Christgau, "New York Dolls," 132–47; both in *Stranded: Rock and Roll for a Desert Island*, ed. Greil Marcus (1979; repr., New York: Da Capo Press,

2007). The Velvet Underground's song "Sister Ray," released on their album *White Heat/White Light*, was about drag queens. On Lou Reed's 1972 solo album *Lou Reed* (RCA Records), Reed posed in drag on the back cover. His second solo album *Transformer* (RCA Records) includes the song "Walk on the Wild Side." Reed also had a highly publicized relationship with the transvestite Rachel. On the New York Dolls and their playing with gender and sexuality, see Clinton Heylin, *From the Velvets to the Voidoids* (London: Penguin, 1993), 188, 78–79.

9. Mark Cline interviews; and Silva Thin, "Interview with the Cockettes," *Interview*, February 1972, 47–49. In a surviving clip of a *Vain Victory* performance, Silva wears a vest without a shirt, a scarf, and makeup as he helps the Warhol superstar Candy Darling move back and forth in a swing as she sings: https://www.youtube.com/watch?v=a-9SilkF4ZI. Silva appears at around 1:40. On Ayers's activities that I have been unable to confirm in other sources, see Brown, *Party Out of Bounds*, 24. On the Factory, see Steven Watson, *Factory Made: Warhol and the Sixties* (New York: Pantheon, 2003). The swing scene in R.E.M.'s "Losing My Religion," whether intentional or not, shares many characteristics with the *Vain Victory* scene.

10. C. Carr, "Bohemian Diaspora," *Village Voice*, February 4, 1992, 29.

11. Brown, *Party Out of Bounds*, 15–16; Mats Sexton, *The B-52's Universe: The Essential Guide to the World's Greatest Party Band* (Minneapolis: Plan B Books, 2002), 30.

12. Brown, *Party Out of Bounds*, 15–16.

13. Cindy Wilson interview; Bill David interview; Robert Croker interviews; and Brown, *Party Out of Bounds*, 23–24.

14. Cindy Wilson interview. Keith Strickland talks about growing up gay in Athens in Scott Dagostino, "Bohemian Rhapsody: How Some Artsy Queer Kids in Georgia Became the World's Greatest Party Band," *Fab Magazine*, March 5, 2008, http://archive.fab magazine.com/features/341/b52.html; and P. J. Maytag, "Funk and Fellini: Meet Keith Strickland of the B-52's," April 28, 2011, http://www.sdgln.com/bottomline/2011/04/28 /meet-b52s-keith-strickland#sthash.mveFzuzk.dpbs; and Sexton, *The B-52's Universe*, 28. See also Aaron Fricke, *Reflections of a Rock Lobster: A Story About Growing Up Gay* (Alyson Publications, 1981), a memoir by a high school student who is inspired by the B-52's' music to take his boyfriend to the prom; James T. Sears, *Growing Up Gay in the South* (New York: Routledge, 1991); and John Howard, *Men Like That: A Southern Queer History* (Chicago: University of Chicago, 2001).

15. Cindy Wilson interview; J. Eddy Ellison, "B-52's Still Feel Like an Athens Band," *Athens Banner Herald*, July 23, 1983; Brown, *Party Out of Bounds*, 48–50, 31; and Tammy Underwood, "Athens' Own B-52's Now Flying High," *Athens Banner-Herald/Daily News*, February 16, 1980. For an early account of the new ironic "flea-marketing" style, see Kennedy Fraser, "On and Off the Avenue: Feminine Fashions," *New Yorker*, April 14, 1975, 80–89.

16. William "Ort" Carlton, "Ort Reviews the Irreviewable [*sic*]," *Tasty World* 5 [April 1985], 9.

17. William Orten Carlton interview; Brown, *Party Out of Bounds*,19–22; and Charles White, *The Life and Times of Little Richard* (New York: Harmony Books, 1984).

18. Ellison, "B-52's Still Feel Like an Athens Band"; Taylor, "B-52's and Me"; Sexton, *B-52's Universe*, 32; and Brown, *Party Out of Bounds*, 17–30.

19. Taylor, "B-52's and Me"; Sexton, *B-52's Universe*, 31–32; and Brown, *Party Out of Bounds*, 26–28.

20. Ellison, "B-52's Still Feel Like an Athens Band"; and James Henke, "Interview: The B-52's," *Rolling Stone*, December 11, 1980. On the back-to-the-land movement, see Jeffrey Carl Jacob, *New Pioneers: The Back-to-the-Land Movement and the Search for a Sustainable Future* (University Park: Penn State University Press, 1997); and Jinny Turman, "Appalachian Alter-Natives: The Back to the Land Migration and Community Change, 1970–2000" (PhD diss., West Virginia University, 2013).

21. The goats (either 4 or 5) appear in Glenn O'Brien, "The B-52s [*sic*]: Beehives Not Bombers," *Interview*, February 1979, 56; Henke, "Interview: The B-52's,"; and Taylor, "B-52's and Me."

22. For an online archive of oral histories, documents, and photographs of the Atlanta Hippie Scene, see http://www.thestripproject.com/; and http://www.messyoptics.com/, the archive of *Bird* photographer Carter Tomassi. On the Allman Brothers and southern rock, see Scott Freeman, *Midnight Riders: The Story of the Allman Brothers Band* (Boston: Little, Brown, 1995). On Carter, see Julian E. Zelizer, *Jimmy Carter* (New York: Times Books, 2010).

23. Ellison, "B-52's Still Feel Like an Athens Band"; and Brown, *Party Out of Bounds*, 26–28.

24. Steve Hendrix, "Touring Athens with the B-52's: Southern College City is Alternative Rock's Hometown," *Washington Post*, July 2, 2003; and Carr, "Bohemian Diaspora." For the first book to chart the history of one of these unlikely scenes, see Barry Shank, *Dissonant Identities: The Rock 'n' Roll Scene in Austin, Texas* (Middletown: Wesleyan University Press, 1994).

25. Judy McWillie interviews; William Orten Carleton interview; and Brown, *Party Out of Bounds*, 28–29.

26. Cindy Wilson interview; Taylor, "B-52s and Me"; Sexton, *The B-52's Universe*; and Henke, "Interview: The B-52's."

27. Jeff Walls interview; and Keith Bennett interviews.

28. Taylor, "B-52's and Me"; Cindy Wilson interview; Keith Bennett interviews; Vanessa Briscoe Hay interviews; Jeff Walls interview; Sam Seawright interviews; Paul Butchart interview; Sean Bourne interview; and Julie House interview.

29. Taylor, "B-52's and Me," photograph of the dancing crowd; Brown, *Party Out of Bounds*, 31–34; Sexton, *B-52's Universe*, photograph of this gig, 36; and Blake Gumprecht, *The American College Town* (Boston: University of Massachusetts Press, 2008), 189–226.

30. Keith Bennett interviews; Sam Seawright interviews; Jared Bailey interview.

31. Beverly Cox, "The Night that Spawned a 'Cosmic Thing,'" *Athens Daily News*, February 14, 1997; Hendrix, "Touring Athens with the B-52's"; and Brown, *Party Out of Bounds*, 35–39.

32. Robert Christgau, foreword to new edition of Marcus, *Stranded*; Legs McNeil and Gillian McCain, *Please Kill Me: The Uncensored Oral History of Punk* (New York: Grove, 1996); Greil Marcus, *Lipstick Traces: A Secret History of the Twentieth Century* (Cambridge: Harvard University Press, 1989); Heylin, *From the Velvets to the Voidoids*; Heylin, *Babylon's Burning: From Punk to Grunge* (New York: Canongate, 2017); and Jon Savage, *England's Dreaming: Anarchy, Sex Pistols, Punk Rock, and Beyond* (New York: St. Martin's Press, 1992).

33. Tom Carson, "Tom Carson Talks Straight," *rockcritics.com*, http://rockcriticsarchives .com/interviews/tomcarson/tomcarson.html.

34. Special thanks to Joey Thompson for pushing me to think more about the Ramones

and for this insight about the Ramones and girl groups. Tom Carson, "Rocket to Russia," in Marcus, *Stranded*, 108. Hell is quoted in Heylin, *Babylon's Burning*, 21.

35. Dana Downs interview; Cindy Wilson interview; Robert Croker interview; Sam Seawright interviews; and Bill King, "The Fans: Not Your Typical Atlanta Rockers," *Atlanta Journal-Constitution*, May 28, 1977. On the history of Talking Heads, see David Bowman, *This Must Be the Place: The Adventures of the Talking Heads in the Twentieth Century* (New York, Harper, 2001).

36. Andy Bennett and Richard Peterson, eds., *Music Scenes: Local, Translocal, and Virtual* (Nashville: Vanderbilt University Press, 2004).

37. McLaughlin interview. On the Fans NYC show, the *Village Voice* ad on January 3, 1977, says Talking Heads are coming soon at CBGB's but does not mention the band playing Max's. Talking Heads played CBGB's January 13, 14, and 15, 1977. A *Village Voice* ad shows the B-52's opening for Teenage Jesus and the Jerks on May 28, 1978.

38. Bourne interview; Dana Downs interview; Betty Alice Fowler interview; O'Brien, "B-52s [*sic*]: Beehives Not Bombers," 56; Brown, *Party Out of Bounds*, 48–49; and Taylor, "B-52's and Me." Knapp was originally from Long Island. See John D. Addario, "Celebrity Photographer Sets Up Shop in Faubourg Marigny," *New Orleans Advocate*, July 22, 2015, http://www.theneworleansadvocate.com/beaucoup/12923762-125/celebrity-photographer-sets-up-shop. Betty Alice Fowler still lives in Athens, where she showed me her films in March of 2016. She has donated her footage to the University of Georgia Special Collections library.

39. Mitchell Cohen, "The B-52's: Climate Control in the Land of 16 Dances," *Creem*, December 1979; and Henke, "Interview: The B-52's." The *Village Voice* ad for Max's lists the B-52's playing on December 12, 1977.

40. Keith Bennett interviews; Cindy Wilson interview; Jeff Walls interview; Dana Downs interview; and Brown, *Party Out of Bounds*, 48–50.

41. Cindy Wilson interview; Keith Bennett interviews; Cohen, "B-52's: Climate Control"; O'Brien, "B-52s [*sic*]: Beehives Not Bombers"; Tom Carson, "B-52's," *New York Rocker*, July 1979, 4–5; Alan Platt, "Beehive Yourself: Will Success Spoil the Wholesome Kids from GA Who Claim They Didn't Know What They Were Doing?," *Soho Weekly News*, August 27, 1980;10–11; Brown, *Party Out of Bounds*, 51–52; and Sexton, *B-52's Universe*, 38–9. On the history of Max's, see Yvonne Sewall Ruskin, *High on Rebellion: Inside the Underground at Max's Kansas City* (New York: Thunder's Mouth Press, 1998).

42. Cindy Wilson interview; Keith Bennett interviews; Sam Seawright interviews; Mark Cline interviews; John Taylor, "New Wave Rock Comes to Town," *Athens Observer*, January 26, 1978, 17; Taylor, "B-52's and Me"; William Haines, "Sex Pistols Hitting Atlanta Scene," *Red and Black*, January 5, 1978, 3; Sullivan, *R.E.M.: Talk About the Passion*, 2; Kurt Wood, "Punk Rock Plays Emory," *Red and Black*, February 22, 1978, 5; and Jeff Calder, "Bruce Baxter: The Boy Who Pressed Buttons," *Georgia Music*, April 16, 2008, http://georgiamusic.org/bruce-baxter-the-boy-who-pressed-buttons/. On the WUOG broadcast, see the bootleg B-52's album *Anola Gay* (London: Monomatapa Records, sometime in the 1980s), which includes WUOG broadcast "The B-52's-Live 1978-02-xx The Last Resort, Athens, Georgia [*Anola Gay*], and the comments here: http://www.bootlegzone.com/album.php?name=b52s197802xx.

43. Cindy Wilson interview; Keith Bennett interviews; Sean Bourne interview; and Henke, "Interview: The B-52's." The Morton Building also housed the then unusable Morton Theater, a former African American vaudeville theater. It has since been restored.

On the El Dorado, see "A Farewell to an Idea That Was the El Dorado," *Athens Observer*, April 9, 1981.

44. McLaughlin interview; Carson, "B-52's"; Henke, "Interview: The B-52's"; and Andy Schwartz, [editorial], *New York Rocker*, February 1978. In the *Village Voice*, the Max's and CBGB's ads list shows for February and March 1978.

45. Carson, "B-52's"; John Rockwell, "B-52's, Rock Band from Georgia," *New York Times*, June 3, 1978, 11; and Stephen Holden, "The B-52's' American Graffiti," *Village Voice*, August 13, 1979. Holden coined the phrase "pop art rock band" here.

46. Van Gosse, "The B-52's Attack," *Village Voice* (October 1, 1980), 95; and Holden, "B-52's' *American Graffiti*."

47. Taylor, "New Wave Rock Comes to Town"; William Haines, "B-52's Are Taking Off," *Athens Observer*, April 13, 1978, 10B; and Jon Savage, "The B-52's: *B-52's* (Island): Yesterday's Sound Tomorrow," *Melody Maker*, June 30, 1979. See also Harry Sumrall, "The B-52's," *Washington Post*, February 26, 1979, which describes the B-52's as "a Southern cross of sci-fi and Beach Blanket Bingo."

48. Tom Carson, "B-52's Take Off," *Village Voice*, June 12, 1978, 49–50; Sumrall, "B-52's"; and Paul Rambali, "The B-52's: Hot Pants Cold Sweat and a Brand New Beehive Hair Do," *New Musical Express*, June 9, 1979.

49. "Interview with Danny Beard," *Tasty World* 3 [April 1985], 11; and Glenn O'Brien, "Beat," *Interview*, October 1978, 53. Robert Christgau was a key exception among white critics. O'Brien first mentioned the group in "Beat" *Interview* (July 1978), 34. Pop and disco were for the most part beneath the notice of self-identified "serious" critics. On the history of conflating "black" and "southern" sounds, see Karl Hagstrom Miller, *Segregating Sound: Inventing Folk and Pop Music in the Age of Jim Crow* (Durham: Duke University Press, 2010).

50. Jeff Clark, "Making It Up as You Go: How DB Recs Chronicled the South in the 80s," *Stomp and Stammer*, August 2003.

51. John Rockwell, "Records: The Disco Fever is Spreading," *New York Times*, February 26, 1978, D14: "homosexual discos and cabarets" have been moving "toward the worlds of cabaret, nostalgia, and theater." On the seventies idea, stylized in glam rock and disco, that gender and sexuality were "constructed and mutable (246)," see Ann Powers, *Good Booty: Love and Sex, Black and White, Body and Soul in American Music* (New York: Dey Street, 2017), 216–29, 246–49.

52. John Rockwell, "B-52's, A 'Tacky' Band," *New York Times*, April 15, 1982; and O'Brien, "B-52s [sic]: Beehives Not Bombers."

53. Cindy Wilson interview. Footage of the B-52's playing at the Downtown Café is online at https://www.youtube.com/playlist?list=PL0AF6372F5B725846. The videos on YouTube are labeled: "Produced by Tom Lure/ Directed and edited by Kelly Mills/ Camera work by Tom Lure and Gary Anderson." See also "1978 B-52's Concert Kicks Off AthFest RockDocs," *Online Athens: the Athens Banner-Herald*, June 18, 2008, http:// onlineathens.com/stories/061808/marquee_20080618021.shtml#.VWXtS0if4Zw. The Downtown Café concert is described in Haines, "B-52's are Taking Off," an article which also mentions that Seymour Stein was there, trying to sign the band. See also Seymour Stein with Gareth Murphy, *Siren Song: My Life in Music* (New York: St. Martin's Press, 2018), 155–56. All these songs performed in this concert appeared on *The B-52's* (Warner Brothers, 1979), except "Devil's in My Car" and "Runnin' Around," which appeared on *Wild Planet* (Warner Brothers, 1980).

On the unique qualities of live music, see Simon Frith, *Performing Rites: On the Value of Pop Music* (Cambridge: Harvard University Press, 1998); Peggy Phelan, *Unmarked: The Politics of Performance* (New York: Routledge, 1993); and Phillip Auslander, *Liveness: Performance in Mediatized Culture* (New York: Routledge, 1999); André Lepeck, *Of the Presence of the Body: Essays on Dance and Performance Theory* (Middletown: Wesleyan University Press, 2004); and Andrea Jones and Adrian Heathfield, *Perform, Repeat, Record: Live Art in History* (Chicago: University of Chicago Press, 2012). It is worth noting that the B-52's to varying degrees "script" and practice their "liveness."

54. For a different take on the B-52's, see Theo Cateforis, *Are We Not New Wave: Modern Pop at the Turn of the 1980s* (Ann Arbor: University of Michigan, 2011), 95–122.

55. Pierson has talked about how Fred Schneider introduced her and Cindy Wilson to Yoko Ono's music. See Will Harris, "Kate Pierson of the B-52s," *The A.V. Club*, November 1, 2011, online at https://music.avclub.com/kate-pierson-of-the-b-52s-1798228355. (Note that in 2008 the group dropped the apostrophe in its name.)

56. On Ricky Wilson's guitar playing, see Keith Bennett's unpublished essay, "Ricky Wilson" circulated on *Facebook* and in the author's possession. Wilson was a pioneer in the use of alternate tunings, a practice that would become widespread in the Athens scene in the 1980s and early 1990s.

57. Gosse, "B-52's Attack." On queer time, see J. Jack Halberstam, *In a Queer Time and Place: Transgender Bodies, Subcultural Lives* (New York: New York University Press, 2005).

58. William Haines, "B-52's at the Georgia Theater," *Athens Observer*, May 18, 1978.

59. Jeff Walls interview; Keith Bennett interviews; Cindy Wilson interview; and Brown, *Party Out of Bounds*, 58, 62–63.

60. McLaughlin interview; and Sexton, *B-52's Universe*. On the East Village scene in New York City in this period and the B-52's' place within it, see Steven Hager, *Art After Midnight: The East Village Scene* (New York: St. Martin's Press, 1986), which includes a photograph of the B-52's at the Mudd Club (58–59); and Marc Masters, *No Wave* (London: Black Dog Publishing, 2007).

61. Michael Lachowski interviews; Vanessa Briscoe Hay interviews; Robert Croker interviews; Brown, *Party Out of Bounds*, 61; and Sullivan, *R.E.M.: Talk About the Passion*, 6.

62. Sources on the firing of McLoughlin include Maureen McLoughlin interview; Carson, "B-52's"; and Brown, *Party Out of Bounds*, 92–94. McLoughlin says Brown is wrong about everything, but Carson provides information that supports Brown's version. Tom Carson, "The B-52's: Mid-Sixties bombers," *Rolling Stone*, September 20, 1979, 96; Paul Rambali, "The B-52's (Island)," *New Musical Express*, June 30, 1979; Andy Schwartz, "Update: The B-52's," *New York Rocker*, April 1979; and Stuart Cohn, "The B-52's: Just Like Us," *Trouser Press*, November 1979, 8. See Stanley Mieses, "B-52s [*sic*]: Bouffant Bob," *Melody Maker*, January 13, 1979, 18, for a Q and A with the band in which members discuss getting their Warner Brothers contract.

63. Holden, "The B-52's' *American Graffiti*."

64. Powers, *Good Booty*, 216–29, 246–49.

65. Gosse, "B-52's Attack,"; and Robert Christgau, "The Pazz and Jop Critics' Poll (Almost) Grows Up," *Village Voice*, February 1979.

66. Tom Carson, "B-52's"; Carson, "B-52's Take Off"; Taylor, "B-52's and Me"; Rockwell, "B-52's, Rock Band from Georgia"; Alan Platt, "Hairdos by Laverne," *Soho Weekly News*, August 9, 1979, 17; and Kory Grow, "Love Shacks, Rock Lobsters, and Wild Parties: The B-52's in Their Own Words," *Rolling Stone*, June 1, 2018, online at https://www.rollingstone

.com/music/music-features/love-shacks-rock-lobsters-and-nude-parties-the-b-52s-in
-their-own-words-627925/.

67. Carson, "B-52's"; and Tom Carson, "Stop 'N' Rock," *Village Voice*, December 3, 1980,
43–48.

68. Glenn O'Brien, "Beat," *Interview* (August 1979).

69. Cindy Wilson interview. On gays and punk music, see Adam Block, "The
Confessions of a Gay Rocker," *The Advocate*, April 15, 1982, 43–47.

CHAPTER 2

1. Vanessa Briscoe Hay interviews.

2. Vanessa started school as Vanessa Briscoe. She became Vanessa Ellison when she
married Jimmie Ellison, future member of Athens band the Side Effects, when she was
around twenty. Then she changed her name again to Vanessa Briscoe Hay when she
married Bob Hay, then a member of Athens band the Squalls, in 1986. Vanessa Briscoe
Hay interviews; Bob Hay interview; Sam Seawright interviews; and Vanessa Briscoe Hay,
"Vanessa's Version," online at http://www.netnik.com/jollybeggars/pylon.html.

3. Vanessa Briscoe Hay interviews; and Briscoe Hay, "Vanessa's Version."

4. Michael Lachowski interviews.

5. Michael Lachowski interviews; Kim Taylor Bennett, "We Talked to Pylon's Michael
Lachowski Because He's a Legend," August 7, 2014, http://noisey.vice.com/read/we
-talked-to-michael-lachowski-from-pylon-because-hes-a-legend; Jason Gross, "Tribute
to Randy Bewley," *Perfect Sound Forever*, February 2010, www.furious.com/perfect/pylon
randy.html; Jason Gross, "Pylon Interview: Part 1 and Part 2," *Perfect Sound Forever*, May
1998, http://www.furious.com/perfect/pylon.html; http://www.furious.com/perfect
/pylon2.html; and Fred Mills, "Everything Is Cool: Form Followed Function for Athens
Postpunk Legends Pylon," *Harp*, December 2007, http://www.rocksbackpages.com
/article.html?ArticleID=13437.

6. Michael Lachowski interviews; Vanessa Briscoe Hay interviews; Sam Seawright
interviews; Judy McWillie interviews; Art Rosenbaum interviews; Richard Olsen
interview; Robert Croker interview; and Bill Paul interview. Through this chapter, I have
benefited from materials collected by Art Rocks Athens, or alternately, ARTROXATH, a
series of events created by former participants to celebrate the role of the arts in starting
the Athens music scene. Art Rocks Athens generated multiple exhibitions in 2014 and 2015
and a website that was previously available at http://artrocksathens.com/VIPGallery
500web/html. The website is no longer active, but I have materials from the site, as
well as other materials given me by participants and documentation of what was in the
exhibitions, in my possession. Special thanks on this front to Robert Croker. I will cite
these materials as the Art Rocks Athens Collection.

7. Copies of flyers for art shows, author's possession; John Martin Taylor, "The B-52's
and Me," *Hoppin' John's*, February 16, 2008, http://hoppinjohns.net/?p=263; and email
correspondence with Robert Croker, January 22, 2016. The show at Memorial Hall was
called "Upstairs Uptown."

8. Judith Rodenbeck, *Radical Prototypes: Allan Kaprow and the Invention of Happenings*
(Boston: MIT Press, 2011); Mildred L. Glimcher, *Happenings: New York, 1958–1963* (New
York: Monacelli Press, 2012); Hannah Higgins, *Fluxus Experience* (Berkeley: University
of California Press, 2002); Vincent Katz, editor, *Black Mountain College: An Experiment in*

Art (Boston: MIT Press, 2013); and Martin Duberman, *Black Mountain: An Exploration in Community* (Evanston: Northwestern University Press, 2009).

9. Simon Frith and Howard Horne, *Art into Pop* (London: Methuen, 1987); Bernard Gendron, *From Montmartre to the Mudd Club: Popular Music and the Avant-garde* (Chicago: University of Chicago Press, 2011), 227–316; and Simon Reynolds, *Rip It Up and Start Again: Postpunk, 1978–1984* (London: Faber and Faber, 2005), 30–49.

10. Michael Lachowski interviews. On the history of *New York Rocker*, see Jesse Jarnow, *Big Day Coming: Yo La Tengo and the Rise of Indie Rock* (New York: Gotham, 2012).

11. Michael Lachowski interviews; Vanessa Briscoe Hay interviews; and "Pylon," *New Musical Express*, September 1980.

12. Vanessa Briscoe Hay interviews; and Michael Lachowski interviews.

13. Vanessa Briscoe Hay interviews; Mark Cline interviews; Michael Lachowski interviews; and "Closeup: Vanessa Briscoe," *Athens Observer*, January 20, 1983.

14. Lester Bangs, "Of Pop, Pies and Fun: A Program for Mass Liberation in the Form of a Stooges Review of, Who's the Fool?," *Creem*, November/December 1970, collected in *Psychotic Reactions and Carburetor Dung*, ed. Greil Marcus (New York: Anchor Books, 2003), 45; and Van Gosse, "Pylon Draws the Line," *Village Voice*, February 25, 1981, 61–62.

15. Curtis Crowe is quoted in Pylon, *Gyrate* (1980; reissue, DFA Records, 2007), liner notes.

16. Stephen Pond, "R.E.M.: America's Best Rock and Roll Band," *Rolling Stone*, December 3, 1987; Velena Vego interview; T. Patton Biddle interview; and Dan Weiss, "Taking Fun Seriously: Pylon's Last Hurrah," *Spin*, August 2, 2016, https://www.spin .com/2016/08/pylon-live-deerhunter-sleater-kinney-rem/.

17. On the ways music can create new worlds, see Barry Shank, *The Political Force of Musical Beauty* (Durham: Duke University Press, 2014); Josh Kun, *Audiotopia: Music, Race, and America* (Berkeley: University of California Press, 2005); and Ann Powers, *Good Booty: Love and Sex, Black and White, Body and Soul in American Music* (New York: Dey Street, 2017).

18. Lachowski quote is from Gross, "Pylon Interview: Part I"; Karen Moline, "Pylon: From Athens, GA: New Sounds of the Old South: Temporary Rock" *New York Rocker*, March 1981, 15–17; Michael Lachowski interviews; and Vanessa Briscoe Hay interviews.

19. Sean Bourne interview; Chris Rasmussen interview; Sam Seawright interviews; Jeff Wall interview; Gross, "Pylon Interview: Part 1," and Jeff Wall memories posted online in the Athens Rewind, a collection of memories, photographs, and flyers collected for a 2006 reunion of participants in the early years of the Athens scene and archived online at http://www.athensrewind.com/play_II.html. Some of the organizers of this event had the idea of creating an oral history of the scene, similar to Legs McNeil and Gillian McCain, *Please Kill Me: The Uncensored Oral History of Punk* (New York: Grove, 1996). The book was never completed. Hereafter, these materials will be cited as Athens Rewind.

20. Jeff Wall interview; and Rodger Brown, *Party Out of Bounds: The B-52's, R.E.M., and the Kids Who Rocked Athens, Georgia* (New York: Plume, 1991), 80–82.

21. Michael Lachowski interview; Mills, "Everything Is Cool"; Gross, "Pylon Interview: Part I"; Moline, "Pylon: From Athens, GA"; Gerald Burris, "Don't Fret: Randy Bewley," *Athens Music Junkie*, April 12, 2011, http://athensmusicjunkie.com/2011/04/12/dont-fret -randy-bewley/; and Brown, *Party Out of Bounds*, 85.

22. Gross, "Pylon Interview: Part I"; and Mills, "Everything Is Cool."

23. Michael Lachowski interviews; Vanessa Briscoe Hay interviews; Mills, "Everything Is Cool"; Gross, "Pylon Interview: Part I"; and Brown, *Party Out of Bounds*, 83–89.

24. Nancy Lukasiewicz interview; Vanessa Briscoe Hay interviews; Sam Seawright interviews; Michael Lachowski interviews; and publication called *The Agora*, section entitled "Art in Athens, No. 3 May," listed shows around town, from "Art in Athens," clipping files, Georgia Room, UGA library. A photograph of Lachowski's sculpture is online at http://michaellachowski.com/.

25. Vanessa Briscoe Hay interviews; Sam Seawright interviews; and Briscoe Hay, "Vanessa's Version."

26. Vanessa Briscoe Hay interviews; Sam Seawright interviews; and Briscoe Hay, "Vanessa's Version."

27. Vanessa Briscoe Hay interviews; Briscoe Hay, "Vanessa's Version"; Mills, "Everything is Cool"; and Moline, "Pylon: From Athens, GA," 15.

28. Lachowski letter to Robert Croker (copy in author's possession); Michael Lachowski interviews; Vanessa Briscoe Hay interviews; Watt King interview; Brown, *Party Out of Bounds*, 58; and Moline, "Pylon: From Athens, GA."

29. Michael Lachowski letter to Robert Croker; Michael Lachowski interviews; Vanessa Briscoe Hay interviews; Moline, "Pylon: From Athens, GA"; and Jimmy Ellison, photograph of Pylon playing at the original non-commercial location of the 40 Watt Club (Curtis Crowe and Bill Tabor's private loft residence, Myers Building, third floor, 171 College Ave.) in 1979 in Athens Rewind.

30. Vanessa Briscoe Hay interviews; Briscoe Hay, "Vanessa's Version"; Michael Lachowski interviews; liner notes for Pylon, *Gyrate* (DB Records, 1980; reissue, DFA Records, 2007); and Craig S. Phillips, "Athens: A Music Mecca," *Red and Black*, November 8, 1999, 1, 3. The name Tyrone's OC linked the current name of the club to the name of the previous business that occupied the space. OC meant "Old Chameleon."

31. Vanessa Briscoe Hay interviews; Vic Varney interview; and Briscoe Hay, "Vanessa's Version." Fouratt was a big supporter of Athens bands at every New York club he booked, including Hurrah and Danceteria.

32. Flyer for Pylon's first New York gig, part of the Sam Seawright collection, photograph of flyer in the author's possession.

33. Karen Stinnett interview.

34. Karen Stinnett interview; Karen Stinnett, "Zak MFA," Art Rocks Athens Collection; Sean Bourne interview; Robert Croker interviews; and email correspondence with and documents sent by Robert Croker.

35. Robert Croker interviews; Andrew Krieger interview; Sean Bourne interview; Michael Paxton interview; and email correspondence with and documents sent by Robert Croker, including photographs of the exhibition.

36. Karen Stinnett Interview; Robert Croker interviews; and Michael Paxton interview.

37. Sean Bourne interview.

38. Mark Cline interviews.

39. Mark Cline interviews; Sam Seawright interviews; and Jennifer Hartley interview. On the influence of art school on the British music scene, from the Beatles and the Stones to punk and new wave, see Frith and Horne, *Art into Pop*. For the influence of art school on postpunk, see Reynolds, *Rip It Up and Start Again*, 264.

40. Andrew Krieger interview; Robert Croker interviews; Karen Stinnett interview; and Judy McWillie interviews.

41. Andrew Krieger interview; Karen Stinnett interview; and scan of the Edible Art show poster by Krieger, in the author's possession. Photographs of Lachowski's piece and his award, http://michaellachowski.com/Edible-Art-Show.

42. Mark Cline interviews; Robert Croker interviews; and Briscoe Hay interviews. Robert Waldrop earned songwriting credits on B-52's songs including "Hero Worship," "Dirty Back Road," and "Roam."

43. Robert Croker interviews; and Sean Mills, "Tooled Education," a web presentation of the history of Art X, online at http://seanmillsartist.com/tooldeducation/index2.html.

44. Robert Croker interviews; Sean Bourne interview; Roy R. Behrens, "Drawing in the Dark: Hoyt Sherman and the Flash Lab at Ohio State University," online at http://www.bobolinkbooks.com/Ames/DrawingInDark.html; and Mills, "Tooled Education." Scholars see "Art X" as an important prototype for virtual reality.

45. Robert Croker interviews; Chatham Murray, published biography from the Studio Group's promotional materials, in the author's possession; and Mills, "Tooled Education."

46. Sean Bourne interview; and Lamar Dodd School of Art's description of its history, online at http://art.uga.edu/about-us.

47. Mills interviewed Richard Olsen for his project and includes Olsen's description of his classes in "Tooled Education." Richard Olsen interview; Sean Bourne interview; and Robert Croker interviews.

48. Robert Croker interviews; Robert Croker, autobiographical notes emailed to the author; and Judy McWillie interviews.

49. Robert Croker interviews; and Robert Croker, autobiographical notes emailed to author.

50. Robert Croker interviews; Mark Cline interviews; Karen Stinnet interviews; Sam Seawright interviews; Sally Speed interview; Briscoe Hay interviews; Michael Lachowski interviews; and Keith Bennett interviews.

51. Mark Cline interviews; Karen Stinnet interview; Sam Seawright interviews; Robert Croker interviews; and images in Croker's drawing notebooks, part of Croker Collection at the Georgia Museum of Art, Athens, Georgia.

52. Mark Cline interviews; and Robert Croker interviews. I am indebted to colleague Lisa Goff for suggesting this connection to gonzo journalism.

53. Sean Bourne interviews; Mark Cline interviews; Michael Lachowski interviews; Jennifer Hartley interview; Annelies Mondi interview; Judy McWillie interviews; and "Campus Life: Georgia, Films by Students Find an Audience Outside of Class," *New York Times*, February 23, 1992.

54. Art Rosenbaum interviews; Jennifer Hartley interviews; and Sam Seawright interviews.

55. Mark Cline interviews; Robert Croker interviews; Sam Seawright interviews; Sally Speed interview; Art Harris, "O Little Town of Rock 'n' Roll," *Washington Post*, August 29, 1984; and Jim Herbert, Bio, Art Rocks Athens Collection, http://artrocksathens.com/VIP Gallery500web/html; and "Georgia, Films by Students Find an Audience Outside of Class." More than one person reported that Herbert had peep holes in his home.

56. Robert Croker, emailed party notes, in author's possession; Robert Croker interviews; Mark Cline interviews; Karen Stinnett interviews; Vanessa Briscoe Hay interviews; and Vanessa Briscoe Hay, "Vanessa's Version."

57. Robert Croker interviews; Judy McWillie interviews; Mark Cline interviews; Sam Seawright interviews; Keith Bennett interviews; Karen Stinnett interview; Vic Varney

interview; James T. Sears, *Growing Up Gay in the South* (New York: Routledge, 1991); and John Howard, *Men Like That: A Southern Queer History* (Chicago: University of Chicago, 2001).

58. Here, I draw on the totality of my interviews. My vagueness in naming names and assigning sexual and gender categories to people who did not then and in many cases have not since claimed those identities is intentional. In cases where I have not talked to a person and/or that individual has not left a public record of their choice, I have not "assigned" them to a category.

59. Karen Stinnett interview; Judy McWillie interviews; Sally Speed interview; Jennifer Hartley interview; Briscoe Hay interviews; Sam Seawright interviews; Keith Bennett interviews; Mark Cline interviews; and Annelies Mondi interview.

60. Judy McWillie interviews.

61. Here, I draw on the totality of my interviews; memories submitted to Athens Rewind, http://www.athensrewind.com/play_II.html; and Vic Varney, "Nineteen Hours from New York: Small Town Makes Good," *New York Rocker*, March 1981, 20.

62. Mark Cline interviews; Lauren Fancher interviews; Michael Lachowski interviews; Sally Speed interview; Sam Seawright interviews; and Keith Bennett interviews.

63. Christopher Bollen, "Michael Stipe," *Interview*, May 4, 2011, http://www.interview magazine.com/music/michael-stipe/; and Mark Cline interviews.

64. Arthur Johnson interviews; David Barbe interviews; Claire Horne interview; Bryan Cook interview; and Lauren Fancher interviews.

65. Michael Lachowski, letter to Croker, April 23, 1979, part of Art Rocks Athens Collection, in author's possession. He never delivered the letter but sealed it in an envelope and did not discover it again until cleaning out his studio in 2014. Michael Lachowski interviews; and Robert Croker interviews. Robert Christgau is wrong when he says they got their name from the Faulkner album.

66. Mills, "Everything Is Cool"; Michael Lachowski interviews; Vanessa Briscoe Hay interviews; Briscoe Hay, "Vanessa's Version"; Art Rocks Athens show of Athens music artifacts at the University of Georgia's Special Collections Library, 2014 (includes Pylon posters); and Sam Seawright interviews and archive.

67. Briscoe Hay, "Vanessa's Version"; Vanessa Briscoe Hay interviews; Gross, "Pylon Interview"; and J. Eddy Ellison, "Athens Success Method Fails for 'Actors,'" *Red and Black*, November 11, 1982, 5. Some sources say Vic Varney handled this kind of business for Pylon in the early days and that he got them their gigs opening for Gang of Four in Philadelphia and headlining at the Ratt in Boston.

68. Briscoe Hay, "Vanessa's Version"; and Michael Lachowski interviews.

69. Vanessa Briscoe Hay interviews; and Briscoe Hay, "Vanessa's Version."

70. Briscoe Hay, "Vanessa's Version"; and Glenn O'Brien, "Beat," *Interview*, September 1979.

71. Vanessa Briscoe Hay interviews; Michael Lachowski interviews; and Cindy Wilson interview.

72. "Georgia Record Labels: Indies Formed from Red Clay," *Flagpole*, September 23, 1992, 6; Briscoe Hay, "Vanessa's Version"; Athens Rewind; and Brown, *Party Out of Bounds*, 126.

73. Briscoe Hay, "Vanessa's Version"; J. Eddy Ellison, "Limbo District Explores Beat," *Athens Banner Herald/Daily News*, March 26, 1983; Blake Gumprecht, "R.E.M.," *Alternative America*, Winter 1983, 35–36; Jim Herbert, "Carnival—Limbo District (1982)," online at

https://beatopolis.wordpress.com/2016/08/24/carnival-limbo-district-1982/; "Limbo District," https://www.chunklet.com/limbo-district-athens-biggest-puzzle-at-least-to -me/; and Athens Rewind.

74. Vanessa Briscoe Hay interviews; Briscoe Hay, "Vanessa's Version"; Jared Bailey, "Pylon Performance Shines Despite Crowd, Delay," *Red and Black*, October 13, 1981, 7; and "Closeup: Vanessa Briscoe." Bailey later founded the weekly free paper *Flagpole* and the annual music festival *Athfest* and was co-owner for years of the music club the 40 Watt.

75. Briscoe Hay, "Vanessa's Version"; Gross, "Pylon Interview: Part 1"; Vanessa Briscoe Hay interviews; and Michael Lachowski interviews.

76. Glenn O'Brien, "Beat," *Interview* (June 1980), 52–53. Robert Christgau, "Pazz and Jop 1980: Dean's List," published in the *Village Voice*, online at https://www.robert christgau.com/xg/pnj/deans80.php.

77. Moline, "Pylon: From Athens, GA"; and Michael Lachowski interviews.

78. The Athens and Bronx scenes evolved at the same time, in the late seventies and eighties, and by 1980, increasing numbers of outsiders had begun to "discover" both places. The mostly white and middle-class Athens scene was often "easier" for many journalists (themselves often white and middle-class) to love. Athens became nationally and internationally known as a key site of alternative culture in the eighties. The Bronx and other sites nurturing hip-hop became in this way the "alternative" alternative, even as hip-hop artists rooted themselves in the local much as Athens scene makers did. Jeff Chang, *Can't Stop, Won't Stop: A History of the Hip-Hop Generation* (New York: St. Martin's, 2005); Tricia Rose, *Black Noise: Rap Music and Black Culture in Contemporary America* (Middletown: Wesleyan University Press, 1994); Blake Gumprecht, *The American College Town* (Amherst: University of Massachusetts Press, 2008), 207; and Ian Svenonius, "The Rise and Fall of College Rock," *New Republic*, October 23, 2015, online at https:// newrepublic.com/article/123187/how-npr-killed-college-rock.

79. Kit Swartz interview; Vanessa Briscoe Hay interviews; and Mark Cline interviews.

80. Julie House interview; and Brown, *Party Out of Bounds*.

81. Moline, "Pylon: From Athens, GA"; posters and photographs, Athens Rewind, http://www.athensrewind.com/play_II.html; Michael Lachowski interviews; Armistead Wellford interview; Mark Cline interviews; and Watt King interview. See the entry "For Your Love" by the Side Effects at Pylon Park, Athens Rewind, http://www.athensrewind .com/play_II.html: "The entire night at this particular Pylon Park party was timeless. Michael's huge clear plastic sheet suspended 20 feet between trees with "Rain" spray-painted on it and sprinkler cascading in fan motion back and forth all night was brilliant. I still get chills down my back remembering Kit, Jimmy and Paul playing 'For Your Love.'"

82. Vanessa Briscoe Hay interviews; and Michael Lachowski interviews. The Plastics had been unable to get into the country.

83. Greg McLean, [untitled piece], *New York Rocker*, June/July 1980, 10.

84. Bill King, "Athens: A City Attuned to New Wave-length," *Atlanta Journal Constitution*, August 30, 1981, 1F, 6F; Danceteria ad that labels bands by where they are from, including in the April 1982 issue of the *Village Voice* and in August 9, 1980, September 4, 1980, July 15, 1981, and July 22, 1981 issues of *Soho Weekly News*; Gross, "Pylon Interview: Part 1 and Part 2"; Michael Lachowski interviews; and Moline, "Pylon: From Athens, GA."

85. "Pylon-1980," online at https://vimeo.com/50389377. See also http://eastvillage .thelocal.nytimes.com/2012/10/15/nightclubbing-pylon/, which described the video

as part of Pat Ivers and Emily Armstrong's archive of punk-era concert footage being digitized for the Downtown Collection at N.Y.U.'s Fales Library.

86. "Pylon-1980," online at https://vimeo.com/50389377.

87. Gosse, "Pylon Draws the Line," describes Briscoe Hay in a performance at the Rock Lounge in New York on Valentine's Day 1981 as, "shoeless with whistle, in a parochial-school blue smock and white blouse" (3).

88. Gosse, "Pylon Draws the Line," 3.

89. "Review of *Gyrate*," *New Musical Express*, December 1980; Robert Holland, "After Hours," *Red and Black*, February 8, 1980, 5; "Interview with Danny Beard," *Tasty World* 3 [April 1985], 11; Jay Watson, "Local Groups Get Boost from DB Records," *Red and Black*, January 13, 1982, 1, 5; Briscoe Hay, "Vanessa's Version"; Vanessa Briscoe Hay interviews; Sean Bourne interview; T. Patton Biddle interview; and Chris Rasmussen interview. Bewley did the cover art for the album and former art student Bourne, then working in Atlanta at Beard's record store, did the art direction and design.

90. Glenn O'Brien, "Beat," *Interview*, March 1981, 62.

91. Gosse, "Pylon Draws the Line," 61–62. Gosse's article offered very high praise considering how much good rock and roll came out in 1980, including Springsteen's *The River*, John Lennon's *Double Fantasy*, Pete Townshend's *Empty Glass*, David Bowie's *Scary Monsters*, Grace Jones's *Warm Leatherette*, Captain Beefheart's *Doc at the Radar Station*, The English Beat's *I Just Can't Stop It*, and Stevie Wonder's *Hotter Than July*, and albums by more underground acts like Talking Heads' *Remain in Light*, Elvis Costello's *Get Happy!*, X's *Los Angeles*, The Clash's *Sandinista!*, and the Dead Kennedys' *Fresh Fruit for Rotting Vegetables*.

92. Moline, "Pylon: From Athens, GA"; and Varney, "Nineteen Hours from New York." For more interesting writing about Pylon, see Robert Palmer, "Critics' Choices," *New York Times*, April 4, 1982; Guy Trebay, "Survey of the Week's Events: Pylon/dB's," *Village Voice*, April 20, 1982; "Pylon/'Crazy,'" *New York Rocker*, June 1982, 43; Steve Anderson, "Pylontechnics," *Village Voice*, November 9, 1982, 66; Stephen Holden, "Music: Pylon at the Ritz," *New York Times*, May 31, 1983; Tom Carson, "Pylon Up Around the Bend," *Village Voice*, June 14, 1983, 84; and Bennett, "We Talked to Pylon's Michael Lachowski."

93. Vanessa Briscoe Hay interviews; T. Patton Biddle interview; Jay Watson, "'Athens' Finest' Play Tonight," *Red and Black*, January 13, 1982, 5; and Moline, "Pylon: From Athens, GA"; T. Patton Biddle, better known as Pat the soundman, has the flyer for the Memorial Hall show with Pylon and Love Tractor on his website at https://www.patthewiz.com/.

94. Cindy Wilson interview; Jon Piccarella, "The B-52's, *Mesopotamia* (Warner Brothers)," *New York Rocker*, April 1982, 43; and J. Eddy Ellison, "Athens Own B-52's Rock the Fox, Still Have Their 40 Watt Charisma," *Red and Black*, May 12, 1982, 2. Of course, the B-52's never played the 40 Watt Club.

95. Vanessa Briscoe Hay interviews; and Michael Lachowski interviews.

96. Poster reproduced as an ad, *Red and Black*, December 1, 1983, 6; Michael Lachowski interviews; and Vanessa Briscoe Hay interviews.

97. Pylon, *Pylon Live* (Chunklet, 2016); and Stuart Berman, review of *Pylon Live*, by Pylon, *Pitchfork*, July 19, 2016, online at https://pitchfork.com/reviews/albums/22125 -pylon-live/.

98. J. Eddy Ellison, "A Fond Farewell: Fans, Followers and Friends Sadly Try to Accept," *Athens Banner Herald-Athens Daily News*, December 2, 1983, 10–11; Michael Lachowski

interviews; Vanessa Briscoe Hay interview; and David Pierce, "The Tasty World Interview: Michael Lachowski," *Tasty World* 2 [no date], 23, 29.

99. Mark Cline interviews; Vanessa Briscoe Hay interviews; and Michael Lachowski interviews.

CHAPTER 3

1. Parke Puterbaugh, "R.E.M.'s Southern Rock Revival," *Rolling Stone*, June 9, 1983, reprinted in *R.E.M.: The Rolling Stone Files*, ed. Anthony DeCurtis (New York: Hyperion, 1995), 30; and Steve Pond, "R.E.M. in the Real World," *Rolling Stone*, December 1987, reprinted in Curtis, *Rolling Stone Files*, 73–84. For scene participants' memories of the church, see Paul Butchart interview; Kit Swartz interview; Sam Seawright interviews; Mark Cline interviews; and Athens Rewind.

2. Paul Butchart interview; Kit Swartz interview; Sam Seawright interviews; Mark Cline interviews; and Athens Rewind. Kurt Wood is quoted about his WUOG experience in David Buckley, *R.E.M. Fiction: An Alternative Biography* (New York: Virgin, 2003), 21. Pete Buck's brother Ken, a music student at UGA, along with perhaps another woman, also lived at the church.

3. Paul Butchart, Athens Rewind; Paul Butchart interview; Puterbaugh, "R.E.M.'s Southern Rock Revival"; Steve Pond, "R.E.M. in the Real World"; and Rodger Brown, *Party Out of Bounds: The B-52's, R.E.M., and the Kids Who Rocked Athens, Georgia* (New York: Plume, 1991), 135–39.

4. Kit Swartz interview; Sam Seawright interview; Denise Sullivan, *R.E.M.: Talk About the Passion, An Oral History* (New York: Da Capo Press, 1998), 8–11; Blake Gumprecht, "R.E.M.," *Alternative America*, Winter 1983, 35–36; Jim Sullivan, "R.E.M.: Shadows and Murmurs," *Record*, July 1983; and Pond, "R.E.M. in the Real World." Patti Smith, a key inspiration for both Stipe and Buck, recorded a cover of Van Morrison's song "Gloria," with new lyrics that described NYC punk life, on her 1975 album *Horses*. Hatred of hippies, characteristic of punk, was not nearly as strong in Athens, even among kids who loved punk music. More than a few bohemians had previously been hippies, including Armistead Wellford, Bob Hay, and Chris DeBarr. Ken Starratt managed to be both simultaneously. Some sources say the third band was the $windles.

5. Sullivan, *R.E.M.: Talk About the Passion*, 5, 7; Howard Pousner, "The B-52s Are No Bomb," *Atlanta Journal-Constitution*, August, 20, 1980; Mitchell Cohen, "The B-52s: Climate Control in the Land of 16 Dances," *Creem*, December 1979; Kevin Bicknell, Jared H. Bailey, and J. Gregg Clark, "Athens Credited with Birth of Modern Music," *Red and Black*, April 23, 1981, 1, 2; and Bicknell, Bailey, and Clark, "Trendiness May Ruin New Wave's Fun," *Red and Black*, April 24, 1981, 1, 2.

6. Tom Carson, "Stop 'N' Rock," *Village Voice*, December 3–9, 1980, 43.

7. Bicknell, Bailey, and Clark, "Athens Credited with Birth of Modern Music"; and Bicknell, Bailey, and Clark, "Trendiness May Ruin New Wave's Fun." This rejection of traditional politics in favor of cultural politics can be traced through Carson, "Stop 'N' Rock"; Barry Shank, *Dissonant Identities: The Rock 'n' Roll Scene in Austin, Texas* (Middletown: Wesleyan University Press, 1994); Michael Azerrad, *Our Band Could Be Your Life: Scenes from the American Indie Underground, 1981–1991* (New York: Little, Brown, 2001); Simon Reynolds, *Rip It Up and Start Again: Postpunk, 1978–1984* (London: Faber

and Faber, 2005); Reynolds, *Totally Wired: Postpunk Interviews and Overviews* (New York: Soft Skull Press, 2009); and Bob Mehr, *Trouble Boys: The True Story of the Replacements* (Boston: Da Capo Press, 2016).

8. Jerrold Seigel, *Bohemian Paris: Culture, Politics, and the Boundaries of Bourgeois Life, 1830–1930* (New York: Viking, 1986); Christine Stansell, *American Moderns: Bohemian New York and the Creation of a New Century* (2000; repr., Princeton: Princeton University Press, 2009); Bernard Gendron, *Between Montmartre and the Mudd Club: Popular Music and the Avant-Garde* (Chicago: University of Chicago Press, 2002); and Carson, "Stop 'N' Rock." On alternative culture as a form of bohemia, see Ann Powers, *Weird Like Us: My Bohemian America* (New York: Simon & Schuster, 2000).

9. Carson, "Stop 'N' Rock"; and C. Carr, "Bohemian Diaspora," *Village Voice*, February 4, 1992, 27.

10. Bill King, "Athens: A City Attuned to a New Wave-Length," *Atlanta Constitution*, August 30, 1981, 1F, 6F; and Chuck Reece, "Resurrect Spirit of Tyrone's," *Red and Black*, February 2, 1982, 4.

11. J. Eddy Ellison, "R.E.M. to Play Athens, Sets Letterman Date," *Athens Banner-Herald/Daily News*, October 1, 1983, 4; Sullivan, "R.E.M.: Shadows and Murmurs"; Tony Fletcher, "R.E.M. Interview with Tony Fletcher," *Jamming!* (1983), republished on the website Remring, http://www.remring.com/?q=node/64; Fletcher, *Remarks: The Story of R.E.M.* (New York: Bantam Books, 1990), 8, 13; and Brown, *Party Out of Bounds*, 136. Part of Buck's reluctance to be in a band may have stemmed from the fact that his younger brother Ken was a talented guitar player and music major at UGA. Much of what appears about the formation of the band in books and articles — especially quotes from band members — comes from Brown's *Party Out of Bounds* and sometimes contradicts in the details if not the broader outlines of what band members told journalists when interviewed years earlier and what other people remember more recently. Over the years, band members, too, changed how they narrated their past. I try here to look at these sources in relation to each other to both reveal disagreements and determine, to the extent possible, what actually happened. Matthew Bannister, *White Boys, White Noise: Masculinities and 1980s Indie Guitar Rock* (Burlington: Ashgate, 2006), describes denial of ambition as a central characteristic of white indie masculinity.

12. David Fricke, "Peter Buck Q & A," *Rolling Stone*, November 15, 1990, reprinted in DeCurtis, *Rolling Stone Files*, 111–21; the Notorious Stuart Brothers, "A Date with Pete Buck," *Bucketfull of Brains*, December 1987, reprinted in John Platt, ed., *The R.E.M. Companion* (New York: Schirmer Books, 1998), 93–104; Rob Jovanovic, *Michael Stipe: The Biography* (New York: Little, Brown, 2007), 30–31; and "R.E.M. about Athens and Starting the Band," interviews with band members Mills, Stipe, and Buck, online at https://www.youtube.com/watch?v=4kkiXUY8Sko.

13. David Fricke, "Michael Stipe: The Rolling Stone Interview," *Rolling Stone*, March 5, 1992), reprinted in DeCurtis, *Rolling Stone Files*, 144–53; and April 4, 2005, episode of Andrew Denton's Australian talk show *Enough Rope*, transcript online at http://www.remrock.com/remrock/archives.php?thepage=news&id=151. In *Rolling Stone*, Stipe claimed he saw a photograph of Patti Smith in the November 1975 issue of *Creem*, but there is none in that issue. Stipe and Buck, like many postpunk and indie musicians, came of age reading rock criticism and probably curated their past influences to fit their current taste and their understanding of the history of underground music.

14. Christopher Bollen, "Michael Stipe," *Interview*, May 5, 2011, online at http://www

.interviewmagazine.com/music/michael-stipe#page2; April 4, 2005, episode of Andrew Denton's Australian talk show *Enough Rope*; "R.E.M. about Athens and Starting the Band"; Fricke, "Michael Stipe: The Rolling Stone Interview," 149; "Losing My Religion," a program produced by the Scandinavian public broadcasters NRK and SVT as part of a series called *The History of the Hit Song*, online at https://tv.nrk.no/program/MKTF57 000016/history-of-the-hit-song-losing-my-religion; Art Rosenbaum interviews; Mark Cline interviews; Sally Speed interview; Judy McWillie interviews; and Armistead Wellford interview.

15. Mark Cline interviews; Sullivan, *R.E.M.: Talk About the Passion*, 41; and Bollen, "Michael Stipe."

16. Sullivan, *R.E.M.: Talk About the Passion*, 2, 3, 8–10; Ellison, "R.E.M. to Play Athens"; John Platt, "R.E.M.," *Bucketfull of Brains*, December 1984, reprinted in John Platt, ed., *The R.E.M. Companion* (New York: Schirmer Books, 1998), 9; Gumprecht, "R.E.M."; Pond, "R.E.M. in the Real World"; and Brad Evans, "An Interview with Mike Mills," *The 11th Hour*, February 19, 2010, http://11thhouronline.com/2010/02/19/fusce-sem-massa-ultrices -vitae-mauris-vel-porta-egestas/.

17. Sullivan, *R.E.M.: Talk About the Passion*, 2, 3, 8–10; Ellison, "R.E.M. to Play Athens," 4; Platt, "R.E.M."; Gumprecht, "R.E.M."; Pond, "R.E.M. in the Real World"; and Ian Copeland, *Wild Thing* (New York: Simon & Schuster, 1995), 213–36.

18. Sullivan, *R.E.M.: Talk About the Passion*, 2, 3, 8–10; Ellison, "R.E.M. to Play Athens," 4; John Platt, "R.E.M.," 9; Blake Gumprecht, "R.E.M."; Pond, "R.E.M. in the Real World"; and Copeland, *Wild Thing*, 213–36. UGA was on the quarter system then, with three terms rather than two during the academic year, plus a summer term.

19. Sullivan, *R.E.M.: Talk About the Passion*, 8–11, 17; David Fricke, "Pete Buck Q & A," reprinted in DeCurtis, *Rolling Stone Files*, 111–21; Brown, *Party Out of Bounds*, 125–28, 157; Marcus Gray, *It Crawled from the South: An R.E.M. Companion* (New York: Da Capo, 1997), 60–63; Mark Cline interviews; Armistead Wellford interview; and Sam Seawright interviews. See Fletcher, *Remarks*, 13, for photo of Stipe before his transformation.

20. Sullivan, *R.E.M.: Talk About the Passion*, 9–11; William Haines, "'Underdog' R.E.M. Upstages the Brains," *Red and Black*, May 8, 1980, 9; and Fletcher, *Remarks*, 26–27. The Side Effects put out one EP called *The Side Effects* with DB Records in 1981. Greg Nicoll filmed them playing at Tyrone's on August 8, 1980, and the documentary is online at https://www.youtube.com/watch?v=r6WwkecWV4Q.

21. Bertis Downs interview; Brown, *Party Out of Bounds*, 140–41; Haines, "'Underdog' R.E.M.," 9; and "the Print Shop" flyer, in the author's possession.

22. Sullivan, *R.E.M.: Talk About the Passion* 11–12, 19; Sean Bourne interview; and William Haines, "'Underdog' R.E.M.," 9. Tommy Boyce and Bobby Hart actually wrote the song "(I'm Not Your) Steppin' Stone," recorded first by Paul Revere and the Raiders and released on their 1966 album *Midnight Ride*. The Monkees' version became a hit that same year.

23. Bobby Bryd, "Brains, R.E.M. Star Tonight in Union's Only Spring Show," *Red and Black*, May 15, 1980; and Kevin Bicknell, "Packed House Agrees That R.E.M. Was the Real Headliner," *Red and Black*, May 20, 1980.

24. Grey, *It Crawled from the South*, 37–39. R.E.M. also made an amateur video that included a soundtrack recorded at the Decatur Wuxtry that year.

25. Fricke, "Pete Buck Q & A," 113; Greil Marcus, *Stranded: Rock and Roll for a Desert Island* (New York: Knopf, 1979); Anthony DeCurtis interview; and DeCurtis, "Rock

Criticism and the Rocker: A Conversation with Peter Buck," in *Rocking My Life Away: Writing about Music and Other Matters* (Durham: Duke University Press, 1998), 41–61. Stipe talks about the influence of the Velvets and the *Nuggets* compilation in Christopher Bollen, "Michael Stipe."

26. Bob Mehr, *Trouble Boys*, 182; "R.E.M. about Athens and Starting the Band"; Sullivan, *R.E.M.: Talk About the Passion*, 20, 41; and Fletcher, *Remarks*, 45.

27. For information on R.E.M.'s October 4, 1980, gig at Tyrone's and the bootleg recorded there and later released as *Bodycount at Tyrone's*, see Gray, *It Crawled from the South*, 41–45; the entry at https://www.discogs.com/REM-Bodycount-At-Tyrones /release/4232849; the entry about the bootleg at Remring, online at http://www.remring .com/?q=REM1980-10-4; and the R.E.M. Timeline for 1980 at https://www.remtimeline .com/1980.html. Stipe's accent in 1978 in the TV news footage of him in Rocky Horror drag is an interesting contrast to his widely varying accent in 1980 in surviving recordings of R.E.M. On Stipe's love of the Cramps, see his comment "anything by the Cramps," in his list of the top records of the 1980s in "Michael Stipe on the Eighties," *Rolling Stone*, November 15, 1990, in DeCurtis, *Rolling Stone Files*, 122–23. On Stipe sounding like Elvis in the early days of R.E.M., see Dana Downs, autobiographical writings in the author's possession and online at Athens Rewind, http://www.athensrewind.com/play.html; and Mark Cline interviews. On Alex Chilton, see Holly George-Warren, *A Man Called Destruction: The Life and Music of Alex Chilton, from Box Tops to Big Star to Backdoor Man* (New York: Viking, 2014).

28. Sullivan, *R.E.M.: Talk About the Passion*, 12, 2–4; John Keane interview; Bill King, "Athens: A City Attuned to a New Wave-Length"; and Gumprecht, "R.E.M."

29. Vic Varney, "'Nineteen Hours From New York': Small Town Makes Good," *New York Rocker*, March 1981, 20; Bill King, "Athens: A City Attuned to a New Wave-Length"; Sullivan, *R.E.M.: Talk About the Passion*, 15; and Chris J. Starrs, "The Sleeper Band: In the Beginning, No One Expected This Sweet Little Band to Get So Big," R.E.M. in the Hall, a special section of OnlineAthens.com, 2007, http://onlineathens.com/rem-hall/stories /sleeperband.shtml.

30. Anthony DeCurtis, "The Athens Scene," in DeCurtis, *Rocking My Life Away*, 25; DeCurtis, "The Corner and the Spotlight: R.E.M. Comes of Age," quotes, 39–40, http:// www.najp.org/publications/articles/decurtis.pdf; Anthony DeCurtis interview; and Fletcher, *Remarks*, 37. While there, Tom Carson read from his novel *Twisted Kicks*, which would be published the next year, at the Night Gallery on Prince.

31. Watson, "R.E.M. Is Serious about Having Fun," *Red and Black*, May 6, 1981, 1; Chuck Reece, "R.E.M. Show Lays Bad Memories to Rest," *Red and Black*, October 26, 1982; Gumprecht, "R.E.M."; and J. Eddy Ellison, "R.E.M. to Play Athens." The i and i club, located near Tyrone's but larger, billed itself as "Athens' Progressive Music Club" and operated for a brief period in the early eighties. R.E.M. played there in 1982 and 1983. In their second TV performance (their first was earlier that month on *Late Night with David Letterman*), R.E.M. appeared on *Livewire* on October 30, 1983, and performed So. Central Rain and Carnival of Sorts. The interview portion of the show is online at https://www .youtube.com/watch?v=60WYma8jc9M, transcriptions mine. See Jared H. Bailey, "Big Turnout says All About REM Show," *Red and Black*, October 13, 1981, for an example of a student reporter repeating the band's own mantra for them: "The theme for the night was a very simple one—have fun at all costs . . . they made every song a carnival. And they had fun doing it."

32. Sullivan, *R.E.M.: Talk About the Passion*, 18, 14, 38–9; and Pond, "R.E.M. in the Real World."

33. Copeland, *Wild Thing*, 165–236; Pond, "R.E.M. in the Real World, 77; and R.E.M. Timeline for 1980, online at https://www.remtimeline.com/1980.html.

34. Sullivan, *R.E.M.: Talk About the Passion*, 32; Fletcher, *Remarks*, 18–19, 28, 38–39; Pond, "R.E.M. in the Real World," 77; Puterbaugh, "R.E.M.'s Southern Rock Revival"; and Copeland, *Wild Thing*, 297–302. Stipe talks about opening for other bands in Ken Garvin, "R.E.M.'s Stipe Isn't Chasing Fame," *Athens Banner Herald/Daily News*, August 6, 1983, 4.

35. Fletcher, *Remarks*, 28, 45; Sullivan, *R.E.M.: Talk About the Passion*, 20–21, 28–30, 61–62; Fricke, "Pete Buck Q & A," 114; Fletcher, "R.E.M. Interview with Tony Fletcher"; and Anthony DeCurtis interview.

36. On the Stipe incident, see Julie House interview. On the hippie scene in Athens, see the documentary project online at http://www.thestripproject.com/. On gay life in Georgia and the South more broadly, see James T. Sears, *Growing Up Gay in the South* (New York: Routledge, 1991); and John Howard, *Men Like That: A Southern Queer History* (Chicago: University of Chicago, 2001).

37. Sullivan, *R.E.M.: Talk About the Passion*, 29; Anthony DeCurtis, "An Open Party: R.E.M.'s Hip American Dream," *The Record*, June 1984, reprinted in DeCurtis, *Rolling Stone Files*, 42; Pond, "R.E.M. in the Real World," 78; Mark Cline interviews; Michael Lachowski interviews; Armistead Wellford interview; and Vanessa Briscoe Hay interviews.

38. Sullivan, *R.E.M.: Talk About the Passion*, 14–15, 21–22; Gene Northcutt, "The 40 Watt: The Original Music Spot Grows Up alongside Bands It Introduced," *Red and Black*, April 22, 1983, 6; Watson, "R.E.M. is Serious About Having Fun"; Bailey, "Big Turnout Says All About REM Show"; Reece, "R.E.M. Show Lays Bad Memories to Rest," 5; Chris Rasmussen interview; Mark Cline interviews; and Sam Seawright interviews.

39. Gene Northcutt, "40 Watt," 6; Chris Rasmussen interview; Mark Cline interviews; Sam Seawright interviews; Julie House interview; Annelies Mondi interview; and William Orten Carlton interview.

40. Watson, "R.E.M. Is Serious About Having Fun"; Chuck Reece interview; Julie House interview; and Annelies Mondi interview.

41. Watson, "R.E.M. Is Serious About Having Fun"; Varney, "'Nineteen Hours From New York,'"; Vic Varney, "Athens Success Method Fails for Actors," *Red and Black*, November 11, 1982; Athens Rewind; Chris Rasmussen interview; Mark Cline interviews; Sam Seawright interviews; and Tony Fletcher, *Remarks Remade: The Story of R.E.M.* (New York: Omnibus Press, 2002), 72–73.

42. R.E.M. played Legion Field with the Fleshtones and Alex Chilton opening on April 22, 1985. Raymond Valley, "R.E.M. Captivates Legion Crowd with Mix of Old Favorites, New Tunes," *Red and Black*, April 24, 1985, 6.

43. The footage of Stipe is online at ahttps://www.youtube.com/watch?v=nvG6Le GWU2g. See also Richard Metzger's post of this footage on Dangerous Minds, http:// dangerousminds.net/comments/teenage_michael_stipe_rocky_horror.

44. The footage of Stipe is online at https://www.youtube.com/watch?v=nvG6Le GWU2g.

45. Mark Cline interviews; Julie House interview; Annelies Mondi interview; Vanessa Briscoe Hay interviews; Velena Vego interview; Athens Rewind; and Kennedy Fraser, "On and Off the Avenue," *New Yorker*, April 14, 1975, 80–89. See also Vanessa Briscoe, "Fred!" (an interview with Fred Schneider), *Tasty World* 3 [no date given but articles seem to be

written in September and the 40 Watt calendar is for December], 7, where Schneider said in Athens when he lived there "every other day was Halloween."

46. Buckley, *R.E.M. Fiction*, 14; Mark Cline interviews; Keith Bennett interviews; and Athens Rewind. "Another Life to Live" [name of regular Athens music news column], *Tasty World* 6 [May/June 1985], 6, described the members of Love Tractor playing in vintage dresses as Wheel of Cheese, their alter ego cover band, and Stipe and Buck joining them: "Mr. Stipe had all the ladies jealous over his snappy spring ensemble." Mills sings this line in the 1983 recording of the Stitchcraft show, online at https://www.youtube.com/watch?v=g54900RafTs.

47. Cindy Wilson interview; Keith Bennett interviews; Mark Cline interviews; Julie House interview; Annelies Mondi interview; Vanessa Briscoe Hay interviews; and Velena Vego interview.

48. On the history of the many uses of secondhand clothes in the United States, see Jennifer Le Zotte, *From Goodwill to Grunge: A History of Secondhand Styles and Alternative Economies* (Chapel Hill: University of North Carolina Press, 2017).

49. Mark Cline interviews; Sally Speed interview; Keith Bennett interview; Sam Seawright interviews; and Shane Harrison, "When Art Made Athens Rock," *Atlanta Journal/Constitution*, April 12, 2014, online at https://www.ajc.com/entertainment/music/when-art-made-athens-rock/ymW74DQWJHpnPqKTIKuDYI/.

50. April Chapman interview.

51. Lauren Fancher interviews; Mark Cline interviews; Andrew Krieger interview; Bill David interview; Vanessa Briscoe Hay interviews; Bob Hay interview; Keith Bennett interviews; Julie House interview; Anthony DeCurtis interview; and Athens Rewind.

52. Lauren Fancher interviews; Mark Cline interviews; Andrew Krieger interview; Bob Hay interview; Keith Bennett interviews; Michael Lachowski interviews; Sean Bourne interview; Chris Rasmussen interview; and Athens Rewind.

53. Blair Dorminey interview; Keith Bennett interviews; and Sam Seawright interviews.

54. Athens Rewind; Julie House interview; Mark Cline interviews; Michael Lachowski interviews; Sam Seawright interviews; Rodger Brown interview; and Brown, *Party Out of Bounds*, 98–99, 103–9.

55. Sally Speed interview; Sam Seawright interviews; Vic Varney interview; Julie House interview; and Mark Cline interviews. On Boat Of, see Steven Garnett, "Tom Smith and Rat Bastard," Ink 19, May 22, 2018, https://ink19.com/2018/05/magazine/interviews/tom-smith-and-rat-bastard.

56. Athens Rewind; and Sam Seawright interviews. The R.E.M. song "Oddfellows Local 151," on *Document* (I.R.S., 1987), is probably about these men.

57. Athens Rewind; Sullivan, *R.E.M.: Talk About the Passion*, 30, 42; Elizabeth Phillip, "Pete Buck Is Bending Over Backwards to Save R.E.M. from the Pimps of Rock," *Summer Northwestern*, July 13, 1984, as reproduced at http://remring.com/?q=peter-buck-and-the-pimps-of-rock; Kit Swartz interview; Sam Seawright interviews; Mark Cline interviews; Rodger Brown interview; and Brown, *Party Out of Bounds*, 163–73. For a Phipps photograph of R.E.M. at their Barber Street house, see Fletcher, *Remarks*, 41.

58. Mark Cline interviews; and Armistead Wellford interview.

59. Sullivan, *R.E.M.: Talk About the Passion*, 15, 30–42.

60. Bryant Simon, *Hamlet Fire: A Tragic Story of Cheap Food, Cheap Government, and Cheap Lives* (New York: New Press, 2017).

61. Lauren Fancher interviews; Julie House interview; and Annelies Mondi interview.

62. Athens Rewind; and Sullivan, *R.E.M.: Talk About the Passion*, 25–42.

63. Fletcher, *Remarks Remade*, 47; Brown, *Party Out of Bounds*, 199; Athens Rewind; and Sullivan, *Talk About the Passion*, 25–42.

64. Mark Cline interviews; Sullivan, *R.E.M.: Talk About the Passion*, 29; Anthony DeCurtis, "An Open Party: R.E.M.'s Hip American Dream," *The Record*, June 1984, reprinted in DeCurtis, *Rolling Stone Files*, 42; and Pond, "R.E.M. in the Real World," 78.

65. On Boat Of, see "Boat Of/ Peach of Immortality: A chronological discography," April 17, 2013, online at http://www.toliveandshaveinla.com/bopoi/bopoibio.htm. On Tanzplagen, see "After Hours," *Red and Black*, January 8, 1982, 6; Gary Sperrazza, "Crib Death," *New York Rocker*, May 1982, 44; "William Lee Self," http://www.william-lee-self .com/tanzplagen/; "Lost Single and Live 40 Watt Club, Athens, Georgia 1981," http:// www.bandtoband.com/band/tanzplagen/the-lost-single-and-live-40-watt-club-athens-georgia-19; and "Tanzplagen," https://en.wikipedia.org/wiki/Tanzplagen. On Gaggle O' Sound, see REM Timeline, http://www.remtimeline.com/1980.html.

66. Sullivan, *R.E.M.: Talk About the Passion*, 25–42; Mark Cline interviews; Armistead Wellford interview; Sam Seawright interviews; and Ira Robbins, "Ten Years Down the Road, Athens, Georgia's Little-Band-That-Could Takes Stock of Fame, Fortune, and Folk Music," *Pulse*, October 1992. For the Mike Mills interview in February 1992, see "R.E.M.'s Mike Mills on 'Live! with Regis and Kathie Lee,'" Dangerous Minds, March 7, 2014, online at https://dangerousminds.net/comments/rems_mike_mills_on_live_with_regis_and _kathie_lee. Mills plays acoustic guitar and sings "Don't Go Back to Rockville."

67. Gray, *It Crawled from the South*, 60–63.

68. Charles Aaron, "R.E.M. Comes Alive," *Spin*, August 1995, 34–40, 110; Mark Cline interviews; Keith Bennett interviews; and Sam Seawright interviews.

69. David Pierce, "Michael Stipe Speaks Clearly," *Tasty World* 4 [February 1985], 24; Garvin, "R.E.M.'s Stipe Isn't Chasing Fame," 4.

70. Kit Swartz interview; Vic Varney interview; Mark Cline interviews; Paul Butchart interview; Armistead Wellford interview; Gumprecht, "R.E.M."; Peter Cline memories in Athens Rewind; and Chris J. Starrs, "In the Beginning: Producer Remembers First Recordings with R.E.M.," in R.E.M.: In the Hall, a special section of OnlineAthens .com, http://onlineathens.com/rem-hall/stories/beginning.shtml. For the DB records discography, see https://www.discogs.com/label/81555-DB-Recs?sort=year&sort_order=. These bands also swapped members. Berry took over Swartz's role as Love Tractor's drummer after Swartz quit to focus on the Side Effects. Later, Swartz returned to Love Tractor and quit the Side Effects, causing that band to break up. When Swartz left Athens in 1983 because the scene had gotten "too serious," Andrew Carter became Love Tractor's drummer.

71. Fred Mills, "Mitch Easter Interviewed: Perfect Sound Forever—the Director's Cut," Rock's Backpages, Summer 2007, https://www.rocksbackpages.com/Library/Article /mitch-easter-interviewed-perfect-sound-forever---the-directors-cut; Erin Amar, "Mitch Easter—Beyond and Back," *Rockerzine*, March 18, 2011; Vanessa Briscoe Hay, "Vanessa's Version," http://jollybeggars.netnik.com/pylon.html; Sullivan, *R.E.M.: Talk About the Passion*, 39; and Puterbaugh, "R.E.M.'s Southern Rock Revival," 29.

72. Richard Buskind, "Classic Tracks: REM, 'Radio Free Europe,'" *Sound on Sound*, November 2009, online at http://www.soundonsound.com/people/rem-radio-free -europe-classic-tracks; Mills, "Mitch Easter Interviewed"; and Amar, "Mitch Easter— Beyond and Back."

73. Sullivan, *R.E.M.: Talk About the Passion*, 26–27; and liner notes to R.E.M., *Dead Letter Office* (I.R.S., 1987). Christgau's mention of the demo in the *Village Voice* is quoted in Fletcher, *Remarks*, 33.

74. Sullivan, *R.E.M.: Talk About the Passion*, 27. On WUOG, see Craig Williams interview; Claire Horne interview; and Manfred Jones interview. R.E.M. released a cover of the Pylon song "Crazy" as the B side of its "Driver Eight" single in 1985.

75. "Pat the Wiz," the 40 Watt's longtime soundman (his real name is T. Patton Biddle), has posted his collection of flyers and recordings of bands playing the 40 Watt online at https://www.patthewiz.com/. T. Patton Biddle interview; Northcutt, "40 Watt"; King, "Athens: A City Attuned to a New Wave-Length"; Varney, "'Nineteen Hours from New York'"; Bicknell, Bailey, and Clark, "Athens Credited with Birth of Modern Music"; Fricke, "Peter Buck Q & A"; Cline interviews; Sam Seawright interviews; and Armistead Wellford interviews.

76. On Limbo District, see J. Eddy Ellison, "Limbo District Explores Beat," *Athens Banner Herald/Daily News*, March 26, 1983; and Ellison, "National Attention Warms Up Hot Bands," *Red and Black*, September 17, 1982, 10; "Limbo District," https://www .chunklet.com/limbo-district-athens-biggest-puzzle-at-least-to-me/; Athens Rewind; and Gumprecht, "R.E.M." Jim Herbert's film *Carnival—Limbo District* (1982), is online at https://beatopolis.wordpress.com/2016/08/24/carnival-limbo-district-1982/. On Boat Of, see "Boat Of/ Peach of Immortality," http://www.toliveandshaveinla.com/bopoi /bogallery8083.htm.

77. REM Timeline, online at https://www.remtimeline.com/1981.html; Lynda Stipe interview; David Pierce interview; Brown, *Party Out of Bounds*, 184; Grace Elizabeth Hale, "The Complete Oh-OK: Music as Child's Play in Athens, Georgia," *Southern Spaces*, September 26, 2011, http://www.southernspaces.org/2011/complete-oh-ok-music-child %E2%80%99s-play-athens-georgia; Sylvia Colwell, "Oh OK is A O-K," *Red and Black*, January 12, 1982, 8; and Jason Gross, "Oh-OK: Interviews," *Perfect Sound Forever*, July 2001, http://www.furious.com/perfect/ohok.html.

78. Lynda Stipe interview; David Pierce interview; Vanessa Briscoe Hay interviews; Jay Watson, "Local Groups Get Boost from DB Records," *Red and Black*, January 13, 1982, 1, 5; Hale, "The Complete Oh-OK"; Briscoe Hay, "Vanessa's Version." Robert Christgau quotes his own *Village Voice* review of June 1982 Danceteria show in Christgau, "Their Tiny Life," liner notes to the reissue *The Complete Oh-OK* (Collectors' Choice Music, 2002), reproduced online at https://www.robertchristgau.com/xg/cdrev/ohok-not.php. Varney is quoted in King, "Athens: A City Attuned to a New Wave-Length."

79. Andy Schwartz, "R.E.M.," *New York Rocker*, January 1982, https://www.rocksback pages.com/Library/Article/rem-5; Watson, "Local Groups Get Boost from DB Records"; Jared H. Bailey, "Energy Is One Side Effect," *Red and Black*, February 12, 1981, 5; Anthony DeCurtis, "The Athens Scene," article commissioned by *Rolling Stone* in 1981 but not run, published in *Rocking My Life Away*, 26–27; Sullivan, *R.E.M.: Talk About the Passion*, 29; Paul Butchart interview; and Kit Swartz interview. Ironically, the other band Stipe says that got to New York on their own is Limbo District, the art noise band that included Jerry Ayers, Athens musicians' original connection to the New York scene.

80. Leslie Berman, "Electric Company: Goodbye R.E.M., Hello Erik Frandsen," EvilTwin Publishing, October 6, 2011, http://eviltwinpublishing.com/articles/2011-10 -06-rem.shtml; Mark Cline interviews; and Garvin, "R.E.M.'s Stipe Isn't Chasing Fame," 4. Michael Azerrad quote is from his bio in the "About the Contributors" section

of the contributors to DeCurtis, *Rolling Stone Files*, 195. Pylon opened for the Gang of Four in New York and Philly in August 1979 and toured the Midwest with them in 1980, but Copeland claims he arranged R.E.M.'s "showcase" dates at the Ritz. He also says "the show received rave reviews in all the music press." I have not been able to locate any of these positive reviews. See Copeland, *Wild Thing*, 298–99.

81. Fletcher, *Remarks*, 37; Gary Sperrazza, "Crib Death"; Schwartz, "R.E.M."; and Bailey, "Big Turnout Says All About R.E.M. Show," 5.

82. Kevin Bicknell, "A Look Back at the 'Musical Pleasures' of Last Year," *Red and Black*, January 20, 1982, 7; Review of R.E.M., "Radio Free Europe"/"Sitting Still," *New York Rocker*, December 1981, 46; and Robert Palmer, "The Pop Life," *New York Times*, December 30, 1981.

83. Schwartz, "R.E.M."

84. Sven Haarhoff, "Tyrone's Had No Insurance," *Red and Black*, January 12, 1982, 2; Reece, "Resurrect Spirit of Tyrone's"; and Sandra-Lee Phipps, "Hot Nights in Athens," *New York Rocker*, April 1982, 6.

85. Garvin, "R.E.M.'s Stipe Isn't Chasing Fame"; Sullivan, "R.E.M. Shadows and Murmurs"; J. D. Considine, "R.E.M.: Subverting Small Town Boredom," *Musician*, August 1983, reprinted in Platt, *R.E.M. Companion*, 22–27; Fricke, "Pete Buck Q & A," 111–21; DeCurtis, "R.E.M.'s Brave New World," *Rolling Stone*, April 20, 1989, reprinted in DeCurtis, *Rolling Stone Files*, 94–106, quote, 100; Sullivan, *R.E.M.: Talk About the Passion*, 25–42; and "R.E.M.'s Mike Mills on 'Live! with Regis and Kathie Lee.'"

86. Robert Christgau, "Music Events," *Village Voice*, April 14, 1982, 62–63; review of R.E.M. show in "NY News," *New York Rocker*, April 1982, 8; musicians and critics push R.E.M. demo tapes and single in sidebar to "NY News," *New York Rocker*, May 1982, 40; mention of RCA tapes and Easter EP in "New York News," *New York Rocker*, June 1982, 8; and Slater, "Athens Band a Hit in New York," *Rolling Stone*, October 28, 1982, reprinted in DeCurtis, *Rolling Stone Files*, 26–27. R.E.M. played New York several times between the poorly attended Mudd Club show in September and the dates described here.

87. Slater, "Athens Band a Hit in New York"; and "New York News," *New York Rocker*, June 1982, 8. The RCA demos are online at https://www.youtube.com/watch?v=aHF-wXmzdN0, https://www.youtube.com/watch?v=3p0_jw8Wabk, and https://www.youtube.com/watch?v=wg02Yep8Owo.

88. Bill King, "Stardom a Blink Away for R.E.M.," *Atlanta Constitution*, October 15, 1982; Fletcher, *Remarks*, 37–38; Sullivan, *R.E.M.: Talk About the Passion*, 32–33; and Anthony DeCurtis interview.

89. Mills, "Mitch Easter Interviewed"; Erin Amar, "Mitch Easter—Beyond and Back"; King, "Stardom a Blink Away for R.E.M."; Fletcher, *Remarks*, 36–38; and Sullivan, *R.E.M.: Talk About the Passion*, 25–62. A video of R.E.M. playing at the Pier in Raleigh, North Carolina, on October 19, 1982, online at https://www.youtube.com/watch?v=9sBVX9kRmBE, makes clear how recording the EP *Chronic Town* shaped the band's live performance.

90. Robert Christgau, "R.E.M." under the heading "Music," events listings, *Village Voice*, April 14, 1982, 62–63; Slater, "Athens Band a Hit in New York"; and Danceteria poster for April 1982, copy in author's possession. When exactly F.B.I. formally signed R.E.M. as a client is unclear, but it happened by early 1982, before the I.R.S. record deal in May, and helped convince Miles Copeland to support I.R.S. president Jay Boberg in offering the band a contract. Ian Copeland and F.B.I. were setting up gigs for the band before early 1982. See Fletcher, *Remarks*, 38–39, and Copeland, *Wild Thing*, 299–301.

91. Fletcher, *Remarks*, 38–40; Sullivan, *R.E.M.: Talk About the Passion*, 32–33; and Copeland, *Wild Thing*, 299–301.

92. Fletcher, *Remarks*, 44; Sullivan, *R.E.M.: Talk About the Passion*, 37–38; and interviews for the *Cutting Edge*, taped in Los Angeles in June 1983 and broadcast in October, included in *When the Light Is Mine: R.E.M.: The Best of the I.R.S. Years* (Capitol Records, 2006).

93. Schwartz, "R.E.M."; Bill King, "Stardom a Blink Away for R.E.M."; Andrew Slater, "R.E.M.: Not Just Another Athens, Georgia, Band," *Rolling Stone*, October 28, 1982, reprinted in DeCurtis, *Rolling Stone Files*, 26; Considine, "R.E.M.: Subverting Small Town Boredom," 23–24; and Phillip, "Pete Buck Is Bending Over Backwards to Save R.E.M. from the Pimps of Rock."

94. DeCurtis, "Athens Scene," 24; and Mark Cline interviews.

95. Chuck Reece, "R.E.M. Makes Big Comeback with New Album," *Red and Black*, September 17, 1982, 11; Sullivan, *R.E.M.: Talk About the Passion*, 35–39; and Fletcher, *Remarks*, 43–44.

96. Billy Altman, "History Lesson," *Village Voice*, October 26, 1982, 84, 94; Greil Marcus, ed., *Rock and Roll Will Stand* (Boston: Beacon, 1969); and Slater, "R.E.M.: Not Just Another Athens, Georgia, Band."

97. Altman, "History Lesson."

98. Richard Grabel, "R.E.M.: *Chronic Town*," *New Musical Express*, November 12, 1982, https://www.rocksbackpages.com/Library/Article/rem-ichronic-towni-2. Christgau's rankings and the annual *Village Voice* poll appeared in the February 22, 1983, issue of the *Village Voice*. His 1982 list is online at https://www.robertchristgau.com/xg/pnj/deans82 .php, and the critics' 1982 list is online at https://www.robertchristgau.com/xg/pnj/pjres82 .php.

99. Robot A. Hull, "R.E.M.: *Chronic Town*," *Creem* (January 1983), https://www.rocks backpages.com/Library/Article/rem-ichronic-towni.

100. The show at the Pier is available online at https://www.youtube.com/watch?v=iPE -l-tfNoI.

101. Brown, *Party Out of Bounds*, 135; Aaron, "R.E.M. Comes Alive"; Joshua Simon, "A Session with Michael Stipe," *Life Special Issue: 40 Years of Rock & Roll*, December 1, 1992, 102–4; Jeff Giles, "Everybody Hurts Sometime," *Newsweek*, September 25, 1994, online at https://www.newsweek.com/everybody-hurts-sometime-188414; Anthony DeCurtis, "Monster Madness," *Rolling Stone*, October 20, 1994, 58–64, 161–63: Stipe says, "In terms of the whole queer-straight-bi thing, my feeling is that labels are for canned food. . . . I think sexuality is a much more slippery thing than that. . . . I've always been of questionable sexuality or dubious sexuality"; Michael Goldberg, "Cybersex, Sex, and the Mysterious Stipe-Man," *Addicted to Noise*, January 19, 1995: this online magazine is no longer available but copy of article in author's possession; Chris Heath, "Michael in the Middle," *Details*, February 1995, 80; Andy Pemberton, "Michael Stipe: Cash for Questions," *Q* (May 1999); and Fred Maus, "Intimacy and Distance: On Stipe's Queerness," *Journal of Popular Music Studies* 18, no. 2 (August 2006): 191–214.

102. The show at the Pier is available online at https://www.youtube.com/watch?v=iPE -l-tfNoI.

103. "The Top 100: The Best Albums of the Last 20 Years: *Murmur*," *Rolling Stone*, August 27, 1987, 68–69; reprinted in DeCurtis, *Rolling Stone Files*; Fricke, "Pete Buck Q & A"; and Mark Cline interviews. The Hague demo is on YouTube at https://www.youtube.com /watch?v=QJNMtXQBG2s.

104. Mills, "Mitch Easter Interviewed," and Fletcher, *Remarks*, 48–49.

105. Richard Buskind, "Classic Tracks"; and Sullivan, *R.E.M.: Talk About the Passion*, 25–62.

106. Mills, "Mitch Easter Interviewed"; Buskind, "Classic Tracks"; and Sullivan, *R.E.M.: Talk About the Passion*, 25–62.

107. Jimmy Tremayne, "After Hours," *Red and Black*, February 25, 1983, 3; Ellison, "Limbo District Explores Beat"; April Chapman interview; Lynda Stipe interview; Armistead Wellford interview; Mark Cline interviews; Kit Swartz interview; Jay Watson, "Love Tractor May Just Be the Best Show in Athens-Town," *Red and Black*, February 17, 1982, 6; Kevin Bicknell, "Pylon and Love Tractor: A Great Show at Memorial," *Red and Black*, January 22, 1982, 6; "After Hours," *Red and Black*, January 29, 1982, 6; "Atlanta Highlights," *Red and Black*, February 18, 1982, 5; "After Hours," *Red and Black*, March 5, 1982, 7; i and i ad, *Red and Black*, June 2, 1982, 2; "Love Tractor," *Tasty World* 2 [late August or early September 1984], 16; Phil Davis, review of *Love Tractor* (DB Records, 1982), in *New York Rocker*, June 1982, 47; and Robert Palmer, "Regional Bands in National Spotlight," *New York Times*, November 6, 1981.

108. "These Days Athens (Ga.) Is a Creative Center," *People*, January 17, 1983.

109. "These Days Athens (Ga.) Is a Creative Center"; and "Elvis' 'Bedroom' Critics' No. 1 Pick," *Red and Black*, January 18, 1983, 5. Maureen McLaughlin says she has outtake images that date the shoot as December 11, 1982. Maureen McLaughlin interview. A copy of another photograph made during this shoot that appeared in a local paper is in the UGA Library's clipping file, "Athens, Music and Musicians," with no other accompanying information. See also photographs taken by Jay Thomas circulated and tagged on Facebook, downloaded and in the author's possession. On the emerging underground network, see Azerrad, *Our Band Could Be Your Life*, 5–14.

110. Brown interview; "Boat Of" website at http://www.toliveandshaveinla.com/bopoi/bogallery8083.htm; Brown, *Party Out of Bounds*, 206; and Christopher Bollen, "Michael Stipe." "Camera" appeared on the band's second album, *Reckoning* (I.R.S. Records, 1984).

111. Jay Watson, "R.E.M. on the Road, Behind the Scenes," *Athens Observer*, June 4, 1983, 1–2; and Watson, "R.E.M. on the Road: Hopes are High for LP 'Murmur,'" *Athens Observer*, June 16, 1983, 1–2.

112. Chuck Reece, "'Murmur' Offers a New, Mesmerizing Sound," *Red and Black*, April 28, 1983, 10; and J. Eddy Ellison, "R.E.M.'s Record 'Murmur' Is an Adventurous Experiment," *Athens Banner Herald/Daily News*, May 21, 1983.

113. Reece, "'Murmur' Offers a New, Mesmerizing Sound"; and Ellison, "R.E.M.'s Record 'Murmur' Is an Adventurous Experiment."

114. Sullivan, *R.E.M.: Talk About the Passion*, 8–57; and Fletcher, *Remarks Remade*, 91–92.

115. R.E.M., *Murmur*, I.R.S., SP-70604, 1983, 33⅓ rpm; Rodger Brown interview; and Sullivan, *R.E.M.: Talk About the Passion*, 48–49.

116. John Piccarella, "Men Without Words," *Village Voice*, May 10, 1983, 65–66; Hull, "R.E.M.: *Chronic Town*"; and Howard Wuelfing, "R.E.M. at the 9:30 Club," *Washington Post*, March 14, 1983: "Michael Stipe lurched toward the mike, collared it and began belting out surreal, muddled lyrics in classic southern pop style—hoarse yet tuneful, more concerned with passion than with precision." For other reviews of *Murmur*, see Steve Pond, "*Murmur* Album Review," *Rolling Stone*, May 26, 1983; and Puterbaugh, "R.E.M.'s Southern Rock Revival"; John Morthland, "R.E.M.'s *Murmur*," *Creem*, July 1983; and Richard Grabel, "R.E.M.: *Murmur*," *New Musical Express*, September 3, 1983.

117. Fletcher, *Remarks Remade*, 123.

118. Amanda Petrusich, "The Road Goes on Forever," *Oxford American*, Winter 2016, online at http://www.oxfordamerican.org/magazine/item/722-the-road-goes-on-forever; and Mark Kemp, *Dixie Lullaby* (New York: Free Press, 2004).

119. Pond, "*Murmur* Album Review," 28; and Puterbaugh, "R.E.M.'s Southern Rock Revival," quotes, 29–30, 31. See also Laura Levine's 1982 New York City photograph of R.E.M. where Buck holds her Patsy Cline album, online at http://lauralevine.com/photography/gallery/rem.php.

120. R.E.M., *Murmur* (I.R.S. Records, 1983); J. Nimi, *Murmur* (New York: Continuum, 2005), 24–54; and Sullivan, *R.E.M.: Talk About the Passion*, 51. There are many errors in the Nimi book, but some of his analysis of the music has influenced my argument here.

121. Sullivan, "R.E.M.: Shadows and Murmurs."

122. Sullivan, *R.E.M.: Talk About the Passion*, 48–57; and Sean Bourne interview.

123. Jon Pareles, "Folk-Rock: Love Tractor," *New York Times*, September 13, 1983, C15; Pareles, "Old and New Acts Ignite a Folk-Rock Comeback," *New York Times*, September 18, 1983, H21; and Sullivan, *R.E.M.: Talk About the Passion*, 57.

CHAPTER 4

1. Arthur Johnson interviews; and Claire Horne interview. Prints of these photos are in Johnson's possession.

2. Arthur Johnson interviews. Robert Burke Warren's blog is called "Solitude & Good Company," and the post with this phrase is dated December 3, 2013; https://solitudeand goodcompany.wordpress.com/tag/the-now-explosion/. Johnson's best friend growing up was Todd Butler, who went on to play in Atlanta bands like Wee Wee Pole, with RuPaul Charles and Robert Burke Warren, the Opal Foxx Quartet, and Smoke. On *Rocky Horror* reenactment, see Jeffrey Weinstock, *The Rocky Horror Picture Show* (New York: Columbia University Press, 2007); and Weinstock, ed., *Reading Rocky Horror: The Rocky Horror Picture Show and Popular Culture* (New York: Palgrave Macmillan, 2008). Pylon played the i and i on September 16 and 17, 1982. See the ad in the *Red and Black*, September 17, 1982, 2.

3. Arthur Johnson interviews; and Craig Williams interview.

4. Arthur Johnson interviews; Craig Williams interview; and Kevin Garvin, "Craig Williams: WUOG Program Director Speaks Out on Athens and Music," *Athens Banner Herald/Daily News*, October 7, 1983, 8.

5. Arthur Johnson interviews; David Barbe interviews; "After Hours," *Red and Black*, May 25, 1984, 6; and "After Hours," *Red and Black*, June 15, 1984, 5. The Kilkenny Cats cover band is listed alternately as the Hollowmen and the Hollow Men.

6. "After Hours," *Red and Black*, July 12, 1984, 5; and After Hours," *Red and Black*, November 30, 1984, 6.

7. Jimmy Tremayne, "Bar-B-Q Killers Bring All Its Talent to 40 Watt During Opening Act Jan. 21," *Red and Black*, January 18, 1985, 5; and Arthur Johnson interviews.

8. Arthur Johnson interviews; Keith Landers interviews; Barry Marler interview; and advertisement for the 40 Watt Uptown in the *Red and Black*, February 23, 1984, 3. Jimmy Tremayne's story is in the Athens Rewind collection, http://www.athensrewind.com/play_II.html.

9. Kelly Noonan interview. 40 Watt Club Uptown ad, *Red and Black*, September 20,

1984, 6, lists a gig by Music School. Uptown Lounge ad, *Red and Black*, November 15, 1984, 8, lists Dark Harvest, formerly Music School.

10. Bob Hay interview; David Barbe interviews; and Dan Matthews interview. My point here is not that either count of the number of scene bands is definitive but that by any set of criteria for counting groups in the scene the number of them was exploding.

11. Grace Elizabeth Hale, "Acting Out: The Athens, Georgia Music Scene and the Emergence of a Bohemian Diaspora," in Shawn Chandler Bingham and Lindsay A. Freeman, eds., *The Bohemian South: Creating Countercultures from Poe to Punk* (Chapel Hill: University of North Carolina Press, 2017).

12. See the twenty-fifth anniversary issue of *CMJ New Music Report*, January 5, 2004, online at https://books.google.it/books?id=zVp_QgtYGGUC&pg=PT5&redir_esc=y#v=onepage&q&f=false; Gina Arnold, *Route 666: On the Road to Nirvana* (New York: St. Martins, 1993); Ian Svenonius, "The Rise and Fall of College Rock: How Yuppies and NPR Gentrified Punk," *New Republic*, October 23, 2015, online at https://newrepublic.com/authors/ian-svenonius; and Nicholas Rubin, "College Radio: The Development of a Trope in U.S. Student Broadcasting," *Interactions: Studies in Communication & Culture* 6, no. 1 (March 2015): 47–64.

13. Arnold, *Route 666*; Garvin, "Craig Williams"; Thomas J. Meyer, "Innovative Campus Radio Stations Shun 'Top-40' Music," *Chronicle of Higher Education*, November 7, 1984; and Harry Weinger, "College Radio Making an Impact at Retail and Concert Level," *Cashbox*, October 1, 1983.

14. Michael Azerrad, *Our Band Could Be Your Life: Scenes from the American Indie Underground, 1981–1991* (New York: Little, Brown, 2001); and Arnold, *Route 666*.

15. Azerrad, *Our Band Could Be Your Life*; Arnold, *Route 666*; Steven Blush, *American Hardcore: A Tribal History* (Los Angeles: Feral House, 2001); Eric J. Abbey and Colin Helb, eds., *Hardcore, Punk, and Other Junk: Aggressive Sounds in Contemporary Music* (Lanham, Md.: Lexington Books, 2014); Dewar MacLeod, *Kids of the Black Hole: Punk Rock in Postsuburban California* (Norman: University of Oklahoma Press, 2010); and Steve Waksman, *This Ain't the Summer of Love: Conflict and Crossover in Heavy Metal and Punk* (Berkeley: University of California Press, 2009).

16. Robert Christgau, "Getting Their Hands Dirty," *Village Voice*, August 14, 2001, online at https://www.villagevoice.com/2001/08/07/getting-their-hands-dirty/.

17. Arnold, *Route 666*; Robert Christgau, "Dreams So Real," *Village Voice*, September 24, 1996, online at https://www.robertchristgau.com/xg/rock/rem-96.php; Christgau, "Getting Their Hands Dirty"; and Holly Kruse, *Site and Sound: Understanding Independent Music Scenes* (New York: Peter Lang, 2003).

18. Pete Buck, "The True Spirit of American Rock," *Record*, October 1984, 19, 62.

19. Buck, "True Spirit."

20. Buck, "True Spirit"; and Kruse, *Site and Sound*, 9.

21. Landers interviews; David Barbe interviews; Arthur Johnson interviews; Bryan Cook interview; and Mike Tidwell, "Legion's Wild Yet Mild Music Style Defies Usual Classification," *Red and Black*, April 13, 1984, 3.

22. Sean Bourne interview. R.E.M. released their cover of "Superman" on their 1986 I.R.S. album *Life's Rich Pageant*. The logo for David Barbe's recording studio is online at http://www.chaseparktransduction.com/.

23. Keith Landers interviews; David Barbe interviews; and Sam Seawright interviews.

24. Cook interview; Lynda Stipe interview; "After Hours," *Red and Black*, April 13, 1984, 3; and the author's own observations in the mid-1980s.

25. Keith Landers interviews; David Barbe interviews; Patton Biddle interview; Kyle Pilgrim interview; and Bryan Cook interview.

26. Keith Landers interviews; James Martinez, "Clubs Try to Accommodate Athens Bands," *Red and Black*, October 25, 1983, 3; and John Alden, "Uptown Lounge Gets Facelift," *Red and Black*, May 8, 1984, 5. The manager of the Uptown then was named Jim Kovach.

27. David Barbe interviews; Keith Landers interviews; Martinez, "Clubs Try to Accommodate Athens Bands"; and Alden, "Uptown Lounge Gets Facelift." Beginning in late October, 1983, the *Red and Black* "After Hours" column begins listing band dates for the Uptown.

28. Velena Vego interview; Arthur Johnson interviews; Julia House interview; and David Barbe interviews.

29. Keith Landers interviews. He remembered the show as being at the Mad Hatter, but the dates—his birthday, the legal drinking age in that time period in Georgia, and R.E.M.'s schedule—suggest the i and i dates in October.

30. David Barbe interviews; Arthur Johnson interviews; and Keith Landers interviews.

31. Keith Landers interviews. "Another Life to Live: Southern Music News" [name of regular Athens music news column], *Tasty World* 6 [May/June 1985], 6.

32. Bryan Cook interview; Chad Radford, "Is/Ought Gap Is a Throwback to Athens' Golden Era," *Flagpole*, May 17, 2017, online at http://flagpole.com/music/music-features /2017/05/17/is-ought-gap-is-a-throwback-to-athens-golden-era; and Is/Ought Gap website, http://isoughtgap.strikingly.com/. In 2014, Is/Ought Gap finally released the EP *Luck Seven*, recorded in 1984.

33. Bryan Cook interview; Radford, "Is/Ought Gap Is a Throwback"; and the author's own observations in the mid-1980s.

34. Bryan Cook interview; Lynda Stipe interview; "After Hours," *Red and Black*, April 13, 1984, 3; and the author's own observations in the mid-1980s.

35. Arthur Johnson interviews; Claire Horne interview; Keith Landers interviews; David Barbe interviews; Beth Lilly, "Athens' Music Scene Changing—as Usual," *Red and Black*, November 1, 1983, 6; Bob Keyes, "Kilkenny Cats Looking for That Big Break," *Red and Black*, November 17, 1983; Charles Aaron, "After Hours," *Red and Black*, July 12, 1984, 5; Aaron, "After Hours," *Red and Black*, August 9, 1984, 5; and Jim Tremayne, "After Hours," *Red and Black*, September 28, 1984, 7.

36. Arthur Johnson interviews; Claire Horne interview; David Barbe interviews; Keith Landers interviews; D. Loring Aiken, "Another Life to Live," *Tasty World* 2 [late August or early September 1984]; and Seven Yates, "Kilkenny Cats: A Walk on the Raucous Side," *Tasty World* 3 [no date given but articles seem written in September and the 40 Watt calendar is for December 1984] 5, 14, 22; and Kilkenny Cats, "Attractive Figure"/"Of Talk," Coyote Records, COY 111, 1984, 45 rpm.

37. David Barbe interviews; Arthur Johnson interviews; and Claire Horne interview.

38. Kelly Noonan interview, Arthur Johnson interviews; and Claire Horne interviews. I also draw throughout this section on my own memories of the Bar-B-Q Killers' shows.

39. Claire Horne interview; and Johnson interviews.

40. David Barbe interviews.

41. David Barbe interviews; Arthur Johnson interviews; and Claire Horne interview.

42. Mark Cline interviews; Armistead Wellford interview; Jeff Walls interview; and Art Harris, "O Little Town of Rock 'n' Roll," *Washington Post*, August 29, 1984, B1, B8.

43. Dan Matthews, "Last Go Van Go Performance Tonight at the Uptown Lounge," *Red and Black*, January 17, 1985, 5. Atlanta musician Robert Warren, formerly a member of RuPaul's Atlanta band Wee Wee Pole, moved to town to play bass in this band.

44. Mark Cline interviews; and Armistead Wellford interview. On Wheel of Cheese, see Jim Tremayne, "After Hours," *Red and Black*, February 24, 1984, 5; "Surprise!," *Red and Black*, March 2, 1984, 1; and Jim Tremayne, "After Hours," *Red and Black*, March 29, 1985, 2.

45. Love Tractor, *Round the Bend*, DB Records, 1984; and Mark Coleman, "Men Without Words," *Village Voice*, August 14, 1984, 69, 73.

46. Love Tractor, "Spin Your Partner" 1983 video directed by Howard Libov, online at https://www.youtube.com/watch?v=U9z9j8eNoukn; Mark Cline interviews; and Armistead Wellford interview.

47. Tony Paris, "The Tony Paris Interview with Mark Cline," *Tasty World* 2 [August or September 1984], 17, 19; Sebastian Cargo, "The Love Tractor Factor," *Tasty World* 2, [August or September 1984], 16; Mark Cline interviews; Armistead Wellford interview; and DB Records discography, online at https://www.discogs.com/label/81555-DB-Recs.

48. Mark Cline interviews; and Armistead Wellford interview.

49. Mark Cline interviews.

50. Bob Hay interviews; Mark Cooper Smith interview; and Justin Gage, "Pylon: A Sonic Remembrance of 1980s Athens, GA," *Aquarium Drunkard*, July 2016, http://www.aquariumdrunkard.com/2016/07/22/pylon-a-sonic-reminiscence-of-1980s-athens-ga/.

51. Mark Cooper Smith interview; J. Eddy Ellison, "Squalls Cry Pop," *Red and Black*, September 30, 1982, 5; "After Hours," *Red and Black*, September 24, 1982, 6; and Chris DeBarr, "The Squalls," *Tasty World* 4 [February 1985], 10.

52. Bob Hay interviews; Vanessa Briscoe Hay interviews; Vanessa Briscoe Hay, "Vanessa's Version," http://www.netnik.com/jollybeggars/pylon.html; DeBarr, "Squalls." DeBarr quotes *Village Voice* critic "Van Gosen's" positive review of the band's show at Maxwell's. As no one named Van Gosen wrote reviews for the *Voice*, this is probably Van Gosse. I asked Van Gosse, now a historian at Franklin and Marshall College, about whether he wrote this review, and he confirmed that he did but has never been able to locate a clipping in the spotty archives of the *Voice*. Email to the author, April 22, 2019.

53. Bob Hay interviews; Mark Cooper Smith interview; and "After Hours," *Red and Black*, April 6, 1984, 6; May 25, 1984, 6; September 21, 1984, 3; and September 28, 1984.

54. Bob Hay interviews; Mark Cooper Smith interview; and Ann Powers, *Good Booty: Love and Sex, Black & White, Body and Soul in American Music* (New York: Dey Street, 2017), xxviii–xxix.

55. Velena Vego interview; Arthur Johnson interviews; David Barbe interviews; Curtiss Pernice interviews; Tony Paris, "Peach Pits: Atlanta News," *Tasty World* 1 [July or August 1984], 4; and Phyllis Heller, "This Butt's for You," *Spin*, June 1986, 82. The *Red and Black*'s 1985 critics' poll, published January 22, 1986, 6, lists the Flat Duo Jets at number two, after Mercyland, in the list of best new local bands. Given some early scene participants' disdain for people who moved to town to play music, it is likely that at least some Athens residents simply did not admit why they had come to town. On Mystery Date, see also Mercedes Delorean, "Mystery Date," *Tasty World* 3 [December 1984], 25, 26, 30.

56. Velena Vego interview; and Delorean, "Mystery Date."

57. Arthur Johnson interviews; David Barbe interviews; Curtiss Pernice interview; and Heller, "This Butt's for You," 82.

58. Grace Elizabeth Hale, "The Complete Oh-OK: Music as Child's Play in Athens, Georgia," *Southern Spaces*, September 26, 2011, http://www.southernspaces.org/2011/complete-oh-ok-music-child%E2%80%99s-play-athens-georgia; Briscoe Hay, "Vanessa's Version"; Robert Christgau talks about his *Village Voice* review of a June 1982 Danceteria show in "Their Tiny Life," the liner notes for the reissue of Oh-OK's music *The Complete Oh OK*, Collectors' Choice Music, 2002, reproduced online at https://www.robert christgau.com/xg/cdrev/ohok-not.php.

59. Hale, "Complete Oh-OK"; Oh-OK playing Such 'n' Such at the Strand, Marietta, Ga., on May 6, 1983, online at https://www.youtube.com/watch?v=zbZ_iRwOT4w.

60. Hale, "Complete Oh-OK"; Oh-OK, *Wow Mini Album*, DB Records, 1982, and *Furthermore What*, DB Records, 1983, were reissued, along with additional material, as *Oh-OK: The Complete Recordings*.

61. Hale, "Complete Oh-OK." Velvet Underground disciple Jonathan Richman was a pioneer of this childlike style, especially with his mid-1970s songs like "Hey There Little Insect" and "Ice Cream Man." Like other bands inspired by the Velvet Underground, Richman did not perform emotional expressiveness straight. See Keir Keightley, "Reconsidering Rock," in Simon Frith, Will Straw, and John Street, eds., *Cambridge Companion to Pop and Rock* (New York: Cambridge University Press, 2001), 109–42; Jonathan Richman, *Jonathan Richman and the Modern Lovers*, Beserkley Records, 1976; and Jonathan Richman, *Rock 'N' Roll with the Modern Lovers*, Beserkley Records, 1977.

62. Rodger Brown interview; handwritten band chronology that Linda Hopper wrote for Rodger Brown, copy in the author's possession; and Rodger Brown, *Party Out of Bounds: The B-52's, R.E.M., and the Kids Who Rocked Athens, Georgia* (New York: Plume, 1991), 210–11.

63. Rodger Brown interview; Julie House interview; Keith Landers interviews; Craig Williams interview; Michael Lachowski interviews; Butchart interview; and Harris, "O Little Town of Rock 'n' Roll," B8.

64. Hale, "Complete Oh-OK"; Sebastian Cargo [pseudonym], "Growing Up with Oh OK," *Tasty World* 1 [July or August 1984], 7, 26; Lynda Stipe interview; David Pierce interview; Mark Cline interviews; Rodger Brown interview; Oh-OK band chronology; and Brown, *Party Out of Bounds*, 210–11.

65. Oh-OK chronology; David Pierce interview; Rodger Brown interview; Craig Williams interview; Lynda Stipe interview; Paul Butchart interview; Michael Lachowski interview; Julie House interview; and Brown, *Party Out of Bounds*, 210–11. Sweet is quoted in Bill Oliver, "Pylon's Studio Debut Brings Buzz of Delight," *Red and Black*, February 21, 1984, 3; and Cargo, "Growing Up with Oh OK," 7, 26.

66. Brown, *Party Out of Bounds*, 210–11; Harris, "O Little Town of Rock 'n' Roll"; and Oliver, "Pylon's Video Debut," 3.

67. Oh-OK chronology; Keith Landers interviews and email to the author; Bryan Cook interview; and Cargo, "Growing Up with Oh OK," 7, 26. Recordings from the band's show at the Peppermint Lounge April 16, 1984 are included in Oh-OK, *Oh-OK: The Complete Reissue*, Happy Birth Day to Me Records, HHBTM141, 2011. Keith Landers sat in on guitar for a few gigs but was too busy with Fashionbattery to join another band.

68. Christgau's review of *Furthermore What* is online at http://www.robertchristgau

.com/get_artist.php?name=oh+ok; Jimmy Tremayne, "After Hours," *Red and Black*, May 11, 1984, 5; and Charles Aaron, "After Hours," *Red and Black*, May 17, 1984, 5.

69. David Pierce interview; Joe Cafiero, "Famous Poets Draw Large Crowds," *Red and Black*, May 9, 1985, 6; and Greg Nicoll, "Jimmy Ellison: Love's Jester," *Tasty World* 4 [February 1985], 4. Ten undated issues of *Tasty World* magazine came out between the summer of 1984 and January of 1986. Information about *Partyline* can be found at http://chipshirleyshow.blogspot.com/. There are also episodes and clips on YouTube.

70. David Pierce interview; and postings by former staffers on the *Tasty World* Facebook page. I purchased issues of the magazine on eBay, but a few libraries have scattered holdings, including UGA Special Collections.

71. Bob Mehr, *Trouble Boys: The True Story of the Replacements* (Boston: Da Capo, 2016); *Tasty World* 1 [July or August 1984]; and Diane Loring Aiken, post on *Tasty World* Facebook page, February 25, 2015.

72. David Pierce interview; and Marcus Gray, *It Crawled from the South: An R.E.M. Companion* (New York: Da Capo, 1997), 66, 161–62.

73. David Pierce interview; and Pete McCommons interview.

74. David Pierce interview; Pete McCommons interview; and *Tasty World* issues 1–9.

75. Charles Aaron interview; Charles Aaron, "After Hours," *Red and Black*, June 15, 1984, 5; August 9, 1984, 6; July 12, 1984, 5; July 19, 1984, 5; and August 2, 1984, 6. Aaron told me he was very embarrassed about the music criticism he wrote as a young man. He thought then that the way to take the music seriously was to judge it harshly. Only later did he realize that the "small" and "fragile" scene needed support, unlike the corporate music industry or the world of professional sports.

76. Aaron, "After Hours," *Red and Black*, July 19, 1984, 5.

77. Aaron, "After Hours," *Red and Black*, August 2, 1984, 6; and Charles Aaron, "Spazz and Dim Report: The The Transcends Trendiness; Buzz Boring," *Red and Black*, May 15, 1984, 6. This regular feature was modeled on Christgau's record review and rating system and his annual polls in the *Village Voice*.

78. Aaron, "After Hours," *Red and Black*, August 9, 1984, 6; and David Pierce, "Music Media: Insiders and Outsiders," *Tasty World* 2 [August or September 1984], 5.

79. Pierce, "Music Media," 5.

80. Anthony DeCurtis interview. Other participants mentioned the story but did not want to go on the record.

81. DJM, "Big Boys at Play," *Tasty World* 1 [July or August 1984], 28; Miguel Des Sequoia [probably a pseudonym], untitled box of text and photograph of Squalls, *Tasty World* 2 [August or September 1985], 7; and Aiken, "Another Life to Live," *Tasty World* 1 [July or August 1984], 5–6.

82. Debi Atkinson, "Getting Out" and "The 5 Box Fashion Show," *Tasty World* 2 [August or September 1984], 5, 8; Michael Paxton interview; and Watt King interview. The rent on the whole building at 199 Prince was $210 a month during the days when the Night Gallery was downstairs and Rat and Duck Playhouse was upstairs. When Rat and Duck was not practicing or performing in their space, bands like Limbo District practiced there. Today, the Grit occupies the downstairs space in this building, which is owned by Michael Stipe.

83. Charles Aaron interview.

84. Charles Aaron, "Rosemary Brings a Divine Package," *Red and Black*, October 3, 1984, 4; Aiken, "Another Life to Live," *Tasty World* 3 [articles seem to be about September

1984 but club calendar is for December 1984], 5; and Jim Tremayne, "It's a Hootenanny: Replacements Have Fun on Their Own Terms," *Red and Black*, September 28, 1984, 1.

85. *Tasty World* 4 [February 1985].

86. Steven Yates, "Bar-B-Q Killers" *Tasty World* 4, 22.

87. David Pierce, "Michael Stipe Speaks Clearly," *Tasty World* 4 [February 1985], 24. The next page prints excerpts of Stipe's travel journal under the headline "My Diary of Japan."

88. Watt King interview; Michael Paxton interview; Neil Bogan, "Stage," and J. Griffith, "Meridian," both in *Tasty World* 5 [April 1985], 7; and Neil Bogan, "The Little World Stage," *Tasty World* 6 [May or June 1985], 8.

89. Dori Cosgrove, "Art," *Tasty World* 4 [February 1985], 6; Cosgrove, "Patrik Keim," *Tasty World* 5 [April 1985], 6; and Cosgrove, "Arty-facts," *Tasty World* 6 [May or June 1985], 8.

90. Jennifer Hartley interview; Annelies Mondi interview; Sally Speed interview; Lauren Fancher interviews; Cosgrove, "Art"; Cosgrove, "Patrik Keim"; and Cosgrove, "Arty-facts."

91. Jennifer Hartley interview; Annelies Mondi interview; Sally Speed interview; Lauren Fancher interviews; Cosgrove, "Art"; Cosgrove, "Patrik Keim"; Cosgrove, "Arty-facts."

92. Cosgrove, "Arty-facts." In May 1985, the Georgia Museum of Art displayed Keim's "3-D paintings enhanced with found objects" and another installation called *Order of the State, Moving,* in which a record of someone saying multiplication tables droned in the middle of a floor covered with broken eggshells and numbered sheets of paper.

93. Sally Speed interview; and Annelies Mondi interview.

94. "Pete Pitches in as Oh-OK Says So Long," *Red and Black*, October 24, 1984, 6. Clips from this show, incorrectly dated as October 11, 1984 — the gig was October 19 — are available on YouTube, including a cover of Let's Active's "Every Word Means No," and a cover of the Velvet Underground's "Pale Blue Eyes," https://www.youtube.com/watch?v =KZv94h_Noao and https://www.youtube.com/watch?v=mfAfRFSyZwQ.

95. Lynda Stipe interview; Vanessa Briscoe Hay interviews; and Dana Downs interview.

96. Special thanks to Arthur Johnson for sharing the episode featuring the Bar-B-Q Killers with me.

CHAPTER 5

1. Art Rosenbaum interviews; and Andy Nasisse interview. The university was not very supportive of the course. Nasisse and Rosenbaum had to teach it as an overload, in addition to their regular offerings. After the art historians at UGA refused to give credit for the course, Nasisse and Rosenbaum got the university to count it as an elective. Because the course was so time-consuming, they only offered it two or three times.

2. Jennifer Hartley interview; and Art Rosenbaum interviews.

3. Jennifer Hartley interview; and Art Rosenbaum interviews.

4. Jennifer Hartley interview; and Art Rosenbaum interviews. On Art Rosenbaum, see Fred C. Fussell, "Art Rosenbaum: An Oral History with the Artist, Author, Musician, and Folklorist," *Georgia Music*, September 15, 2006, http://georgiamusic.org/a-conversation -with-art-rosenbaum/. On Andy Nasisse, see his website, http://www.andynasisse.com /html/index.php?cat=16.

5. Jerry Cullum, "R.A. Miller: More Than Cute-Looking Whirligigs, or Why Even

Simple-Looking Folk Art Required Multidisciplinary Investigation," *Art Papers* 18, no. 5 (September/October 1994): 23–27; and Jonathan Williams, Roger Manley, and Guy Mendes, *Walks to the Paradise Garden: A Lowdown Southern Odyssey* (Lexington, Ky.: Institute 193, 2019).

6. Chuck Reece interview.

7. Grace Elizabeth Hale, "Black as Folk: The Folk Music Revival, the Civil Rights Movement, and Bob Dylan," in *Nation of Outsiders: How the White Middle Class Fell in Love with Rebellion in Postwar America* (New York: Oxford University Press, 2011).

8. Hale, "Black as Folk"; and Robert Cantrell, *When We Were Good: The Folk Revival* (Cambridge: Harvard University Press, 1996). On R.E.M.'s interest in sixties music, see Mitch Easter's comments in Denise Sullivan, *R.E.M.: Talk About the Passion, An Oral History* (New York: Da Capo, 1998), 39.

9. Blake Gumprecht, "R.E.M.," *Alternative America*, Winter 1983, 35–36. Special thanks to Gumprecht for sending me a copy of this piece in the first and only issue of this publication. On Hartley, see http://jenniferhartley.com/. On Joni Mabe, see Erika Doss, "The Power of Elvis," *American Art* 11, no. 2 (Summer 1997): 4–7; and Joni Mabe, "Obsessions, Personalities, & Oddities," *Georgia Review* 42, no. 2 (Summer 1988): 320–28.

10. April Chapman interview; Julia House interview; Mark Cline interviews; Jennifer Hartley interview; and Armistead Wellford interview.

11. Art Rosenbaum interviews; Sullivan, *R.E.M.: Talk About the Passion*, 49–50; J. F. Turner, *Howard Finster, Man of Visions* (New York: Knopf, 1989); Norman Girardot, *Howard Finster: The Religion and Art of a Stranger from Another World* (Oakland: University of California Press, 2015); and Matthew Sutton, "Little America: R.E.M., Howard Finster, and the Southern 'Outsider Art' Aesthetic," *Studies in Popular Culture* 30, no. 2 (Spring 2008): 1–20. For an overview of the scene in the spring and summer of 1986, see the articles in the one issue published of what was supposed to be a local magazine called *Open City*, June–July 1986, in the author's possession.

12. Anthony DeCurtis interview. On Warhol and the Factory, see chapter 1. On the Mercer Arts Center scene, see Paul Nelson, "Moonstruck over the Miamis," *Village Voice*, December 16, 1974, 132; and Lisa Robinson, "Rebel Nights," *Vanity Fair*, February 14, 2014, http://www.vanityfair.com/culture/2002/11/new-york-rock-scene-1970s. I am indebted here to Anthony DeCurtis, who helped me think through the meaning and the cumulative effect of all the references to Athens bands I have been able to find in the *Village Voice*, *New York Rocker*, *Interview*, *Soho Weekly News*, and *Trouser Press*.

13. Jennifer Hartley interview; and Art Rosenbaum interviews.

14. Art Rosenbaum interviews; Art Rosenbaum, "Welcome Hinges," *Oxford American* 91 (Winter 2015), posted online on February 16, 2016, http://www.oxfordamerican.org/item/718-welcome-hinges; Sullivan, *R.E.M.: Talk About the Passion*, 49–50; Turner, *Howard Finster*; Girardot, *Howard Finster*; and Sutton, "Little America."

15. Andy Nasisse, "Howard Finster: Man of Visions," *Tasty World* 4 [February 1985], 6–7; and David Pierce, "Michael Stipe Speaks (Clearly)," *Tasty World* 4 [February 1985], 24.

16. Fred Mills, "Mitch Easter Interviewed: Perfect Sound Forever—the Director's Cut," *Rock's Backpages*, Summer 2007, https://www.rocksbackpages.com/Library/Article/mitch-easter-interviewed-perfect-sound-forever---the-directors-cut; Erin Amar, "Mitch Easter—Beyond and Back," *Rockerzine*, March 18, 2011; "Vanessa's Version" http://jollybeggars.netnik.com/pylon.html; Sullivan, *R.E.M.: Talk About the Passion*, 39; Parke Puterbaugh, "R.E.M.'s Southern Rock Revival," *Rolling Stone*, June 9, 1983, reprinted in

Anthony DeCurtis, ed., *The Rolling Stone Files* (New York: Hyperion, 1995), 29–32; and Ingrid Schorr, "Rockville Girl Speaks," *Hilobrow*, September 23, 2011, reprinting of article first published in *Hermenaut* 15 (Summer 1999), online at http://hilobrow.com/2011/09/23/rockville-girl-speaks/.

17. Anthony DeCurtis interview; Anthony DeCurtis, "R.E.M.: An Open Party," *Record*, June 1984, online at https://www.rocksbackpages.com/Library/Article/rem-an-open-party; J. D. Considine, "R.E.M.: Subverting Small Town Boredom," *Musician*, August 1983, reprinted in John Platt, ed., *The R.E.M. Companion* (New York: Schirmer Books, 1998), 22–27; Robert Palmer, "Poplife [review of R.E.M.'s *Reckoning*]," *New York Times*, May 30, 1984, C17; "R.E.M. – interview – 6/8.84 – Capitol Theatre," online at https://www.youtube.com/watch?v=f-AQP1VpxqM; "Bill Berry R.E.M. interview – 1985," WRBN FM radio station, Warner Robbins, GA, on online at https://www.youtube.com/watch?v=NOpVO4QPy1Y; and Ryan Dombal, interview with Michael Stipe and Mike Mills, *Pitchfork*, November 21, 2011, https://pitchfork.com/features/interview/8712-rem/.

18. Jonathan Richman playing with various versions of his group the Modern Lovers was a pioneer in reviving old rock sounds in the seventies when he lived in Boston, California, and Maine.

19. Robert Palmer, "Young Bands Make Country Music for the MTV Generation," *New York Times*, June 10, 1984, http://www.nytimes.com/1984/06/10/arts/young-bands-make-country-music-for-the-mtv-generation.html; and Barry Shank, *Dissonant Identities: The Rock 'n' Roll Scene in Austin, Texas* (Middletown: Wesleyan University Press, 1994). X played at the Tate Student Center November 30, 1983.

20. Sandy Robertson, "Jason and the Scorchers: Meanwhile, Back at the Ranch," *Sounds*, May 19, 1984; Jon Pareles, "Old and New Acts Ignite a Folk Rock Comeback," *New York Times*, September 18, 1983, H21; Gina Arnold, *Route 666: On the Road to Nirvana* (New York: St. Martin's Press, 1993); Ann Powers, *Weird Like Us: My Bohemian America* (New York: Simon & Schuster, 2000); Michael Azerrad, *This Band Could Be Your Life: Scenes from the American Indie Underground, 1981–1991* (New York: Little, Brown, 2001); and Simon Reynolds, *Rip It Up and Start Again: Postpunk 1978–1984* (London: Faber & Faber, 2005).

21. On the song "Little America," see Pop Songs (blog), https://popsongs.wordpress.com/2007/03/27/little-america/.

22. Helen Fitzgerald, "Tales from Black Mountain," *Melody Maker*, April 27, 1985, reprinted in Platt, *R.E.M. Companion*, 29–35; and Marcus Gray, *It Crawled from the South: An R.E.M. Companion* (New York: Da Capo, 1997), 273. It is worth noting here the sexism of Stipe's fantasy, the way the woman plays the support role of cooking and caring for the man who makes the music.

23. "Annelise" is most likely Annelies Mondi, a scene participant and art history major at UGA who often attended early R.E.M. shows. Annelies Mondi interview. Video of R.E.M.'s 1984 *Cutting Edge* performance circulates on YouTube: R.E.M., "Rockville," https://www.youtube.com/watch?v=4zghoy9vTgY&list=PLBA8466AB374AE43A&index=4; and R.E.M., "Time after Time," https://www.youtube.com/watch?v=4EzXYsZfur8&index=3&list=PLBA8466AB374AE43A.

24. Gray, *It Crawled from the South*, 277.

25. R.E.M., *Fables of the Reconstruction/Reconstruction of the Fables* (I.R.S. Records, 1985); Gray, *It Crawled from the South*, 69, 276.

26. R.E.M., *Fables of the Reconstruction*; Gray, *It Crawled from the South*, 69, 226, 276;

Tony Gayton, dir., *Athens, GA: Inside/Out* (Spotlight Productions and Subterranean Films, 1987), around 54:40; and Matthew Perpetua, "Life and How to Live It" (July 22, 2008), Pop Songs, https://popsongs.wordpress.com/2008/07/22/life-and-how-to-live-it/. Brivs Mekis's book was for sale at https://www.ebay.com/itm/LIFE-AND-HOW-TO-LIVE -BRIVS-MEKIS-RARE-REM-CULT-BOOK-WHERE-REM-GOT-THE-SONG -TITLE-/200405494476. I knew Jeff Gilley and remember him talking about going to visit Finster with Stipe.

27. Anthony DeCurtis interview; DeCurtis, "The Price of Victory," *The Record*, July 1985, 46–51; and David Fricke, "R.E.M.'s Southern-Fried Art: The Thinking Fan's Rock Band Just Wants You to Dance," 52–56, both reprinted in DeCurtis, *Rolling Stone Files*; and Gray, *It Crawled from the South*, 69–74, 102, 176–78, 224–26, 272–88, 292–94, 389, 411–14.

28. "Alex Chilton, Pop's Reluctant Hero," *Tasty World* 5 [April 1985], 16.

29. Raymond Valley, "R.E.M. Captivated Legion Crowd with Mix of Old Favorites and New Tunes," *Red and Black*, April 24, 1985, 6.

30. Valley, "R.E.M. Captivated Legion Crowd"; and Shelia Jones, "Concert Cut Short by Noise Complaints," *Red and Black*, April 24, 1985, 6.

31. Valley, "R.E.M. Captivated Legion Crowd"; and Jones, "Concert Cut Short," 6.

32. On the album's cover, an old book bursting into flames sat on a wooden ledge that might have been part of a pulpit or an altar. Moody color photographs of the band members' heads shot in front of projected films filled the four corners. On the back, a wooden block fitted on its sides with metal rectangles featuring an imprint of a human ear swung on a cord. The sleeve, too, featured one of the metal ear molds attached to a wooden carving of a human figure propped among wooden architectural fragments, Stipe's version of visionary folk art. On the front of one t-shirt, a band photo caught Mike Mills gesturing at the sky like a preacher calling down the spirit, while on the back, what looked like a torn page of doodled song titles in alternately scratchy and blocky letters listed the album's contents. A color graphic from an antique ad in which a monkey and a green parrot rode a bicycle together appeared on other materials and t-shirts. R.E.M., *Fables of the Reconstruction*; and Eric Heiman, "The New, Weird America," *Eye*, Summer 2008, 33. A t-shirt from this tour was for sale online at https://thecaptainsvintage.com /products/80s-r-e-m-fables-of-the-reconstruction-1985-t-shirt-extra-large.

33. Jon Pareles, "The Pop Life: R.E.M., the Rock Band, Thrives on Ambiguity," *New York Times*, August 28, 1985. R.E.M. manager Jefferson Holt described the "small, homey, hokey, *Mayberry R.F.D.* kind of feel to the way we live our lives" to Anthony DeCurtis for the latter's article "R.E.M.'s Brave New World," *Rolling Stone*, April 20, 1989, reprinted in DeCurtis, *Rocking My Life Away: Writing About Music and Other Matters* (Durham: Duke University Press, 1998), 28–40.

34. Karl Hagstrom Miller, *Segregating Sound: Inventing Folk and Pop Music in the Age of Jim Crow* (Durham: Duke University Press, 2010).

35. Gray, *It Crawled from the South*, 226; Joe Sasfy, "Reckoning with R.E.M.," *Washington Post*, May 10, 1984, online at https://www.washingtonpost.com/archive/lifestyle/1984 /05/10/reckoning-with-rem/bb929767-c59c-4ca9-ac56-3338bb5f9824/?utm_term =.4fd3035dc382; Fred Mills and Todd Goss, "R.E.M. '86 — Dogged Perseverance," *The Bob*, June 1986, reprinted in Platt, *R.E.M. Companion*, 41–71; Anthony DeCurtis, "The Price of Victory: Confident but Confused, R.E.M. Comes All the Way Home," *Record*, July 1985; and "Interview with Pete Buck," *Record*, January–February 1986.

36. Legs McNeil and Gillian McCain, *Please Kill Me: The Uncensored Oral History of*

Punk (New York: Grove, 1996), 278; and Tony Fletcher, *Remarks Remade: The Story of R.E.M.* (New York: Omnibus Press, 2002), 214.

37. Lester Bangs, "The White Noise Supremacists," *Village Voice*, April 30, 1979, reprinted in Greil Marcus, ed., *Psychotic Reactions and Carburetor Dung* (New York: Anchor Books, 2003), 272–82, quotes, 278; and the Notorious Stuart Brothers, "A Date with Peter Buck," *Bucketfull of Brains*, December 1987, reprinted in, *The R.E.M. Companion*, 98.

38. Bangs, "White Noise Supremacists," 276, 277. A photograph of Bangs wearing this shirt appears in McNeil and McCain, *Please Kill Me*, unnumbered page before 204.

39. Bangs, "White Noise Supremacists," 279.

40. Jeff Walls interview; Lynda Stipe interview; and Bill Cody interview. On Marietta and the history of school integration there, see Ruth Yow, *Students of the Dream: Race and Inequality in the Resegregating South* (Cambridge: Harvard University Press, 2017). Bill Berry talks about this incident in Barry Walters, "Visions of Glory," *Spin*, October 1986, 52–58, 78.

41. Kelly Noonan interview; and Arthur Johnson interview. On the integration of the Westminster Schools, see Michelle A. Purdy, "Blurring Public and Private: The Pragmatic Desegregation Politics of an Elite Private School in Atlanta," *History of Education Quarterly* 56, no. 1 (February 2016): 61–89.

42. Every year, the UGA Office of Institutional Research publishes an official book of statistics and other information called the *UGA Fact Book*, and they are online at https://oir.uga.edu/factbook/pastfactbooks/.

43. Robert Burke Warren, "Southern Belles, Latchkey Kids, and Thrift-store Crossdressers: Notes from the New Wave Queer Underground," *Bitter Southerner*, online at https://bittersoutherner.com/southern-belles-latchkey-kids-and-thrift-store -crossdressers#.XQUsFNNKjdd; and "Larry Tee's Celebrity Club: Nightclub or Nightmare?" *Tasty World* 5 [April 1985], 17.

44. Dana Downs interview; Charlayne Hunter-Gault, "Once Segregated, This Georgia Neighborhood Finds New Life by Welcoming New Communities," *PBS News Hour*, May 18, 2017, online at https://www.pbs.org/newshour/show/segregated-georgia -neighborhood-finds-new-life-welcoming-new-communities; and Richard Cromelin, "The Return of the Love Shack's House Band : The B-52's Hot 'n' Sweaty Party Hit Recalls Athens, Ga., Beginnings," *Los Angeles Times*, December 31, 1989, http://articles.latimes .com/1989-12-31/entertainment/ca-263_1_love-shack.

45. Miller, *Segregating Sound*.

46. Mike Mills, "Our Town," *Spin*, July 1985, 21–23.

47. Mills, "Our Town."

48. Mills, "Our Town."

49. Jeff Chang, *Can't Stop, Won't Stop: A History of the Hip-Hop Generation* (New York: St. Martin's, 2005), 141–65; *Downtown Punkrock Meets Uptown Hip Hop* (blog), http://downtownpunkrockmeetsuptownhiphop.blogspot.com/2010_05_01_archive.html; Michael Lachowski interviews; and Sean Bourne interview. Robert Christgau's annual *Village Voice* polls are online at https://www.robertchristgau.com/xg/pnj/index.php.

50. Wini Brienes, *Community and Organization in the New Left, 1962–1968: The Great Refusal* (New York: Praeger, 1982).

51. On the sexism of the members of R.E.M., hard evidence is difficult to come by, but a great deal of talk about it circulated in the scene at the time, in situations where women spoke privately to each other. It was not hard to catch Buck, Mills, and Berry, when they

were in town, ogling attractive young women at the Georgia Bar or the 40 Watt and even making sexually suggestive comments that would today warrant the label of harassment. At times, I witnessed this behavior myself. On the other hand, this kind of behavior was so *very common* then in places where alcohol was served that most groups of heterosexual men out drinking were engaging in these behaviors. Accusations of sexist behavior in the R.E.M. office also circulated widely in the 1980s, but no one has been willing to go on the record about it. Many people in Athens claimed Jefferson Holt, R.E.M.'s longtime manager, was guilty of sexual harassment, that a longtime R.E.M. office employee had made the complaint, and that Holt resigned for this reason in May 1996. See Chuck Philips, "R.E.M.'s Former Manager Denies Allegations of Sex Harassment," *Los Angeles Times*, June 21, 1996, http://articles.latimes.com/1996-06-21/business/fi-17183_1_sexual -harassment. Although the terms of his settlement prevent him from speaking publicly, Jefferson Holt did name the company he founded after he left R.E.M., a kind of hybrid press, management and record company, Daniel 13, which just happens to be a reference to a Bible story about a woman who is falsely accused of sexual misbehavior. I reached out to Holt, who I knew a bit in the past, through a mutual friend, to get his take on the scene and R.E.M., whatever he could talk about outside his legal agreement with the band. He politely declined.

52. Bill Cody interview; Errol Morris, dir., *Vernon, Florida* (Errol Morris Films, 1981); and R.E.M. Timeline for 1985, online at http://www.remtimeline.com/1985.html.

53. Bill Cody interview.

54. Bill Cody interview; and Gayton, *Athens, GA: Inside/Out.*

55. Bill Cody interview.

56. Bill Cody interview. See the credits for Gayton, *Athens, GA: Inside/Out*, at the end of the film and online at http://www.imdb.com/title/tt0092591/fullcredits?ref_=ttrel_sa_1. See also the following video on YouTube, which includes footage from the documentary as well as footage made around the release of the documentary, of Cody and Gayton talking about making *Inside/Out*, https://www.youtube.com/watch?v=lJCoik8NsZ4.

57. Perhaps the experience of these failed interviews remained with him. Before he died, he always politely rebuffed my attempts to interview him.

58. Bill Cody interview; and Gayton, *Athens, GA: Inside/Out.*

59. Bill Cody interview. According to Cody, R.E.M. finished writing the song the night before the filmmakers shot the band playing it on January 29, 1986. Other sources suggest it was written in November 1985. See Gray, *It Crawled from the South*, 72. Also according to Cody, the inclusion of two, previously unrecorded R.E.M. songs "made the film" as the band was at the height of their college-rock fame in 1987 when the completed documentary was released and played in theaters and later on MTV.

60. Bill Cody interview; Mark Cooper Smith interview; Barry Marler interview; Bryan Cook interview; Craig Williams interview; and Terry Allen interview. On Dreams So Real, see also Charles Aaron, "After Hours," *Red and Black*, June 15, 1984, 5; July 18, 1984, 5; and August 9, 1984, 6; and Charles Aaron, "Bourbon Street Offers New Venue for Bands," *Red and Black*, June 28, 1984, 6; [No author], "Another Life to Live," *Tasty World* 6 [May or June 1985], 6; and Philip Campbell, "Another Life to Live," *Tasty World* 9 [September 1985].

61. Bill Cody interview.

62. See the interview Jeff Arndt, "Dexter Romweber: Beyond the Flat Duo Jets," *Perfect Sound Forever*, September 2001, http://www.furious.com/perfect/flatduojets.html; and

Gretchen Wood, "Dexter Romweber Duo: It's a Family Affair," *Perfect Sound Forever*, June 2009, http://www.furious.com/perfect/dexterromweber.html.

63. Gayton, *Athens, GA: Inside/Out.*

64. Gayton, *Athens, GA: Inside/Out*; Bill Cody interview; and Lynda Stipe interview. Stipe makes similar moves, minus the spindle, in the video that he helped direct for the song "Can't Get There from Here," filmed in and around Philomath in prime folk-artist territory in May 1985. There is more than a hint of blackface in these performances.

65. Gayton, *Athens, GA: Inside/Out*; and Melanie Haner Reynolds interview. In 1990, Haner married Tom Reynolds, the brother of Athens photographer and musician Ben Reynolds, and changed her name. Love Tractor later turned Seawright's poem "I Broke My Saw" into a song. The scene's celebration of eccentric, crazy personas sometimes made it difficult to tell that some people were not just eccentric but also had serious mental health issues.

66. Rittenbury means the Butthole Surfers. Michael Stipe did not share his bandmates' love for Walter's BBQ because he was a vegetarian.

67. Gayton, *Athens, GA: Inside/Out*; Vanessa Briscoe Hay interviews; and Briscoe Hay, "Vanessa's Version." Briscoe Hay was filmed by her then-landlord and former professor Jim Herbert. She remembers the date — January 28, 1986 — because it was the day of the Challenger disaster.

68. I make my *brief* appearance around 59:40 in Gayton, *Athens, GA: Inside/Out.*

69. Mark Cooper Smith interview; Keith Landers interviews; Bill Cody interview; Arthur Johnson interviews; Claire Horne interview; I.R.S. Records, *Music from the Film Athens GA Inside/Out* (I.R.S 6185, 1987); Will Ostick, "Film to Explore the Cultural Essence of Athens Inside and Out through Its Artists and Musicians," *Red and Black*, November 1986, 1; and Julie Carey, "'Athens Inside/Out' Cool Scene," *Red and Black*, December 4, 1986, 4. In Athens, the Georgia Theater hosted a concert called "Athens, GA/Outside the Movie." See the advertisement "Athens, GA/Outside the Movie," *Red and Black*, May 28, 1987, 2.

70. Mark Cooper Smith interview; and Scott Cain, "Musicians' 'Athens' Is Full of Zest," *Atlanta Constitution*, April 24, 1987, 1P, 6P.

71. David Barbe interviews.

72. David Barbe interviews; Chuck Reece interview; Raymond Valley and John McMahon, "Spaz and Dim Report," *Red and Black*, August 11, 1986, 6; and Raymond Valley, "Summer Revolves Around Local Cassette," *Red and Black*, September 23, 1986, 22. The *Red and Black* described Eat America as ex–Kilkenny Cat "Haynes Collins and Errol Stewart's newest project" in early 1986 when they played at the Uptown on a Monday night for a $1 cover. Haynes played bass and Stewart guitar. Other members then were Dru Wilbur on vocals and Gene Lyon on drums. Michael Koenig, "After Hours," *Red and Black*, February 21, 1986, 6. By the fall of 1986, Stewart had quit and was replaced by Matt Hansen and "Jolly" John Rogers, friends who had recently moved to Athens from Seattle. See Gordon Lamb, "That Beat in Time: Local Bands Unforgotten: Eat America," *Flagpole*, May 9, 2007, 32. Porn Orchard then was a quartet with Curtiss Pernice on guitar and vocals, Ted Hafer on vocals, Rob Hargrove on bass, and Sam Mixon on drums. After Hargrove left, Hafer took over on bass. The Primates included Greg Reece and brothers Eric and L. H. Sales, who had all moved to Athens from the tiny North Georgia town of Ellijay. They had a practice space for years at Stitchcraft and started out as a cover band.

The La Di Das had a changing line-up that included Todd McBride, Rob Veal, and Vic Chesnutt.

73. This entire section about the "Better Than TV Tour" is drawn from interviews with David Barbe, Arthur Johnson, and Bryan Cook, and my own still-vivid memories of this trip. On Mercyland, see also Noah Arceneaux, "Band's Popularity Grows in Athens," *Red and Black*, April 17, 1987, 6. Many thanks to Arthur Johnson for getting me a copy of Erica McCarthy's documentary *Some: The 1986 Better Than TV Tour*. Though this film has been screened on occasion by McCarthy, it has never been commercially released. I pop up in the film doing things like sleeping on the bus and watching bands — you get to see my back more often than my face. I do make one brief speaking appearance (around 31:30), talking in a southern accent so thick I don't recognize my own voice.

74. Bryan Cook interview.

75. McCarthy, *Some: The 1986 Better Than TV Tour*.

76. David Barbe interviews; Bryan Cook interview; and McCarthy, *Some: The 1986 Better Than TV Tour*.

77. McCarthy, *Some: The 1986 Better Than TV Tour*.

78. Bryan Cook interview; and McCarthy, *Some: The 1986 Better Than TV Tour*.

79. Bryan Cook interview, Arthur Johnson interview; and David Barbe interviews.

80. Bryan Cook interview; David Barbe interviews, and Greg Shelnutt, "The Grit Holds Benefit for DRG Groups Displaying Art Created by Bandmembers," *Red and Black*, January 21, 1987, 5.

81. Cook interview; and Barbe interviews. The captioned photo of Bryan Cook and Andrew Donaldson included in Greg Shelnutt, "Grit Holds Benefit," describes the music benefit.

82. McCarthy, *Some: The 1986 Better Than TV Tour*.

83. Jessica Greene and Ted Hafer, *The Grit Cookbook* (Chicago: Chicago Review Press, 2007), ix–x; Jennifer Hartley interview; Melanie Haner Reynolds interview; and Sam Seawright interviews.

84. Jennifer Hartley interview.

85. Jennifer Hartley interview.

86. Jennifer Hartley interview. There is a short clip near the beginning of *Athens, GA: Inside/Out* of an African American man in a suit and hat entering True Confections.

87. Jennifer Hartley interview; and Andy Smith, "Downtown Show Gives Artists Rare Opportunity," *Red and Black*, April 11, 1986, 3.

88. Melanie Haner Reynolds interview.

89. Jennifer Hartley interview; and Melanie Haner Reynolds interview.

90. Jennifer Hartley interview; and Melanie Haner Reynolds interview.

91. Jennifer Hartley interview; and Melanie Haner Reynolds interview.

92. Jennifer Hartley interview; and Melanie Haner Reynolds interview.

93. Sam Seawright interviews. Years later, Stipe contacted Seawright to get the rights to use some of those doodles in the movie projected behind R.E.M. during the "Work" tour that accompanied the release of *Document* on I.R.S. in 1987. On Starbucks and the creation of new kinds of commercialized social spaces where people can work as well as socialize, see Bryant Simon, *Everything but the Coffee: Learning About America from Starbucks* (Berkeley: University of California Press, 2011).

94. Melanie Haner Reynolds interview; and Gray, *It Crawled from the South*, 73–77.

95. Jennifer Hartley interview; Melanie Haner Reynolds interview; and Sam Seawright interviews.

96. Jennifer Hartley interview; Melanie Haner Reynolds interview; and Sam Seawright interviews. The writer John Seawright, who carried around a book in which he wrote poems and lyrics, ended up collaborating with Vic Chesnutt on five songs, including one Chesnutt later recorded called "Elberton Fair."

97. Jennifer Hartley interview; Sam Seawright interviews; and Andy Nasisse interview.

98. Andy Nasisse interview.

99. Andy Nasisse interview. Photograph on the front page of the *Red and Black* with the caption, "On second thought, make it a Bud Light," February 12, 1988, 1. Nasisse sent me a copy of this photograph.

100. Melanie Haner Reynolds interview; Jennifer Hartley interview; and Gray, *It Crawled from the South*, 246–47.

101. Jennifer Hartley interview; Melanie Haner Reynolds interview; Art Rosenbaum interviews; and Joe Willey interview.

102. Jennifer Hartley interview; Melanie Haner Reynolds interview; Sam Seawright interviews; and Art Rosenbaum interviews; Five Eight Facebook page, online at https://www.facebook.com/fiveeightathens/; and Greene and Hafer, *Grit Cookbook*.

103. In this way, the Grit joined the El Dorado/Bluebird and non-vegetarian places like Wilson's Soul Food and Weaver D's in popularizing the kind of cuisine now celebrated by the Southern Foodways Alliance.

CHAPTER 6

1. The lyrics quoted here are reproduced as Vic Chesnutt wrote them in the liner notes for *Little*, with the caveat that his handwriting sometimes makes it hard to tell what letters are capitalized. A transcription of the lyrics he sings on this record would be slightly different. See Vic Chesnutt, *Little*, Texas Hotel Records, 1990.

2. My analysis of Vic Chesnutt is based here and throughout on my own experience — I saw him play many times and knew him and his wife Tina Whatley Chesnutt well. I also draw on published sources, especially interviews, and on my own interviews with people who knew him well. Vic died before I started working on this book.

3. "Speed Racer" and "Giupetto" [*sic*] appear on Vic Chesnutt's first album, *Little*.

4. On Vic Chesnutt, see John Herman, *The Life and Songwriting of Vic Chesnutt* (master's thesis, University of Mississippi, 2014). John "Jo Jo" Herman was the keyboardist for Athens jam band Widespread Panic. As part of this study, he hired Scott Stuckey, who had been a friend of Chesnutt's and for a time ran a recording studio in his house in Athens, to shoot hours of interviews with Chesnutt. Other useful sources on Chesnutt include David Peisner, "When the Bottom Fell Out," *Spin*, July 2010, online at https://books.google.com/books?id=9Cu_K00ObfsC&pg=PA68&lpg=PA68&dq=athens+band+the+la+di+das&source=bl&ots=87kA7EjP6G&sig=cyb23wBSsj6c5xsjpSyLdhqpUjw&hl=en&sa=X&ved=0ahUKEwjS2efbxNPbAhVls1kKHT1pChYQ6AEIbDAO#v=onepage&q=vic%20chesnutt&f=false; Bob Townsend, "Vic Chesnutt: The Life You Save May Be Your Own," *No Depression*, February 28, 2005, http://nodepression.com/article/vic-chesnutt-life-you-save-may-be-your-own; Mark Kemp, "Vic Chesnutt: Famous by Association," *Rolling Stone*, September 9, 1986, available at https://www.rocksbackpages.com/Library/Article/vic-chesnutt-famous-by-association; Terri Gross, "Songs of Survival and Reflection: 'At

the Cut,'" *Fresh Air*, National Public Radio, December 1, 2009, online at https://www.npr
.org/templates/story/story.php?storyId=120978388; Charles Fontaine's blog *Debriefing:
The Music and Art of Vic Chesnutt*, online at http://debriefingthemusicandartofvicchesnutt
.blogspot.com/; *A Tribute to Vic Chesnutt*, online at http://www.vicchesnuttrelief.com
/index.html; and Rabbits Are Cooking Breakfast: A Vic Chesnutt Page, online at http://
vicchesnutt.cupantae.com/. See also the documentary film Peter Sillen, *Speed Racer:
Welcome to the World of Vic Chesnutt* (Dashboard Dog Pictures, 1994). One source I do not
rely on is Kristen Hersh, *Don't Suck, Don't Die: Giving Up Vic Chesnutt* (Austin: University
of Texas Press, 2015). As someone who frequently visited Vic and Tina in their home, I was
troubled that the descriptions of the layout and look of this home were off. When I asked
Athens people who knew Chesnutt well about the book, including people who toured with
him in his backing band, they all raised questions about the accuracy of many of the book's
details.

5. Lance Bangs, "Made in Athens," Vice Media, 2014, online at https://flagpole.com
/blogs/homedrone/posts/watch-vice-s-made-in-athens-video; Steve Pond, "R.E.M.
in the Real World: Rock's Most Influential College Band Graduates," *Rolling Stone*,
December 3, 1987; Katy Linfield, "A Romantic Review of Athens, Georgia," *Flagpole*,
September 6, 1989, 14–15; Scott Cain, "Musicians' 'Athens' Is Full of Zest," *Atlanta
Constitution*, April 24, 1987, 1P, 6P; and Marcus Gray, *It Crawled from the South: An R.E.M.
Companion* (New York: Da Capo Press, 1996), 374.

6. Jennifer Hartley interview; Melanie Haner Reynolds interview; Sam Seawright
interviews; Julie House interview; Curtiss Pernice interviews; and Velena Vego interview.
In the past, many early scene folks rented rooms in Buck's house at 748 Cobb, nicknamed
the Jester House. The Porn Orchard house was at 255 Elizabeth Street and then on Finley.

7. Arthur Johnson interviews; and Sam Seawright interviews. Mona Hawkins and
Mary Beth Mills ran the literary magazine *Lift Archaic*. Cathy Hestor edited *Blue Plate
Special*. Theron Case, "New Club to Open at Previous Lunch Paper Location," *Red and
Black*, April 30, 1987, 4. Thomas had owned Lunch Paper, a performance space in the old
Stitchcraft factory building, with Chris DeBarr. See chapter 4. When he opened his first
store on Hull Street he called it Lunch Paper. Then the business was called the Club-with-
No-Name for a while before becoming Spend Money Here. Taken together, Jim Stacy's
cartoons in the *Flagpole* in 1989 form a pictorial history of the scene. On Pat Cardiff, see
Hillary Meister, "Of Boomerangs and Transcendentalists," *Flagpole*, June 26, 1991, 10–11.

8. Bryan Cook, "Whatever," *Flagpole* 1, October 1, 1987, 8; and Jared Bailey interview.
When I began this "little" book, the *Flagpole* was hard to find. I got it on microfilm and
printed out every copy up until my cutoff date, the end of 1991. Since then, it has been
added to the Digital Library of Georgia's Georgia Historic Newspapers collection,
searchable online at https://gahistoricnewspapers.galileo.usg.edu/lccn/sn94029049/.
Sometime between June 1987, when Jared Bailey and Barrie Buck reopened the 40 Watt
at its former Clayton Street location and October 1, 1987, when Bailey published the
first issue of *Flagpole*, Bailey had a fight with the publisher of the *Classic City Live*, a free
weekly then providing club calendars and other listings for stuff happening in town, plus
a few articles and lots of ads. Bailey pulled the 40 Watt's ads, in his telling because of poor
production and coverage, and the owner of *Live* called him a "fucking asshole" in front of
a crowd of tourists. See Erik D. Immanuel [probably a pseudonym], "Media Assassin,"
Flagpole, June 7, 1989, 20–21; and Noel Murray, "Jared Bailey: Man on the Local Music
Scene," *Red and Black*, December 3, 1990, 14–15. See Josh Rosenbaum, "Classic City Live

Fades Away," *Red and Black*, May 25, 1992, 3, on the history of that weekly. For the most part, the *Red and Black* was the only paper that regularly published thoughtful and serious music criticism in the eighties, but that coverage ebbed and flowed according to the degree of student journalists' interest in local music.

9. On R.E.M.'s politicization in the second half of the 1980s, see Gray, *It Crawled from the South*, 385–430.

10. Natalie Merchant claims credit for Stipe's turn toward writing more political songs. James McNair, "How We Met: Michael Stipe and Natalie Merchant," *The Independent*, November 8, 1998, online at https://www.independent.co.uk/arts-entertainment/how -we-met-michael-stipe-and-natalie-merchant-1183710.html; and Erle Norton, "R.E.M. to Buy Athens Building," *Red and Black*, February 14, 1986, 1.

11. See https://www.discogs.com/ for information about the discographies of all these bands. On Texas Hotel Records, see David Wharton, "Talent Search: Texas Hotel Records May Be a Small Label, But It's Had Big Success in Launching Promising Young Bands," *Los Angeles Times*, June 11, 1989, online at https://www.articles.latimes.com/1989–06–11 /entertainment/ca-3163_1_texas-hotel-labels-bands.

12. Scott Stuckey, *What Doesn't Kill Me*, rough cut of a Vic Chesnutt documentary, online at https://www.youtube.com/watch?v=QI_wIZdy4Rs; Peisner, "When the Bottom Fell Out"; and Sillen, *Speed Racer*. A dispute between the producer and Chesnutt's widow Tina Whatley Chesnutt had halted release of this film. Stuckey says he had access to about 400 hours of Chesnutt interviews and performances.

13. Stuckey, *What Doesn't Kill Me*; Herman, *Life and Songwriting of Vic Chesnutt*; Townsend, "Life You Save"; and Peisner, "When the Bottom Fell Out." Zebulon had a population of about 1,400 in the 1980 census.

14. Kemp, "Famous by Association."

15. Herman, *Life and Songwriting of Vic Chesnutt*.

16. Gross, "Songs of Survival and Reflection"; and Townsend, "Life You Save."

17. Townsend, "Life You Save."

18. Townsend, "Life You Save."

19. Herman, *Life and Songwriting of Vic Chesnutt*; Nick Hasted, "Vic Chesnutt: Dark Side of the Tune," *The Independent*, April 4, 2003, available at https://www.rocksbackpages .com/Library/Article/vic-chesnutt-dark-side-of-the-tune-; Ian Fortnam, "Vic Chesnutt," *New Musical Express, April 1995*, available at https://www.rocksbackpages.com/Library /Article/vic-chesnutt; and Travis Nichols, "It Weren't Supernatural," *Flagpole*, October 20, 1999, 22–25, 34, and October 27, 1999, 27–29, a two-part interview with Chesnutt.

20. Townsend, "Life You Save," 82.

21. Herman, *Life and Songwriting of Vic Chesnutt*, 78.

22. Herman, *Life and Songwriting of Vic Chesnutt*, 65, 29, 41; and Stuckey, *What Doesn't Kill Me*.

23. Andrew Donaldson interview; and Deonna Mann interview.

24. Andrew Donaldson interview.

25. Deonna Mann interview.

26. Nichols, "It Weren't Supernatural."

27. Kemp, "Famous by Association"; and Herman, *Life and Songwriting of Vic Chesnutt*, 38.

28. Townsend, "Life You Save"; Curtiss Pernice interviews; David Barbe interviews; and Arthur Johnson interviews.

29. *NINETOGETOUT* is online at Samizdat: Nine To Get Out (Athens 80's Tape

Comp Series), https://www.chunklet.com/samizdat-nine-to-get-out-athens-80s-tape-comp-series/. Thanks also to Arthur Johnson for sharing his copy of this tape.

30. Stuckey, *What Doesn't Kill Me*; and Sam Seawright interviews.

31. Herman, *Life and Songwriting of Vic Chesnutt*, 28–9; Townsend, "Life You Save"; J. M. Davidson, entry on Vic Chesnutt in *Concert and Chaos: A Documentary of the Athens Music Scene: Volume 1* (self-published, no date but sometime in 1989), no page numbers. Curtiss Pernice told me the La Di Das broke up in 1987, yet they played multiple gigs at the 40 Watt in early 1988. Perhaps they were just playing gigs they had already booked. I saw them perform multiple times in these days, but don't remember when they broke up.

32. Joe Willey interview; Herman, *Life and Songwriting of Vic Chesnutt*, 51–52; and photographs of Chesnutt at the concert taken by Rick the printer, Rick Hawkins, which have been periodically for sale on eBay. The show occurred on June 24, 1988. Most likely, he got the idea from the poet Stevie Smith who often created little drawings to accompany her poems.

33. Mark Kemp, "Michael Stipe: What Are Friends For," *Option*, September 1990, available at https://www.rocksbackpages.com/Library/Article/michael-stipe-what-are-friends-for.

34. Kathy Kirbo interview. Nichols, "It Weren't Supernatural"; Peisner, "When the Bottom Fell Out"; Kemp, "Famous by Association"; Fortnam, "Vic Chesnutt"; and Townsend, "Life You Save." Chesnutt's mother died of cancer as well, around 1994. Chesnutt named his publishing company Ghetto Bells in tribute to his favorite store. In 2005 he released an album with this name too.

35. Kemp, "Famous by Association."

36. Kemp, "Michael Stipe: What are Friends For." I think this "Brenda" is Brenda Roberson, who co-owned the Grit in its original location for a brief period with Jessica Greene. I asked people who knew Vic well in this period, but people either do not remember her last name or thought it might be Roberson but were not sure.

37. "Isadora Duncan" appears on Chesnutt, *Little*.

38. In the liner notes, Chesnutt actually writes "Linda Limner" instead of Lynda Limner, the actual pseudonym Lynda Stipe used for a while.

39. Davidson, entry on Vic Chesnutt in *Concert and Chaos*, no page numbers.

40. Ian MacKaye was a member of D.C. punk bands Minor Threat and Fugazi and founder of Dischord Records. He is quoted in Stuckey, *What Doesn't Kill Me*.

41. Armistead Wellford interview; Mark Cline interviews; Jeff Walls interview; Mark Cooper Smith interview; and Mark Cooper Smith, "Take the Stage: Access and Participation in a Music Counter-Culture" (master's thesis, University of Georgia, 1989), 44.

42. Noel Murray, "After Hours" [photograph and mini-review], *Red and Black*, October 12, 1990, 8; Noel Murray, "After Hours" [highlighted "Best Bet" at top of the listings], *Red and Black*, January 25, 1991, 6; and Gordon Lamb, "Threats & Promises: Music News and Gossip," *Flagpole*, January 6, 2010, 11. A sampling of our *Flagpole* coverage includes: "Cordy Lon Double Dates with Vic," *Flagpole*, June 7, 1989, 11; "Mr. and Mrs. Cordy Lon," *Flagpole*, January 3, 1990, 22; "Hey Kids, It's Cordy Lon," *Flagpole*, January 24,1990, 10; "Umbilical Cordy Lon, Navel of the Universe," *Flagpole*, March 7, 1990, 15; "Cordy Lon on TV," *Flagpole*, June 6, 1990, 30; and "Mystery Man" [our drummer Rob], *Flagpole*, August 29, 1990, 11. See also Davidson, *Concert and Chaos*, entry on "Cordy Lon," no page numbers. "*Misanthropic* On Sale Now. Wuxtry and Downtown Records" [an ad for our

tape], *Flagpole*, May 8, 1990, 29; and Jeff Payne, "What Jeff Saw, What Jeff Heard...," *Flagpole*, February 7, 1990, 35. "Rock A' Lon," *Flagpole*, November 7, 1990, 30, announces an upcoming show and our recent appearance on election day on WUOG, which I also own a tape of. After we sent Island Records our demo tape, Chris Blackwell wrote to tell us how much he liked the band but that he could not sign us because David sounded too much like Michael Stipe circa *Murmur* when he sang. Despite the praise, the comparison to Stipe crushed David.

43. I had no idea then that Hartley, too, was inspired by her own study abroad experience.

44. Don Chambers interview.

45. I did not know that Jennifer Hartley and Melanie Haner went through a very similar experience opening the Grit until I interviewed them for this book.

46. Opening night was October 7, 1987.

47. The person who was technically our first employee did not last more than a few weeks.

48. In Jim Stacy's own accounts of his past available online, he often says he started the Downstairs. See publicity about his Cooking Channel show *Offbeat Eats* and his Facebook page, https://www.facebook.com/pg/bigjimstacy/about/?ref=page_internal. This is not true. We did promote him to manager in our second year and give him a small ownership stake in recognition of his importance in our success.

49. Donna Ashley interview.

50. Deonna Mann interview; and "Evening with the Downstairs," *Flagpole*, May 31, 1989, 23. Chris Debarr wrote a regular column on local and Atlanta art shows under the alias Comrade Pulchritude. Comrade Pulchritude, "Art Bureaucrat," *Flagpole* (January 10, 1990), 8–9, quote, 8.

51. Arthur Johnson interviews; and Craig Williams interview.

52. Denise Pfannkuche, "Happy Birthday, Downstairs," *Red and Black*, October 4, 1988, 8. "Sometimes, ads spelled the band's name "Gaen Ainm" and other times "Gan Ainm," which means "no name" in Irish. I am not sure whether these are typos or whether the band spelled their name "Gaen" to start. "Song Swap Swaps Sites or Song Swap Site Swap," *Flagpole*, October 11, 1989, 17.

53. Pfannkuche, "Happy Birthday, Downstairs"; Rand Pearson, "The Downstairs Captures the Essence of Athens with Food and Art," *Red and Black*, June 16, 1988, 3; and Maura Corrigan, "Underground Café Celebrates Birthday Tonight," *Red and Black*, October 9, 1990, 7. On the Cabbagetown bands, see Scott Freeman, "The Triumph and the Tragedy of the Cabbagetown Sound," *Creative Loafing*, June 24, 2010, online at https://creativeloafing.com/content-168324-The-triumph-and-tragedy-of-the-Cabbagetown-sound; Nathan P. Owens, "Dust and Drag," *Oxford American*, March 2, 2016, https://www.oxfordamerican.org/item/773-dust-and-drag; Abigail Covington, "When the Fire Broke Out," *Oxford American*, January 25, 2016, online at https://www.oxfordamerican.org/magazine/item/755-when-the-fire-broke-out; "Deacon Lunchbox, 41, A Performance Artist," *New York Times*, April 22, 1992, 23; Jody Grind, *One Man's Trash is Another Man's Treasure*, DB Records, 1990; and Opal Foxx Quartet, *The Love That Won't Shut Up*, self-released, 1993. The Jody Grind made a video for "Behind the Eight Ball," a song on the first album, at the Downstairs. It is online at https://www.youtube.com/watch?v=hUiCTm XY8_w.

I saw all of these Cabbagetown musicians perform often in Athens in this period. Sometimes, club calendars list "An Evening with the Garbagemen" as "An Evening with the Garbageman."

54. "Sculptural Butts," *Flagpole*, October 19, 1988, 12; Cooper Smith, "Take the Stage," 45, 50–45; Mark Cooper Smith interview; and Bill David interview. On the Rockfish, see Nicole Gustin, "New Music Club Opens in Athens This Summer," *Red and Black*, June 4, 1987, 6.

55. The performance artist and poet Deacon Lunchbox was Tim Ruttenber. Kicked out of a small North Carolina college in the seventies, Ruttenber lived alone in the mountains for a few years where he learned to meditate, explored Eastern religions, and smoked a lot of homegrown pot. Shy as hell then, he invented the Deacon persona for an assignment in an English class at Georgia Tech. Kelly Hogan's account of the accident that killed Ruttenber and other band members and ended the Jody Grind and Opal Foxx is online at http://hoganhere.tumblr.com/post/10118062681/this-is-my-favorite-picture-of-my-first-real-band#me.

56. Douglas Wood and Bill Kenyon, "Nightlife," *Flagpole*, October 12, 1989, 12–13.

57. "After Hours," *Red and Black*, June 9, 1989, 6; Lisa Gilmore, "Greenpeace Tours to Fight Toxic Waste Dump," *Red and Black*, June 12, 1989, 7; "Clean Air and Good Music," *Flagpole*, June 21, 1989, 16; "Greenpeace Benefit," *Flagpole*, June 14, 1989, 9; and "The Downstairs Turns 2," *Flagpole*, October 11, 1989, 2. Dan Matthews got a lot of criticism for revealing who was playing. David and I never would have told anyone, but the truth is we might not have survived without that night, and I was grateful to Widespread Panic and Dan, too, for making it happen. I treat jam bands like Widespread Panic and White Buffalo as part of the scene here because they played the same places and worked the same kinds of shit jobs and were friends with some of the same people. The scene was always diverse in terms of sound and in this period the range of genres people were reinterpreting and playing with grew even larger.

58. Cindy Wilson interview; Keith Bennett interviews; Lynda Stipe interview; Craig Williams interview; Curtiss Pernice interviews; Barry Marler interview; and Cooper Smith, "Take the Stage," 45. Many bands that moved to town often changed their names and/or added a new member or two. For some, that meant they were formed in Athens. Others believed this was yet another way of taking advantage of the scene. If a band survived a few years, though, these issues usually disappeared. After Mike Mantione saw *Athens, GA: Inside/Out* in New York City, he convinced his bandmates and friends from SUNY Binghamton Dan Horowitz and Mike Palmatier to move to Athens in 1988. They called their group Five Eight, a reference to the fact that everyone in the band was that height. By the early 1990s, no one questioned whether the group was an "Athens" band. On the place-based nature of indie America, especially the hardcore scene, see Kelefa Sanneh, "How Hard Was Their Core? Looking Back at Anger," *New York Times*, September 21, 2006, E1; and Steven Blush, *American Hardcore: A Tribal History* (Port Townsend, Wash.: Feral House, 2010).

59. Cooper Smith, "Take the Stage," 54. For a while, before he became too sick, a friend and regular customer became our door person. He had lost his job cooking in a downtown restaurant after his bosses learned he had AIDS and despite years of experience and a stellar work ethic, no one would hire him. Then, he did not want me to reveal his status, and he died without revoking that request so I will not name him here. He had rural family members who did not approve of his being gay.

60. Tony Paris, "R.E.M.: The Year of Living Quietly," *Spin*, February 1989, 58; Mills and Buck's episode of WUOG's *Sound of the City* was broadcast on February 16, 1988. R.E.M. timeline includes the set list, but gets the name of the show wrong: Porn Orchard, "Our

Band"; The Side Effects, "Through With You"; Mercyland, "Black On Black On Black";
Primates, "Hitler Youth"; Dark Harvest, "Back To Back"; White Trash, "Fear"; Squalls,
"Cindy"; Pylon, "Crazy"; Art in the Dark, "Tell Me"; La Di Das, "Isadora Duncan";
B-52's, "Give Me Back My Man"; Method Actors, "Eye"; El May Dukes, "Life Goes On";
Kilkenny Cats, "Hands Down"; Bar-B-Q Killers, "Mark E. Smith"; Doubts Even Here,
"Imagine This"; Love Tractor, "Fun To Be Happy"; R.E.M., "Perfect Circle," online at
https://www.remtimeline.com/1987.html. See also the WUOG archives, UGA Special
Collections library.

61. R.E.M. Timeline, online at http://www.remtimeline.com; Gray, *It Crawled from the
South*, 194–215, 351–8; and *Flagpole*, October 5, 1988, 7 (for an announcement of Pylon's
Legion Field show on October 19, 1988).

62. Curtiss Pernice interviews; and Gordon Lamb, "That Beat in Time: Local Bands
Unforgotten: Porn Orchard," *Flagpole*, October 11, 2006, 36.

63. Curtiss Pernice interviews; Larry Tenner interview; and Curtiss Pernice interview
of Sam Mixon for the Athens Music Project, online at https://kaltura.uga.edu/media/t
/1_mzr6jpzn.

64. Curtiss Pernice interviews; Curtiss Pernice interview of Sam Mixon for the Athens
Music Project; and Gordon Lamb, "Porn Orchard."

65. Raymond Valley, "Summer Revolves Around Local Cassette," *Red and Black*,
September 23, 1986, 22; Gordon Lamb, "Porn Orchard"; and Curtiss Pernice interviews.

66. Curtiss Pernice interviews; David Barbe interviews; Deonna Mann interview; and
Arthur Johnson interviews.

67. Curtiss Pernice interviews; and Curtiss Pernice interview of Sam Mixon for the
Athens Music Project.

68. Curtiss Pernice interviews.

69. Ben Reynolds interviews; Lynda Stipe interview; Mark Kemp, "Michael Stipe:
What Are Friends For"; and Gray, *It Crawled from the South*, 335–39. On the rumored Stipe
solo project, see Christopher Dawes, "Michael Stipe No Go Solo," online at http://www
.pushstuff.co.uk/mminfofreakos/michaelstipe051292.html.

70. Ben Reynolds interviews; and Kemp, "Michael Stipe: What Are Friends For."
Other sources on the Chickasaw Mudd Puppies include Tom Popson, "Those Old-time,
Postmodern Chickasaw Mudd Puppies," *Chicago Tribune*, November 23, 1990, https://
www.chicagotribune.com/news/ct-xpm-1990-11-23-9004080138-story.html; Russ DeVault,
"How 'Bout Them Puppies: As in Chickasaw Mudd Stompin' Boys," *Atlanta Journal/
Constitution*, April 12, 1991, F1, F6; Karen Schoemer, "Delta Blues and Girl Groups in
2 New Incarnations," *New York Times*, January 18, 1991, C6; Joseph Gallivan, "Critics'
Choice: Rock," *The Independent*, March 3, 1991, SR5; and David Toop, "Chickasaw Mudd
Puppies," *The Times* (London), March 11, 1991.

71. "Out Mud Puppying," *Flagpole*, February 3, 1988, 18–19. I saw the Chickasaw Mudd
Puppies play multiple times in Athens.

72. "Out Mud Puppying"; Davidson, "Chickasaw Mudd Puppies," in *Concert and
Chaos*," no page numbers; and *Atlanta Constitution* April 12, 1991, F1, F6.

73. "Puppies O' Mudd," *Flagpole*, June 15, 1988, 3; Kevin Ward, "After Hours," *Red and
Black*, September 30, 1988; and "Mudd Puppies in the Studio," *Flagpole*, January 25, 1989,
11. On February 2, 1990, the Mudd Puppies played a gig under the alias "Boot Lip" at
the Downstairs with the gospel-loving and -parodying group the New Iberian Gospel

Contingency that featured Vic Chesnutt, Kim Stacey, Deonna Mann, and other members. This group could be accused of similar blackface moves for performing a musical style created by African Americans.

74. "Chickasaw Mudd Puppies on their way to Austin," *Flagpole*, February 8, 1989, 2–3; and Holly [no last name given], "Mud, Blood, and Money," *Flagpole*, November 1, 1989, 24–25; and Ben Reynolds interviews. Polygram even released a promo single plus live bonus tracks in a burlap sack with the band name stenciled in black on the front.

75. Ben Reynolds interviews; Polygram promotional video for *8 Track Stomp*, online at https://www.youtube.com/watch?v=6az_4UngKfA; Gray, *It Crawled from the South*, 199–201; and m. m. bumble, "We Came, We Saw, Etc.," *Flagpole*, March 21, 1990, 19. *8 Track Stomp* featured a photograph of a drawing by folk artist R. A. Miller sitting on a worn quilt on the front and a photograph of raggedy and handsome Ben and Brant on the back.

76. Popson, "Those Old-time, Postmodern Chickasaw Mudd Puppies." On white guys performing the blues during the folk music revival, see Grace Elizabeth Hale, *A Nation of Outsiders* (New York: Oxford University Press, 2011), 84–131. On blackface minstrelsy, see Eric Lott, *Love and Theft: Blackface Minstrelsy and the American Working Class* (New York: Oxford University Press, 1993); and Lott, *Black Mirror: The Cultural Contradictions of American Racism* (Cambridge: Belknap Press, 2017).

77. Schoemer, "Delta Blues and Girl Groups." In a review of a Chickasaw Mudd Puppies performance in the Atlanta paper *Creative Loafing* on December 23, 1989, music critic and record label owner David T. Lindsay accused the band of copying the Atlanta trio the Chowder Shouters. There is no evidence that anybody in the Chickasaw Mudd Puppies ever saw this Atlanta group perform or heard their record *No Tongue Can Tell How Bad I Feel*, which Atlanta independent Landslide Records released in 1987. Instead, both groups offered raw and intense interpretations of the same kinds of materials.

78. For footage of Mr. Crowe's Garden in 1987, see https://www.youtube.com/watch?v=Rv2Wath1OFM. At the margins as well as within the more commercial currents of the scene where the Indigo Girls, Michelle Malone, and Mr. Crowe's Garden (the original name of the Black Crowes) played, Atlanta bands had finally escaped from the age-old rivalry that turned Athens crowds against them.

79. "Negroes and Whites: Athens Police Arrest Five After Protests, *Valdosta Daily Times*, August 5, 1963; "Athens Begins Racial Study," *Macon Telegraph*, August 16, 1963, "Athens Arrests 25 Protestors," *Atlanta Journal*, March 19, 1964; and "Athens Restaurants Drop Racial Bars," *Atlanta Journal*, July 8, 1964; clippings found in the old vertical file folder marked "Athens: Race Relations" in the Georgia Room of the Hargrett Rare Book and Manuscript Library, UGA, Athens.

80. By 1970, the *Athens Banner Herald* (the afternoon daily) and *Athens Daily News* (the morning daily) had the same ownership and an overlapping staff and published one merged paper on Sundays. They provided extensive coverage of the protests in the spring of 1970, including "Youngsters March: Won't Condone Disorder — Mayor," *Athens Banner Herald*, April 30, 1970; Sharon Bailey, "Sources of Unrest: Desegregation: Disorder, Dispute," *Athens Banner Herald/ The Daily News*, May 10, 1970; Hank Johnson, "200 March Downtown; No Disorder," *Athens Banner Herald*, May 11, 1970; "On Standby; Mayor Orders 200 Guardsman; City Takes Legal Steps For Curfew," and "Firebombs Found: Police Arrest 75; Five Fires Reported," *Athens Banner Herald*, May 13, 1970; "Quiet Night Saturday; 263 Protestors Freed from Jail," *Athens Banner Herald/ The Daily News*,

May 17, 1970; and the series of interviews published under "Black Athens: Triumph and Tragedy," *Athens Banner Herald/ The Daily News*, May 31, 1970. In May and June of 1975, the *Athens Banner Herald* published a series of articles revisiting the events of 1970, kicked off by Hank Johnson, "Five Years Later: Have We Made Progress?" *Athens Banner Herald/ The Daily News*, May 25, 1975. See also Terry Adamson, "Blacks, Whites to March Tonight in Athens," *Atlanta Constitution*, May 15, 1970; Ron Taylor, "Athens Beginning to Look Like Racial Testing Ground," *Atlanta Constitution*, May 17, 1970; and Lee Shearer, "Economics Keys Black Activism: Social Gains of Last Decade Undercut by Loss of Buying Power," *Athens Observer*, June 12, 1980, quote. All of these clippings are in the vertical file folder marked "Athens: Race Relations" in the Georgia Room of the Hargrett Rare Book and Manuscript Library, UGA, Athens.

81. Ed Tant interview; Ed Tant writings and photographs, including information about the history of the Athens Human Rights Festival and information about past festivals, at http://edtant.com/Collected_Writings_and_photos_by_Ed_Tant/Collected_Writing _and_Photos_by_Ed_Tant.html. I knew Chris DeBarr and Deb Bernstein during the period they worked with the festival.

82. H. M. Gelfand, "Phinizy Spalding (1930–1994)," *New Georgia Encyclopedia*, August 15, 2013, https://www.georgiaencyclopedia.org/articles/history-archaeology/phinizy -spalding-1930-1994. Sven Haarhoff, "Residents Attend Rally for 'Freeze,'" *Athens Daily News*, March 10, 1983; Valerie Ready, "Community Debates 'Freeze,'" *Athens Banner Herald/Daily News*, March 6, 1983; and Phil Sanderlin, "A Compromise on the Freeze," *Athens Observer*, March 3, 1983.

83. McNair, "How We Met: Michael Stipe and Natalie Merchant"; and Gray, *It Crawled from the South*, 71, 385–430.

84. Rockfish advertisement, *Flagpole*, March 2, 1988, 21; Cara May, "Local bands Will Showcase First Athens Music Festival September 25," *Red and Black*, July 28, 1988, 1; Nicole Guston, "Athens Musicians to Play Fundraiser," *Red and Black*, September 20, 1988, 6A; full-page advertisement for the Athens Music Festival, *Flagpole*, September 21, 1988, 3; Cara May, "Organizer Michael Collins Declares Athens Music Festival a Great Success," *Red and Black*, September 27, 1988, 7; and Cara May, "Music Festival Helps Charities," *Red and Black*, November 30, 1988, 3.

85. On the B-52's Athens show on October 14, 1989, see "Soundtrack," *Red and Black*, October 5, 1989, 3; and Douglas Wood, "The Original 'Rock Lobsters' Wig Out," *Red and Black*, October 16, 1989, 11–12. On our birthday bash, see "The Downstairs Turns 2," *Flagpole*, October 11, 1989, 2.

86. Bertis Downs interview; and Fran Taliaferro Thomas, *Historic Athens and Clarke County*, 2nd ed. (Athens: University of Georgia Press, 2009), 247–49, 252–54. I am grateful to Fran Thomas, an often-overlooked heroine of preservation activism in Athens, for teaching me most of what I know about historic preservation in the town, both during these fights in the eighties and nineties as well as in writing this book.

87. Jim McKay, "Not an Olympic Commentary," *Flagpole*, March 2, 1988, 19–20.

88. Jared Bailey interview; Erik D. Immanuel, "Media Assassin," *Flagpole*, June 7, 1989, 20–21; and Jared Bailey, "Mr. Pole's Ramblings," *Flagpole*, April 12, 1989, 3.

89. Thomas, *Historic Athens and Clarke County*, 247–49, 252–54.

90. Kathy Kirbo interview; Jared Bailey interview; and Gwen O'Looney interview, parts 1 and 2, Athens Oral History Project, Russell Library, UGA; "Who to Vote for: Part 4," *Flagpole*, October 31, 2018, 6–31.

91. Gwen O'Looney interview; and Monty Greene, "Letter #1," *Flagpole*, November 14, 1990, 4.

CONCLUSION

1. Mark Cooper Smith interview; Mark Cooper Smith, "Take the Stage: Access and Participation in a Music Counter-Culture" (master's thesis, University of Georgia, 1989), 45; and J. M. Davidson, *Concert and Chaos: A Documentary of the Athens Music Scene: Volume 1* (self-published, no date but sometime in 1989). Smith counted "roughly 90" bands in March 1989. In the winter of 1988–89, Jimmy Davidson documented only 35 bands and admits he did not get all the bands at that time. One hundred is a good but conservative estimate for 1991.

2. David Barbe interviews.

3. David Barbe interviews.

4. Bertis Downs interview. Commissioner John Barrow, a preservationist, had been given the chance to prove that a design incorporating the old fire hall and the historic warehouse that housed the Athens Flea Market could be built without reducing the functionality or increasing the construction costs. While scene participants wanted to hear what Barrow had to say, we were mostly there to show the other government officials that a lot of voters wanted to keep the old buildings. I remember seeing Bertis's wife Katherine Downs come into the meeting and speak to her husband who then leaned over and whispered something to Michael Stipe. Over twenty-five years later, I learned from Bertis what they were talking about. At their house on Cobb Street, Katherine had answered the phone, learned the news, and driven downtown to tell the guys. Jeff Giles, "Number One with an Attitude," *Rolling Stone*, June 27, 1991, reprinted in Anthony DeCurtis, ed., *The Rolling Stone Files* (New York: Hyperion, 1995), 129–39, gives a slightly different version of the story Downs told me.

5. "Longbox," episode 124 of *99% Invisible*, online at https://99percentinvisible.org/episode/longbox/; and Robert Christgau, "Strummers for Life," *Village Voice*, March 26, 1991, online at https://www.robertchristgau.com/xg/rock/rem-91.php. The PSA is online at https://www.youtube.com/watch?v=5vrXUIeuZTQ.

6. Parke Puterbaugh, *Out of Time* album review, *Rolling Stone*, March 21, 1991, 124–26; Anthony DeCurtis, "Performance Review: Shocking, Milan, Italy, March 22, 1991," *Rolling Stone*, May 16, 1991, 127–28; and Giles, "Number One with an Attitude," 129–39; all reprinted in DeCurtis, *Rolling Stone Files*.

7. R.E.M., *Out of Time*, Warner Brothers, 1991; and Vic Chesnutt, *Little*, Texas Hotel Records, 1991.

8. David Browne, "Seattle Rock: Out of the Woods and Into the Wild," *New York Times*, November 18, 1990, 31; Mark Kemp, "Michael Stipe: What Are Friends For," *Option*, September 1990, https://www.rocksbackpages.com/Library/Article/michael-stipe-what-are-friends-for; and David Fricke, "Artist of the Year: R.E.M.'s Michael Stipe on the Band's First Decade," *Rolling Stone*, March 5, 1992, online at https://www.rollingstone.com/music/music-news/artist-of-the-year-r-e-m-s-michael-stipe-on-the-bands-first-decade-83283/.

9. Marcus Gray, *It Crawled from the South: An R.E.M. Companion* (New York: Da Capo, 1997), 194–215.

10. Kemp, "Michael Stipe: What Are Friends For"; Fricke, "Artist of the Year"; Vic

Chesnutt, *West of Rome*, Texas Hotel Records, 1992; Craig S. Phillips, "Athens: A Music Mecca," *Red and Black*, November 8, 1999, 1, 3; Philips, "Athens Music Comes of Age," *Red and Black* (November 9, 1999), 1, 3; and Philips, "1980s Usher in a New Wave of Music Popularity," *Red and Black*, November 10, 1999, 1, 6, a multi-part series on the history of Athens music clubs.

11. Robbie Ethridge interview.

12. Robbie Ethridge interview.

13. Robbie Ethridge interview; and Watt King interview.

14. Robbie Ethridge interview; and Mark Cooper Smith interview. Special thanks to David Varricchio, who I met when I gave a talk at Montana State University, for this information and for copies of the cover and sleeve of a cassette featuring four songs by 28 Days that was released locally in 1988.

15. Robbie Ethridge interview; Mark Cooper Smith interview; and copy of 28 Days guest list at the Downstairs, from an original owned by Sam Seawright, author's possession.

16. Robbie Ethridge interview.

17. The "Gaffney Peach" is a peach-shaped water tower in South Carolina beside I-85.

18. Rodger Brown interview.

19. Rodger Brown interview.

20. Rodger Brown interview; Rodger Brown, *Party Out of Bounds: The B-52's, R.E.M., and the Kids Who Rocked Athens, Georgia* (New York: Plume, 1991); Steve Dollar, "Brown goes 'Out of Bounds' with look at Athens rock scene," *Atlanta Journal*, August 18, 1991, UGA library clipping, no page number; and Helen A. S. Popkin, "When Athens Was Sincere," *St. Petersburg Times*, September 1, 1991, 7D.

21. Bob Townsend, "Vic Chesnutt: The Life You Save May Be Your Own," *No Depression*, February 28, 2005, 84, 86; and Chesnutt, *West of Rome*.

22. Chesnutt, *West of Rome*.

23. Townsend, "Life You Save."

24. Vic Chesnutt thanks the Albany Mission in the liner notes for *West of Rome*. Curtiss Pernice told me this story at his house in Athens, Georgia, on June 11, 2018, after the two of us interviewed Don Chambers for the Athens Music Project. Vic shared it with Curtiss, who knew the singer songwriter well and frequently toured with him, playing guitar in his backing band along with his former Porn Orchard bandmate Sam Mixon. Curtiss also played guitar and sang backing vocals on some tracks on two of Vic's albums, *Merriment* (Backburner Records, 2000) and *Dark Developments* (Orange Twin Records, 2008). When Curtiss and Sam and various drummers backed Vic, they were often called the Amorphous Strums.

25. For information about Vic's struggles with depression, I have relied on multiple interviews as well as more informal conversations with people who knew him well and/or toured with him, including Curtiss Pernice, Robbie Ethridge, Deonna Mann, David Barbe, Rob Veal, and Arthur Johnson, as well as my own memories. I have also used Chesnutt's statements over the years in multiple articles and interviews cited in chapter 6. People's memories differ, and I have tried to reconcile differences. Tina Whatley Chesnutt declined to be interviewed.

26. Dudley Clendinen, "Thousands in Civil Rights March Jeered by Crowd in Georgia Town," *New York Times*, January 25, 1987, 1, 21.

Index

Page numbers in italics refer to illustrations.

Atlanta Punk Festival, 34, 42
Atlanta Rising (market and tearoom), 26
At the Cut (Chesnutt), 290
"Attractive Figure" (Kilkenny Cats), 153–54
"Auctioneer" (R.E.M.), 196
Austin, Texas, 5, 27
Automatic for the People (R.E.M.), 282
Ayers, Jerry (Jeremy; Silva Thin), 24, 25,
    28, 33, 64, 85, 180, 186, 203, 268, 290;
    charisma of, 15, 208, 226; documentary
    film project and, 207, 208, 210, 212, 213;
    extravagant dress of, 20–21, 75, 108,
    109–10; finances of, 114; at the Grit, 224,
    225–28, 229; Limbo District cofounded
    by, 121, 207; as mentor, 118, 151, 280; in
    New York underground, 16–19, 20, 23,
    26, 121, 189; sexuality of, 19, 20–21, 70, 75,
    96, 153, 292; as songwriter and lyricist, 38,
    194, 207, 266
Ayers, Robert, 15
Azerrad, Michael, 11, 122, 145–46, 192
Aztec Camera (band), 137

Babb, Beverly, 241, 241, 244, 261
Back Door Band, 95
Bad Brains, 204
Bad Energy Ranch, 240, 241
Baez, Joan, 185
Bailey, Jared "Mr. Pole," 235–36, 259, 275–76
"Bakersfield" (La Di Das), 243
Bambaataa, Afrika, 77
Bangs, Lester, 35, 51, 95, 98, 198–99, 275
Banned 37 (band), 144, 149, 203
Barbe, David, 154, 155, 209, 215, 220, 240–41,
    242, 243, 263, 279–80; Bar-B-Q Killers
    viewed by, 141, 156; Laura Carter viewed
    by, 148; record label formed by, 188, 214;
    R.E.M. viewed by, 151
Bar-B-Q Killers (Emotional Female), 72,
    149, 176, 181, 203, 205, 214, 215, 216, 219,
    234, 252, 257, 261, 263; amateurism of, 142,
    147, 154; in documentary film, 209, 213;
    formation of, 141–42; musical style of,
    143, 151, 155–56, 191
Barnes, Doc, 185, 186, 207
Barnes, Lucy, 207
Barrow, John, 351n4

Batman theme (Pylon), 58, 75, 86, 148
Baumgartner, Sunny, 61
Beach Blanket Bingo (film), 36
Beard, Danny, 94, 97, 174; B-52's and, 33, 34,
    38, 75, 76; DB Records headed by, 37, 38,
    75, 76, 118, 121, 166; Pylon and, 76, R.E.M.
    criticized by, 100
Beasley, Darin, 254, 258
Beat Atlanta (periodical), 169
Beatles, 22, 31, 68, 112
"Beep" (Pylon), 131
Beggar Weeds (band), 261
Bennett, Keith, 34, 64, 67, 69, 71, 111
Berman, Leslie, 121
Bernstein, Deb, 255
Berry, Bill, 4, 53, 95, 108, 113, 115–16, 153,
    164, 262; as Love Tractor member, 117;
    in music business, 102, 103; political
    activism and, 273, 286; as producer, 282;
    as R.E.M. member, 89, 90, 93, 96, 99, 100,
    101, 104, 109, 113, 117, 118, 123–31, 133, 189,
    192–93, 197, 210; southern background
    of, 135, 191, 200; touring renounced by,
    280–81; as UGA student, 96, 111
Beuys, Joseph, 178
Bewley, Randy, 80, 113, 181; as art student,
    48, 50, 67; as Pylon member, 16, 51, 52,
    54–59, 74, 77, 79, 81–82, 86, 117
B-52's, 3, 8, 22, 29, 75, 87, 98, 101, 115, 131,
    136, 138, 173, 261, 269, 274; anti-gay
    sentiment and, 103; art-school links
    of, 57, 64, 71; Athens links maintained
    by, 90; in Atlanta, 39–40, 42, 48, 94;
    at Atlanta Punk Festival, 34; Bar-B-Q
    Killers influenced by, 156; black music
    influence on, 198; debut of, 28–30; in
    documentary film, 209; formation of, 10,
    15; in New York and environs, 16, 33–38,
    45, 50, 79, 121; record contract sought by,
    41–42; R.E.M. contrasted with, 99–100;
    slumping popularity of, 85; stylistic
    evolution of, 46; on UGA campus, 42,
    43, 51
—recordings: "Cosmic Thing," 236; "Dance
    This Mess Around," 39, 40; "Deadbeat
    Club," 236–37; "Devil in My Car," 37,
    39; "Downtown," 36, 39; "52 Girls," 15,

37, 38, 39, 118; "Hero Worship," 37, 39;
"Killer B's," 27, 30; "Love Shack," 236–
37; *Mesopotamia*, 85; "Planet Claire,"
36; "Rock Lobster," 30, 37–38, 39, 59;
"Runnin' Around," 39; *Whammy!*, 85;
Wild Planet, 39, 85
Big Star (band), 196
Big Time (record label), 159
Bilheimer, Chris, 254
Billboard, 236, 281
Billy James (band), 186, 209, 252
Bingo Hand Job (alias of R.E.M.), 268
Black, Daryl, 254
Black Crowes (Mr. Crowe's Garden; band),
269
Black Flag, 106, 146, 191, 262
Black Mountain College, 49
Black Narcissus (band), 23, 27
black power movement, 205
Blakey, Lynn, 167, 168–69, 180
Blasters (band), 191
Bleecker Bob's (record shop), 38
Bloch, Ernst, 13
Blondie, 30, 45, 57, 68
Bloods (band), 122
Bluebird Café, 105, 115, 160, 208, 266
Blue Oyster Cult, 32
Blue Plate (magazine), 235
Boat Of (band), 112, 117, 160
Boberg, Jay, 134, 325n90
"Body Count" (R.E.M.), 180
Bogan, Neil, 176, 177
bohemianism, 3, 5, 13, 61, 99, 106, 131, 142–
44, 151, 153, 157, 158, 167, 177, 180, 286;
Ayers as exemplar of, 16, 118, 186, 187, 280;
bourgeois sexuality vs., 9, 71, 103, 292;
Chesnutt as exemplar of, 239, 246–48;
clothing and, 109; club culture and, 110;
commercialism and professionalism vs.,
10, 87, 114, 115, 130–31, 201, 224, 239, 293;
exclusivity of, 11, 175; gentrification
and, 291; hierarchies within, 150; living
arrangements and, 112, 113, 290, 291;
origins of, 12, 91–92, 283; ossification of,
294; politics and, 188, 192–93, 235, 272,
273, 275, 292; punks and, 36, 46; race
and, 103, 202, 292; R.E.M. and, 93, 100,

104, 105, 116, 124, 130, 162, 189, 249; self-
transformation linked to, 168; urban
orientation of, 17, 31, 36, 80, 92, 111, 249;
vernacular culture and, 145–46, 183, 185,
210, 214, 230, 266; women and, 115, 116
Boles, Ann, 113, 115
Boling, Terry, 221, 224
Bongos (band), 196
Booker T. and the M.G.'s, 28
Bourne, Sean, 32–33, 55, 57–58, 60–61, 97,
136, 137
Bowie, David, 20, 24, 50, 199
Bow Wow Wow, 102, 140
Boxtops, 196
Boyd, Joe, 195
Brains (band), 97–98
Bread for the World, 236
Brienes, Wini, 205
Briscoe Hay, Vanessa (Ellison), 89, *116*, 152,
156, 203, 239, 280, 286; as art student,
47–48, 67–68; in documentary film, 212,
213; as Pylon member, 51, 52, 53, 55–59,
73–77, 79–83, 85, 86, 117, 120, 129, 164
Brite, Poppy Z., 258
Brooklyn, N.Y., 5
"Brother" (Oh-OK), 133, 164
Brown, James, 28, 37, 77, 112
Brown, Rodger Lyle, 22, 166, 169, 285–86
Brown v. Board of Education (1954), 270
Bruce, Lenny, 199
Bruce, W. Guy, 184, 268
Buck, Barrie Greene, 228, 262, 282
Buck, Ken, 317n2, 318n11
Buck, Peter, 4, 8, 34, 95, 113, 150, 153, 166–
67, 180, 181, 189, 234, 235, 276, 282, 290;
commercialism decried by, 146, 147;
country-music influence on, 191; in
documentary film, 210, 211; political
activism and, 137, 273; as R.E.M. member,
88–89, 90, 93–94, 96, 98, 99, 101, 102, 103,
109, *113*, 118, 122–31, 133, 134, 192–94, 197,
198, 262; R.E.M.'s reputation recalled by,
117; southern stereotypes viewed by, 135;
touring renounced by, 280–81; whiteness
of, 205–6
Bugden, Kelly, 29
Bullock, George, 277

Man Student (Keim), 179–80
Mantione, Mike, 234, 347n58
Mapplethorpe, Robert, 20
"Maps and Legends" (R.E.M.), 194
Marcus, Greil, 98, 127
Marcus, Larry, 113, 133, 160–61, 283
"Mark E. Smith" (Bar-B-Q Killers), 214
Marler, Barry, 143, 174, 180
Marriott, Bill, 72
Martin, Doc. 22
Mason, Frank, 205
Matthews, Dan, 170, 260
Maximum Rocknroll (magazine), 265
Max's Kansas City (nightclub), 20, 30–34, 35–36, 39, 45
Maxwell's (nightclub), 124, 159, 161
Mbrella (record label), 161
McArthur, Neil, 55, 57, 111, 113, 117
McBride, Todd, 237–38, 239, 340–41n72
McCarthy, Erica, 218, 220
McCarthyism, 191
McCommons, Pete, 170
"McIntosh" (Chickasaw Mudd Puppies), 268
McKay, Jim, 262, 266–68, 275
McLaughlin, Maureen, 16, 32, 33, 35, 44
McMahon, Debbie, 25, 49, 111
McManus, Alex, *287*
McNair, David, 164, *165*, 180
McWillie, Judy, 49, 67, 68, 70, 71, 188
Meaders, Lanier, 183, 187
Meat Puppets, 192
Meister, Michael, 266
Mekis, Brivs, 195
Mekons (band), 50, 192
Melody Maker, 37, 50, 82–83
Memorial Hall (UGA student center), 22, 42, 43, 51, 56, 84, 177
Men in Trees (band), 89, 123
Mercer Arts Center, 189
Merchant, Natalie, 273
Mercyland (band), 141, 149, 188, *215*, 216, 234, 242, 252, 261, 263, 274, 279; debut of, 209; grassroots fan base of, 3; musical style of, 151, 214, 241
Meridian (theater troupe), 177

Mesopotamia (B-52's), 85
"Mess Around" (Charles), 41
Method Actors (band), 8, 23, 74, 98, 104, 112, 121, 132, 157, 174; breakup of, 131; cross dressing and, 109; debut of, 75, 96; formation of, 90; in *New York Rocker*, 80; record contract of, 100, 118, 126; R.E.M. contrasted with, 99–100
Michel, Leslie, 113, 121, 152
Middle Earth (head shop), 26
Miller, R. A., 183, 186, 349n74
"Miller's Tale, The" (Chaucer), 70
Mills, Kelly, 39
Mills, Mary Beth, 235
Mills, Mike, 4, 95, 113, 153, 202–4, 211; political activism and, 273, 276; as producer, 282; as R.E.M. member, 89, 90, 93, 96, 99, 100, 101, 104, 109, *113*, 117, 118, 123–31, 133, 189, 190, 193, 197, 210, 262; southern background of, 135, 191; touring renounced by, 280–81; as UGA student, 96; whiteness of, 205–6
Minor Threat (band), 191
Minutemen (band), 106, 147
Misanthropic (Cordy Lon), 251
Mr. Crowe's Garden (band; Black Crowes), 269
"Mr. Riley" (Chesnutt), 242–43
Mrs. Atkins (band), 284
Mitchell, Joni, 22
Mixon, Sam, 263, 264, 352n24
Moe's (nightclub), 95
Molina, Juan, 7, 157, 161, 205
Moline, Karen, 286
Mondale, Walter, 192
Mondi, Annelies, 71, 336n23
"Money Changes Everything" (Brains), 97
Monkees, 112
Morehouse College, 201
Morris, Errol, 206
Motor Voter Act (1993), 281
Mould, Bob, 242, 287, 288–89
"M-Train" (Pylon), 77, 84, 86, 119, 131
MTV, 157–58, 159, 213, 234, 281
Mudd Club, 42, 122, 204
Munkacsi, Kurt, 124

124; Oh-OK and, 121; R.E.M. contrasted with, 99–100, 104

—recordings: "Altitude," 131; *Batman* theme, 58, 75, 86, 148; "Beep," 131; *Chomp*, 84; "Cool," 76–77, 131; "Crazy," 77, 84, 119, 120, 131; "Danger," 53, 74, 81; "Dub," 76–77, 131; *Gyrate*, 58–59, 82, 83, 125; "The Human Body," 76; "M-Train," 77, 84, 86, 119, 131; "Piece of My Heart," 76; "Working Is No Problem," 86

Pylon Reenactment Society, 280

Radar Records, 42

"Radio Free Europe" (R.E.M.), 117, 119, 122, 126, 190

Ramone, Joey, 199

Ramones, 30, 40, 50, 68, 95, 198–99; influence of, 28, 31, 44, 56, 57, 61, 98

Randolph, Teresa, 16, 30, 32, 33

Rank and File (band), 192

rap, 5, 77–78, 168, 170, 202, 279

Rasmussen, Chris, 50, 55, 99

Rat (nightclub), 74

Rat and Duck Playhouse, 177, 212, 221, 284

Ratcliff, Charles, 222

Ray Ugly (band), 261

RCA Corporation, 124–25, 151, 159

Reagan, Ronald, 41, 83, 107, 188, 192, 270, 271, 273, 275

Reckoning (R.E.M.), 186, 189, 190, 192, 193, 198

Record (periodical), 146

Red and Black (student newspaper), 91, 170, 258, 269; Bar-B-Q Killers coverage by, 142; B-52's coverage by, 34–35, 51; DRG compilation reviewed by, 214; Fashionbattery coverage by, 151; Is/Ought Gap coverage by, 153; local bands disparaged by, 172–73, 175; Oh-OK coverage by, 131, 166, 180, R.E.M. coverage by, 97–98, 104, 134, 220; Squalls coverage by, 160, 161; *Tasty World* vs., 172–74

Redcoat Band, 152

Reece, Chuck, 104–5, 123, 134, 173, 184–85

Reece, Greg, 340–41n72

Reed, Lou, 20, 35, 98, 199

Reed, Ralph, 271

Reflection Sound Studios, 130, 166

R.E.M., 1, 3, 4, 8, 34, 88, 90, 113, 140, 143, 165, 173, 182, 184, 203, 239, 268; amateurism vs. professionalism reconfigured by, 93, 174; bohemians and, 93, 100, 104, 105, 116, 124, 130, 162, 189, 249; "college rock" exemplified by, 144–45; covers performed by, 96–97, 105, 209; debut of, 78, 276; divided opinions of, 99–101, 116–17, 122–24, 133–34; documentary film project and, 208–9, 210–11; female fan base of, 115; folk and country-music influence on, 186, 189–97; formation of, 89, 96–97; free concerts by, 106; gender ambiguity of, 109, 129; growing popularity of, 10, 53, 84, 116, 117, 127, 157, 159, 260, 280–83; indie rock exemplified by, 146–47; mimicry of, 154; musical style of, 98–99, 128–29, 134–38, 282; political engagement of, 236, 273, 275; as producers, 262; record contract sought by, 118–19, 124–26; at the Ritz (New York), 121–22, 134; *Rolling Stone* coverage of, 53, 117, 126, 136, 234; southern stereotypes linked to, 198–99, 202; studio homogenization of, 130; touring strategy of, 102, 104, 280–81; Warner Brothers contract with, 236, 249

—recordings: "All I Have to Do Is Dream," 209, 211; "Auctioneer," 196; *Automatic for the People*, 282; "Body Count," 180; "Camera," 133, 198; "Can't Get There from Here," 195, 198; "Carnival of Sorts," 124; "Catapult," 124, 130, 134; *Chronic Town*, 117, 126–28, 131, 134–35, 147, 150, 151; *Country Feedback*, 282; "A Different Girl," 89; *Document*, 228, 236, 249, 265; "Does Your Mother Know," 105; "Don't Go Back to Rockville," 190, 193; "Dream," 212; "Driver 8," 193–94, 196; *Fables of the Reconstruction/Reconstruction of the Fables*, 16, 193, 195, 196–97; "Feeling Gravity's Pull," 195, 196; "Femme Fatale," 193; *Green*, 236, 249, 262, 282; *Half a*

Seawright, Sam, 34, 69, 113, 159, 224, 225, 266; as art student and artist, 55, 67, 226, 227, 284; Athens viewed by, 61; Chesnutt recalled by, 243–44; Lachowski viewed by, 57

"Second Guessing" (R.E.M.), 109

Seeger, Mike, 185

Segel, Jonathan, 147

segregation, 185, 198, 200, 202, 204, 242, 270

Selby, Melissa, 284

Self, Will, 117

Severe Driving Problems (band), 260

sexism, 115

Sex Pistols, 34, 47, 92, 94, 98, 152

Shadowfax (band), 95

"Shaking Through" (R.E.M.), 124

Shangri-Las, 36

Shank, Barry, 11

Shepard, Sam, 177

Sherman, Hoyt, 65, 67

"Shiny, Happy People" (R.E.M.), 282

Shipp, Edna Lori, 74, 75

Shipp, Jean, 177

Shirley, Chip. 167–68, 181

Shiva Gondi (band), 229

Side Effects (band), 89, 96, 113, 120, 121, 123, 126, 132, 283; breakup of, 131; debut of, 78; female fan base of, 115; in New York Rocker, 84; record contract of, 118

Silva Thin. See Ayers, Jerry

Singerman, Bob, 159

Siouxsie and the Banshees, 102

Sire Records, 40, 43

"Sitting Still" (R.E.M.), 117, 119, 126

688 (nightclub), 85, 101, 102, 131, 143, 177, 201

Skelton, Todd, 220

Skin Pops (band), 261

Slash Records, 146, 153

Slater, Andrew, 125

Slay, Brant, 16, 222, 266–69

Slay, Chris, 108, 177, 187, 189, 210, 266

Slayton, Jackie, 72

Slotin, Moe, 32

Smith, Calvin Orlando, 205

Smith, Chris "Crow," 209–10

Smith, Mark Cooper, 156, 160, 161, 162, 214, 284

Smith, Patti, 20, 30, 32, 35, 82, 94, 177; influence of, 28, 31, 98, 99, 176

Smith, Richard, 303n3

Smith, Stevie, 239, 247

Smith, Tom, 112

Smithereens (film), 133

sofa club, 110

"Soft Picasso" (Chesnutt), 232, 244, 247

Some (compilation recording), 216, 218

Some: The 1986 Better Than TV Tour (documentary film), 218–20

Songbird Studios, 152

Sonstock festival, 153

Sorry Ma, Forgot to Take Out the Trash (Replacements), 175

Sound Castles (Buzz of Delight), 166, 172

Sound of the City (radio program), 106, 262

South by Southwest Music Festival, 268

"South Central Rain" (R.E.M.), 196

Southern Christian Leadership Conference, 270

southern rock, 134–36

Spalding, Margie, 272–73

Spalding, Phinizy, 272–73

Speed, Sally, 69, 70–71

"Speed Racer" (Chesnutt), 244, 246

Spelman College, 201

Spencer, Jean, 284

Sperrassa, Gary, 122

Sphinx, Terry, 240

Spin (magazine), 173, 202, 273

"Spin Your Partner" (Love Tractor), 157

"Sponge" (Chesnutt), 288

Squalls (band), 139, 156, 159–62, 163, 203, 205, 272; debut of, 143, 160; grassroots fan base of, 3; older membership of, 157; recordings by, 161, 174, 188, 209

SST (record label), 145, 146

Stacy, Jim, 255, 256, 258, 260

Stacey, Kim, 348–49n73

Stafford, Sally, 29

Stamey, Chris, 135, 196, 210

"Stand" (R.E.M.), 236

Stapler, Phyllis, 42

Starratt, Ken, 159, 160, 161, 162, 272

Star Trek, 36

Steele, Rick, 240

mekwerk gears in the depths churned and rolled. Mia saw siege towers made of wood, a battering ram covered with a pavilion of thick hide, a heavy ballista, and two catapults stocked with barrels of burning pitch. Scarlet banners unfurled on the stone keep's walls, set with the sigil of the old Kingdom of Vaan. Mia looked at the red crown daubed on her shield, the scarlet plumes on the helms around her.

"O, shit," she breathed.

". . . What?" Matteo asked.

"They're reenacting the Siege of Blackbridge," she realized. "The battle between Itreya and Vaan that marked the beginning of King Francisco's empire." Mia tapped the red crown on Matteo's shield, the scarlet plume on his helm. "*We're* the Vaanians."

The boy tilted his head. Mia inwardly sighed.

"The Vaanians *lost*, Matteo."

". . . O, shit."

The mekwerk gears slowly ground to a halt, all the pieces of the battle to come laid out on the field. The editorii's voice rang across the sands.

"Behold! The troops of King Brandr VI, the besieged defenders of Vaan!"

The portcullis shifted, rolled up. Guards shoved Mia and her fellows, prodding them with spears until they emerged blinking into the sunlight. They were met with jeers, the mostly Itreyan crowd roaring with disapproval at the sight of their ancient foes.* The guards marched the competitors across the arena floor, toward the open gates of the small keep. And ushering them inside, they sealed its doors behind them.

The keep stood perhaps twenty feet high, fifty feet square. Taller towers loomed on every corner, crenelated battlements crested the walls. From the inside, Mia saw the structure wasn't stone at all, but a thick plaster facade reinforced with a heavy timber frame. The group milled about in confusion, most unsure what came next.

"Man the walls, for fucksakes!" someone hollered.

"Get up there, you bastards!"

Trumpets rang across the arena as Mia, Matteo and Sidonius scrambled up a wooden ladder and claimed their place on one of the towers. She saw two shortbows made of ashwood, two quivers full of arrows.

"Can either of you shoot?" she asked her fellows.

"I can," Matteo replied.

---

*The Vaanians in the audience kept their mouths on the safe side of shut.

Mia took up one bow and slung a quiver over her shoulders, handed the other to Matteo. She squeezed his hand as he took it, looked him in the eye.

"Don't be afraid," she said. "This is not where we die."

The boy nodded. All around them, an ocean of people were on their feet in the stands. The arena walls stood fifteen feet high, boxes containing the marrowborn and politicians studded around the edges. In one, Mia saw Dona Leona, seated with other sanguila. She was dressed in a golden gown, her long auburn hair coiled around her brow like a victor's laurel. But for all her beauty, the legacy of her name, her property had still wound up playing the roles of the conquered.

Not the politician your father is by half, Mi Domina.

In a great booth on the western edge, Mia saw a man she presumed was the city governor, surrounded by officials, administratii, pretty women in beautiful gowns. The games' editorii stood at the edge of this booth, clad in a blood-red robe, the waist and sleeves trimmed with dozens of small golden daggers. A white capuchin monkey sat on his shoulder. He spoke into a long curling horn, his voice amplified by other horns around the arena's edge.

"Citizens!" he cried. "Behold the noble legions of Itreya!"

A portcullis at the other end of the arena yawned wide, and the guards escorted in another cadre of competitors. They were armed and armored the same as Mia and her fellows, but the plumes on their helms were golden, the three eyes of Aa painted on their shields. The crowd roared in approval at the sight of them, stamping their feet and shaking the floor. Most of the group took up position by the wooden siege towers, others manned the ballista and catapults on the arena's edge.

"The contest ends when only one color remains!" cried the editorii. "To the victors, the right to stand as full-fledged gladiatii upon the sands of the *venatus*! To the defeated, the eternal sleep of death! Let the Winnowing . . . begin!"

Roars from the crowd. Movement from the golden troops, dozens of them bracing against the base of the siege towers and pushing them forward. Mia looked about the red troops manning the walls, searching for a leader and finding none. Turning her eyes back to the approaching towers, she called above the mob.

"Any of you fine gentles serve in the legion?"

"Aye," said a burly man on the tower opposite.

"You wouldn't be experienced in siege warfare by any chance?"

"I was a fucking cook, lass."

Mia looked at the approaching army. Down to the little sword in her hand.

"Well, shit," she sighed.

"Archers, lay down fire on those incoming towers! I need six of you ready at the gate for that battering ram, the rest of you on the walls to repel their troops! Two men to a station, lock your shields and keep your backs to each other, clear?"

Mia raised an eyebrow, looked about to see who was shouting.

It was Sidonius. But not the smart-mouthed, lecherous Sid she'd kicked in the bollocks and punched in the jaw. This man was fierce as a whitedrake, his voice booming, radiating an aura of command that brooked no dissent.

"O, aye?" someone yelled. "And who the fuck are you?"

"Aye," Mia murmured. "Who the fuck *are* you?"

"I'm the bastard who's going to save your miserable lives!" Sid bellowed. "Unless one of you pathetic sheepfuckers have a better plan? Now see to your swords and send these bastards to the 'byss where they belong!"

Mia stared a moment longer, eyebrow raised. But seeing Sid was in no mood to argue, and being counted among the pathetic sheepfuckers with no better plan, she aimed her bow at the incoming towers. Matteo nocked an arrow beside her, speaking from the corner of his mouth as he smirked at Sid.

"Well, *that* was unexpect—"

The ballista bolt hit him like an anvil. Blood spattered Mia's face as Matteo was flung off the tower with a "*whufff*," toppling headfirst into the sand below. The boy hit the ground with a sickening crunch, two feet of steel and wood in his chest, neck twisted the entirely wrong way around.

"'Byss and blood," Mia breathed.

A shattering boom shook the castle as one of the catapults flung a barrel of burning pitch. The projectile shattered on the wall, liquid fire raining down on the men and women inside. The crowd roared approval as the second catapult fired, the barrel smashing into the facade and setting the wooden gate ablaze. Men fell from the battlements covered in flaming oil, screaming as they tried to douse themselves on the sand. Mia and Sidonius ducked low, looking at each other with wide eyes.

"Four fucking Daughters," the big man breathed.

"Suggestions, General?" Mia asked.

"Archers! Have at those towers!"

Mia and a few of her fellows rose up from cover, unleashed a volley into the approaching siege towers. Several of the gold troops fell, the crowd howling as a second volley dropped a handful more. Black smoke billowed from the rising flames, clawing at Mia's eyes and throat as she fired again.

"Battering ram!" she shouted. "Coming hard."

"Brace the doors!" Sidonius roared.

Half a dozen of the Golds rushed forward between the troop towers, the battering ram between them. Mia fired again, but the team were protected by a cover of thick hide. The walls shook as they hit the front gate, shaking further as another barrel of blazing oil hit one of the keep's rear towers to the crowd's delight. The explosion bloomed, bright and fierce, immolating another three Reds on the walls. They fell screaming, a fourth among them tumbling back with a ballista bolt through her chest.

"Those siege weapons are killing us!" Mia shouted.

"Well, we've little to throw at them but harsh language!" Sidonius roared. "The Vaanians lost the siege of Blackbridge, little Crow! These dice are rigged!"

The gate boomed again as the ram struck home. Mia twisted up from cover, firing through the rolling smoke and putting an arrow through the foot of one of the battering team. It was all she could see of them under that blasted hide, but it had the desired effect; the man dropped, howling, and Mia ducked a ballista bolt as she loosed another shot, her arrow striking him clean through the throat.

Another barrel exploded, the crowd now howling drunk with fury. The castle was ablaze, the gate coming off its hinges. The first siege tower struck the battlements, spilling half a dozen men onto the defenses with bloodthirsty cries. Sidonius charged along the wall and put his sword through a man's belly with a roar. Mia rose without a sound, reaching out to one Gold's shadow and fixing him in place, battering aside another man's sword and slamming him off the wall with her shield before burying her blade in the first man's chest. Blood spattered, warm and copperish on her lips. She'd wondered how she might use her gifts without the crowd getting wise, but in all the chaos and smoke and flame, nobody could see a thing of her shadowerking.

The gate shuddered again, the wood splitting. One more good thrust and they'd be home. Another Red sailed off the battlement with a ballista bolt through his belly, another barrel burst on the ground in front of the keep, spraying the walls with burning oil. It was all well and good to stay here and defend the walls—Mia cut down another Gold, slicing his belly wide open and spilling his guts across the deck as he fell screaming—but those catapults would eventually set the whole place ablaze.

Conquer your fear, and you can conquer the world.

She thought back to her lessons in the Hall of Masks with Shahiid Aalea. The assassin inside her rising to the fore. She could swing a sword with the best of them, she knew that true, but the advantage she truly had over the people fighting and dying around her was her training in the Red Church. Her wits. Her guile.

Don't think like a gladiatii. Think like a Blade.

She looked at the faces around her. The face of the man she'd just killed, sealed inside his helm. And tearing the helm off the dead Gold's head, she shoved her hand into his sundered guts, and pulled out a great, steaming handful. Pulling off her own headgear, she slammed on the golden-crested helmet and shouted to Sidonius.

"Don't let them shoot me on the way back!"

Mia smeared blood down her neck and chest, slapped her handful of ruptured intestines against her belly, and taking a deep breath, dropped off the wall. She hit the sand outside the keep with a grunt, wobbled and fell onto her side. Black smoke boiled all around her, timbers breaking and folk roaring as the gate shattered. A boom echoed across the arena as another barrel exploded against the wall, Mia curling up tight to shield herself from the flaming globules of oil.

She rose to her feet, holding her fistful of torn guts against her own stomach. And with her sword dangling from her other hand, she staggered toward the first catapult.

The crowd paid her little mind—from the look of her wound across the arena, she was a dead girl walking. The crew on the catapult paid no heed either; her golden helm marked her as one of their own, but each of them was fighting to save their own skins. And so, nobody ran to help her or stop her as she staggered across the sand, blood and guts drenching her front, dripping at her feet.

She stumbled to sell it better, rising with a gasp. Closer now, the catapult and the three men manning it just a few feet away. She dragged herself up with a groan, limping ever closer. And a few feet from the team, she came to life, slinging her handful of guts into the first Gold's face and plunging her gladius into his chest.

The man fell back with a cry. Before the other two could process what had happened, Mia had gutted one, his insides spraying across the sand as he fell with a bloodcurdling scream. The last fumbled for his blade but Mia smashed it aside, weaving left, right. And with a flash of her blade, she gifted him to the Maw.

"*Hear me, Mother,*" she whispered, snatching up one of the fallen men's swords.

"*Hear me now,*" she breathed, sprinting toward the second catapult.

"*This flesh your feast.*"

One of the team saw her coming out of the smoke

"This blood your wine."

opening his mouth, perhaps to cry warning

"Hold them close."

but her blow severed his throat all the way to the bone, lodging in his spine. She tore it free, chopped another's legs out from under him, hurling her second blade at the last man's chest. The sword punched through flesh and ribs, knocking the man off his feet in a spray of red, and the second catapult fell silent.

The crowd began to notice something amiss. The Golds had broken through to the keep, a bloody brawl now erupting at the gate, upon the walls. But more and more were pointing at the short, pale girl, drenched in red among the now silent machines. She knelt by the bodies of those she'd killed, took off her helm and dipped the gold plume in the blood pooled on the sand, staining it red. And slamming it back on her head, she dashed with swords in hand, right at the ballista crew.

They saw her coming, swiveling the weapon and firing off a bolt at her. But smoke was rolling across the sands from the burning keep, and after all, she was only a little thing, fast and sharp as knives. Mia tumbled aside, rolling back up to her feet as one of the crew charged her down. He was a giant of a man: a Dweymeri with long saltlocks, two feet taller than she. Mia met his blades with her own, taking a glancing blow to her helm, and being so much shorter than him, slipped her blade lower than his shield could reach. His hamstring was sliced through to the bone, Mia grabbing a handful of his saltlocks as he fell to one knee. She twisted him around as the ballista fired at her again, shielding herself behind her foe as the bolt punched through his shield and into the chest beyond.

The crowd roared as she climbed up on the falling man's shoulder and sprang at the two women crewing the machine, twisting the shadows at the first one's feet as she sliced the second's chest open. The woman fell with a scream, her own strike cutting deep into Mia's arm, blood spraying. The girl staggered, crowd and pulse and thunder deafening in her ears as she hurled her second sword at the other woman's head.

With her boots fixed to the floor, the woman could only fall backward to dodge the blow, landing on her backside in the dust. She cursed, eyes wide with fear as she pulled at her boots, still stuck fast in the sand. Mia loomed up over her, one arm hanging limp, drenched head to foot in blood, second sword raised.

"No," the woman breathed. "I have a baby girl, I—"

No mothers.

No daughters.

Only enemies.

Her sword silenced the woman's plea. The crowd around her bellowed. With a pained wince for her wounded arm, she loaded another bolt into the ballista, ratcheted back the drawline to fire another shot. But the battlements behind her were now clear, the only fighting seemed to be going on inside the keep walls.

Mia picked up a sword with a weary sigh. Her right arm was bleeding freely from a deep gash in her bicep, her head swimming. Adjusting her helm on her head and slinging a shield onto her wounded arm, she stalked back across the bloodied, burning sands to face whoever was left alive in there. The crowd were chanting, stamping their feet in time with her tread—though the girl wore the color of the enemy, the fancy of the reenactment had given way to a purer kind of bloodlust, and this small slip of a girl had just murdered almost a dozen people in a handful of minutes.

She stopped twenty feet before the gate in a veil of smoke, the stench of sundered bowel and burning blood. She saw four figures in the haze, marching toward her. Drawing a deep breath, picturing all she stood to lose if she failed, she raised her sword. And squinting through the smoke, she made out the color of their plumes.

Blood red.

Mia dropped her shield, laughing loud as she saw Sidonius, battered and bleeding among the men. Beyond them, Mia could see the bottleneck at the gate had become a slaughterhouse, Golds and Reds lying dead by the dozen. She saw Matteo among them, pretty eyes open wide and seeing nothing at all.

She tried to push the sorrow aside, knowing she had no use for it. This was her world now. Life and death, with just a sword stroke between them. And with every stroke, she stood one step closer to revenge.

No room for anything but enemies.

"Citizens!" cried the editorii. "Governor Valente presents to you, your victors!"

The crowd bellowed in answer, a fanfare of trumpets splitting the air. Smeared head to foot in blood, Mia limped forward, held out her hand to Sidonius. The big man grinned, clasped her forearm, then dragged her into a crushing hug.

"Come here, you magnificent little bitch," he laughed.

"Let me go, you great fucking lump!" she grinned.

Sidonius raised the knuckles into the air, roared at the crowd. "Take that, you bastards! No man can kill me, you hear? NO MAN CAN KILL ME!"

Mia looked to the marrowborn boxes, saw Dona Leona on her feet applauding. Beside her stood Executus, his arms folded, glowering as always. But ever so slightly, the man inclined his head. The closest thing to praise he'd ever given.

She turned in a circle, taking in the ocean of faces, the blood-drunken cheers, the thundering feet. And for a tiny moment, she ceased being Mia Corvere, the orphaned girl, the darkin assassin, the embodiment of vengeance. She held her arms wide, dripping red onto the sand, and listened to the crowd roar in response. And just for a breath, she forgot what she had been.

Knowing only what she'd become.

Gladiatii.

EPIPHANY

"Did you know?"

The bishop of Godsgrave leapt near three feet out of his chair. His teacup of goldwine slipped from his fingers, spilled across the parchment on his desk. Heart rattling about his chest, Mercurio turned and found his old pupil behind him, swathed in the shadows of his bookshelves.

"'Byss and bl—"

His heart stilled as he saw the gravebone stiletto in his former protégée's hand. A blond girl was standing in the gloom behind her, dressed in dark leathers. She looked vaguely familiar, but damned if Mercurio could place her . . .

A low growl made him turn, and he saw a wolf made of shadows coalescing near his open chamber door. As if in a soft breeze, it slowly creaked shut.

"Did. You. Know?" Mia repeated.

Mercurio turned his eyes back to his former pupil.

"I know lots of things, little Crow," he said calmly. "You'll have to be m—"

She moved in a blur, across the space between them in a blinking. He hissed as she seized his throat, pressed her blade to his jugular.

"Get that bloody pigsticker off my neck," the old man demanded.

"Answer me!"

Mercurio tapped his own blade—which he'd drawn as he dropped his goldwine—against Mia's femoral artery.

"One good twitch and you'll be bled out in moments," he said.

"That makes two of us."

"I gave you that knife," he said, swallowing against the gravebone blade.

"No, Mister Kindly gave it to me."

Mercurio eyed the not-cat now coalescing on Mia's shoulder.

". . . you just gave it back, old man . . ."

"Still. Never thought I'd find it against my own throat, little Crow."

"I never thought you'd give me a reason," the girl said.

"And what would that be?"

"They killed my father, Mercurio," she said, voice trembling. "Or as good as. They handed him over to Scaeva and let him hang!"

"Who did?" the old man scowled, glancing over Mia's shoulder at the blonde.

"The Ministry!" Mia spat. "Drusilla, Cassius, the rest of them. My father and Antonius were captured in the middle of a camp of ten thousand men. Who could do that if not a Blade of Niah?"

"That makes no blo—"

"Did you know?"

The old man looked at his pupil, saw no fear of the blade in his hand. No fear of dying reflected in her eyes. Only rage.

"Six years, I trained you for the Church's trials," he said quietly. "Why in the Black Mother's name would I do that, if I knew the Church helped Scaeva murder your da?"

"Well, why would the Church train me at all if they helped kill him, Mercurio?"

"That's what I mean about this not making sense, Mia. Think on it."

Mia hands trembled on her stiletto, and she stared into his eyes. He could see the Blade in her, the killer they carved from the girl he'd given them. He knew that was what she'd become, sending her there. He knew the mark it would leave. You don't gift someone to the Maw without gifting a piece of yourself, also. But beneath, he could still see her. The waif he'd saved from the Godsgrave streets. The girl he'd sheltered beneath his roof, taught everything he knew. The girl who, even after she failed, he'd still thought of as his kin.

"I'd never hurt you, little Crow. You know that. On my life, I swear it."

She stared a moment longer. The killer she'd become warring with the girl she'd *been. And slowly, ever so slowly, Mia withdrew the knife. Mercurio lifted his blade away from her leg, slipped it back into his armrest, and leaned back in his chair.*

"You want to tell me what all this is about?" *he asked.*

The blond girl produced a book from beneath her cloak, placed it on the desk before him. It was black. Leather. Unadorned.

"The fuck's this?" *he asked.*

"The Red Church ledger," *Blondie replied.*

His eyes grew wide. Suddenly, it made sense. Suddenly . . .

"I recognize you now," *he breathed.* "We met at the Church, when I came to get Mia. You're Torvar's girl. You're Ashlinn fucking Järnheim."

"Well, my middle name's actually Frija, but—"

"We've been hunting you for eight bloody months!" *Mercurio turned to Mia, voice rising.* "Have you taken complete leave of your senses? Thanks to this traitor and her da, most of our Blades are in the fucking ground!"

Ashlinn shrugged. "Live by the sword . . ."

"It was a miracle they never got me!"

"Bullshit," *the girl replied.* "When the Luminatii purged Godsgrave, they never kicked in the door of your little Curio Shop, did they?"

"O, and why's that, pray tell?" *the old man growled.*

Ashlinn looked toward Mia. Back to the red-faced bishop.

"Because I didn't want her hurt."

Silence fell in the room, Mia looking anywhere but into Ashlinn's eyes. After a long, uncomfortable quiet, she turned to the ledger, flipping through the pages until she found a name listed among the many patrons and their payments. A name written in a bold flowing script, stark black against the yellowing parchment.

Julius Scaeva.

"You knew, didn't you?" *Mia asked.* "The Ministry would have to tell bishops who can and can't be touched, if only to avoid breaches of Sanctity."

"Of course I knew," *the old man snapped.* "They told me as soon as they made me bishop. Why the 'byss do you think I haven't sent one of my Blades to cut the bastard's throat? Standing for a fourth term as consul? He's a fucking king in all but name. And I've said so all along, remember?"

Mia tapped the entry with her finger.

"Ten thousand silver priests," *she said.* "Sent to the Church by Scaeva himself, dated three turns after my father's execution. Paid by the man who stood to gain the most from the rebellion's failure. And the name of my father's right-hand man is carved at Niah's feet in the Hall of Eulogies. Explain that to me, Mercurio."

The old man stroked his chin with a scowl.

Looked down at the names and numbers, blurring in the dim light.

It couldn't be . . .

Of course he knew Scaeva was secretly paying the Church. Truth told, it made sense for people who could afford the cost to be stuffing Niah's coffers. That was one of the beauties of Sanctity, you see—gift the Church enough money to be considered a patron, you'd be protected under the Red Promise. The King of Vaan had been doing it for years. Stroke of genius, really. Niah's faithful could get paid without lifting a finger.*

Of course, Scaeva went further than just a retainer—he'd used the Church to rid himself of a dozen thorns in his side. But Mercurio had never suspected the Church had been involved with the end of the Kingmakers. Everything he'd ever heard led him to believe Corvere and Antonius had been betrayed by one of their own men.

Could it be . . . ?

"The Red Church captured my father," Mia said, her voice thick with pain. "Handed him over to the Senate. They as good as murdered him themselves."

Mister Kindly tilted his head, purring soft.

". . . what I do not understand, is why scaeva had remus attack the mountain, if scaeva already has the church in his pocket . . . ?"

". . . AS IF THAT IS THE ONLY THING YOU DO NOT UNDERSTAND . . ."

". . . hush now, child, the adults are talking . . ."

"*Remus attacked the Mountain without Scaeva's consent,*" Ashlinn said.

"Bullshit." Mercurio turned on the Vaanian girl with a scowl. "Remus didn't take a squirt without asking Scaeva's permission first. The Senate, the Luminatii, and Aa's Church are the three pillars of the whole fucking Republic, girl."

"Don't call me girl, you crusty old prick," Ashlinn snapped. "My father was the one in league with Remus, remember? The justicus hated Scaeva's guts. O, aye, he took the consul's orders, but Remus was one of Aa's faithful, just like Duomo. Using the Red Church for his dirty work made Scaeva a heretic in Remus's eyes.

---

* Aye, aye, I can hear your question, gentlefriends. Just as if I were sitting behind you. (No fear, I am not sitting behind you.) But you find yourself wondering, if the Red Church won't murder anyone they're currently employed by, why doesn't everyone simply pay them a retainer and sleep soundly in the nevernight? An excellent question, gentlefriends, with a very simple answer:

It's *fucking* expensive.

A king or consul might afford to keep the Church on permanent retainer. But you must remember, gentlefriends, the Red Church is a cult of assassins, not extortionists. And it'd be quite difficult to maintain a reputation as the most fearsome murderers in the Republic if they spent all their time being paid to *not* murder anyone.

And shutting down the Church would've cut Scaeva's access to his pack of hired murderers."

Mercurio scratched his chin. "I thought Remus and Duomo—"

"Duomo's a patron of the Church too."

"I know that," Mercurio snapped. "I'm not some simpleton fresh in from the rain, I'm a bishop of Our Lady of Blessed fucking Murder."

"Except our illustrious grand cardinal never hires the Church to blessedly fucking murder anyone." Ashlinn flicked through the ledger, showed exorbitant payments from Duomo dating back six years. "He just pays an annual stipend out of Aa's coffers. Protects him under Sanctity, see? That way, he knows Scaeva can't just have his throat cut while he sleeps. The cardinal and the consul hate each other, and both of them would do almost anything to see the other dead."

". . . IT OCCURS TO ME THAT RECORDING THIS IN A LEDGER WAS A FANTASTICALLY FOOLISH IDEA . . ."

"They kept it in a locked vault," Ashlinn said to the shadowwolf. "Inside a den of the most feared killers in the Republic. And the only key was hung around the neck of one of the most accomplished assassins the world has ever known. Considering what I had to go through to get hold of it, perhaps it's not as foolish as you think."

". . . speaking of which, little traitor, why, pray tell, have we not murdered you yet . . . ?"

"My winning personality?" Ashlinn glanced at the not-cat on Mia's shoulder. "Or perhaps it's just because I'm the only one with half a clue what the fuck is going on around here."

"So what is goi . . ." The old man blinked, looked about the room. ". . . Wait, where the 'byss is Jessamine?"

Mia and Ashlinn exchanged a long, uneasy glance. Ash's lip was split and swollen from her brawl on the roof, her eye bruised black.

". . . there was some . . . unpleasantness . . ."

"Fucking wonderful." Mercurio glared at Ashlinn. "And you're responsible for it?"

"If it makes you feel better, Jess stabbed me first." Ashlinn shrugged. "I just stabbed her last. And . . . repeatedly."

"So what are you doing here?" the bishop demanded. "Mia got sent out seven turns ago to kill a braavi and steal a map. She comes back here with the most wanted traitor in Church history. Where do you fit into all of this?"

Ashlinn shrugged. "I have the map."

". . . you had the map. it exploded, remember . . . ?"

The girl smirked. "You don't think I'm stupid enough to let something that valuable go up in flames, do you, Mister Know-it-all?"

"You'd best start talking, then," Mercurio growled.

"Aye," Mia nodded. "Where did you get it? Where does it lead? And who are you working for? The braavi said you were selling the map to Cardinal Duomo."

"He hired me to get it," Ash said, leaning against the wall and folding her arms. "After the attack on the Church went tits up, da and I spent the next eight months dodging Blades sent to kill us. By the time da died, we'd burned most of our coin. Duomo and Remus plotted together to bring the Church down, so I knew how to get in touch with the cardinal. Turns out he was looking for someone with my . . . skill set."

"For what? Back-talking and smart-arsery?" Mercurio spat.

Ashlinn's lips twisted in that maddening smirk. "Locks. Traps. Dark work. He'd learned of another way he might tip the balance and undo the Red Church once and for all. Without them in the way, he'd be free to take down Scaeva, install a pliant new consul, and have the pot for himself."

Mia's eyes narrowed. "What kind of 'other way'?"

Ash shrugged. "He never said. I never asked. My job was to travel with a pack of sellswords and a bishop of Aa's ministry. To a temple ruin on the north coast of Old Ysiir. That's where we found the map. And . . . other things."

"What kind of other things?" Mercurio asked.

Ashlinn's face was stone, but Mia saw a sliver of fear in her eyes.

"The dangerous kind."

"What happened to your comrades?"

The girl shrugged. "They didn't make it."

"So you came back to the 'Grave alone to sell the map to Duomo?" Mia asked.

Ash nodded. "The Toffs act as his middlemen. Duomo has the coin to carry a lot of people in his pocket. I didn't know if he'd try to shiv me in the back, but I presumed the worst. I'm a loose end. One of the only people alive who knew the cardinal was working against Scaeva to take the Church down."

"Well, someone knew Duomo is working with the Toffs," Mercurio said. "And that the map was being delivered to them this eve. And that someone hired Mia to . . ."

Mia met Mercurio's stare. The old man's eyes growing wide.

"You don't think . . . ," he began.

Mia searched the floorboards as if looking for a truth she'd dropped. Dragging her hair behind her ear. The sinking in his stomach reflected on her face.

"My patron for this offering requested me specifically," she breathed. "'She who slew the justicus of the Luminatii Legion.' Or so the Ministry said. And I've offered up three others at the same patron's request."

". . . Who did you kill?"

"A senator's son, Gaius Aurelius. The mistress of another Liisian Senator, Armando Tulli. And a Galante magistrate named Cicerii."

"Black Mother," Mercurio growled.

"What is it?" Ashlinn asked, looking between them.

"Gaius Aurelius was rumored to be planning a run for consul against Scaeva," Mercurio said. "And Cicerii was organizing an inquest into the constitutionality of Scaeva sitting a fourth term."

Mia sank to her haunches, steadied herself against the flagstones. Eclipse coalesced beside her, Mister Kindly licking her hand with his insubstantial tongue.

"O, goddess . . . ," she breathed.

"Scaeva is pulling people into line," Mercurio realized. "Intimidating opponents or killing them. Making sure he's elected again."

"And I've been helping him . . . ," Mia whispered.

". . . bastard . . ."

"Which means he knows Duomo is working against him. He knows whatever this map leads to is a threat to the Church, and he's using the Church to eliminate it."

"Protecting his little cult of assassins." Ashlinn looked at Mia, shaking her head. "What did I tell you? Whores, all. And not content with helping to murder your father, the Church made you slit throats for the bastard responsible for his hanging. Solis. Mouser. Spiderkiller. Aalea. Drusilla. They need a killing, Mia. Every last one of them."

"Scaeva."

Mia spat the word like a mouthful of poison. Lips peeling back from her teeth. She glared at Ashlinn, slowly shaking her head.

"Scaeva and Duomo first."

Ashlinn stepped forward, eyes glinting like steel.

"Duomo is probably at the Basilica Grande right now."

Mia shook her head. "I can't get in there. I tried once before. The trinities . . ."

"I can get him for you," Ashlinn offered. "He might bathe with one about his neck, sleep with one under his damned pillow, there's no trinity that can stop me. I steal inside and cut his throat, then we get Scaeva and the Ch—"

"No," Mia said. "They're mine. The pair of them."

She rose slowly from the floor, black hair draped about a ghost-pale face.

"Those bastards are mine."

"Hold now," Mercurio counseled. "Let's not speak hasty."

"Hasty?" Mia snarled. "The Red Church helped kill my father, Mercurio. Just as Scaeva and Duomo did. The Ministry are as guilty as the other two."

"But why would the Red Church train you if they helped kill your father?"

"Maybe they thought I'd never find out? Maybe Cassius ordered them to train me, knowing I was darkin? Maybe that fucker Scaeva found it amusing? Or maybe they thought once I'd killed enough, grown cold enough, I just wouldn't care anymore?"

The old man steepled his fingers at his chin, staring at the ledger.

"Feed someone to the Maw, you also feed it a part of yourself," he murmured.

"Are you with me?" she asked.

He looked at the ledger. Scaeva's name. The man who'd crafted himself a throne in a Republic that had rid itself of its kings centuries ago. A man who thought himself above law, honor, morality. But truthfully, Mercurio himself had cast most of those aside himself, years ago. All in the name of faith.

"I've devoted my life to the Red Church," the old man said.

Mia stepped forward, her eyes burning.

"Are you with me?"

The bishop of Godsgrave looked at his former pupil. She seemed carved of stone, jaw set, fists clenched in the soft arkemical glow. He searched those dark eyes, looking for something of the girl he'd taken under his wing for six long years. He'd been angry with her after she failed her initiation. After she failed him. But in truth, she'd been his daughter those six years. And she always would be.

The Church had already taken one father from her.

Could he let them take another?

"I'm with you."

The answer hung in the room like a sword above their heads. Mercurio knew what it would mean, and where it would end. How big the foe they were pitting themselves against truly was.

"We have to do this unseen, Mia," Mercurio said. "The Church can't know it's you when you get Scaeva, or they'll retaliate. And you'll have to get Duomo with the same stroke, or else he's going to be ten times as hard to hit."

"That's the least of our problems," Mia replied. "The Church are going to want me back. The Dona is dead. Scaeva could have another offering for me."

"They still don't have the map," Mercurio said. "I can weave a story. Say the map slipped your grasp, but you're chasing it now. Strictly speaking, that could take months."

"The Ministry won't be pleased with that," Ashlinn said.

"Fuck them," Mia scowled. "The Ministry aren't pleased with me anyway."

"Wonderful," Ashlinn said. "So now all we need do is ponder a way for you to murder a cardinal you can't physically get close to, while at the same time killing the most highly guarded consul in the history of the Itreyan Republic."

Mia and Mercurio were silent. The old man's brow creased in thought. Mia's

eyes were narrowed, roaming the bookshelves and finding no answer along their
spines. She turned her gaze to the other wall, Mercurio's collection of weapons. The
Luminatii sunsteel blade, the Vaanian battleaxe, the gladius from a gladiatii arena
in Liis . . .

  Her eyes narrowed farther. The wheels behind them turning.
  She glanced to her old teacher, her breath coming quick.
  "What is it?" he asked.
  Idiotic.
  Insane.
  Impossible.
  "I think I have an idea . . ."

Thirteen gladiatii were gathered in a circle in the training yard. The walls
of Crow's Nest rose about them, banners of the Familia Remus fluttering in the rising wind. They'd arrived back from Blackbridge late, and it was
near the turn of nevernight. But before evemeal, time would be taken to welcome their new brother and sister into their fold—the most sacred of rites,
conducted here on the sacred ground of their collegium.

The *votum vitus.**

The twin suns beat down on the yard, and Mia felt sweat dripping down
her bare belly and arms. She was on her knees in the circle, Sidonius beside
her. Arkades stood before them, clad in a gleaming breastplate embossed with
twin lions, scratched and scored from years of combat. Dona Leona watched

---

*The origins of the Vow of Blood are shrouded in antiquity, but many believe they lay
in the Old Ysiiri Empire, and the mythology of the famed warrior-prince Andarai.

  Andarai's exploits were so well known, his legend survived even the fall of the
empire itself. He was a typical brand of hero for the age—peerlessly wise, undefeated
in battle, and reputedly hung like a mule. He spent much of his time running about
rescuing princesses, slaying beasts, and siring bastards, though he also apparently
found time to invent the lyre, the loom, and, strangely enough, the birthing stool. His
most hated foe was the legendary Thief of Faces, Tariq, who, among his other exploits,
stole Andarai's blacksteel sword, and bedded Andarai's mother, sister, *and* daughter,
all reportedly on the same evening.

  Andarai was somewhat put out about this. Particularly the bit about his mother.

  The pair's rivalry spanned decades, and looked surely to end in the death of one or
both. But when the daemon-king, Sha'Annu, rose in the north and threatened all the
empire, the pair joined forces to defeat him. Bound by the kinship found only in battle,
the pair declared themselves brothers, and vowed in blood they would remain so 'til the
end of their days. Tariq even refrained from bedding Andarai's mother again.

  His daughter, however . . .

from the balcony in a beautiful silken yellow gown. When she looked down at the executus, she smiled, and the sapphire of her eyes seemed to say, "I told you so."

"Gladiatii," the executus said. "We stand here on sacred ground, in sacred rite, to welcome these two proven warriors into our fold. We bind ourselves not with steel, but with blood. For blood we are, and blood we shall remain."

"Blood we are," came the voices around the circle. "And blood we shall remain."

Executus drew a dagger from his belt, drew the blade across his palm, let the red drip upon the sand. And then he passed the blade to his left.

The Butcher of Amai took the dagger. He repeated the ritual, cutting his palm before passing it to Bladesinger. The woman looked Mia in the eye as she cut her palm. And so it went, around the thirteen. To the Vaanian twins, Bryn and Byern, the male Dweymeri, Wavewaker, to the rest of the gladiatii in the circle, until finally, the bloody blade was passed to their champion, Furian, the Unfallen.

The Itreyan watched Mia with dark, clouded eyes, a new silver laurel resting on his brow. She'd watched him fight at Blackbridge, and his victory ("peerless," the editorii had called it, "flawless") had only inflamed her curiosity. She felt her shadow tremble as he cut his palm, mingling his blood with his gladiatii familia on the razored edge. He let the scarlet droplets fall to the sand, then walked across the circle to stand before Sidonius and Mia. Glancing from that handsome jaw, those burning eyes, down to the darkness at his feet, she saw his shadow was trembling too.

He stands in your way, she reminded herself.

All of them.

In your way.

"Blood we are," he said, passing her the blade. "And blood we shall remain."

Mia took the knife, her belly thrilling as her fingertips brushed his. And chiding herself for a fool, she turned to the executus, looked him in the eye.

"Not too deep," he cautioned. "You will ruin your grip."

Mia nodded, drawing the blade across her palm. The pain was bright and real, bringing all the world into focus. She was here. A blooded member of the collegium. Before her lay a desert of sand, an ocean of red. But at the end, she saw Grand Cardinal Duomo in his beggar's robes, no trinity about his throat. Consul Scaeva, reaching up to place the victor's laurel upon her brow.

Her shadow, reaching toward theirs . . .

"Blood we shall remain," she said.

Sidonius took the blade, cut his palm, and repeated the vow.

"Blood we shall remain."

A rousing cheer went up around the circle. Executus motioned for Mia and Sidonius to rise, and the gladiatii closed in. Bladesinger smiled at Mia, and the Vaanian girl Bryn crushed her to her breast, whispering, "You fought well." Butcher slapped her on the back so hard she almost fell over, the others offering their bloody hands or giving her friendly thumps on the arm. Only Furian held himself apart—but whether out of his lofty status as champion or the enmity between them, Mia had no idea.

"My Falcons," came a voice from the balcony.

"Attend!" snapped the executus, and all eyes turned upward.

Dona Leona smiled at them like a goddess upon her children, arms spread wide. "Our victories at Blackbridge earn us yet more renown, and berth at the *venatus* four weeks hence in Stormwatch!"

The gladiatii cheered, and Sidonius wrapped his arm around Mia's neck, squeezing as he bellowed. Mia laughed and pushed the big man off, but she couldn't help but find her voice caught up among them.

"The contests shall only grow fiercer as we approach the *magni*. On the morrow, you return to training. But for now, never let it be said your domina does not reward your valor, or the honor you do her each time you take to the sands!"

Leona clapped her hands, and three servants wheeled a large barrel out among the tables and chairs on the verandah.

"Is that wine?" Sidonius breathed.

"Drink, my Falcons!" Leona smiled. "A toast to your new brother and sister. A toast to glory! And a toast to our many victories to come!"

Three hours later, as she lay down in her cell, Mia's head was swimming. She'd tried to drink frugally, but Sid had bellowed every time she slacked her pace, and every one of the other gladiatii seemed to drink as though their lives depended on it. It made perfect sense, she supposed—for folk who owned nothing, their lives at risk every time they took to the sands, a moment of respite and a full cup must seem like a paradise. And so, she'd done her best to play her role, drinking hard with her new familia and smiling at their praise.

The Dweymeri woman, Bladesinger, seemed to have taken a particular liking to her, though most of the collegium had a kind word. Her ploy in the arena—wearing the enemy's colors and playing wounded to get close enough to bring them down—had struck most of her new kin as a stroke of small genius.

Bryn, the blond Vaanian girl, had raised her cup in toast.

"A fine ruse, little Crow."

"Aye," her brother Byern replied. "When I saw you clutching those guts and realized what you were up to, I almost shouted loud enough to give the game away."

"Crow my arse," Butcher had grinned. "We should call her the bloody Fox."

"The Wolf," Bladesinger smiled.

"The Snake," came a voice.

All eyes had turned to Furian, glowering at the head of the table. Mia had met his stare, watched his lip curl in derision.

"Gladiatii fight with honor," he'd said. "Not with lies."

"Brother, come," Bladesinger had said. "A victory won is a victory earned."

"I am champion of this collegium," the Unfallen had replied. "I say what is earned. And what is stolen."

Bladesinger had glanced at the torc around Furian's neck, the laurel at his brow, nodded acquiescence. The Unfallen returned to his cup, speaking no more. Festivities ended soon after, and in truth, Mia had been thankful. She wasn't accustomed to so much wine, and a few more cups and she'd have been painting the walls.

She sat in her cell now, the bars slowly spinning. She'd heard that same singing from Bladesinger's cell before the lights died, supposing it might be some sort of prayer. But now darkness had descended, all she could hear was the sound of sleep.

Sidonius was on his back snoring like a dying bull, pausing only long enough to fart so loud Mia felt it through the floor. She scowled and kicked the big Itreyan, who rolled over with a grumble.

"Fucking pig," she cursed, covering her nose. "I need my own bloody cell."

"*. . . i seldom find myself ungrateful that I do not need to breathe . . .*"

Mia's eyes widened as she heard the whisper.

"*. . . at this moment, doubly so . . .*"

"Mister Kindly!"

"*. . . she cried, loud enough to wake the dead . . .*"

Two black shapes coalesced from the shadows at the other end of the cell.

"*. . . IF THIS LUMP'S SNORING HASN'T DONE SO, NOTHING WILL . . .*"

Mia grinned as the pair of daemons bounded up to her, diving into her shadow as if it were black water. A rush of soothing chill washed over her, rippling down the length of her body, leaving an iron calm in its wake. She felt Mister Kindly stalking across her shoulder, weaving among her hair without disturbing a single strand. Eclipse curled around Mia's back, put her insubstantial head in the girl's lap. Mia ran her hands through both of them, their shapes rippling like black smoke. She hadn't realized how badly she'd missed them until she had them back.

"Black Mother, it's good to see you two," she whispered.

"*. . . I MISSED YOU . . .*"

"*. . . o, please . . .*"

"*. . . I MISSED THE MOGGY LESS . . .*"

Mia ran her hands down the length of the shadowwolf's body. There was no sensation of being able to touch her, but petting Eclipse was like petting a cool breeze.

"When did you arrive?"

"*. . . YESTERTURN. BUT YOU WERE NOT YET RETURNED FROM THE* VENATUS *. . .*"

"*. . . things went well, i take it . . .*"

"I'm not dead, if that counts for anything."

Mister Kindly nuzzled against her ear, and Mia's skin tingled. It felt like being kissed by cigarillo smoke.

"*. . . everything . . . ,*" he whispered.

The trio sat in the gloom for a while, simply enjoying each other's company. Mia curled her fingers through their gossamer bodies, felt any trace of the fear she'd felt over the past weeks fading to nothing. She'd done it, she realized. The first step toward Duomo's and Scaeva's throats was complete. And with her passengers beside her, the remaining steps seemed not so far at all.

"*. . . lovely as this is . . .*"

"*. . . ALWAYS WE CAN COUNT UPON YOU TO SPOIL THE MOOD . . .*"

"No, he's right," Mia sighed. "Is she waiting?"

"*. . . AYE . . .*"

"Take me to her, then."

Her passengers faded into the black. Mia felt them coalesce in the shadows of the antechamber, and just as she'd done the nevernight she visited Furian, she closed her eyes, reached into the dark. Perhaps it was the wine, perhaps the practice she'd had, but she found the Step a little easier this time, the sudden rush, the vertigo. Opening her eyes, she found the room spinning wildly, but she was in the shadow of the stairwell beside them.

Bending double, she retched a few cups' worth onto the stone, covering her mouth to stifle the sound. She felt a few gladiatii stirring in the barracks, sinking back into the shadows and fighting the urge to vomit again. She clutched the wall to help it stop spinning. Wiped her hand across her lips, and spat onto the stone.

"Black Mother, remind me not to do that when I'm half-drunk again."

"*. . . COME . . .*"

"*. . . the viper waits, mia . . .*"

She glanced to the mekwerk control on the wall, pondering how it worked. On unsteady legs, she stole out through the keep, into the shadows of the verandah. Fang was sitting beneath a table, watching with curious eyes. As Mister Kindly and Eclipse flitted past, the dog's hackles rose. Mia offered her hand to calm the mastiff, but with a low whimper, Fang scampered away.

"*. . . dogs are fools . . .*"

"*. . . SAYS THE FOOL WHO GOT LOST ON THE WAY UP HERE . . .*"

"*. . . i was not lost, dear mongrel, i was exploring . . .*"

"*. . . IT IS AN ENORMOUS KEEP ATOP A CLIFF OVERLOOKING THE WHOLE CITY, HOW DO—. . .*"

"Hsst," Mia hissed, ducking into an alcove. Swift footsteps marked the approach of the magistrae, a serving girl in tow. The pair were in deep discussion about travel arrangements to Stormwatch, the girl marking notes in a wax ledger. Mia waited 'til the pair were out of sight, slowly crept along the corridor to the front doors, open wide to cool sea breeze. Squinting against the sunlight, she peered out at the high keep walls, red stone against a sky of burning blue.

Gathering handfuls of shadows, Mia draped them about her shoulders. Her fingers were a little clumsy from the drink, but finally all the world was shrouded in muzzy black and muffled white, and she was almost as blind as the turn she was born. With soft whispers, her two passengers guided her through the courtyard, past the patrolling guards and into a shadowed alcove just beside the main gates. And from there, she closed her eyes

and Stepped

into the

shadow

across

the road.

Mia fell to her knees, clutching her belly and fighting the urge to vomit with all she had. After a few minutes in the dirt, she caught her breath, wiping tears from her eyes.

"*. . . are you well . . . ?*"

"Next silly question, please," she whispered.

"*. . . WE DO NOT HAVE TO SEE HER NOW . . .*"

"No, we should. But we can't be gone too long. They don't rouse us 'til early morn, but if they somehow miss me in the nevernight . . ."

"*. . . THE WINE WILL KEEP YOUR CELLMATE DREAMING 'TIL THEN . . .*"

"Still, we need to be swift."

"*. . . it is not far . . .*"

She rose on shaking legs and staggered along the dusty road, winding down the sheer hill upon which Crow's Nest stood. Mia didn't need Mister Kindly or Eclipse as much out here—she knew the road well enough to walk it blind. But she didn't dare risk casting off her shadow cloak just yet. She was still clad as a gladiatii, and the twin circles branded on her cheek marked her as property. Though masters might often walk in the company of armed warrior slaves, it would be a rarity to see one wandering alone. Best to remain hidden, and avoid questions entirely.

Mia could hear the sea to the south, the ringing of port bells below, smell the familiar scents of the town in the keep's shadow. Known as Crow's Rest, it was home to three or four thousand—a bustling trade port that had sprung up under the keep's protection. The buildings were red stone and white plaster, crammed together on the steep hillsides leaning down to the water. The air rang with the song of gulls.

Her passengers led her into the tangled warren of dockside. She threw off her cloak here, stole down twisted alleys, ripe with garbage and salt air. They arrived at a small alehouse, Mister Kindly nodding to the guest rooms above.

"*. . . second floor, third window . . .*"

Mia glanced about to ensure all was clear, and began to climb. She reached the second-floor terraces, slipped over the iron railing, rapped once upon the glass.

The window opened and she stole inside, quiet as whispers.

Mia's eyes took a moment to adjust after the sunslight outside. But finally she saw a figure dropping herself into an old divan, stretching long legs out before her. She was dressed in black, leather britches and a short leather corset, a long-sleeved shirt of dark silk beneath. She'd dyed her hair to cover the telltale blond, now as bloody-red as Jessamine's had been. But there was no mistaking those eyes.

The girl leaned back in her chair, looked Mia up and down.

"Hello, beautiful," she smiled.

"Hello, Ashlinn," Mia replied.

BLOOD AND GLORY

CHAPTER 13

EGRESS

Clove-scented smoke curled in the sea air, slipping out in thin trails from Mia's nostrils. She dragged the last breath from the cigarillo, crushed the life out of it against the wall and breathed a contented sigh.

"'Byss and blood, I needed that."

"I knew you'd be missing them."

Ash smiled, dragged a lock of blood-red behind her ear. She'd dyed it for subterfuge—if by some horrid stroke of fate, someone from the Church saw her and Mia together at a distance, Ash might be able to pass for Jessamine. It was a thin ruse, but as Mister Kindly was so fond of telling Mia, this whole game was so thin it was practically translucent.

Still, Mia inclined her head in thanks, and closing her eyes, she leaned back against the old leather couch, listening to the tobacco buzz in her blood.

"It's good to see you again," Ash said.

Mia opened her eyes, staring at Ash through her lashes. Mister Kindly hopped up onto the lounge, tail draped over Mia's shoulder. Eclipse wrapped herself around Mia's waist, head in her lap. Neither of her passengers trusted Ashlinn, and even after setting all this in motion together, Mia couldn't bring herself to either. Ash killed Jess. She'd killed Tric. Killed anyone who stood in the way of her revenge.

Is she so different from you?

She'd not given the Luminatii the location of Mercurio's shop, after all . . .

Ashlinn peered at the rags Mia was clad in.

"Nice to see you dressed up for the occasion."

"Take you much trouble to get here?" Mia asked.

Ash shook her head. "Mister Grumpy found us quick enough."

Eclipse's laughter came from beneath the floor. Mister Kindly tilted his head at Ashlinn and whispered with a voice like smoke.

"... *insolence*..."

Ashlinn smirked at the shadowcat, slipped a dagger from her belt, and skewered an apple from the bowl of fruit on the table beside her. With a deft flick of her wrist, she tossed it into Mia's outstretched hand.

"We waited at Whitekeep as planned," Ash said. "Once Leonides arrived and you weren't among his purchases, I knew something had gone balls up. Though I didn't imagine jewels were facing so proudly skyward until Mister Smart-arse found us."

"... *stop that*..."

"... *NO, DO CONTINUE, PLEASE*..."

Ash ignored the shadows, instead quirked an eyebrow at Mia. The girl took a noisy bite out of her apple, chewing for a good while before she answered.

"I admit, the plan has suffered a few ... setbacks."

"You always had a talent for understatement, Corvere." Ashlinn stabbed another apple from the bowl, began peeling it with deft strokes of her blade. "Living in the keep that belonged to your father before he was hanged for treason. Under ownership of the wife of the justicus you murdered. In a stable that can only be a half-year old at most, and only has one laurel to its name. How's that faring?"

"I survived the Winnowing," Mia shrugged.

Ash slipped a sliver of apple between her lips. "I *had* noticed you weren't dead."

"And I've taken the blood vow," Mia continued. "I'm full-fledged gladiatii now. The plan remains the same. I'll just have to do it through a different collegium is all."

"You're going to have to fight twice as hard," Ash pointed out. "Leonides has already assured his collegium a berth in the *magni* from previous years' victories. Leona doesn't have anything like the political capital her father does. She needs to win at least three more laurels before she can even fight in the grand games."

"If I need someone to state the bleeding obvious, I already have Mister Kindly, Ashlinn."

"... *some things are important enough to point out twice*..."

"Listen, nobody knows better than me how deep the shit we're in is," Mia snapped. "But if one of you can think of a better way to get Duomo and Scaeva at once, without the Red Church getting a whiff of it, I'm all fucking ears."

"I've told you before, Mia," Ash said. "*I* can get Duomo for you. I trained at the Church, same as you. We can sail back to Godsgrave right now and—"

"No, I told *you*," the girl scowled. "Duomo is mine. Scaeva is *mine*. I want to look those bastards in the eye as they die. I want them to *know* it was me."

"*. . . BLOOD MUST HAVE BLOOD . . . ,*" Eclipse growled.

Ash popped another slice of apple between her teeth, raised an eyebrow at Mister Kindly. The pair might have been at odds about everything else, but as far as the insanity of Mia's plan went, they were of one accord.

"*. . . mia, perha— . . .*"

"No!" she snapped. "This is the way. And this was the deal, Ashlinn. You help me get Scaeva and Duomo, Mercurio and I help you get the Ministry."

"You wouldn't just be getting them for *me,* Mia. Let's be honest."

"Are you certain you know what honesty even looks like anymore, Ashlinn?"

The girl sucked her lip, slowly nodded. "A fine thrust."

"I've been practicing."

"I should point out that I *am* here helping you, Mia."

"I get Duomo. *I* get Scaeva. That was the bargain struck."

And so it was. Insane as the plan had seemed, sitting for hours in the Godsgrave Chapel, neither Mercurio nor Ashlinn could ponder a better one. Scaeva rarely made public appearances anymore, and Duomo spent most of his time in the Basilica Grande. For the pair of them to be together at the *magni,* within striking range, all while Duomo wouldn't be wearing a cursed trinity about his neck . . . No matter how hard it would be to get there, the opportunity was too ripe to waste.

And so, Mercurio had reported to the Ministry that the deal with the braavi had gone south, and that Mia was now pursuing the map on the mainland. The trio had then set about researching the best collegia to see Mia through to the *magni,* although Mercurio wasn't exactly happy about Ashlinn being involved. True, the girl wanted revenge on the Red Church, almost as badly as Mia. True, she was a better liar than Mia; she and her brother had almost brought the Church down all by themselves. But, the fact was, Mia and her old mentor trusted her about as far as they could spit her.

Still, Mia had Eclipse around to keep Ash under watch—the girl couldn't breathe without the daemon there to hear it. And when swimming in drake-infested waters, it never hurt to have company, if only so the drakes had someone to eat other than you.

Ashlinn stretched like a cat, ate another slice of apple.

"Fair enough," she said. "I'm just pointing out other options. But the deal was struck, and I'll hold to it. Never let it be said I'm not a woman of my word."

Mister Kindly scoffed, tail curling about Mia's throat.

"... *on the contrary, i feel it should be said as loudly and often as possible* ..."

Ashlinn flipped the knuckles. "Nobody was talking to you, Mister Positivity."

Eclipse raised her head, her whisper echoing through the floorboards.

"... AS YOU MAY HAVE GUESSED, DONA JÄRNHEIM AND I HAVE BEEN GETTING ALONG FAMOUSLY IN YOUR ABSENCE ..."

"... *color me unsurprised* ..."

"... HAVE YOU NOT MICE TO CHASE, LITTLE MOGGY ...?"

"... *have you not crotches to sniff, dear mongrel* ...?"

"All right, enough, enough," Mia said. "I need to get back to my lovely stinky cell in Crow's Nest before I'm missed. We need to find out as much about Leona as we can. We knew the book on her father, but the dona herself is something of a mystery."

"A good thing I've been asking around, then," Ash smiled.

The girl sliced off another sliver of apple, pressed it to her tongue.

Mia raised an eyebrow. "Out with it, then."

"Say please," Ashlinn smiled.

"Ash ... ," Mia growled.

The girl grinned, leaned back in her chair. "I've only been here a turn. So there's more to learn. But I know Leona married Remus around three years back. She caught his eye at the last *magni,* and Remus sought her hand from her father soon after. Quite a coup, for the daughter of a mere sanguila to be married off to the justicus of the Luminatii Legion. Shows how much political clout her da has, I suppose."

Mia took a bite of the apple, spoke around her mouthful.

"Their marriage was arranged?"

"They always are at that level." Ash sliced a thin wafer, popped it between her lips. "Though from what I can tell, Leona wasn't forced into it. Remus was rich. Handsome. His political star on the rise. She stood to gain a lot from slipping into bed with him. So I'd not let it slip you slit his throat were I you."

"O, damnation, because I was planning on it."

Ashlinn smirked and pressed another sliver to her tongue.

"What about Arkades?" Mia spoke around another noisy bite. "He was Leonides's champion for years. Why does he serve Leona as executus instead of her father?"

Ashlinn shrugged again. "I've only been here a single turn. Give me time."

"Well, I need all the leverage I can get." Mia wiped her lips, stood, and stretched. "So the more you can find out about my domina, the better."

Ash nodded to the rags Mia was wearing, staring pointedly at her bare midriff and legs. "I like her fashion sense, if nothing else."

Mia ignored the comment, slipped to the window, peered out to look for unfriendly eyes. Finding none, she swung her leg over the sill, made to climb out.

"Mia."

She turned to look at Ashlinn, one eyebrow raised. The girl's hands fluttered at her sides, picking at the hem of her britches.

"Be careful in there," she said.

Mia glanced at Eclipse, still curled on the divan in a puddle of black.

"Keep an eye out," Mia said.

"... AS MUCH AS THE EYELESS CAN ... ," the not-wolf replied.

And with that, she was gone. Down the wall, to the alley, dragging the shadows about her head. Stealing back up the way to Crow's Nest with Mister Kindly to guide her to her rest.

She thought about the way Ashlinn looked at her. The kiss they'd shared the turn Mia left the Mountain. That had all been for show on Ashlinn's part, she was sure of it. Just a play to further the girl's plan to take down the Ministry. Mia knew it. Everyone knew it. Ashlinn Järnheim was poison. But thinking on that kiss, her mind drifted to that nevernight in Gaius Aurelius's bed, the way that Liisian beauty had tasted on his lips. Wondering if that had been all for show on *her* part—just another ruse to get within striking distance of the senator's son. Wondering if part of her hadn't enjoyed it, or if it mattered, even if she had.

Wondering why she was wondering *at all*.

Eyes on the fucking prize, Corvere . . .

Back at Crow's Nest, she found the portcullis still sealed, the guards watching. The hour was late, and there was little hope a servant might be sent down to the Rest until after the gladiatii were roused for mornmeal. And so Mia reached out to the shadows at her feet, the shadows in the courtyard, and drawing a deep breath, she

Stepped

     across

         the space

             between them.

She fell to her knees in the dust, head swimming, the burning light of the two suns overhead pounding upon her skull. At least the wine had worn off, and she wasn't tempted to spew, but the sensation was still far on the south side of pleasant. The captain of the dona's houseguard, a sharp-eyed fellow named Gannicus, turned at the sound of her hitting the dirt. But with Mia hidden beneath her cloak in the shadow of the wall, he saw nothing of account, and slowly turned back to his watch.

It was several minutes before Mia felt steady enough to rise, creeping slow across the courtyard at Mister Kindly's whispers, down the building's flank to the open verandah at the rear. Stealing down the stairs, groping blind, she finally found the iron bars that sealed off the barracks from the rest of the villa. Taking a moment to ready herself, dreading the incoming vertigo, she felt for the shadows of her dingy little cell. And closing her eyes tight she

Stepped

down into the black

at her feet

and into the cell beyond.

The heat of the suns was nowhere near as intense in the barrack's dark, but still, she was almost sick, puke bubbling up from her gullet and welling in her cheeks. She was getting better at shadow-stepping since the basilica roof—like any muscle, she supposed it grew stronger the more she used it. But a second Step so soon after the first was apparently too much, especially with the suns burning so bright in the sky. She swallowed thickly, crouched upon the straw, clutching the stones beneath to stop the world from spinning. Listening to the cells around her, she heard nothing but soft snoring and sighs.

"*. . . all looks clear . . . ,*" came a whisper in her ear.

She waited a moment longer, the world slowly steadying itself. And finally, safe inside her cell, Mia threw her shadowcloak aside and blinked around the cellar's gloom, right into Sidonius's opening eyes.

"Fuck me," he murmured. "Look wh—"

Mia crossed the cell in a flash, seized the man by the throat, one hand over his mouth. Sidonius clawed her back, muscles bulging, growling as the pair struggled. Sid was bigger, Mia faster, the pair scuffling silently in the straw.

Each had the other in a choke hold, veins bulging at their throats, Sid's eyes welling with tears.

"P-pe . . . ," he gurgled.

Even as Mia choked him, his own hold tightened. Mia's throat cinched closed, her chest burning, blood cut off to her brain. She was still dizzy from her shadow-stepping, she'd no idea if the big Itreyan would succumb before she did. No idea what he'd do if she did . . .

"P . . . peace," he managed to gasp.

Mia eased off her hold a fraction, looking into Sidonius's eyes. The big man did the same, letting just a whisper of breath into her lungs. Slow as melting ice, she released her grip, the big man's fingers unwinding from about her neck. Mia rolled off the big Itreyan, retreated to one corner of their cell.

"'Byss and b-blood," Sid whispered, rubbing his throat. "Wh . . . what was that for?"

"You saw," Mia whispered.

"So what?"

"You know. What I *am*."

Sid winced, trying to swallow. He whispered almost lower than she could hear.

"Darkin."

Mia said nothing, dark eyes locked on his.

"And that deserves a bloody strangling?" he pressed.

"Keep your fucking voice down," Mia spat, looking about the other cells.

"*. . . advice best followed by everyone concerned . . . ?*"

Sidonius's eyes grew wide as the shadowcat faded into view on Mia's shoulder.

"Bugger me . . . ," he breathed.

"*. . . a generous offer, but no, thank you . . .*"

"And thank *you* for telling me all looked clear," Mia whispered.

The not-cat tilted his head.

"*. . . i can't be perfect in every way . . .*"

Mia and Sidonius looked at each other across the straw. There was fear in the man's stare—fear of the unknown, fear of what she was. But, despite it, Sidonius held his peace, held his tongue, looking her over with curious eyes.

"Shouldn't you be screaming for the guards right now?" Mia asked. "Blathering that they should be nailing me up for witchery?"

"Witchery?" Sid scoffed. "Do I look like some addle-witted peasant to you?"

"*. . . I admit, you're taking the news better than most.*"

"I've seen a lot of this world, little Crow. And you're not the strangest of it.

Not by a long ways." The Itreyan leaned back against the bars, folded his arms. "It's true, then . . . what they say about you lot?"

"That we spoil milk where we walk and deflower virgins wher—"

"That you walk through walls, you little nonce. I woke up to piss a half-hour ago and you weren't here. Then, *pop,* you appear right out of the fucking air?"

"That's not what happened, Sid."

"I know what I saw, Crow."

Sounds of waking could be heard in the villa overhead. The cook's footsteps on the boards, the watch changing outside. Executus would be down here soon, rousing them for their first round of brutal calisthenics.

Mia looked Sidonius in the eye, studying him with care. The man was a smart-arse, a thug, an utter lackwit when it came to women. But he was no fool. She didn't trust him, not by half. But they'd bled together on the sands of Blackbridge, and that counted for something. Still, there was no chance she was willing to share anything of herself without him giving something in return . . .

She looked at the scarred knuckles and heavy muscle that spoke of a man who'd spent a life fighting. The cold blue eyes that spoke of long miles and longer years. The word *COWARD* burned into his skin.

"Just how much of the world *have* you seen?" she asked.

"Liis," he replied. "Vaan. Itreya. Anywhere the banner took me."

Mia raised an eyebrow. Remembering the way Sid had conducted himself during the Winnowing. Barking orders like a man used to command. Thinking tactics, like . . .

"You were in the Itreyan legion," she said.

Sid shook his head. "I was *Luminatii,* little Crow. Served the justicus five years."

Mia's eyes narrowed, belly turning to ice. "You served Marcus Remus?"

"Remus?" Sid scoffed. "That treacherous shitheel? 'Byss, no. I served the justicus before him. The *true* justicus, girl. Darius fucking Corvere."

Mia's heart lurched in her chest. Tongue cleaving to the roof of her mouth. Black Mother, this man had served her *father.*

But that makes no sense . . .

"I . . ." Mia cleared her throat. "I heard the Kingmaker's army were all crucified . . . on the banks of the Choir. They paved the Senate house steps with their skulls."

"I wasn't there when Corvere and Antonius's army fell apart." Sid rubbed the brand at his chest, his voice growing distant. "Always wondered if I might have done some good had I been . . ."

Sid ran a hand over his dark cropped hair. He nodded at the walls around them. The bars that held them in.

"This used to be Corvere's house, you know," he sighed. "He and his familia used to spend summers here, I think. Little girl. Baby son. Before they gave it to that snake, Remus. To think this is where I'd end my turns. Locked in that fucker's basement. Winning blood and glory for his widow until my guts paint the sand."

So. Sidonius had done more than serve her father. He'd remained loyal, when the whole Republic turned against him . . .

Maw's teeth, she'd never imagined it. To think she'd meet one of her father's men, under this very roof? If she'd felt no kinship before for this man she'd bled beside at Blackbridge, she felt it flooding inside her chest now. The way Sidonius spoke about her father made her want to kiss the stupid sod.

"The true *justicus,"* he'd said.

When everyone else just called Darius Corvere "traitor."

Mia rubbed her bruised throat, her shadow rippling as Mister Kindly drank her fear. She'd not spoken of her gift much, not to anyone. People feared what they didn't understand, and hated what they feared. But for all the strangeness of it, Sidonius didn't feel anything close to afraid anymore.

He's an odd one . . .

"I can't walk through walls," she confessed.

Sid's eyes came into focus, looking at her across the cell.

"I just sort of . . . Step. After a fashion. Between shadows, I mean."

" 'Byss and blood," the big man breathed.

"But it makes me want to puke afterward," she added. "And I can make myself unseen. But I'm almost blind when I do. It's not the most wondrous gift, truth told."

"And your passenger?"

"Say hello, Mister Kindly."

". . . hello, mister kindly . . ."

"So you can leave these cells any time you want?"

Mia shrugged. "After a fashion."

The Itreyan shook his head in bewilderment. "Then what in the name of the Everseeing and all Four fucking Daughters are you still doing here, little Crow?"

The portcullis shuddered upward as a guard pulled a mekwerk lever. Executus marched into the barracks, graying beard bristling, whip curled in his hand.

"Gladiatii!" he barked. "Attend!"

With a shrug to Sid, Mia rose to begin her turn's work.

CHAPTER 14

BREATHING

Two suns burned the skies clear, Shiih's smoldering yellow and Saan's bloody red against a curtain of endless, beautiful blue.* The heat shimmered against the endless ocean, and Mia cursed the Everseeing for the hundredth time that turn.

She danced across the circle, dodging Bladesinger's strikes, weaving in and out of range. The woman's face was set like stone, her wooden sword whistling as if it knew her name.

"No!" Executus bellowed from the circle's edge. "You're bouncing like a damned blackrabbit. You'll wear yourself to fainting if you keep dancing in this heat. A shield is a weapon, just like your blade. Batter your foes' strikes aside, send her off-balance."

Mia raised the great curved rectangle of wood and iron on her right arm. It was heavy as a pile of bricks, affixed with a band of old rope. She hated the fucking thing, truth told, but it was true what Arkades said—she was sweating like a pig from dodging about so much. She tried to mark his tutelage, but as Bladesinger raised her sword and bore down on Mia like thunder, the girl instinctively skipped past Bladesinger's guard and slapped her blade against the woman's hamstring.

"Shit," Bladesinger spat. "Quicker than a drakeling, this one."

---

*Though the Ysiiri Empire ended in a mysterious magikal calamity millennia previous, remnants of the language survive in the Itreyan Republic to this day. The names of the three suns, Shiih (*the Watcher*), Saan (*the Seer*), and Saai (*the Knower*) are the most obvious example, but it may be of interest to note that the names of the Itreyan pantheon are also Ysiiri words.

Aa is the Ysiiri word for "all" and *Niah,* Ysiiri for "nothing." Itreyan academics spend a great deal of time arguing with each other at dinner parties, debating whether both Aa and Niah were worshipped in Old Ysiir, and whether the religion of the Republic is far older than the Republic itself. Preferably while consuming enormous quantities of wine.

Aa himself has made no comment on the topic, pissed or otherwise.

"*No!*"

Executus limped across the circle, drawing out the steel gladius he always wore to session.

"If you'll not stop dancing like a bride at her wedding, I'll bloody hobble you . . ."

Mia bristled, thinking perhaps Arkades was set to strike her. But instead, he stabbed the sword into the dirt, right in the center of the ring. He snapped his fingers at Maggot, waiting as always in the shade of the small shed in the corner of the yard.

"Rope," Arkades commanded.

The girl dashed to the weapon racks, unslung one of the pull ropes the gladiatii used for their calisthenics. Dragging it back to Arkades, Maggot watched with curious eyes as the executus fixed one end around his blade hilt, the other to Mia's leg.

"Dance with that, blackrabbit," he scowled.

Arkades retired to the circle's edge, barked at Bladesinger to attack. Unable to dodge, Mia was forced to use her shield, Bladesinger's strikes landing like thunderclaps. The impacts jarred Mia's arm, until finally the old rope affixing the shield to her forearm snapped clean in half, snagging up her hand in the knotted leather grip. And with a series of damp, snapping sounds, three of Mia's fingers popped right at the knuckle.

"'Byss and fucking *blood*!" she bellowed, dropping her shield.

The other gladiatii in the yard turned to stare, watching as she bent double, clutching her hand. Butcher laughed, Wavewaker broke into a round of applause. Fixing her broken shield in her glare, Mia aimed a savage kick at it ("Fucking thing!"), sent it flying across the yard before dropping onto her backside in the dust.

"Owww," she moaned, clutching her now-sprained toes with her one good hand.

"Show me," Executus said, limping over to kneel beside her.

Mia held up her trembling hand. Her smallest finger was jutting out at entirely the wrong angle, her ring and middle finger were both crooked. Arkades turned her hand this way and that as Mia writhed and cursed.

"You broke my fingers!" she said, glaring at Bladesinger.

The woman shrugged, slinging her long saltlocks over her shoulder.

"Welcome to the sand, Crow."

"Stop whining, girl," Arkades said, squinting. "They're just dislocated. Maggot!"

The girl perked up from her shady seat near the shed, dashed over to Mia. Untying the rope at her ankle, Maggot helped Mia up, the older girl rising with a wince. The other gladiatii returned to training as Maggot led Mia by the hand across the yard. She saw Furian sparring with Wavewaker, watching from the corner of his eye. His face was a mask, her belly, as always, a knot of sickness and hunger when he was near.

Do I make him feel the same?

Maggot took Mia into a long room at the rear of the keep, set with four sandstone slabs. The stone was the same burned ochre as the cliffs about them, but it was stained a deeper red, spatter-mad patterns on the surface.

Bloodstains, Mia realized.

"You can sit," Maggot said in a small, shy voice.

Mia did as she was bid, holding her throbbing hand to her chest. Maggot toddled across the room, fishing about in a series of chests. She returned with a handful of wooden splints and a ball of woven brown cotton.

"Hold out your hand," the girl commanded.

Mia's shadow swelled, Mister Kindly drinking her fear at the thought of what was to come. Maggot looked her digits over, stroking her chin. And gentle as falling leaves, she took hold of Mia's smallest finger.

"It won't hurt," she promised. "I'm very good at this."

"All riiiiiaaaaaaaaaaaaAAAGHH!" Mia howled as Maggot popped her finger back into place, quick as silver. She rose from the slab and bent double, clutching her hand.

"That *HURT*!" she yelled.

Maggot gave a solemn nod. "Yes."

"You promised it wouldn't!"

"And you believed me." The girl smiled sweet as sugar-floss. "I told you, I'm very good at this." She motioned to the slab again. "Sit back down."

Mia blinked back hot tears, hand throbbing in agony. But looking at her finger, she could see Maggot had worked it right, popping the dislocated joint back into place neat as could be. Breathing deep, she sat back down and dutifully proffered her hand.

The little girl took hold of Mia's ring finger, looked up at her with big, dark eyes.

"I'm going to count three," she said.

"All riiiiiaaaaaaaaaaaaa*FUCK*!" Mia roared as Maggot snapped the joint back into place. She rose and half-danced, half-hopped about the room, wounded hand between her legs. "Shit cock twat fucking *fuckitall*!"

"You swear an awful lot," Maggot frowned.

"You said you were going to count three!"

Maggot nodded sadly. "You believed me again, didn't you?"

Mia winced, teeth gritted, looking the girl up and down.

". . . You *are* very good at this," she realized.

Maggot smiled, patted the bench. "Last one."

Sighing, Mia sat back down, hand shaking with pain as Maggot gently took hold of her middle finger. She looked at Mia solemnly.

"Now this one is *really* going to hurt," she warned.

"Wa—" The Blade flinched as Maggot popped the finger back in.

Mia blinked.

"Ow?" she said.

"All done," Maggot smiled.

"But that was the easiest of the lot?" Mia protested.

"I know," Maggot replied. "I'm—"

"—*very good at this,*" they both finished.

Maggot began splinting Mia's fingers, binding them tight to limit their movement. The three circles branded into the little girl's cheek weren't so much of a mystery anymore . . .

"Why do they call you Crow?" she asked as she worked.

Mia looked at the girl carefully, trying to ignore the warm, throbbing pain in her hand. Maggot was Liisian; tanned skin and dark, tangled hair, big dark eyes. She was skinny, thin dress hugging her thinner frame.

Not a turn over twelve, Mia guessed.

Perhaps it was seeing her in the keep where she'd grown up. Perhaps it was the mischievous intelligence glittering in those dark eyes, or the way she spoke so brazenly to her elders. But truth told, the little girl reminded Mia a little of herself . . .

"Why do they call you Maggot?" Mia replied.

"I asked first."

"Crow is a nickname."

Mia thought back to the first turn anyone had called her by it. Her first meeting with Old Mercurio. The old man had beaten seven shades of shit out of some alley thugs who'd stolen Mia's brooch. The very turn after her father was hanged. She was the daughter of a traitor, wanted by the most powerful men in the Republic. And Mercurio had thought nothing of taking her in, giving her a roof, saving her life.

Black Mother, the things he risked for me . . .

Mia shook her head, thinking about this insane plan of hers.

The things he still *risks for me.*

"A friend gave it to me," Mia said. "When I was a little girl. I had a piece of jewelry with a crow on it. He named me for it."

"I've never owned jewelry," Maggot mused.

"I've not owned any since. That one was a gift from my mother."

"Where is your mother now?"

The dona looked at her daughter, wide eyes and a broken yellow smile, far, far too wide. Mister Kindly materialized on the cell floor beside Mia, and the Dona Corvere hissed like she'd been scalded, shrinking back from the bars, teeth bared in a snarl.

"He's in you," she'd whispered. "O, Daughters, he's in you."

Mia stared at the stone floor. The old blood, spattered and brown.

"She's gone," Mia said.

Maggot looked at Mia, nodded sadly as she tied off the bandage.

"Mine, too," she said. "But she taught me all she knew. And so, whenever I stitch a wound or set a bone or mend a fever, she's still with me."

A fine thought, Mia mused. One no doubt sung to orphans across the world since the beginning of time. But even if there *were* some semblance of her father in the way she fought, her mother in the way she spoke, they were still dead and gone. If they were with her at all, it was as ghosts upon her shoulder, whispering in the nevernight of all that might have been.

If not for *them* . . .

Mia turned her wounded hand this way and that. It was still sore, but the pain had eased. In a week or so, it'd be as new.

"You still haven't told me why they call you Maggot," she said.

The little girl looked deep into Mia's eyes.

"Pray you never find out," she said.

The girl walked out of the infirmary, Mia behind her. Maggot retreated to her seat in the shade as Executus limped over to Mia, taking a small pull from the flask at his hip as he came. Grabbing her wrist, he scowled at her wounded hand.

"You'll not be sparring with that for a few—"

"Executus," came a soft call.

Arkades looked up to the balcony. Dona Leona stood there, auburn hair in long flowing ringlets, her silken dress as blue as the sky above. Beside her stood a rather dapper-looking Liisian man in a frock coat far too fine for the surroundings and far too warm for the weather. He was flanked by two heavyset bodyguards in leather jerkins.

"Attend!" Arkades barked.

The yard fell still at the call, the gladiatii turning toward their mistress.

"Executus, see to Matilius." The dona glanced to a big Itreyan man, sparring with a Liisian named Otho. "He is to accompany these men to the home of his new master."

Arkades's gray brows drew together in a frown. "New master, Mi Dona?"

"He has been sold to Varro Caito."

The gladiatii shared uneasy glances, Mia noting the sudden fall in mood. Matilius set aside his practice blades, brow creased as he looked up at Leona.

"Domina," the Itreyan said. "Have . . . I displeased you?"

Leona stared at the big man, blue eyes shining. But with a glance at the dapper man beside her, her gaze became hard as the red stone beneath her feet.

"I am no longer your domina," she said. "But you still have no right to question me. Know your place, slave, lest I have Executus gift you a parting reminder."

The big man lowered his gaze, bewilderment swimming in his eyes.

"Apologies," he grunted.

Leona's cold blue stare fell on Arkades. "Executus, see to his transfer. The rest of you, back to training."

Arkades bowed. "Your whisper, my will."

Though he hid it well, Mia could still see the confusion in the executus's eyes. Whatever the nature of this "sale," Leona clearly hadn't consulted him about it.

The big man straightened, looked at Mia, down at her wounded hand.

"You'll not spar for the next three turns, girl." He nodded to the blond Vaanian twins, working the training dummies across the yard. "Accompany Bryn and Byern to the equorium amorrow. You can help them with their practice, at least."

Turning on his heel, the Red Lion limped across the yard. Matilius was speaking swift goodbyes among the other gladiatii in the few moments he had left. He grasped Furian's forearm, squeezed tight. Bladesinger wrapped him in a crushing hug, Butcher and Wavewaker and Otho clapped him on the back. Matilius looked across the yard to Mia, nodded once, and she nodded in reply. She'd not known him well, but he seemed a decent sort. And it was clear he had friends here among the collegium; brothers and sisters he'd fought and bled with, and was now being forced to farewell.

Mia cruised over to the training dummies, slipped up beside Bryn and Byern. The Vaanian girl was short, almost pretty, her long topknot drenched in sweat. Byern was taller, better looking, his jaw square and his shoulders broad. His training sword hung limp in his hand as he watched Matilius say his goodbyes. The Vaanians were around Mia's age, but each seemed older somehow.

Something in the eyes, maybe.

"Who is Varro Caito?" Mia asked softly.

The twins startled—they'd not heard Mia's approach. With a scowl, Bryn turned back to the farewells, shooting a poison glance to the dapper Liisian on the balcony.

"A fleshmonger," she replied. "He runs Pandemonium."

Mia raised an eyebrow in question.

"A fighting pit," Bryn explained. "Underground. Not sanctioned by the administratii. But the battles are bloody. And popular. Former gladiatii fetch a fine price."

"So it's a kind of arena?"

Byern shook his head. "No honor there. No rules. No mercy. Pandemonium is closer to a human dogfight than the *venatus*. And the contests, ever to the finish. Most warriors perish in a few turns. Even the best only endure a month."

Mia watched Matilius, now being manacled by Executus and handed over to the Liisian fleshpeddler. The bodyguards checked the irons, nodded once. And with one final glance, the man was marched from the yard in the keeping of his new master.

Bryn sighed, shook her head. "He walks to his death."

"Then why does he walk?" Mia asked.

"What else would he do?" Byern replied.

"Run," she said fiercely. *"Fight."*

"Fight?" Bryn looked at Mia as if she were a child. "There was a slave revolt down in Crow's Rest. Maybe seven, eight months back. Did you hear tell of it?"

Mia shook her head.

"Two slaves fell in love," Byern said. "They wished to wed, but their domini forbid it. So the pair slit their master's throat in the nevernight and fled. They made it to Dawnspear before they were caught. Do you know what the administratii did?"

"Crucified them, at a guess," Mia said.

"Aye," Bryn nodded, smoothing back her topknot. "But not just them. They flogged and crucified every slave in their domini's house beside them to set example. The only one they spared was the slave who told the administratii where the murderers could be found. And for her loyalty to the Republic, that slave was forced to wield the lash during the floggings."

"Such, the price of defiance in Itreya," Byern said.

Mia's lips curled at the thought. Sickness in her belly. She'd known the life of a slave in the Republic was cruel, often short. She knew punishment for those who rebelled was horrific. But Black Mother, the brutality of it . . .

"Did you see?" she asked softly. "The executions?"

Byern nodded. "We all did. The administratii commanded every slave from every household in the Rest come and bear witness. The youngest boy they strung up couldn't have been more than eight years old."

"Four Daughters," Mia breathed. "I never imagined . . ."

"As gladiatii, your lot is better than most," Bryn said. "Blood. Glory. Be grateful."

Mia peered at the girl sidelong. "Are *you* grateful?"

Bryn looked at the wooden sword in her hand. Her brother, Byern, standing tall beside her. She looked to the sky above her head, down to the sand at her feet.

"We endure," she finally replied.

Mia watched Matilius being marched to the front gate. He paused before the portcullis, throwing one last glance back at his brothers and sisters, raising his hand in farewell. Bryn waved in reply, Byern closed a fist, placed it over his heart. And with a shove in Matilius's back, the man was gone.

Mia shook her head, wondering what she would do in his place. Fight in some futile gesture of defiance and get her brothers and sisters killed? Or march quietly to her death? How would it feel if life in this collegium was truly her lot? If instead of being able to Step outside the walls whenever she chose, she was actually trapped here? No control. No say in her own future?

"How?" she asked. "How do you endure the unendurable?"

"We have a saying in Vaan," Byern replied. "In every breath, hope abides."

Bryn turned to Mia.

A quick smile to cover her pain.

A slap on Mia's back to break the ugly stillness.

"Just keep breathing, little Crow."

CHAPTER 15

RIGHT

Evemeal was sullen that nevernight, none of the bawdy jokes or friendly banter that usually marked dinner around the long verandah tables. All minds seemed turned to Matilius's sale. Thinking about the fate that awaited the man in Pandemonium, Mia found herself without appetite, and instead of the usual scraps she gave when Fang came snuffling around, she gave over almost her entire meal.

The big mastiff licked her wounded fingers, his stubby tail all a-wag. She ruffled his ears and tried her best not to dwell on it. To think instead of the contests to come, the revenge awaiting her at the end of them. She was here for one reason, and one alone. And vengeance wouldn't be served by getting too close to any she fought beside. No matter how crushing the thought of it all was.

As if echoing her thoughts, she felt a cool breeze on the back of her neck. Fang whined softly and scampered away from Mia, ears pressed flat, tail tucked. Mister Kindly entwined himself in the shadows of her hair and whispered, soft as shadows.

"*. . . these people are not your familia, and not your friends. all of them are only a means to an end . . .*"

The other gladiatii seemed in no mood to speak on it, chewing their food in silence. Butcher was dark, though, muttering to himself and shaking his head. And near the meal's end, he could keep his tongue in his head no longer.

"This is horseshit," he growled, pushing his bowl aside.

"'Tis beef, I think," Wavewaker said, picking his teeth.

"I mean Mati, you bleeding cunt," Butcher said, glaring at the bigger man. "Selling him to that devious shitbag Caito? He deserved better than the damned pit."

"Mind your language, brother," Wavewaker waved a warning finger, his baritone growing deeper. "There are ladies present."

Bladesinger raised her eyebrow. "Where?"

"Enough," Furian growled. The champion stared hard, dark eyes burning. His jaw was set. Muscles taut. "Eat your food, Butcher."

"It's not right, Furian."

The Unfallen slammed a fist down on the table, and all eyes turned to stare.

"It is Domina's will," he said. "She is mistress of this collegium. You seem too apt to forget that. But remind me, brother, what were you, before she and Executus dragged you up from the shit?"

"A bodyguard," Butcher said, squaring his jaw.

"A bloody *mule* is what you were," Furian spat. "Carrying bags to market for some wrinkled old dona, and fucking her on command. And what of you, Wavewaker?"

"I was a thespian," the big man replied proudly.

"Thespian? You were a damned doorman in a two-beggar theater, bouncing drunks and mopping shit out of the privy between shows."

Wavewaker looked a little crestfallen. "I was set to play the Magus Ki—"

"Byern was headed for an Ysiiri copper mine." The Unfallen gestured about the room. "Bryn, a Liisian brothel. Aa's bleeding cock, Bladesinger was set to be fucking hanged! And Domina raised all of us up and forged us into *gods*!"

The champion's dark glare roamed the mess, inviting dissent.

"Domina feeds us," he said. "Shelters us. Gives us the chance to fight for glory and honor in the *venatus* instead of living on our knees or on our backs. And you name it not right? We all owe our lives to her. Including Matilius. That *makes* it right."

Mia sat in silence, listening to the Unfallen's tirade. None in the room voiced disagreement. She wondered at the man again; who he was, what made him breathe. She was a good judge of character, but Furian was a mystery. He fought like a daemon in the arena, true enough. And yet, he seemed perfectly content to bend his knee to this life of blood and servitude, and deny the truth of what he really was.

Why, just once, can't I meet a darkin who's not a bastard or a fool?

Evemeal ended, the gladiatii were marched to the barracks and bathed, four at a time. She was often thrown in with Sidonius, Butcher, and Bladesinger, though she preferred bathing with Wavewaker best. The man had a beautiful voice, and he often sang as he washed—songs learned from his brief spell in the theater, apparently.

Mia had already abandoned any notion of decency, what with walking about all turn wearing two strips of padded cloth and a pair of sandals. She found it strange, how easily she was becoming accustomed to life in the collegium. No privacy. No modesty. And when she closed her eyes, she could still hear the sound that had lingered in her mind since the games at Blackbridge. The roar, lifting her up on wings of thunder.

The crowd.

Her skin thrilled to think of it, despite herself. The memory burned in the black behind her eyes. Still, she reminded herself she was here for a reason, and that reason was the *magni*. Leona had sold Matilius without discussing the matter with Arkades. If there was some jeopardy for the collegium, she'd best learn the truth of it.

Sid seemed of a mood when Mia returned to their cell after her bath, and she didn't press him. Instead she lay against the bars and snoozed, wondering how she might turn the big Itreyan's allegiance to her father to some kind of advantage. There in the dark, she listened to the soft murmuring under Bladesinger's door, sitting in silence until she was certain the rest of the gladiatii were asleep. She whispered Sid's name, but he didn't stir. Feeling a cool whisper on back of her neck.

"*. . . where do we go . . . ?*"

"You tell me," she whispered in reply.

"*. . . i have been roaming the house since evemeal . . .*"

"So tell me a story."

"*. . . arkades requested a meeting with leona. he was told to come after she had bathed . . .*"

Mia nodded. "Lead the way."

Her shadow rippled and Mister Kindly was gone, flitting over to the portcullis, now locked tight for the nevernight. Mia reached out to the shadows in the antechamber, just as she'd done yestereve. They were no easier to grip, her hold slipping for a moment as she scowled in concentration and drew a long steady breath and

      Stepped

           into

                the shadow

                      beyond the portcullis.

The world turned on its head and she almost fell, biting down on a curse as she steadied herself with her wounded hand. Head hung low, long dark hair draped over ink-black eyes.

"...come..."

The not-cat flitted ahead, keeping watch for the houseguards. Slipping through her old home like a knife between ribs, Mia passed the rows of armor, up the wide stairway to the first floor. Her mind swimming with memories of her childhood here.

She remembered her father working his horses in the yard. Her mother reading by the bay windows in her room. She remembered the nevernight her brother Jonnen was born, under this very roof. Her father had wept as he held the babe in his arms.

She could recall him so clearly. The way he smelled. The way he kissed her mother, first on one eyelid, then the other, then finally upon her smooth, olive brow.

A good man.

A loving husband.

A faithful soldier.

What kind of king would he have made?

Mia shook her head, cursing herself a fool. It didn't matter. Her father's kingdom was two feet wide and six feet deep, and two of the men who'd killed him were still talking and breathing. That was all that mattered. *That* was all she should care about.

Up to the fourth floor. The level had been used for storage when Mia's parents had owned the Nest, but with her Falcons kept secure in the basement, the upper level now belonged to the mistress of the house. Quiet as a whisper, Mia stole down the long hallways toward soft voices coming from the bathhouse.

Peering in through the door, she saw Dona Leona emerging from a deep, steaming pool, water running in rivulets down her bare body. Her hair was damp, her face bereft of paint. It occurred to Mia that she was a beauty; full hips and fuller lips. Her eyes roamed Leona's curves, wreathed in steam, and she wondered at the thrill of it. Why, downstairs in the barracks, seeing naked bodies meant nothing, but here, her skin was prickling. Heart beating faster. Thinking, perhaps, of another beauty on Aurelius's bed, her taste on the young don's mouth, her golden kisses sinking ever lower.

She thought of Ashlinn, then. The kiss they'd shared when Mia left the Church. That kiss that lasted a moment too long. Maybe not long enough?

Mia shook her head. Cursing herself for a novice. Ashlinn Järnheim killed Tric. Ashlinn Järnheim betrayed the Church and her sacred vows to avenge her father ...

She looked across the hall, caught her reflection in a small mirror on the wall.

Remind you of anyone else you know?

Magistrae was waiting faithfully beside Leona's bath, slipping a long robe about her mistress. Leona seemed pensive, chewing her fingernail and staring at the small statue of Trelene that also served as the water spout. She sighed as Magistrae tried to rub the tension from her shoulders.

"What troubles, love?" the older woman asked.

Leona smiled. "How do you know I'm troubled?"

"These were the hands that delivered you into the world," Magistrae smiled in return. "This was the bosom that nursed you. Though I'll not claim to always know your mind, I know when dark thoughts fill it, sure and true."

Leona closed her eyes as Magistrae worked a knot in her neck.

". . . I'm having dreams again, Anthea. About Mother."

"O, love," Magistrae cooed. "Long years have passed since then."

"I know that, as I sit here now. But I'm always a child in the dreams. A little girl, small and afraid. Just as I was when . . ."

Leona chewed a fingernail and shook her head, silence ringing in the bathhouse.

"It's an awful thing," she finally sighed. "To live in fear."

"Then do not, love. Look how far you've come. Look at all you've built."

"I *do*. But all I've built stands at the edge of ruin, Anthea." The dona breathed deep, clenched her jaw. "I need *coin*. Marcus left me with little beyond these walls and the funds I spent reshaping them. He was not a careful man with his money."

"You two were well suited, then."

Leona smiled sadly. "I deserve that, I suppose."

"Do you miss him, love?" Magistrae asked, swiftly changing subjects.

". . . No," Leona sighed. "Marcus was fair enough, but I never loved him. And . . . I hated needing him. Does that make me awful?"

"It makes you honest," the older woman smiled.

Silence fell again, Leona gnawing at her fingertips and staring at the wall. The dona seemed younger in here than she did in the yard, her armor cast aside with none but trusted eyes to see. Almost like the little girl she spoke of being in her dreams. Magistrae kept kneading her shoulders, occasionally chewing her lip. When the woman spoke again, it was with obvious trepidation.

"Leona, I know you and your father—"

"No, Anthea."

"But he has coin aplenty, surely if you—"

"*No!*" She turned on her nurse, blue eyes flashing. "You forget your place. And I'll not hear another word of it. I will *die* before I accept a single copper beggar from that man, do you understand me?"

The magistrae's eyes found the floor.

"Aye, Domina," she said.

Watching from the shadows, Mia found herself saddened. She could sense Anthea was truly concerned for Leona, could see the barrier between them had been worn thin over decades. But as much as Anthea cared for her mistress, she'd always be a servant. Though she'd fed Leona at her breast, Anthea would never be her mother.

Still, it was one thing to listen in on a conversation that might decide her fate, entirely another intrude on such a private moment. Information was power, and power was advantage. But Mia had learned enough here.

Stealing down the corridor behind Mister Kindly, she found the broad dining hall. All the old furniture was still here—the long dining table where her parents had entertained, the wooden chairs she'd crawled and hid among as a little girl. Some of the same tapestries hung on the walls—Goddess Tsana wreathed in flame, Goddess Trelene cloaked in rolling waves.

Footsteps. Approaching. *Clink* thump. *Clink* thump.

Mia and Mister Kindly slipped behind one of the long, heavy drapes. She could have just cloaked herself in shadows and listened to Executus and Leona talk, but in truth she wanted to see their faces. See if the armor Leona wore outside these walls was the same armor she wore for this legend of the arena, who served her instead of the man who'd raised him up a champion.

Arkades limped into the room, found it empty. Jaw clenched, he sat at the long table to wait. Mia saw he'd bathed, brushed his beard and his long salt-and-pepper hair. The scar at his face and his weathered skin made it hard to tell, but she supposed him in his mid-thirties. Life on the sand hadn't been kind, but his physique, the sheer magnetism from a life spent winning victories before the adoring crowd . . .

He'd put aside the leather armor he wore in the yard, dressed in finery instead. His dark doublet was embroidered with the Falcons of Remus and the Lions of Leonides. His walking stick was also set with a lion's head. Mia again wondered at his loyalties. Here he was, serving Leona. And yet he still wore her father's lion on his chest.

Looking about, Arkades lifted a flask from inside his doublet like a thief, took a long, deep pull.

"We have goblets if you prefer, Executus."

Arkades startled, rising to his feet as Leona appeared in the doorway behind, carrying a bottle of wine and two goblets. His eyes widened a touch at the sight of her, and Mia couldn't help but raise an eyebrow herself. Leona's hair was wet, she was barefoot and still clad in her bathrobe, which was tied only loosely. If one looked hard enough from the right angle, very little was being left to the imagination.

"Mi Dona," Arkades said, bowing with his eyes to the floor and studiously avoiding looking hard from any kind of angle at all.

Mia noted the small smirk on Leona's face as she walked to the head of the table, flopped into a chair. She poured herself a glass, putting her foot up on the wood. Her robe slipped up, exposing her leg all the way to the thigh.

"Help yourself," she smiled.

". . . Mi Dona?"

Leona motioned to the second goblet, the bottle.

"It's awful, I'm afraid. But it cleaves to the task. Here." Leona leaned forward, poured a glass and pushed it across the table. Arkades kept his eyes fixed anywhere but on her chest, practically writhing as he returned to his chair.

She keeps him off-balance with it, Mia noted. *He's ten years her senior. Twice her size. A warrior of a hundred battles, champion of the* magni, *and the poor bastard doesn't even know which way to look when she walks into the room.*

"So," Leona said, leaning back and sipping from her cup. "You have thoughts. Ones most pressing that simply *must* be shared."

Arkades nodded, his embarrassment evaporating as talk turned to the collegium.

"Matilius, Mi Dona."

"What of him?"

"His sale to Caito—"

"Was a necessity," she interrupted. "The purse at Blackbridge was not enough to cover expenses this month. Our creditors press, and they will have their coin."

"But Caito . . . ," Arkades began. "Pandemonium is no place for a man to die."

Leona downed her cup with one swallow.

"Matilius was not a man," she said, pouring another. "He was a slave."

"You do not truly believe that, Mi Dona."

Arkades stared at the younger woman across the table. Mia could see a moment's softness in her stare, replaced quickly with iron.

"Do I not?" she asked.

"Matilius was gladiatii," Arkades said. "He won glory and honor for this collegium. For *you,* Dona. He was not our finest blade, true, but he served you with all he had."

"It was not enough. I have mouths aplenty and they all cost money. Our debts mount with every turn and my purse is all but empty."

"And how came that to be, I wonder?" Executus scowled. "When you spend a living fortune on a single recruit?"

"Ah," Leona sighed. "We come to the rub quickly this time."

"For the thousand silver pieces you paid for that girl, you could have fed this collegium for the rest of the year!"

Mia's ears pricked up at her mention, eyes narrowing.

"Did you watch her at Blackbridge?" Leona asked. "Did you see the way she ignited the crowd?"

"We have Furian for that!" Arkades all but shouted, rising from his chair. "The Unfallen is this collegium's champion! That slip can't even lift a damn shield!"

"Then we fight her Caravaggio style. Twin blades. No shield. The crowd will adore it, and her. A girl her size, gutting men twice as big? And looking the way she does? Four Daughters, the crowd won't be able to see for the swelling of their cocks."

Arkades sighed, pushing his knuckles into his eyes.

"When you started this collegium, Dona, you asked for my aid."

"I did." Leona toyed with the neckline of her robe. "And I am ever grateful for it."

"So with all respect, my counsel must carry weight. I have known you since you were a child. I know you grew up around the *venatus.* But there is a world of difference between watching from the boxes, and running a collegium."

Leona's eyes and voice turned cold. "Think you, I do not know that?"

"I think you wish to spite your father."

Leona's eyes narrowed, her lips thin. "You overstep, Executus."

Arkades raised a hand in supplication at Leona's outrage. "Daughters know, I remember how he treated you and your mother. And your rage has no lack of merit. But I fear outbidding him on that girl so steeply proves your mind is clouded on matters of *familia.* Mine is clear. I fought for years on the sand, trained your father's gladiatii years after that. And I tell you now, that girl is no champion. She has a fox's cunning, but she's not half the gladiatii Furian is. There will come a time when guile and wit won't serve her. When it's only she, and a sword, and a man she has to kill."

Arkades leaned on the table, staring into Leona's eyes.

"And she. Will. Fail."

Mia's stomach sank to hear Arkades talk so. She thought she'd impressed him with her showing at Blackbridge, but the man seemed utterly blind to her merits.

Leona's eyes fell and Arkades remembered himself, sat back in his chair with an apologetic grunt. The dona downed the rest of her wine, stared into the empty goblet for endless minutes. When she spoke, her voice was so soft Mia almost couldn't hear.

"Perhaps it was ill advised, spending such a sum. But I . . . I didn't want to see him win again. Mother warned me when I was a little girl. 'Never stand against your father,' she told me. 'He *always* wins.'"

She looked up at her executus, eyes bright with fury.

"But not this time," she spat. "Never again. I want him on his knees. I want him to look up into my eyes and know it was me who put him there. I want to drink his suffering like the finest wine." She hurled the bottle into the wall just beside Mia's head, shattering it into a thousand splinters. "Not this fucking slop."

She hung her head and sighed.

"Even selling Matilius, we owe another dozen creditors."

". . . How much?"

"*Much.* And the points accrue by the turn." Leona curled a fist, knuckles turning white. "Daughters, if only Marcus hadn't died. Another few years on a justicus's stipend, I'd have had enough to do this properly. If I find the ones who took him from me . . ."

"It matters not," Arkades said. "We can pay whatever is owed with the coin we make from the Crow's sale. And from there, we will drive Furian all the way to the *magni*. We have three *venata* between now and truelight, three laurels to win a qualifying berth. You *will* have your victory, Dona," Arkades vowed. "*If* you let me give it to you. Have faith in me. As I have faith in you."

Mia looked at the pair of them, each alone, and then together. Leona's robe, the brazen sexuality, the way she used her body to put Arkades off guard—it made a kind of sense, knowing she'd grown up in the home of a domineering father.

But Arkades . . .

The fire in his eyes. The fervor in his voice when he made his vow. He was champion of the most brutal competition the Republic had devised. Ten years her senior. Separated by the barrier between the wealthy born and former property.

And yet . . .

Mia shook her head. Five minutes with them alone and she knew exactly why Arkades had left Leonides and come to serve his wayward daughter.

The poor fool's actually in love with her.

Leona placed her empty goblet on the table and sighed.

I wonder if she knows?

"You are my executus," the dona said. "I know you gave up much to come here. And I would see that faith rewarded."

Leona toyed with the lip of her cup, nodded, as if to herself.

"I will heed your counsel. We will fight the Crow at the *venatus* in Stormwatch at month's end. Not the Ultima, we have our champion for that. Some minor bout, so as not to damage her. With good fortune, she'll comport herself in fashion fine enough to regain some measure of the cost we paid for her."

Mia's stomach dropped into her boots.

Black Mother . . .

"You will sell her, then?" Arkades asked.

Leona looked to the tapestry on the wall. The goddess of fire, sword in hand, shield raised and wreathed in flame.

"Unless she proves herself Tsana made flesh?"

Leona heaved a sigh.

"Very well. I will sell her."

Arkades nodded, Leona poured herself another glass.

"Now, if you are well satisfied?" she asked.

The executus grunted apology, stood slow. With a deep bow to his dona, the man limped from the room, his walking stick and iron leg beating a tired retreat down the stone stairs. Leona sat alone, swallowing deep from her cup, clouded eyes fixed on some nothing only she could see. Running idle fingers across her collarbone, down the pale skin of her throat. Taking another draft and licking her lips.

Mia stood silent in the shadows, watching close. Trying to ponder this woman, a way to sway her mind. If she could fashion some way for Furian to lose favor, poison him before a bout, perhaps? If Mia could raise herself in the dona's esteem . . .

One thing was certain—she could *not* be sold.

Leona chewed her lip, blinking as she woke from her reverie. She looked to the open door, stilled herself as if listening, The hour was late, the villa was quiet. Finishing her wine, Leona stood, gathered her robe about herself and, almost on tiptoe, quietly stole out into the corridor.

Mia frowned, narrowed her eyes.

Leona was mistress of this place.

Why creep about like a thief in her own house?

Mia slipped from behind the curtain and crept to the doorway, silent as death. Peering beyond the frame, she saw Leona at the stairs leading down to the third level. She ducked out of sight as the dona looked about, then stole quickly downward.

"*. . . perhaps we have risked enough this eve, mia . . .*"

Ignoring the shadowcat's warning, Mia followed on whisper-soft feet. Moving like a shadow, she followed Leona down to the third, then second level. Here the dona paused, waiting for Captain Gannicus and another houseguard to walk past, murmuring among themselves. When the guards were gone, Leona crept on, Mia following like a wraith until she reached the first floor.

Mia watched from the stair above as the dona peered about, listening in the still for the guards. Sneaking out from the stairwell, Leona crept to a single wooden door at the far end of the corridor. Out of sight. Out of earshot.

Ah. It makes a kind of sense now.

The tirade at dinner. The insistence that their domina's will alone was what mattered, despite the sale of Matilius. The fervor in his eyes when he spoke of his mistress, his devotion to these walls.

Furian.

Leona reached into a pocket for an iron key, unlocked the door. The Unfallen was waiting on the other side, long dark hair framing his beautiful face, the smile that curled his lips as he saw his mistress. With one last glance the way she'd come, Leona threw her arms around Furian's neck, dragged him down into a hungry kiss. And stepping inside, the dona of the house shut the door behind her.

"*. . . interesting . . . ,*" came a cool whisper at her ear.

"Aye." Mia scowled in reply. "But just once, I'd like to look about and find my life was a little *less* interesting."

"*. . . o, what fun would that be . . . ?*"

Mia raised the knuckles to the shadowcat. Mister Kindly only chuckled in reply. And without another sound, the pair stole off into the shadows they so loved.

CHAPTER 16

HONEY

Wsssshhthunk.

The arrow struck the strawman, close to his heart.

Wsssshhthunk.

Another struck closer than the first.

Wsssshhthunk.

A third struck the target, right in its featureless face.

Mia lowered her bow, the fingers on her right hand throbbing.

"Fine work," Bryn said beside her. "Where'd you learn to shoot like that?"

"Read about it in a book," Mia growled. "When I was done fucking your father."

The Vaanian girl chuckled, lifting her own bow and drawing back the string.

"Rough nevernight, little Crow?"

Mia set her bow aside, wincing at the pain. "I've had better."

"Not with my poor old da, I'll wager," Bryn grinned.

The blonde let half a dozen arrows fly in quick succession. Three punched through the strawman's heart, two into its throat, the last in its head.

"Maw's teeth . . . ," Mia breathed.

"You should see her shoot with her good hand," Byern said, walking past the pair with a bunch of leather tackle slung over his shoulder.

"Ah, that'd just be showing off," Bryn replied.

The twins had left Crow's Nest early that morning, just as they did every second turn. Per Executus's command, Mia had accompanied them, trailing behind like a dog with no bone. Arkades limped with them to the gates of the keep, Mia trying to keep the scowl from her face as she remembered how the man had spoken about her the nevernight before. Arkades had made no mention of her impending sale, the sword hanging over her head. It wasn't as if he were offering a chance to prove herself, no. It was clear Executus simply wanted her gone.

It stung her pride, truth told. More than it should have. Mia didn't know why she wanted his approval. But in the intervening hours, hurt pride had turned to burning rage. She didn't have time to waste anymore—being sold to another master was a risk she simply couldn't take. She needed to prove herself. Not to Arkades, but to Dona Leona.

The fact that she was bedding Furian aside, Mia suspected the dona still saw some measure of value in her. Mia had ignited the audience at Blackbridge, and the crowd's reaction had set some small ember of respect burning in Leona's breast. Mia needed a way to coax that spark into flame.

The *venatus* at Stormwatch would decide her future, in this collegium, and in the arena. Her plan to murder Duomo and Scaeva hung in the balance.

She'd no idea, yet, how to tip the scales.

Mia, Bryn and Byern had been escorted by four of Dona Leona's houseguards into the rough scrubland behind Crow's Nest. After half a mile, they'd reached an oblong track, perhaps a mile long, marked in the ochre sand with flat stones. A stable stood to one side, and Byern marched inside with his harness and tackle while Bryn loosed quiver after quiver of arrows into the three strawmen targets.

The houseguards stood in the shade, paying no mind. Mia realized how easy it would be for Bryn and Byern to escape—a few arrows into each guard's chest, two horses, and the pair would be dust on the horizon. But, even if they somehow made their way in the Republic with brands on their cheeks, the twins would be condemning every other gladiatii in Leona's stable to execution in the arena.

She had to hand it to the administratii—the heartless bastards knew their trade.

Mia's fingers were bruising badly, and it hurt to hold the bow for long, so she mostly contented herself watching Bryn's form. The girl could shoot blind, left-handed as well as right. After emptying another quiver, she took off her boots, clutched her bow between her toes. And, in what might have been the most astonishing display of dexterity Mia had ever witnessed, slowly stood on her hands, arched her spine and loosed a shot with her *feet,* skewering the strawman in the heart.

"Speaking of showing off . . . ," Mia said.

Bryn curled smoothly over and stood, brushing the dust off her palms.

"It's child's play when you and the targets aren't moving," she shrugged. Turning to the stable, she called to her brother. " 'Byss and blood, Byern, are you rigging those horses or asking them to marry you?"

"I've asked before, they both said no," came the reply.

"Well, they have excellent taste."

Bryn's twin emerged from the stable, carrying a great shield and leading a pair of horses harnessed to a long, sleek chariot. The beasts were white as clouds, muscles carved in marble. Despite herself, Mia felt a small pang at the sight of them, thinking of her own stallion, Bastard. After he'd rescued her from near death in the Ysiiri desert, Mia had set him free rather than lock him up in the Red Church stable. She hoped he was wandering somewhere pleasant, siring as many of his own bastards as he could.

She missed him.

She missed a lot about that time, truth told . . .

"Sister Crow," Byern waved to the horses with a flourish, "meet Briar and Rose."

Mia studied the pair pulling Byern's chariot. Like every horse she'd ever met, the beasts were skittish around her, so she gave them a wide berth. The fact that she called the only horse who'd ever tolerated her "Bastard" spoke to her feeling about the beasts in general, but she knew a fine specimen when she saw it.

"They're mares," Mia noted. "Most equillai I've seen run stallions."

"Most equillai you've seen are idiots," Byern replied.

His sister nodded. "Stallions think with their cocks. Mares know how to keep their heads in a crisis. As with horses, so with humans, eh, brother mine?"

Byern raised a finger in warning. "Respect your elders, pup."

"You're *two minutes* older than me, Byern."

"Two minutes and fourteen seconds. Now, are you coming or no?"

"Stand out in the center," Bryn directed Mia, nodding at the dusty track. "When I give the word, you let fly with the best you have."

". . . You want me to shoot you?" Mia asked, eyebrow raised.

Bryn laughed aloud. "I want you to try. And remember to breathe."

With that, the Vaanian jumped into the chariot beside her brother. With a snap of the reins and a wink to Mia (met with a punch in the arm from his sister), Byern led the horses onto the track.

The chariot was two-wheeled, broad and deep enough to allow the siblings to trade sides. It was red, trimmed in gold paint, carved with the falcon of the Remus Collegium. The great shield Byern carried was also painted with a red falcon, and its edges were crenelated like the walls of a fortified keep.

Mia walked until she stood in the island of ochre dirt, surrounded by the oblong track. Strawman targets were arranged in a single row down the middle of the island, to Mia's left and right. At a real *venatus,* those strawmen would be *real* men—murderers and rapists set to be executed *e equillai* before the adoring crowd.*

---

*Equillai are a subset of gladiatii, a tradition imported from Liis and adopted by the Itreyan Republic with enormous enthusiasm—equillai races are a highlight at any

Mia watched as the twins tore around the track, faster and faster. Bryn's topknot whipped in the wind behind her, Byern's bronze skin gleaming in the sunlight.

"Ready?" Bryn called to Mia.

"Aye," the girl replied.

"Let fly, little Crow!"

Mia sighed, drew a bead on Byern's chest. She tracked the chariot, breathing slow as Bryn had instructed despite the ache in her wounded fingers. And as the pair wheeled around the corner, she loosed a shot right at the handsome Vaanian's chest.

Byern raised his shield, blocked the shot easily. Firing through the crenelation in the raised shield, Bryn loosed four shots, two of which struck the dirt at Mia's sandals, the other two striking the strawman closest to her.

"I said shoot us, not ask us to dance!" Bryn shouted.

"I can dance with you later, if you wish," Byern called.

Bryn punctured another strawman, and her brother leaned out of the chariot at a precarious angle, scooping up a small stone off the track with his free hand. Mia scowled, trying to shake the feeling she was being made a fool of.

"All right, fuck this . . . ," she muttered.

Mia began firing, shot after shot as the pair galloped around the track. And

---

venatus, and the men and women who take to the track can win renown as great as any warrior on the sands.

Equillai fight in pairs: a charioteer, known as the *sagmae* (saddle), and an archer, known as the *flagillae* (whip). Equillai contests are held on an oblong track, marked in the center of the arena, and traditionally involve four teams. The contest is run over nine laps of the circuit, and the winners decided on points accrued over the entire course.

Points are scored in a number of ways. First, a kill shot on any of the prisoners in the center of the track. The prisoners are lashed to posts and cannot run, so the points scored are low—only two apiece.

A successful lap of the circuit also earns two points. A wounding shot on a member of an opposing equillai team is worth three points, a kill shot, five. Laurel wreaths, known as *coronae,* are also thrown onto the track at random intervals, and an equillai team scores one point for every *coronae* scooped up from the dirt. However, a shot to the opposing teams' horses is penalized by ten points—the contests are meant to be between the equillai themselves, and the softhearted among you will be pleased to learn attacking their mounts is deemed unsporting.

Murdering fellow equillai as dramatically as possible is perfectly acceptable and, indeed, encouraged.

though her aim was true, she soon realized Bryn and Byern were both masters. Byern's shield was impregnable, and his skill at driving his horses was almost equal to his sister's archery. At the most humiliating point, Byern blocked a shot whistling straight for Bryn's throat, while simultaneously leaning out of the chariot to scoop up a stone, holding the reins in his damned *teeth*. Meanwhile, Bryn peppered every strawman with a dozen shots, pausing occasionally to make Mia dance by loosing a shot at her toes.

Nine laps later, the pair pulled to a stop in front of her. Byern hopped out of the chariot, bowed low. "Do you prefer the waltz or the Balinna, Mi Dona?"

Bryn punched her brother's arm again, smiled at Mia. "Fine shooting. You almost got me there, once or twice."

"Liar," Mia said. "I never came close."

Bryn winced, nodded sadly. "I was trying to make you feel better."

"Where did you learn to do that?"

"Our da raised horses," Byern said. "And Bryn's been a daemon with a bow since she could walk."

Mia shook her head. She knew she shouldn't ask. Shouldn't get close. But truth was, she liked this pair. Byern's easy smile and Bryn's self-assured swagger.

"How did you come to be here?" she asked, looking at the track about them, the silhouette of Crow's Nest in the distance. "This place?"

Bryn sniffed. "Bad harvest. Three years back. Village didn't have the grain to pay our tithe to the Itreyan administratii. They locked our laird in irons, had him and his whole familia flogged in the stocks."

"We didn't like that," Byern explained. "Me and Bryn were too young for our da to let us go, but anyone big enough to swing a sword marched up to the magistrate's door. Dragged him down to the stocks and gave him a flogging right back."

"He didn't like *that*," Bryn said. "You can imagine what came next."

"Legionaries," Mia said.

"Aye," Byern nodded. "Five centuries of the bastards. Killed every rebel. Burned every home. Sold everyone left standing. Sis and me included."

"But you weren't even involved," Mia said. "Your da didn't let you rise."

"You think the Itreyans care?" Byern smiled lopsided. "This whole Republic, the Kingdom before it, even. It's built on the back of free labor. But now, Liis, Ysiir, Vaan, they're all under Itreyan control. So where do the new slaves come from? When there are no lands left to conquer?"

"They build a Republic that's unfair in its bones," Bryn said. "That bene-fits the few, not the many. But the few have *steel*. And men they pay to wield it, unthinkingly. So, when someone among the many rises against the injus-tice, the brutality, the system locks them in irons. Makes of them an example for others, and with the very same stroke, sends one more body to be branded. One more pair of hands to build their roads, raise their walls, work their forges, all for a pittance and fear of the lash."

Mia shook her head. "That's . . ."

"Bullshit?" Byern offered.

"Aye."

"That's life in the Republic," Bryn shrugged.

Mia sighed, strands of raven black stuck to the sweat on her face.

All her life, she'd never questioned the rightness of it. Never stopped to look about her and see the people below her. The folk who'd walked like voice-less ghosts about their home, their apartments in the Ribs. The men and women who'd dressed her, made her meals, taught her numbers and letters. Her mother and father had cared for them, no doubt. Rewarded those who served well. But still, they'd *served*. Not because they wanted to. Because the alternative was the lash, or death.

She felt as if scales were falling from her eyes. The true horror of the Re-public she'd been raised inside unveiled in all its awful majesty.

But still . . .

Scaeva.

Duomo.

Their names burned like flame in her mind. Like a lighthouse, ever guid-ing her way no matter how dark the world became. The injustice, the cruelty of this system, aye, she could see it. But what in truth could she actually do to change it? Without risking all she'd worked for? Closing her eyes, she could still see her father, swinging on the end of his rope in the forum. Her mother in the Philosopher's Stone, light fading in her stare as she pushed Mia's bloody hand away, and with her dying breath whispered:

"Not my daughter . . . Just . . . her shadow."

The memories brought rage, and the rage tasted good. Reminding her of who she was, why she was here. To defeat the greatest gladiatii in the Repub-lic. To stand before her familia's murderers triumphant and open their throats, one by one. And she was going to have a hard time doing that if she was sold off like a leg of beef at market.

Excelling in the *venatus* at Stormwatch. That was her concern.

Her first, her *only* concern.

And so, despite the pain in her injured hand, she nocked another arrow to her bow and nodded at Bryn.

"All right. Tell me what I'm doing wrong. And then, we'll go again."

So she's apparently hocked herself to the eyeteeth," Mia said, dragging on her cigarillo. "And Arkades has convinced her to sell me to fend off her creditors."

Ashlinn leaned back in her divan, popped a grape in her mouth. "Bastard."

"After I killed a dozen people at Blackbridge. He's got no thought for anyone on the sand, save Furian. '*He* is the champion of this collegium.' '*He* will bring you your victory, Mi Dona.' O, aye, he'll bring her victory all right, you dozy fuck. Right after he brings her to climax. Should've heard the pair of them going at it . . ."

Mia breathed a lungful of gray smoke as if it were flame.

"Arkades stuck me on a leash in the circle, yesterturn. Near broke my hand with those ridiculous shields. Calling me 'girl' as if the word were kin for 'dogshit.'"

"*Fucking* bastard," Ash said, eating another grape.

Mia's eyes narrowed at the girl sitting opposite her.

"Look, are you just agreeing to humor me?"

"Mostly," Ash smirked. "But it's good to get these things off your tits, Corvere."

"*. . . i trust you are feeling better now . . .*"

Mia looked at the not-cat curled on her shoulder. "You're starting in on me too?"

"*. . . moaning or thinking. which is more productive . . . ?*"

"It seems Mister Jolly and I agree on something for once," Ashlinn said.

"*. . . had i true claws, little viper, i would cut the tongue fr— . . .*"

"Eclipse and I have been snooping about," Ash continued as if the shadowcat hadn't spoken. "Your domina's debts certainly aren't common knowledge. She buys the finest at market. Dresses like a queen. I suspect that's half her problem."

Eclipse raised her head from Mia's lap, voice echoing through the floor.

"*. . . TOO ENAMORED BY WHAT FOLK THINK OF HER BY FAR . . .*"

"Probably doesn't want word getting back to her father," Mia said, crushing out her smoke. "Doesn't want to give him the satisfaction of seeing her struggling."

Ash tossed a bunch of grapes to Mia, speaking around her mouthful.

"So the way I see it, we have a few options," she said.

"*. . . THE SIMPLEST IS TO PUT LEONA'S CREDITORS IN THE DIRT . . .*"

"Aye," Ashlinn nodded. "It'd take some asking about, but I know for a fact the only place she'd be getting her grain is a merchant named Anatolio. It just so happens he's fond of his whores, and I know exactly where he dips his—"

"We're not going to top some poor bastard whose only crime is extending a line of credit to my domina," Mia scowled.

"*. . . IT SOUNDS AS IF WE WOULD NEED TO END MORE THAN ONE . . .*"

Ash nodded. "She's almost certainly in hock to the harbormaster. Maybe the builders who worked on the Nest. And her seamstresses wou—"

"Aye, aye, I understand," Mia said. "We'd probably need to murder half the Rest. Which we're not going to do. If the collegium puts in a good showing, Leona might be able to secure patronage from some rich marrowborn bastard after the next *venatus*. So for now, it's smarter to just turn our eyes to—"

"Stormwatch," Ash nodded. "Aye. The only way to ensure your place in the Remus Collegium is to win at Stormwatch *venatus*. And win grand."

"We don't even know what shape the *venatus* there will take."

"*. . . NOT YET . . .*"

Ashlinn nodded. "That's why you've got me and wolfie, here. There's a ship bound for the 'Watch leaving amorrow. We can be there in a week, can scout the workings at the arena and know exactly what you're in for. Then, we plan accordingly, give you a victory that will outshine even Leona's little fuckboy."

"I'd never have picked it if I'd not seen it," Mia sighed. "She acts far too proper."

Ash shrugged. "She wouldn't be the first rich woman to pay for a fine stud to scratch her itches. Having to keep it secret is probably half the thrill."

Mia chewed her grapes, brow creased in thought. The fruit was delicious, and a welcome change from the endless array of stew and porridge the gladiatii were served for eve and mornmeal every turn.*

"Good grapes, these," she muttered.

---

*In the weeks since Blackbridge, Mia had learned the emaciated cook who served Dona Leona was named "Finger," though nobody among the stable seemed to know why. Most of the gladiatii assumed he'd earned the name by being finger thin, though Butcher insisted that he'd been a member of a braavi gang whose favored means of thuggery involved chopping off people's less-essential digits and stuffing them in orifices not usually designed for stuffing.

Whatever the origins of his moniker, Finger's culinary skill was only slightly more impressive than a drunken blind man's skill at finding the pisspot. His porridge had

"Never let it be said I don't love you, Corvere."

Mia looked up sharply at that, but Ash was leaning back in her chair, dropping grapes into her mouth. Her boots were up on the divan's armrest, legs crossed, leather-clad. Her hair was getting longer, falling down her back in red waves.

Red. Like the blood on her hands.

And yet, here Mia was. Trusting her. She knew Ashlinn wanted the Ministry dead. And Mia and Mercurio were Ash's best chance back into the Mountain to see the deed done. But was that mutual hatred of the Red Church enough? Was Ash playing a longer game? It wasn't like she hadn't done so before.

Ashlinn Järnheim had lied to her.

Ashlinn Järnheim was poison.

So why had her lips tasted like honey?

Mia ran her hand over her eyes, nodded slow.

"Head to Stormwatch with Eclipse," she said. "The more we know, the better the chance I'll have at a victory Leona can't help but reward. I imagine we'll be arriving a few turns before the *venatus* begins. I'll need to know everything by then."

Ash nodded, finishing her mouthful and wiping her lips on her sleeve.

"So," she said. "Leona's stud. Furian, the Unfallen."

"*. . . THE DARKIN . . .*"

"Is he going to be a problem?"

Mia shook her head. "Nothing you need worry yourself with."

"But I *do* worry."

"Because without me, you don't get the Church, aye?"

Dark eyes stared into glittering blue. Looking for the lies behind them.

"Look, I know we've blood in our past," Ashlinn said. "But there's more than just red between us. I'm not just here for the Church. And I'm surely not cooped up in this dingy little shithole for the glamor of it. And you must know that, or you'd not be here with me, no matter how many shadowwolves you have watching over my shoulder."

Mia stared. Ashlinn's eyes. Ashlinn's hands. Ashlinn's lips. The girl simply stared back, letting the silence ask her questions for her.

---

the consistency of runny snot, and one evemeal, Mia found a suspiciously human-looking toe bone in her stew.

Needless to say, Fang, who always nosed about the table looking for scraps, was growing fonder of Mia by the nevernight.

Mia ignored them all.

"Good luck in Stormwatch," she finally said. "Keep an eye on the harbor. Send Eclipse when we arrive and let me know the lay of the games." She stood swift, dragging her hair over her shoulder and avoiding Ashlinn's stare.

"You're leaving already?"

Mia nodded. "I'd best be off before I'm missed. Sidonius is a decent sort, but I've no wish for anyone else to find out what I am."

Ashlinn said nothing, watching Mia walk to the window, climb over the sill and disappear from sight. Without a final word. Without a parting glance.

Shaking her head, Ash dropped another grape into her mouth.

"That much is obvious, Corvere," she sighed.

CHAPTER 17
STORMWATCH

Mia paced back and forth in her cage, eyes fixed on the sand.

She, Sidonius, Bladesinger, Wavewaker and Butcher were all locked in cells at the edge of Stormwatch arena, sunken beneath the floor. Small barred windows let them watch the *venatus* while they waited for their turn before the crowd, Mia stalking about the cage and pondering the events that led her here.

Just as she'd told Ashlinn, the gladiatii of the Remus Collegium had trained another week in the sweltering suns before setting out for Stormwatch. Mia's hand was mended enough to go back to practice after a few turns, though for all the attention Arkades gave, she mightn't have bothered—it was clear all hopes were being pinned on Furian, Bryn, and Byern to win their berth in the *Venatus Magni*. Eavesdropping on Dona Leona and the magistrae, Mister Kindly had learned inquiries were already being made about Mia's sale. There were a few interested parties—a pleasure house in Whitekeep, a local magistrate in need of a bodyguard he could occasionally slip his cock into, and of course Varro Caito and his Pandemonium. Not a real sanguila among them.

Mia's entire plan hung upon victory at Stormwatch.

They'd traveled to the city via the *Gloryhound,* arriving a few turns before the *venatus* was set to begin. The port was abuzz with excitement, and folks had journeyed from miles about for the games; every inn, bedsit and outhouse was filled to bursting.* Ashlinn had sent Eclipse to visit Mia in her cell, and the shadowwolf had spoken of all she and Ashlinn had learned about the upcoming games. Over the next few nevernights, passing messages via the daemon, Mia and Ashlinn had formulated their plan.

Now, all that remained was to execute it.

Mia watched the equillai roar around the track, the percussion of their horses' hooves vibrating through the stone walls. Bryn and Byern were doing well—placed second with five laps to go. But if Mia thought the Vaanians were skilled, she was amazed watching Leonides's team in action. Leona's father fielded only the best, and his equillai were no exception; a Dweymeri *sagmae* whose lion-crested shield seemed impenetrable, and a pretty Liisian *flagellae* whose bowmanship was equal to Bryn's, if not better.

"Stonekiller and Armando," Bladesinger murmured, standing at the bars beside Mia. "The b-best equillai in the Republic. The . . . crowd adore them."

Despite a stunning kill shot from Bryn on another team's *sagmae*, the Lions of Leonides simply proved the better, and after nine laps, they stood the victors. Stonekiller and Armando dismounted their chariot together, fingers

---

*Stormwatch is a port in the northwest of Itreya, and one of the oldest cities in the Republic. Its beginnings were humble—a simple lighthouse on the northern banks of the Bay of Tempests, meant to warn ships away from treacherous reefs. Despite best efforts, enough wrecks still occurred that a community of beachcombers built up on the coast nearby, and eventually raised a city known as Stormwall.

Scandal struck some years later, when Stormwall's lighthouse keeper, Flavius Severis, was accused by his friend, Dannilus Calidius, of steering ships onto the rocks to further his own fortunes. Calidius built a second lighthouse on the southern mouth of the bay, and founded a second city, naming it Cloudwatch.

The rivalry between the familia Severis and Calidius, and thus, Stormwall and Cloudwatch, was legendary. Several bloody conflicts broke out over the years, and both lighthouses were destroyed. King Francisco I, the Great Unifier, who gave no shits for "rights" and "wrongs" but just wanted his "bloody ships to stop crashing on the bloody rocks," threatened to crucify every Severis and Calidius he could find to ensure peace was restored.

The solution, however, did not lay in violence. Unbeknownst to their parents, a daughter of the Familia Severis and a son of the Familia Calidius met and, in defiance of all common sense, fell madly in lust. Though the story had all the makings of a classic Itreyan tragedy, the tale resolved itself remarkably peacefully, and only one best friend, a second cousin (who nobody much liked anyway), and a small terrier named Baron Woofsalot were murdered in the resulting drama. The pair married, peace was brokered, and many babies were had. Over time, the newly named Stormwatch became one of the wealthiest ports in Francisco's kingdom.

The city stands to this turn—an enduring testament, gentlefriends, to the power of teenage hormones and parents' desire for adorable grandchildren.

intertwined and hands held aloft in victory as the crowd around them thundered. It was well known that the pair were lovers, and their astonishing skill coupled with the affection they showed each other made them crowd favorites. The fact that they were undefeated didn't hurt either.

Mia felt bad for Bryn and Byern, worse that the Remus Collegium was still absent its third laurel. But, in truth, her mind was elsewhere. She looked sidelong at Bladesinger, the ghastly greenish hue of the woman's skin beneath her tattoos.

"Feeling better?" she asked.

"Think s-so," the woman nodded. "The w-worst seems . . ."

Bladesinger's eyes widened and she fell to her knees, once again vomiting all over the floor. Sidonius lay where he was, barely able to groan as the puke spattered his sandals. Butcher rolled away from the splashback, his own cheeks ballooning.

"At least empty your g-guts outside . . . the cell, sister," he moaned.

"Fuggoff," Bladesinger groaned, a long string of drool and puke dangling from her lips. "Before I s-slap your ugly . . ."

Another fountain of vomit exploded from Bladesinger's mouth, this time hitting Wavewaker, who in turn lunged up onto his knees and aimed a spray of puke out through the bars. The stench rolled over Mia in warm, cloying waves and she stood on tiptoes, pressed her lips between the bars and breathed deep of the comparatively pleasant aroma of blood and horseshit outside.

"Four fucking Daughters," she swore.

"Pray all you like," came a growl. "I fear they're not listening."

Turning, Mia saw Executus Arkades, standing outside the cell with hands on hips. Surveying the puke-soaked straw, his best gladiatii lying about like wounded after a war. Maggot stood beside him, nose screwed up at the stench as she looked the fallen gladiatii over. Dona Leona hung back, wearing a gown of beautiful scarlet silk and a thoroughly disgusted expression.

"Blessed Aa," she said. "All of them?"

"Save Bryn and Byern," Arkades replied, glancing at Mia. "And the Crow. Even Furian is bursting at both ends. Everseeing only knows what caused it."

Mia kept her face as stone, met Arkades's eyes with an expression innocent enough to shame a sister in the Sorority of Flame.* Of course, she knew exactly what had caused the bout of intestinal distress among her brothers and

---

*An offshoot of Aa's ministry, fully sanctioned by the Church, devoted to worship of the goddess Tsana. Consisting entirely of women, the sorority's vows include

sisters of the collegium. Ashlinn had snuck rather more Mishap into their evemeal than Mia would have liked—the results didn't need to be quite so explosive, truth told. But Ash had never been Spiderkiller's finest student.

"Food poisoning," Maggot declared, kneeling by a puddle of vomit. Reaching through the bars, she pressed her palm to Butcher's sweat-filmed brow. "Not fatal, I think. But they'll wish they were dead before the ending."

"F-far ahead of . . . you, my d-dear," Wavewaker moaned, stifling a belch.

"How is it you're not ill?" Dona Leona asked Mia.

"I didn't eat yestereve, Domina," Mia replied. "Too nervous about the games."

"'Byss and blood," Leona spat. "I should have that cook *flogged*. We're three laurels shy of the *magni,* this is the first *venatus* me and my father pit gladiatii against one another, and my sharpest blades are all sick as sailors with no sea legs?" Her eyes narrowed with a sudden thought, and she turned to Arkades. "You don't think *he* orchestrated this, do you?"

Executus rubbed his chin in thought. "Possible, thou—"

Sidonius leaned back against the wall as a spray of puke erupted from his gut, Maggot and Leona both skipping back in disgust. The dona fished a scented kerchief from her dress, pressing it to her mouth as the big Itreyan groaned an almost-indecipherable apology, and promptly shit his loincloth.

"They can't fight like this, Domina," Maggot said softly.

"Aye," Arkades nodded. "It'll be a slaughter. Not a one of them can stand."

"*I* can stand," Mia replied.

The trio looked to her silently. Leona's eyes narrowed.

"I can *win,*" Mia swore.

Arkades shook his head. "Set eyes through those bars, girl. Does anything about this arena strike attention?"

Mia peered out to the sands, eyes scanning the walls, the crowd. The remains of the equillai match were being packed up, targets broken down, markers removed. The crowd were stamping their feet, impatient for the next match to begin.

"Broken glass," Mia said, turning to look at the executus. "And firepots. On the wall skirting the arena's edge."

"And that tells you what?"

"Either the editorii don't want the crowd getting onto the sand, or they

---

Chastity, Humility, Poverty, Sobriety, and Generally Having No Fun Whatsofuck-ingever.

don't want whatever they're about to release on the sand getting into the crowd," Mia replied.

"Menagerie," Arkades said. "The theme for this *venatus*. Beasts from all corners of the Republic, set to do battle with each other and gladiatii for the crowd's amusement." The big man folded his massive arms, the scar on his face deepening as he scowled. "Do you have any idea what you'd face out there?"

Mia shrugged, feigning ignorance.

"Whatever the 'byss it is, it can't smell worse than in here." She looked at Leona, her jaw set. "Your equillai just lost to your father's men, Domina. And only one of your gladiatii can lift a sword. If you've a thirst for a victor's laurel at all, or anything to prove, it seems you've but one choice."

Leona's eyes had narrowed at the words "anything to prove." But Mia spoke truth—there was only one way Leona would see a victor's purse this *venatus*. Only one way she might recoup some of her costs, win some glory, accrue another laurel for her collegium's berth at the *magni*.

Mia and Ashlinn had orchestrated it that way, after all.

Part of Mia still didn't trust her coconspirator. She was still waiting for the hammer to drop. But Ash had spoken truth; Eclipse had confirmed it. She'd dosed the other gladiatii, left Mia on her feet, all the better to convince Leona that Mia was the only hope she had of winning the victory she so desperately needed. But still . . .

But still . . .

"Executus," Leona said, eyes never leaving Mia's. "Tell the editorii our Crow will fight for Remus Collegium in the Ultima. We will field no other gladiatii this turn."

"Mi Dona, Furian was slated for the Ultima. A change at this final hour—"

"I paid for berth at this *venatus*," Leona snarled. "I will be *damned* if fate's cold hand robs me of my victory. If the editorii take issue with my arrangements, tell them they can bring them to me personally. But, by the Everseeing and all four of his holy fucking Daughters, you'd best warn them to bring an extra pair of balls, because I'll be ripping off the first and wearing them for earrings." She indicated her gown with a sweep of her hand. "The red should complement my dress nicely."

Maggot grinned, and Arkades tried to hide his smile in his beard.

"Your whisper, my will," he murmured.

With a hand-to-heart bow, the executus limped off in search of the editorii, and Maggot in search of some water to wash away the mess. Leona remained behind in the damp, the stink, staring at Mia through the bars with glittering blue eyes.

"I risk much on you, little Crow."

"It's only a risk if I don't win, Domina," Mia replied. "And in all truth, you've nothing to lose."

"I'll not forgive it," Leona warned, "if you fail me."

Putting her hand to her heart, Mia bowed low.

"And I trust you'll not forget it," she replied, "when I don't."

The matches had been brutal, bloody, beautiful. The crowd were drunk on it—the wine, the slaughter, their roars reverberating through the stone above Mia's head. The guards were already proclaiming the *venatus* the finest that Stormwatch had ever seen, that the editorii had outdone themselves again.

Spectators had thrilled as a mob of gladiatii hunted a three-ton saberwolf through a sea of long grass that had grown up from the sands upon command. They'd howled in delight as gladiatii from the collegia of Leonides, Trajan, and Phillipi clashed upon a web of shifting wires hung over the arena, while a pack of Vaanian whitebears prowled below, tearing any warrior who fell into bloody pieces. Prisoners of the state had been tied to stakes and executed by a flock of starving Ysiiri bloodhawks; gladiatii with tridents and nets had fought an actual live sand kraken before the bellowing mob.* And now, as nevernight winds blew in from the ocean and the turn drew near its close, they were ready for the Ultima.

None knew what could possibly top the sand kraken, though all were salivating at the prospect. They stamped their feet in time, the rhythm echoing down into the mekwerk pits beneath the sands. And then, as if in answer, rumbling up from the depths, came a shuddering, spine-chilling roar.

"Citizens of Itreya!" came the call across the arena horns. "Honored administratii! Senators and marrowborn! We give thanks to our honored consul, Julius Scaeva, for providing the funds for the Ultima to close this most glorious *venatus*!"

The crowd roared approval, and Mia grit her teeth to hear them chanting Scaeva's name. She pushed thought of the consul from her mind, focusing only on the task ahead. None of the fighters in the staging cell around her had an inkling, but Mia knew exactly what awaited them beneath the floor. And even

---

* Only a twelve-footer, but the beast still killed seven men before being sent to its grave.

with the advantage she'd bought herself, she still knew this would be a fight for her very life.

She wore a sleeve of mail rings on her right arm, iron spaulders and greaves to protect her shoulders and shins, a leather skirt and breastplate. The armor would count for next to nothing against the foe she'd face, but still, it was better than fighting bare-arsed with a grin on her face. Her helm was plumed in red—the color of her domina's standard. *Remus's* standard. The thought chafed, but again, she pushed it aside. No place for pride here. No place for pain. Only steel. And blood. And glory.

The swords in her hands felt like home—good Liisian steel, sharp as razors. She'd need them, and all her strength, if she was to survive what was to come.

"Citizens!" came the cry. "Behold, your gladiatii! Chosen from the finest collegia in the Republic, here to fight and die for the glory of their domini! From the Tacitus Collegium, we present to you, Appius, bane of the Werewood!"

The portcullis before them shuddered upward with a metallic groan. A huge man strode past Mia, up into the arena, raising his spear and shield to the din of the roaring crowd. His helm was fashioned like a wolf's head, sunslight glinting on his sleeves and breastplate of steel.

"From the Livian Collegium, Ashbringer, Terror of the Silent Sea!"

A Dweymeri gladiatii strode up to the sand, raised a twin-handed mattock longer than Mia was tall. He prowled about the arena's edge, stamping his feet upon the sand, and the crowd fell in time until the entire world seemed made of thunder.

And so it went. Each collegium was announced, fearsome gladiatii with equally fearsome titles marching up to take their places, riling the crowd with their theatrics. Mia noticed with interest that Leonides wasn't fielding a warrior in the Ultima—unusual for a collegium of stature. She wondered if he had some inkling of the nature of their foe . . .

More than two dozen warriors stood on the sands before Mia heard the editorii call, "From the Remus Collegium . . ."

"Furian!" came a cry.

"Unfaaaaallen!" came another.

". . . the Crow!" roared the editorii.

Mia marched up into the sunslight, raising her twin swords above her head. She was met by bemusement, scattered applause, a few jeers from folk who'd been expecting the champion of Remus Collegium rather than some skinny girl half his size. Not a one of them had any clue who she was.

Soon.

Mia grit her teeth, silently vowing to herself.

Soon, the sky itself will know my name.

In a grand booth on the arena's edge, Mia saw the governor of Stormwatch, the city's elite gathered about his chair. An editorii stood in a separate booth, clad in the traditional blood-red robe trimmed with golden daggers. A smoke-gray cat was curled on his shoulder, eyeing proceedings with an air of distinct boredom. The man spoke into a great horn, voice amplified across the vast space.

"And now!" he cried. "Gentlefriends, steady your hearts. Children, avert your eyes! Dragged from the depths of the Ysiiri Whisperwastes at the command of our glorious consul, a horror polluted by the corruption that brought the old empire to its knees. Behold, citizens of Stormwatch, your *Ultima!*"

Mia felt the floor tremble, heard the great mekwerk beneath the sand begin to move. Rocky outcroppings rose from the sand like teeth, tall and wicked-sharp. The arena's heart split apart, sand cascading into the depths as a pit opened wide. And, as if from the abyss itself, up rose a horror unlike anything Mia had ever seen.

"'Byss and blood . . . ," said a voice beside her.

Mia looked to the Dweymeri gladiatii; the man named Ashbringer. His eyes were wide. His great mattock trembling in his hands.

The monster roared, shaking the very earth. The crowd answered, rising to their feet, cheering, howling, giddy. Not a one among them had ever seen the like, but all had heard the tales. Nightmare of the deepest deserts. More terrifying than the sand kraken. More fearsome than a hundred dustwraiths. A word that struck panic into every caravaneer and trader who ran the Ysiiri wastes.

"Retchwyrm . . . ," Ashbringer whispered.*

---

*Although commonly considered the apex predator of the Ysiiri wastes, the sand kraken *does* run a poor second to the true masters of the deepest desert. A creature so awful that it almost defies belief, the retchwyrm does its level best to shatter the illusion that there is any kind of benevolence in the creator of the universe at all.

Stretching up to two hundred feet long, the retchwyrm is a serpentine creature with no discernible eyes or nostrils, and only the most rudimentary of ears. Loresmen at the Grand Collegium in Godsgrave have theorized the beasts sense prey by vibration, or perhaps through a kind of echolocation, similar to various breeds of flying mice. However, since any bastard foolish enough to study them usually ends up dis-

The beast roared again, raising the end of its body that Mia supposed was its head. Its skin was pitted, cracked and browned like old leather. It moved like some obscene caterpillar, lunging toward the crowd as they screamed. But an iron collar and thick lengths of chain bound the monster to the arena floor, prevented it from getting anywhere close to the audience. Once they realized they were in no danger, the crowd burst into applause, cheering and chanting.

With all eyes on the beast, Mia turned and strode across the sand, thirty more steps, until she stood beneath a statue of Tsana on the inner wall. Stabbing her swords into the earth, she knelt, bowed her head as if in prayer to the goddess. But with her right hand, she began searching beneath the sand at the arena's edge.

She felt nothing at first. Her shadow rippling as her stomach ran cold, as the thought that Ashlinn had betrayed her rose like a dustwraith in back of her—

No.

Her fingers felt softness. Leather.

There it is.

She pulled the object from the sand—a leather pouch filled with spherical objects—tucking it beneath her spaulder.

The editorii raised his hands, calling for silence.

The crowd fell still as a millpond.

The man drew a breath, heard across the arena. His cat simply yawned.

"Ultima!" he cried. *"Begin!"*

The crowd roared, deafening and rapturous. The beast chained in the arena's heart writhed in response, its blind head swinging side to side as its

---

solved in a pool of concentrated sulfuric acid, this theory has largely remained untested.

The retchwyrm has two puckered mouths, one at each end of its body, which also serve as its backsides (which orifice serves which purpose at any given time seems to be entirely arbitrary, and dependent on the mood of the retchwyrm in question). It has no jaw or teeth, and is incapable of seizing prey in its mouth. Instead—in what may be the most disgusting method of consuming nourishment in the entire animal kingdom—the retchwyrm projectile vomits its *entire stomach* out of its mouth, engulfing its prey in a tangle of writhing tendrils and corrosive acid, then noisily sucks the entire mess back up again, hapless prey included.

Do you see what I mean?

Honestly, what kind of sick *bastard* thought this thing up?

stomach bubbled up in its throat, desperate to consume the prey it could sense but couldn't reach. And in answer, it let out another sky-shaking roar.

And not a single gladiatii

moved

a

single

muscle.

"*. . . can't blame them, really . . . ,*" came the whisper in Mia's ear as she took her place back alongside her fellows.

The crowd began to get restless, several starting to boo as the gladiatii all stood paralyzed, a few circling the retchwyrm as it thrashed and growled.

"*Kill it!*" someone roared.

"*Fight, cowards!*"

Standing beside Mia, Ashbringer prickled at the word "coward." He looked about the bleachers, up to his domini in the sanguila's boxes. And hefting his mattock, he bellowed, "With me!" at the top of his lungs and charged the beast with weapon raised. Several other gladiatii took up the call, Mia among them, rushing forward with bloody cries. They attacked the wyrm from four sides, hewing and stabbing with spear and sword. Preferring the flank, Mia darted out from behind one of the fangs of stone, burying her blades to the hilt. Ashbringer charged head-on, swung his mattock, pulping a great hole in the beast's hide. And with a revolting wet burping sound, the retchwyrm reared up and spewed its stomach all over the men in front of it.

The flesh was a rotten pink, almost liquid, splashing on the ground and stretching out with finger-like tendrils. Appius was completely buried under the deluge of guts, Ashbringer was engulfed to the waist, screaming as his flesh began to burn in the acid slicking the wyrm's insides. He swung again with his hammer, pounding on the spongy mass. The stomach continued to crawl over the ground, almost like a thing with a mind of its own, stretching out sticky strands and snaring the gladiatii about it. And finally, with a hollow, rushing slurp, the beast inhaled its guts back inside itself, dragging half a dozen screaming men with it. The crowd roared in delight and disgust.

On the beast's flank, Mia stabbed her blade hilt-deep again, feeling the monster shiver. Its blood was deep red, almost black, slicking her to the elbows. As the behemoth rolled and bucked, she reached up to her spaulders— the pouch Ashlinn had hidden in the sand. Groping inside, she grabbed a handful and drew it out; three spheres of bright red glass in the palm of her hand.

A gift from Mercurio before they'd departed.

Wyrdglass.*

Dragging her sword free, she pushed her fist into the wound, burying the spheres into the beast's muscle. The retchwyrm roared in pain, rolled over on its side to crush Mia. The girl dove free, narrowly avoided getting pulped against one of the stone fangs as the wyrm whipped its tail. Wyrdglass was activated by pressure, usually by throwing it at the wall or floor, but Mia hoped the press of the beast's own muscles and weight would be enough to break the arkemical bonds that held the glass in solid state. As she stumbled to her feet, dashed away, she heard a dull pop, almost lost beneath the crowd baying, the monster's roars. A bubbling gout of blood and flesh burst up from the retchwyrm's side as her wyrdglass exploded.

The crowd cheered—they'd no idea what the girl had done, only that she'd wounded the beast. The retchwyrm howled, gullet bubbling in its throat, the stench of blood and ashes and acid washing over Mia in waves.

"... I THINK YOU MADE IT ANGRY ..."

"... ever the observant one, dear mongrel ..."

"... EVER THE SMART-ARSE, LITTLE MOGGY ..."

"... flattery will get you nowhere ..."

The retchwyrm turned its blind head toward Mia, let loose a terrible howl. The girl dashed back toward the cluster of other gladiatii, seeking cover among the rocks, trying to get beyond the reach of the retchwyrm's chain. The monster snaked after her in pursuit, slamming its massive bulk onto the dirt in an attempt to crush her. The ground shook, Mia stumbled. Other gladiatii were hacking and chopping at the beast, but it seemed largely intent on the girl who'd wounded it worst. In desperation, Mia turned, held up her hand as she

---

* One of Shahiid Spiderkiller's finest inventions, you may remember wyrdglass comes in three variants:

Black creates smoke, useful for diversions.

White creates a cloud of the toxin known as Swoon, useful for knocking people unconscious.

Red simply explodes, useful for making people dead.

Three colors, three flavors. All rather simple, though you'd be surprised how often a novice Blade has reached into the wrong pouch and grabbed the wrong color in the heat of the moment. It can be a little embarrassing when you realize the black wyrdglass you threw at your feet to cause a distraction is actually white, and you've accidently knocked yourself cold—although not quite as bad as throwing down a handful of red glass and realizing you've accidentally blown your own legs off.

It does tend to be the kind of mistake Blades only make once, however.

scrambled backward, trying to snare the monster with its own massive shadow until she was beyond the reach of its chain.

The reaction was instantaneous. Terrifying. The behemoth stilled, as if its every muscle went suddenly taut. With a spine-chilling roar, it lunged across the sand right at Mia, mouth distended, corrosive spittle hissing as it thrashed against its bonds. And with a shriek of tortured metal, the bright sound of shattering steel, the chain binding the beast to the floor snapped clean in two.

"... *o, shit* ..."

"... *O, SHIT* ..."

"O, *shit*!"

The beast whipped about, far too huge for Mia to hold it still with her shadowerking. The girl dove aside as its tail swept across the arena in a great scything arc, crushing stone to splinters and the gladiatii about it to pulp. Mia was clipped as she dove free, smashed into an outcropping, black stars bursting in her eyes. She lost her grip on the shadows as she collapsed, the retchwyrm roaring in incandescent rage.

"It ..." Mia blinked hard, spitting dust off her tongue. "... It heard me?"

"... *WHEN YOU CALLED THE DARK* ..."

"... *interesting* ..."

The beast howled again, seemingly furious, skin rippling as its guts bubbled and burped in its throat. But with no shadows now to distract it, and realizing it was suddenly free of its bonds, the retchwyrm turned its blind head toward the vibrations of the chanting, roaring crowd. And as the audience also realized the behemoth's chain was broken, they broke into screaming, frothing panic.

Mia reached up to her spaulders, blood running cold as she realized the pouch of wyrdglass was no longer there. She searched the sand about her as the retchwyrm snaked toward the arena wall, the broken glass and firepots ringing the enclosure now seeming pitiful in the face of the monster's sheer size and rage. A cadre of half a dozen Luminatii legionaries rushed into the arena, sunsteel blades drawn, crying, "For the Republic!" and "Luminus Invicta!" as they charged. Seemingly giving no shits for Republics, Light, or Anything Much at All, the beast vomited its gullet again, engulfing the entire cadre in a tangled mess of rotten pink and burning acid.

Sweat burned Mia's eyes, the screams of the crowd almost deafening. The arena around her was sheer bedlam now, people rushing for the exits, others sitting paralyzed in their seats and crying out in terror.

The retchwyrm reared up and bellowed, its broken collar hanging loose about its throat. Twenty fresh legionaries with swords and shields charged out from one of the iron portcullises, but with a single sweep of its massive tail, the monster smashed them all to pulp against the arena wall. Its thick, leathery hide was pierced in a dozen places by spears and blades, dark blood dribbling from the wounds.

"*. . . well, this is going splendidly . . .*"

"You know, it's very easy to sit back and criticize," Mia gasped, rolling onto her belly, her head still ringing.

"*. . . strangely satisfying, too . . .*"

"*. . . TELL THAT TO THE PEOPLE ABOUT TO BE DEVOURED . . .*"

"*. . . what would be the point of that, exactly . . . ?*"

The retchwyrm had reached the arena wall, its eighty-foot length undulating like some grotesque moth spawn. It loomed over the ten-foot barricade easily, featureless head swaying above a pack of terrified spectators, its gullet burbling as it inhaled. Mia dragged herself up out of the dirt, skull throbbing, the bodies of dead gladiatii spattered and smeared all about her. Searching among the corpses, she found a longspear, its haft still intact. Her damned helmet only interfered with her vision, but she dare not remove it in the off chance some random servant of the Church saw her face. And so, with a silent prayer to the Black Mother, she drew back her arm and hurled the spear with all her strength.

The weapon sailed through the air in a perfect arc, steel head gleaming in the sunlight as it pierced the retchwyrm's throat. The monster bellowed, shaking its head to dislodge the toothpick, black blood spraying. And reaching out once more to the dark puddled beneath it, Mia seized hold of the monster's shadow.

"Oi!" she yelled. "*Bastard!*"

The retchwyrm shuddered, a deep, rumbling whine shivering its entire length. The people in the bleachers forgotten, the beast turned its blind head toward Mia and split the air with a hollow, deafening roar.

"*. . . now you have its attention . . .*"

"Excellent."

Mia picked up two swords from the bloody dirt around her.

"But what the fuck do I do with it?"

CHAPTER 18

GLORIA

Try as she might, Mia couldn't hold the beast still.

Like a giant pushing aside a helpless infant, the retchwyrm broke free of Mia's shadowerking, swung its massive bulk away from the crowd, and snaked toward her. Its mouth yawned wide, a trembling roar rolling up from the dark of its belly. The twin swords of Liisian steel in Mia's hands might well have been butter knives, and her shadow rippled as her passengers drank down her fear.

Leaving her cold.

Hard.

Unafraid.

Mind racing. Eyes scanning the arena walls, the broken rocks, the bloody sand, the monster bearing down on her. And finally, there, she saw it, half-buried in a tumble of shattered stone and dirt between her and the charging monstrosity.

Her bag of wyrdglass.

A thought took seed—insane, suicidal. But with no fear, no pause, no breath to waste, the girl raised her swords. Sweat in her eyes, hair stuck to dusty skin, lips peeling back from her teeth, Mia charged with a bloodcurdling cry, right *toward* the enraged retchwyrm.

The panicked crowd fell still in amazement, watching the tiny speck of a girl running headlong at the horror of the deepwastes. The beast reared back its colossal bulk, a horrid belch spilling up from its gullet. Mia sprinted through a mash of broken bodies, broken stone, broken weapons littering the sand, leaping carefully over her small leather sack of 'glass, half-buried in the dust. And the retchwyrm opened its maw, spewing its guts all over the floor.

Completely engulfing her.

In turns to come, the next few moments would be the topic of countless taverna tales, dinner table debates, and barroom brawls across the city of Stormwatch.

There were those who swore they saw the girl dive aside, simply too swift to mark, entirely avoiding the spray of the beast's innards. There were those who claimed that with all the dust and blood and chaos, it was simply too hard to tell *what* happened, only that she moved quick as silver. And there were those—discounted as madmen and drunks, for the most part—who swore by the Everseeing and all four of his Holy Daughters that this little slip of a girl, this daemon wrapped in leather and mail, simply *disappeared*. One moment buried in the retchwyrm's guts, the next, standing ten feet away in the long shadow cast beside it on the sand.

Mia swayed on her feet, the rush of vertigo almost sending her to her knees. Only adrenaline and stubborn will kept her upright, half-staggering, half-running, chest burning as her head spun. The beast inhaled its innards, slurping up the mashed gladiatii corpses and fallen weapons and the small leather pouch full of shining wyrdglass globes. Mia stumbled up a broken outcropping of stone and launched herself onto the thing's back, burying her swords in its flesh to steady herself. The behemoth thrashed beneath her as she groped her way upright, stumbled along the creature's length, up toward its rearing head. The crowd bellowing, the retchwyrm roaring, her own pulse thundering and beneath it all, through that cacophony, that deafening chaos, she thought perhaps she heard it, deep inside the monster's belly.

A series of tiny, wet pops.

The retchwyrm paused, a tremor running through its body. Mia scrambled onto its neck, throwing one of her blades aside, clinging to a broken spear embedded in its leathery hide. Gripping the beast with her thighs and fingernails and sheer bloody-mindedness, she drew back her Liisian steel and with a cry, plunged it into the flesh behind the monster's tiny ear.

The creature bellowed, a bubble of blood welling up from its gullet and bursting at its mouth. The crowd had no inkling about the 'glass it had swallowed; no clue the explosion had turned a goodly section of the retchwyrm's gullet to bloody soup. All they knew was that as they watched dumbfounded, mouths open in awe, the girl plunged in her blade, the beast swayed back and forth like a drunkard at the privy, and with a bubbling sigh, crashed dead and still to the ground.

The *thuddd* echoed across the arena, dust rising as the creature collapsed. But as the nevernight winds blew across the bleachers, across the blood-soaked sand, the pall cleared to reveal a single figure, standing alone on the dead beast's head.

Panting, bleeding, Mia bent down and dragged her blade free. And turning to the dumbfounded spectators, she slowly raised it to the sky.

Silence rang across the sands. Hollow and still. No one in the crowd could believe their eyes, let alone speak. Until finally, a small boy in his mother's arms pointed at the bloodstained girl at the arena's heart, his brown eyes grown wide.

"Crow!" came his tiny cry.

A man beside him looked to the boy, then shouted to those around him.

"Crow!"

The word began repeating, like an echo, more and more folk taking up the call. Dozens, then hundreds, then thousands, all chanting in time like a vow, like a prayer, "Crow! Crow! Crow!" as Mia limped the length of the retchwyrm's carcass, sword held high, the audience stamping their feet in time with their chant, faster and faster now, the word and the thunder of their feet burring into "CrowCrowCrowCrowCrow!"

Mia roared with them, elation and bloody pride welling inside her chest.

"What is my name?" she screamed.

"CrowCrowCrowCrowCrow!"

"WHAT IS MY NAME?"

"CROWCROWCROWCROWCROW!"

Mia closed her eyes, drinking it in, letting it soak into her skin.

Sanguii e Gloria.

She turned to the sanguila boxes, saw Dona Leona on her feet, cheering. She looked to the gladiatii cells, saw Sidonius and Bladesinger and Butcher at the bars, howling her name and pounding the iron. And finally, up in the crowd, amid the sea of smiling faces, she saw a girl. Long red hair. Eyes as blue as empty skies. And with her smile beaming bright as the suns overhead, Ashlinn raised her hand, fingers spread.

And she blew Mia a kiss.

T he Remus Collegium dined like marrowborn that night. A long table in the cells beneath the arena was laden with food and wine, Mia's gladiatii brothers and sisters toasting her victory like the lords and ladies of old. Furian sat at the table's head like a king, as was his place as champion. But if this was a kingdom, it now had a queen. Sat at the table's foot, a silver victor's laurel crowning her long dark hair, Mia Corvere raised her wine and grinned like a madwoman.

The gladiatii were recovered enough from their poisoning, and buoyed by the adrenaline of Mia's victory. They drank a great deal and ate very little, recounting the battle again and again. Sidonius crowed so loud about it, you'd think he'd defeated the beast himself, wrapping his ham-hock arm around Mia's neck and declaring it the greatest triumph he'd ever seen on the sands.

"This magnificent little bitch!" he roared.

"Get off me, you great oaf," Mia grinned, pushing him away.

"I've never witnessed the like!" Sid bellowed. "Have you, 'Singer?"

"Nay," the woman smiled, raising her cup. "Never the like."

"Wavewaker?"

"A victory worthy of Pythias and Prospero!" the big man declared.*

"And you, Butcher? What about you, Otho?"

"Nay," they replied. "Never."

"To the Crow!" Sid roared, and the room raised their cups in answer.

Only Furian was silent, sipping his wine as if it were poisoned.† His eyes never left Mia's, filled with accusation and cold fury. Sick as he'd been, she knew he must have watched her battle, probably felt her calling the dark. But still, there was no denying her victory had been glorious, and no matter how

---

* "The Tragedy of Pythias and Prospero" is a saga penned by the famous bard, Talia. Though banned by the Ministry of Aa, it remains one of the oldest and most renowned plays in history, predating the Itreyan Kingdom by centuries. The play is based on an ancient myth and is set in the time before the Mother of Night had been banished from the Itreyan sky.

It follows the adventures of two lovers: Pythias, captain of the guard, and Prospero, son of the Sorcerer King, who are separated by Prospero's father when he learns of their affair. Pythias is banished to the far corners of the earth, and in their quest to be reunited, the pair conquer armies, nations, and finally the Sorcerer King himself to be together again.

Sadly, when a tale has the word "tragedy" in the title, it's probably folly to expect a happy ending; Pythias is poisoned in the final confrontation. Dying in his lover's arms, he delivers a stirring speech on the enduring power of hope, fidelity, and love— widely regarded as the finest monologue ever put to vellum. Prospero, inheritor of his father's magiks, sets his lover's body in the heavens as a constellation, and names it in his honor.

Not a dry eye in the bloody house, gentlefriends.

Though banned by the Ministry, and most copies of it destroyed in the Bright Light book burning of 27PR, Pythias's monologue is still quoted in modern times. A few complete versions of the play are rumored to exist in secret—handwritten from memory by actors who performed it, or secreted away from the puritans of Aa's church. The copies are rare, however, and have almost become myth among Itreyan theater groups. Any actor claiming to have read one is more than likely just a lying tosser.

Although now I think about it, most actors I've met were lying tossers anyway . . .

† To be fair, the last wine he'd drunk *had* been.

much the sight of that silver laurel on her brow burned his craw, the Unfallen wisely kept his bile behind his teeth.

Occasionally, Mia would stare across the feast with ink-black eyes, boring into the champion's own, the illness and hunger she felt whenever she was around him swelling in her belly. Glancing at his seat at the table's head, she silently promised.

Soon.

"Attend!"

The gladiatii fell silent, rising to their feet as Executus Arkades marched into the room, along with Magistrae. Dona Leona walked behind them, beaming.

"Domina!" the gladiatii barked.

"Be still, my Falcons," she raised her hands, urged them to take their seats. "I'll not part you from your revels. The streets ring with the name of the Remus Collegium, and you've earned this moment's joy, all of you."

The dona smiled as they raised their cups, toasted her health. She'd taken time to change into an off-the-shoulder dress and matching corset in beautiful crushed velvet, the same rust-red as her hair. Mia wondered exactly how much silver the woman had spent on it. How many dresses she'd hauled here from the Nest. How much this damned celebration feast was costing her and where the 'byss she got the coin. For someone who was so strapped she'd been willing to sell Mia to a pleasure house a mere turn ago . . .

Mia glanced at Arkades, saw the Executus eyeing the food and wine with the same concern. Mia looked at the jewels about the dona's throat, the gold at her wrists, the realization only sinking deeper.

She's awful with money. Raised rich, so she's never learned the real value of a coin, or truly understood the life that awaits you when you run out of them. All she cares about is how she appears to others.

To her father.

Mia looked Leona up and down, sighing inside.

Could I have grown up the same way, if mine hadn't been killed?

Mia saw Furian look to his domina from the corner of her eye, perhaps seeking some gesture of acknowledgment. But true to her ruse, tall and proud and O, so *proper*, Leona did not even grace him with a glance.

"My Crow," the dona said, smiling at Mia. "A word."

"Domina."

Mia followed Leona from the room, conscious of Furian's burning gaze on her back. Arkades and Magistrae followed, the older woman shutting the door as Sidonius started recounting the battle again, using a jug of wine and a tooth-pick for props.

"You are well?" Leona asked.

"Well enough," Mia replied. "My thanks, Domina."

"'Tis I who should be thanking you," Leona said, her eyes dancing. "Our collegium is the talk of the entire *city*. The governor of Stormwatch, Quintus Messala himself, has declared this the finest contest the Republic has ever seen, and *you*"—Leona squeezed Mia's shoulders—"you, my bloody beauty, are the heart of it all."

"I live to honor you, Domina," Mia said.

Arkades narrowed his eyes at that, but Leona seemed almost giddy.

"Governor Messala holds a traditional feast the nevernight after the *venatus*," the dona said. "Every marrowborn and administratii attends his palazzo, and he invites every sanguila who fields gladiatii in the games, along with their champion." Leona's eyes twinkled with fierce delight. "But he has sent personal missive, asking that in addition to Furian, I bring *you*, that all may gaze upon the Savior of Stormwatch."

". . . The Savior of Stormwatch?" Mia murmured.

"It has a fine ring to it, neh?" Leona chuckled. "The minstrels are already singing of your victory in taverna across the city. You will be the pride of the feast, the jewel in my crown. And we'll be showered in coin—the elite of the city will be throwing offers of patronage at my *feet*. The eyes of every sanguila upon you, *burning* with jealousy."

Every *sanguila* . . .

"Messala has always favored fighters from my father's collegium," Leona said. "For years, he has heaped accolades upon the Lions of Leonides. How badly it will burn, to see me in the seat of favor at Messala's right hand."

The dona pressed her fingers to her lips, smothering her mad grin.

"Imagine the look on the old bastard's face."

"Mi Dona," Magistrae warned, glancing at Mia. "You should not speak so . . ."

"Mmm, aye." Leona remembered herself, nodding and smoothing down the lines of her dress. "I keep you from your revels, my Crow. Go and celebrate your victory. But not too much wine, neh? I want you looking your best at the feast amorrow."

Like a prized pet, Mia realized. *Like a dog at her mistress's feet. To be sold in an instant if she fails to bark on command.*

Sit.

Roll over.

Play dead.

Be *dead.*

Mia pressed her lips tight. Thinking of her father, swinging at the end of his rope. Her mother bleeding to death in her arms. Her baby brother, taking his first steps in some lightless pit and dying there in the dark.

Thinking of Duomo.

Thinking of Scaeva.

Eyes on the prize, Corvere.

And looking into Leona's eyes, she bowed, hand to her heart.

"Your whisper, my will," she said. "Domina."

B lack fucking Mother, you were *brilliant!*"
Ashlinn crashed into Mia as soon as she climbed through the taverna window, arms wrapped around her tight. Mia nodded, "Aye, aye," and extricated herself from the girl's grip, drew the curtains behind her. She was the most well-known person in Stormwatch, after all, and the streets were still filled with revelers celebrating the *venatus.* The suns were burning her eyes, the beating she'd taken that afternoon was leaving its bruises, and after the feast with her brother and sister gladiatii, Mia was feeling more than a little drunk. Looking about the tiny room, she saw there were no chairs to sit in—just a single cot with a mattress as thin as a slice of fine cheese.

"Not exactly the consul's villa, is it?"

"Every inn, outhouse and brothel was full because of the *venatus,*" Ash shrugged. "The Mother smiled on me to even get a berth in this hovel. Don't ask how much we're paying for it. Good thing Mercurio gave us so much coin. But anyway, to the 'byss with the room, you just killed a colossus! The whole city is talking about you!"

Mia slumped down on the bed, massaged her aching ribs.

"Aye," was all she mustered.

"'Byss and blood, Corvere," Ash said, flopping down on the mattress beside her. "You slew a retchwyrm! Saved the lives of hundreds of people in front of ten thousand more! Leona would have to be three shades mad and five bottles drunk to even think about selling you now! Aren't you happy?"

Mia had asked herself that same question on the way here, sneaking out from the arena cells and Stepping through the shadows. She *should* be happy. Aside from the retchwyrm breaking its chain, all had gone more or less to her design. Leona's favor won. Patronage for the collegium assured. Her name ringing in the streets. One laurel closer to the *magni,* Scaeva's and Duomo's throats.

But the wrongness of it was creeping on her like a cancer. Every turn she spent with this brand on her cheek made it harder and harder for her to ignore the folk who couldn't just skip away from their chains through the shadows like she could. Not just gladiatii. The whole Republic was oiled by the machine of human misery. Now that her eyes were opened to it, she couldn't unsee it. Didn't *want* to.

But she also knew she couldn't fix it. She couldn't even help the other members of the collegium without dooming her plan to failure. She'd gambled too much to be here already. And not just her. Mercurio. Ashlinn, too. And all for the greater good, aye? Couldn't she truly say that? That the Republic would be better off without a tyrant in the consul's chair?

That *everyone* would be better off once Julius Scaeva was dead?

But what would happen to her brothers and sisters in the collegium, if somehow her plan succeeded? Two slaves kill their master, and the administratii murder every slave in their house. What would they do to the ones she left behind in Crow's Nest, if she killed a cardinal and a fucking consul? Even if she managed to pull off her miracle, Sidonius, Bryn and Byern, Bladesinger . . . they'd all be executed.

Mia looked at the girl, staring back at her with those bright blue eyes.

"A long turn is all," she sighed. "Got a smoke?"

Ash grinned, fished inside her shirt and produced her thin silver cigarillo case. It was embossed with the sigil of the Familia Corvere—a crow in flight over two crossed swords. It had been a present from Mercurio, the nevernight Mia turned fifteen. The metal was warm from the press of Ashlinn's skin.

Mia lit the cigarillo with a flintbox, sighed gray.

"Where are Eclipse and Mister Know-it-all?" Ash asked.

"Eclipse is watching the street. Mister Kindly is trailing Dona Leona. There's a big soiree at the governor's palazzo amorrow. Leona's attempting to secure patronage, end her money troubles once and for all. The governor asked to bring me with her."

"Of course," Ash nodded. "You should've seen yourself. Damned retchwyrm looked set to devour half the crowd, and you call it a rude word and it just turns on you like a snake. Unbelievable."

"Aye," Mia muttered. "I can scarce believe it myself."

She took another drag of her cigarillo, shaking her head. Ash was still grinning, blue eyes shining with the memory of her victory. She reached across, rubbed at the scowl between Mia's brows as if attempting to erase it. Mia battered her hand away.

"Maw's teeth, what's wrong?" Ash sighed, exasperated. "You're the toast of the city. You won a laurel, gained your dona's favor, and guaranteed the future of the collegium. Everything went your way, and you're scowling up a summer storm."

Mia chewed her lip. Debating if she should say anything at all. She looked at Ashlinn, dark eyes picked out with a pinprick of flame as she dragged on her cigarillo. The wine in her belly had loosened her tongue, but the distrust in her veins was keeping her jaw firmly clenched.

". . .'Byss and blood, Mia, what is it?" Ashlinn asked.

"The retchwyrm," Mia finally said.

"What of it?"

". . . In the desert outside the Quiet Mountain, back when was I chasing you and Remus to Last Hope . . ." She exhaled gray, waiting for some kind of reaction at talk of their confrontation last year, but Ashlinn was only listening. "A sand kraken attacked the Luminatii wagon. Killed scores of Remus's men."

"I remember."

Mia drew a deep breath, held it for a long, pregnant moment.

"I made it do that," she exhaled at last.

Ashlinn blinked. "How?"

Mia shrugged. "I've no idea. I just know that anytime I called the shadows in the Whisperwastes of Ysiir, sand kraken would come, and they'd be angry. And that retchwyrm in the arena reacted the same way. I tried to hold it in place with its own shadow, and it near lost its fucking mind."

Mia shook her head, took another drag on her smoke.

"Loresmen say that sand kraken and other beasts of the Ysiiri wastes were twisted by the magikal pollutants left over from the empire's destruction."

The Crown of the Moon.

The fall of the Ysiiri Empire.

The monstrosities left in its wake.

"I'm wondering . . . could all of it be connected?"

"To the empire's fall?" Ashlinn asked. "The darkin?"

Mia shrugged, a now familiar frustration welling up inside her. Cassius hadn't learned a thing of himself. Furian didn't want to. Mercurio and Mother Drusilla had told her she was Chosen of the Mother, but what the 'byss did that actually mean?

No one she'd ever met had any real answers for her. But that thing in the Galante necropolis . . . it seemed to know more.

"*YOUR TRUTH LIES BURIED IN THE GRAVE. AND YET YOU PAINT YOUR HANDS IN RED FOR THEM, WHEN YOU SHOULD BE PAINTING THE SKIES BLACK.*"

"I'm just fucking sick and tired of not knowing what I am, Ashlinn."

"Well, that's easy," the girl declared, reaching across and squeezing Mia's hand.

"O, aye?"

"Aye," Ashlinn smiled. "You're brave. And you're bright. And you're beautiful."

Mia scoffed, shaking her head and gazing at the wall.

"I mean it," Ashlinn said, leaning in and kissing Mia's cheek.

Mia turned to stare, dark eyes fixed on sunburned blue. Ashlinn was still close, drifting closer, ever so slow. The scent of lavender coiled on her skin, red hair cascading around her lightly freckled face, Mia's stomach thrilling as she realized the girl was about to kiss her.

"You're beautiful," Ash whispered.

And closing her eyes, she leaned in and—

"Don't," Mia said.

Ashlinn stopped, lips just a breath from Mia's. Looking from her eyes, down to her mouth.

"Why not?" she whispered.

"Because I don't trust you, Ashlinn," Mia replied. "And I don't want you thinking you can drag me into bed just to get me in your pocket."

Ashlinn leaned back on her haunches, looked at Mia in disbelief.

"You think I'd—"

"Do anything to get your way?" Mia asked. "Lie? Cheat? Fuck? Murder?"

Mia took a long drag of her smoke, eyes narrowed. Her tongue felt a little too thick for her mouth from the wine she'd drunk at dinner, but she'd set it loose now.

"Aye, Ash, that's the problem," she said. "I think I do."

Ashlinn reared up off the bed like Mia had struck her. She walked across the room, far as the tiny space would allow. Hands on hips and staring at the wall. She was silent a long moment, finally turning on Mia with a snarl.

"Fuck you, Mia."

Stamping back across the room, she raised the knuckles in Mia's face.

"Fuck *you*!"

"Get your hand out of my face, Ashlinn," Mia warned.

"I should knock that cigarillo out of your mouth!" she yelled.

Mia shook her head, taking another drag. "Have you ever noticed how people start to shout when they've nothing worthwhile to say?"

"Maw's teeth, you've got some stones. In case you haven't noticed, there's one person in the entire world right now who's on your side, and—"

"Mercurio's on my side, Ashlinn. Long before you."

"I don't see him anywhere around here, do you?" Ash shouted. "I don't see him dragging his arse from Godsgrave to Whitekeep to Stormwatch. I don't see *him* sneaking into arenas and planting wyrdglass in the sands and sending you warning about the monstrosity set to melt the flesh off your damned bones. He did nothing but try to talk you out of this, and I've done nothing but fucking help you!"

Mia shook her head, grinding her cigarillo into the wall. "Not because you hate the Ministry as much as I do. Not because you stand to gain from all this, O, no, Mother forbid. Because you care *so much* about me."

"And that just fucking terrifies you, doesn't it?"

Mia scoffed. "I have two shadow daemons who quite literally eat my fear, Ashlinn. I'm not terrified of anything."

"Mister Shithead and Wolfie aren't in the room," Ash snapped. "It's just you and me, now. And for all your bluster, that thought scares you witless. By the smell of you, you had to smash a bottle of goldwine just to muster the courage to send them away. But you *did* send them away. And you're too much a coward to admit why."

"Fuck you, Ashlinn."

"I thought you'd never ask, Mia."

Mia tensed, springing up off the bed, hands in fists. Ashlinn stood her ground, staring Mia down, jaw clenched. Their faces were only a few inches apart, the air between them crackling with arkemical current.

"Don't pretend you don't feel it," Ash said. "Because it's written in your every line and curve. You might know me, Mia Corvere, but I know *you* just as well. And I know what it is you want."

Mia grit her teeth, one hand curling into a fist. She didn't know whether she wanted to punch the girl or . . .

There was an ocean of lies between them. Ash's betrayal. Tric's murder. The certainty the girl *would* do or say anything to get what she wanted. But there was truth in her words too. Of every person she knew in the world, the only one here helping her in her darkest need was Ashlinn Järnheim.

Ashlinn Järnheim was made of lies.

Ashlinn Järnheim was poison.

And Ashlinn Järnheim was beautiful.

Mia couldn't deny it. Soft lips parted in the smoky light. Long red hair spilling about her shoulders in waves. Her skin was smooth, a hint of anger in her cheeks, turning them to rose. Big blue eyes framed by dark curling lashes, the look in them making Mia's fingers tingle, her belly flip. Wine humming in her veins, she stared into those pools of sunburned blue and saw her reflection, saw the same thing in her eyes as she saw swimming in Ash's own.

Want.

Want.

But . . .

. . . without her passengers beside her, Mia *was* afraid.

Not of wanting a girl, like perhaps Ash suspected. She'd had one before, after all. Even though that golden beauty in Aurelius's bed was simply a means to an end, Mia could admit she might have found a way to kiss the senator's son sooner. Might have ended him quite some time before she felt those golden lips between her legs, tasted the girl on Aurelius's tongue.

No, if Mia was afraid, it wasn't of wanting a girl.

It was wanting *this* girl.

Ashlinn Järnheim.

Thief.

Liar.

Killer.

Traitor.

"How can I trust you?" Mia asked. "After all you've done?"

"If I wanted you dead, Mia . . ."

"I'm not talking about trusting you with my life, Ashlinn."

Mia looked at Ashlinn's heaving breast, pictured the heart beneath it. Wondering if it thundered as hard as hers, or if all this was simply a means to an end.

Ashlinn lifted her hand, bringing it up to Mia's face. Her fingers brushed Mia's skin, eliciting a dizzying rush of warmth that had nothing to do with the sunlight or the wine she'd drunk. She inched closer, eyes flitting from Mia's own, down to her lips. Breathing harder, moving closer, just an inch away now, just a heartbeat. And Mia looked across the room and

Stepped

to the shadow

of the curtains

pulling them aside, throwing the window open, her head spinning from the drink, from the shadowalking, from all of it. Ash called her name, but she ignored it, scrambling over the sill and climbing down the wall, swift as a morning-after goodbye.

Calling Eclipse to her side, she dragged the darkness about her shoulders and over her head, stealing off into the nevernight streets. Celebrations of her victory were still ringing from taverna windows, from smokehouse doors, echoing in the very air. The fear draining from her like poison from a wound as Eclipse coiled inside her shadow, leaving her cold and hard and unafraid.

She couldn't trust Ashlinn Järnheim. That much was certain. But the thought of standing over the corpses of the men who'd destroyed everything she loved? The feel of cold steel in her hand and warm blood on her face and the knowledge that everything she'd worked for over the past seven years was now finally within her reach?

That she could trust.

And nothing else mattered.

She ran her hand down her cheek where Ashlinn had touched her, her skin still tingling.

Nothing at all.

YIELD

They called for Mia before dessert.

Dona Leona had commanded her to wait in a small antechamber, down in the servants' wing of the governor's palazzo. A guard was posted at her door, she was given a simple meal and some watered wine, while the guests in the banquet hall enjoyed aperitifs of stuffed quail hearts doused with brandy butter, followed by a main of roasted honeyfish and kingclaw braised in goldwine.

Mia knew Quintus Messala had served as governor of Stormwatch for six years—he'd been appointed soon after the Kingmaker Rebellion. As a childhood friend of Consul Scaeva and a scion of one of the twelve great familia of the Republic, his wealth and power were the envy of everyone who met him, and it seemed Messala lived to stoke that envy. Mia couldn't recall an affair as lavish, or a house quite as opulent. The antechamber she sat in was decorated with intricate stucco reliefs, gold leaf, and Dweymeri crystal chandeliers. The man who served her meal was dressed in clothes most marrowborn dons would envy.

She'd sat in the room brooding about her argument with Ashlinn until Arkades had come to fetch her. He was dressed in his finery, falcons and lions on his doublet. Mia was dressed in the armor she'd worn yesterturn, though it had been polished to within an inch of its life. They'd not given her helmet back, but there was little she could do about that. The chances of a Red Church servant being at the feast were low, but still, walking toward the banquet hall, Executus in front and two guards at her flanks, Mia felt as if she were bucknaked and strolling into a scabdog's den.

"Hold," Arkades told her, stopping at the door to the dining hall.

The big man turned to look at her, raised a finger in warning.

"Do not speak unless you are spoken to. Remember that all eyes are upon you. You may never have seen the like before, but the people in this room are *serpents,* girl. They slay with a whisper. Bestow fortunes or end reputations with a word. If you shame your domina's name, I swear by the Everseeing, I'll see you suffer for it."

Black Mother, the torch he's carrying for that woman could light up truedark . . .

Truth was, Mia knew the machinations of the marrowborn all too well—she'd seen her mother play their power games for years. The Dona Corvere could reduce men to hollow shells and women to tears when she put her mind to it. But Mia wasn't about to let Arkades know that. Instead, she simply bowed her head.

"Aye, Executus."

Satisfied, the man opened the door to the dining hall and limped inside. Mia waited, hands clasped. She could hear string music, voices in the room beyond.

"Fine match yesterturn," one of the guards beside her murmured.

"Aye," another said. "Bloody spectacular, lass."

Mia nodded thanks, grateful word of her victory was still spreading. If there had been any chance of Leona selling her off before the *venatus,* it was as dead as that retchwyrm now. Her domina would have to ponder some other way to pay her creditors—though if all went well this eve, that should prove no difficulty. Wealthy marrowborn often offered patronage to favored collegia, and with the Falcons of Remus the toast of the city, Leona should have no trouble securing investment.

The future of the collegium was assured.

All that remained was securing her place at the *magni*.

Mia soon heard the clinking of a ring upon a crystal goblet, a lull in conversation. A voice called out in the room beyond; a silk-smooth baritone Mia guessed must belong to Governor Messala.

"Esteemed guests, honored friends, I thank you for visiting my humble home this nevernight. It gives me and my good wife no end of pride to see so many of you here. May the Everseeing watch over you, and the Four Daughters bestow their blessings."

Messala waited for the polite applause to die before continuing.

"We hold this feast every *venatus,* to give thanks to friends who grace our city but rarely, and yet, leave their mark indelibly on the hearts and minds of our citizens. It is with no hyperbole that I declare yesterturn's *venatus* the greatest seen in our fine city, and I thank each and every sanguila here present who toiled to make it so!"

Messala paused again for applause. It was a rarity for sanguila to be invited to a governor's home—blood masters could never hold the status of the true marrowborn. But Mia could see Messala's acumen in arranging it. The sanguila were popular with common folk, and the love of the citizenry had seen Julius Scaeva flout all convention and sit in the consuls' chair for three terms. It made sense for Messala to court the men who owned the favor of the mob.

A snake this one, sure and true.

"Now," Messala continued. "Each sanguila has brought their champion, that we may marvel. But for you, dear friends, I've arranged a gift more marvelous still. Through the generosity of Dona Leona of the Remus Collegium"—Mia heard a murmur ripple through the guests—"I am pleased to present the victor of yesterturn's Ultima, and one of the finest warriors to set foot upon the sands . . . Crow, the Savior of Stormwatch!"

The doors were flung wide, and Mia looked out into a sea of curious faces. Hundreds of people were in attendance—the cream of society, gathered in pretty knots or lying on divans around the vast room. The hall was marble, frescoed, tall windows thrown open to the let in the cool nevernight breeze. Plates were laden with food, goblets overflowed with wine, wealth dripping off the walls.

Mia recognized this world. She'd grown up in it, after all. Daughter of a marrowborn familia, raised in opulence just like this. So much wealth held in so few palms. A kingdom of the blind, built on the backs of the bruised and the broken.

And nobody born to it ever questioning a thing.

Governor Messala stood at the center of the room—a handsome Itreyan man with dark, piercing eyes. The divans were arranged about his own, and guests were seated according to their status. Mia saw Dona Leona at a place of honor on Messala's right side, Arkades beside her. Furian loomed behind, dressed in a breastplate of iron, bracers and shin guards crafted like falcon's wings. The champion was practically seething, staring at Mia with hatred in his eyes.

But when she looked at him, still . . . that hunger . . .

That *want*.

Mia noted other sanguila around the room, recognizing their sigils. A heavyset man wearing the sword and shield of the Trajan Collegium. A one-handed man that could only be Phillipi, a former gladiatii who'd started his own stable. And there among them, Mia saw an overweight man wearing a frock coat embroidered with golden lions. She recognized him immediately—the man who'd offered to buy her for a thousand silver priests, and been bested by a single coin.

Leonides.

He was still sat close to Messala, Mia noted, even though he hadn't fielded a fighter in the Ultima. She wondered again at that, and at Leona's revelation that the governor had long favored the Lions of Leonides. Looking about the room, another might have seen a simple banquet. But Mia saw a spiderweb, sticky strands spun among the guests, vibration thrumming to the center of the web. And at the heart of it was Dona Leona, a goblet to her lips, sitting blithely at the spider's right hand.

Leonides himself seemed unremarkable in many ways. Too fond of his food and drink perhaps, but no kind of monster. He sipped his wine and affected a yawn, pretending not to notice Mia had entered. But she saw how he watched, the glittering blue eyes he'd gifted his daughter not missing a thing.

Thus, the greatest monsters get their way, she realized.

By looking just like the rest of us.

Beside Leonides stood his hulking bald executus, Titus, the girth of his arms straining his silken shirt. And behind Titus, Mia saw an ominous figure, at least seven feet tall, cloaked and cowled despite the heat.

. . . His champion?

"Good Crow."

The governor's voice snatched Mia from her reverie.

"Come forward," he beckoned. "Let Stormwatch see its savior."

Mia marched into the room as commanded, the guards in step beside her.

The guests weren't so crass as to applaud her presence—Mia was property, after all, and quality didn't clap when a pet successfully performed a trick. But she could feel an arkemical current in the air nevertheless; curiosity, admiration, even desire. Just a turn ago, she'd had tens of thousands of people on their feet, roaring her name. That gave her a kind of gravity, she realized. The same kind of magnetism Arkades wore like armor, the other gladiatii in the room fought to attain. Primal, perhaps. Steeped in blood.

But power nonetheless.

"I commend you, good Crow," Messala said, "and give thanks on behalf of the citizens of our city. Not only did you treat us to a spectacle unlike any other, but through skill and courage, the lives of no few of our citizens were rescued from calamity." The governor raised his goblet, joined by the many guests around the room. "Aa bless and keep you, and Tsana ever guide your hand."

Mia bowed. "You honor me, Governor."

"You honor *us*, as does your domina." The governor turned with a smile to the woman at his right, raised his goblet to Leona. "My thanks to you, gracious Dona, for allowing opportunity to see our savior up close."

Leona inclined her head. "I am your humble servant, Governor."

"She *is* quite magnificent, aye?" Messala said to his guests, walking around Mia and admiring the view from every angle. "The goddess Tsana made flesh. 'Tis one thing to bear witness from the boxes, quite another to see her here, neh?"

Leona smiled. "Who'd have thought one so fair could be so fierce?"

"I'd wager she could best any three of my houseguards."

Leona smiled wide, basking in the adoration. She shot a poison glance at her father, Mia noting Leonides's face was flush with anger. And as a thought seized her, Mia saw the dona look to her executus, lips curling in a devious smile.

"Perhaps you and your guests desire a demonstration, Governor Quintus?"

The man tilted his head, playful. "Would you indulge us, Mi Dona?"

"It would be my honor to pit my Crow against your finest man," Leona said. "*E navium*, of course."*

---

*Matches in the calendar leading up to the *Venatus Magni* are often fought *e mortium*, or to the death. Little else will satisfy the appetites of the crowd, and it's not as if anybody could talk a sand kraken out of their breakfast anyway. But many gladiatii matches are fought *e navium*, or to submission.

Though real steel is still employed, a wounded gladiatii may appeal to the editorii for the match to end at any time by holding out a palm in supplication, and death

Messala raised an eyebrow, looked among his guests. "What say you, friends?"

Arkades frowned at the suggestion, obviously displeased. Mia herself didn't much fancy the thought of performing for the elite's amusement—she was black and blue from her battle against the retchwyrm yesterturn. But the marrowborn were well charmed with the dona's suggestion, and impressing with a simple bout *did* seem a sensible way for Leona to secure the patronage she so needed.

Still . . .

Mia looked to Leonides. Back to Messala. Trying to shake the ill feeling crawling on her skin.

The governor turned to one of his guards—a burly lump with biceps as thick as his neck. "Varius, perhaps you'd be kind enough to oblige?"

The big man nodded, took a gladius from the guard beside him, and tossed it to Mia. Snatching it from the air, she looked to Dona Leona, who simply gave an encouraging nod while Furian—obviously incensed at being overshadowed—glowered in the background. Space was cleared by the governor's servants in the center of the room, and Mia took up her place, sword raised, trying to shake her misgivings. The guard drew his own blade and bowed to the governor, set his eyes on Mia.

"I beg pardon, honored Governor," came a voice. "If I might interject?"

All eyes turned to Sanguila Leonides, standing by his divan and bowing low.

"Good Leonides?" Messala asked.

"Gracious host, I mean no offense to your man," Leonides said. "But if we are to see the Savior of Stormwatch at her finest, might I suggest she cross steel with one trained in the arts of the sand?" Leonides turned glittering eyes to his daughter. "Unless the Crow's sanguila feels she is not fit for the task?"

---

blows aren't meted to a fallen foe at the match's end. Injuries still abound, but accidental fatalities are rare in *e navium* bouts. Thus, sanguila can test the mettle of their opponent's stables and build a reputation for their collegia while avoiding the inconvenience and expense of losing a fighter every time they lose a match.

In times past, crafty sanguila employed bladders of chicken's blood and fake blades in order to give appearance of fatalities, even in official *venatus* matches. But such subterfuge can only last so long—the crowds tended to notice when their slaughtered favorites kept returning from the grave. Such cheap theatrics were banned by the editorii in 34PR, and relegated to the realm of mummers and theaters where they belong. If one attends a death match of the *venatus* these turns, gentlefriends, if you can be assured of one thing, it is this:

The dead stay fucking dead.

Leona stared at her father across the crowd, her face a mask of perfect calm. But Mia's hackles were raised. She could see the trap now. With a few buttered words, Messala had manipulated Leona into putting a sword in Mia's hand, and Leonides could make his daughter look the coward if challenge was refused. And yet, Mia knew the man wasn't fool enough to propose a match without some advantage.

It seemed finally the dona had a sense of the danger herself now, eyes flickering to her host, back to her father, remaining mute a moment too long.

"She hesitates?" Leonides smiled to the other guests. "Understandable, of course. Remus Collegium has only three laurels to its name, and our Crow here is but a babe upon the sands. Perhaps our savior needs a few turns to rest her wings before she is fit to fight again, neh?"

Mia saw Arkades whisper in his dona's ear. But Leona raised her hand in annoyance, and the man fell silent. She glanced once more about the room, the faces of the assembled marrowborn—folk she might have sat among as an equal were she still married to a justicus. Patrons she now needed to keep her collegium afloat. Mia could see that desperate need to impress in her eyes. The same desire that saw her bid at the Gardens without thought, spend beyond her means, dress as if she were attending a gala every turn. And as Mia's heart sank to see her so easily goaded, warning trapped behind her teeth, Leona inclined her head and smiled.

"I thought only to spare you embarrassment, Sanguila Leonides. But I gratefully accept your offer. My bloody beauty will meet any man from your stable, steel to steel."

"Man? O, no, my dear, you misunderstand." Leonides motioned to the robed and hooded figure looming beside him. "I'd thought to keep my Ishkah here in lieu until the next *venatus,* as I've only just secured her purchase. But in honor of good Governor Messala, and fighting *e navium,* I see no risk in a small preview to whet appetites now."

He turned to the figure, speaking softly.

"Be gentle with her, my lioness."

A murmur of excitement rippled across the room as Leonides's fighter stepped forward into the sparring space. This was a treat no one had expected— to see champions cross blades for the marrowborn's own private amusement. The guests smiled wide, teeth stained dark with wine, pulses quickening at the thought of blood in the water. Mia raised her sword, sunlight glinting on the edge.

"Ladies and gentlefriends, honored hosts," Leonides said with a dramatic sweep of his hand. "May I present the latest addition to my pride. A foe fiercer than the Black Mother herself, a terror among her kind, whose very name means 'death' in the tongue of the Dominion. It has taken me years to secure a prize like her, but in all my time beside the sand, I have never seen her equal. I give you my next champion, and the next victor of the *Venatus Magni* . . . Ishkah, the Exile!"

Leonides dropped his hand. And as the crowd gasped in wonder, his challenger sloughed off its robe to reveal the figure beneath.

"Four Daughters . . . ," someone breathed.

"Almighty Aa . . . ," another whispered.

Maw's teeth . . .

Mia swallowed thickly, shadow rippling at her feet.

A silkling.

Mia had read about the denizens of the Silken Dominion in Mercurio's books as a child, but she'd never thought to see one in the flesh. Looking at Leonides's fighter, Mia could see she was almost certainly female, hips curved beneath her studded leather skirt, six arms folded over the subtle curve of her breasts. She was seven feet tall, her skin chitinous, a green so dark it was almost black. Her lips were painted white, two large, featureless orbs set in a smooth, oval face, six smaller eyes scattered across her cheeks like freckles. She had no eyelids with which to blink. From her readings, Mia guessed the silkling was young, but in truth, she had no real way to tell.*

The silkling reached up to her back, drew forth six glittering blades, each

---

*Native to the Drakespine Mountains bordering Vaan and Itreya and, despite their rather pretty name, the arachnid silkling are a species renowned as . . . somewhat unneighborly. The Silken Dominion is scattered over thousands of miles of inhospitable crags, and its conquest by the Itreyan legions proved extraordinarily costly; it was only after every War Walker in the Iron Collegium was brought to bear that the silkling BroodQueen was brought to heel.

Though the silkling have ostensibly sworn loyalty to the Itreyan Republic, their seat in the Senate House has remained empty since it was explained that only males can hold the title of Itreyan senator (male silkling are smaller than their counterparts, and venomless). The Senate themselves are content to leave the silkling mostly alone, and the threat of a posting as Itreyan ambassador to the Dominion is often used as a stick to keep unruly younger members in line. As a general rule, the silkling have nothing to do with the Republic or its citizenry if they can help it.

Silkling females mark their cheeks with ritual scarification for every brood they've hatched. They murder their mates postcoitus with alarming regularity. And if you're tempted to ask how it is the species continues to thrive under such circumstances, I can only assure you that, yes, the females possess vaginas, and yes, the males have penises.

The rest should be self-explanatory.

gently curved and razor-sharp, etched with strange glyphs. As the assembled marrowborn murmured in astonishment, she wove the weapons through the air in an intricate, twisting dance, the steel whistling as it sliced the air. Finishing her display, Ishkah spread her arms like fans, blades poised and pointed directly at Mia.

The girl glanced to Leona, Arkades, Furian. The dona's face was stone, but her eyes were dark with fear, seeing now how simply she'd been played. And yet, with the marrowborn now awash with excitement, she dare not make an overture to end the bout prematurely. Leonides looked to his daughter and smiled like a cat who'd stolen the cream, the bucket, and the maid to boot.

He played her like a lyre. If I lose here, the people of the city might still sing my name. But the people of influence and power . . . they'll sing only of the Lions of Leonides. And Leona's chance of patronage goes up in flames.

Mia saw the trap revealed. Paused a moment to admire its simplicity. She saw the strands of the web between the governor and Leonides, the invitation that had brought Leona here with her guard down. Plying her with a wine or two and a bevy of compliments from folk above her station, manipulating her into a fight she couldn't afford to lose, and yet supposing she couldn't ever win.

We'll see about that, bastards . . .

"*. . . are you certain about this . . . ?*" came a whisper from her hair.

"Are you certain you could shut up for the next minutes so I don't get killed?" she muttered.

"*. . . ah . . . probably not . . . ?*"

"Exactly."

Truthfully, Mia had never been less certain about anything in her life, but she had no choice—to lose here would mean the collegium would still be up to its neck in debt, all her work still at risk. And so, she turned to one of the guards who'd praised her victory before they entered the hall, glanced to the blade at his waist.

"Might I trouble you for a loan, good sir?"

The guard drew his sword, handed it over dutifully. "Tsana guide you, lass."

Mia took the blade with a nod of thanks. And cutting her swords through the air, Mister Kindly doing his level best to shut up for a few minutes, Mia took her place in the sparring ring, eyes locked on the silkling's.

"This contest will be fought *e navium*," Governor Messala reminded them. "A hand raised in submission will signal an end to the bout. Fight with honor, and for the glory of your collegium. Aa bless and keep you, and Tsana guide your hand."

The crowd hushed, the music stopped, and all Mia could hear was the thunderous beating of her own heart.

"Begin!" Messala cried.

Quick as silver, Mia struck with both blades, steel ringing as the silkling parried with four of her own. Dancing forward, she struck again at head and chest, but her foe blocked again with ease. Countering this time, the silkling launched a flurry of strikes at Mia, the air a whispering blur. Mia was pushed back, desperately blocking the incoming blades, until she was forced beyond the edge of the sparring circle. The marrowborn around her skittered aside, eyes on her swords. But the silkling didn't press, returning to the center of the ring and waiting with her weapons poised in a glittering fan.

Mia tilted her head, felt her neck pop. Tossed her hair from her eyes. And stepping up to her foe, she launched another salvo.

She'd always prided herself on her skill with a blade—she'd trained hard under Mercurio, and harder still in the Red Church, her natural speed combined with utter fearlessness and an uncanny aim. But even her best foes had only met her with two blades of their own—never six of the cursed things. Wherever she struck, the silkling's steel was waiting. Whenever she left a gap, Ishkah forced her back. The silkling had the size, the reach, the speed. And worse, Mia knew she wasn't giving her all. Just as Arkades had warned the first turn she set foot on the sand in Crow's Nest, Ishkah was studying her form in readiness for her final assault.

And so, seeking to even the scales (how is six blades against two fair, she reasoned), Mia reached out to shadow at the silkling's feet.

None in the room would have noticed it—the dark shivered only a little. But as the silkling stepped forward to strike, she found her boots fixed fast to the mosaic tile at her feet, the long shadows cast by the sunlight outside. A moment's hesitation from her foe was enough, and Mia struck hard, a blinding series of strikes that broke through Ishkah's guard and opened a long, ragged wound on her shoulder, just shy of her throat. The crowd gasped in astonishment, blood as green as poplar leaves sprayed from the wound. Mia knocked another of the silkling's swords flying, and aimed a blow low to sweep her foe off her feet.

And then, just like the first turn she set foot on the sand in Crow's Nest,
she lost her grip on the shadows
and her foe stepped aside.

Mia's strike went wide, the silkling's blades flashed, opening up a shallow cut across the girl's knuckles and sending her sword spinning from her hand.

Mia tried to counter with her other blade, but was met by a wall of steel, Ishkah striking with an empty fist, driving the breath from the girl's lungs. Mia staggered, the silkling twirled behind her, smashing her across the back of the head with the flat of her blade. Cathedral bells rang in Mia's skull, the whole world blurring to double as her legs were knocked out from under her and she crashed senseless to the floor.

The silkling stood above her, blades poised to strike.

"Yield," she demanded, with a voice like dry cicada wings.

Mia's brow had split on the tile, her head still ringing. Fingernails clawing the ground, she blinked the blood from her eyes and struck out with her feet, trying to knock the silkling down. Ishkah sidestepped like a dancer, pressing her blades to Mia's throat.

"Yield," she said again.

Mia looked to Leona's crestfallen face. To Arkades, shaking his head in disdain. And finally to Furian. Staring into his dark eyes, she knew, sure as she knew the turn she'd faced Arkades—the bastard had wrested her grip on the shadows, allowed her foe to slip free.

Teeth bared.

Rage boiling in her belly.

"Even a dog knows when it is beaten," came a voice from among the sanguila.

"Perhaps the fault lies not with the dog," Leonides replied, "but with its mistress?"

Leona's cheeks were spotted with rage as she looked at her father, stepped toward him with clenched fists. Arkades whispered—some word Mia couldn't hear—and the woman fell still, face flushed, eyes burning.

"Yield," she commanded.

"*. . . yield, mia . . .*"

Just a turn ago, she'd stood triumphant among tens of thousands of people, every one of them chanting her name. And now, she lay on her belly like a whipped pup, the marrowborn around her tittering with amusement. Mia looked to Furian, hate boiling in her chest, the edges of her shadow rippling. She could feel the dark in her, the black, wanting to stretch out toward the Unfallen and tear him limb from bloody limb. But the blades at her throat, the memory of her familia, the thought that none in this room could know what she truly was—all of it helped her to fight down the rage, stow it in her breast to cool. Not forgotten, no. Nor forgiven. Never.

And slowly, Mia raised one trembling, bloodstained hand to the governor.

". . . Yield," she whispered.

Satisfied, the silkling removed her blades from Mia's throat, sheathed them at her back. Governor Messala looked among his guests, the mood now shifted, tinged with red. Tension was thick in the air, not just from the bloodshed in the circle, but the obvious enmity between Dona Leona and her father. If there was one thing that entertained the rich and idle more than bloodshed, it was scandal. To see it played out in front of them was better sport than any *venatus* under the suns.

"You deceived me," Leona said, voice trembling.

"You deceived yourself," her father sneered. "When you started that backwater collegium. I warned you, Leona. The sands are no place for a woman, and the sanguila's box is no place for you."

Leona glanced to the silkling. "Don't look now, Father, but your champion appears to have breasts."

The crowd tittered as Leona scored her point. Emboldened, she continued.

"But perhaps you don't intend to field her on the sand at all? I noted your collegium's absence yesterturn in the Ultima, when mine was claiming the victor's laurel. All the better to unveil her like some cheap mummer in a two-beggar corner show, and cheat me of my glory behind closed doors?"

Leonides's face darkened.

"If you think yourself cheated," he declared, "let Aa and Tsana decide. The next *venatus* is at Whitekeep, five weeks hence. I will field my Ishkah against your Crow. And since you so desperately need it, dear daughter, I shall wager one of my berths in the *magni* against the winner. But a fight to the death this time, neh?"

Leona looked to the marrowborn about her, opened her mouth to sp—

"I fear the contest unbalanced," said a voice. "And the crowd would cry the same."

All eyes turned at the growl. Arkades, the Red Lion of Itreya, stood by his mistress's side, glaring at his former master. His face was twisted in a scowl, his scar cutting a deep shadow down his features. Mia could see the cold enmity in his eyes, looking at the man he'd once fought and bled for.

"I commend you on your find, Sanguila Leonides," Executus continued, glancing at the silkling. "I have never seen her equal either. Not in all my years *upon* the sand. But six blades against two? What honor lies in contest such as that?"

Arkades looked at Mia still sprawled on the floor, then to Furian behind him.

"Especially when our collegium's best is absent the match."

Leonides looked his former champion over with a calculating smile.

"A fair point. Never let it be said Leonides does not know the will of the crowd." Glancing around the assembled marrowborn, the showman in him rose to the fore. "Bring your best *three* champions to Whitekeep, then. Ishkah will face them all. Six blades to six. No quarter, no submission. A match for the ages, neh?"

Arkades shook his head. "I wou—"

"Done."

The marrowborn looked to Leona. The sanguila stood still as stone, glare locked on her father. Mia could see the hate there, pure and blinding. She knew that hatred well. The fire of it. Keeping you warm when all else in the world was black and cold. Keeping you moving, when all else in the world seemed simply to drag you down.

She wondered what Leonides had done, exactly, to earn it.

"Done," Leona repeated. She glanced about the smiling marrowborn, the wine-stained teeth, eyes glittering. "I will see you in Whitekeep, Father."

Leona swept from the room, Furian following close behind. Arkades and Leonides stared at each other a moment longer, former master and former champion, now bitter rivals. The executus limped over to Mia, loomed above her expectantly. The girl struggled to her feet with a soft groan, blood gumming her lashes shut, her head pounding with pain. Stumbling behind the big man as he strode from the room.

"Arkades," Leonides called.

The man stopped, turned to look at the smiling sanguila.

"When next you speak to her, thank your domina for sparing me the mistake of your little Crow's purchase. If your mistress seeks to recoup some of her losses, I've a pleasure house in Whitekeep always looking for new quim."

Leonides looked Mia up and down with a sneer.

"Perhaps she'd fare better with a different kind of sword in hand."

An amused ripple flowed through the crowd. Arkades turned and limped from the room without a word. Mia followed, head hung low, dark hair draped about her bloodstained face. She knew it was foolish, that she shouldn't let this pompous fool get to her. That in winning the *magni,* she'd have to defeat Leonides's best fighters and see him taste the shame of defeat anyway. But still . . .

But still . . .

Rubbing this prick's face in his own shit had now become a burning priority.

Personal now, bastard.

CHAPTER 2⁰

THREE

"Furian, certainly," Arkades said.

"That goes without saying," Leona replied. "He is our champion."

"Are you certain, Mi Dona? I thought perhaps you'd forgot him."

Leona steepled her fingers at her chin and glowered at her executus.

"I forget nothing, Arkades. And I forgive even less."

The pair were sat in a small cabin aboard the *Gloryhound,* the ship rolling and creaking with the ocean's swell. They'd set sail the turn after the banquet at Governor Messala's home, and four turns out from Crow's Nest, Leona and Arkades were still trying to decide who would stand against his silkling. Magistrae sat behind her mistress, weaving Leona's hair into artful plaits while the pair argued. And below her chair, puddled in the shadow, sat a cat who was nothing close to a cat at all.

"We could refuse the match," Arkades said. "Throw our dice in the Ultima."

"We need two laurels between now and truelight, Executus," Leona replied. "And Whitekeep is the last *venatus* in the calendar before the *magni.*"

"Our equillai could win us a laurel. Bryn and Byern ran a close second t—"

"Aye, and if they lose?" Leona asked. "Even with victory in the Ultima after that, we'd find ourselves a laurel short. We wager twice by refusing challenge against my father. We wager but once if we accept. The only way we can be *assured* of fighting in Godsgrave is to best that fucking silkling."

"Language, Domina," Magistrae warned.

"Aye," Leona sighed. "Apologies."

The older woman's brow creased in thought as she went back to work on Leona's hair. "Beg pardon, Domina, but even if you win contest against your father's champion, will the editorii honor the wager?"

"Precedent has long been set," Arkades replied, toying with the handle of his walking stick. "Well-established collegium often lure more inexperienced sanguila to compete in one-sided matches with the promise of a seat at the *magni.*"

Leona aimed a withering glare. "Well, that was unusually tactful."

"He is *playing* you, Mi Dona," Arkades replied. "This berth the bait, and those games the noose. Not content with denying you patronage, your father wants you to send your three best gladiatii to be butchered, and with them, this collegium's future."

"Without the *magni*, we have no future!" Leona snapped. "Our Crow was flogged in front of every marrowborn in Stormwatch! No one with a purse will touch us now!"

Silence rang in the room, broken only by the creak of timbers, the incessant pounding of waves upon the hull. Mister Kindly yawned and licked his paw.

"Furian, then," Arkades sighed.

"Aye," Leona nodded. "And the Crow beside him."

Executus leaned forward, shaking his head. "Mi Dona—"

"Unless the next words to leave your mouth are 'that's a splendid notion, Mi Dona, and by the by, your hair is looking magnificent,' I do not wish to hear them, Arkades."

Executus scratched his beard, tried unsuccessfully to hide his smile.

"Ah, he can still laugh," Leona preened. "I thought perhaps you'd forgot how."

"All due respec—"

"She is the Savior of Stormwatch," Leona sighed.

"That silkling almost cracked her fucking skull open!"

"Language!" Magistrae scowled.

Arkades mumbled apology as Leona continued.

"She was bested in Messala's palazzo, aye, but the common folk don't know that. The citizenry will expect to see her draw steel under our banner. Four Daughters, Arkades, she butchered a retchwyrm almost single-handed. You yourself declared the match against the silkling unbalanced. Crow won a laurel for this collegium, and did honor to my name in front of the entire arena. She deserves *some* credit, surely?"

The big man hung silent a moment, finally gave a grudging nod.

"She can't lift a shield to save herself. But her Caravaggio was . . . passable."

"Such praise," Magistrae sighed. "Pray, don't let the girl hear you sing like that, she'll never get her head through the door."

Leona and Arkades shared a smile as the older woman began a new braid.

"So," the big man finally sighed. "Furian and the Crow. Who shall be our third?"

Leona pouted, tapping her lip.

". . . Butcher?"

"He plays badly with others."

"Wavewaker?"

"He's a fine blade, but I fear he's too much the brawler."

"If you'll permit me an opinion, Domina?" said Magistrae.

"O, aye, here's a turn," Arkades sighed. "Advice from the nurse. And who shall we seek counsel of next? The cabin boy?"

Leona shot him a withering glance. "Speak, Magistrae."

The old woman raised one graying eyebrow at Arkades before continuing. "Granted, I am no expert. But the Crow's strength seems to lie in her speed. It seems you need someone to bridge the gap between her pace and Furian's brawn."

Leona and Arkades looked at each other, spoke as one.

"Bladesinger."

Arkades leaned back in his chair, staring into space.

"She has the reach Crow lacks, the speed Furian needs. It could work."

Leona leaned forward, squeezed his hand.

"It *must* work," she replied.

Arkades looked down at her hand in his. Her skin was pale, her fingers tapered and delicate, soft as silk. His hand was browned by the suns, cracked like old leather, callused from sword grips and the press of life on the sands.

He swallowed thickly. Pausing, as if gathering his nerve. And wrapping her hand in his own, he leaned down and placed a soft kiss on her knuckles.

"It *will* work, Mi Dona," he murmured. "I vow it."

Leona blinked, hand trapped at Arkades's lips, uncertain where to look. Magistrae simply looked aghast. But without giving his dona a chance to respond, Arkades released his mistress and stood, took up his cane, and limped toward the door. Stopping at the threshold, he turned toward Leona.

"Your hair *is* looking magnificent, by the by."

Executus turned on his heel and left the room.

N o!"
The practice blade slammed into Mia's side, sending her to her knees. Bladesinger lunged with a fierce cry, but Arkades was already twisting aside, bringing his second blade down on the woman's forearm. She stumbled back into Furian, and a riposte from Arkades sent the pair of them sprawling.

The trio lay panting in the dirt, drenched to the bones in sweat.

"You listen, but you do not hear!" the executus bellowed, limping back and forth between them. "The Exile is unlike any foe you have faced. Six blades wielded with a single purpose. Eight eyes to track your every move. I have but a pair of each and you cannot best me. How in the name of the Four fucking Daughters do you hope to stand the victors against her?"

They had been drilling all turn, every turn since they'd arrived back at Crow's Nest. The other gladiatii trained around them, but in truth, all eyes were on the four in the circle, watching Arkades kick his opponent's arses up and down the sand. The two suns hung heavy in the sky, blistering with all the heat of summersdeep, burning gold and bloody red. And if one looked hard enough, a subtle hint of brighter blue could be seen on the horizon, heralding the slow arrival of the third eye of Aa.

Truelight was approaching, and with it, the *magni*. And the Falcons of Remus Collegium were only a little closer to those sands than they'd been three months ago.

"Get up," Arkades barked. "Move with resolve and strike as one."

"A difficult task," Bladesinger growled, "when two of us attack at cross-purpose."

Mia wiped the sweat from her brow, glowered across the sand at Furian. The Unfallen stared back at her, black eyes gleaming like obsidian. He dragged himself to his feet and offered his hand to Bladesinger, pulling her up from the dust. Ignoring Mia completely, he gathered his sword and shield and took up a ready stance.

Mia stood, practice blades in hand.

"Attack!" roared Executus.

Without waiting for the others, Furian launched his assault on Arkades, battering him back across the sands. In practice, Executus had always held his own, teaching his sparring partners their weaknesses without seeking to punish them. But over the last few turns, Mia began to realize how much the former champion had held himself back. Arkades was a god on the sand—even with his missing leg, he moved like water, struck like thunder, stood like a mountain. His blows left the air bruised behind them, his guard knew no flaw, and he punished every mistake with a blow close to bone-breaking.

Battering Furian's attack aside, Arkades smashed the champion onto his backside and turned on Bladesinger and Mia. The pair moved well together, Mia weaving below the taller woman's blows and striking at Arkades's belly and legs. She landed a passing blow to his gut, but as she twisted aside from the Red Lion's riposte, she crashed right into a charging Furian, who'd dragged himself to his feet and thrown himself back into the fray.

"Watch your fucki—"

A wooden blade cracked across Mia's temple, sent her flying. Arkades disarmed Bladesinger and locked up Furian's guard, toppling the man with an elbow to the jaw. Rolling across the sand to scoop up her weapons, saltlocks flying, Bladesinger cursed as Arkades hurled both his weapons and struck her in the throat and above the heart.

He stood, empty-handed, chest heaving as he glared at the vanquished trio. "Pitiful," he spat.

"That stupid bitch got in my way," Furian growled.

"O, Furian," Mia sighed, fixing him with a withering stare. "If I've learned anything in this life, it's how not to care when a dog calls me bitch."

"Dog, am I?" Furian rose out of the dust, Mia standing just as swift.

"Enough!" Arkades barked.

The pair hung still, eyes locked and poised to strike. Mia could feel her shadow straining at its edges, like water behind a dam. If she weren't holding it in check, she knew without a doubt it would be reaching across the sand toward Furian's own, hands twisted to claws. Her teeth were gritted, and she fought for calm, blinking the sweat from her eyes. For her to lose her grip here, for everyone to mark her for what she was . . .

"Enough sparring for one turn," the executus declared. "Crow, Bladesinger, go work the woodmen. You must strike harder if you're to break the silkling's guard. Furian, attend your footwork. You need better pace to best this foe."

Mia and Furian glared at each other, not moving a muscle.

"Move!" Arkades roared.

Bladesinger gathered up her fallen swords and marched across the yard, began furiously battering the training dummies. Mia followed slower, narrowed eyes still aimed at Furian, feeling cold hate burn along with the sickness and hunger she felt in her belly whenever he was near.

Pigheaded fucking idiot . . .

Taking up position beside Bladesinger, Mia pictured Furian's head atop her woodman, started beating it mercilessly. Sweat soaked her skin, bangs hanging in her eyes as she smashed her blade into its belly, chest, shit-eating face.

"You're going to get me killed," Bladesinger muttered, shaking her head.

"It's Furian sowing discord, not I."

"It's the pair of you," the woman spat. "I don't know why you don't just find a nice dark corner to fuck in and get it over with."

Mia scoffed. "I'd rather have Butcher slip his cock into me."

"Then what lies between you two?" Bladesinger paused to bind her floor-length saltlocks up. "Your tongues spit venom but your eyes never stray far from the other."

Mia knew the woman spoke truth. She'd have bested that silkling if not for Furian's interference. Instead she'd taken a public beating and Leona had lost all chance at patronage among the Stormwatch marrowborn. And yet . . .

She couldn't deny it. Despite her tangle of feelings for Ashlinn, she was *drawn* to Furian. And though the Unfallen was doubtlessly attractive, this was something beyond desire. Something bone-deep. The same thing she'd felt when Lord Cassius was near her. Something beyond lust and more like . . . longing. Like an amputee for her missing limb. Like a puzzle, searching for a piece of itself.

But why?

Cleo had spoken of it in her journal. Walking the earth, being drawn to other darkin as a spider to a fly, and then . . .

. . . then eating them.

But what the 'byss did that mean?

"The many were one. And will be again; one beneath the three, to raise the four, free the first, blind the second and the third.

"O, Mother, blackest Mother, what have I become?"

Mia shook her head, spat into the dust.

"I've no fucking clue," she said.

"Well, you'd best ponder on it, and fashion a solution," Bladesinger warned. "Because if we step into a contest for our lives the way we are now? All three of us will be sitting by the Hearth before truelight, little Crow."

The woman began beating the strawman again, eyes narrowed. Mia stared at Furian across the yard, her belly tangled in hateful knots.

"There's no reasoning with him. I've tried before. He's an ignorant fool."

Crack! went Bladesinger's sword against her target.

"Furian is many things," she grunted. "Stubborn, perhaps. Arrogant, most definitely. But never a fool."

"Bollocks." Mia struck her woodman's neck. "Have you ever tried talking to him?"

"O, aye," Bladesinger nodded. "Like bashing your head against a stone wall. Honor." *Crack!* "Discipline." *Crack!* "Faith. These are the principles that define him. But above all, the Unfallen is a champion, and you are a threat to that." The woman shrugged. "The greatest gulf between people is always pride, little Crow."

Mia sighed, glanced over at Furian.

"That sounds suspiciously like wisdom to me."

Crack! went Bladesinger's sword against her target.

"Not mine," she grunted. "It's from the Book of the Blind."

Mia stabbed at her woodman's chest. "Isn't that old Liisian scripture?"

"Aye," Bladesinger nodded. "I know it by heart. We had to read holy texts from all over the Republic." *Crack! Crack!* "The suffi at Farrow like you to have a worldly perspective before you're inducted into the order. Know the world, know yourself."

Mia tilted her head, looked sidelong at her comrade. It made sense now. The full-body tattoos. The singing she occasionally heard under Bladesinger's door.

". . . You were a priestess?"

"Just a novice." *Crack!* "Never got to take my final vows."

"Then what the 'byss"—*Crack! Crack!*—"are you doing here?"

Bladesinger shrugged. "Pirate raid. A quick sale. A common tale."

Mia shook her head, sickened. "Too fucking common."

"The suffi named it so"—*Crack!*—"when I was born."

Mia bent double, hands to her knees as she panted.

Black Mother, this heat . . .

"Named it so?"

Bladesinger stopped drubbing the woodman, wiped the sweat from her brow. "Do you know how Dweymeri are named, little Crow?"

Mia nodded, remembering Tric's tale to her in the Quiet Mountain.

"You're taken to Farrow when you're young," she replied. "To the Temple of Trelene. The suffi holds you up to the ocean and asks the Mother about the path before you, and gives you a name to match it."

"Bladesinger, she named me," the woman said. "Not Hymnsinger. Not Prayersinger. *Blade*singer. And I'll be damned," she said, pointing her practice sword at Mia's face, "if the last my blades sing is because you and Furian can't agree on the color of shit. Fuck him. Stab him. Stab him while you fuck him, I don't give a damn. But get it sorted before you get us all killed."

Mia looked across to Furian, speed training in one corner of the yard. As Mia stared, he glanced up, meeting her eyes with that burning black gaze.

The greatest gulf between people is always pride.

"You two!" Arkades roared. "Back to work!"

Mia sighed. But as always, she obeyed.

I suspected I'd be seeing you, witch," Furian said.

Mia looked up and down the hallway, just to be safe. Mister Kindly was trailing the guard patrol—there was no chance they might catch her. But without her passenger, her belly was a tangle of hunger and trepidation, made all the worse by the presence of the man she'd come to see. She tucked her stolen fork/lockpick into her loincloth and stood expectantly on the threshold of the Unfallen's room.

Waiting.

Wait

ing

"Can I fucking come in or not?" Mia finally snarled.

"If it please you," Furian said with a sour look. "Though if the breath were mine, I'd not trouble myself in the wasting of it."

Mia scowled and stepped inside, closing the door behind. Looking around the room, she saw it was the same as when she'd last visited—the shrine to Tsana, the crude trinity of Aa scribed on the wall, the incense burning.

Furian was at least dressed this time, though within these walls, that didn't count for much. His torso was bared, rippling with muscle, his skin bronzed from working beneath the suns. He was a golden god, fresh from the forge. And he was an intolerable prick, spat from the depths of the abyss.

She hated him. She wanted him. Neither and both at the same time.

Mia looked to her shadow, saw it drifting like smoke across the wall, reaching out with translucent hands toward Furian's own. The Unfallen's shadow trembled in response, but with visible effort, he held it in check, glowering at Mia with those bottomless black eyes.

"Take hold of yourself," he growled.

Mia clenched her jaw, pulled her shadow into check. It retreated reluctantly, hair blowing as if in a breeze, hand stretched out like a lover saying farewell. She thought of Ashlinn, then. A pang of momentary, inexplicable guilt. Wanting two people, and wanting neither, promises made to none. But in comparison to Furian, a traitor and her honeyed lips and her poison tongue seemed a downright simple proposition . . .

"What do you want, witch?" the Unfallen asked.

"I'm no more a witch than you are, Furian."

"I hold no truck with the darkness," he spat. "I do not step between the shadows and sneak about our domina's house like a thief."

"No, you just threaten to bring the walls down about her ears, you dozy shit."

"You dare . . . ?"

"O, I dare," Mia replied. "That's the difference between me and most."

"I fight for the glory of this collegium. The glory of our domina."

"You cost our domina her patronage at Stormwatch!" Mia hissed. "All you needed to do was keep your cock in your loincloth and let me drub the silkling, and Leona would have been up to her tits in gold."

"You werked the darkness in your match against the Exile," Furian said, folding his arms. "If I'd allowed you to win at Messala's palazzo with your devilry, you'd have set a taint at the heart of this place. I'd starve before I ate food bought with dishonest coin, and die before I claimed a laurel I'd not earned."

"Didn't earn?" Mia was incredulous. "Fuck *you,* you arrogant prick. How many retchwyrms have you slaughtered lately?"

"A victory without honor is no victory at all," he replied. "I'll not allow you to win more false accolades for this collegium with your witchery."

"So you use the same witchery to fuck with me?" Mia caught herself raising her voice, tried to pull her temper into check. "*You* called the dark when you stopped me besting the silkling. That doesn't strike you as the least bit hypocritical?"

Furian stalked toward her, fists clenched.

"Get out of here, Crow."

His shadow flared, slithering across the wall toward her own. Mia's shadow rose to meet it, twisting and rearing up like a serpent, hands twisted into claws. She swore the room turned chill, hackles raising on the back of her neck, hunger flaring in her belly and threatening to swallow her whole . . .

"No."

She closed her eyes, shook her head. Forcing the darkness back inside herself. This wasn't going the way she'd planned it. She was meant to be holding her temper, speaking sense. She didn't know what Furian's presence was doing to her, why he made her so eager for violence, what any of it meant. All she knew was . . .

"We must come to accord," she said, opening her eyes, palms out in supplication. "Furian, listen to me, if we fight together on the sands as we are now, you, Bladesinger and I will all be butchered. How will that avail our domina?"

"You may hold yourself of no account without witchery to aid you, girl," the man said, thumping his chest. "But I am the Unfallen. I fought for almost an hour in the burning suns at Talia, slew two dozen men to win my laur—"

"Ishkah isn't a fucking man! You saw her fight at Messala's palazzo. With two blades in her hands she'd be a match for any one of us. With six? Fighting to the death? She'll cut us to bloody pieces!"

"How is it you live with yourself?" The Unfallen shook his head. "No faith in the Father or his Daughters, no faith in yourself? Only shadows and darkness and deceit."

"Don't make the mistake of thinking you know me, Furian." She glanced at his trembling shadow and shook her head. "You don't even know yourself."

"Get out."

"Expecting another guest, are you?" Mia glanced to his bed.

Furian's eyes widened at that, rage darkening his brow. He raised his hand to shove her backward, and Mia moved, battering his hand aside and locking up his arm. He seized her wrist, slammed her back against the door, the pair snarling and cursing as they struggled. This close, Mia could smell his fresh sweat, feel the warmth of his skin pressed against hers, rage and lust and hunger all intertwined. Through his loincloth she could feel the heat of his cock, hardening against her hip. She wanted to kiss him, bite him, hold him, choke him, fuck him, kill him, teeth bared in a snarl, heart hammering in her chest, his lips just an inch from—

"Merciful Aa . . . ," Furian breathed.

She followed his eyeline to their shadows on the wall, breath catching in her throat. The shadows were tangled like serpents, twisting and writhing and curling like smoke. They'd lost their shapes utterly, two amorphous slivers of blackness, each entwined in the other. Mia realized they were twice as dark as they should have been, just as when Mister Kindly or Eclipse rode with her. The room was noticeably colder, her skin prickling with goosebumps, desire making her tremble.

Furian pushed her back, stepped away, horror on his face. Their shadows continued to tie themselves in knots, and the man held up three fingers—Aa's warding sign against evil. Like locks of knotted hair, the shadows slowly tore themselves apart, resuming their human shapes. They clung to one another, arms, hands, then fingertips, Furian's shadow snapping into place as he backed farther away. Mia's shadow ebbed and pulsed on the wall, like the ocean in a swell.

"What are we?" she breathed.

Furian's chest was heaving, his long dark hair moving as if of its own accord. He snatched it up, tied it in a knot behind his head, snarling.

"We are nothing, you and I."

"We're the *same*. This is who we *are*, Furian."

"*That*," Furian spat, pointing to the trinity on the wall, "is who I am. A faithful, god-fearing son of Aa. Bathed in his light and taught by his scripture. *That*," he said, pointing to the wooden swords, "is who I am. Gladiatii. Undefeated. Unbroken. Unfallen. And so I would remain, if a thousand silklings stood between me and the *magni*."

"So the *magni* is all that matters? If freedom is so important to y—"

"This is not about *freedom*," he spat. "And that is just one more difference between you and me. Being gladiatii is a masque you wear. For me, the sand, the crowd, the glory, it is a reason to wake. A reason to breathe."

Furian marched across the room, and listening briefly at the door, he opened it. He glared at Mia, seemingly unwilling to touch her again.

"Get out of here, Crow."

She'd not convinced him. Not even come close. His stupid pride. His idiotic sense of honor. His fear of who and what he was. She didn't understand any of it. And though they were both darkin, in truth, Mia realized they were completely different people. That whatever kinship they might know in the shadows, this here, this life, this flesh, they were as alike as truelight and truedark.

If you can't see your chains, what use is a key?

And so, with a sigh, she stepped beyond the threshold of his room, into the corridor beyond.

"What made you so?" she asked softly. "What were you before this?"

"Exactly what you will be when the *magni* is done, girl."

Furian shut the door in her face with a parting jab.

"Nothing."

CHAPTER 21

PLEASE

"Well, well," Sidonius said. "Look what the shadowcat dragged in."

Mia crouched on the cell floor, still dizzy from her Stepping. The barracks were almost pitch black, the quiet broken only by the soft snoring and fitful murmurs of the gladiatii around them. Sidonius lay on his side in the straw, eyes open only a sliver. Mister Kindly had warned Mia that the man was awake, but he knew her secret anyway. Well, *some* of her secrets . . .

No sense in hiding what he already knew.

"You pinch me some grub, or what?" Sid asked.

Mia smiled, tossed the man a hunk of cheese she'd stolen from the kitchen.

He grinned, tearing off a bite and speaking around his mouthful. "Sneakier than a fart in Church, you are."

"Were you waiting up for me? Awfully sweet of you."

"No, in fact I'll have you know you interrupted a lovely dream involving me, the magistrae, a riding crop and a featherdown bed."

"The magistrae?" Mia raised her eyebrow.

"I've a penchant for older women, little Crow."

"You've a penchant for anything with two tits, a hole and heartbeat, Sid."

"Ha! You know me well." The big man grinned, raising his cheese in toast. "But Four Daughters, I do like your style."

"A pity Furian can't say the same."

"Ah, that's where you were. How's he hung? A man swaggers around with that much bravado, he's usually compensating for the peanut in his britches."

Mia remembered the feel of Furian's cock against her hip, pressed her thighs together to heighten the ache. She was feeling edgy after her encounter with the Unfallen. Restless and overflowing. Trying to ignore all of it and think clear.

"I wasn't bedding him, Sid," she scowled. "I was trying to convince him not to get me fucking murdered."

"Well, speaking as a former world traveler, you'd be surprised how far a quick wristjob will go toward mending strained foreign relations."

Mia kicked the straw at her cellmate and grinned despite herself. "You're a pig."

"As I say, you know me well, little Crow."

"If Furian and I don't learn to fight together, that silkling is going to be using my lower intestines to make her sausages."

"She that fearsome?"

"I'm not afraid of her, no. But she's the best I've ever seen with a blade."

"O, aye? And how many others have you seen with a blade?"

"My fair share."

"Mmf," Sid grunted, leaning against the wall and looking Mia up and down. "Secrets within secrets with you. Not eighteen years old, I'd wager. Skinny slip of a thing, and better with a sword than I am. But you do realize there's always an alternative to becoming a silkling's suppertime, don't you?"

"And what's that?" Mia sighed. "Murder Furian in his sleep and hope Leona pairs me and Bladesinger with someone who's not an insufferable cockhead?"

Sidonius lifted his hands and made the motion of flapping wings.

"Fly awayyyyy, little Crow."

"Not an option."

Sid scoffed. "You step in and out of this cell more often than a fourteen-year-old boy spanks his chaplain. You can leave this place anytime you choose. So if Champion Cockhead is going to get you stone-cold murdered, why don't you just escape?"

Mia sighed. "If I did, every one of you would be executed."

"Bollocks," Sid said. "I watch you, Crow. I watch you watching *us*. Arkades. Leona. Furian. Me. Those little wheels behind those shady eyes always aturn. And though I don't think you're quite the coldest fish in this pond, you can't honestly say you give a damn whether any of us lives or dies. Especially when we're all likely to perish in the *venatus* anyways. So what's your game?"

"Believe me, Sidonius," Mia replied. "The last thing I'm doing here is playing."

"Have it your way, then." Sid took another bite of cheese, shook his head, wistful. "I tell you true, you remind me of a woman I used to know. It's bloody uncanny. Same eyes as you. Same skin. Secrets within secrets on her, too."

"Some old flame? Break your heart, did she?"

"Neh," Sid shook his head. "I never loved her. But most men who knew her did. She almost brought the Republic to its knees. But in the end, she and her shady eyes and her secrets within secrets got her whole familia killed. Husband. Young daughter. Baby son. And a lot of my friends besides."

Mia's stomach turned cold. Eyes narrowing.

"Who are you talking about?"

"Former dona of this house, of course," Sid said, gesturing to the walls. "Wife of the true justicus. Alinne Corvere." He shook his head. "Stupid fucking whore."

Afterward, Mia couldn't remember moving. All she could recall was the satisfying crunch as her fist landed on Sidonius's jaw, the sharp crack as his head bounced off the wall behind him. The big man cursed, tried to batter her away as she clawed at his throat, punching his cheek, his temple, his nose.

"Have you lost your—"

"Take it back," she spat.

"Get off me!"

Mia and Sidonius fell to struggling, the bigger man wrestling her onto the floor as her knuckles played a tune on his face. "*Take it back!*" she roared, the pair rolling about in the straw, flailing and punching. A few other gladiatii woke up at the commotion, Bladesinger peering out from the slit in her cell door, Otho and Felix cheering as they realized a brawl had erupted, straining at their cell bars for a better look.

"Shut the fuck up in there!" Butcher bellowed from the cell across the way.

"Peace, Crow!" Sidonius cried.

"*. . . mia stop this . . .*"

"*Take it back!*"

"Take *what* back?"

Sidonius cracked Mia across the jaw, Mia punched him in the throat. Choking, the big man grabbed a fistful of Mia's hair and slammed her head into the bars, ringing all the world like a gong. Lashing out blind, stars in her eyes, she landed a brutal kick to his bollocks. Both gladiatii fell to the stone floor, gasping, bleeding, the cut on Mia's brow from her silkling brawl split anew, Sid groaning and clutching his jewels.

"*. . . mia, stop, arkades will hear . . . !*"

Mister Kindly's whisper cut through the red haze in her head, dragged her to her senses. The not-cat spoke truth—if they kept brawling, Executus would surely hear the commotion, and they'd likely be flogged. She aimed one last kick at Sidonius, who rolled away across the floor with a curse. The big man dragged himself into a corner like a whipped dog, Mia into the opposite, the pair gasping and glaring at each other across the bloodstained stone.

"What th-the 'byss . . . was that?" Sid managed, his voice almost an octave higher.

Mia dragged bloody knuckles across her bloody nose.

"*Nobody* talks that way about her."

"About wh—"

Sidonius blinked. Ice-blue eyes narrowing as he looked across the cell to the girl panting and wheezing in the corner. Dragging her long dark hair away from her dark eyes—the eyes that reminded him of . . .

"Can't be . . . ," he breathed.

Sidonius looked to the walls around him. Back to the girl. Mia could see the slow puzzle of it, the impossible math, all of it falling into an insane kind of place in his eyes. This girl who wouldn't escape these walls, despite being able to leave whenever she chose. This girl who seemed determined to fight in the most vicious contest yet devised in Republic history, just to attain a freedom she could have anytime she chose. So, if it wasn't about the freedom . . .

"The Crow," he breathed. "And here we sit, in Crow's Nest."

. . . it must be about the winning.

"You're . . . You're their . . . ?"

She felt it welling up inside her. Behind the pain of Sid's beating, the pulse throbbing in her head and spilling blood into her eyes. The weight of it. Being surrounded every turn by reminders of who she'd been, what might have become, all that had been taken from her. The frustration and hunger she felt around Furian, the confusion and desire she felt around Ashlinn, the sheer magnitude of the task before her. She didn't feel fear in the face of it all, no, the thing in her shadow wouldn't allow that. But she did feel sorrow. Regret, for all that was and might have been.

And just for a second, just for a moment, the weight of it felt too much.

The other gladiatii had realized the show was over, shuffled back to their places in the straw. Mia sat hunched, hugging her scuffed knees, glaring at Sidonius through her ragged fringe. Lip trembling. Eyes burning in the dark.

"Take it *back*," she whispered, tears welling in her lashes.

"Peace, Crow," the man murmured, swabbing his bleeding lip. "If offense was given, I beg pardon. I didn't . . . I *couldn't* . . ."

He stared at her bewildered, once more glancing at the walls around them. Red stone, iron bars, rusty chains. None could hold her. And yet, here she still was . . .

"Four Daughters, I'm sorry . . ."

Mia sat there in the dark, feeling his eyes, feeling his pity, crawling like lice on her skin. She couldn't stand it, the weakness she'd shown, the sorrow in Sid's gaze, dragging her bleeding knuckles across her eyes and feeling her temper swell once more. Feeling angry felt better—far better than feeling sorry for herself. The adrenaline from her brawl tingled in her fingertips, left her legs shaking. She wanted to run, wanted to fight, wanted to close her eyes and still the tempest inside her head, for time to stand still for just one second.

Is that what she wanted?

What do *you want?*

It had been stupid to let it slip. To let her rage get the better of her, let Sid guess who she was. But had it been a mistake?

He'd known her father. Served him loyally. Still revered him, after all these years.

Maybe she'd *wanted* him to know?

Maybe she wanted to know someone who knew them too? Who understood a fraction of what being here must be like.

The future loomed before her, the empty sands of Godsgrave arena. All the blood that awaited her, all the blood behind her. Every moment of her life had led her to this path, this vengeance, this unbending, unbranching road.

But what did she want, besides revenge?

It was still hours until nevernight's end.

She didn't want to sleep.

She didn't want to dream.

She didn't want to lay her head down in this place that had been her home, and now served only as a fading reminder of all that could have been.

So what do you want?

"Crow?"

She looked up at Sid, quietly bleeding in his corner.

"Blessed Aa, I'm sorry, girl," he said.

She didn't want him looking at her, that much was certain. And as he rose from his straw and sat down beside her, wrapping one of those big, ham-hock arms around her shoulder, she realized the last thing on earth she wanted was him consoling her. She didn't want pity. She didn't want to fall into some lump's clumsy, slightly uncomfortable hug and cry like some frightened child. That time was long behind her. Dead and buried like her familia. She was a Blade of the Red Church now. Not weak and fragile glass. She was steel.

But she didn't want to be alone, either.

She thought of her time as an acolyte. The forgetting and solace she'd found in Tric's arms. But he was dead and buried too, now. An empty tomb in a hollow hall, carved with the only memoriam he'd ever know. She'd told Shahiid Aalea that she missed him, and there was truth in that. But more, she realized she missed the clarity of it; the simple joy of wanting and being wanted in kind. The lingering ache from her visit with Furian wasn't helping any.

The brightest flames burn out the fastest, Aalea had told her. *But in them, there is warmth that can last a lifetime. Even from a love that only lasts the nevernight. For people like us, there are no promises of forever.*

Looking up into Sidonius's eyes, she finally realized what she wanted.

Not forever, perhaps.

But for now.

". . . Why're you looking at me like that?" the big Itreyan asked.

And without a word

she looked over his shoulder

to the shadow in the stairwell

and disappeared right out of his arms.

Sounds of the harbor. Soldiers calling "all's well" as they patrolled the nevernight streets. The wind blowing in off the ocean into Crow's Rest was blessedly cool, Mia shivering after the dank heat of the barracks. Her hand hovered above the window glass, just shy of knocking.

"... *this is unwise* ..."

"Go back to the keep," Mia whispered. "And tell Eclipse to watch the street."

"... *mia, i—* ..."

"Go."

Without a sound, the not-cat left her, her shadow growing thin and pale. As soon as Mister Kindly departed, she felt it, sneaking and creeping inside her belly—the fear she'd have *always* felt without him beside her. Fear of being here. Fear of what it meant, or where it could lead. Fear of who and what she was. And before it could sink its cold claws too far into her skin, she knocked, once, twice, knuckles striking sharp upon the glass.

No sound from the room inside. Mia felt a deepening dread, thinking perhaps she wasn't in there, that she'd stolen away after their argument, betrayed her and left her behind, proved that all the mistrust and sus—

The window opened. Ashlinn Järnheim stood beyond the sill, pillow-mussed and befuddled by sleep. Her eyes were the blue of sunburned skies.

"Mia?" the girl asked, stifling a yawn. "What time is it?"

Those blue eyes widened as she saw the scrapes on Mia's knuckles, the split above her bruised eye, the bruise at her jaw.

"Black Mother, what happened to ... ?"

The question trailed off as Mia reached out, pressed a finger to Ash's lips. They hung there a moment; two girls, barely touching, all the world around them holding its breath. The confusion in Ashlinn's eyes began to melt as Mia moved her finger, gentle as feathers. She traced the smooth bow of Ashlinn's upper lip, the plump softness of her lower, slow and soft. The arc of her cheek, the line of her jaw, Ash's breath coming quicker as she came fully awake, aware, awonder, the skin on her bare arms prickling. And as she parted her lips to speak, perhaps to protest, Mia leaned in and silenced her with a kiss.

She'd not kissed a girl before. At least, not like this. The kiss between them in the Mountain had been of farewell—lingering perhaps, but still a goodbye. This kiss was an invitation; a gentle, desperate plea for a beginning, not an ending. A question without words, Mia's mouth open and melting against Ashlinn's own. And as she felt Ashlinn shiver, the feather-light brush of her tongue in kind, Mia had her answer.

She climbed in through the window, their lips never parting. Arms entwined, hands exploring, Mia breaking the kiss only long enough to drag Ashlinn's nightshirt up over her head. She was naked beneath, stripped gloriously bare with a single gesture. Mia paused a moment to drink in the sight; the sunlight caressing the line of her throat, the swell of her curves, the shadow between her legs.

"Mia, I . . ."

Mia sank back, pressing her mouth to Ashlinn's neck. The girl's chest was heaving, her cheeks flushed, whispering soft nothings and letting her head drift back as Mia sank lower, down to her breast, teasing one pebble-hard nipple with her tongue.

The pair collapsed onto the bed, Ash's hands tearing at the bindings about Mia's chest, her hips, groaning as Mia's teeth nipped at her neck. Any questions she might have had were drowned now, breath coming too quick to speak, lips parted as she crushed Mia to her, skin on skin, every sweet secret at her fingertips. Down her ribs, over the swell of her hips to the curve of her arse as Mia wrapped one leg about her, dragging her in closer.

Mia felt Ash's fingers brushing the inside of her thigh, an arkemical thrill sizzling up her spine and sparking in the dark behind her eyes. Her own hand quested lower, down across Ash's taut belly to the downy blond between her legs. Their hands found their marks at the same time, their kiss deepening, their sighs smothered. Mia's back arched as she felt Ashlinn drawing tight, firm circles on her with clever fingers. She kneaded a breast with her free hand, the other setting to work between Ashlinn's legs, mimicking her slow, agonizing rhythm and listening to her moan in time.

It was like nothing she'd ever known. Jolting current and sweet softness and kisses, endless, paralyzing kisses that filled her with a warmth all the way to her fingertips. Time stood still, nothing but teasing tongues and breathless sighs, a heat building between her legs, setting her whole body aflame.

"O, Goddess, yes," Mia whispered.

"Don't stop," Ashlinn pleaded.

Her lips were honey, warm and soft, her body writhing as Mia's fingers rolled back and forth across her swollen bud. She was so hot down there, slick and shivering, the hunger in Mia rising until she could stand it no more.

"I want to taste you," she breathed, nuzzling Ashlinn's neck.

"O, yes . . . yes . . ."

Descending, slow as melting ice. Running her tongue down the line of Ashlinn's throat, smiling as the girl's back arched, toes curled. Down to the swell of her breasts, Mia took one in her mouth, licking, suckling, her hand still strumming between Ashlinn's thighs. A thirst was burning inside her, desert-dry, and Mia could think of only one way to sate it. Dragging her like some sweet, dark gravity. Down.

Always down.

Ash was splayed on the mattress, groaning as Mia continued her descent, long, languid kisses running over her ribs, her belly. Mia paused, tracing slow,

burning circles around her navel with the tip of her tongue, fingernails tracing gentle lines across Ashlinn's skin. Inhaling a soft hint of lavender and the
dizzying scent of Ash's desire.

"Please, Mia," the girl breathed.

Down, down to the smooth length of Ashlinn's parted legs, running her
tongue closer to that intoxicating heat. There was a small dark mole at the divot
of Ash's thigh and her sex, and Mia licked it slow, smiling dark.

"Please what?" she whispered.

"*Please,* Mia . . ."

She pursed her lips, blew softly on her mark as Ashlinn shivered. She'd been
tasted before, but never done the tasting, anticipation curling in her belly and
making her tremble. She wanted to take her time, to savor every second, the
thrill of it all, but Ash snarled her fingers in Mia's hair, and with a shivering
gasp, dragged her in.

Silken softness, drenched with lust, parting under the press of her kiss. Mia
moved slow, running her tongue through Ashlinn's folds, flickering in and out.
Ashlinn mewled and sighed, hips grinding in time, the hands in Mia's hair
pulling her in tighter. Mia found herself consumed by it, thirsty, starving; the
taste of her, the flood of warm nectar across her tongue. Delighting in Ashlinn's moans as she pinched her swollen nipples, ran her hands down the girl's
breasts, clawed her arse.

Ashlinn lost herself as Mia went to work in earnest, eyes rolling back in
her head, half-hanging off the bed as she urged Mia on, *don't stop, don't stop.*
Mia had never felt so much power; her every movement, every flick of her
tongue or touch of her lips eliciting a groan, a whispered plea, a tremor running
the length of Ashlinn's entire body.

Time lost all meaning, each second a year, each year a heartbeat, the heat
building between them, dragging Ash ever higher, hotter, brighter, her moans
growing louder, longer, until she went tense as a bowstring, spine arching,
thighs clamped either side of Mia's head, every muscle taut and straining as
she pointed her toes skyward and screamed as if the world were ending.

Ash's whole body went limp in the breathless aftermath, Mia tracing light
circles, still savoring her taste, the power of her little triumph. She grinned
as she sank her tongue deeper into Ash's petals, making her groan, "Enough,
Goddess, enough," relenting as the girl gently pulled her up. Ash enfolded Mia
in her arms, their bodies melding into one, slender legs wrapped around Mia's
waist as they sank into another long, hungry kiss. Ash's taste mingled upon
their tongues, and Mia found herself drowning in it, eyelashes fluttering against
her cheeks, so right and sweet and heaped in bliss she never wanted it to end.

But then she gasped, Ashlinn smacking her arse, biting her lips, almost hard enough to draw blood.

"Ow," Mia flinched. "What was that for?"

"Making me beg," Ashlinn scowled.

"O?" Mia smiled, lips brushing Ashlinn's own. "I heard no complaints at the time."

"Don't get a big head on me now, Corvere. That was beginner's luck."

"O, really?"

Soft laughter turned to warm shivers as Ash nuzzled her neck.

"Really," the girl breathed, teeth brushing her skin.

"Then . . . perhaps the dona would give the novice a demonstration?"

"Say please."

"I—ah!"

Mia gasped as Ashlinn dragged her head back by her hair, landed another firm smack on her backside. The girl's lips drifted along Mia's throat, teeth grazing her jugular, fingernails tracing lines of fire and ice up her soaking thighs.

"Say," Ash whispered, nipping Mia's throat, "please."

In her heart, Mia had never bowed to anyone. Not in the Church, not in the arena, not in the bedchamber. And though she'd delighted in the control of a moment ago, her every touch, her every move setting the girl in her arms aflame, Mia wondered if there might be a deeper joy found in some small moment of surrender.

Ash's fingers danced over her, light as the breeze. Mia's belly tightened as the girl sank lower, her tongue drawing a tightening spiral around her heaving breast.

"Say it," the girl whispered, flicking Mia's nipple with her tongue.

Smoky light filtered through the curtain, and Mia closed her eyes as Ashlinn descended, not wanting to see or hear or speak, but only to *feel*. A waterfall of kisses, cascading down her body, Ash's hands seemingly everywhere at once. Mia found her legs parting of their own volition, the ache between them a sweet agony, her breath growing ragged, heart pounding with anticipation. A feeling like nothing she'd ever known was budding inside her—not with Tric, not with Aalea, not with Aurelius and that golden beauty, desire swelling to a burning pitch as she felt Ashlinn kneel between her legs, hot breath against her swollen lips.

"Say . . ."

A brush of the girl's tongue, impossibly light, making Mia buck and shiver.

". . . please."

Mia lifted her head, looking down the length of her body to Ashlinn, poised to devour her. Heart hammering, not enough breath in her lungs, dizzy. And eyes fluttering closed once more, she let her head fall back and the tension flee from her bones as she gave herself over to it utterly.

"*Please,*" Mia breathed.

A long, low moan escaped her lips as Ashlinn went to work, lips and tongue dancing in the dark. She'd no idea where the girl had learned her skills; Aalea, some new lover, some old flame. But Goddess, it was blinding. Ash was a maestro, the tune between them, older than time. The heat in her pulsed hotter with every brush of the girl's tongue, Mia barely able to breathe, bedsheet twisted in her tightening fists. She almost lost her mind when she felt Ashlinn slip a finger inside her, curling, coaxing, stoking that smoldering heat, arkemical current crackling to the tips of her toes.

"O, Goddess . . ."

Helpless before it, caught up and swept away, a hurricane of lust and longing, the heat inside her almost impossible to bear. Ashlinn was merciless, the rhythm of her tongue matched by her touch, Mia's back arching, lifting her hips high off the bed, mouth in a perfect O, fingers snarled in the red river of Ashlinn's hair and dragging her deeper, harder, more, *more.* She was shaking so hard she couldn't breathe, couldn't think, couldn't speak save to wordlessly beg an ending to it all. And as she felt Ashlinn's hand move, a second finger joining the first, Mia's hips bucked uncontrollably, black stars blooming behind her eyes, the heat inside her bursting into ravenous flame and she lost herself, screaming soundlessly, blinded by the fire of a thousand suns.

She felt soft lips on her own, wet and darkly sweet. Mia opened her eyes and saw a girl above her, beautiful, smiling.

A girl she shouldn't trust.

A lover she shouldn't love.

She tried to find her breath, heart hammering against her ribs.

"That was . . . impressive . . ."

"That was overdue," Ashlinn grinned.

Mia dragged her in for a kiss, their lips crushed together, the ripples of her climax still tingling in her bones. Breaking apart after a long, sweet forever, Ashlinn flopped back on the mattress, breathing a contented sigh.

Mia climbed out of the bed, legs still shaking. Atop the drawers, she found her silver cigarillo case, lighting one with her flintbox before slipping back between the sheets. Ashlinn threw her arms around her, took her hand and kissed her wounded knuckles before snuggling closer, nuzzling her neck. Mia took a drag of the cigarillo, inhaling deep and feeling the sweet, heavy gray fill her lungs.

"You smoke a lot," Ash murmured.

"Settles the nerves," Mia replied.

"Make you nervous, do I?"

Mia held out her hand in answer. She was usually rock-steady, never a tremor to weaken her swordgrip. But her hands were shaking now.

"O, you're all aquiver, love," Ash cooed. "First times will do that to a girl, neh?"

"Let's see yours then, smart-arse."

Ash held up her own hand, and though she tried to hide it, Mia could see she was shaking too. She could feel the girl's breast pressed against her, the heart beneath running to the same thunderous tune. Threading her fingertips through Ashlinn's own, she sensed the current crackling between them. Realizing she was still thirsty.

"Perhaps *you* should take up smoking."

Ash made a face. "Don't enjoy the taste, I'm afraid."

"I can make it sweeter . . ."

Dragging deep on the cigarillo, Mia inhaled another warm lungful. And tipping up Ashlinn's chin with her fingertips, she leaned in close and kissed her, lips parted, breathing into her mouth. Her lips were sugared from the cigarillo paper, the clove-scented smoke drifting around their tongues as the kiss deepened. Ash tilted her head and sighed, pressing the length of her body against Mia's own. Mia's hands roamed her back, feeling the goosebumps rising on Ashlinn's skin, the sweet ache rising once more between her legs. Ashlinn closed her mouth, sucking on Mia's tongue before breaking the kiss.

"Not bad," she smiled, exhaling gray. "But I'm still not taking up smoking."

Mia shrugged, taking another drag. Ashlinn settled in against her side again, Mia's arm around her shoulder. They lay in silence for a time, listening to the sounds of the nevernight outside. She took a good look at the girl in her arms, the slender curves, the twin divots at the base of her spine, fingers pushing the long tresses of blood-red aside and exposing . . .

. . . the inkwerk crawling across her back.

". . . What's that?" Mia whispered.

Ashlinn tensed, sitting up and tossing her hair back over her shoulder.

She'd only caught a glimpse, but Mia had seen intricate lines and shading, a hint of strange writing, the shape of a curved blade on Ash's left shoulder . . .

"One stipulation," Solis said, holding up his finger. *"An item of import to your patron. A map, written in Old Ysiiri and set with a seal shaped like a sickle's blade."*

. . . *Goddess.*

"The map," Mia realized. "Duomo's map."

"Is that why you came here?" Ash asked softly.

Mia frowned, cigarillo bobbing on her lips. "What?"

"Eclipse is always skulking about. Maybe she caught a glimpse." The girl fixed Mia in her blue-sky stare. "So you figure the only way you'll get a better look is to get my clothes off? Smart play, Corvere."

". . . Is that what you think?"

"I don't think anything." Ash squared her shoulders, making sure the tattoo was hidden from sight. "That's why I'm asking."

"Ash, I had no idea. Why do you have Duomo's map tattooed on your back?"

"Not tattooed," she said, nodding to the double circles marked on Mia's cheek. "It's arkemical, just like your brand."

Mia blinked as realization struck her. "So if they kill you . . ."

"The brand disappears. No map for them." The girl shrugged. "People who play with fire do better if they expect to get burned."

A dozen questions burned in Mia's mind. What was so important about this map that Ashlinn had it indelibly branded on her skin? What did Duomo and Scaeva want with it, that they were set to move so openly against each other to obtain it? Where did it lead? Where did the girl she'd just been holding in her arms fit in with all of it?

"There's a lot about this you're not telling me, Ashlinn."

"I could say the same for you, Mia."

"Such as?"

Ashlinn looked deep into her eyes, swallowing hard.

"Why did you come here? Why now?"

"Because I wanted to be with you."

"But why?"

Mia took a drag of cigarillo, mulling it over.

"Because I was thinking. About all the things that brought me to this point. The things that made me what I am, and all the things I could've been if I'd been given a choice. And then I didn't want to think anymore."

"So that's all this was?" Ashlinn kept her face steady, her voice cool, but Mia could see the storm building in that sunburned blue. "Just a distraction?"

"The sweetest distraction," Mia smiled.

"No jesting," Ashlinn said. "You run hot and cold as a faulty bathhouse, and if this was just a quick roll to fuck unpleasant thoughts away, that's fine. I'd rather that than a ruse to see the ink on my skin. But whichever it was, I need to know."

"It was neither, Ash."

"I know a lie when I taste it, Mia."

Mia sighed, shook her head. She'd pondered it on the way here, stealing down through the nevernight streets. Why it hadn't been right before, why it felt right now. Her fight with Furian had left her enflamed, her fight with Sid had done nothing to sate it. But it wasn't simply that, wasn't the thought of her parents or the painful reminders of being locked up in that place or the thought of where she'd been or what was to come.

"I thought about all the things I could've been if I'd been given a choice," she finally said. "And I realized that mostly I've never had one. Ever since my father was killed, my feet were set upon this course. No denying it. No escape. So I wanted to choose something for myself. Something that could just be mine. *My* choice."

Mia looked at Ash, running trembling fingertips across her cheek.

"And I chose you."

Ashlinn simply stared, bee-stung lips parted as she breathed, and Mia found herself falling, down into a long, sweet kiss. Ashlinn surged against her, hands cupping her face, lost in the sweetness of a kiss that seemed to shiver all the way to Mia's soul. She pulled away only with reluctance, dark eyes searching Ashlinn's own.

"Do I taste like I'm lying?" she asked.

Ashlinn smiled soft, shook her head.

"No. Do I?"

Did she? Had anything changed here? Wasn't everything still the same? The question of this map—where it led, why Duomo wanted it, what it all meant—still hung between them. Ashlinn Järnheim was still a girl who'd do anything to get what she wanted. Lie, cheat, steal, kill. She had secrets. She was *dangerous*.

But was Mia so different?

The more time they spent together, the more kinship she saw with this girl she supposed she should despise.

"You taste like honey," Mia whispered.

Ashlinn smiled, pressed her forehead to Mia's. Mia closed her eyes, listening to the sounds of the streets outside, to the cool nevernight winds, now slowly dying. She had questions. Too many questions. But the turn would soon begin, Executus would rouse them for another session of sweat and beatings and bloody Furian, and all of it—for a blessed moment forgotten in the arc of this girl's arms—came flooding back. Mia remembered who she was. What she was. Opening her eyes and sighing.

"We need to talk on this some more. But I have to get back."

"I know," Ashlinn said, leaning in for another brief kiss.

"I want to stay."

"I know," Ash breathed, nibbling her lower lip. "Just promise to return."

"Say please."

Ashlinn's nibble turned into a painful bite.

"Fuck you, Corvere," she smiled.

"Thought you'd never ask."

"I *didn't* ask, remember?"

Grinning, she kissed Ashlinn's eyes, Ashlinn's cheek, Ashlinn's lips, steeling herself against the moment. And then she rose from the bed, *their* bed, wrapping herself in her scraps of cloth, dreading the sunlight that awaited her just beyond the curtain. But still, she pulled the fabric aside, squinting against the brightness, turning to take one last look at the beauty she was leaving behind.

Has anything changed here?

With a sigh, she climbed out into the waiting light.

Nothing would ever be the same again.

QUIET

" 'Byss and blood, that's *hot*."

Mia sighed, closing her eyes and sinking farther down into the steaming heat. The water closed over her head, sounds of the bathhouse momentarily muted, all the noise of the world falling away.

She hung there in the dark and the warmth, enjoying the sensation on her aching muscles. The last two weeks had been spent training under the blazing suns with Furian and Bladesinger, and the trio were no closer to learning to fight together as a unit. Knowing the silkling would give no quarter, Arkades was showing no mercy in the circle, and Mia ached in muscles she never even knew she had. She was black and blue all over, and growing more frustrated with Furian by the turn.

Holding her breath beneath the water, she floated weightless. She was reminded for a moment of Marius's pools, and blood walks from the Quiet Mountain. Thinking of Solis, Drusilla and the others. The role they'd played in her familia's fall.

What were they doing right now? Helping Scaeva secure his fourth term, no doubt. Rolling in their coin like hogs at trough. But the consul, and thus the Ministry, must be growing impatient at her lack of progress recovering Duomo's map. How was Mercurio fending them off?

Not for the first time, she realized what a risk her old mentor was taking for her. Thinking of it, she found herself ashamed she'd ever thought Mercurio might betray her. She missed him, truth told. Missed his counsel, his smoker's growl, even his bastard of a temper. But soon enough, she'd be back in Godsgrave, standing on the sands of the arena. She'd see him then. And after, when the deed was done.

Presuming I don't get murdered at Whitekeep first . . .

Mia surfaced with burning lungs, shrouded in steam. Blinking the water from her eyes, she was greeted by the sight of Wavewaker walking into the bathhouse. The man was gleaming with sweat from his turn's training, dusted with dirt and grime from the circle. He was singing a duet called "Mi Uitori" all by himself; the female's lines in falsetto, the male's in his traditional baritone.* Stripping off his loincloth at a suitably dramatic *noooooooooote,* he stepped into the bath and Mia gave him an impromptu round of applause.

---

*An infamous Itreyan opera commissioned by King Francisco XII (known by his subjects as "the Proud" in life, and "the Wanker" in death). Francisco was an enthusiast of musical theater, and after his triumph during a rebellion by King Oskar III of Vaan, he commissioned an ode to his glory. His court's premier composer, Maximillian Omberti, toiled for over a year on the composition, naming it "Mi Uitori" (My Victory).

Francisco was convinced his opera was a path to everlasting fame and popularity with his subjects. He spared no expense in assembling the production, and fancying himself as something of a singer, decreed he would play the role of himself at the premiere. Held at Godsgrave arena, every member of the nobility was in attendance, along with ninety thousand citizens. To ensure the crowd would appreciate every moment of his masterpiece, Francisco XII ordered the arena exits locked as the overture began.

Sadly, though the opera does feature the aforementioned titular "Mi Uitori" in its final act—considered Omberti's finest piece, and still played centuries later—the king

"Too kind, Mi Dona," the big man bowed.

"Quite a set of pipes you've got on you there."

"I studied at the feet of the best."

"Were you *really* an actor in a theater?" she asked, head tilted.

"Wellll," the big man said. "I worked in one, on the door. In happier turns. I always wanted to stride the stage, marveling the crowd, but . . ." He shrugged at the walls around them. " 'Twas not to be."

She looked the man over with a critical eye as he reached for the soap. Wavewaker was a daemon on the sand, a little undisciplined perhaps, but strong as a bull. She'd wager those hands of his could encircle her throat easily, crush her skull if he squeezed hard enough, and she could no more imagine him wearing tights and mumming in some pantomime than she could imagine herself sprouting wings.

"Let me guess." He raised an eyebrow. "I don't strike you as the theater type."

"Forgive me," she chuckled. "But not at all."

"You're forgiven," Wavewaker grinned. "My father said much the same. He raised me in the art of steel, you see. Taught me from the time I was a boy how to break men with my bare hands. He intended me to be an honorguard of the Bara, like his father before him. Called me a fool when I told him I wanted to be a thespian. The suffi hadn't named me 'Stagestrider,' after all. But I didn't fancy the thought of being told what I could or couldn't be. So I tried anyway. It was my dream. And one best dreamed awake."

Mia found herself nodding, admiration budding in her chest.

"So I traveled to the City of Bridges and Bones," Wavewaker continued, with dramatic flair. "Found a troupe who'd take me in. A little theater called the Sanctuary."

---

had demanded the composer include *every detail* of his Vaanian triumph. The premier performance was over seventeen hours in length, its duration made all the worse by Francisco's singing voice, which was described by the historian Cornelius the Younger as "akin to two cats fucking in a burning bag."

The performance went so long, two women gave birth during it, and several hundred citizens risked broken legs and execution by leaping from the arena's walls to the street outside. A particularly wily baron of the king's court, one Gaspare Giancarli, faked a heart attack so that the guards would permit his familia to remove his lifeless corpse from the premises.

Francisco was reported to be "quite disappointed" with the opera's reception.

Omberti committed suicide shortly after the premiere.

There was no repeat performance.

"I know it!" Mia gasped, delighted. "Down near the Nethers!"

"Aye," Wavewaker smiled broad. "Grand old place. I had no training, so they started me slow. I was only standing the door and cleaning up after shows at first, but it was still magikal to me. Listening to the great old dramas, watching poetry float in the air like gossamer, and scenes come alive before the crowd's wondering eyes. That's the power of words: twenty-six little letters can paint a whole universe." Wavewaker's voice grew wistful. "They were the happiest turns of my life."

Mia knew she shouldn't open her mouth. Shouldn't let herself know more about the man. But still . . .

"What happened?" she heard herself asking.

Wavewaker sighed.

"Aemillia, one of our actresses. She caught the eye of a some rich man's son. Paulus, his name. The dona made it clear she was uninterested in his affections, and I was forced to see him off a few times after he'd had too much goldwine, but that wasn't so unusual. It was a rough part of town. All was going well, really. The troupe was making coin, crowds were growing. I'd studied hard, and was set to play my first role in one of the productions—the Magus King in *Marcus and Messalina,* do you know it?"

"Aye," Mia smiled.

"It was the turn of my maiden performance. But it seemed even after Aemillia's refusals and the drubbings I gave him, little Paulus wasn't used to taking no for an answer."

"Rich men's sons often aren't," Mia said.

"Aye. I found the bastard backstage after dress rehearsal, trying to force himself on Aemillia. Her costume torn. Her lip bloodied. You can guess the rest. Father taught me from the time I was a boy how to break men with my bare hands, after all."

Wavewaker looked down at his sword-callused palms.

"But he was a rich man's son. It was only the testimony of my fellow players saved me from the gallows. I was sold into bondage instead, the price of my sale paid to Paulus by way of compensation for the broken hands I'd gifted him."

"Four Daughters," Mia breathed. "I'm sorry."

"Don't be sorry, love," Wavewaker smiled. "I'm not. State I left him in, he'll never place those hands anywhere without invitation again."

"But this is the price you pay?" Mia waved to the stone walls, the iron bars.

"A man must accept his fate, little Crow. Or be consumed by it. As gladiatii, our lot is better than most. A chance to win our freedom. *Sanguii e Gloria*, and all that."

"But it's not fair, Wavewaker. You didn't do anything wrong."

"Fair?" The big man scoffed. "What Republic are you living in?"

Shaking his head and smirking as if Mia had said something funny, the big man kept on soaping himself like all was right in the world. Mia reached for another perfumed bar as Bryn and Byern walked into the bathhouse, stripping off their loincloths and kicking their sandals loose. It'd been their turn to train down by the equorium, and Mia could smell the sweat and horse on the pair of them at ten paces.

"Ah, our brave equillai," Wavewaker smiled. "The twin terrors, unequaled on the track, welcome. The Crow and I were just discussing the theater."

"Four Daughters, what for?" Bryn scowled, sinking below the water.

"I knew an actress once," Byern said, his voice wistful.

"What, that sugargirl who'd come through the village in the summers?"

"She wasn't a sugargirl, sis, she was a thespian."

"If she tugged you for beggars, she was a sugargirl, darling brother."

Byern glanced at Mia and Wavewaker. "She's talking rot now. Smearing my good name to make me look bad. I've never paid for it in my life, and the lass in question was as at home on the stage as a fish in water, I assure you."

"The only acting she did was pretending that she fancied you," Bryn scoffed.

"Respect your elders, pup!" Byern said, splashing his sister in the face.

The twins engaged in a brief water fight, Mia and Wavewaker backing away across to the other side of the bath so they didn't get caught in the crossfire. Byern dunked Bryn's head below the surface and she punched him in the stomach. The pair retreated to opposite corners, Bryn raising the knuckles at her brother and scowling.

"Are you two done?" Wavewaker asked.

"Aye," Bryn said. "No, wait . . ."

She snatched up a bar of soap and bounced it off her brother's head.

"Ow!"

"Now I'm done."

"One turn," Wavewaker declared, once hostilities had died, "when we're out of this hole, I'll take you all to a proper theater. Show you some culture."

"Daughters know some of us could use it," Bryn said.

"Keep it up, and I shall see you before the magistrate for slander." Byern warned, splashing his sister again. Bryn retaliated with a sweeping arc of her hand, a great scythe of water hitting her brother and Wavewaker in the face.

"Sorry," she smirked.

"O, you will be," the big man replied, wiping his chin.

Wavewaker curved his massive hand and slung a shot of bathwater right into Bryn's eyes. Byern stepped in to defend his sister, slapping water back and catching Mia in the crossfire. The girl joined in, and soon all four were going at it, fierce as whitedrakes, splashing and cursing and laughing. Wavewaker slung Mia clear across the bath into Byern's bare chest, grabbed Bryn in a head-lock, and proceeded to dunk her below the surface as she kicked and flai—

"What in the Everseeing's name goes on here?"

Mia slung her sodden hair from her eyes, looked up to find Magistrae standing at the bathhouse door, hands on hips. She was dressed immaculately as always, long gray braid swept over one shoulder. Her voice bristled with indignity.

"You are gladiatii of the Remus Collegium, and here I find you, caterwauling and fooling like a pack of brats. This is how you honor your domina?"

"Apologies, Magistrae," Wavewaker said, releasing Bryn's neck. "A moment's jest is all. The weather grows hot and the turns long, and—"

"And there are only a handful of those turns left before the Whitekeep *venatus,* and from there, the *magni,*" Magistrae snapped. "Do you know what it will cost your domina if you fail? The shame she will endure? Perhaps you think it wise to spend your time jackanaping, but were I you, I would set mind to the games, and what awaits you all if this collegium falls."

The smile on Mia's face died, the momentary joy she'd felt evaporating. The gladiatii hung their heads like scolded children. It was true what the magistrae said, and all knew it—if the collegium failed, they'd probably be sold off like cheap meat, and only the Everseeing knew who to. New sanguila perhaps, but more likely to Pandemonium. All their lives hung in the balance.

Maw's teeth, it had been grand to forget it all for a moment. But Mia clenched her jaw. Hardened her resolve. She was growing soft here. Not physically—under Arkades's training, she'd grown harder and fitter than she'd ever been in her life. But letting herself grow close to her fellow gladiatii was a mistake. Likeable as they might be, the men and women in the collegium were only pawns on a board. Pawns that would likely be sacrificed before she got to the king.

These people are not your familia, and not your friends, she reminded herself.

All of them are only a means to an end.

H arder."

Leona braced her palms against the wall and pushed her knees into the mattress, head thrown back. Furian had hold of her waist, his grip slippery with their sweat, her whole body shuddering with every thrust of his hips. The bedframe shook from the force of it, stone dust drifting off the wall and down to the floor.

"*Harder,*" Leona groaned again.

Her champion complied, bucking like a stallion. The dona reached back, clawing his skin, urging him deeper as he took a handful of her auburn hair and pulled her back, farther onto his burning length. Leona closed her eyes, rocked to her core and quivering, mouth open wide.

"Fuck me," she breathed.

"Domina . . ."

"O, Daughters, yes."

"Domina, I can't . . ."

"Yes, finish it," she gasped. "Fuck me, fuck me, *fuck me.*"

Furian slammed himself home a few more times then dragged himself free, his whole body rigid as he spent himself across her buttocks and back. Leona hung her head, fingernails digging into his skin, biting her lip to stifle her cry. Breathless, she collapsed facedown onto the bed, purring like a cat.

The Unfallen lowered himself down beside her, chest heaving, his body drenched. Though the bed was small, he took care not to touch her—it seemed the dona had little taste for postcoital affections. Leaning his back against the wall, he licked his lips and sighed, heart pounding.

"A fine performance, my champion," the dona murmured.

"Your whisper, my will," he replied.

Leona chuckled, rolled over onto her back. Wriggling her hips, she arched her spine and looked up at the man above her.

"Four Daughters, I needed that," she sighed.

"No less than I," Furian said. "I'd begun to suspect you'd forgot me."

Leona cooed, smoothing his long dark hair away from his face, running her fingertips down his rippling abdomen. "Did you miss me, my champion?"

"It has been weeks, Domina."

"No need to fear, lover," the dona smiled. "Ever I'll return."

"Until you find favor in another?"

"Another?" Leona's lips twisted. "And who would that be, pray?"

"The Savior of Stormwatch," he muttered with mock theatricality.

"Ah," Leona sighed, rolling her eyes. "We arrive at spear's tip. But I've no taste for women, Furian. And even less for jealousy."

"You fight her on the sands beside me," he muttered. "As if she were my equal. But she has no honor. She has—"

"She has a victor's laurel," Leona said. "She has the favor of the crowd. And she has one-third the key to unlock the gates of the *magni* for us."

"I can best your father's silkling alone, Domina," Furian growled. "I need help from no one, least of all some conniving slip that my enemy has already defeated."

Leona sighed. Rising from the bed, she gathered up the sheet and casually wiped his seed off her skin.

"This conversation bores me."

Furian reached out his hand. "Leona . . ."

"Leona?" The dona glanced up sharply. "You forget yourself, slave."

"O, slave, aye," Furian nodded. "Until you've a thirst again. And then it's all 'lover' and 'my champion' and honeyed words until you've had your fill."

"And you complain so bitterly at the time?"

"I've a mind to be more than just your stud."

"And what more would you be?" Leona asked. "You may stand a champion in the arena, but other laurels, you've far from won. I am domina of this house. Think not that simply because I bed you, I hold you in my counsel. Or that when command is given, I do not expect it to be obeyed."

"When your nightmares wake you from your sleep, do you think I comfort you because I'm commanded to do so? Do you think I hold you because—"

"You overstep, Champion."

Furian pressed his lips together, anger darkening his brow. But he spoke no more. Looking at him a long, still moment, Leona's face softened. She sank down onto the bed beside him, pressed her hand to his cheek.

"I care for you," she murmured. "But I cann—"

A knock sounded at the door.

"Champion?"

Leona's eyes widened as she recognized the voice.

"Almighty Aa . . . ," she hissed. "Arkades!"

Furian rose off the bed, his face running pale. "I thought he was in his cups?"

"He was! Passed out in the dining room, dead to the damned world."

Another knock. "Furian?"

Leona searched the room desperately. The shrine to Tsana. A small chest. Wooden swords and a practice dummy. Nowhere to hide. Finally, the dona of the house dropped to her knees. Crawling under the bed with Furian's aid, she drew her legs up and hugged them to her chest. Satisfied she was out of sight, the Unfallen tied his loincloth and opened the door.

Arkades stood on the threshold, his face blotched from drink. He was swaying slightly, goldwine thick on his breath as he looked the champion up and down.

"Apologies," he said. "Were you asleep?"

"Only resting, Executus."

"Mmf."

Arkades shouldered past and limped into the room, his iron leg ringing on the stone, *clink,* thump, *clink,* thump. He looked about for somewhere to sit, finally thumping down on the bed. The straw mattress sagged under his weight, Leona smothering her cry as it smacked into the back of her skull and bounced her head off the floor. Cursing under her breath, she hunkered lower, like a disobedient child hiding from her parents.

Arkades sniffed the air, raised an eyebrow, his voice thick from drink.

"Stinks in here."

"The heat, Executus. Saai crawls closer to the horizon every turn."

Arkades wrinkled his nose. "I'll have a word to the magistrae. That soap she's got you using smells like a woman's perfume."

Furian's eyes widened slightly, and looked to the shadow below the bed. The executus didn't notice, pulling out his trusty flask and taking a long pull. He offered it to the Unfallen, who declined with a silent shake of his head.

"Mmf, good man," Arkades said, stowing the drink away. "Makes you soft on the sands."

"But it makes you forget the blood that stains them, too," Furian replied softly.

Arkades nodded, almost to himself, a faraway look in his eyes. Staring down at his hands. Up into the Unfallen's dark stare.

"I like that about you, Furian. You see. You *understand*. The pain we endure. The red rivers we must wade through."

"On our way to glory."

"A heavy weight."

"I welcome it. If it brings me victory."

Arkades scoffed softly. "I like that about you, too."

"Forgive me . . . But do you need something, Executus?"

Arkades sighed and shifted his weight, the sagging mattress pushing Leona into the floor. The dona was breathing soft and thin, chest pressed hard to the stone, panic on her face. If she made a sound, if her executus discovered her there . . .

"I need you to stop working at odds with the Crow," Arkades replied, slightly slurred from the drink. "I need you to fight beside her, not against her."

Furian scowled. "That girl is on every tongue this nevernight, it seems."

A blink. ". . . What?"

"She is a liar and a cur, Executus. Her glory is undeserved."

"How can you say so?" Arkades frowned. "Aa's cock, I hold no more fondness for her than you, but you saw her fight at Stormwatch. Her victory over the retchwyrm—"

"Was steeped in treachery. She is not a victor, she is a thief."

Arkades sighed, reaching for his flask before he caught himself. He stood, unsteady for a moment, Leona sighing in relief now she could breathe again. Regaining his balance and limping around the room, Arkades motioned to the walls around them.

"What do you see?"

"My domina's house," the Unfallen replied.

"Aye. The walls that shelter you, the roof that keeps the suns off your back. Know you what will happen, if we fail to secure berth at the *magni*?"

"I need no aid besting the silkling, Executus," Furian growled, bristling. "And I will not fight alongside an honorless dog who steals what should be earned."

"Because you'd know all about being an honorless dog, neh?"

Furian's eyes grew wide. "You dare—"

"Spare me your indignity," Arkades growled, raising one callused hand. "You forget I was the one who found you, brought you here. I alone know where it is you came from, what it is you *did* to find yourself in chains."

Furian glanced to his bed. The figure lurking beneath it.

"That was many a turn ago," he said. "I am that man no longer. I am a god-fearing son of the Everseeing, and a gladiatii who lives to honor his domina."

"You live to honor *yourself*," Arkades replied, shaking his head in exasperation. "To prove yourself better than the man you were. And I see to the heart of that. But say not that you fight for your domina. If you truly thought for one moment of Leona, if you felt one drop of what I feel for h—"

Arkades blinked and caught himself. Swaying on his feet. Glancing up at the champion, Executus cleared his throat, rubbed at bleary eyes.

"You have the skill and the *will* to see us all the way to the *magni,* Furian. I did not pluck you from the mire to redeem you from the sins of your past. I did it because I see in you a *champion,* just as I was. You can win your freedom. Walk among us as a man once more, not the animal you were. But those who stand for nothing die for the same. And if you stand only for yourself, you fall alone."

"Stand for myself?" Furian repeated, incredulous. "I stand for these walls!"

"Then prove it," Arkades growled. "Fight *with* the Crow, not against her. And when the silkling is bested and our berth assured, when you face the Crow in the grand games *e mortium,* you can prove yourself the man I know you to be."

Arkades placed one hand on the champion's shoulder.

"Or fall alone," he repeated. "And bring this house down with you."

Executus swayed like a tree in a storm, the grip on Furian's shoulder more to steady himself than prove a comfort. But though the goldwine hung heavy on his breath, though he could barely stay upright, it seemed he'd aimed true.

Furian clenched his jaw. But finally, he nodded.

"I will stand with her at Whitekeep," he said. "But in Godsgrave, she dies."

Arkades nodded, limped toward the door, *clink,* thump, *clink,* thump, turning at the threshold to look Furian over once more.

"Perhaps before? Who can say?"

Executus smiled, closing the door behind him. Furian stood still, listening to the sound of his limping tread fade down the hallway. Sinking to his knees, he offered a hand to Leona, helped her drag herself out from under the bed. Once standing, the dona snatched her hand away from his, dragged her dress over her head to cover herself. Indignity written in every movement.

"So," she glared. "You'd disobey my command to fight beside the Crow, but Arkades speaks a handful of words and you see the right of it?"

"Domin—"

"You told me you were a trader before this," she said, fixing the champion in her glittering blue stare. "A merchant."

"I was," Furian replied.

"Arkades did not make it sound so. He named you animal. How many sins can a simple merchant accrue, that he fights so fierce to redeem them?"

The Unfallen made no reply.

"What did you do, Furian?" she asked. "What lies have you told me?"

The champion only stared at the trinity of Aa on the wall, refusing to meet her gaze. She stood there long moments, searching his eyes, looking for answers. Finding only silence. And with a disgusted harrumph, she turned, stomped toward the door. Listening for a moment, she tore it open, almost heedless, and strode out into the hallway, slamming it behind her.

The Unfallen slumped his shoulders and softly cursed.

Sitting on the bed, he saw Leona had left her underslip behind. Gathering it up in his hands, he stared at it for long moments, lost in thought. Running his fingers across the silk, the lace. Inhaling her perfume. And finally, he bent down and stuffed it under his mattress, hiding it in the shadows beneath his bed.

The shadows where a not-cat sat and listened.

Trying terribly hard not to roll his not-eyes.

"... *sigh* ..."

CHAPTER 23

WHITEKEEP

The crash of waves on a stony shore.

The screams of gulls in sunburned skies.

The roar of seventy thousand voices, joined as one.

A lone gladiatii stood in the arena's heart, bathed in thunder. The blinding scorch of the two suns glittered on the twin lengths of razored chain he twirled about his body. He was clad in gleaming steel, arm wrapped in scaled mail, greaves at his shins. His face was hidden behind a polished helm, fashioned like a roaring drake's maw.

The prisoners around him wore no such protection—a few scraps of piecemeal leather, rusty swords in hand. Execution bouts were meant to entertain the crowd between the major events, but there were a dozen condemned men and women in the arena, fighting against a single gladiatii; it wouldn't do to give the criminals much of a chance at surviving. They were meant to die here, after all.

A convicted rapist charged with a cry, the gladiatii whipping his spike chain across the man's belly, spilling coils of purple guts onto the now-scarlet sand. The crowd roared in approval. An arsonist and a murderer struck at the gladiatii's rear, but both were met with a whistling wall of steel, slicing their sword arms off at the elbows and their throats to the bone.

As the mob's cheers swelled louder, as the walls of Whitekeep arena near shook with the stomping of their feet, the gladiatii went to work in earnest. Opening windpipes and stomachs, severing hands and legs, and as a thrilling finale, taking the last prisoner's head clean off his shoulders.

"Citizens of Itreya!" came the call across the arena horns. "Honored administratii! Senators and marrowborn! Your victor, Giovanni of Liis!"

The gladiatii roared, raising his bloody chains. As he strode about the sand, whipping the crowd to frenzy, the criminals' mutilated corpses were dragged away for disposal. Only an unmarked grave and the abyss awaiting them.

Mia stood in her cell, staring out through the bars to the sands beyond. The games were almost done—only the equillai race and their feature match against the silkling remained between now and the Ultima. Butcher had fought earlier in the turn, but he'd been soundly thrashed by a swordsman from the Tacitus Collegium—only a plea for mercy from the editorii had seen his life spared. Wavewaker and Sidonius had fought in a bestiary match with two dozen other gladiatii and a pack of Vaanian scythebears. The pair had slain three beasts between them, though they'd been bested in the final points tally by a pair of stalkers from the Trajan Collegium. Only two marks shy of victory.

So close to a laurel, yet so far away.

The pair sat in the cell with Mia now, nursing their wounds and stung pride. Butcher was with Maggot, getting his head and ribs stitched up. Bladesinger sat with her back to the sand, listening to the furor die outside. She was busy tying a handful of hooked knives into the ends of her saltlocks, humming to herself. The blades were three inches long, razor-sharp. She was clad in a boiled leather breastplate, spaulders and greaves of dark iron. A helmet with the crown cut away sat on the bench beside her.

"Bryn and Byern will be up soon," Mia said.

Bladesinger nodded, saying nothing.

"Nervous?" Mia asked.

"Always," the woman replied.

"Courage, sisters," Wavewaker smiled. "This match is yours."

Bladesinger nodded slow. In the weeks leading up to their departure from Crow's Nest, their training with Furian had improved no end, and in the long sessions beneath the burning suns, the trio had reached a kind of synchronicity. Moving as one, they'd begun to best Arkades regularly. Mia's speed. Furian's brawn. Bladesinger the bridge between. Though the Unfallen was kept apart from them in his champion's cell, as was tradition before the match, they were as close to a team as they would ever be.

"We have a chance," Bladesinger admitted.

Truth told, they had more than one. Ashlinn had arrived in Whitekeep a week before the gladiatii of the Remus Collegium, and had been skulking about the arena ever since. Passing messages through Eclipse, she'd told Mia exactly how the editorii planned to spice up the spectacle of the clash between the champions of the Leonides and Remus Collegia. But moreover, Ash had arranged a special gift to tip the scales further in their favor.

Mia closed her eyes, listened to the sound of the distant ocean.* Godsgrave was just across the water—if she climbed the city walls, she'd be able to see it from here. She was just one step away from the *magni*.

One match away from revenge.

Trumpets sounded, the crowd roaring in response. The stone beneath her feet trembled, the great mekwerk apparatus beneath the arena floor churning. Mia looked out through the bars, saw the center of the sands split apart, an oblong island rising in the heart of the arena. Almost forty crucifixes were lined up in a neat row along the island's length, convicted prisoners lashed tight to the crossbeams.

"It's starting," Mia said.

Bladesinger joined her by the bars, Wavewaker beside her. She glanced at

---

* The city of Whitekeep is a sprawling metropolis on the southern shores of Itreya, and sister city to Godsgrave. The City of Bridges and Bones can be seen from its shoreline, and the mighty aqueduct that feeds water to Itreya's capital runs from the mountains at Whitekeep's back, down through the metropolis, over the bay, and on to Godsgrave.

Set with statuary of Aa and his Four Daughters and guarded at either end by the towering figures of Itreyan War Walkers, the aqueduct is a marvel of engineering, and one of the wonders of the Itreyan Republic. Its chief architect was a resident of Whitekeep named Marius Gandolfini, who was commissioned to oversee the project by King Francisco II, the Great Builder.

The aqueduct allowed the Itreyan capital to blossom from a squalid cesspool into a water-rich marvel, overflowing with fountains, a complex sewer network, hundreds of public baths, and all manner of waterworks. Though Gandolfini died of old age before the aqueduct was complete, his name is still venerated in the City of Bridges and Bones to this turn. A statue of him stands proudly in the Visionaries' Row of the Iron Collegium, marble busts of his likeness are found in bathhouses across the city, and certain specialist brothels offer a "Gandolfini" to their more . . . adventurous clientele.

Use your imagination, gentlefriends.

Sidonius as he muscled up next to her. They'd not spoken about the revelation of her parentage since the nevernight they'd fought in their cell—Sid seemed a man content to wait until Mia approached him, to talk when she was ready. But she noted he never strayed far from her anymore. Sitting next to her at meals, training nearby, never more than a few feet away. As if he felt protective of her now. As if the news she was the daughter of Darius Corvere—

"Citizens of Itreya!" came the editorii's booming call. "We present to you, the equillai race of this, the Whitekeep *venatus*!"

The crowd roared in answer, waves rippling across the mob. The White-keep arena wasn't quite the size of its sister in Godsgrave, but Mia reckoned there were at least seventy thousand people in the stands. The clamor of them, the heat, the pulsing rhythm of their chants swept her up, back to the sands of Stormwatch as she prowled up and down the retchwyrm's corpse.

"What is my name?" she screamed.

"CrowCrowCrowCrowCrow!"

"WHAT IS MY NAME?"

They knew it now, sure and true. Word of her victory had spread across the Republic; Ashlinn had heard pundits telling tales in a taverna just two nevernights ago. "The Bloody Beauty," they called her. "The Savior of Stormwatch."

She looked in the direction of Godsgrave. Listening to the sound of the ocean above the crowd's clamor.

Soon, all will know my name.

She clenched her fists.

My real *name . . .*

"And now, our equillai!" the editorii called. "From the Wolves of Tacitus, the Colossi of Carrion Hall, Alfr and Baldr!"

Two huge Vaanian men rode out from the rising portcullis at the southern end of the arena. They stood astride a chariot embossed with snarling wolves, the wings on their helms and the blond of their beards gleaming in the sun-light as they raised their hands to the cheering crowd.

"From the Swords of Phillipi! Victors of Talia, the Ninth Itreyan Wonders, Maxus and Agrippina!"*

---

* Despite claims to the contrary from enthusiastic editorii, there are only eight Itreyan Wonders:

- The Ribs of Godsgrave.
- The Godsgrave Aqueduct.

A second chariot rode out after the first, drawn by chestnut stallions. The equillai were mixed sex like Bryn and Byern, but by the bow in his hand, the male looked to be the *flagellae* of the pair. In an impressive acrobatic display, he stood astride the horses, arms spread wide, whipping up the crowd.

"From the Falcons of Remus Collegium . . . !"

"Here we go," Sidonius breathed.

". . . the twin terrors of Vaan, Bryn and Byern!"

The siblings burst forth on their chariot, hooves thundering on the packed dirt. Not to be outdone by the Phillipi's *flagellae*, Bryn was astride Rose's and Briar's backs in a handstand, her bow in her toes. She loosed her arrow into the air, the shaft falling to earth and piercing the track right at the finish line.

Mia and her fellows whooped as Bryn and Byern's chariot swooped past their cell. Byern flashed them a winning grin, Bryn blowing a kiss as they passed, Wavewaker reaching out as if to snatch it from the air.

"Trelene ride with you, my friends!" he bellowed. "Ride!"

"And now, from the Lions of Leonides, Victors of Stormwatch and Black-bridge, the Titans of the Track, your beloved . . . Stonekiller and Armando!"

The equillai charged forward onto the track to deafening applause, smiles wide. Their hands were joined, held aloft. They wore golden armor, their

---

- The Mausoleum of Lucius I—the final resting place of the first Liisian Magus King, this ziggurat looms near five hundred feet tall, and baffles contemporary engineers with the genius of its construction.
- The Dust Falls of Nuuvash—a series of massive cliffs found in southern Ysiir, which spill vast avalanches of dust off the Whisperwastes into the oceans below.
- The Statue of Trelene at Farrow—found in the high temple of the Dweymeri capital, this marble-and-gold sculpture of the Mother of Oceans performs miracles when credible sources aren't looking.
- The Thousand Towers—a series of natural stone spires, rising hundreds of feet from an ancient riverbed in Ysiir. In truth, there are only nine hundred sixty-four. "Thousand Towers" just sounds better.
- The Temple of Aa in Elai—constructed by the Great Unifier, Francisco I, to commemorate his conquest of Liis. At its heart stands a ten-foot statue made of solid gold—the material acquired by melting the personal fortunes of every nobleborn Liisian familia who stood against Francisco in battle.

Honorable mentions to the List of Wonders include the Great Salt; the Tomb of Brandr I; a courtesan named Francesca Andiami, who can do extraordinary things with a bowl of strawberries and a string of prayer beads; and my own personal astonishment that any of you took the time to read this when they're about to start the bloody horse race.

shoulders draped with the pelts of mighty lions. Armando reached into the quiver at his side and began firing arrows into the air. Through some arkemy, the arrows exploded into confetti and ribbon, falling in rainbow-colored showers among the delighted audience.

Rhythmic chanting filled the stands as the equillai took up their positions, each at an opposite point of the oblong. Mia watched Bryn and Byern with no fear in her heart, but she knew their odds were long. With Leona fielding no one from her stable in the Ultima, even if the twins won, the Falcons would still be one laurel short of a berth at the *magni*—only Mia's feature match with the silkling could guarantee them a place now. Bryn and Byern were competing simply for the purse, and perhaps for their own glory. But it was a great deal to risk for a handful of coin and some pride.

Mia wasn't the only one who knew the odds. Bladesinger stood beside her, tense as steel. Wavewaker was gripping the bars tight, Sidonius holding his breath. Mia recalled Bryn and Byern's words to her back at the Nest. The saying from their homeland they'd shared.

"In every breath, hope abides."

She reached out, squeezed Sidonius's hand.

"Keep breathing," she whispered.

"Equillai . . . ," came the editorii's call. *"Begin!"*

The crack of reins. The percussion of hooves. Mia grit her teeth as the race began, each of the teams building up a swift head of speed. As the chariots roared around the track, gaining speed, the archers released shot after shot at the helpless prisoners, trying to kill as many as possible in order to rack up points. The crowd bellowed, the condemned screamed, scarlet painted the sands.

Editorii stood in the crowd with spyglasses, marking the different colored feathers from each team and noting who scored the kill shots. Two tally boards stood in the west and eastern stands, spry children marking each team's total by slotting stones into divots in the board. Sidonius pointed to the score.

"We're in the lead."

The crowd roared, dragging Mia's attention away from the points. The Phillipi team had adopted an aggressive early strategy, neglecting the prisoners and quickly engaging instead. Their archer was firing at Bryn and Byern, black-feathered shafts whistling through the air. Byern protected his sister behind his shield as she put a shot into one of the last prisoners, and spinning on her heel, she returned fire, forcing the Phillipi archer back into cover. Meanwhile, the Lions of Leonides were trading shots with the Wolves of Tacitus, the crowd thrilling as Armando landed a clever shot into the Wolf archer's thigh.

"First blood to the Lions of Leonides!" cried the editorii.

Trumpets sounded.

Eight laps to go.

Four *coronae* were randomly flung onto the track, the silver wreaths gleaming in the dust. They were worth a single point, but with only a few points between first and last place, every one would count. Bryn loosed three shots at the Phillipi archer as her brother leaned out of their chariot, scooping up one *coronae*. The Swords took the second, the Lions another. The riders thundered about the track, arrows cut the air, Mia and her fellows watching on, cheering with the rest of the mob.

Six laps to go.

More *coronae* fell. Trumpets rang, the ground rumbled as the sands split apart. Wooden barricades rose out of the sands along the track, set with vicious tangles of razorvine. As if the risk of collision weren't enough, the barricades simultaneously burst into flame. The *sagmae* were now forced to focus more on steering their chariots and less on protecting their partners, and with the pace lessened, it was easier to close distance. The arrows flew thick and fast, Mia cursing as Bryn was grazed by a shot that Byern failed to deflect in time. And as the crowd thrilled, the Wolves of Tacitus managed to score a hit on Stonekiller, a white-feathered arrow sinking deep into his shin.

Stonekiller staggered, sinking to his knees and lowering his shield as their chariot skidded wildly. The Wolf archer fired again, the crowd howling as Armando was struck in the shoulder. With the skill that had made them champions, Stonekiller brought the chariot back under control, Armando tearing the arrows from his arm, his *sagmae*'s leg. But the blood was flowing thick, and the Wolves used the time to scoop up another three *coronae*, putting them in the lead.

Mia shook her head, watching Bryn and Byern falling further behind.

Four laps to go.

More wreaths were showered onto the track—half a dozen this time. The Wolves held first place, the Falcons and Lions tied for second. Bryn was like a woman possessed, firing shot after shot at her foes. The Swords were coming last in the tally, their situation desperate. In his haste to scoop up a *coronae*, the Sword *sagmae* ran their chariot too close to a barricade, their wheel clipping the burning razorvine with a hail of sparks. Off-balance, the *sagmae* fell to his knee, and Bryn loosed a stunning shot, her red-feathered arrow swishing right through the driver's throat.

The man gurgled, a second shot thudding into his chest. The horses clipped another barricade, snapping the crossbar clean, and the chariot flipped over and crashed into a tangled ruin.

"First kill for the Falcons!" the editorii crowed. *"Sanguii e Gloria!"*

Bryn raised a fist in triumph and Byern scooped up another *coronae*, Mia and her fellows hollering. With those five points, the Remus Collegium was back in first place. Victory in sight.

"Two laps remain!" came the call.

Smoke from the burning barricades drifted over the track, the sands red with blood. With the foes that had dogged them all match now dead, Byern whipped his mares into a burst of speed, closing in on the Lions from behind. Armando was pressed low behind Stonekiller's shield, the pair bleeding heavily. The crowd howled, wondering if the beloved Lions were being set up for the kill, but Mia's eyes were narrowed. Armando and Stonekiller were no fools, and a big cat is never more dangerous than when wounded.

"Be careful!" she shouted as the Falcons wheeled past their cell window.

Bryn raised her bow and took aim, the Wolves' archer did the same from their lead. The crowd was on their feet, thinking Stonekiller and Armando were about to fall in the crossfire. But with astonishing skill, Stonekiller seized one wheel with his bare hands, locking it tight. The drag whipped the chariot sideways, their enemies' shots going wide. Armando rose up from cover and loosed a shot at the Wolves, the arrow whispering right past the surprised *sagmae*'s shield and into her archer's neck. The mob howled, the archer staggered, topping into the dirt.

"Third kill, Lions!" came the cry.

The Wolf chariot clipped a barricade, rocking it sideways. As three of Bryn's shots thudded into Stonekiller's shield, Armando fired again, striking the Wolf driver in the knee and chest. She collapsed, her leg catching as she fell from the chariot, dragged for a few hundred feet before she was torn loose.

"Lions, Fourth kill! *Sanguii e Gloria!*"

The mob bellowed, drunk on the carnage. Byern scooped up another *coronae*, Briar and Rose both drenched in sweat. Stonekiller whipped his stallions, trying to keep distance from the Falcons. With their two kill shots against the Wolves, the Lions were now in the lead—all they needed to do was maintain distance and keep pace with the Falcons in scooping up wreaths, and victory would be theirs.

"Final lap!"

The entire arena was on its feet, the noise crawling on Mia's skin and down her spine. Sidonius was muttering beneath his breath, urging the twins on,

Bladesinger quietly praying, Wavewaker silent as stone. Horses frothing, crowd baying, flames crackling, Mister Kindly swelled in Mia's shadow as fear tried to take root in her belly, her jaw clenched tight. She watched Byern whipping his horses hard, trying to close distance so his sister could score a kill shot. Desperation on their faces. Blood on their skin. Death in the air.

Watching the crowd, Mia felt sick to her stomach. The euphoria, the red glaze in their eyes. Four people were out there on the sands, fighting for their lives. But the crowd didn't see men and women with hopes and dreams and fears.

She wanted Bryn and Byern to triumph. Despite knowing better than to think of them as friends, she *knew* them. She *liked* them. She didn't want them to die. But she was surprised to realize she didn't want Stonekiller and Armando and all their hopes and dreams and fears to die either. Just for the sake of a laurel that didn't matter anyway?

The Lions were closing on the finish line. The crowd, all open mouths and shapeless howls. Rounding to the final straight, Stonekiller leaned down to scoop up another *coronae*. The Falcons flew around the corner behind, running so hard their chariot went up on one wheel. Bryn fired through the dust and smoke and flame—a miracle shot, slipping past the man's shield and into his arm. Stonekiller slipped in the blood, dragging the reins. The chariot slewed sideways, the crowd bellowing as it collided with a barricade, smashing the equillai inside like glass. The axle shattered, one wheel snapping loose from the ruin and bouncing back down the track.

Right at the Falcons of Remus.

Byern hauled on the reins, trying to steer his horses left, but their momentum was too much. The tumbling wheel sheared through Briar's legs, the mare screaming as she toppled. The chariot's crossbeam struck the sand, and as Mia and her comrades gasped

O, no . . .

the whole rig crumpled like dry vellum and flipped high into the air.

Bryn and Byern were tossed like rag dolls, the crowd groaning as the twins crashed to earth. Bryn landed shoulder first in the sand, but her brother wasn't as lucky. Byern flew headfirst into one of the burning barricades, Mia wincing at the wet crackle of shattering bone. The Vaanian crashed clean through the obstacle and tumbled to a rest twenty feet down the track, lying in a tangled heap just beyond their cell window.

"Mother of Oceans," Bladesinger breathed.

The crowd was stunned—both equillai teams had crashed before the finish line. Stonekiller and Armando lay motionless in the wreckage of their chariot, the young archer's back twisted at a ghastly angle, his partner motionless beside him. But in the ringing aftermath, the mob soon began to cheer.

"Almighty Aa, look!" Sidonius cried.

Mia squinted through the smoke, realizing that Bryn was moving. Slow at first, the girl stirred, pushing herself up onto her knees and slinging off her plumed helmet. As Mia watched, as the crowd began roaring again, the archer swayed to her feet.

Bryn stood perhaps fifty feet from the finish line. All she needed to do was walk across, and the Falcons would have their victory. She began limping toward it, holding her ribs and hobbling, stumbling, the mob began chanting, "Bryn! Bryn! Bryn!" The young archer spat blood onto the sand, face twisted, eyes locked on the line.

Until she caught sight of her brother.

Mia held her breath as the girl stopped, the entire arena falling still. Confusion flitted across Bryn's face. And then she was stumbling, limping, gasping toward Byern. He lay facedown, just a stone's throw from where Mia and the others were caged. Bryn fell to her knees beside him, rolling him over gently.

"Byern?" Bryn asked, her voice trembling.

Mia saw blood at his lips. Blue eyes open wide to the burning sky above. Bryn reached out with bloody hands to shake him.

". . . B-brother?"

"O, Daughters . . . ," Sidonius breathed.

"Keep breathing," Mia prayed.

Bryn leaned close, pressed her ear to her brother's lips. Hearing nothing, she shook him again, face twisting as she screamed.

"Byern?" she cried, shaking him. *"Byern!"*

Guards marched into the arena, arrayed all in black. As they checked the bodies of the fallen Lions, Bryn gathered her twin up in her arms and started wailing, weeping, howling. Mia felt her heart aching, tears slipping down her cheeks. Sidonius was as still as a statue. Wavewaker hanging his head as Bryn screamed.

"BYERN!"

The guards marched to where the girl knelt in the dust, dragging her up by the arms. Coming to her senses, Bryn fought back, kicking and screaming, "No! *NO!*" It took four men to drag her off the sand, thrashing and howling her brother's name.

"Citizens of Itreya!" came the call across the arena horns. "We regret to declare . . . no victor!"

Mia closed her eyes. After all that, it was for nothing. No laurel. No glory. Just nothing. And then, as her belly burned, a chill creeping across her skin, she heard the crowd begin to boo. Staring out through the bars, she saw the mob on their feet, throwing food and spitting on the sand. That sand stained with the blood of eight men and women, seven of whom had just died for their amusement. Seven people with hopes and fears and dreams, now, nothing but corpses.

And the crowd? They cared not a drop.

All they wanted was a victory.

Mia took a deep breath. Clenched her jaw. Sidonius and the others remained at the bars, but Mia turned her back, walked away. Stare fixed on the stone at her feet. The path before her. The vengeance awaiting her at the end of it.

"*. . . i am sorry, mia . . .*"

"You?" she whispered. "Why?"

"*. . . he was your friend . . .*"

"They're not my familia, remember?" she replied. "They're not my friends." She looked down at her hands. Blurred almost shapeless by her tears.

"All of them are only a means to an end."

OBSIDIAN

Hollow.

That's how Mia felt inside. Listening to the mob stamping impatiently on the bleachers as Byern's corpse was dragged away. Long hair hanging about her eyes, she busied herself strapping the leather breastplate to her chest, the iron greaves about her shins. Every movement cold.

Methodical.

Mekanical.

"*. . . ARE YOU WELL . . . ?*"

A whisper in her ear, beneath the shadows of her hair.

"*. . . mia . . . ?*"

Guards arrived at their cell door to collect them, dressed all in black. Furian stood behind them in his gleaming armor, a Falcon helm on his head, his silver champion's torc glittering around his neck. Arkades limped beside the

Unfallen, his face a masque. Dona Leona walked before all of them, resplendent in a long, sky-blue gown, tears smudging the kohl about her eyes. As the guards unlocked the cell door, Mia met her domina's stare, trying to weigh her grief.

Was it sincere? Or as hollow as her chest felt at that moment?

"Domina?" Bladesinger asked quietly. "Is Bryn . . . ?"

"She is with Maggot," the dona murmured. "She is . . . not well."

"Her brother died out there, Domina," Sidonius said. "How else should she be?"

"I . . ."

"Enough," Arkades growled. "Byern died with honor, as gladiatii. Set your mind to the match and troubling thoughts aside. Your foe will not be hindered by them."

Mia still stared at Leona. Pondering all she knew of the woman. The dona had grown up around the violence of the arena. But though she kept a stable of men and women to fight and die for the amusement of the mob, some humanity might remain in her breast. She'd seen hints of it in the bathhouse with the magistrae, even perhaps in her backward affections for Furian. There was more to her than a simple thirst to best her father. Would the dona show true grief now, or urge them to "avenge their fallen brother," and just happen to win her berth at the *magni* besides?

Leona took Mia's hand. Bladesinger's also.

"I . . ."

She shook her head, trying to speak. Tears welling in her eyes.

"Be careful out there," she finally whispered.

Bladesinger blinked in surprise. Looking to Arkades.

". . . Aye, Domina."

"The match awaits, Mi Dona," the guard captain warned.

Leona nodded, wiping her face. "Very well."

They were marched through the arena's bowels, the thrumming clamor of the crowd echoing in the rafters overhead. They reached a large staging area, black stone and an iron portcullis, four broad steps leading down to the arena floor. The sounds of the crowd washed over her and Mia clenched her jaw, eyes to the sand.

"This is the hour," Arkades said. "Immortality within your grasp. A chance to carve your name into the earth, to honor your domina, and win your freedom. Only one foe stands between you and the *magni*. A foe who can bleed. A foe who can die." He fixed each in his ice-blue stare. "You are gladiatii of the Remus Collegium. Stand together, or fall alone."

Furian nodded. "Executus."

"Aye, Executus," Bladesinger murmured.

Mia only stared, remembering what Mister Kindly had told her of Arkades's words to the Unfallen in his room. Knowing that she was only an inconvenience to this man, a stone to be stepped upon on the way to the *magni*. He was only using her to see Furian elevated, his ends attained.

All right then, bastard. Let's use each other.

Mia spoke, her voice cold as wintersdeep. "Executus."

Leona said nothing more, and the pair left the staging area, the door locked behind them. Furian looked at her sidelong, expression hidden behind his Falcon helm. Bladesinger's eyes were fixed on the arena as she threaded her saltlocks through her helmet's crown, slipped it over her head. Hefting a heavy iron shield embossed with a red falcon, she tossed her head, the razor-tipped blades she'd woven at the tips of her locks glinting in the sunlight.

Mia clenched and unclenched her empty hands, shadow trembling, all the hunger and desire and breathless energy she felt when she was near Furian rising to her surface. She didn't bother grabbing a shield—she was useless with them anyway. Mister Kindly and Eclipse swelled in her shadow, pouncing on the butterflies trying to take wing in her belly and murdering them, one by one.

She knew this would be the hardest fight of her life.

Trumpets sounded, hushing the crowd, anticipation dripping from the very walls.

"Hold . . . ," Furian said, looking to the guard captain. "Where are our swords?"

"Waiting for us," Mia answered softly. "Out there."

"Citizens of Itreya!" The editorii's words echoed in the quiet. "Honored administratii! Senators and marrowborn! We present to you, a feature bout between the Lions of Leonides and the Falcons of Remus!"

An excited murmur rippled through the crowd.

"This match shall be fought *e mortium,* no surrender, no quarter given! Sanguila Leonides has placed a berth in the *Venatus Magni* in ante! Should the Falcons of Remus stand the victors, his daughter, Sanguila Leona of the Remus Collegium, shall be permitted to enter her gladiatii in the grand games at Godsgrave, six weeks hence."

The murmur became a rising swell.

"Entering from the Coast Gate for the Falcons of Remus, we present to you, Bladesinger, the Reaper of Dweym! The Bloody Beauty and Savior of Stormwatch, Crow! And the Champion of Talia, the Unfallen himself, Furiaaaan!"

The crowd came to their feet, roaring in approval. The portcullis drew up, and with a final glance to each other, the three Falcons strode out into the sand, guards marching beside them. Bladesinger and Furian raised their hands in greeting, the crowd bellowing in response, thousands upon thousands. Mia only scowled. She remembered not so long ago, when that applause had thrilled her soul. Now, she knew they cheered not for *her,* but the bloody spectacle she provided. It mattered not who swung the blade. Only that someone's neck was there to meet it.

She wanted to be done with this, wanted this bloody gala ended and Duomo and Scaeva gone and a thousand years in a hot spring to wash the blood and stink of it away . . .

The great island that had marked the equillai track had sunk back down into the mekwerk beneath the arena floor. The sand before them was featureless, off-white, streaked with fresh red.

"Wait here," the guard captain commanded. "Do *not* move until commanded by the editorii, or you will be disqualified."

The guards marched back to the portcullis, and sealed them in.

"What the 'byss is happening here?" Bladesinger muttered.

"Just hold still," Mia replied. "And brace yourself."

"Do you know something we do not, Crow?" the Unfallen growled.

"Furian," she sighed. "The things I know that you don't could just about fill the Great fucking Salt."

"Entering from the Tower Gate for the Lions of Leonides, we present a terror from the Drakespine Mountains! A pariah among her own kind, her very name, death in the tongue of the Dominion! Behold, Ishkah, the Exiiiiile!"

A wondering murmur rolled through the crowd, the portcullis in the arena's northern wall grinding open. Out of the shadow walked Leonides's silkling, flanked by a half-dozen guards. She was decked in a suit of magnificent golden armor, highlighted with emerald green. A lion's pelt was draped about her shoulders, its head and great mane fitted around her helm. As the crowd cheered wildly, the silkling strode into the arena. The guards marched back in formation, the portcullis slamming behind them.

Mia stared across the sand to their enemy, dust blowing in the rising wind. Ishkah stood seven feet tall, all gleaming chitin and muscle, her lips painted cloud-white. She sloughed off her lion's pelt, six arms unfolding like a flower in bloom. Her dark green skin gleamed in the sunlight, those featureless eyes staring down her foes.

"Mother of Oceans," Bladesinger murmured. "She's a sight."

"Just brace yourselves," Mia said.

"Citizens, behold!" cried the editorii. "Your battleground."

A deep rumbling sounded beneath the sands, the grinding of colossal gears. The floor shuddered, but Mia's comrades held steady as a large, wedge-shaped section of the floor they stood on began to rise. Sand cascaded down, Mia looking over the edge into the massive mekwerks below. She smelled oil, sulfur, salt.

Other sections of the sand were moving, the entire arena floor breaking up into a series of wedged platforms. Differing heights and dimensions, the platforms began slowly rotating around the central plinth, spinning, twisting, passing above and beneath one another like the interlocking pieces of some enormous clockface. Furian, Bladesinger and Mia exchanged glances, Bladesinger whispering a prayer to Trelene.

"You can't say they don't know how to put on a show," Mia muttered.

The gobsmacked crowd were cheering for all they were worth. Mia and her comrades were perhaps twenty feet above ground level now. She glanced down again into the arena's mekwerk guts—to slip off the edge would be to tumble into those great, grinding gears, and be mashed to pulp between greasy metal teeth.

"Weapons!" cried the editorii.

The great circular platform in the center of the arena groaned, and Mia saw a dozen blades of differing lengths rise hilt-first from the sands. There were shortswords, longblades, and the cruel, curved scimitars that the Exile favored. All of them were black, razor-edged, gleaming in the sunlight.

"We have to run for our swords?" Bladesinger muttered.

"Aye," Mia nodded. "But be warned—they're all made of obsidian, not steel. They'll be sharp as glass, but they're fragile. You'll only get a few swings before they're useless. Block with your shields, not your blades."

"How do you know this?" Furian demanded.

"Does it fucking matter?" she snarled. "Let's just get this done."

"No witchery, Crow," he warned. "We will earn this laurel, or a glorious death."

Bladesinger looked between the pair. "Stand together or fall alone, remember?"

"Gladiatii!" the editorii called. "Prepare!"

Mia coiled like a sprinter, eyes on a pair of twin swords in the center of the ring.

"Good luck, sister," Bladesinger said. "Brother. Lady of Oceans protect you."

"Aye," Furian nodded. "Aa bless and keep you, Tsana guide your hands."

Mia blinked the sweat from her eyes. The crowd was thunder in her ears. She looked out into the seething mob, searching for a girl with dyed red hair and eyes blue as sunsburned skies. Her shadow was trembling at its edges, ebbing like water toward Furian's own.

"Mother watch over us," she whispered.

"Gladiatii!" the editorii roared. "Begin!"

Mia took off, sprinting hard as she could. Breath burning in her lungs, glare fixed on those swords, the silkling sprinting at them from the opposite end of the arena as the crowd bellowed. Bladesinger charged just a few steps behind her, long legs pumping smoothly, Furian bringing up the rear.

Mia reached the edge of their platform, vaulting the gap to the next. The wedge shifted under her feet, swinging clockwise, those colossal gears grinding below her. Sand crunched under her boots and she leapt across to the next tier of smaller wedges, closer to the arena's heart. Her eyes were on the silkling, running hard, drawing ever closer to those gleaming, black blades. Heart sinking as she realized . . .

. . . *she's going to get there first.*

Mia reached out across the shifting platforms, the swirling sands, the mighty gears. Her shadow trembled as she took hold of the silkling's own, snarled it in her boots. Ishkah hissed, stumbling momentarily as Mia dashed toward the central plinth. But with a curse, she felt her grip on the shadows break, and Ishkah's feet slip free.

Fucking Furian . . .

"No witchery!" he shouted behind her.

Ishkah made the central platform, six hands snaking out and seizing the hilts of six cruelly curved scimitars. The crowd roared, sunslight gleaming on obsidian. The silkling wheeled about as Mia leapt onto the plinth, three of her swords glittering as they scythed through the air, right at Mia's throat. With a gasp, the girl dove left, hit the sand with her shoulder and rolled, under the whistling blades and behind Ishkah. And with a gasp, Mia seized hold of two swords and dragged them free.

She turned just as Ishkah struck, her blades a blur. Mia dare not block the strikes edge on edge—the obsidian might shatter if she struck at the wrong angle, and Ishkah had swords to spare. Instead she danced away, sand flying, twisting left and right and bending backward, spine extended, one of the strikes whipping just over her chin. Tumbling back, she rolled up into a crouch right at the platform's edge, wobbling precariously over a shifting sea of grinding metal cogs.

Bladesinger roared as she barreled into Ishkah from behind, shield crunching into the silkling's back and sending her flying. Ishkah fell forward, off the platform and onto another passing below, rolling up to her feet. Those pale, featureless eyes glinted as she watched Mia regain her balance, Bladesinger snatch up an obsidian longblade. Ishkah took a few steps toward Furian, but he was too far out of reach, finally vaulting up to the central plinth and snatching up another obsidian sword. The Unfallen raised his blade in the air, the crowd bellowing in reply. The race was over, the competitors all armed. Now, the battle could begin in earnest.

Ishkah opened her arms, scimitars poised in a glittering fan, and without a sound, leapt back across to the central plinth. The three Falcons moved to meet her, Mia dashing out first, quick as silver and striking low. Bladesinger struck mid, her shield guarding Mia, while Furian swung at the silkling's head. Ishkah moved with stunning grace, slipping aside from Bladesinger and Mia's strikes. But as she raised one of her blades to counter Furian, the haft shattered like the thinnest ice.

The silkling rallied, scimitars cutting the air. She put a savage kick into Bladesinger's shield, knocking the smaller woman off-balance. Her swords opened up a shallow cut on Furian's arm. One of her blades whistled past Mia's throat and scraped her breastplate, splitting the leather wide. And drawing a breath, Ishkah parted those cloud-white lips in a snarl, and spat a mouthful of bright green venom right at Mia's face.

"... *beware* ... !"

Mia gasped, twisting desperately and turning her head. The liquid hit the side of her helm, spattering thick. As it touched the metal, the venom hissed, eating through the iron like a heated blade into snow. Mia rolled out of reach, tearing her helm loose and blinking hard. None had got in her eyes, on her skin, but Goddess, that was close ...

The Unfallen struck back with a furious cry, swinging his sword in a brutal overhand strike. Ishkah raised two blades, cross-guard, but her swords simply shattered against the Unfallen's. Mia shielded her eyes from the obsidian shards as the silkling hissed in frustration. Bladesinger swung her own sword, her strike glancing off Ishkah's armor. As Mia climbed to her feet, Furian pummeled Ishkah with his shield, forcing her back toward the platform's edge as another of her scimitars fractured on Bladesinger's armor. Mia lunged, feinting high and striking low, the crowd bellowing as she opened up the silkling's thigh. Green blood sprayed on the sand, obsidian splinters flying as Ishkah parried one of Mia's blades into the dirt and stomped on it with her boot. She swung her scimitar and Mia rolled aside, the silkling's forth sword splintering on the dirt.

Furian's blade was still intact, Mia had one blade left, and Bladesinger's was only slightly fractured. Ishkah had but two swords remaining, and three foes.

She struck simultaneously, forcing the Falcons back, the air hissing where she struck. Furian was on the defensive, bashing away with his shield where he could. Bladesinger and Mia fought side by side, the woman catching one of Ishkah's strikes on her shield and driving the sword into the ground, snapping it in half. Ishkah struck with her last blade, the broken haft of another, the blows whistling toward Bladesinger's belly and throat. Furian blocked the high strike on his shield, Mia parried the low, breaking Ishkah's final blade off at the hilt. With a furious war cry, Bladesinger charged, striking the silkling in the belly with her shield and knocking her backward off the platform. Ishkah made a desperate clicking noise, seizing the lip of a passing platform to halt her fall, and dragging herself up to safety.

The three Falcons stood together, gasping for breath. The silkling revolved around the central plinth on her own platform, featureless eyes locked on theirs. She still held the hilts of her broken swords, pale eyes fixed on the weapons of her enemies. Obsidian was fragile, but it wasn't supposed to be *this* fragile. Though the Falcons' weapons were chipped and scratched, Ishkah's scimitars had proven to be delicate as autumn leaves. Almost as if . . .

As if . . .

A slow smile curled Mia's lips.

"She looks upset."

". . . *the viper managed it, then* . . ."

"I wish you wouldn't call her that."

Mia risked a glance into the crowd, heart swelling in her chest, looking once more among the mob for blood-red hair, a pair of pretty blue eyes. She didn't truly know the concoction she'd devised—one part calcite acid, two parts boric oxide—would prove as effective on the silkling's weapons as it had. Didn't know whether Ashlinn would be clever or quick enough to sneak down into the arena's bowels and treat Ishkah's scimitars with the solution before the match began. But looking at the shattered blades in the silkling's hands, the relatively unscathed sword in her own, she knew somehow Ash had done it. The silkling was all but disarmed, and now, even with the venom and the frightening speed, the scales between them were somewhere close to even.

The crowd roared, urging the Falcons in for the kill.

Furian scowled at Mia. "The match proves easier than any supposed."

"Fancy that," Mia replied.

"*Crow* . . . ," Furian growled.

Mia looked at Furian sidelong, and winked.

"Enough talk," Bladesinger spat. "Let's just gut this ugly bitch."

The Falcons raised their weapons, made ready to charge.

"Blades!" cried the editorii.

Mia heard a rumble, turned to a platform at the arena's edge. Her heart sank as the sand shivered, and ten new obsidian blades rose up out of the dirt.

"Shit . . . ," she breathed.

"*. . . i take it you and the viper didn't know about those . . .*"

"Shit, shit, *shit*."

"*. . . o, this is maaaarvelous . . .*"

The crowd bellowed as Ishkah dashed toward the fresh swords, leaping from one shifting platform to the next. Mia took off after her, her comrades sprinting behind. The platforms wheeled and turned, a great mekwerk dance that was hard to judge, sweat burning Mia's eyes.

She supposed Ashlinn should've suspected there'd be backup plans in case every competitor broke their weapon, but there was no time to whine about it now—those new scimitars hadn't been weakened by her concoction. If Ishkah got her hands on them, the fight might end up being fair, and *that* couldn't happen. But as she ran, Mia realized with a sinking heart that again, the silkling would reach the blades before her.

"Furian?" she gasped.

"No!" the Unfallen spat, leaping across a rumbling chasm.

Spitting dust from her mouth she shook her head, and despite the burning heat of the two suns above, reached out toward Ishkah's shadow anyway. She felt it in her grasp, cool and tenebrous, slipping up like snakes to entwine itself with Ishkah's feet. The silkling stumbled, fell to her knees, her helm tumbling off her head and into the mekwerks below. But with a sharp, tearing sensation, Mia found her grip ripped away, the darkness slithering through her fingers.

"Mother fucking damn you!" she spat, face twisted.

"Victory is earned!" Furian shouted in reply. "Not stolen!"

Ishkah reached the swords, casting her chipped blades into the abyss and drawing six new ones—longblades this time, not scimitars. Turning to face the trio as they tumbled and leaped across the platforms toward her, she cut an awesome sight, blades whistling through the air in an almost hypnotic pattern. Mia reached the platform first, tumbling and hurling a handful of sand into Ishkah's face. She had only one sword, so as the silkling staggered back, pawing at her eyes, Mia dove toward the remaining blades to snatch a second, replace her first. She rolled aside as the silkling's swords struck the sand, the crowd gasping as her boot collided with Mia's ribs. The impact was thunderous, Mia feeling her ribs crack, burning fire in her chest. Spit spraying from her lips, Mia's face twisted as Ishkah raised her blade and—

Crack! came the sound as Bladesinger hurled her shield into the silkling's face. Ishkah shrieked, staggering, the audience bellowing as they saw the shield's edge had struck one of the silkling's eyes, smashing it like an eggshell. Green fluid dribbled from the wound, Mia dragging herself to her feet with a pained gasp and snatching up a new pair of blades. Bladesinger leapt across the chasm and Ishkah *screeeeeeched*, the Dweymeri raising her cracked sword and meeting her charge.

Bladesinger's blade shattered with the first blow, the enraged silkling scoring deep wounds on her shoulder, and shattering one of her swords on the side of Bladesinger's helm. The woman fell to her knees, skull ringing. But as Ishkah raised her blades to strike the deathblow, Furian arrived, leaping across the gulf with a howl and crashing shield-first into his foe. The pair fell to the ground in a tangle of limbs, Furian's shield skidding across the dirt.

The Unfallen sat atop the silkling, fingers hooked into her bleeding eyehole, pounding his knuckles on her face again and again.

"Fucking bitch!" *Crack!* "Do you know who I am?" *Crack!* "I am the Un—"

Ishkah shrieked, and spat a mouthful of venom. The bilious green fluid spattered over Furian's breastplate, up his unprotected throat, the man screaming as it began to burn. He fell backward, clawing at his neck, rolling in the sand as the crowd bellowed. Ishkah scrambled to her feet with a gargling growl, snatching up her blades and raising them above her head to end him.

Mia's sword flashed, striking Ishkah's blow aside. Ishkah struck back, cracking Mia's sword at the hilt and lashing out at her head. The girl pulled back, crying out as the blow sliced down through her brow, opened up her cheek, blood in her eyes. Staggering backward, she fell to one knee, and Ishkah kicked her savagely in the chest again, the fire in Mia's broken ribs burning white. Winded, she tumbled backward along the dirt, barely stopping herself from plummeting off the platform's edge.

With a shapeless cry, Bladesinger whipped her neck, her long saltlocks scything through the air. The razored blades she'd woven at the ends of her braids tore into Ishkah's face, her forearms. Bladesinger charged, a sword in each hand, clashing toe to toe with the towering silkling over Furian's prone body. Her blades cut the air, whistling, whirling, *singing*, shattering one of Ishkah's weapons and plunging deep into the silkling's side. Bladesinger *twisted* her wrist, shattering the obsidian sword inside the wound, green blood spraying. Ishkah screeched, stabbing back, opening up Bladesinger's forearm to the bone as she tried to ward off the blow. An empty fist pummeled the woman's face, a blade scythed at her throat, and as Bladesinger ducked, the silkling brought her knee up into her foe's face.

Bone crunched, Bladesinger's spine arching as she flew back, helm flying from her head, nose pulped. Holding her sundered guts in with one hand, Ishkah followed through, driving a brutal kick into the woman's solar plexus and sending her rolling back across the platform. Mia rose to her feet, blood drooling from her split cheek, gasping as she realized Bladesinger was about to tumble over the edge.

"*. . . MIA, NO . . . !*"

It was foolish. Idiotic, really. Victory was her goal here, not heroics, and Bladesinger was not her friend. But with a desperate cry, Mia hurled herself across the platform, plunged her remaining sword deep into the sand and seized hold of Bladesinger's wrist. Bladesinger cried out as she went over the edge, dragging Mia with her. The girl screamed as she arrested their fall, holding tight to Bladesinger with one hand, the sword hilt with the other, the fire of her broken ribs blooming inside her chest. The crowd roared in amazement, Mia's bleeding face twisted in agony. Her ribs were pressed against the side of the platform, the colossal gears churning ten feet below as it continued its revolution around the arena's heart. Her grip was slippery with blood, her body drenched in sweat.

"Hold on!" she cried.

Bladesinger gasped in agony, her face a bloody pulp. She glanced down to the shifting mekwerk below, up to Mia, shaking her head.

"Let me go!"

"Are you mad? Climb!"

"I'm too heavy, you skinny little shit! Let me go!"

"Stand together or fall alone!"

Ishkah was on her knees, two hands pressed to the terrible wound Bladesinger had carved in her side, green ichor dribbling from her shattered eye, her slashed face. Features twisted, she scrabbled in the dust, took hold of a fallen sword. And with the strength of a mountain, crowd murmuring in awe, she rose.

"Kill!" the crowd roared. "Kill!"

"O, shit . . . ," Mia breathed. "Bladesinger, *climb*!"

Ishkah began stalking toward her, sunslight gleaming on her sword. Mia winced, trying to keep her grip as Bladesinger pulled herself up. Her ribs were screaming, face throbbing, teeth gritted at the pain. Her hands were full, she couldn't clutch the shadows, couldn't reach out to the dark as she'd done so many times before . . .

"*. . . mia, look . . . !*"

Beyond the silkling, stalking closer, Furian was stirring. Sloughing off his helmet, the flesh of his chin and jaw and throat a bubbling, weeping ruin, breath rattling in his chest. The crowd's cries became a chant, a rhythm, pulsing with every beat of her heart.

"Kill! Kill! Kill!"

"Furian!" Mia screamed.

The Unfallen looked up, saw Bladesinger trying to drag herself up Mia's shoulder, the girl's face smeared in blood, the silkling a few steps away from ending them both.

"Furian!" Mia roared. "The dark!"

Ishkah snarled, needle teeth bared as she stepped closer.

"Kill! Kill! Kill!"

"*Do it!*" Mia screamed.

Bladesinger dragged herself up over the edge, reached out to Mia. Ishkah raised her blade, only two steps away. And fingers curled, teeth bared, the Unfallen reached out to the shadow beneath her, and tangled up the silkling's feet.

Ishkah stumbled, hissing in confusion. The crowd ceased their chanting, held their breath. Mia dragged herself up over the platform's edge, face twisted in agony. Furian gasped, collapsing onto his belly as he lost his grip on the darkness, Ishkah stepping up and slashing Bladesinger across her back, splitting the leather, blood spraying. Bladesinger collapsed with a cry, and with a desperate gasp, Mia dragged her obsidian sword from the earth, twisted away from Ishkah's sword, and hacked the silkling's arm off at the elbow.

Ishkah screamed, green blood fountaining. The crowd were alight, howling their fury. Mia twisted, dropping low and hewing at the silkling's leg, bringing her to her knees. The arena erupted, the noise deafening, seventy thousand voices rising in crescendo, "*Kill! Kill! Kill!,*" the suns burning overhead, blood thrumming in her veins, heart thundering in her chest as Mia screamed and swung her sword double-handed, all her strength, all her fury, all her pain, taking Ishkah's head clean off her shoulders.

Blood sprayed, spattering Mia with warm, sticky green. Ishkah's body trembled, six arms twitching as she toppled off the platform's edge and down into the grinding gears below. Mia winced at the bubbling crunch, averted her eyes, bloody obsidian still clutched in her hand.

But still . . .

. . . *I did it.*

Trumpets blared, silver and bright, the platforms ground to a shuddering halt. The editorii's voice rose over the blood-mad roar of the crowd, bouncing off the arena walls.

"Citizens of Itreya! Your victors! The Falcons of Remus!"

The crowd went wild, the applause deafening. Bladesinger staggered to her feet, face alight with pain and triumph, blood streaming from her wounds. But still, she grinned, throwing her good arm around Mia's shoulder and kissing her bloody cheek.

We *did it . . .*

Turning, Bladesinger grasped Mia's hand in her own, raised it high into the sky, bellowing at the crowd.

"What is her name?"

"Crow!" they roared.

"What is her name?"

Feet stamping, hands clapping, the word reverberating across the sands.

"Crow! Crow! Crow! Crow!"

Mia looked down at the bloody sword in her hand. Over to Furian, curled in a ball in the dirt, hands to his savaged throat. She raised her eyes to the sanguila's box, saw Leona on her feet, horrified stare locked on Furian. Arkades stood beside her, hands raised in somber applause.

She thought of Godsgrave, of the *Venatus Magni,* the berth her victory had now assured. She thought of Bryn, her dead brother cradled in her arms as she wailed. She thought of her father, holding her hands as he whisked her around some glittering ballroom, her feet atop his as they danced. Her mother, making her watch as he was hanged, as she whispered the words that would shape Mia forever, as the hope children breathed and adults mourned withered and fell away, floating like ashes on the wind.

"Never flinch. Never fear. And never, *ever* forget."

What is my name?

"Crow! Crow! Crow! Crow!"

What is my name?

"CROWCROWCROWCROW!"

Dark delight in her belly.

Warm blood on her hands.

Mia closed her eyes.

Raised her blade.

O, Mother, blackest Mother, what have I become?

THE GAME

CHAPTER 25

ROT

"Hold him still!"

"Almighty God, it burns!"

"Hold his legs, damn you!"

"Aa, help me! Help me!"

Mia sat in a dark corner of the cell, ribs burning, a blood-soaked rag held to her split cheek. She could feel the adrenaline from the match souring in her veins, hands trembling. The crowd bellowed above, the Ultima in full swing, the stone beneath her vibrating with the fury of the final bout. Bladesinger sat beside her, arm swaddled in red-soaked cloth, Mia pressing a sodden bandage to the ragged wound across the woman's back. The pair of them were in need of stitching, blood pooling on the stone around them. But Maggot's hands were more than full.

"Tie him down!" the girl yelled. "He's only making it worse!"

Furian screamed again, full-throated and trembling, his agony echoing through the arena's bowels. He was laid out on a stone slab, Executus and three of Leona's houseguards trying to keep him still. The flesh of his throat, jaw, and chest was blistered and weeping from the touch of the silkling's venom. He seemed to have gone mad from the agony, muscles corded in his arms and chest as he screamed.

Dona Leona stood by the door, horror in her eyes.

"Almighty Aa . . . ," she whispered.

"Tie him down!" Maggot cried again.

Arkades snapped heavy iron manacles about Furian's arms, feet, and waist, securing him to the slab. But the Unfallen continued to thrash, cutting his wrists and ankles on his bonds, smashing the back of his head against the stone.

Mia had seen pain before—the blood scourging in the Mountain, her branding in that cell in the Hanging Gardens. But she'd never seen agony the likes
of this in her life.

"You need to put him under, Maggot," she said.

"I don't have any slumberweed!" the little girl cried, pointing to a chest of
herbs and remedies. "It all spoiled on the way here!"

"Do you have any Swoon?"

"I used it all on Butcher!"

"Four Daughters," Leona cursed. "Did you only bring a thimbleful?"

"All respect, Domina, but you've not given me coin to restock in months!"

"Well, you must do something!" Leona cried. "Listen to him!"

Furian screamed again, mouth open wide, his throat bleeding with the force
of it. With a wince at her cracked ribs, Mia rose and limped to Maggot's herb
chest. Fingers sticky with blood, she rifled through the phials and jars of powder and liquid, all the lessons from Spiderkiller's hall buzzing in her head.

"What the 'byss are you doing?" Arkades growled.

Mia ignored the executus, handed Maggot a half-dozen jars. "Grind the
scalpweed with the maidenhead and a pinch of allroot, mix it with some goldwine."

"No," Maggot frowned. "The alcohol will calcify the maidenhe—"

"That's what the mireleaf is for," Mia interrupted. "Steep the leaf in the . . .
in fact, let me do it. You go stitch up Bladesinger. She's bleeding all over the
fucking floor."

"Crow?" Leona asked.

Mia turned to the woman by the door. "Trust me, Domina."

Leona looked to Furian, still writhing in agony. Eyes brimming, she nodded, and Mia set to work mixing her concoction. Maggot took a needle and
silken thread, set to work stitching the awful wound on Bladesinger's forearm.
The silkling's blade had sliced the woman down to the bone, and the blood
was flowing like cheap wine at a truelight feast. Bladesinger grit her teeth, eyes
locked on the Unfallen.

"Can you save him?"

"I can make him sleep," Mia replied. "Executus, I need your flask."

Arkades raised an eyebrow as Mia held out one bloody hand.

"Your goldwine, now!"

Arkades reached into his tunic, pulled out his silver flask. Mia poured her
concoction into the whiskey, shook the mixture thoroughly.

Furian was still bucking, screaming, begging. And as Mia stepped closer, flask in hand, his shadow began bleeding over the stone, reaching out toward her own. It was only the dim light of the cell and the drama unfolding on the slab that prevented any from noticing right away, and Mia moved quickly, shouldering one of the guards aside. The Unfallen's shadow melted into her own, all the sickness, all the hunger she felt when she was near him rising in her gullet and almost making her vomit. She staggered, nearly dropped the flask, Arkades grabbing her shoulders to stop her fall.

Black Mother, I can feel him . . .

"Are you well?"

. . . as if he were part of me.

"Hold his m-mouth open," Mia said.

The pain from her split cheek and broken ribs was awful, but she could feel pain at her throat and chest, too; Furian's agony was somehow bleeding into her, worsening her own.

"Furian, you must drink!" Mia shouted. "Do you hear me?"

A gurgling wail of agony was his only reply, and so Mia upended the flask into the man's mouth. He gargled, tried to spit the dose out, but Mia clamped her hand over his blistered lips and roared, "Swallow!"

Furian bucked, straining against his bonds, tears spilling from his eyes. But finally he did as commanded, his mangled throat bobbing as he drank the burning draft. It took a few minutes for the herbs to take effect—Mia wasn't working with the finest materials, after all. But slowly, the Unfallen's struggles slowed, his screams became moans, and finally, after what seemed an age in the lightless bowels beneath that bloody sand, Furian's bloodshot eyes fluttered closed.

Mia fell to her knees, hair plastered to her split brow and cheek, head swimming.

"Where did you learn to do that?" Maggot asked, bewildered.

Mia hung her head, vision swimming.

". . . Crow?" Leona asked.

"*. . . mia . . . ?*"

"*. . . MIA . . . !*"

Blood on her hands, in her eyes, the taste of bitter medicine she'd never drunk on her tongue. She looked down to her shadow. The shadow that should have been dark enough for three. But as the room swam before her eyes, as the pain of her wounds and the trauma of her ordeal in the arena and the shuddering aftermath rose up to sweep a black curtain over her eyes, she realized . . .

Dark enough for four . . .

———

"... *Mia* ..."

She woke in the hold of a ship, creaking beams above and the sound of the waves all around. As she opened her eyes, she felt a cool, featherlight touch on the back of her neck, a whispered sigh of relief in her ear.

"... *at last* ..."

The hammock she lay in ebbed and rolled, her mouth dry as dust. Garish light filtered in through a small glass porthole, a glimpse of two blues framed beyond; sunburned bright and ocean deep. Her ribs burned like a dying fire. Mia reached up to her face, felt a bandage over her cheek and brow, crusted with dried blood.

"Don't touch it," came a voice. "It'll heal best when let alone."

Mia looked up and saw Maggot, her dark eyes and pretty smile. She was hovering over Furian, the man swinging in a hammock beside her. Glancing to her shadow, Mia saw Furian's had apparently left hers somewhere as they slept. But still, that sickness lingered, the ache of a missing piece of herself swelling in her chest.

She took a deep breath, signing in Tongueless so only Mister Kindly might understand.

Where?

"... *the gloryhound* ...," came the whispered reply. "... *bound for crow's nest* ..."

Eclipse? Ashlinn?

"... *they follow, a handful of turns behind us* ..."

Furian?

"... *not good* ..."

Mia nodded to herself, looking about the cabin. She'd not been up here before—every trip she'd taken had been spent locked down in the hold. The room was cramped, a chest full of Maggot's implements and herbs and some wooden crates were the only decor. Three hammocks hung from the ceiling, Mia in the middle. Bladesinger was belly-down to her left, eyes closed, sword-arm and back swathed in bloody bandages. To her right, the Champion of Remus Collegium lay unconscious, soaked through. Furian's torso and throat were swabbed with a greenish salve, but the wounds from the silkling's venom still looked awful. Above the bilge and the sea and the sweat, Mia could smell the beginnings of a high, ripe decay.

Maggot held a cup of fresh water to her lips, and Mia drank all she was given despite the pain, sighing with relief.

"Bladesinger . . . ," she began, licking at dry lips. "H-how does . . ."

"Passing fair," Maggot whispered, so as not to disturb the sleepers. "The tendon and muscle in her swordarm are badly cut. But she stitched up well. I think she'll wake."

"And . . . F-Furian?"

Maggot sighed, looking the Unfallen over. "Not so well. Infection is taking root, and I fear it will turn to blood sepsis. I need to get him back to the Nest."

"We sail as fast as Lady Trelene and Lady Nalipse allow."

Mia looked up to see Dona Leona at the doorway, eyes locked on the Unfallen. Magistrae stood beside her, ever the dutiful second.

As usual, the magistrae's appearance was immaculate, but Mia was surprised to see the turn Leona had taken. The dona usually dressed as if she were attending some grand salon, but now, she wore only a simple white shift. Mia could see her fingernails were chewed down to the quick. In her right hand, she held the silver torc that had once encircled Furian's neck. The metal was melted slightly by the silkling's venom.

"Domina," Mia nodded.

"My Crow," the woman answered. "I am heartened to see you wake."

Mia sat up with a wince, head swimming. Her cheek felt swollen, and she could feel the pinch of sutures in her skin. Ribs aching, she took a second cup from Maggot, drank until it was empty.

"H-how long did I sleep for?"

"Three turns since your triumph," Leona said.

"It is ours, then?" she asked, stomach thrilling. "The *magni*?"

"Aye," the dona replied, stepping into the room. "It is ours. My father is many things, little Crow. A snake. A liar. A bastard. But no sanguila would dare renege on a wager made so publicly. With the laurels he has won, he had berths to spare. He can afford to lose one to us. But now, thanks to Bryn and Byern's sacrifice, he has no equillai. And thanks to your valor, he has no champion."

The woman fixed her eyes on Furian.

"All we have desired is now within our reach."

"How is Bryn?" Mia asked.

The dona's haunted glance was Mia's only reply. But Bryn had lost her twin brother, right before her very eyes. Crushed and bled out before a booing mob. And all for nothing. No purse. No glory. Nothing at all.

How the 'byss do you expect her to be?

"How are your wounds?" Leona asked.

Mia gingerly touched the bandages at her cheek, looked to Maggot.
"You tell me."

"Your ribs are cracked," the young girl replied. "The bruises will be awful, but you'll mend. The cut to your face is healing well. Though I'm afraid it will scar."

Mia focused on that thought, briefly burning hotter than the pain of her wounds. She'd never been pretty when she was a girl—she'd only discovered what beauty was once Marielle wove her face into a portrait in the Quiet Mountain. And truth was, she'd reveled in the power it bestowed.

She wondered what Ashlinn might say. How the girl might look at her now, and whether she'd hate the reflection she saw in those pools of sunburned blue. For a moment, she wished she were back in the Mountain, where Marielle could mend all hurts with a wave of her hand. She supposed that option would be forever denied her now she'd set herself against the Church. That this scar, the brand beside it, would be hers to cherish until she died.

Mia pictured her father, swinging and choking before the mob. Her mother, weeping and bleeding out in her arms. Her brother, dying as a babe in a lightless pit.

And, hand falling away from her face, she shrugged.

"The choice between looking plain and pretty isn't really a choice at all. But any fool knows looking dangerous is preferable to both."

A mirthless smile curled Leona's lips, and she slowly shook her head.

"I like you, Crow. Everseeing help me, but I do. I know not what you were before this, but for the assistance you offered our champion and your courage in the arena, I will be forever grateful."

"I wonder if your champion will say the same, Domina . . ."

The dona's eyes returned to Furian, fingers clasped so tight about his silver torc that her knuckles were white. Mia wondered how often the dona had visited his side since they left Whitekeep. Wondered if perhaps she did truly care for him. Wondered what Arkades would be making of it all if he knew . . .

"Perhaps we should head back up to the deck, Domina?" Magistrae murmured, squeezing the woman's hand. "Let them rest."

Leona blinked as if waking from a dream. But she nodded, allowed herself to be led away. As she reached the cabin door, she stopped, turned to Mia.

"Thank you, Crow," she murmured.

And with that, she was gone.

Turn after turn, the *Gloryhound* cut through the Sea of Swords, a trader's wind at their backs. The Lady of Oceans was merciful, and the ship pulled into the harbor at Crow's Rest a good twenty hours before schedule. But even with Mother Trelene on his side, it seemed Furian the Unfallen's luck was all but spent.

Just as Maggot predicted, his wounds had turned septic. By the time they arrived at Crow's Rest, the flesh about his chest and throat was dark and weeping, and the sweet stink of rot hung over him like fog. Maggot and Mia did their best to keep him sedated, though he slipped in and out of consciousness frequently. He was barely lucid when awake, and murmured fever-dream nonsense while sleeping. What it would mean for the collegium and Leona if he died, Mia had no idea.

A waiting wagon rushed them up to Crow's Nest, hooves pounding on the hillside. Mia's knowledge of herbcraft seemed to have impressed the dona, and she rode with Maggot and the dazed and groaning Furian, Leona and Magistrae beside her. Arkades and the other gladiatii were left to tromp up the hill on foot.

Captain Gannicus met them at the gates, Leona's houseguards carrying Furian to the rear of the house. Despite the ache of her broken ribs, once inside Maggot's infirmary, Mia began looking for ingredients that might quell his blood poisoning. Maggot herself disappeared into the shed in the corner of the yard. Leona hovered like a mother hen, a kerchief pressed to her nose and mouth to stifle the stench, pale with worry.

"Can you save him?" she asked.

Mia only scowled, sighing as she rifled through Maggot's chests and cupboards. It was true what the girl had said—it looked to have been months since Leona allowed her to restock. Even with all she'd learned from Spiderkiller and her beloved, dog-eared copy of *Arkemical Truths,* there wasn't enough to work with.

"We need hollyroot," Mia declared. "Maidenhead. Something to kill the swelling, like tinberry or pufferfish bladder. And ice. Lots of ice. This fever is burning him out like a fucking candle."

"Can you write?" Leona asked.

Mia raised an eyebrow. "Aye. I can write."

"Make a list," Leona commanded. "All you need."

Maggot returned from the shed, waddling under the weight of an old tin bucket. She thumped it on the bloodstained slab beside Furian's head, tied up her hair and began peeling off the pus-soaked bandages from his throat and chest.

"What are you doing?" Mia asked.

"You remember when you asked how I got my name?"

"You told me to pray I'd never find out," Mia replied.

The girl dragged her nose along her arm, wincing at the stench of Furian's wounds. "Well, you didn't pray hard enough."

Mia peered into the bucket and saw a great wriggling mass; hundreds of tiny white bodies, black heads, chewing sightlessly at the air. She put her hand to her mouth, gorge rising at the sight of those crawling, squirming . . .

"Four Daughters," she gagged. "Those are . . ."

"Maggots," the little girl replied. "I breed them in the shed."

". . . What the 'byss for?"

"What do maggots eat, Crow?"

Mia looked at the flesh of Furian's neck, his torso. The infection was dug deep; the wounds streaked with pus, muscles and skin gone putrid with decay. The veins about the wound were dark with corruption, every heartbeat only spreading it farther.

"Rotten meat," she whispered. "But what stops them eating . . ."

"The good bits?"

"Aye."

"Two jars on the shelf behind you. Bring them here."

Mia did as she was bid, peering at the spidery writing on the sides. She looked at the little girl, a smile creeping to her lips despite herself.

"Vinegar and bay leaves. You *are* very good at this."

Maggot offered a mirthless smile and began applying the larvae to the wounds, sprinkling them like salt onto the rancid flesh. Sickened despite the genius of it, Mia began writing on a wax tablet, making a list of all they'd need to keep Furian sedated, stop the sepsis spreading, kill his fever. She showed the list to Maggot, who looked up long enough to grunt assent, then handed the list to Leona.

The dona looked over the tablet once, gave it to her magistrae.

"Anthea, head to town," she commanded. "Gather all that Crow bids you."

Magistrae looked over the list, raised her eyebrow. "Domina, the cost of—"

"Hang the bloody cost!" Leona snapped. "Do as I command!"

The woman glanced to Mia and Maggot, pursed her lips. But still, she looked to her mistress and bowed low. "Your whisper, my will, Domina."

Magistrae marched out into the yard, wax tablet in hand. Dona Leona remained behind, eyes locked on Furian, chewing her tortured fingernails.

"He must live," she whispered.

A command.

A hope.

A desperate prayer.

But whether it was because she cared about the man, or cared about the *magni,* Mia had no idea.

They worked into the nevernight, Maggot applying the squirming flyspawn over Furian's wounds, smearing the edges with vinegar and bay leaves to repel the larvae from the hale flesh, and then gently wrapping it all in gauze. Mia stood by, helping when she could, but mostly observing with a churning belly.

Finger brought their evemeal to them, the emaciated cook peering at Furian as if he were already dead. Fang came snuffling about looking for scraps soon after, and with the pain of her ribs, the nausea at Maggot's treatments, Mia fed the mastiff most of her meal, scruffing him behind his ears as he wagged his stubby tail. Dona Leona also refused to eat, sitting and staring at the Unfallen, not saying a word. Her eyes were wide and bloodshot. Her cheeks hollow.

The other gladiatii arrived back at the Nest, marching down to the barracks accompanied by the houseguards. Arkades limped into the infirmary, dusty and sore from his long walk. He looked Furian over, pressed a hand to the man's sweat-slicked brow, watched the rapid rise and fall of his chest. The long scar bisecting his cheek deepened as he scowled. Mia touched the bandage at her own face. Once more thinking of Ashlinn.

Wondering.

"How does he fare?" Arkades asked.

"We've done all we can 'til Magistrae returns," Maggot replied. "The herbs and brews she's fetching will help. But it's no sure thing, Executus."

Arkades nodded. "Crow, return to the barracks. Maggot will call if she has need."

"I'd prefer to sta—"

"And I'd prefer a villa in southern Liis and my real leg back," Arkades growled. "It is after nevernight. Your place is under lock and key in the barracks."

Mia glanced to Dona Leona, but the woman was paying no attention at all, stare fixed on Furian. Touching Maggot's shoulder in farewell, Mia limped out into the yard, flanked by two houseguards. Arkades remained, staring at his mistress, brow creased in thought. A small, cat-shaped piece of Mia's shadow stayed behind also.

"Mi Dona, you should rest," Arkades said.

"I will stay."

"Maggot can inform you if there is any cha—"

"I will *stay*!" Leona snapped.

Maggot glanced up at the shout, returned quickly to work. The executus looked between his mistress and the fallen gladiatii on the bench. Nodding slow.

"Your whisper, my will."

Turning on his heel, he limped out from the infirmary into the yard. Staring up at the nevernight suns, the blue glow budding ever deeper on the horizon. Truelight was close now—just a few weeks until all three of the Everseeing's eyes burned bright in the sky. Scorching the world pure. Exposing all their sins.

Sins.

Arkades glanced back over his shoulder to his mistress, watching her watching her champion, lips pursed. And then he was walking, into the keep and along the halls, *clink* thump, *clink* thump, the tune of his tread. His brow was a dark scowl, his lips a thin line, those mighty, sword-callused fists clenched.

He did not notice the small, dark shape following him, flitting from shadow to shadow behind. Silent as cats.

Arkades limped passed paintings on the walls of old gladiatii battles, the suits of armor and gleaming helms, the marble busts of Marcus Remus's ancestors, paying them not a moment's mind. And finally, he arrived at a single door at the end of the hall, unlocking it with an iron key.

Arkades walked into Furian's room. Folding his arms and surveying the scene. The shrine to Tsana beneath the small window. The trinity of Aa on the wall. A practice dummy and some swords. A small chest for the Unfallen's meager belongings.

Closing the door behind him, Arkades limped to the chest. Kneeling with a wince, he began rifling through it—two silver laurels won at Talia and Blackbridge. The hilt of a broken sword. A moldy deck of cards and some dice. Spare loincloth. A fishbone comb. A handful of copper beggars.

Arkades stood, scowling about the room. His face was darkening, eyes glinting with anger. He limped to the bed, searched inside the pillow and threw it to the floor, tore off the sheets, pawed at the straw mattress. With a frustrated curse, he flipped the mattress over and hurled it against the wall. And there, on the bedframe, he saw it.

A silken underslip.

The executus stooped, lifted the slip to his nose and inhaled. The faint scent of jasmine perfume. The same scent he'd inhaled when he'd visited here before the *venatus,* warning the Unfallen that his soap was making him smell like a woman.

"You fucking bastard . . ."

Arkades clenched the slip in one white-knuckled fist.

"You ungrateful . . ."

Arkades returned the room to its former state, remaking the bed, smoothing the sheets. His face was pale, jaw clenched. With the bedchamber as it was, he turned and stormed from the room, *clink* thump, *clink* thump. Limping down the corridor, storm clouds over his brow, he arrived at his bedchamber and slammed the door.

Enraged as he was, the Executus failed to notice Magistrae standing by the storeroom, her arms laden with the remedies she'd fetched from town.

But the old woman certainly noticed the silk slip clutched in his hand.

". . . *interesting* . . . ," the shadows whispered.

SILVER

They gathered in the yard after mornmeal.

Seven turns had passed, and little had changed—Furian's fever burned the lesser, but still hadn't burned out entirely. The fly larvae were doing . . . well, they were doing exactly what maggots do. The process was beyond disgusting, the sight when Maggot pulled back those bandages was almost more than Mia could stomach. And there was still no telling whether it was doing any good.

The gladiatii were of a mood. Buoyed by their victory in the arena and the berth the Falcons of Remus had won in the *Venatus Magni.* But the price they'd paid . . .

Bryn stayed in her cell, speaking to no one, even at mealtimes. Bladesinger might never fight again. Furian hovered close to death's door, and Byern was simply dead. If this was the tithe they paid for a chance at freedom, it was drenched in more blood than most would have preferred.

Arkades had summoned them at the command of their domina, the suns beating down on the sand like hammers as the gladiatii of the Remus Collegium assembled. Mia's ribs ached abominably, the slice on her face itching beneath the crusted gauze. It was odd seeing the world with one eye under a bandage, the lack of depth, the loss of balance. She knew she should go see Ashlinn—Eclipse had appeared in her cell late last nevernight, informing her that their ship had arrived back in Crow's Rest. But with the situation in the keep the way it was, Mia dare not risk a visit. Furian might wake at any moment, and if Maggot called on her to help with some herbcraft in the middle of the nevernight and the guards discovered her missing . . .

She touched the bandage at her face. She'd not yet mustered the will to look underneath it in a mirror. Wondering what she'd see when she did.

Wondering what Ashlinn would see.

Butcher stood with hands clasped behind his back, shifting his weight from one foot to the other as always. Despite losing his match at Whitekeep, he seemed pleased that he'd earned himself a few more scars to add to his collection.

Sidonius waited silently, arms crossed over the COWARD branded on his broad chest. His cropped hair was getting longer, his blue eyes sparking in the sun. As always, he stood right beside Mia, never straying far if he could help it. He'd sung her praises in their cell, declaring her match against the silkling the greatest he'd ever seen. And still, he didn't press about her parents. Didn't ask questions she wasn't yet prepared to answer. For all his bluster and thuggery, for all his foolery around women, he knew when to talk, and when to keep his mouth shut.

Mia liked him more and more with every passing turn.

But he is not my friend.

Wavewaker stood at Sidonius's other side, feet planted in the earth like the roots of mountains. He'd fought like a daemon against those scythebears in the arena; he and Sid had fallen shy of their own laurel by only two points. Again, Mia found it hard to imagine the man strutting about the stage in silken hose, talking in rhyming couplets. Standing tall, skin gleaming in the sunlight, he seemed a warrior born.

And he is not my friend.

Bryn stood beside Otho and Felix, looking as though she'd not slept a wink since Whitekeep. It was so strange to see her without her twin—Mia actually caught herself glancing about for Byern. The Vaanian girl walked like a ghost. Bloodshot and empty stare, arms wrapped about herself.

And she is not . . .

Bladesinger leaned at the door to the infirmary. Her face was bloodless beneath her tattoos, swordarm slung around her neck with blood-soaked gauze. The slice to her back had been vicious, but the gouge to her arm had been horrendous. None knew if the woman would ever wield a sword again. Mia could see fear in her eyes.

But she is . . .

And Furian?

He lay sleeping on the infirmary slab, Maggot by his side. Mia could feel his pain whenever she strayed too near, as if it were bleeding through the dark at her feet. She had no idea why. Even with all her herbcraft, with Maggot's remedies, none knew his future, save perhaps the Mother.

"Gladiatii!" Arkades barked. "Attend!"

The assembled warriors straightened, fists to their chests. Leona and Anthea marched out from the verandah, the dona one step ahead of her magistrae.

Leona looked tired, but at last she'd dressed in a manner more like her usual self. She was clad in a flowing white dress, the fabric rippling about her sandals as she took her place on the burning sands. Her hair was plaited about her brow like the victor's laurel she held in her right hand.

"My Falcons!" she called, raising the laurel high. "Behold!"

The assembled gladiatii cheered, but circumstances being what they were, Mia felt their enthusiasm rang a little hollow.

"Though the tithe we paid was steep, we have the victory we have so long sought. With this laurel comes a berth in the *Venatus Magni*, five weeks hence. Freedom is within your reach, and soon, the City of Bridges and Bones shall ring with the name of the Remus Collegium!"

A second cheer rang in the yard, much louder than the first. It seemed no matter how deep they ran, the promise of liberty could make any gladiatii forget their sorrows. Wavewaker clapped his hand on Sid's shoulder, Butcher slapped his thighs and roared. The thought of fighting in the *magni* was enough to thrill their hearts, and Mia found her blood quickening along with the rest. Picturing Scaeva and Duomo in her mind's eye.

Soon, bastards . . .

"Three among you stand tall," Leona declared. "The best and bravest yet trained within these walls under the careful eye of our noble Executus."

Leona inclined her head to Arkades, who responded with a stiff, formal bow.

"And yet," she continued, "there was only one who struck the killing blow against the Exile. Only one whose valor and skill have paved our way to glory."

Leona looked to Mia.

"Crow, step forward."

Mia glanced to Bladesinger, but did as she was bid, bowing before her mistress. Leona fixed her in that glittering blue stare.

"Kneel," she said, curtly.

Mia grit her teeth at the reminder of her station, but did as commanded, wincing at the pain of her broken ribs. Taking care not to snag her bandaged brow, Leona placed the silver laurel on Mia's head. And reaching inside the folds of her dress, she held out Furian's silver torc on her open palm. It was slightly melted, the metal discolored from the kiss of Ishkah's venom.

"This is yours now," Leona said.

Mia frowned toward the infirmary, looking up into the dona's eyes.

"If we are to have victory in the *magni*," Leona continued, "if the Falcons of Remus are to claim the glory that is rightfully ours, I think it shall be by your hand, no other. But in all truth, regardless of what comes, you have earned this, Crow."

Leona fixed the torc about the girl's throat.

"My Champion," she declared proudly.

Sidonius roared, and the other gladiatii followed suit, stamping their feet and pounding their hands together. Mia looked once again to Bladesinger, struck by the injustice. 'Singer and Furian had fought just as hard as she, risked just as much—she'd not have triumphed over Ishkah without them. But only Mia was being named in the glories. Only Mia was being called Champion.

This is what you worked for, she reminded herself.

You only need play the game a few weeks longer.

She bowed her head, her voice soft.

"You honor me, Domina."

"You honor us, Crow. And you will continue to do so in the City of Bridges and Bones. But you'll not do it clad in leather scraps and offcuts of steel, no. You fight beneath our banner a champion now. And you should look the part."

Leona clapped her hands.

"Behold."

Two of the dona's houseguards wheeled out a wooden dummy from inside the keep, out onto the verandah. The figure was wearing one of the suits of armor that had stood in the entry hall, but Mia realized it had been refitted to her size.

The iron was almost black, polished to a dark luster. The breastplate was engraved with a soaring falcon, and the greaves and spaulders were also crafted like falcons in flight. The breastplate was trimmed with a pleated skirt and sleeves of plated iron, and a cloak of blood-red feathers was draped about its shoulders. The helm was fashioned in the likeness of the warrior goddess

Tsana, her expression fierce and merciless. Twin blades were sheathed at its belt; Liisian steel, by the look. A double-edged gladius and a long razored dagger, ideally suited for fighting Caravaggio style.

It was one of the finest suits of armor Mia had ever seen, sure and true. But it must have cost a fortune. A fortune Leona could ill afford.

"You fight beneath our banner a champion now."

Mia glanced at Leona, holding back her sigh.

"And you should look the part."

"I thank you, Domina," Mia said.

"You may thank me in the *magni*," Leona replied. "By bringing me the vic . . ."

The dona's voice trailed off as a houseguard marched into the yard, a young boy in a feathered cap beside him. The lad's cheek was branded with the single circle, but he wore expensive livery, a little dusty from the road. His doublet was embroidered with the Lion of Leonides.

"Messenger, Mi Dona," the guard said. "The boy claims the matter urgent."

"I bring missive from my master, your father, gracious Dona," the boy said bowing low. "I am instructed to read it aloud, under pain of the lash."

"Speak, then," Leona commanded.

The boy produced a sheaf of parchment set with Leonides's seal. He glanced at the assembled gladiatii, clearly unnerved. But with a loud, clear voice, he began to speak.

"Beloved Daughter,

"It is with a happy heart that I congratulate you upon your victory at White-keep. I confess surprise that you did not seek audience to gloat afterward, and it gladdens me to think that the humility I sought to teach you in your childhood has begun to take root. Would that I had . . ."

The boy faltered, glancing up at Leona and swallowing thickly.

"Continue," she demanded.

The boy stammered a moment before he found his voice.

". . . W-would that I had beaten you harder, and more often."

Several of the gladiatii stirred, glowering at the boy. Mia felt her fingernails cut into her palm, her eyes on the dona. Leona's expression didn't change at all.

This is why she hates him so . . .

The lad was sweating now, pawing at the collar of his doublet as if it choked him. Desperate to finish, his cleared his throat and plunged on.

"I have been reliably informed by my business acquaintances that Remus Collegium is in serious arrears with its suppliers. To spare myself the humiliation

*of seeing a daughter of my line dragged before the debtor's court, I have taken
the liberty of purchasing all debts from your creditors, and consolidating them
into a single sum, which is now owed to Leonides Collegium and accrues points
weekly."*

Leona's eyes widened. "What?"

*"Your first repayment of three thousand two hundred forty-three silver priests
is due at the turning of the month, three weeks hence. Should you fail to deliver
the required sum, I will have no choice but to seek punitive compensation through
the magistrate's court, and claim possession of your collegium, properties, and
other financial holdings by way of reimbursement.*

*"Please do not think I hold wrath or rancor in my heart for you, my dearest.
This is, as you once told me, just business."*

The boy glanced up at Leona, voice trembling.

"If only your dear mother were here to see just how far you have come," he finished. *"With all the respect you are due, your loving f-father, Leonides."*

The courtyard was so still, Mia could have heard Mister Kindly breathing.
Looking at the messenger, she realized the poor bastard had no idea about the
contents of the letter he was delivering. Glancing at Wavewaker and Otho's
faces, the lad probably fully expected to be dragged down to the cliffs and
thrown into the sea.

"H-he also wished me to convey you a gift, Mi Dona," the boy said. "To
celebrate your victory."

Reaching into his pack, the boy produced a bottle of goldwine and placed
it on the sand. A blood-red label denoted the vintage on the side.

Albari, seventy-four.

As Leona saw the label, her entire body stiffened with rage. Mia had no
idea why, but to the dona, the sight of that bottle was like blood to a whitedrake. With clear effort, Leona drew a deep breath, only the trembling of her
clenched fists to bely her fury. And standing tall, she addressed the boy with
customary formality.

"Convey all thanks to my father," she said. "Inform him the magistrate's
involvement will be unnecessary. He will have his coin by month's end. I do
here vow it."

"Yes, Mi Dona," the boy bowed, relief flooding his features.

"You may go," she said, her voice turning to cold steel.

The boy doffed his cap and scurried away as fast as his legs could carry him.

"O, and boy?" Leona said.

The messenger turned, half-wincing, eyebrow raised. "Y-yes, Mi Dona?"

Leona ran her hand over Mia's new armor, her fingers lingering at the dagger's hilt. "Please convey condolences to my father at the slaughter of his champion. Tell him that I look forward to watching my Crow butcher his next offering in Godsgrave."

"Y-yes, Mi Dona," the boy stammered, and scampered out of sight.

Silence reigned in the yard, only the call of distant gulls and the faint song of the sea to break it. Leona walked across the sand, picked up the bottle of goldwine and held it in her hand, staring at that label. She looked among her gladiatii, fury spotting her cheeks. They had fought so hard, come so far, and even now, on the brink of victory, they still stood at the precipice of disaster. Where in the Daughters' names would she get that kind of money?

"Back to training, my Falcons," she commanded. "We have work to do."

The gladiatii marched to the racks, took up their practice weapons.

The dona turned and walked back into the keep.

Arkades watched her leave.

His eyes were narrowed.

His hands, fists.

L eona sat in her study, bent over her ledgers, bathed in sunlight spilling through the bay window. The shadows were long and dark, and if one beneath her desk was of a peculiar shape, the dona was too intent on her work to notice.

A guard knocked softly on the door, stepping inside at her command.

"Mi Dona," the guard said. "Executus begs a word."

"Send him in," Leona replied.

Arkades entered, *clink* thump, *clink* thump, the guard closing the door behind him. Leona's gaze didn't stray from her bookwork, a quill poised in her fingers, scribing figures in her neat, flowing hand. The Albari seventy-four was sat on the desk beside her, unopened. Arkades stood before her, staring at that bottle, shifting his weight.

"What is it, Executus?" the dona asked, not looking up.

"I . . . I wished to see if you were well, Domina."

"And why would I not be?"

"Your father's missive . . ."

Leona stilled, finally looking up.

"I thought his gift was a lovely touch." The dona glanced to the bottle beside her. "I'm surprised he remembered the vintage."

"I knew him to be the cruelest of men, but . . ." Arkades sighed, his voice soft with sorrow. "Your mother was a fine woman, Mi Dona. You do not deserve such insult. And she did not deserve what he did to her."

"He beat her to death with a bottle of goldwine, Arkades," Leona said, her voice beginning to tremble. "Because she knocked over his glass at dinner. Who exactly *does* deserve that?"

The executus searched the floorboards as if looking for the right words. He might be a god on the sands, but here, in the privacy of his dona's chambers, under her pale blue stare, he seemed as helpless as a newborn.

"If ever . . ."

He paused, swallowed hard. Drawing a deep breath, as if before the plunge.

"If ever you seek comfort . . . that is to say, if ever you wish to talk . . ."

Leona tilted her head, looking her executus in the eye.

"That is very kind of you, Arkades. But I do not think it appropriate."

He glanced out the window into the yard, to the infirmary where Furian lay.

". . . Appropriate?" he repeated.

"I am no longer the girl who spent her childhood on tiptoe, for fear of what might set the monster she lived with off next. I am not the girl who cowered beneath the table as that bottle fell, again and again and again. I am sanguila. I am domina of this collegium. You are my executus. And my father's cheap theater serves in only one regard: to harden my resolve to stand victorious in Godsgrave."

Arkades simply stared at her, grief and anger plain on his face.

"I need no comfort," Leona continued, rage shining in her eyes. "I need that bastard on his fucking knees. If you'd serve me, Arkades, I pray you, serve me in the matter I pay you for. Bring me my victory."

Leona bent back over her bookwork, resting her head in one hand.

"You may go," she said.

Arkades stood for an empty moment, utterly mute. But finally . . .

"Your whisper," he murmured. "My will."

The big man turned and limped from the room, shutting the door behind him. Leona dropped her quill as soon as he was gone. Pressing her lips together and drawing one shuddering breath after another. Swiping a hand across her eyes in rage.

Her tears bested, she turned her stare to the bottle on her desk. The sunslight glinting on the glass. The label, painted in blood red.

Leona hung her head, waves of auburn hiding her eyes.

"*Father,*" she spat.

A knock came at the door.

"Four Daughters, who is it now?" Leona demanded.

"Apologies, Mi Dona," the guard said, peering inside. "Magistrae seeks audience."

Leona sighed, smoothed her hair back from her face.

"Very well."

The older woman entered, pushing the door closed behind her. Leona sat tall in her chair, quill in hand, a fresh picture of poise. Her magistrae stood before her, twisting her braid of long gray hair and bowing her head.

"What is it, Anthea?"

". . . Domina, you know that ever I have served you faithfully." Trepidation shone in Magistrae's eyes as she glanced to that bottle of goldwine. "And I would never seek to do you hurt."

"Of course."

"I know your father presses your finances. I did not wish to place one more trouble upon your brow. I've struggled with whether or not to bring this to you, bu—"

"Anthea," Leona said calmly. "Speak your piece."

". . . It is Arkades, Domina."

Leona looked to the door her executus had just left by.

"What of him?"

"He knows."

Leona put aside her quill and sat back in the chair, frowning.

"Knows what?"

"Leona," Magistrae said. "He *knows.*"

M ia sat in the infirmary, listening to the nevernight winds blowing off the ocean. The turn in temperature was a welcome relief, but not nearly enough to let her breathe easy. Squinting at the horizon earlier, she'd fancied she could see the third sun, poised at the world's end. Soon it would rise, truelight would begin; awful heat and thrumming crowds and oceans and oceans of blood.

The sounds of the other gladiatii at evemeal filtered through the stone walls, and Mia could hear Butcher complaining about the quality of Finger's "stew."

To the hoots and cheers of their fellows, the emaciated cook loudly informed the Butcher of Amai where he could stick said stew if he didn't like it.*

Mia's smile became a wince as Maggot swabbed her cheek with aloe and evermint, the vague sting crawling in her wound. Maggot nodded to herself, wrapping Mia's face in fresh bandages and tying a gentle knot.

"It's healing well," she said. "We can leave the wrappings off next time."

"Aye," Mia said. "My thanks."

"Cheer up, little Crow," came a groggy voice behind her. "Pretty as you were, you're not true gladiatii without a few scars."

Mia turned to Bladesinger, yawning and sitting up on the slab beside her.

"Well, if that's the case," the girl smiled, "you're the truest gladiatii that ever walked the sands, 'Singer."

"Aye," the woman smirked. She held up her swordarm, still wrapped in bandages. "It's going to be a beaut, that much is sure."

"Can you move it yet?" Mia asked softly.

Bladesinger looked to Maggot, shook her head.

"It's early turns," the little girl declared. "Far too early to tell."

Mia and the older woman exchanged an uneasy glance, but said nothing. Finger shuffled into the infirmary, carrying four steaming bowls on a wooden tray. As he set down his burden with a flourish, Mia looked the cook up and down, wondering how many people parts he'd used in his creation this time.

"Dinner," he declared. "Eat it while it's hot."

"Scrumptious," Maggot smiled. "Thank you, Finger."

The man scruffed the girl's hair and shuffled back out. Mia raised an eyebrow.

"*Scrumptious?*" she said, once the cook was out of earshot. "Of every word in creation, the last I'd use to describe Finger's cooking is 'scrumptious,' Maggot."

"Depends how you grew up," the girl shrugged. "Once you've eaten raw rat with your bare hands, you become far less choosy about cookery, believe me."

Mia nodded, sucked her lip. Again she was struck by how much this little girl reminded her of herself. Growing up rough and brash, just as Mia had done after her parents were taken. Unafraid to speak her mind. Maybe a touch too clever for her own good. She knew she shouldn't. Knew it was weakness.

---

*I am not a physician, nor an expert in anatomy. However, Finger's suggestion would seem to require an unearthly amount of flexibility on Butcher's part.

But Mia liked her.

"Fair point," she smiled. "Apologies."

"You want any or not?"

"Give it over, then."

Maggot passed Mia a bowl, raised an eyebrow at her second patient. "Bladesinger?"

"My thanks."

The woman set the bowl on the slab beside her. Mia watched her carefully spoon a mouthful with her off-hand. Wondering what would become of her if she never regained use of her swordarm. How quickly would this world dispose of a gladiatii who couldn't lift a blade?

Fang wandered into the infirmary, the big mastiff looking up at Mia's bowl and wagging his tail hopefully. She leaned down and scruffed his ears, but kept her dinner to herself.

"How does Furian fare?" Mia asked.

Maggot nodded at the Unfallen, speaking around her mouthful. "Take a look."

Mia set her bowl aside and rose with a wince—her ribs were still bothering her, and there was no real remedy save working them as little as possible. She stepped to the sleeping Furian's side, shadow trembling, a familiar hunger rising in her belly that had nothing to do with her waiting meal.

Truth told, the Unfallen looked a little better. Color was returning to his face, and touching his brow, Mia found his fever lessened. Wincing with trepidation, she pulled back the bandages to take a peek. The injuries were ghastly, no doubt about it; the silkling's venom had burned through muscle and skin across his chest and throat. But instead of the rotten, weeping mess she'd last seen, the wounds were clean, healthy, pink. The sight of fat, wriggling maggots crawling over the fissures in Furian's skin still made Mia sick to her stomach, and the smell was far from roses. But Black Mother be praised, the blighted flesh was all but gone.

"It's incredible," Bladesinger murmured.

"It's disgusting," Mia said.

Utterly nauseated, she finally surrendered her bowl of dinner to Fang, who *wuff*ed and began chowing down with relish.

"But aye, it's incredible," Mia admitted. "Fine work, Maggot."

The girl waved her wooden spoon like a queen. "Too kind, Mi Dona. Too kind."

"What comes next?"

"It's more an art than a science, aye?" Maggot replied, wiping her nose on her arm. "I think in few turns we might rid him of the larvae. My ma told me to drown them in hot vinegar, but I feel bad about that with all the work they've done. After that, we keep it clean, keep it salved, keep him dosed. His fever is still fluxing, and the infection could creep back with bad luck. He's a long way from out of the desert, but between you and me, his odds are passing fair."

"Will he be able to fight in the *magni*?" Bladesinger asked.

"Steady on," the little girl said. "I'm not a bloody miracle worker."

"Seems like a miracle to me." Mia shook her head in admiration, smiled at the girl. "Your ma really taught you all this?"

"Aye. She could have taught me more, if she was given time to. Sometimes I wonder about all the knowings she took to her grave."

"Aye," Mia sighed. "I know what you mean."

Maggot spooned her stew around the bowl, sucking her lip. "It's funny, but I was thinking . . . when you take a person out of the world, you don't just take *them,* do you? You take everything they were, too." The little girl squinted at Bladesinger. "Do you ever think about that? When you kill someone in the arena?"

"No," the woman said. "That way lies madness."

"What do you think about, then?" Maggot asked, taking another bite.

"I think better them than me," Bladesinger replied.

The little girl turned to Mia, talking with her mouth full. "What about you, Crow? Do you think about the things you're taking away?"

Mia parted her lips, but found no words to speak.

Truth was, she *did* think about those she'd ended. More and more, it seemed. The Luminatii she'd killed at the Mountain, those she could justify easily. But everyone after that? The senator's son and magistratii she'd unwittingly murdered in Scaeva's employ? Those men in the Pit at the Hanging Gardens? The gladiatii she'd killed in the arena? In some way, they all paved the way for her to be here, just a few weeks from the consul's and the cardinal's throats. But did that truly vindicate her?

"I think the end justifies the means," she replied. "As long as the end isn't mine."

"Do you truly believe that?"

"I have to."

"Well," Maggot smiled sadly. "Better you than me."

Fang whined, licked at Mia's fingers with his flat, pink tongue.

"I'm sorry, boy," she said, kneeling to scruff the dog's chin. "You already ate it all. Surprised you've got room for more."

The mastiff whined again, deeper this time, licking at his chops. He snuffled Mia's hand, walking in a small circle with his stubby tail between his legs. Sitting on his haunches, he made a hacking noise, as if from a hairball. And looking at Mia with his big brown eyes, the dog coughed a spray of bright red blood all over the floor.

"Maw's teeth," Mia cursed, flinching away.

Maggot's bowl of stew fell from her hand, spattered over the stone.

"Crow . . ."

Mia looked up, saw a trickle of blood spill from the girl's lips.

"I don't feel w-well . . . ," she whispered.

"O, shit," Mia breathed.

Maggot slipped down off the slab, coughed a mouthful of blood. Mia rushed to her side, caught her before she fell. She looked to Bladesinger, the woman wiping at her lips and bringing her knuckles away red. As she watched, the woman clutched her belly and coughed a spatter of blood onto the stone.

Mia looked at Fang, curled up in a puddle of gore.

The empty bowl the dog had eaten her dinner from . . .

"O, *shit* . . ."

Poison . . .

"Help me!" she roared. *"Help!"*

She heard cries of pain from the verandah, bewildered curses, hacking coughs. Clutching Maggot in her arms, Mia staggered to the infirmary door and saw every gladiatii in the collegium on their knees or on their backs, mouths and hands smeared with blood, bowls of stew spilled over the tables and floor. Maggot moaned, coughed another mouthful of blood onto Mia's chest. A gobsmacked Finger was staring at the carnage, several guards standing around dumbfounded.

"Don't just stand there, fucking *help me*!" Mia roared.

Finger saw Maggot in Mia's arms, hobbled to her side. Somewhere in the house, someone began clanging the alarm. Between the pair of them, Mia and Finger carried Maggot back into the infirmary, laid her on a slab. Bladesinger had collapsed, blood leaking from her mouth. Mia looked about the room, mind racing. Kneeling by Maggot's bowl, she dipped her finger into the stew, tasted and spat. Beneath the seasoning, she could sense a bitterness, a metallic tang. Her mind racing, all the knowledge that had made her Spiderkiller's favored student spinning in her memory, repeating the four principles of venomcraft to herself, over and over.

Delivery: Ingested.

Efficacy: Lethal.

Celerity: Five minutes or less.

Locality: Stomach and intestines.

Mia's eyes widened, the answer coming to her in a flash.

"It's Elegy," she said, turning to Finger.

"Are you—"

"Yes, I'm fucking sure. Do you have cow's milk in the kitchen? Or cream?"

". . . I've goat's milk for the dona's tea."

"Set it boiling. All of it. Now."

"But I—"

"Now, Finger!"

The cook hobbled off, and Mia started sorting through Maggot's jars and phials. Elegy was a deadly poison, relatively difficult to concoct unless you knew what you were about. But it was one of the first toxins Mercurio had taught her how to brew, and while the antidote wasn't well known, it was easy enough for a Blade of Our Lady of Blessed Murder to fix. Grateful the dona had allowed Maggot to restock, Mia ransacked the shelves, grabbing the ingredients she needed.

Brightweed. Lopsome. Milkthistl—

"Four Daughters . . ."

Mia turned and saw Dona Leona in her nightshift, standing by the infirmary door. Magistrae stood beside her, horror on her face as the alarm continued to ring.

"What in the Everseeing's name . . . ," Leona breathed.

"Poison," Mia said. "Elegy, mixed with their evemeal. We don't have much time. I can't find the fucking silver nitrate . . . Do you have a mirror?"

The dona's face was fixed on Maggot's, watching the blood leaking from her lips.

"Leona!" Mia barked. "Do you have a looking glass?"

The woman blinked, focused on Mia. "A-aye."

"Bring it to the kitchen. Now!" She turned to the guards hovering beside their mistress. "You, carry Maggot, you two bring Bladesinger. Hurry!"

"Do as she says!" Leona barked.

Mia gathered her armful of phials and jars, rushed across the yard with the guards in tow while Leona dashed up to her room. She could hear Maggot coughing again, Bladesinger groaning. The verandah looked like a war zone, gladiatii laid out in pools of blood. Wavewaker was facedown, Bryn leaning on a table, thick ribbons of gore and mucus spilling from her lips, Sidonius on his back. Executus stood amid the carnage, wide-eyed and horrified.

"Arkades, turn Sidonius on his side," Mia shouted, rushing past. "Roll everyone off their backs or they'll drown in their own blood!"

In the kitchen, Finger was leaning over a large pot, stirring the steaming milk inside. Mia pushed him out of the way, began adding her ingredients, measuring carefully despite her haste. She had no seconds to waste—every moment would drag Maggot and the others closer to death. But as always, the passenger in her shadow kept her nerves like steel, her hands steady. First rule of venomcraft: a poorly mixed antidote was as bad as no antidote at all.

The guards placed Maggot on the kitchen bench behind her. The girl was ghastly pale, moaning and bringing up another gout of blood.

"Keep her throat clear, she needs to breathe!"

Sweat in her eyes. Pulse hammering under her skin. Maggot coughed again, a bubble of bright red popping at her lips.

"Maggot, you keep breathing, you hear me?"

Leona arrived with a large oval looking glass from her bedroom wall.

"Will this d—"

Mia grabbed it off her, seized a kitchen knife and pried the mirror's frame away. Taking the blade to the back of the glass, she began furiously shaving away the reflective layer of silver nitrate, gleaming flakes of metal spilling onto the kitchen bench. Maggot coughed again, head lolling on her shoulders as if her neck were broken.

"Crow, she's stopped breathing!" Magistrae cried.

"Maggot, don't you die on me!" Mia shouted over her shoulder.

She gathered the flakes of nitrate, crushed them to powder with a mortar and pestle. Shoving Finger aside again, she added the powder to the boiling concoction on the stove, the scent of burning metal in the air. She looked over her shoulder, saw Maggot convulsing in Leona's arms. Prayers to the Black Mother, the Four Daughters, whoever was listening spilling over her lips.

"Please," she whispered. "Please please *please* . . ."

It was ready, the concoction set. Mia scooped a healthy dose into a clay-cup, turned to the girl behind her. Maggot was pale as death, still as a millpond. The dona's eyes were wide, her nightshift and hands spattered in the girl's blood.

"Take a cupful to everyone affected," she told Finger. "The unconscious ones first. Make them drink at least three mouthfuls, take a funnel if you have to, go *go*!"

Mia wrangled Maggot from Leona's arms, breathing quick. Laying the girl on her back, Mia wiped the bloody foam from Maggot's lips, forced her mouth open. Holding the cup in steady hands, she poured a goodly dose into the girl's mouth.

"Swallow it, baby," she whispered, massaging her throat. "Swallow."

Maggot wasn't listening. She surely wasn't swallowing. Mia pulled her up to sitting position, the antidote spilling from the little girl's lips. Leona and Magistrae helped prop up Maggot between them, and tilting her head back, Mia poured more of the draft into her open mouth.

"Swallow, Maggot," she begged. *"Please."*

Mia massaged the girl's throat, shook her gently. Maggot wasn't responding, wasn't moving, wasn't breathing. Hanging limp in their arms like some broken doll. The Blade in her had seen all this before. But the girl in her, the girl who looked at Maggot and saw a pale reflection of herself, she refused to believe it. Praying for some miracle, like in the books she used to read as a child. Some prince to ride in on a silver charger to wake Maggot with a kiss. Some fae godmother with her pockets full of magik and wishes to spare.

Mia felt hot tears in her eyes, a crushing weight on her shoulders. A scream was building in her belly, but her voice was only a whisper.

"Please, baby."

"It's funny, but when you take a person out of the world, you don't just take them, *do you?"*

Leona looked at Mia, eyes wide with shock, tears spilling down her cheeks.

". . . Crow?"

"You take everything they were, too."

"Please," Mia begged.

"Do you ever think about that?"

The cup slipped from Mia's fingers, shattered on the floor.

Do you ever think about that?

SEVERING

Mia couldn't remember the last time she really cried.

She'd spilled a tear or two here and there along the road, but it was never the primal kind of grief. The kind where the sobs are being torn out of you, shaking you to your bones and leaving you hollowed out inside. She hadn't cried when she failed her initiation. Hadn't cried when Ashlinn murdered Tric.

Hadn't cried when the Ministry said a quiet mass and sealed the boy in an empty tomb in the Hall of Eulogies.

She wasn't very good with grief, you see.

Mia preferred rage instead.

She stood in the infirmary over Maggot's lifeless body, belly knotted with fury. The girl's hair had been combed, the blood wiped from her face. She looked almost as if she were asleep. Otho lay beside her, just as peaceful. The big Itreyan's eyes were closed, the lines of care that had creased his features as he fought upon the sands now smoothed away.

It was a miracle only two of them had died—as if "only" had a place anywhere in that thought. Maggot was simply too small, and had imbibed too much toxin. Otho was a grown man, strong as an ox. But he'd wolfed his entire meal down and been on the way for seconds before the effects kicked in, and by then, it was too late. More of the Falcons would have succumbed—all, in fact—if Mia hadn't been there. She supposed whoever poisoned their meal wasn't expecting a trained assassin to be on hand to boil up the antidote. As it was, most of the gladiatii suffered varying degrees of internal hemorrhaging, but the remedy she'd mixed had saved them all from death.

Almost all, anyway . . .

Fang lay on a bloodstained blanket, the dog's eyes forever closed. Executus had almost wept when he found the mastiff curled up in a pool of blood on the infirmary floor. He sat beside Fang now, running one callused hand over the dog's flanks. His fingers were shaking. From anger or grief, Mia couldn't tell.

"How in the Everseeing's name did this happen?" Leona demanded, looking over the bodies with her hands on her hips.

"Simply enough," Mia murmured, eyes never leaving Maggot's body. "Somebody dosed the onions in the pantry with Elegy, and Finger used them in the stew. Onion is porous, acts like a sponge. And the smell and flavor does a fine job of masking the toxin's. Good delivery method. The killer knew what they were doing."

Leona turned to Finger. The cook stood trembling between two houseguards, steel grips on both his arms. His lank hair hung over his eyes, his body shaking.

"What do you know of this?" the dona asked.

"N-nothing, Domina," the cook replied. "I serve you faithfully!"

"Any snake would hiss the same," Leona snarled.

Finger shook his head, his voice shaking.

"Domina, I . . . Ever you've treated me well and fair. I've no cause to harm your flock. Nor would I ever hurt the lass. She was like kin to me. I served the meal to her with my own hands." Tears filled his eyes, snot at his lips as he looked to Maggot's lifeless corpse. "You think me cold enough to look in her eyes and smile as I p-passed the blade that would end her?"

The man's chest heaved, face twisting as tears spilled down his cheeks.

"Never. By the Everseeing and all his Daughters, *never*."

Leona's eyes narrowed, but she could see it in his face, plain as Mia. His thin frame trembling. Eyes swimming with grief. Either Finger was an actor worthy of the greatest theater in all the Republic, or the man was genuinely gutted at Maggot's death.

"Who had means to get into the larder?" Leona asked.

Finger pawed his eyes, sniffled hard. "Anyone with access to the keep could get to the provisions, Domina. They're not locked of a nevernight . . . I-I'd have kept them with more care, but I had n-no inkling a serpent lived among us."

"Nor I," Leona said. "But I've suckled one at my breast, sure and true."

"Elegy isn't easy to make," Mia said. "Dangerous. Messy. But in a city as big as Crow's Rest, there's bound to be a way to buy it, if you've the coin."

"And how do you know this, exactly?" Arkades growled.

"I've made no secret of my knowledge of herblore," Mia replied. "The difference between a remedy and a requiem can be as little as half a dram. And if we're taking tally, my meal was dosed too."

"Then how comes it you were not poisoned with the rest of your fellows?"

"I didn't eat my dinner," Mia spat.

"The second time in as many months you've dodged a suspicious meal."

"Have you looked under Furian's bandages?" Mia demanded. "It's fucking sickening. The smell would put a scabdog off its meal, let alone the sight."

"And so you just happen to give your draft to *my* dog and watch him die? Then just *happen* to have the ingredients to save the lives of your fellows?"

Mia turned to fully face Arkades, teeth clenched. "You accuse *me* of this? Poisoning an eleven-year-old girl?"

Arkades ignored her, turned to Leona. "I say if we seek a serpent among us, begin with the one who best knows poison, neh?"

Rage took Mia then, bright and blinding, and she took a step toward Arkades with her fists clenched. The big man rose with that surprising speed, shoulders squared, chin low. She could feel his growl in her chest.

"Try," he said. "Just *try* . . ."

"Executus, enough," Leona snapped. "Crow is champion of this collegium. She already stands atop the mountain. What in the Everseeing's name would she gain by murdering all my Falcons, let alone Maggot besides?"

"What would *anyone* gain?" Magistrae asked, looking around the room. "If we seek the killer, first we must find the motive. How does *anyone* profit from this?"

"Your father would profit, Domina," Mia said.

Leona shook her head. "He would not dare . . ."

"Think on it," Mia replied. "He owns all your debts. You owe him coin that you simply don't have. How have you made up your shortfalls to creditors in the past?"

". . . I am still working the figures," Leona replied.

"Aye," Mia nodded. "But even with the Whitekeep purse in consideration, have you pondered any way to conjure over three thousand silver pieces that doesn't involve selling at least a few of your gladiatii to Pandemonium?"

Leona looked to Arkades, then to Magistrae.

"No," she admitted.

"So what happens if all your gladiatii are dead and you've none to sell?"

"Then I lose everything," Leona said. "The *magni*. This collegium. Everything."

"Is your father the kind of man who murders to get his way? And would it be so hard for a man with that much money to hold sway over one of your guards? Or perhaps someone even closer to you?"

"Impertinent wretch," Arkades spat. "Just what are you implying?"

"Only that there's two kinds of loyalty," Mia replied. "The kind paid for with love, and the kind paid for with silver."

"Domina, this—"

Leona held up her hand, cutting her magistrae's objection off at the knee. She turned to her houseguard captain, her voice cold with command.

"Gannicus, I want every bedchamber in the keep searched. Every chest, every cupboard, every crack. You and your fellow houseguards will search by threes, and you will not search your own belongings, am I clear?"

The captain slapped a fist to his chest. "Aye, Domina."

Gannicus spun on his heel, gathered the other houseguards and marched across the yard. Scowling dark, Arkades cast one last look at his murdered dog, the murdered girl, and began limping after them.

"Where are you going, Executus?" Leona asked.

". . . To assist the search, Domina."

"Gannicus has the matter in hand. Take Finger and gather firewood for a pyre." She glanced briefly at Maggot's body. "It would not do to allow them to linger in this heat. They must be sent to the Hearth, and the gentle keeping of Lady Keph."

Looking Arkades up and down, Mia could see his pupils were dilated, his breathing quickened. Fight-or-flight instinct kicking in.

"... *he fears* ...," came the whisper in her ear.

But finally, as always, the executus bowed.

"Your whisper, my will."

M ia had never smelled a burning body before.

She'd smelled death, certainly. The noxious stench of sundered bellies. The sweet, high perfume of decay. But until she stood in the courtyard of Crow's Nest, listening to dry wood crackle and snap over the song of the sea, she'd never smelled a funeral pyre. She'd read stories as a child—grieving lovers or orphaned children, sending their loved ones off to the hereafter atop a pillar of flame. There was a kind of romance to it, she'd thought. Something fierce and bright and enduring. But the books never talked about the smell. The burning hair and boiling blood and blackening skin.

It was hideous.

They'd laid Maggot atop the firewood that Arkades and Finger had gathered, Otho beside her. It wasn't the grandest bier ever created, but they'd used all the fuel the kitchen had, stacked in neat rows over three feet high. The pair were wrapped in simple cotton shifts, faces uncovered to the sky. Dona Leona spoke quiet prayers to the Everseeing over their bodies. A wreath of flowers was placed upon their chests. A small mahogany coin beneath their tongues.*

And then, they were set aflame.

Most of the gladiatii held their grief back, but Bryn was weeping openly—this was the second funeral she'd attended in a week, all the wounds from her brother's loss torn open and bleeding fresh. Sidonius was the only other gladiatii to let tears fall, those big brawny shoulders heaving up and down. Mia

---

* Known as *reparii,* these coins are paid to the Goddess Keph in return for a succor by her Hearth in the hereafter.

Since the Earth Goddess has been slumbering for eons and has no use for currency, the wooden coins are thrown into the Hearth to keep it burning. The fire within the Hearth was a gift from Keph's sister, Tsana, the Lady of Flame, who thought it unfair that their mother, Niah, be given sole dominion over the dead. Thus, she created the fire to give righteous souls a place to gather and warm themselves against the chill of the hereafter's endless night.

Tsana hates her mother, you see. Almost as much as her father does.

One is forced to wonder if she was hugged enough as a child.

wondered at the riddle of him, that brand on his chest, the lecherous buffoon-ery, all at odds with the fellow who'd spoken with such adoration of her father, and tried to comfort her in the dark.

The flames burned brighter, the smoke rising into the blinding sky. The crash of distant waves. The cry of circling gulls. Dona Leona's plaintive prayer to Aa.

With the rites spoken, Leona hung her head, walked solemnly from the pyre. Mia watched her trudge across the yard, the smoke stinging in her unbandaged eye. She knew now Leona was a product of the violence she'd grown up with, that at their hearts, the two of them weren't so dissimilar. If Mia's childhood had been a different one, it could just as easily have been her sitting as mistress of this keep. But a part of her couldn't help but blame the dona for this. If only this collegium didn't exist, if only Maggot had never been sold here . . .

No. You have no time for "if only" . . .

Leona stepped up to the verandah, just as the guard she'd placed in com-mand of the search returned from inside the keep. Mia watched them side-long, Gannicus speaking softly, glancing to Arkades. He handed what looked to be a folded piece of fabric to his mistress, and Mia's stomach turned.

"Arkades?" Leona said, turning to her executus.

The man looked up from the burning pyre. The same fear she'd seen in the infirmary lingered in the man's eyes.

"Mi Dona?"

"Explain this," the dona said, holding out her hand.

Clutched in her fingers was a silken underslip, edged with fine lace.

The gladiatii turned to stare, the pyre still blazing in the background. Arkades looked to the warriors he'd trained, his expression darkening. He could barely meet Leona's eyes, his voice edged with shame.

"Mi Dona, if we could speak in private—"

"It was found in your room," Leona said. "Beneath your mattress. Now I see why you were so eager to aid Gannicus and his guards in their search. But tell me, noble Arkades, how comes it that my underclothes are found among your possessions?"

"Mi Dona, I—"

"And what is this?"

Leona held up a small phial of clear liquid, gleaming in the sunslight.

Arkades blinked. "I have never seen that before in my life."

"It was found wrapped inside my underslip. Hidden among your little trove. Perfume, perhaps? Or a little liquor to make the nevernights easier?" Leona turned to Mia, held out the phial on her palm. "Crow?"

Glancing at Arkades, seeing the fear swelling inside him, Mia took the phial from the dona's hands. Unstopping it, she sniffed, dabbed her finger and tasted, immediately spat once, twice. Lips curling as she looked to Leona.

"It's Elegy, Domina. No question."

Leona's glare welled with tears as she looked at Arkades, lip trembling, her entire body shaking with rage.

"You."

Horror welled in Arkades's eyes. "Mi Dona, I would never . . ."

"Then how comes it to be in your room?" Leona demanded. "Wrapped in the underslip you stole from me? Or do you deny the keeping of that, too?"

"I do not deny it, I fou—"

"You have known me from a child, Arkades! I thought you a man of honor, who saw the righteousness of my cause. I thought your infatuation harmless, but now I see it turned to poison before my eyes." She shook the silk in his face. "Now I see to the heart of you! *Now* I see the reason you have walked with me all these years!"

"Infatuation?" Arkades was pale, his voice trembling.

"How much does my father pay you?"

". . . What?"

"How much?" she screamed. "Ever I wondered at the lions you wore on your doublet, the lion's head on your cane. I thought it simple homage to where you'd been and who you were, but now I see it for truth! You were *always* his man! *Always!*"

Magistrae placed a gentle hand on her mistress's shoulder. "Domina, please."

Leona snarled, threw off the woman's grip. "Did he promise me to you, perhaps? Some broken trophy to hide beneath your mattress with all your other dirty little secrets? You'd poison my flock, murder an eleven-year-old girl to have your way? After what he did to my mother? Smiling like a snake and offering me your *comforts*?"

Tears gleamed in Arkades's eyes. "You think me capable . . ."

"I think you a liar," Leona spat. "I think you a murderer. I think you a sad old man ruled by lust and accursed drink and memory of past glory gone wrong and rotten." Leona dragged ragged breath through gritted teeth. "I think you every inch the bastard my father is. I want you out of my collegium."

"Leona, I—"

"Get *out*!" Leona roared. "Or I swear by the Everseeing and all four of his Daughters, I will show you the mercy you showed the child on that pyre!"

The woman stood trembling, tears pouring down her cheeks. But her jaw was set, teeth bared in a snarl. Arkades hung like a broken mirror, chest heaving, his face pale. Looking among the gladiatii, he found only disdain and rage. He turned back to Leona, agony in his eyes, one final, desperate plea on his lips.

"Please—"

"GET OUT!" Leona screamed, launching herself at him and flailing with her fists. Scratching his face, clawing at his eyes. "GET OUT! GET *OUT*!"

Arkades staggered back, and Magistrae pulled the flailing, screaming Leona off him. The guards stepped forward to separate them, hands on their swords, glowering at the executus. Gannicus placed a hand on his chest and shoved him farther away, warning plain on his face. The captain obviously had no wish to draw, but the wishes of his mistress were clear, and the smell of that burning child hung heavy in the air.

Arkades looked around the yard and found no friends. Tears brimming in his eyes. He opened his mouth to speak, but found no words to save him. He searched the faces of his former charges, and found none to vouch for him. Mia could see words struggling behind his teeth, but looking into Leona's eyes, he found only hatred and rage. And with no other real choice, he turned and began limping for the gate.

"Take this!" Leona cried, flinging the slip at his back. "May it keep you warm in the nevernight!"

The executus paused, looking back over his shoulder. But without a word, he hung his head and simply kept walking. Mia watched him leave, uncertain what to think. Jealousy could drive a man to any lengths, and Arkades *did* still wear the lions of his former master on his chest. To discover the woman he so clearly loved was bedding Furian must have been an awful blow, and love could turn to cancer when watered with betrayal. But a part of Mia found it hard to believe he'd betray Leona so cruelly . . .

Leaning on her magistrae, the dona left the yard, still weeping. Mia looked to the pyre once more, watching the flames rise higher. Heat caressing her skin. Smoke kissing her tongue. So much in the balance. So close to the end. So much to risk before she got there, and so keen to arrive.

She couldn't wait 'til this was all over.

"Goodbye, Maggot," she whispered. "I'll miss you."

And she still couldn't remember the last time she cried.

The bathhouse swirled with steam, the heat of it scalded her skin. Mia sank into the water with a sigh, the ache in her ribs soothed by the warmth. Slipping below the surface, she tried to shush her thoughts, silence her doubts and rage and enjoy a moment's silence. For just a breath. Just a second.

Bryn entered the bathhouse, walking like she were sleeping. Her eyes were bloodshot, her cheeks red raw. Without looking at Mia, she stripped off her clothes and sank into the water, washing the tears from her skin. She stayed under almost a breath too long, Mia about to reach out toward her, when Bryn finally surfaced, sodden blond framing her face. Drifting to the corner, the girl sat still as stone, as a statue, as a corpse, staring at the ripples on the surface and saying nothing at all.

"A hard turn," Mia said.

"Aye," Bryn murmured.

"Domina spoke the service well."

"Aye."

". . . How are you feeling?"

Bryn looked up a moment, eyes gaining focus.

"How do you think?" she whispered.

Mia hung her head, stared at the swirling steam.

". . . Aye."

Wavewaker trudged into the bathhouse, unwrapped the cloth from his waist. Mia couldn't remember a single turn where they'd bathed together and the big man hadn't gifted her a song, but Wavewaker didn't hum a note this time. His uncharacteristic silence hung heavy in the air, sorrow welling in Mia's chest. Thinking of the water fight they'd had, here with Byern, just a few weeks ago. Thinking of that little girl burning on that pyre, and all that had been lost along with her.

These people are not your familia and not your—

"Four fucking Daughters . . ."

Mia looked up, saw Sidonius stride past the guards posted on the bathhouse entrance. Shutting the door behind him, he stripped off and sank into the water, eyes wide, breathing quick.

"You seem of a mood," Wavewaker said.

"There's no 'seems' about it, brother."

"What troubles?"

"Our fucking domina," the big Itreyan growled. "I just heard from Milaini, one of the serving lasses. Leona has sent missive to Varro fucking Caito, invited him for evemeal tomorrow."

"Why does she dine with a fleshpeddler?" Wavewaker asked.

"She's planning to sell us to Pandemonium, why do you think?" Sidonius spat. "She's already drawn up a list, apparently. Milaini saw it on her desk."

". . . Who's on it?" Mia asked.

"Bryn, for starters," Sid said, nodding at the Vaanian girl.

Bryn blinked, as if hearing the conversation for the first time.

". . . Domina would sell me to Varro Caito?"

"She needs coin," Sidonius growled. "She can't afford a new charioteer to form a new equillai team. But after your showing at Whitekeep, you'll fetch a fortune."

"Who else?" Wavewaker growled.

"Bladesinger," Sidonius spat. "Felix. Albanus. Butcher. And me."

"She's going to sell 'Singer?" Mia breathed.

"She's going to sell anyone with a fucking pulse," Sid replied. "She needs three thousand silver priests, and she's thrown all in on you winning the *magni*, Crow. The rest of us are just sacks of coin to her."

Bryn shook her head, whispering, "Shit."

"That's all you've got to say?" Sidonius whispered, gobsmacked.

"And what else would you have me say?" the girl growled.

"Say you'll not be sold like chaff to die in Pandemonium," Sidonius growled. "Because by the Four fucking Daughters, I won't be."

"And what choice do we have?"

Sid cast an eye to the closed door, lowered his voice further.

"There's always one other choice," he said.

A chill ran over Mia's skin as she looked Sid in the eye. "Meaning what?"

"Meaning Executus is gone, and his lash along with him," Sidonius replied. "Meaning these houseguards are softer than baby shite, and we're full-fledged gladiatii. We could beat them to death with practice swords if we'd a mind to. Especially with surprise on our side."

Wavewaker scowled, rubbing his chin.

"Aye," he muttered. "We could at that."

Bryn's eyes widened, voice dropping to a furious whisper. "You speak of rebellion? Have you lost your mind? You want to end up executed at the *magni*?"

"You'd rather die in Pandemonium?" Sidonius demanded. "In case you've no eyes to see it, sister, this house is coming down around our fucking ears. I've a mind to absent myself before the roof falls in."

"This isn't right," Wavewaker agreed. "Bladesinger fought with honor. Crow would be the first to admit she'd not have stood victor against the Exile if not for 'Singer, aye?"

Mia nodded slow. "Aye."

"And now she's to be sold like meat? Because her swordarm is ruined?" The big man looked to Bryn. "Your brother gave his life for this house. And this is how Leona honors that sacrifice? By hocking his sister to a bastard like Varro Caito? I'll not stand by for this," Sid spat. "I can't. I won't."

Wavewaker looked to Sidonius, shook his head.

"Nor I."

Mia licked her lips, spoke soft. "Hold now."

The three gladiatii looked to her, waiting for her to speak. After the showings she'd put in at the arena, there wasn't a one among them who didn't respect her. And while she could see the injustice of it, while she knew that if she were in their position, she'd almost certainly be arguing for the same . . .

If the gladiatii of the Remus Collegium rebelled, she'd never see the *magni*. Never have her revenge. If she aided them, at best, she'd be a fugitive, on the run in a Republic where such rebellion was brutally punished. At worst, she'd simply be killed in the attempt. And if she didn't participate, but allowed it to happen, she'd probably still be crucified by the administratii for belonging to a house in revolt.

But to sit back and do nothing while Bryn and 'Singer and Sid were sold . . .

"Hold?" Sidonius asked. "Hold for what?"

". . . Let's not speak hasty," Mia said. "The wounds from Maggot's funeral are fresh. I say think on it a few turns before we do anything rash."

"Rash?" Sidonius scowled. "We're talking about our lives here!"

"It may be fine for some," Wavewaker said. "But not all of us are champions in the dona's favor."

"And that favor changes like the wind, Crow," Bryn said, seemingly warming to the idea. "Look how swift she casts Arkades aside."

"I only counsel patience," Mia insisted. "Leona and Caito dine on the morrow, but no sale will be brokered for a turn or two. Domina's blood is running as hot as the rest of us. Perhaps in time, she'll see her folly and seek another way. Perhaps she'll find some trick in her ledger that yet avoids anyone's sale. I'm certain she has no wish to part with any of us."

"If you think that woman has a hint of loyalty inside her," Wavewaker said, "you are the fool I never took you for. Leona thinks of her own glory, none other's."

"Patience," she begged. "Please."

The three gladiatii looked among each other, scowling. But it seemed there'd be no more argument for the moment, each falling into a sullen, scowling silence. And with little else to say and no comfort to offer, Mia finally climbed out of the bath and toweled herself off, tying her wraps about herself and padding softly from the room.

Stalking down the hall to her cell, her mind was whirling. She knew she couldn't allow a rebellion against Leona to happen—her entire plan would be undone if she did. But if she allowed the dona to have her way, if Leona couldn't be swayed, Sid and 'Singer and Bryn were as good as dead. Nobody survived Pandemonium. Even the greatest warriors lasted a few months there, at best.

A slow quiet settled over the barracks, the gladiatii bedding down for the nevernight. Sidonius returned from the bathhouse, sitting opposite Mia in their cell. She'd not been moved upstairs yet—with all the drama of the last few turns, she supposed Leona had more pressing concerns than finding her new champion's quarters. And so, Mia was still stuck in her cage. Feeling Sid's eyes on her as the arkemical lamps were turned down, as the talk of the other gladiatii softened and then stilled, finally replaced by the sounds of sleep.

As always, the man stayed quiet when they were alone. Never pressing.

Simply staring.

Minutes ticking by like days. His blue eyes fixed on her.

Unblinking.

Mute.

"Black Mother, what?" she finally hissed.

"I said nothing," Sidonius whispered.

"So you plan to sit there and stare at me all nevernight?"

"Would you rather me speak?"

"Yes, damn you, say your piece. You weren't shy about it in the fucking bathhouse. We're alone and all of a sudden the cat has your tongue?"

"And what would we speak of? You've made feelings clear enough."

"You've been following me like a fucking bloodhawk since you found out who I was. And you've never asked me of it, not once. Yet at the first whisper of . . ."—Mia glanced about, lowered her voice—". . . of *rebellion*, your tongue is all aflutter."

"The action we take about my impending sale concerns me direct, Crow. But as far as your parentage goes, it's not my place to speak. And if you were wondering, all you needed do was ask. I follow you out of respect for your father. He'd have wanted me to look after you."

"And what do you know of what my father would have wanted?"

Sidonius laughed softly. "More than you realize, little Crow."

"You were a soldier. Branded for cowardice and kicked out of the legion. You weren't in his counsel. You didn't know him."

Sidonius shook his head, hurt shining in his eyes.

"I know he'd be ashamed of what this house has become."

Mia fell quiet at that. Took a deep, shivering breath and looked to the walls around her. The iron bars and the human misery. She'd scrubbed herself hard in the bath, but she could smell the smoke from Maggot's funeral pyre in her hair.

"Your name is Mia, aye?"

She looked up sharply, eyes narrowed.

"It took me a while to remember it," Sid said. "The justicus spoke of you sometimes, but he kept talk of his familia mostly to himself. I think he felt closer to you all that way. Not sharing you with others. Not staining thoughts of you with all the blood and shit we saw on campaign."

"Aye," she finally answered. "Mia."

"Your little brother was Jonnen."

". . . Aye."

Sid nodded, sucking his lip, saying nothing.

"Daughters, spit it out," Mia sighed.

"Spit what out?"

"The rebuke so obviously churning behind your fucking teeth. '*You can leave these walls anytime you like, Crow, you've no right to stop us trying the same. Even if we fail, the administratii will never catch you. No cell can ever hold you.*'"

"Is that what I was thinking?" Sid asked. "Or what *you* were thinking?"

"Fuck you, Sid."

"It took me a while," the big man said. "To ponder it. Why you were here, why you'd want to fight in the *magni*. And then I remembered who'd be standing on the sand with you when you were declared the victor. The same men who stood in judgment over him, aye? The same men who smiled as he hanged."

Mia said nothing. Simply stared.

"I wasn't there when it happened," Sid said. "I was already in chains by then. But I heard about it, afterward. Heard the Dona Corvere stood on the forum walls, above the howling mob. A little girl in her arms. Must have been you, aye? Quite a thing to make your daughter watch."

"She wanted me to see," Mia said. "She wanted me to *remember*."

"Your mother."

"Aye," Mia spat. "What was it you called her? The *stupid fucking whore*?"

"Aye, that was unkind of me," Sid sighed. "But it's hard for me to find too many kind words for your ma, Mia. Knowing what I know of her."

"And what is it you think you know?"

"Just that Alinne Corvere had more ambition than Justicus Darius and General Antonius put together. Half your father's centurions were in love with her. She had a third of the Senate wrapped around her finger." Sid steepled his hands at his chin. "How do you suppose she did that? She wasn't quite the swordswoman her daughter grew up to be. She was a politician. You think a woman like that could almost bring a Republic to its knees without dropping once or twice to her own?"

Mia glowered at Sidonius. "Don't you dare."

"I know you're trying to avenge them," Sidonius said. "I know you think it righteous. I just wonder if you'd think the same if you knew the kind of woman your mother was. Or, the kind of man your father was."

"I *know* what kind of man he was. He was a *hero*."

"We all think that of our parents," Sid said. "They give us life, after all. It's easy to mistake them for gods."

"You speak one ill word of my father," Mia whispered, "and I swear by the Black Mother I will fucking end you right here in this cell. He was doing what he thought was best for the Republic and its people. He was a man who followed his heart."

"I loved your father, Mia. And I served him as well as I could. He had that way about him. The loyalty he inspired in his men . . . I think all of us loved him in our own way." Sid fixed Mia in his stare. "And aye, he was a man who followed his heart. Just not in the way you think he did."

". . . What are you talking about?"

Sid sighed.

"Your father and General Antonius were lovers, Mia."

Mia flinched as if she'd been slapped in the face.

Breath trembling.

The whole world shifting under her feet.

". . . What?"

"Everyone knew it," Sid said. "All their men, anyways. Nobody cared. Not even your mother, so long as they kept it quiet. She'd married the position, not the man. Their marriage was one of friendship. Perhaps even a strange kind of love. But first and foremost, it was one of ambition. Your father commanded loyalty among the Luminatii. It didn't bother us that the would-be king and the Kingmaker occasionally slipped into each other's beds. Some even found it romantic." Sidonius leaned closer, his voice heavy and hard. "But don't tell me the rebellion was about Darius Corvere's love of liberty or the people, Mia. It was about his love for Antonius. The general wanted to be a king. And your father wanted to be the man who placed that crown upon his head. Plain and simple."

Mia remembered the nights in Crow's Nest when the general would visit. She'd always called him "Uncle Antonius." Her mother and father and he all dining together, the wine flowing, their laughter echoing down halls of long red stone.

And afterward . . .

Perhaps under this very roof . . .

"Lies," Mia whispered. "You're speaking lies."

"No, Mia," Sid said. "I'm just speaking difficult truths."

Mia sat still, silent, heart pounding in her chest. Blinking hard.

She couldn't rightly remember the last time she cried . . .

"Hurts, doesn't it?" Sid sighed. "When you find out the ones who gave you life are just as mortal and frail as the rest of us? That the world isn't what you thought it was?"

Mia wiped at her tears with shaking hands. Remembering the way her father kissed her mother. First on one eyelid, then the other, then finally upon her smooth, olive brow.

But never on the lips.

Could it be true?

. . . Did it matter if it was?

If there was no deceit between them, why did she care who her parents lay with? Though they may not have loved each other, they'd both loved her; she knew that if nothing else. They'd taught her to rely on her wits, to be strong, to never be afraid. And she missed them both, even now, like a hole had been carved in her chest the turn they were taken away.

But if her father hadn't been the hero of the people she supposed him, if he'd only been trying to overthrow the Senate for his own selfish ends . . .

. . . what was all this murder and blood for, exactly?

No.

No, Scaeva and Duomo still deserved a killing. They'd still imprisoned her mother and brother, left them to die in an oubliette inside the Philosopher's Stone.

"I will give your brother your regards . . ."

"I know what it will cost you," Sidonius whispered. "To let rebellion happen under this roof. But think of Bryn. Of Bladesinger. Of Butcher and me. Do we truly deserve to die in some godless pit because Leona hates her father, and you love yours too much?"

Silence between them, heavy as lead. Mia looked the man over; this man she'd mistaken for a lecherous fool, a thug, perhaps even the coward his brand told the world he was. She saw he was none of those things. But still . . .

"Why weren't you there when my father and Antonius were captured?" she asked, her voice hollow. "Why aren't you dead with the rest of their men?"

Sidonius sighed deep, hung his head.

"The Luminatii centurions and their Second Spears were informed of Darius and Antonius's plan the nevernight after we mustered. Antonius made a grand speech, spoke of corruption, of hubris, of the Republic being under the control of weak and impious men. And when all the shield beating and chest thumping was over . . . I just couldn't do it. The Republic is rotten, Mia, I'll brook no argument there. A cancer eats at the bones of this place, and Godsgrave is the heart of it. Julius Scaeva is twice the tyrant Antonius would have been. But we were the Luminatii Legion. Soldiers of God. The war that would've come if we marched on our own capital, the suffering that would have ridden in our wake . . .

"Thousands would have died. Tens of thousands, maybe. And for what? So one man could wear a crown, and another could place it on his head? I couldn't do it. I went to my centurion and told him so. He listened patiently as I tried to tell him the wrong of it. And when I was done, he had me beaten near to death, branded a coward, and sold off to the first bidder on the blocks."

Sidonius shook his head.

"Six years in chains for one moment of principle. That's the tithe I paid. But you know what I learned in all the years between then and this, little Crow?"

". . . No."

Sid fixed Mia in his ice-blue stare.

"There's no softer pillow than a clear conscience."

Mia sat in the dark, trembling head to foot. Tears spilling down her cheek. And without another word, Sidonius lay down in the straw, rolled over onto his side, and closed his eyes.

"Sleep well, Mia."

CHAPTER 28

SCARS

"*. . . this is unwise . . .*"

"As you're so fond of reminding me."

"*. . . if i don't, who will? that fool eclipse . . . ?*"

"If I didn't know better, I'd say you were jealous of her and Ashlinn."

"*. . . it is a good thing you know better, then . . .*"

Mia knelt in the alleyway, found the cloak Ash had left for her and wrapped it about her shoulders. Though skulking about Crow's Rest in this heat while wearing a hood and cloak wasn't exactly the best way to avert suspicion, it was easier than blundering around blind beneath a mantle of shadows.

"I need to talk to her, Mister Kindly," Mia said, pulling the hood up over her head. "She's been back two turns and things are moving quick at the collegium."

"*. . . once upon a time, you used to talk to me . . .*"

"I still talk to you."

"*. . . mmm . . .*"

Mister Kindly hopped up onto her shoulder, curled his tail about her throat. Mia made her way out of the alley, stalking down Fisher's Row toward the inn. The hour was late, the winds blowing in off the ocean almost pushing her hood off her head. A few scattered folks ran about in their errands, and she could hear bells tolling down in the harbor, but aside from ne'er-do-wells like her, the streets were all but empty.

"All right, then," she muttered. "What do you want to talk about?"

"*. . . where to begin . . . ,*" came the whisper in her ear. "*. . . that thing that saved your life in galante? your theory that the darkin are somehow connected to the fall of the Ysiiri empire? the map inked on ashlinn's back? and let us not forget your match with the silkling, and the second set of blades she so conveniently forgot to weaken . . .*"

"Anyone could have made that mistake, Mister Kindly."

"*. . . you are a fool to trust her . . .*"

"If Ash wanted me dead, she could have ended me ten times over by now."

"... *be that as it may, her involvement is clouding your judgment. there are so many questions about what is happening here, and you seem to be looking for answers to none of them* ..."

"There's only so much I can do behind the walls of the bloody collegium," she hissed. "The *magni* comes first. We have one chance at this."

"... *do you remember what that shadowthing in galante told you* ... ?"

"That I should be painting the skies black. Whatever the fuck that means."

"... *it said your vengeance serves only to blind you, mia* ..."

"Are you saying I should forget what Scaeva and Duomo did?"

"... *i am saying there may be larger things at play here* ..."

"You think I don't know that?"

They rounded the corner to the inn's back alley, the scent of garbage and rot in the air. Mia threw off her hood and Mister Kindly hopped down onto a broken crate, began cleaning his translucent paws as Mia continued.

"Look, I've felt like a pawn that can only see half the board for months now. And the questions in my head are near deafening. But all those questions will still need answers when truelight is over, and the chance to end Scaeva and Duomo will be gone. Our plan is one rebellion shy of ruin. Everything hangs on the next few turns."

"... *well, if thought of the gladiatii rebelling is all that troubles you, the answer is obvious* ..."

"O, aye? Pray tell, then."

"... *you cannot allow it to happen* ..."

"It's not that simple, Mister Kindly."

"... *it is that simple. if you still wish your vengeance, you must win the* magni. *and you cannot win the* magni *if you have been executed for rebellion against the republic. you talk constantly of how much you have given up to get this far. you cannot fall now, at the last few feet* ..."

"So I'm just to let Sid and the others perish?"

"... *they are not your friends, mia* ..."

"Who are you to tell me that?"

The not-cat tilted his head.

"... *i am* your *friend. your oldest friend. who helped you when scaeva ordered you drowned? who saved you on the streets of godsgrave? who stood beside you through your trials in the church? and in all that time, have i ever steered you wrong* ... ?"

Mia felt a rebuke rising on her lips, but before she could speak it, she sensed her shadow rippling, a familiar chill prickling her skin. A dark shape coalesced at her feet, sleek and lupine, weaving around and in between her legs.

"... *YOU RETURN* ..."

"... Hello, Eclipse."

"... *I MISSED YOU* ..."

"... *o, please* ..."

Eclipse snarled, shadow claws digging into the dirt.

Mister Kindly affected a yawn.

"... *stop, you're frightening me* ..."

"... *I THINK YOU TOO STUPID TO BE FRIGHTENED OF ME, LITTLE MOGGY. BUT ONE TURN, I SHALL TEACH YOU THERE IS A PRICE FOR OWNING TOO MUCH MOUTH AND NOT ENOUGH TEETH* ..."

"... *tell me, dear mongrel, do you practice these blunt little threats when you're alone, or do you simply improvise* ... ?"

Mia frowned, her tolerance of the not-cat's sarcasm at an all-time low.

"Mister Kindly, go watch the Nest. Come fetch me if Furian stirs."

"... *you send me away* ... ?"

"... *O, MY HEART BLEEDS* ..."

"... *we have no hearts, you idiotic mutt* ..."

"... *BE SURE TO REMIND ME OF THAT, WHEN I AM EATING YOURS* ..."

The shadowcat hissed, and the shadowwolf growled. But with a ripple in the black about her feet, Mia felt her passenger depart. She knelt and ran her hands through Eclipse, fancying the slightest whisper of cool velvet beneath her fingertips.

"All is well?"

Eclipse's hackles were still up, but under Mia's touch, she slowly quietened. Licking her mistress's hand with a translucent tongue, the shadowwolf spoke softly.

"... *IT IS WELL. BETTER NOW THAT YOU ARE HERE. HOW ARE YOUR WOUNDS* ... ?"

Mia touched the bandage at her face, grimacing. "Well enough."

"... *YOU SEEM SAD* ... ?"

"Perhaps a little."

"... *DO WE NEED TO HURT ANYONE* ... ?"

"I need you to stay here, Eclipse. Keep watch on the street, aye?"

"... *AS YOU WISH* ..."

Mia smiled, began trudging down the alleyway, glad at least one of her daemons was content to do what it was told. As she walked farther and farther away, climbed up the downspout to the balcony outside Ashlinn's window, she felt Eclipse's hold on her begin to fade, and butterflies begin creeping into her belly. It was still an unfamiliar sensation, cold and sickly and slick. It made her feel small. It made her feel weak.

Black Mother, she loathed being afraid.

She crouched by the window, fist poised over the glass. The hateful sensation of lice crawling in her belly. Cold sweat stinging in the stitches at her cheek. Gritting her teeth, she dragged up the nerve from the bottom of her feet and knocked softly.

The window opened and Ashlinn stood there, bathed in the burning sunlight. For a moment, Mia forgot the blood, the death, the fear, simply drinking in the sight of her. This girl who'd risked her life again —gathering information in Whitekeep, weakening the Exile's blades to even the odds, following Mia across the Republic and back without flinching.

"O, Goddess," Ashlinn breathed, pressing her lips to Mia's own.

Mia closed her eyes, slipping her arms about Ashlinn's waist, letting the girl shower her face with kisses. Taking her by the hand, Ash led Mia to the bed, pulled her down and threw her arms about her, squeezing tight. Despite the ache of her cracked ribs, the pain of the last few turns, Mia breathed easier, inhaling lavender and the scent of henna in Ashlinn's hair. Simply being held and holding in turn.

"I missed you," Ash breathed.

". . . I missed you, too."

They kissed again, long and blissful and soft. Ashlinn pulled her closer, face buried in her neck. They lay like that for an age, bodies fitting together like the strangest of puzzle pieces. Of all the places she expected to find herself on her road, wrapped up in this girl's arms was the last. The warmest. The sweetest.

After a long, peaceful nothing, Ash finally pulled back from Mia's arms, looked her over, from the top of her head to the shadow beneath her.

"Where's Mister Mockery?" she asked.

"I sent him back to the keep," Mia sighed.

"He didn't like that, I'll wager."

Mia shrugged, toying with the end of one of Ashlinn's braids. "He was pissing me off. He's always got something sarcastic to say. Always questioning. Always pushing. He's never just . . . nice."

"Sounds like someone else I know," Ash smiled.

Mia raised an eyebrow, fixed Ashlinn in a withering stare. "O, really?"

"Truth is the sharpest knife, Corvere," Ash grinned.

"You wound me, Dona. I'm fucking lovable, I'll have you know."

Ash grinned. "I've been thinking about that, actually."

"How fucking lovable I am?"

"No," Ashlinn rolled her eyes. "About your passengers. How different they are. Spending all this time traveling with Eclipse, I've gotten to know her quite well. She and Mister Congeniality are like truelight and truedark. He's sarcastic, mean-spirited, a fucking pain in the arse. Eclipse is simpler, more direct. She doesn't question. And I realized those traits are a lot like you and Lord Cassius. You said yourself he never sought the truth of what it was to be darkin."

"You think . . ."

"I don't think anything," Ash shrugged. "It's just interesting. Maybe a passenger inherits the mannerisms of the darkin they first imprint upon?"

Mia chewed on that for a moment, and it tasted like sense. Thinking on it honestly, her two passengers *were* an awful lot like the ones they'd first rode with. The shadowcat's bitter, black humor and biting wit. The shadowwolf's unquestioning loyalty, her propensity for violent solutions to any situation.

Could it be Mister Kindly was just a dark reflection of her?

And if that were true, weren't his thoughts the best measure of what *she* thought?

. . . *they are not your friends, mia* . . .

"I was worried about you," Ashlinn whispered. "During the *venatus* at Whitekeep. I'm sorry I missed that second set of blades. That was stupid of me."

Mia blinked, thoughts coming back into focus. Looking into Ashlinn's eyes.

Wondering . . .

"Sneaking around down there unseen can't have been easy," she finally said. "And it turned out well enough in the end."

Ash sucked her lip. "She hurt you."

"I'm all right," Mia sighed. "Cracked ribs. A few scratches."

Ashlinn leaned up on her elbow, ran gentle fingertips over the bandage on Mia's brow and cheek.

"Didn't look like a scratch when she opened you up."

"It's fine, Ash."

". . . Show me."

Mia shook her head, belly churning. "Ashlinn, I don—"

"Mia," Ash said softly, taking her hand. "Show me."

The fear. Welling in her belly like poison. She wanted Mister Kindly and Eclipse back, right now. Life was so much easier with no regard for consequence, no thought for pain. Her passengers were what made her strong, allowed her to be a terror of the sands, to spare no thought for hurting or being hurt in kind. She was steel when they were inside her. Without them . . .

Without them, what am I?

For all her talk of preferring to look dangerous rather than pretty, she was still afraid of what she looked like beneath that bandage. Of what she'd see in Ashlinn's eyes when she took it off. But just as swift, she felt her old temper rising. The anger that had been her companion through all the years between the turn her father was killed and this one. What did she care how she looked?

What difference did it make to who she was?

Mia reached up to the bandage, untied it from her brow. It was stuck to the wound, dried blood crusted in the gauze, and she had to tug it free, wincing at the pain. Ashlinn sat still, staring with those beautiful blue eyes. Mia glanced at her reflection in the looking glass. The gash cut down through her brow, curling in a cruel hook shape along her left cheek, laced with stitches by Maggot's iron-steady hands.

"It's not that bad," Ashlinn murmured.

"Liar," Mia replied.

"I am at that," Ashlinn smirked. "But not about this."

The girl leaned forward, and with featherlight lips, she kissed Mia's brow. Sinking lower, she placed a half-dozen gentle kisses along the line of Mia's wound, and finally, she pressed her lips to Mia's own.

"Our scars are just gifts from our enemies," Ashlinn whispered into her mouth. "Reminding us they weren't good enough to kill us."

Mia smiled faintly, entwining her fingers in Ashlinn's own.

"You fought bravely in the arena," Ash said.

"It's easy to do that with Mister Kindly and Eclipse by my side."

"And yet you come here alone. That couldn't have been easy."

Mia shook her head. "It wasn't."

"So don't sell yourself cheap, Corvere. There's no one alive who can do the things you do. You're the bravest person I know. Goddess, when you leapt after Bladesinger, I was so afraid . . ." Ashlinn shook her head, gave Mia a playful slap on the leg. "Don't do anything that stupid again, you hear me?"

"I couldn't let her fall, Ashlinn."

The girl's gaze softened, a slow frown forming between her brows.

"Why not?"

"She saved my life."

"And in saving hers, you risked your own." Ash shook her head, blue eyes glittering. "That's not why we're here, Mia. This is bigger than the life of one gladiatii. This is the future of the entire Republic. The end of a tyranny that's been allowed to fester for far too long. The end of the Red Church, the end of—"

"I know why we're here, Ashlinn. I'm no hero. I'm no fucking savior. This is *my* plan, remember?"

". . . I don't seem to be the one who needs reminding."

Mia scowled, pulled herself free of Ashlinn's embrace. Prowling to the bureau, she found her cigarillos, struck her flintbox. She inhaled deep despite the pain in her ribs, feeling the sugared warmth spread over her tongue, tingling on her lips.

"Maggot's dead," she sighed.

". . . What? How?"

"Arkades apparently dosed our evemeal with Elegy. He was working with Leonides. Leona has to sell a bunch of gladiatii to stave her father off long enough to fight me at the *magni*. But the gladiatii have caught wind of their sale."

". . . And how do they feel about that?"

"How the fuck do you think?" Mia folded her arms and leaned on the wall, cigarillo hanging from her mouth. "They're set to rebel. Sidonius is trying to convince me to help. He knows I can escape the cells, let the rest of them out. If they struck in the nevernight, they'd cut through Leona's guards like piss through snow."

"Shit," Ashlinn breathed. "How are you going to stop them? Tell Leona?"

Mia looked at Ash, dragging hard on her smoke.

"Who says I'm going to stop them?"

". . . What?"

"They don't deserve to die, Ash. Not a one of them. Not for this."

"Mia," Ashlinn said. "I know you feel a kinship for these people, believe me, I do. But you were always too mindful of others, even as an acolyte. I warned you then, and I'm warning you now."

Mia scowled at the girl on the bed. That old, delicious anger eating all her fear.

"Ash, if I'd not spared that boy's life in my final trial, I'd have been there when you poisoned the initiation feast. I'd have been trussed up like Hush and the others, completely at the Luminatii's mercy."

"I wouldn't have let that happen."

"You couldn't have stopped them," Mia replied. "Remus would have gutted me as soon as he got his hands on me. So don't fool yourself. If I'd not shown mercy and failed my trial, I'd be dead just like Tric."

Ash flinched. Drew a long, shaking breath.

"You throw that at me every time we argue. It's not fair, Mia."

"O, and what you did to him was?"

"Look, I'm sorry Tric had to die," Ash said. "I know you cared for him. I liked him too. But that's my *point,* Mia. *Everyone* has someone who cares for them. The gladiatii you've killed in the arena, the Luminatii you slaughtered at the Mountain—each of them was someone's daughter or someone's son. Each of them had someone to mourn them. This is bigger than one person, or even a thousand. This is the future of the Republic. And this is *everything* you've worked for."

Mia scowled, dragging hard on her cigarillo. Ashlinn climbed off the bed, walked to Mia, and took hold of her hand.

"You were born for this. And I think you know that. The moment your father chose to rise against the Republic, you were fated for great and terrible things. But fate wouldn't have chosen you if you weren't strong enough to bear the weight of it. I know you're frightened. I know you're hurting. But we're *so* close now. You can do this. You're the strongest person I know. That's one of the reasons I love you, Mia Corvere."

Clove-scented smoke curled through her fingers, floating into the air and weaving with the words that still hung heavy about her head.

". . . What did you say?"

Ash leaned in and entwined her hands with Mia's. Pressed her body to Mia's. Placed her lips on Mia's. The kiss was soft and sweet and dizzying, the floor falling away from her feet, wrapping her up in the scent of lavender and burning cloves and an aching, sighing want. All the world stopped spinning. All of time stood still.

"I said I love you, Mia Corvere," Ash whispered.

For people like us, there are no promises of forever . . .

". . . mia . . ."

Mia caught her breath, heart pounding in her chest. Tearing her gaze from Ashlinn's eyes, she saw a familiar shape sitting on the windowsill. A not-cat, cleaning his paw with his not-tongue.

"What is it?" she asked.

". . . furian . . . ," Mister Kindly replied.

She'd run like a mad thing back up the hill, cloak flapping behind her, not even bothering to hide beneath her mantle of shadows. If someone from the Rest marked her, so be it, but the repercussions from the collegium's champion being spotted by some random stranger in the street would pale in comparison to what would happen if the guards found her missing from her cell. She'd been a fool, risking a visit with so much in flux. Cursing herself an idiot and trying to forget the fact that Ashlinn Järnheim . . .

Ashlinn Järnheim said she loves me.

Mia pushed the thought aside, pain jarring her ribs every time her foot struck the road.

"He's awake?" she gasped.

". . . he is stirring. if they call on you . . ."

"I know."

". . . you risk too much, mia. all now hangs in the balance . . ."

"I *know.*"

". . . do you really . . . ?"

Mia grit her teeth and ran, cursing herself again. Mister Kindly was right. Ashlinn, too. She *was* growing soft. The Mia she knew had been driven. Singleminded. Burning with desire for one thing, and one thing alone. She couldn't afford these kinships anymore. The risks they made her take, all that would be undone if she failed here . . .

A safe distance from the Nest, she slung on her mantle of shadows, Stepping across the portcullis as she'd done a dozen times now and feeling her way down to the barracks. Reaching out to the dark, she Stepped across to the shadows of her cell, falling to her knees and clutching her burning chest. Her breath was fire, head swimming, skin filmed with sweat. But after her desperate dash, all seemed quiet—if Furian had woken, it seemed Leona or her guards hadn't yet seen a need for her.

Goddess, that could have been bad . . .

She threw aside her mantle, faded into view there in the dark of the barracks, amid the sighs and snores and sounds of sleep. Lying in one strawlined corner, Sidonius slowly opened his eyes—the man seemed to have an uncanny knack for sensing when she'd returned. Or perhaps when she'd left.

"Trouble sleeping?" he murmured, pawing at his lashes. "I've just the cure."

Mia scowled and didn't reply, not feeling like another lesson on the benefits of a clear conscience. She heard heavy footsteps coming down the stairs, the keys being turned in the mekwerk beside the barracks gate. Sidonius sat up a little straighter, eyes narrowed as three guards approached, fully armed and armored.

"Rest easy," she said. "They're here for me."

"I rest easy enough, Mia," he whispered. "And I've faith you will too."

The trio of guards arrived at her cell, led by Captain Gannicus.

"The Unfallen has woken," the guard said. "He is in pain. Dona Leona left orders you were to be roused if he did, and afforded all courtesy. With Maggot gone . . ."

"Aye, I'll see to it," Mia sighed. "Take me to him, if it please you."

The guards unlocked her cell and Mia stood. Sidonius watched as she was marched out through the barracks, up into the keep and out to the infirmary. Her mind was still whirling, trying to ponder what to do about Sidonius's budding rebellion, the right and wrong of it all. Ashlinn's and Mister Kindly's words swimming in her head. Her heart was torn—the vengeance that had driven her all these years weighed against the thought of allowing Sid and the others to die.

What was more important?

Revenge for a mother and father it turns out she barely even knew? Or the lives of folk who, try as she might to deny it, had become her friends?

The hour was late, but as she approached, Mia could hear choice cursing from within. Stepping inside, she saw Furian on his slab, damp with sweat. His arms and legs were strapped down, the bandages around his chest spotted with blood.

"Fool tried to tear off the dressings," Gannicus muttered. "We had to bind him."

"There's fucking *maggots crawling on me*!" Furian moaned.

"Leave me with him," Mia told Gannicus. "I'll see to his hurts. If you could tell Finger to set some vinegar boiling, I'd be indebted."

"Aye, Champion," the guard said.

Nodding to his cohorts, Gannicus left a pair stationed outside the infirmary door, and strode off to wake the cook. Mia walked into the infirmary, noted that Bladesinger wasn't lying on her slab. She must have been moved back down to her cell sometime in the nevernight—it was still too soon for her to have been sold off to Caito. Which meant she and Furian would be alone . . .

The man looked her up and down, a dark scowl on that handsome brow. The hunger in her surged as it always did when he was near. He still looked on the south side of awful, his long hair lank with sweat, his skin sallow. But he was awake, alert, dark eyes fixed on the silver torc around her neck.

"She named you champion?" he whispered.

"I didn't ask her for it," Mia replied. "But truthfully, none knew if you'd awaken."

"So she gives away my torc before I'm even cold, and leaves me here to rot?"

"You're not rotting," Mia sighed.

"I've fucking flyspawn crawling all over me!"

"The maggots are removing flesh turned septic by the Exile's venom. They saved your life. And if you don't calm down and stop thrashing against those straps, you're going to start yourself bleeding again." Mia poked among the shelves, collecting ingredients. "The pain can't be pleasant, though. I'll fix you something for it."

Furian's head sank back against the slab, voice heavy with fatigue. "Has Domina named you nursemaid, as well as champion? Where is Maggot?"

Mia pressed her lips together, grinding the ingredients with a mortar and pestle.

"Maggot's dead."

Furian's scowl softened, bewilderment in his eyes. "How?"

"Arkades slipped a dose of Elegy into everyone's evemeal. Maggot and Otho both succumbed before I could brew an antidote."

". . . Arkades?"

"Aye."

"Horseshit," Furian whispered. "Arkades was gladiatii. A man like him looks his enemies in the eye and delivers them with a sword, not a bitter mouthful."

Mia shrugged, and carefully sniffing a cup of water, mixed her powder into it. Carrying the cup to Furian, she put it to his lips, watching his shadow tremble and ripple about its edges. Her own shadow edged closer, like iron to a magnet. All the questions swimming in her mind. What am I? What are we? Why? Who? How?

"It's only fadeleaf and a bit of ginwort," she said. "It will ease the pain."

The Unfallen stared with narrowed eyes.

"You saved my life, Furian," Mia said. "That's a debt not soon forgot. If I wanted you dead, I could have fixed it so you never woke. Now drink."

The former champion grunted assent, and swallowed the draft as Mia poured. His head drifted back to the slab and he sighed, staring at the ceiling and flexing his wrists against his restraints.

"I remember . . . after the match . . . you took my pain away."

"A home remedy," Mia shrugged. "Easy enough to brew."

"No," Furian said, shaking his head. "Before you gave me the sleeping draft. When I was on the slab, screaming. When your . . . when our shadows touched."

Mia frowned, remembering that moment beneath Whitekeep arena. As her shadow had darkened, she'd felt *more* pain, not less—Furian's agony mixed in with her own. She supposed that she might somehow be sharing his burden, but apparently she'd lessened his pain by taking it upon herself?

Why?

Who?

How?

"I didn't know I could do that," she confessed. "I've never done it before."

Furian said nothing, watching her with those dark, pretty eyes. She could see the draft she'd given him taking effect, smoothing the lines of pain away from his face.

"I . . . wanted to thank you, Furian," Mia said. "For calling the dark in the arena. The Exile would have ended me and 'Singer if not for you."

"You cheated," he replied. "You did something to the silkling's blades."

"You twisted her shadow. I suppose that makes us both cheaters, neh?"

The Unfallen remained mute for an age, simply staring. When he finally spoke, it was with hesitation, as if compliments didn't sit well upon his tongue.

"You risked your life for a sister gladiatii," he said. "You risked your life for *me*. Trickery aside, you still showed loyalty to this collegium. Only fitting that it be repaid."

"Was that a compliment?" Mia asked. "'Byss and blood, perhaps I mixed too much fadeleaf in with your tea?"

Furian allowed himself a small smile. "Don't let it swell your head, girl. I'll be reclaiming my torc as soon as I'm able to lift a blade. When I fight at the *magni,* make no mistake—it will be as champion of this collegium."

Mia shook her head, again trying to figure out the puzzle of this man. He'd treated her with nothing but disdain, spoken of their gifts with the darkness as witchery. But when push came to shove, he'd werked the shadows so that the Falcons could best the Exile. Morality aside, it seemed he was prepared to sacrifice anything for victory.

"Why is all this so important to you?" she asked.

"I have told you before, Crow. This is what I *am*."

"That's no kind of reason," Mia sighed. "You weren't *born* gladiatii. You must have had a life before all this."

Furian shook his head. Blinking slow.

"I'd not call it such."

"So what were you? Murderer? Rapist? Thief?"

Furian stared, hidden thoughts swirling behind those bottomless eyes. But the fadeleaf was kicking in now, and the sliproot she'd mixed in with the concoction was loosening his tongue. She felt guilty about dosing him in the hopes he'd open up, but she wanted to understand this man, try to gauge where he'd stand if Sidonius and the others rose in rebellion.

"Murderer, rapist, thief," Furian replied, his voice thick. "All that and more. I was a beast who lined his pockets with the miseries of men. And women. And children."

"What did you do?"

Furian looked to the walls around them, the rusted steel and iron bars.

"I filled places like this. Flesh, my bread, and blood, my wine."

". . . You were a slaver?"

Furian nodded, speaking soft. "Captained a ship for years. The *Iron Gull*. Ran the Ysiir coast all the way to Nuuvash, eastern Liis from Amai to Ta'nise. Sold the men to the fighting pits, women to the pleasure houses, children to whoever wanted them." A heavy shrug. "If that turned out to be no one, we'd just put them over the side."

"'Byss and blood," Mia said, lip curling in revulsion.

"You judge me."

"You're fucking right I do," she hissed.

"No harsher than I judge myself."

"I find that hard to believe," Mia said, her voice turning to steel.

"Believe what you will, Crow. People always do."

"So how came you to be here, then?"

Furian closed his eyes, breathing long and deep. For a moment, Mia thought perhaps he'd drifted off to sleep. But eventually he spoke, his voice heavy with fatigue and something darker still. Regret? Shame?

"We raided a village in Ysiir," he said. "One of the men we brought aboard was a missionary of Aa. Rapha, his name. I let the men have their sport with him. We weren't really that fond of priests, you see. We beat him. Burned him. In the end, we chummed the water for drakes, and I told him to walk the plank. Looking down into that blue, you see the measure of a person in their eyes. Some beg. Some curse. Some don't even have the legs to carry them. You know what Rapha did?"

"I'd not guess," Mia shrugged. "I'm not that fond of priests either."

"He prayed Aa would forgive us," Furian said. "Standing on that plank, a thirty-foot stormdrake circling beneath him. And the bastard starts *praying* for us."

The Unfallen shook his head.

"I'd never seen the like. So I let him live. I didn't really know why at the time. He sailed with us almost a year. Taught me the gospel of the Everseeing. Taught me that I was lost, nothing but an animal, but that I could find my humanity again if I embraced the Light. But he also told me that I must atone for all the evil I'd done. And so, after a year of it, of reading and arguing, of hating and blustering and crying to myself in the long hours of the nevernight, I accepted the Everseeing into my life. Turned my back on the darkness. I sailed us to the Hanging Gardens. And I sold myself."

"You . . ." Mia blinked.

"Seems mad, doesn't it? What kind of fool would choose this?"

Mia thought of her own plight, her own plan, slowly shaking her head.

"But . . . *why*?"

"I knew Aa would give me a chance to redeem myself if I placed myself in his keeping. And he put me here. A place of tribulation, and purity, and suffering. But at the end, on the sands of the *magni,* when I kneel before the grand cardinal drenched in my victory, he will not only declare me free, but a free *man*. Not an animal, Crow. A *man*.

"And there, I will be redeemed."

Furian nodded, took a deep breath, as if he'd purged a poison from his blood.

Mia folded her arms and scowled.

"So that's it?" she demanded. "You think you can atone for selling hundreds of men and women by murdering hundreds more? You can't clean your hands by washing them in other people's blood, Furian. Trust me, that only gets them redder."

Furian shook his head and scowled. "I do not expect you to understand. But *magni* is a holy rite. Judged by the hand of God himself. And if Rapha taught me anything, it was that the things we *do* are more important than the things we've *done*."

Mia heard footsteps behind, a knock at the infirmary door. Gannicus marched into the room, two more guards beside him, carrying a steaming pot between them.

"Your vinegar, boiled as requested."

Mia nodded, turning to Furian.

"I'm going to get rid of the maggots now. This is going to be painful."

"Life always is, little Crow. Life is pain, and loss, and sacrifice."

Furian grit his teeth and closed his eyes.

"But we should welcome that pain. If it brings us salvation."

———

S he returned to her cage, flanked by two of the houseguards. Sidonius
opened his eyes as the cell door closed behind her, the mekwerk lock
twisting closed. Mia had watched carefully from beneath her lashes on the
way in here, noting which key on the iron ring opened the barracks gate, controlled her cell door.

Was this the right thing to do?

Would they understand, at the end, that she'd done it all for the best?

"I spoke to Furian," she whispered once the guards were gone.

"About what?" Sidonius muttered.

"Who he is. How he thinks. Where he's from." She shook her head. "He
dreams only of the *magni*. He'd never do anything to put it at risk. I think
he's still too ill to stand in our way, but when we rise, there's no chance he'll
stand with us."

"When *we* rise?"

"Aye, brother."

Mia reached out in the dark, squeezed Sidonius's hand.

"We."

RISE

It was a lot to risk on a single girl.

Sidonius's belly was a knot of raw nerves, his appetite a distant memory.
Five turns had passed since Mia proposed her plan in the gloom of their cell,
and Sid hadn't slept much since. Instead, he'd paced back and forth in his cage
through the nevernight, staring at the mekwerk lock on the door and counting the hours until it began.

Mia had been moved into her champion's quarters three turns back, so Sid
found himself alone for the first time since moving to Crow's Nest. Alone with
the fear of what was to come, the risk they were all taking, the fate that awaited
them if they failed. He was placing so much faith in Mia, and so much rode
on her shoulders. He'd served Darius Corvere faithfully, saw the traits he'd
admired in the man looming large in his daughter. Courage. Intelligence. Fe-

rocity. But Mia had lost her father when she was only a child, and since then, fallen into the company of shadows and killers.

Sidonius liked her. But could he truly say he knew her?

Could he *trust* her?

Dona Leona had met with Varro Caito three nevernights back, and skulking beneath their table as they drank and dined, Mia's daemon had overheard their every word. Leona had apparently plied the fleshpeddler with honeyed words and honeyed wine, brokering sale of Bryn, Butcher, Felix, Albanus, Bladesinger, and Sidonius himself. The price was a rich one, and Leona would be able to meet the first of her father's repayments, but the cost was steep. The collegium would be gutted, with only Mia, Wavewaker, and Furian remaining. Leona would risk all on one final throw at the *magni*. But she hadn't reckoned on her Falcons throwing dice of their own.

Evemeal had been quiet, the gladiatii subdued. Whispers of the plan had been passed on in the bathhouse, around the practice dummies. All agreed the chances of success were so thin they'd fall through a crack in the cobbles, and Sid could smell fear in the air. It was one thing to risk death in the arena, another thing entirely to pit yourself against the Republic. The administratii. The Senate itself. Every one of them knew this was a step that could never be taken back. The brands on their cheeks would begin to fade only a few minutes after their deaths, so there was no hiding who and what they were if they wanted to keep breathing. To be an escaped slave in the Republic was to be forever on the run.

Still, better to run than die on your knees.

Even with the few extra turns' rest, Bladesinger was still wounded, her back and arm wrapped in heavy gauze. Mia's ribs were yet bruised, but at least she could use both eyes again. Wavewaker and Sidonius had yet to fully recover from their last arena bout, and Butcher was still limping—they weren't the most fearsome fighting force ever arrayed, to be sure. But they'd have surprise on their side if all went well, and they were trained gladiatii, each and every one.

Their sale was set to happen on the morrow.

Caito had already paid the deposit.

Truth told, it was now or never.

Nevernight had fallen, cool winds kissing ochre walls, dust devils dancing in the yard. After Arkades's betrayal, Dona Leona had doubled the patrols around the house, and the guards were omnipresent. But still, whispers and secret nods were exchanged among the gladiatii, and all seemed in readiness.

But Daughters, the waiting . . .

They sat in the dark, no one speaking, no one moving. Watching the arkemical globes slowly dim, the sounds of the keep above gradually fading. Sid could hear Bladesinger chanting inside her cell—some final prayer to Mother Trelene for good fortune, no doubt. Looking at the cell across the passage, he saw Butcher on his haunches, rocking back and forth and raring to go.

He was reminded of his time in the legion. The nevernight before a battle was always the worst. He'd had his faith in Aa to sustain him back then. His loyalty to his justicus. The solace of his brother Luminatii, and the certainty that what they did was Right. All that was gone now—just a clean conscience and a coward's brand upon his chest to show for it. Instead of brother Luminatii, he had brother and sister gladiatii. Instead of faith in the Everseeing and the commands of his justicus, he was placing all his faith in his seventeen-year-old daughter.

It was a lot to risk on a single girl.

Sidonius heard a soft thud, the faint ring of metal on stone. Butcher heard it too, rising to his feet, hands wrapped around the bars of his cell. Mia had two options to break them free once she stole out from her room; either somehow brute force the mekwerk controls to release the inner cell doors, or acquire the master key from the guard patrol. Sid had no idea which way she'd go. But his stomach thrilled as he saw a silhouette creeping down the stairs to the cellar antechamber, a wooden truncheon clutched in one hand, and what looked to be an iron key in the other.

"'Byss and blood, she did it," Butcher grinned.

Twisting the key in the mekwerk, Mia unlocked the cell doors, raised the portcullis, Sidonius wincing at the soft grinding of stone on iron. The gladiatii stole out of the barracks, gathering in the antechamber, all fierce grins and bundled nerves. Sidonius gave Mia a quick embrace, his voice a whisper.

"No trouble?"

Mia shook her head. "Four guards down. The other two are in the front yard."

"Let's be about it, then," Wavewaker whispered.

"Aye," the girl nodded. "And quietly, for fucksakes."

Mia led the group up the stairs, where the bodies of four of Leona's houseguards were laid out on the tile. The men were armored in black leather, falcon feathers pluming their helms, Captain Gannicus among them. Each had been bludgeoned into unconsciousness. The gladiatii quickly stripped their armor, Sidonius, Wavewaker, Butcher, and Felix donning the garb instead. Not only would the boiled leather protect them if things turned ugly, but the high cheek guards would do a fine job of covering the brands on their cheeks.

Weapons were handed out—wooden truncheons and shortswords. In the far distance, Sid heard fourbells being rung down in Crow's Rest, the crash of waves upon a rocky shore. The garish light of the two suns streamed in through the open windows, silken curtains rippling as the rebel gladiatii stole through the keep.

They moved quietly as they could, down the entrance hall to the locked front doors. Butcher and Wavewaker lifted the bar aside, the gladiatii gathering in a small knot at the threshold.

"Ready?" Sidonius asked.

"Aye." Bladesinger raised her sword in her off-hand.

Mia opened the door, and the gladiatii charged soundlessly toward the front portcullis. It took a few moments for the guards to process what they were seeing, and by then, it was too late. One reared back gurgling as Sidonius clubbed him square in the throat. Wavewaker crashed into the other guard, smashing him into the guardhouse wall. The man raised his truncheon, his shout becoming a muffled whimper as Mia clapped her hand over his mouth and buried her knee in his bollocks. He dropped like a stone, and the girl snatched up his club as it fell, cracked it across his head and laid him flat out in the dirt.

Butcher ratcheted up the portcullis as Bladesinger and Albanus stripped the last two guards, began strapping on their breastplates. Mia was too small to wear any man's kit, and besides, there weren't enough unconscious guards to go around. Instead, she threw a cloak she'd gotten from only Aa knew where about her shoulders, pulled the hood low over her eyes.

"Right," she whispered. "We make for the *Gloryhound* in the harbor."

"Walk tall, look folk in the eye," Bladesinger reminded them. "We win this game by appearing as if we belong, aye?"

The gladiatii nodded, and calmly as they could, marched out from the portcullis in neat formation and started tromping down the road. Mia brought up the rear, hood pulled low. Wavewaker's armor didn't fit too well across his broad shoulders, Bladesinger's arm was still swathed in bandages and spotted with blood—under scrutiny, their disguises wouldn't last. But the hour was late, and the port below the Nest was quiet. Hopefully the subterfuge would hold long enough for them to get aboard.

Marching out in front, Sidonius tried to keep his nerves in check. This die was cast, and whatever happened now was in the hands of fate, but Daughters, it was hard not to just break into a run, get as far as he could as fast as possible. The troupe walked down the dusty road encircling Crow's Nest, Sid staring out at the blue waters of the Sea of Swords. Marching into the town, they passed a few farmers on the way to market, a messenger rushing about on his master's business, a handful of urchins gathered around a loaf of stolen bread. Not a one of them paid any mind.

He could see the tall masts of ships looming over the harbor now, his heart beating faster. Thinking of that vast blue ocean, the places they could sail, any place but here. He looked to the other gladiatii, risked a smile, Bryn grinning back, Wavewaker whispering, "Hold steady." Marching closer, the smell of salt in the air, the screeching of gulls like music in his ears, every step bringing them ne—

"Look alive," Bladesinger muttered. "Soldiers ahead."

Sid grit his teeth but didn't break stride, noting the quartet of legionaries from the Crow's Rest garrison marching down the other side of the street. He'd no clue if the local soldiery mixed with Leona's houseguards—men of the sword had a tendency to gather and gripe no matter who they worked for. But at a distance, their disguises should pass, and it was only a few hundred feet to the harbo—

"I know you," said a voice.

Sidonius stopped, looked behind them. A young redheaded girl wearing the feathered cap and pack of a traveling peddler had stopped in the street, pointing at Mia.

"Four Daughters, I *know* you," she repeated. "You're the Savior of Stormwatch!"

Mia shot a warning look to the others, gave the girl a small smile. "Aye, Dona."

"I saw you slay the retchwyrm!" the girl cried, her blue eyes shining. "Merciful Aa, what a fight! I've never seen the like!"

"My thanks, Mi Dona," Mia muttered. "But I've ma—"

"Look here!" the peddler cried to the street. "The Savior of Stormwatch!"

"Here they come," Wavewaker muttered.

Sid's stomach flipped as he realized the legionaries had overheard the peddler, and all four were now crossing the street. Their centurion saw the ornate plume on Sidonius's helm and called out in greeting.

"Ho, Gannicus! What brings you lazy bastards down here at this . . ."

The centurion stopped, squinting at Sidonius's face through the slits in his helm.

". . . Gannicus?"

"Go!" Mia cried.

The gladiatii charged, weapons drawn. The centurion and his men fumbled with their swords, faces bleached with panic. It had been truncheons and fists for Leona's houseguards, but there was no room for mercy here—these were fully armed and armored Itreyan legionaries, trained to kill. Wavewaker drove his blade through the centurion's chest, skewering him like a pig at spit. Butcher smashed another's blade aside, spun, and took his throat clean out, scarlet spraying in the air with the salt. The peddler started screaming, running down the street crying, "Murder! *Murder!*" as Sidonius finished off another legionary with a flash of his sword. Albanus ended the last of them, cutting the legionary's legs out from under him before burying his blade in the join between the man's shoulder and neck.

"Make for the harbor," Mia cried. "Go! Go!"

They broke into a run, all semblance of propriety gone. Sid's sandals pounding the cobbles, folks turning to stare as they dashed past, the cries of *Murder!* from up the street growing louder. They reached the docks, barreling past sailors and merchantmen unloading their stock, fishermen on the wharf. Wavewaker was running beside him, Bryn out in front, Mia bringing up the rear, all of them splashed with blood. He could see the *Gloryhound* at anchor, perhaps a hundred yards out in the bay.

"There she is," he gasped.

Sid dropped over the side of the wharf into the *'Hound*'s longboat. The other gladiatii jumped in beside him, Butcher and Wavewaker taking up the oars and rowing as if their lives depended on it. Sid could hear bells ringing now, the alarm spreading through Crow's Rest and waking the residents from their sleep, the fearful cry echoing up and down their quiet streets.

"Rebellion!"

"The Falcons in revolt!"

Butcher and Wavewaker leaned hard on the oars, each stroke bringing them closer to the *'Hound*. Bladesinger shielded her eyes against the water's glare, nodding at the empty masts.

"Sails are stowed."

"We can set them swift enough," Wavewaker grunted.

"Are you certain?" Butcher gasped.

"Rest easy, brother," Wavewaker nodded. "I was learning to sail while you were still suckling at your mother's teats."

"You only learned to sail last year?" Bryn grinned.

"Let's leave my mother's teats out of this, aye?" Butcher growled.

"Talk softer, row harder," Sidonius said.

They reached the *'Hound*, scrambling up the rope ladder and onto the deck. The ship rolled and swayed with the sea, sunlight burning in that endless blue sky. A lone watchman came down from the bow, demanding to know what they were about, but a backhand from Wavewaker sent him to the boards, moaning and bloodied. From up on deck, Sid could see movement around the docks; a handful of legionaries, mariners pointing in their direction.

"We need those sails up now, 'Waker."

"Aye," the man nodded. "They'll be down in the hold. All of you, with me."

Wavewaker threw aside the large oaken hatch that sealed the '*Hound*'s hold, climbed swiftly down the ladder into the ship's belly. Bladesinger hopped down second, Sidonius and the other gladiatii following while Mia and Bryn remained on deck to keep watch. Sunlight filtered through the timber lattice above their heads, illuminating the ship's belly, and the gladiatii spread out, searching for the great sheets of canvas that would see them under way. Crates and barrels, coils of salt-crusted rope and heavy, iron-bound chests. But . . .

"I can't see them," Bladesinger said.

"They must be here somewhere," Wavewaker growled. "Keep looking."

"Why the 'byss would they stow the sails anyw—"

Sid heard scuffling footsteps, a soft curse above their heads. Squinting up through the lattice, he saw two struggling figures, silhouetted against the light. Bryn was one of them—he could tell from the topknot. But the figure behind her, arm wrapped around her neck, looked like . . .

"Mia?" he whispered.

He heard a gasp, a wet thud as Bryn toppled into the hold and landed atop a great coil of rope with a groan. And as Sid opened his mouth to shout warning, the trapdoor above them slammed closed, sealing them all in the '*Hound*'s hold.

"What the 'byss?" Wavewaker hissed.

Sidonius was kneeling beside Bryn, the girl barely conscious, red marks at her throat. He looked up through the latticework hatch, belly churning, his mouth suddenly dry as dust.

"Crow?" he called. "What are you playing at?"

"I'm sorry, Sidonius," he heard the girl reply, voice thick with sorrow. "But I told you once already. The last thing I'm doing here is playing."

Butcher climbed the ladder, pounded at the hatch with his sword, trying to break it open. "What the fuck goes on here?"

The gladiatii met each other's eyes, confusion and dread in every stare. They were sealed in the '*Hound*'s belly like fish in a barrel, no one to fight, no way out.

"This is how you repay me?" came a voice.

Sidonius looked up, drawing a shivering breath as he saw Dona Leona walking the deck above his head. Instead of nevernight attire, she was dressed in black, her eyes kohled, hair braided as if for war.

"After all I have done for you," Leona said, staring down at the gladiatii trapped in the hold. "Raising you up from the mire. Feeding and sheltering you beneath my roof. Drenching you in glory and the honor of my collegium's name. This is my thanks?"

"Crow," Wavewaker spat, prowling in circles and looking up at the deck. "Crow, what have you *done*?"

"She has done what no other among you had the courage to do," Leona said. "She has remained *loyal* to her domina."

"You bleeding fucking *cunt*!" Butcher roared, slamming his arm against the hatch. "I'll fucking *kill you*!"

"You'll do no such thing," Leona answered. "You will languish in that hold until I decide your fate. And I fear it shall be an unpleasant one, traitor."

"You call us traitors?" Bladesinger shouted. "I brought you honor at White-keep. Crow would *never* have stood victor if not for me! And you give me thanks by selling me to that shitheel Varro Caito before my wounds are even healed?"

The woman spat onto the wood at her feet.

"You faithless fucking bitch."

Leona sneered, shook her head.

"All I hear are treacherous rats, squeaking in a hole of their own making."

Butcher was smashing at the hatch with his sword. Wavewaker pushing at the timbers above their head. A half-dozen houseguards spilled out from the 'Hound's main cabin to surround the dona—the second shift, all of whom should have been slumbering right now in their bunks. There could be no doubt now that Leona had known this was coming, that all the faith they'd put in the daughter of Darius Corvere . . .

Sidonius clenched his fists as he looked up through the lattice. Mia met his stare, dark eyes clouded, her expression grim and bloodless. The scar cutting down her cheek lent her a vicious air, a cruelty and callousness he'd never noticed until now. But still, he fancied he could see tears in those dark lashes, her long dark hair caught up in the nevernight winds and playing about her face like some black halo.

"Crow?"

"It just meant too much to me, Sid," she whispered.

She shook her head, hands fluttering helplessly at her sides.

"I'm so sorry . . ."

It had been a lot to risk on a single girl.

But he'd never thought for a moment they'd actually lose.

"Aye, little Crow."

Sidonius hung his head, pawing at his aching chest.

"I'm sorry too . . ."

INTERLUDE

Two passengers met in a dirty alley, in a little city by the sea.

The first was small, thin as whispers, cut in the shape of a cat. It had worn the seeming for over seven years now. It could barely remember the thing it had been before. A fraction of a deeper darkness, with only enough awareness to crawl from the black beneath Godsgrave's skin and seek another like itself.

Mia.

She'd lost her father, the turn they met. Hanged and dancing before the hoi polloi. She'd screamed, and made the shadows tremble, and he'd followed her call until he found her at her mother's side. The image of her father burned bright in her mind as he reached out and touched her. But she'd lost her kitten, too. Its neck broken in the hands of the justicus who'd stolen her father's title along with his life. A tinier wound. The kitten seemed a far more sensible shape to steal, in the end. Far better than the father. Far easier to love a simple thing.

She'd named him Mister Kindly. It fitted well enough. But somewhere deep inside, the cat who was not a cat knew that was not his name.

The second passenger was larger, had worn its shape for longer. She'd found her Cassius when he was but a boy. Beaten. Starving. Abused beyond reckoning. A child of the Itreyan wilds, dragged to the City of Bridges and Bones in chains, and there, almost drowned in misery. The boy's folk had hunted wolves—he'd remembered that much, even in his nadir. And the boy remembered wolves were strong and fierce. So she became a wolf for him, and together, they'd hunted all who stood in their way.

He'd named her Eclipse. It was close to the truth. But somewhere deep inside, the wolf who was not a wolf knew that was not her name either.

She missed him.

"... HELLO, MOGGY ...," the not-wolf said, resting on the wall of a lean-to inn.

"... hello, mongrel ...," the not-cat replied, atop a stack of empty barrels.

"... IT IS DONE, THEN ...?"

"... it is done ..."

The shadowwolf turned her not-eyes to the ocean, nodded once.

"... I WILL TELL ASHLINN SHE CAN REMOVE THAT RIDICULOUS TINKER'S PACK, THEN ..."

"... if you could convince her to drown herself in the ocean at the same time, i would sincerely appreciate it ..."

"... YOUR JEALOUSY FASCINATES ME, LITTLE MOGGY ..."

"... careful, dear mongrel, i do believe you just used a three-syllable word ..."

"... HOW COMES IT THAT ONE WHO FEASTS ON FEAR CAN BE SO AFRAID ...?"

"... i fear nothing ..."

"... YOU REEK OF IT ..."

"... be a darling and fuck right off, would you ...?"

"... NOTHING WOULD PLEASE ME MORE ..."

The wolf who was not a wolf began to fade, like a whisper on the wind. But the not-cat's plea held it still.

"... wait ..."

"... WHAT ...?"

Mister Kindly hung still for a moment, searching for the words.

"... are ... are you not afraid ...?" he finally asked.

"... OF WHAT ...?"

"... not of. for ..."

"... YOUR RIDDLES BORE ME, GRIMALKIN ..."

"... are you not afraid for her ...?"

The shadowwolf tilted its head.

"... WHY WOULD I BE ...?"

The not-cat sighed, searching the horizon.

"... i wonder sometimes, what we are making of her ..."

"... WE ARE MAKING HER STRONG. STEEL. RUTHLESS AS THE STORM AND THE SEA ..."

"... the thing we take from her ... i wonder if she does not need it ..."

"... YOU SPEAK OF FEAR ...?"

"... no, i speak of fashion sense ..."

"... WHAT NEED HAS SHE OF FEAR, MOGGY ...?"

"*. . . those who do not fear the flame are burned. those who do not fear the blade are bled. and those who do not fear the grave . . .*"

"*. . . ARE FREE TO BE AND DO WHATEVER THEY WISH . . .*"

"*. . . she is different than she once was. she was never this cold. this reckless . . .*"

"*. . . AND YOU BLAME ME FOR THAT . . .*"

"*. . . two of us feast where only one once fed. perhaps we take too much. perhaps we make* her *like this. callous. conniving. cruel . . .*"

"*. . . AND I AM CERTAIN THAT RECENT REVELATIONS ABOUT THE RED CHURCH, HER FAMILIA, HAVE NOTHING TO DO WITH HER CHANGE IN DEMEANOR . . .*"

"*. . . three-syllable word again . . .*"

"*. . . ARE WE FINISHED HERE, LITTLE MOGGY . . . ?*"

The not-cat looked to the sky, burning red and brilliant gold and blinding blue.

"*. . . a reckoning is coming, eclipse. it waits for us in the city of bridges and bones. i can feel it. like that accursed sun on the horizon. drawing closer with every breath . . .*"

"*. . . A GOOD THING, THEN, THAT WE DO NOT BREATHE . . .*"

Mister Kindly sighed.

"*. . . i hate you . . .*"

Eclipse laughed.

"*. . . GOOD . . .*"

And without another sound, she was gone.

A lone passenger sat in a dirty alley, in a little city by the sea.

It could barely remember the thing it had been before. A fraction of a deeper darkness. A larval consciousness, dreaming of shoulders crowned with translucent wings.

And she who would gift them.

Mia.

CHAPTER 31

TRUELIGHT

Godsgrave.

Mia stood on the deck of the *Gloryhound,* the ocean wind in her hair, staring out at the City of Bridges and Bones. The harbor was full, hundreds of sails scattered across that carpet of rolling blue, folk traveling from all corners to celebrate the greatest of Aa's feast turns in the glorious capital of the Republic.

Truelight, at last, was upon them.

Saai had finally crested the horizon as they sailed from Crow's Nest, that pale blue globe joining its gold and red siblings in the sky. The heat was blistering, and Mia was sickened by it, Mister Kindly curled up in her shadow, just as miserable as she. She could feel all the Light Father's fury, beating down upon her like hammers to the anvil. Bowing her head and walking the decks above people who'd once called her friend.

Sidonius and the others were chained in the hold, manacles about their wrists and ankles. They'd put up a courageous front, vowing to kill any of Leona's guards who came down into the hold to get them, but after three turns with no water in this awful heat, they were too weak to resist. The guards stormed the hold on the fifth turn, shackled them in irons. They'd been fed and watered every turn since then; they needed to be fit enough to wield weapons in their execution bouts, after all.

Mia had only avoided arrest because she'd aided in the insurgents' capture, and Furian, only by dint of his sickbed and Leona's sworn testimony before the administratii. The dona had taken a deposit from Varro Caito for the sale of her crop, but with word spreading through Crow's Rest about the uprising, she couldn't actually complete the transaction—no one would be fool enough to buy a pack of gladiatii who'd rebelled against their mistress.

And so, the dona had simply stolen Caito's deposit and put out to sea, taking the scenic route to Godsgrave and fixing to worry about the outraged fleshpeddler when she returned from the capital in triumph. With the coin she'd filched, along with the purse from Whitekeep and the small stipend she'd be paid for the execution bout, she had enough to manage the first repayment to her father. But if she didn't leave Godsgrave with the *Venatus Magni* won, she'd be utterly ruined.

Everything rested upon that single match.

Everything.

Mia rested her hands against the 'Hound's railing, the sunlight blazing on the ocean's face. She tried twisting the shadows at her feet, but it was near impossible; her grip on the darkness was weak, and trying to hold it was like holding smoke. It made sense, she supposed. Her powers had been at their height at truedark, and it was logical they'd be weakest when the Father of Light was strongest in the sky. But that didn't make her feel any better about her chances in the *magni*.

She stared out at the great Itreyan capital, heart in her throat. It had been months since she'd laid eyes upon it. Months of sweat and blood and tears. All the city was laid out before her, the broken archipelago shimmering in the sunlight. Every square foot was encrusted with tenements and shanties and graceful villas, clinging to the shoreline like barnacles on an old galley's hull. Above the cathedral spires and the looming War Walkers and the Senate House, rose the Ribs—those great, ossified towers stretching high into the sky, their bleached white glare almost blinding.

She'd spent much of her childhood inside her parents' apartment there. Far more than in Crow's Nest, truth told. Sitting with her mother and their servants, playing with her baby brother. If Crow's Nest had been their refuge, Godsgrave had been their world. She'd never managed to escape its pull for long.

The thought of her familia made her chest hurt, her eyes mist, all she'd broken and stolen, all the lives she'd taken and miles she'd run and years she'd studied, all of it would soon be justified. In two short turns, the *magni* would begin. In two short turns, she'd fight for her life and stand before Duomo and Scaeva upon that bloody sand, and scream her name as she slit their throats, ear to fucking ear.

It will be worth it.

She looked over her shoulder, down in the shadows of the hold beneath her feet. She could feel their stares upon her. The ones who'd called her friend.

All of it will be worth it.

"I knew you were a cold one, Crow," said a voice behind her. "But I never knew just how much ice flowed in your veins until now."

Mia stared at the Godsgrave skyline as Furian joined her by the rails. The Unfallen's long black hair blew in the sea breeze, bronzed skin glistening with a faint sheen of sweat. His chest was pitted and scarred, the flesh still scabbed, but with the three weeks he'd rested aboard ship, he was almost hale. Despite the three suns burning above, Mia's shadow trembled as he leaned closer. Glancing to their feet, she saw Furian's did the same.

"What do you mean?" she asked.

Furian looked out at the City of Bridges and Bones, dark eyes narrowed against the light. "I'm told you're to wield the blade in the execution bout."

"Domina needs the purse."

"O, I know it," Furian nodded. "And I know it is Domina's right to designate their executioner. I just didn't think you'd be willing to put Sidonius and the others in the dirt."

"We're the only two gladiatii Domina has left standing, Furian. Your wounds are barely healed enough to risk you in the *magni*. Unless Domina wants the execution purse to go to another collegium, who is she going to field? Should she stick a sword in Magistrae's hand and ask her to do the deed?"

Furian smiled. "Now, that would be a sight."

"Aye," Mia sighed. "It would at that."

Furian's smile died slow on his lips, his voice dropping to a murmur.

"Why did you do it?" he asked. "I've been meaning to ask."

Mia glanced at him sidelong, lips pursed. "Do what?"

"You know what I mean," he growled. "Bladesinger and the others thought of you as a friend. Yet Domina tells me that as soon as you got wind of their plan, you brought it straight to her. And not only did you foil their escape, but you fashioned a way they'd be captured *alive,* so they might be brought before the mob for justice."

"If they'd just been killed in their escape, Domina wouldn't have recouped a single coin for their loss," Mia said. "Leonides would have shut down the collegium. We wouldn't *be* here. But now, between the Whitekeep purse and the execution bou—"

"Aye, aye, I know all that," Furian growled, his temper fraying. "What I don't understand is why you didn't *help* them."

"Because I'm not a fucking hero, Furian. They want help, they can help themselves."

Mia turned to walk away, but the Unfallen grabbed her arm, teeth bared.

"Who the 'byss *are* you?" he demanded. "No nameless slip from Little Liis, that much is sure. I look in your eyes and I see intent. I see *design*. Ever since you set foot in our collegium, I've felt your hand at work. Like some shadow puppeteer ever pulling the strings, and we, the marionettes."

Mia snatched her arm free with a snarl. "Don't touch me."

"You've no loyalty to Leona," Furian growled. "I know it now. Even in our match at Whitekeep, risking your life to save Bladesinger, all of it was to further your own ends. You've betrayed those who called you sister. Murdered and lied and stole, all to stand here on the sands of the *magni* when you could just slip between the shadows and claim freedom anytime you choose. So *why in the Everseeing's name are you here?*"

Mia stared into those bitter, chocolate eyes, the darkness trembling at her feet. She'd once thought she and Furian were as much alike as truelight and truedark. But she saw that was a lie now. Saw the similarities between them, as deep as blood and bone. Both prisoners of their past. Both obsessed beyond reason with winning the *magni,* Furian for the sake of redemption, and Mia for revenge.

Mia clenched her jaw, shook her head. Tempted to speak. To look into his eyes and see if he'd grant her some measure of understanding. He of all people should. But this was pointless and she knew it. Furian sought absolution for his sins from the hands of a god. Mia sought to strike down the hands of that same god for their own sins. For one of them to stand the victor, the other would have to fall. And neither would be willing to step aside so that the other might win. This was no storybook. There was no love between them. No fellowship. Only rivalry.

And there was only one way it would end.

"Get your rest, Furian," Mia said.

She turned her eyes back to that blinding skyline.

"You're going to need it come weeksend."

D *rip.*
          Silver at her throat.
Drip.
Stone at her feet.
Drip.
Iron in her heart.

Mia sat in the dark beneath the arena, simply listening. Salt water fell from the ceiling above, splashing on the cell floor. All the years. All the miles.

On the morrow, one way or another, it would all end.

They'd been brought ashore yesterturn, once the administratii had sent approval for the execution bout. The calendar was packed—there had already been five full turns of games, and hundreds of prisoners had already been murdered by the state. The editorii were hard-pressed to find room for another execution bout in the morrow's festivities, but an entire gladiatii stable turning rotten could set a vile example for other collegia. And so, the Falcons of Remus were to be delivered to justice in a five-minute window after the final equillai race. Their lives snuffed out as folk waited for food, or dashed off to the lavatory before the main event.

And after midmeal, after their murders, the *magni* would begin.

Drip.

Drip.

Mia had sat alone in her cell and listened to the festivities, the roar of the colossal crowd shaking the very stone at her feet. Champions of each collegium were afforded a little privacy—her walls were stone, her bed was clean, two small arkemical globes shedding a warm, constant light. A small hatch in her heavy oaken door let in a whisper of fresh air, the smell of the kitchens, of blood, of oil and iron. She wondered what kind of conditions Sidonius and the others were being kept in. How much more they'd be forced to suffer before they walked onto the sand for the final time. Mister Kindly sat in her shadow, watching her with his not-eyes. Whispering that soon, one way or another, all this would be over.

She made no reply.

As she and Furian had been marched through the crowded marrowborn district and into the belly of Godsgrave Arena yesterturn, she'd been awed at the sheer size of the structure. She'd seen it as a younger girl, of course, but never this close. The arena's great oblong was carved directly out of the Spine itself, stretching a thousand feet, concentric rings of bleachers reaching four tiers high. Graceful arches and fluted buttresses, solid marble and gravebone throughout, statuary of the Everseeing and his Four Daughters encircling the outer ring. It was a marvel of engineering, testament to the ingenuity of the folk who'd designed it, the suffering of the slaves who'd built it, a monument to the awesome power, vision, and, above all, cruelty of the Itreyan Republic.*

---

*Godsgrave Arena was commissioned late in the reign of the Great Unifier, King Francisco I, though construction was not completed until his grandson, Francisco III, took the throne some thirty-six years later.

The principal architects were a husband and wife; Don Theodotus and Agrippina of the Familia Arrius. Theodotus was a man of sheer brilliance when it came to mekwerk, but his wife was simply a genius. The pair toiled their entire lives on the structure—it was rumored that Agrippina gave birth to their son, Agrippa, at her drafting table.

Agrippina died three turns after the final stone was placed in the arena's outer ring. Heartbroken at his love's passing, Theodotus joined her barely a week later.

The *venatus* was done for the turn, the crowd pouring out into the street with bright smiles and wide eyes. Cathedral bells tolled all over the city, calling the faithful to mass. With all three of the Everseeing's eyes open in the sky, the more devout citizens of the Republic were preparing for a nevernight of prayer and public piety, and the less religious sorts, an eve of private debauchery.

The excitement was arkemical, anticipation for the *magni* at a dizzying high. Mia could hear the thrum of the great mekwerks beneath her, as the priests of the Iron Collegium tested all would be ready for the morrow. This was the greatest event in the Itreyan calendar, a celebration of the Republic, and the God of Light. Tomorrow, the grandest spectacle beneath the suns would play out before the crowd's wondering eyes, the consul himself would crown Itreya's mightiest warrior with a laurel of gold, as the Hand of God himself granted that warrior their freedom.

It was the stuff legends were made of.

Drip.

Mia stared at nothing.

Drip.

Saying nothing.

Drip.

Listening instead to the echoes of the retiring crowd, the legionaries patrolling the arena's bowels, the swish of a broom as a slave made his way up the corridor outside. And most of all, to the thoughts inside her head.

This is not where I die.

She shook her head, clenched her fists.

I've far too much killing to do.

The broom stopped outside her door. She heard a whisper of cloth, the soft tune of metal on metal, the gentle click of the mekwerk lock at her door. A man entered, sweeping as he came, his back bent with age, gray hair standing in an unruly shock above a pair of piercing, familiar eyes.

"Well," the old man said, closing the door. "The accommodations are noth-

---

Statues of the pair stand side by side in the Visionaries' Row of the Iron Collegium, hands entwined, testament to the power of persistence, ambition and passion.

The script at the statues' base reads, "In love and stone, immortal."

That's the story, gentlefriends.

No punchline.

No sarcasm.

I thought you might want to hear something sweet, given what's about to happen . . .

ing to write home about, but the residents in this place are downright deplorable."

"Mercurio!"

Mia rose from the floor and crashed into his arms. The bishop of Godsgrave grinned wide, wrapped her up in a fierce embrace. She almost sobbed, feeling all the sorrow and pain of the last few turns suddenly weigh a little lighter. The tension bleeding out through her feet into the uncaring stone beneath her. She held on to him so tight he struggled to breathe, and he patted her on the back until she eased her grip, dragged her knuckles across her eyes.

" 'Byss and blood, it's good to see you," she breathed.

"And you, little Crow," her old mentor smiled.

"You look good," she said.

"You've looked better," he replied, touching the scar at her cheek. "How you faring in here?"

"Well enough," she shrugged. "Truelight is making it hard to werk the shadows. The food is shite. And I'm dying for a smoke."

"Well, the first two, I've no remedy for," the bishop said. "But the third . . ."

Mercurio reached into his threadbare tunic, pulled out a thin silver case. Mia's face lit up as he pulled out two cigarillos, lit them with a small flintbox. She practically snatched the offering out of the old man's hand, dragging the smoke into her lungs as if her life depended on it. Groaning, she leaned against the wall and tilted her head back, breathing a plume of clove-scented gray into the air and licking the sugar from her lips.

"Black Dorian's," she sighed.

"Best cigarillos in the 'Grave," Mercurio smiled.

"Maw's teeth, I could kiss you . . ."

"Save your gratitude for the morrow," he said. "You can thank me by not getting your fool self killed."

"That's the trick of it," she replied.

"Our young Dona Järnheim has filled me in on the particulars of your adventures while you've been absent the 'Grave," Mercurio said. "Thank the Black Mother she wasn't sending me regular updates or I'd have had a fucking heart attack."

"I'll admit the plan went slightly . . . awry . . ."

"Awry? It's all over the shop like a madman's shit, Mia. Solis has been on me like cheap silk on a two-beggar sweetboy. I've fended him off well enough 'til now, but his patience is worn thin." Mercurio grimaced, dragging on his cigarillo. "You're traveling in northern Vaan as we speak, just so you know. You missed catching the map bearer in Carrion Hall by a single turn."

"That was sloppy of me," Mia murmured.

"Aye, well, you were never my brightest student."

Mia smirked, inhaling another lungful of warm, sweet gray.

"I received a visit a few turns after you left, by the by," Mercurio said. "A friend of yours came poking around the necropolis."

". . . I don't have friends, Mercurio, you know that."

"A girl named Belle? She said to say you sent her."

Mia blinked, a slow remembering creeping up on her like a thief. She recalled the fourteen-year-old girl in the braavi pleasure house, with the bruise on her lip and too much hurt in her eyes.

"She came looking for you?" Mia smiled. "Good for her."

"I'm not in the business of taking in every stray that walks in off the street, Mia," he growled. "I'm a bishop of Our Lady of Blessed Murder, not a fucking charity worker."

Mia folded her arms, fixed Mercurio with her dark stare.

"I recall a stray who walked into the parlor of Mercurio's Curios not so long ago," she said. "A girl without a friend in the world, and a whole Republic arrayed against her. You took *her* in. You gave her a place to belong. You gave her love in a world where she'd thought there was nothing left but shit. And thinking on it now, I don't ever think she said thank you."

Mia placed a gentle kiss on the old man's cheek.

"So, thank you. For everything."

"Get off," he muttered, pushing her away.

"I know what it's cost you to help me," she said. "I know what you've risked to get me here. Scaeva and Duomo took my familia away, but I found another in you."

The old man cleared his throat, scowling.

"You're not going soft on me, are you, little Crow?"

"Wouldn't dream of it."

The old man blinked furiously, wiped his face.

"Fucking dusty in these cells."

"Aye," she smiled, pawing at her eyes. "It is at that. Is Ashlinn ready?"

"All's prepared. Do you still trust her?"

"With my life."

"I think she's got a soft spot for you."

Mia grinned around her cigarillo. "She always had bad taste."

Mercurio sighed, looked her deep in the eye.

"Are you certain you know what you're doing?"

"If I'm not, it's a little late to switch the song now," she shrugged. "I'll just dance until the music stops, and see where the steps take me."

"It's *not* too late, Mia. You can still change your mind."

"But that's the thing, Mercurio," she said. "I don't *want* to. Even if Mister Kindly and Eclipse weren't with me, I wouldn't be afraid. Every turn of the last seven years has been leading to this moment. I'll play the role that fate has given me. And amorrow, when the curtain falls on the final act, Scaeva and Duomo fall with it."

"Just remember," Mercurio scowled, "the play's final act needn't be your own."

"I've no wish to die," Mia sighed, crushing her smoke out against the wall. "To be honest, it sounds far more interesting to be the most wanted murderer in the Republic."

"A noble goal for any lass to aspire to," Mercurio smiled.

Mia grinned. "Well, you told me once I'd never be a hero."

Mercurio's eyes filled with tears. He wrapped her up in a tight embrace, pulled her close to his chest. And there in the dark, just the pair of them, holding the girl he thought of as his own, the old man whispered.

"I might have lied."

CHAPTER 32

GENTLY

Furian followed the path of a twisting canal through the marrowborn district, flanked on all sides by houseguards of the Remus Collegium. The hour was late, the heat only slightly eased by the cool nevernight winds blowing off the Sea of Silence. Revelry spilled from every taverna, smokehouse, and bordello, handsome dons and donas walking arm in arm, song and merriment ringing in the air.

The Unfallen had stomach for none of it.

The guards escorted him over the Bridge of Solace, along the edge of the Spine to a row of fine villas. They stood in the shadow of the fifth Rib, pale stone and ochre tile, flowers in the windowsills. Not the finest abodes in all of

Godsgrave, to be sure, but closer to a palace than any place he'd slept in his life.

The guards escorted him to the front door, where Magistrae awaited in a flowing gown of ocean blue, a sour look on her face.

"The domina requests your presence," the old woman said. "If it please you."

With a last glance at the guards, Furian stalked into the villa, up the winding stair. The walls were polished white marble, silken curtains rippling in the breeze, rich red carpet beneath his feet. He walked slow, unsure of the way, finally arriving at a set of double doors at the end of the hall.

She lay on the bed inside, long auburn hair streaming in delicate ringlets about her face. Her lashes were kohled ink black, her lips blood red. She was dressed in a gown of white silk, thin as gossamer, her soft curves and the delicious shadow between her thighs visible through the sheer fabric. Her wrists were wrapped in thin gold chains, her eyes glittering like the face of the ocean.

Leona opened her arms, beckoned him to the bed.

"Hello, lover."

M ia sat in the dark of her cell, on a simple cot made of straw, the gloom lightened only by a small arkemical globe. The hour was late, the heat only slightly eased by the cool nevernight breeze blowing in through the bars in the door. She could hear the distant sounds of steel on steel, mekwerk churning beneath the arena sands, the thunder of the crowd still echoing up in the bleachers.

Mia had stomach for none of it.

Guards patrolled the corridor outside, walking the row of champions' cells. They weren't the finest abodes in all of Godsgrave, to be sure, but the cells allowed a moment's privacy before the turn that would decide their occupants' lives.

Mia heard the mekwerk lock twist on her cell door, looked up to see a female guard standing upon the threshold.

"A moment of your time," she said. "If it please you."

The guard walked into the cell, closing the door behind her. The light was dim, her features hidden, but Mia still recognized her at once. The guard pulled off her helm, long red hair tumbling about her face. Her lashes were unpowdered, her lips bereft of paint. She was dressed in a black leather breastplate and skirt, the triple suns of the Itreyan legion on her breast. Her wrists were wrapped in thick leather bracers, her eyes as blue as sunburned skies.

Mia opened her arms, beckoned her to the cot.

"Hello, lover."

Leona pressed her lips to Furian's, mouth open, hungry. Her hands roamed his back, arkemical thrills running down his spine as she explored the troughs and valleys of muscle. Hands tangled in his long dark hair, Leona dragged him down onto the bed, sighing into his mouth. Her hands were everywhere, stroking, teasing, burning, Leona's sighs on his skin, hot as the sunlight outside.

"I want you," she breathed.

She straddled him, hair tumbling about his face, her kiss deepening as she moved her hips, grinding against him. Taking his hands, she placed them on her breasts, the heat of her skin, the scent of her perfume, the music of her sighs filling the room.

"I need you," she whispered.

Her kisses drifted lower, hands descending to unbuckle his belt, whisk off his loincloth. She left a trail of burning kisses down his scarred chest, across the rippling muscle at his belly, her tongue lapping at the sweat on his skin as she sank farther and farther down.

"I own you," she sighed.

"Stop," he whispered.

He took hold of Leona's chin, and gently pushed her away.

"*Stop.*"

Ash pressed her lips to Mia's, mouth open, hungry. Her hands roamed her back, arkemical thrills running down Mia's spine as she explored the smooth lines and graceful curves. Hands tangled in her long dark hair, Mia dragged her down onto the cot, sighing into her mouth. Her hands were everywhere, stroking, teasing, burning, Ash's sighs on her skin, hot as the sunlight outside.

"I want you," she breathed.

Ash straddled her, hair tumbling about Mia's face, their kiss deepening as they moved their hips, grinding against each other. Taking Mia's hands, Ash placed them on her breasts, the heat of her skin, the scent of her sweat, the music of her sighs filling the cell.

"I need you," she whispered.

Her kisses drifted lower, hands descending to unbuckle Mia's belt, whisk off her loincloth. She left a trail of burning kisses down her heaving breasts, across the taut muscle at her belly, tongue lapping at the sweat on Mia's skin as she sank farther and farther down.

"I love you," she sighed.

"Don't stop," Mia whispered.

She took hold of Ash's hair, and gently pulled her in.

"*Don't stop.*"

L eona blinked up at Furian, confusion clouding her eyes.

". . . What's wrong?"

Furian climbed off the soft bed, the thousand-thread sheets, wishing for all the world he were back in his cell. He tied his loincloth about his waist, avoiding her gaze.

"Slave," Leona demanded. "I asked you a question."

He spoke gently then, his words sharp as steel.

"This was a dream. And I was a fool to dream it."

He met her eyes then.

"This is not love," he said.

And without a backward glance, he turned and stalked from the room.

A sh lay in Mia's arms, drenched in sweat, looking up into her dark eyes.

". . . What's wrong?"

Mia only shook her head, held Ashlinn tighter. They lay together on the tiny straw bed in that gloomy pit, the taste of the other still lingering on their lips. Ash's cloak beneath them. Stone and iron around them. All the world against them. Death looming large on a vicious horizon. And for that single, simple moment, none of it mattered.

None of it mattered at all.

"This feels like a dream," Mia whispered. "And I don't want to wake."

She met her eyes then.

"This is love," Mia said simply.

And leaning in, she closed her eyes and gifted Ash a gentle kiss.

CHAPTER 33

BEGIN

The sound was impossible.

A living, breathing, colossal thing, pressing on Mia's skin, so real she felt she could almost reach out and touch it. A weight on her shoulders, rooting her to the earth. A tremor in the stone around her, a physical sensation in the air. In all her years, even in Stormwatch, even in Whitekeep, she'd never heard the like of it.

She sat in her cell, listening to the song of murder above, the verse of steel on steel, the percussion of hooves, the chorus of the blood-mad crowd. Mister Kindly and Eclipse both swam in her shadow, rippling at the edges, trying to devour the fear swelling in her chest. It was hard not to feel it now, try as she might. The daemons did their best, but still, she could sense it, like those hateful suns above her. The scent of Ashlinn's sweat lingering on her skin. Reminding her of all she now had to lose.

"I'm afraid," she whispered.

"... WE ARE SORRY, MIA ..."

"... we try, but the suns ..."

"... THEY BURN US ..."

She clasped her hands together to stop them shaking. Reminding herself of who she was. Where she sat. All that would be undone if she failed.

"Conquer your fear," she whispered, "and you can conquer the world."

The mekwerk lock clicked, the door swung aside. Dona Leona stood there, tall and proud, surrounded by her houseguards and Itreyan legionaries. She was clad in shimmering silver, the gown flowing off her shoulders like summer showers. Her plaited hair was interwoven with metallic ribbon, like a victor's laurel about her brow.

"My champion," she said.

"Domina," Mia replied.

"You are prepared?"

Mia nodded. "Are you?"

Leona blinked. "Why would I not be?"

"These are your gladiatii about to die, Domina," Mia replied. "I wondered if perhaps you felt some regret about that."

Leona raised her chin, pride tightening her jaw. "My only regret is that I fostered a nest of traitors for so very long. Next season, it shall be different, I vow it. With the coin I make from the *magni*, I shall stock my collegium with only the finest gladiatii, and an executus who may be counted upon to forge them into true gods."

"Arkades forged Furian, did he not? Arkades forged me."

"Arkades was a cur. An honorless dog who—"

"Arkades was in love with you, Domina."

Leona lips parted, but she found no words to speak.

"Surely you sensed it?" Mia pressed. "He was champion and then executus of one of the richest, most accomplished collegia in the history of the *venatus*. Why else would he have followed you to Crow's Nest, if he wasn't following his heart?"

"Arkades *betrayed* me," Leona hissed.

Mia shook her head. "Arkades was gladiatii. A man of the sword. Even if he discovered you were bedding Furian, do you honestly think he'd look to poison the whole collegium? Knowing how he felt about you, and what it would cost you if your father got his way?"

". . . I scarce know where to begin," Leona said, blustering. "First of all, how dare you imply—"

"Look to your own house, Leona," Mia said. "Look to those closest to you, and ask yourself who truly stood to gain if you were forced to limp back to civilization and beg forgiveness at your father's feet. Who encouraged you to ask him for coin? Who was the first to object, whenever you spoke ill of him in public?"

The dona stood rooted to the stone, a small frown forming on her brow.

"Sanguila Leona," said a legionary in the hall. "The Crow must be prepared for the execution bout."

Mia stepped closer to her mistress, speaking so only they could hear.

"I might have been like you, if fate were kinder, and crueler. I know what happened to your mother. I know what kind of childhood you had. All the things you are, you are for a reason. Vicious and generous. Courageous and pitiless. I like you, and I hate you, and I couldn't have done this without you. So when the turn is done, I'll give you all the thanks I can muster. You won't think it nearly enough, I'm sure. But it's all I can fashion for you, Leona."

The dona's eyes were narrowed to papercuts, filled with indignant fury.

"You will address me as Domina!"

The crowd roared above them, trumpets rang bright and clear in the air, signaling the end of the equillai race. Mia looked to the older woman, and slowly nodded.

"Aye," she said. "But not for much longer."

S he stood before a portcullis of iron, wrapped in black steel. Falcon wings at her shoulders, a cloak of red feathers at her back. The face of a goddess covered her own, only her eyes visible through the helm's facade.

She was glad no one would be able to see if she wept.

The temperature was soaring, the audience baking in the suns. Many had taken the opportunity after the final (spectacular) equillai race to seek some shade or refreshment. But there was still no shortage of eyes to watch her. Tens of thousands in the stands, stamping their feet and waiting for the main event to begin.

"Citizens of Itreya!" The editorii's words echoed across the bloodstained stone. "We present to you, our final execution bout!"

The crowd's reaction was tepid, some applause, no shortage of jeers from those who simply wished the *magni* to get under way. After five turns of ceaseless butchery, the thought of a few more reprobates sent to slaughter seemed positively pedestrian.

"These are no common criminals!" the editorii insisted. "These are the basest cowards, the vilest wretches, slaves who betrayed their masters!"

The crowd perked up at that, resounding boos echoing around the arena.

"We give thanks to Sanguila Leona of the Remus Collegium, for providing the cattle for this righteous slaughter! Citizens, we present to you . . . the condemned!"

A portcullis opened in the northern end of the arena, and Mia's heart sank to see seven figures stagger out into the sunlight to the crowd's jeers. Sidonius and Wavewaker. Bladesinger and Bryn. Felix and Albanus and Butcher. They'd not been treated kindly in their captivity—all looked weak and starved. They were armed with rusted blades and dressed in piecemeal armor. Just a few scraps of leather on their chests and shins that would avail them not at all against someone even half-skilled with a blade.

They were meant to die here, after all.

The guard beside Mia handed her a razor-sharp gladius and a long, wicked dagger, polished to a blinding sheen. Mia looked into the guard's eyes, blue as the sunburned sky.

"No fear," Ash whispered. "Strike true."

Mia nodded, turned her gaze back to the sand. Sickness in her stomach. Horror at the thought of what was to come. Certainty that it was the only way, that everything she'd sacrificed would soon be worthwhile, that all the death, all the blood, all the pain would be justified once Scaeva and Duomo were in the ground.

This was the end of a tyranny. And the ends justified the means, didn't they?

As long as the end isn't mine?

"And now," the editorii cried. "Our executioner! Champion of the Remus Collegium, victor of Whitekeep, the Savior of Stormwatch, citizens of Godsgrave, we present to you . . . the Crow!"

The crowd rose to their feet, curiosity finally alight. All had heard the tales of the girl who slew the retchwyrm, who saved the citizens of Stormwatch from certain doom, who'd bested a warrior of the Silken Dominion.

The portcullis rose and Mia marched out into the merciless heat, her shadow shriveling as both Mister Kindly and Eclipse hissed in their misery. The crowd roared at the sight of her, blood-red feathers and armor black as truedark, her beautiful, pitiless face wrought in polished steel. On cue, the sands around her spat forth rippling flame, the crowd bellowing in approval. She followed the pillars of fire, out into the center of the arena, awestruck by the scale of it all.

The pale sands stained red with blood. The gravebone walls rising into the blinding sky. The barrier separating the crowd from the arena floor loomed over twenty feet high, hung with banners of the noble houses, the collegia, the trinity of Aa. In the premium seats at the barrier's lip, Mia could see a collection of ministers and holy men arrayed in their bloody red robes and tall, pompous hats, her heart thrilling as she spied the grand cardinal among them. Duomo sat at the heart of his flock, solid as a brick shithouse, looking as ever like a thug who'd beaten a holy man to death and stolen his kit. His robe was the color of heart's blood, his smile like a knife in her chest.

Beside the church, she could see the ringside marrowborn and the sanguilas' boxes. Mia spied Leonides and his hulking executus, Titus. She could see Magistrae in a dazzling scarlet gown. But of Leona, she saw no sign. She turned her eyes upward to the stands, to the rippling, roaring, swelling ocean of people.

"Crow!" they roared. "CROW!"

She looked to the consul's box, set with fluted pillars and shaded from the sun. The Senate of Godsgrave were seated about it, old men with twin-

kling eyes, white togas trimmed with purple. A small army of Luminatii surrounded it, sunsteel swords blazing in their hands. She could see a great chair,
trimmed in gold, dangerously close to what might be called a throne. But the
chair stood empty.

No Scaeva.

Trumpets sounded, dragging Mia's attention back to the sand. Sidonius
and the others were stalking toward her, rusty swords in hand. These matches
weren't supposed to be even, but the former Falcons of Remus were still gladiatii. And though they were beaten, bruised, starving, they were seven, and
she was one. A rusted blade could still cut to the bone if wielded with enough
skill, and a poisoned tongue could cut deeper still.

"So," Wavewaker said, stopping twenty feet away. "They send you to swing
the axe, Mi Dona? Fitting, I suppose."

"Almighty Aa," Sidonius breathed. "Where is your heart, Mia?"

"They buried it with my father, Sidonius," she replied.

"You treacherous fucking cunt," Bladesinger spat.

Mia looked the seven over, the faces of folk who'd once called her friend.
Mouth as dry as dust. Skin drenched with sweat.

Soon, all of this will be worth it.

"I'd tell you exactly why I consider that word a compliment and not an
insult," she said. "But I'm not sure we've time for a monologue, 'Singer."

She drew her heavy sword, her razored dagger, saluted the consul's box.

"Now let's get this over with."

Trumpets blared, the crowd roared, and Dona Leona made her way to her
seat in the sanguila's box. Her magistrae greeted her with a smile, lifting
a parasol over her mistress's head to shield her from the Light Father's burning
eyes.

She looked about the seats around her, saw Tacitus, Trajan, Phillipi, the
other usual suspects. Surrounded by their executi and staffers, decked in
the bright colors of their collegia, their sigils emblazoned on banners at their
backs. And in the box directly to her left, beneath a roaring golden lion,
dressed in an extravagant frock coat and popping a grape between his teeth . . .

"Father," she nodded.

"Dearest daughter." Leonides smiled, raising his voice over the thrum of
the crowd. "My heart gladdens to see you."

"And you," she nodded. "My first payment arrived, I trust?"

"Aye," Leonides called. "It was received with gratitude and, I confess, no small degree of surprise."

"You'll find I'm full of surprises, Father," she called back. "Your Exile could testify to that, I'm sure, had my Crow not separated her head from her body."

The sanguila around them smiled and murmured, updating the score in their mental ledgers. But Leonides only scoffed, popped another grape into his mouth.

"We didn't think we'd be graced with your presence for the execution."

"I'm sorry to disappoint you."

"I'm used to it by now, my dear," he sighed. "But I was just saying to Phillipi here, I'm not certain if shame wouldn't keep me from showing my face, if the best portion of *my* collegium were to be executed for rebellion."

"Have you still shame, Father?" Leona asked. "I thought it buried with the wife you beat to death."

The mood around them dropped, sanguila exchanging uncomfortable glances. Leonides's face darkened, and Magistrae put a restraining hand on Leona's arm.

"You go too far, Domina," she whispered. "Is it wise to insult him so?"

Leona looked to Anthea, the slow frown that had been planted in the Crow's cell returning to her brow. But a peal of trumpets dragged her eyes to the sand, and she found herself squinting at the preliminaries through the awful glare. The Crow and her traitorous gladiatii were exchanging poisoned words, but she could only hear scraps.

She knew it was a risk, fielding her champion to mop up some traitorous dregs. But she simply needed the coin too badly to allow another sanguila to wield the axe. Crow was one of the finest she'd seen on the sand, and the traitors had been beaten and starved to the point of exhaustion. With Aa's grace, the Crow would still stand with Furian in the *magni,* still bring the glory and coin Leona so desperately needed.

Craved.

Trumpets blared again, the match began, the Crow moving swift as her namesake. She had to even the numbers quickly, weed out the weakest of the Falcons before sheer numbers overtook her. Thus, the girl went straight for Felix, skipping under his broad, scything blow and slipping inside his guard. The man was clearly the worse for his captivity, slow to react, and with the speed that had made her the collegium champion, the Crow plunged her dagger into his leather breastplate and the heart beyond.

The crowd roared, Felix clutched his skewered chest and toppled to the sand, the blood spraying bright and red. The Crow moved in a blur, kicking a toeful of sand up into Wavewaker's face and charging at Bryn. The Vaanian girl might have been a daemon with a bow and arrow, but with a sword, she was less the prodigy. The Crow smashed aside her strike with her heavy gladius, opened a small cut on her thigh. As Bryn cried out, staggering, the Crow spun behind her and plunged her blade under the Vaanian girl's spaulder and up into her back.

Blood. Gushing from the wound. Glinting on the Crow's steel. Reflected in the crowd's eyes. They roared as the Vaanian toppled forward in a pool of scarlet, Wavewaker bellowing and running at the Crow like a madman. He swung his rusty blade in a terrifying overhand strike, the steel whistling as it came. But the weeks of starvation in the *Gloryhound*'s hold had weakened his legs, left him slightly off-balance and late to recover, and a swift strike sent him to his knees, hands to his chest, blood welling between his fingers.

"No!"

Bladesinger charged, the crowd thrilling as her strike opened up a shallow cut on the Crow's arm. Sidonius struck from the side, Butcher and Albanus from behind, Crow rolling aside and rising again with shocking speed. Her dagger flashed, Butcher cried out, fell back in a spray of red, Bladesinger falling on the Crow in a frenzy. The girl rolled back across the sand, flinging a handful of dirt into the woman's eyes. Flipping to her feet, she met Sidonius's blade on her own, her legs almost buckling under the bigger man's strength. But as every man in the stands winced in sympathy, the Crow drove her knee up into Sidonius's bollocks, dropping him to the sand with a high-pitched wail. Her counterstrike whistled past Albanus's guard, her dagger buried to the hilt under his armpit, the blood a scarlet waterfall.

Blinking the grit from her eyes, Bladesinger stuck again, the Crow bending backward as the blow skimmed past her chin. The woman's long saltlocks seethed as she followed through, knocking the Crow's gladius flying. Armed only with her knife now, the Crow struck back, punching the woman in the face with her free hand, ducking beneath another strike and snatching up one of Bladesinger's long locks. Dragging the woman off-balance, she pulled Bladesinger backward and onto her blade. The audience howled in approval, Bladesinger stumbled to her knees, blood spilling from her ruptured breastplate and down her belly, collapsing face-first on the sand.

Only Sidonius remained. The man was bent double, clutching his jewels. The Crow moved toward him, merciless, the bigger man trying to fend her off. He was screaming at her, but the pair were so far away, Leona only caught a handful of words.

"... traitor ..."

"... father ..."

"... *no* ..."

And the Crow?

She said nothing at all.

Instead, she feinted sideways and slashed at his wrist, his sword spinning to the sand. She kicked out at his legs, sending him onto his knees. And as the crowd roared, she spun around to his back, long hair streaming behind her, plunging her dagger past the collar of his breastplate and down into his spine. Sidonius's face twisted in agony, a gout of glittering scarlet spraying from the wound. He toppled forward, red spilling across the sand, the mob bellowing in delight.

Leona saw his lips move.

A whispered prayer, perhaps?

A curse for the girl who'd slain him?

And then, his eyes closed for the final time.

Leona sat still, peering at the Crow. The bloodstained blades in her hands. That slow frown deepening on her brow.

The sanguila about her gave polite applause. Tacitus glanced at her and offered an approving nod at her champion's form. She looked to her father, but couldn't catch his eye. Instead, Leonides was staring at that blood-soaked slip of a girl out there on the sand. The girl who'd bested his Exile. The girl who'd just murdered seven gladiatii and barely gotten a scratch. His scowl was black. His eyes, narrowed.

He turned to his executus, Titus. Whispering in the big man's ear.

Leona's frown only deepened.

"Citizens of Itreya!" the editorii called. "Your victor!"

The Crow retrieved her fallen gladius, pointed the bloody blade to the empty consul's chair, then held it to the sky. She was wrapped in black steel. Falcon wings at her shoulders, a cloak of red feathers at her back. As she walked a circuit of the arena, the corpses of the murdered gladiatii were dragged off the sands. The face of a goddess covered her own, only her eyes visible through the helm's facade.

No one could tell if she wept.

MAGNI

Not long now.

Mia had been ushered off the sand after the execution bout, taken straight to a large staging cell, still drenched in blood. Her wound was dressed, she was given a ration of water, then told to wait. Though her mouth was bone dry, instead of drinking, she wasted her water trying to wash the gore from her shaking hands.

By the end of the cup, her fingers were still sticky.

She watched a cadre of Ironpriests scurry past, guards delivering gladiatii to the staging cell a few at a time. She recognized a few from Governor Messala's palazzo; Ragnar of Vaan, Champion of the Tacitus Collegium; Worldeater, Champion of the Swords of Phillipi. But soon there were dozens, then hundreds of others, standing about the chamber, clad in leather and steel.

The temperature was stifling, the walls dripping with sweat. Attendants moved about with buckets and ladles of water, the fighters drinking greedily, but Mia only asked for more water for her hands. Scrubbing away at the stains of the execution, refusing to look at her reflection in the red puddling beneath her.

She could hear mekwerk groaning under her feet; some colossal engine ever hungry for blood. Trying not to think of Bladesinger and Bryn, Wavewaker and the others. They'd chosen their fates. Written them in red. She couldn't afford to spare a thought for them. Their trials were over now, where Mia's greatest lay before her. She could still hear Sidonius's parting words as he lay facedown in the sand.

Eyes fixed on hers.

So quiet, none but she could hear.

"Good luck, Mia," he'd whispered.

Her hands were still sticky.

". . . we are with you . . ."

". . . WE WILL ALWAYS BE WITH YOU . . ."

"You fought well."

She didn't look up. Didn't need to know who it was who stood before her. The sickness in her belly told her that. The lust and the hunger, the ache of longing. Her shadow moved, inching ever closer to his, like iron to the lodestone. Her lips twisted in a bitter smile as she replied.

"I fought against seven starving prisoners who could barely swing their swords."

"Such, the price of defiance in Itreya," the Unfallen replied.

"So they tell me."

"I was not sure . . . how I would feel watching you. They were my brothers and sisters too. When they fell beneath your blades . . ." Furian sighed. "I could scarce believe it. I think I expected some ruse. Some ploy or play or last-minute reprieve."

"Play?"

Mia shook her head, bewildered.

"Why is everyone still acting like this is a fucking game?"

"Gladiatii!" a guard cried. "Attend!"

The eyes of the assembled warriors turned to the iron portcullis. Mia saw three editorii, silhouetted against the glare outside. The eldest of the trio stepped forward, peering among the gladiatii. His long dark beard was plaited, his eyes mismatched, one brown, one green. A banded python was draped around his neck.

"Gladiatii of the collegia of Itreya," he said. "Each of you and your masters have earned, through right of trial and combat, your place upon the sands of the *Venatus Magni*. The greatest spectacle in the Itreyan calendar is about to unfold, and you shall fight and die for the glory of the Republic before an adoring crowd. Those who fall shall still stand as legends. And the one among you who remains at *magni*'s end shall be granted freedom by the Hand of God himself.

"This *magni* is a battle grande; every warrior will begin the match upon the sands. Each will be given a colored armband, to designate initial loyalties. Gladiatii from the same collegia will be grouped together, though you are under *no* obligation to adhere to these allegiances throughout the match. Never forget; all must fall so one may stand."

The man let his words hang in the air a moment, ironhard and cold.

"Once this portcullis opens," he continued, "proceed to your designated starting position, and await instruction from the grand editorii. May Aa bless and keep you, and Tsana guide your hands."

Mia sheathed her blades, still trying to rub the red off her fingers. As the guards roamed among them, handing out strips of cloth in red, blue, gold, and white, she could feel it. The fear. Welling in the hearts and minds of the warriors around her, leaking through the stone and hanging thick in the air. Every one of them was staring into the eyes of death, and all knew only one would survive. Some stalked up and down, pounding their chests, muttering to themselves. Some stood mute, battling their fear in silence. Others looked to comrades for some moment of solace, knowing all loyalties would fail before the final trumpet sounded.

Not long now.

A guard muscled through the mob, tied a strip of fabric around Furian's arm to show his allegiance. Demanding that Mia stand, he bound another strip around her bicep. Both were as red as the stains she'd failed to wash away.

Trumpets sounded, the floor rumbling beneath their feet. The call of the editorii echoed across the arena, the crowd roaring in answer.

"Citizens of Itreya! Honored administratii! Senators and marrowborn! Welcome to the *Venatus Magni* of Godsgrave! From the finest collegia in the Republic, we present to you the mightiest warriors beneath the three suns! Here to do battle before your wondering eyes, to bathe themselves in blood and glory to honor the Everseeing, almighty Aa. We present, the Drakes of Trajan!"

The iron portcullis ratcheted open, and the first group of gladiatii strode out onto the sand, escorted by a cadre of Itreyan legionairies. There were perhaps two hundred and fifty warriors assembled in staging cells by now—far too many to call out individually. Stables were being marched out en masse: the Wolves of Tacitus; the Swords of Phillipi; the Lions of Leonides, one after another striding forth to the welcome of the crowd. As each collegium took their places in the arena, punters in the stands recognized favorites and honored champions, the volume steadily rising.

"The Falcons of Remus!" came the announcer's cry.

"So it begins," Furian whispered.

"And so it ends," Mia replied.

She walked out into the blinding light, the Unfallen beside her. The crowd cheered, some for the Savior of Stormwatch (*"Crow! Crow! Crow!"*), others for the Champion of Talia (*"Unfaaaaaaaallen!"*). As the pair took their places among the other red armbands, the editorii's voice rang in the air.

"Citizens of Itreya, please be upstanding!"

A bright peal of trumpets sounded as the crowd rose to their feet, the fanfare thrilling along Mia's skin.

"Seven years have passed since the traitorous Kingmakers sought to bring our glorious Republic to its knees! Seven years of a glorious peace, seven years of reason and prosperity, seven years of justice and light!"

Mia's heart beat quicker, her mouth suddenly dry. She knew what was coming, *who* was coming. Seven years since he'd destroyed her world, standing over her father's scaffold like a vulture on a cairn. Seven years of bloodstained promises, of murder and steel, of wondering and praying. Furian looked to her, his shadow rippling as hers ebbed and flowed, reaching out with black tendrils toward the Senate, toward the Luminatii, toward . . .

"Your savior! Your consul! Julius Scaeva!"

It was like a punch to her stomach. The sight of him. After all this time, she thought perhaps it might have dulled. But the pain was a knife in her chest, making her stagger, her shadow ripple and seethe despite the three suns burning above.

He was tall, painfully handsome, his dark hair now shot through with the faintest streaks of gray. He wore a long toga of rich purple, a golden laurel at his brow. When he smiled, it seemed the suns shone brighter, the crowd roaring in rapture. Beside him stood a beautiful woman, dark of hair and green of eye, dripping in fine silk and golden jewelry. In her arms, she held a boy, six or seven years old. He had his mother's dark hair, his father's bottomless black eyes. He wore the emblem of the Luminatii Legion embroidered on his chest, though no trinity around his neck.

Scaeva put one arm around his bride, three fingers outstretched in the sign of Aa. The crowd returned the gesture, a hundred thousand people raising their hands and calling his name. Mia felt her jaw clench so tight her teeth ached. Holding her breath because it was simply too painful to breathe. To see him smiling beside his familia when he'd so casually put hers in the ground . . .

Surrounded by that sea of Luminatii, iron and sunsteel, Scaeva stepped forward to a pulpit in the consul's box.

"My people!" he called, his words reverberating among the human sea. "My countrymen! My friends! On this most holy feast, we gather beneath the eyes of the Everseeing in this, the greatest Republic the world has ever known!"

The consul paused for a burst of giddy applause.

"My friends, these are troubling times. When I announced my intent to stand for a fourth term as consul, I was plagued with doubt. But continued attacks against our magistrates, our administratii, even the *children* of our noble senators overseas, have convinced me the threat to our glorious Republic is not yet ended. And I will not abandon Itreya, or *you,* in such an hour of need."

Scaeva called louder as the crowd erupted.

"We must stand together! And with your support, we *shall* stand together! From myself, my beloved wife Liviana, my son Lucius . . ."—Scaeva was forced to pause as the cheers overwhelmed his voice—". . . from my familia to yours, friends, we thank you for your vigilance, your courage, but most of all, your faith! In God, and us!"

Mia's eyes were locked on Scaeva, boiling with hatred. Her fingers slipping unconsciously to the gravebone dagger hidden beneath the iron encircling her wrist. The gravebone dagger Alinne Corvere had once pressed to Scaeva's throat, the turn he took Mia's world away.

Patience.

Mia's fingers slipped away from the dagger. She could taste blood in her mouth.

Patience.

Scaeva beamed in the crowd's adoration, playing the part of the humble one, the grateful one. Reaching out to his wife, the consul placed his son Lucius on his shoulders, held out his three fingers again in blessing. Mia watched the little boy lean down, whisper in his father's ear.

"My son says ever I speak too long," he smiled, laughter rippling among the crowd. "He reminds me we are here at purpose. So, shall we begin?"

The crowd roared as one.

"My friends, I asked, *shall we begin?*"

A single, deafening cheer, rising all the way to the sky.

"I will now hand over to our beloved grand cardinal, and my dear friend, Francesco Duomo, to lead us in prayer."

All eyes turned to the ministry of Aa in their ringside seats. Grand Cardinal Duomo stood at another pulpit, dark eyes fixed on Scaeva, glittering with veiled malice as he bowed low. He spoke into a mekwerk horn, his voice ringing across the arena, thick as toffee, sweet and dark.

"My thanks, glorious Consul," he said, bowing deep. "May Aa ever keep you in the Light. May your *reign* be long and fruitful."

Scaeva's smile turned sharper as he returned the bow.

"Beloved citizens, please bow your heads," Duomo said.

The entire arena fell still, silence ringing in the air and on the wind.

"Almighty Aa, Father of Light, creator of all, on this your most holy feast, we thank you for your love, your vigilance, and your many blessings upon us. Remain ever watchful of our hearts, and bless those who here die for the glory of our Republic.

"In your name, this we pray."

The crowd replied as one.

"In your name, this we pray."

Duomo spread his arms, a smile brightening his eyes.

"Let the *magni* begin!"

The crowd roared, stamping and hollering as Duomo returned to his flock of cardinals and bishops, smug as a groom after his wedding night. Mia's gaze returned to Scaeva, watching as he took his seat, the consul's dark eyes fixed on Duomo. The pair watched each other like a pair of vipers over the corpse of a single mouse. But Scaeva's son whispered something in his ear, and the consul suddenly laughed, bright and loud. His bride leaned over, kissed him on the cheek. Scaeva broke his gaze from Duomo's, instead beaming at his familia. Mia felt her legs trembling.

They didn't deserve to be so happy. For Scaeva to have a wife and child when he'd left her with nothing. For Duomo to play at piety and speak of love when he'd destroyed her entire world. She looked to the gladiatii around her, every one of them an obstacle, every sword a hindrance, every throat a stepping stone on the way to those bastard's hearts.

"I can feel it . . . ," Furian breathed. "Your hatred . . ."

Mia blinked, looked to the man beside her. Furian was looking at her with a mix of horror, fear, pity. Glancing down to the shadow at her feet.

"Almighty Aa . . . what did they do to you?"

"Citizens of Itreya!" came the cry. "Behold, your battleground!"

The crowd stilled as a great, trembling groan ran the length of the entire arena. The four groups of gladiatii, red, white, gold, and blue, were positioned at opposite points around the arena's oblong, clustered together in mobs of sixty or so. As Mia watched, the ground before her split apart, sand cascading down into the arena's mekwerk belly. The crowd were on their feet, straining for a better look as four great shapes loomed up from beneath the floor. Fifty feet long, heavy ironwood hulls, fantastical beasts carved at their prows, their flanks studded with dozens of gleaming oars.

"Those are war galleys," one bewildered gladiatii murmured.

"But . . . ," another said. "But . . ."

"Gladiatii, attend!" the centurion barked, pointing at the rope ladders dangling from their ship's flank. "All of you, climb! Now! Move!"

Mia did as she was told immediately, and Furian followed without question, scrambling up the ladders to the deck above. Others climbed along behind, but yet more gladiatii simply stared at the centurion in undisguised bafflement.

"Ships?" one asked. "Almighty Aa, we're standing on fucking sand!"

The ground groaned again, trumpets blaring.

"I'd do as commanded, were I you," the centurion said.

The man turned, and with the rest of his cadre, beat feet back across the sand. Some gladiatii began climbing onto the galleys, others looking about in bewilderment. Mia heard another mekwerk moan, the groan of metal under pressure. Heavy iron shutters clanked down over the cells skirting the arena's edge, a series of circular grates rose from beneath the sand. And as the crowd watched in wonder, those grates shivered and, with a last hollow metal cough, began spewing water high into the air.

The mob sighed, cheered, water vapor caught on the swirling breeze and bringing a merciful cool to the arena's oppressive heat. But within moments, those sighs became delighted roars as the water began gushing forth harder, higher, flooding over the arena floor and swirling about the ships. Soon it was six inches deep. Eight. A foot, rising up the gladiatii's shins in an inexorable flood.

"This is salt water," one said.

A Lion of Leonides leaned over the railing, shouting at the top of his voice.

"It's a naval battle, you stupid bastards, climb, climb!"

The gladiatii obeyed now, dashing to the ladders and scrambling up the sides. Mia stood at the prow, watching the water rushing and crashing around their keel. Ten feet deep and still rising, their ship beginning to rock in its wooden scaffold as it was buoyed up on the flood. Thanks to Ashlinn's reconnaissance, Mia had some inkling of what was in store for her on the sands, but to stand among it all . . .

The girl shook her head, simply awed by the power on display. The ingenuity. The sheer fucking hubris. Instead of sending its citizens to the ocean, the great Republic of Itreya had brought the ocean to its citizens.

"Citizens of Itreya!" cried the grand editorii. "The Senate and Iron Collegium of our glorious Republic are proud to present to you, the battle of Seawall!"*

The water was fifteen feet deep now, growing deeper. A great plinth rose in the center of the arena, a stone keep atop it—presumably representing the

---

* An infamous clash in the earliest years of the Republic, and probably the largest sea battle ever fought under the three suns. The Battle of Seawall involved four massive fleets; the Itreyan Navy under command of the Great Unifier, Francisco I, and a tithed fleet from the vassal state of Vaan clashed with Dweymeri clan ships under command of Bara Sundancer of the Threedrake clan, and an armada of pirate lords who had sworn to resist Itreyan dominance of the seas.

As you might have guessed, resistance lasted about as long as a bottle of top-shelf goldwine in a brothel full of pissheads.

mighty fortifications at Seawall itself. Mia could see mekwerk catapults atop the crenelated walls, loaded with burning pitch. And looking down into swirling eddies below, Mia saw dozens of dark shapes cruising around their hull.

Furian peered over the railing, squinting at the serpentine shadows.

"Are those . . . ?"

The crowd roared as one of the shapes breached the surface, all blunt snout and dead black eyes and row upon row of razored teeth. Almost fifteen feet long, it cut the water with its massive forked tail before disappearing below the surface.

"Stormdrakes," the Unfallen breathed.

Mia shook her head. Catapults ahead. Enemy ships around. Monsters below.

And as she looked to the sigils on breastplates and shields on the gladiatii around them, she realized she and Furian were surrounded by Lions of Leonides. At least a dozen, all as big as houses and hard as the iron at her chest.

"Well," Mia murmured. "Isn't this cozy."

"Foes on all sides," Furian whispered.

"At least my life is consistent."

"If it comes down to you and I . . ."

"I know."

"But until then?" He glanced to the blades in her hands, still stained with the blood of those who'd called her friend. "You had duty enough to defend the collegium, put those who betrayed it in the ground. I am hoping perhaps I was wrong about you. That you have learned something of honor, and the way of the gladiatii. Need I worry about your blade at my back?"

Mia looked at him sidelong, the water about them rising ever higher.

"There's only one way this ends," she said. "And you and I both know it. But I'll come at you frontways. I can promise you that, at least."

The Unfallen nodded, tightened his grip on his blade.

"So be it. *Sanguii e Gloria.*"

Mia shook her head. "You can keep the glory, Furian."

She turned her eyes to the consul's chair.

"I'm just here for the blood."

Down in the arena's belly, Mercurio finished loading the wheelbarrow, dragging the heavy bucket into the tray with a wince. Truth was, he was too old for this kind of rot. His bloody arthritis was playing up again, and walking about down here dressed in rags for the past two turns wasn't helping his shingles any, either.

"Next time, *I* get to dress up in the guard's kit," he growled.

Ashlinn rolled her eyes.

"Who the 'byss is going to believe you're a guard, you grumpy old prick?"

The girl was lurking by the antechamber door, eyes on the hallway outside. She was still dressed in her stolen armor, black leather breastplate and skirt, a plumed helm to cover her face. Mercurio could hear the audience roaring above his head, belly filling with ice and butterflies as he realized the *magni* was under way.

Though she kept her face like stone, Järnheim's daughter seemed to share his concern. She looked to the arena above their heads, sighing.

"I should be up there," she whispered.

"This is important to her," Mercurio replied.

"Be that as it may, this whole plan is fucking lunacy."

Mercurio sighed. "I'm not sure if you've noticed yet, girl, but Mia Corvere and lunacy go together like cigarillos and smoke."

Ashlinn smiled. "O, aye, I noticed."

The bishop of Godsgrave joined her by the doorway, peered out into the corridor.

"I realize this isn't the time or place," he muttered. "But just know, if you hurt her, there's no place under the suns you can hide that I won't find you."

Ash raised an eyebrow, looked the old man up and down.

"You know, you really are very sweet for a grumpy old prick."

"Fuck off," Mercurio growled.

"Sounds like a plan to me. Shall we?"

"Aye. But as you're so fond of noting, I'm a senior citizen."

"So?"

"So you push the bloody wheelbarrow."

Applause echoing on the stone about them, Ashlinn pushing a barrow before them, the pair stole off into the dark.

The crowd thundered as the trumpets rang, every man, woman, and child on their feet. After five turns of slaughter, five turns of blazing sunlight, five turns of blinding spectacle, the *Venatus Magni* was under way.

Leona watched as the catapults in the Seawall keep loosed their barrels of flaming pitch. The first rounds were simply warning shots, tumbling through the air before plunging into the water with a vicious hiss. But the threat of immolation was enough to send the gladiatii scrambling, chaos breaking out on the decks as brief struggles for command got under way.

Ragnar of Vaan quickly took leadership of the Gold ship, the crowd thrilling as he ended a brief mutiny from another Wolf of Tacitus by putting his sword through the man's throat and kicking him over the side. The water beneath the railing turned to foaming red as at least four stormdrakes tore the man to screaming pieces. Roaring to the oarsmen, Ragnar took the helm and steered his ship for the keep.

Worldeater of the Phillipi took command of the Blue ship soon after, the crew also bending their oars for the fortifications. The deck of the White ship had broken into complete chaos, with the Drakes of Trajan fighting for dominance with gladiatii from three other collegia. The crowd roared as the vessel became a slaughterhouse, blood slicked over the boards.

Looking to the Reds, Leona saw their galley was under way, the Bloodhawks of Artimedes at the helm. She could see the Crow and Furian at the bow, blades drawn, their ship headed for the fortifications. But as she watched, she saw more than a dozen Lions of Leonides forming up at their backs. Not content to wait until they'd reached the keep, Leonides's gladiatii looked set to end Leona's hopes of victory here and now.

The dona looked to her father, found the man staring back at her, smiling.

"Just business," he whispered.

"They come," Furian murmured.

"I know," Mia replied.

"Don't die before I can kill you."

"This is not where I die."

The Lions charged without ceremony, and Mia and Furian turned to meet them, steel crashing against steel. The crowd thrilled at the sudden and bloody betrayal, Mia and Furian forced across the deck until their backs were to the figurehead at the bow.

Though outnumbered, they'd chosen their battleground well—the prow was narrow, bottlenecking the Lions and making their numbers count for less. Mia reached out to the shadows at a charging Lion's feet, but simply couldn't hold them with all three suns blazing overhead. She was forced to rely on her speed instead, the training she'd endured under Mercurio, Solis, and then Arkades, the turns, weeks, months she'd spent with some kind of blade in her hands.

That, and the measure of Swoon that Ashlinn had mixed in with the glad-iatii's water supply, of course.

It hadn't been a huge dose; not enough to send them dreaming. But she knew anyone who'd swallowed a ladleful would be feeling it by now, and it seemed the Lions charging them had been thirsty before the match. Mia feinted left, the Lion stumbled, cursed as Mia opened up a deep gouge on his thigh with her gladius. He lunged, but she slipped sideways, her blows glancing off his shield, his blade knocked from clumsy fingers and sent clattering to the deck.

Furian moved like water, long black hair flowing behind him as he bat-tered the charging Lions backward with his broad shield. He met a thrust with his own blade, his counter sending the sword spinning from its owner's grip and off into the water. The catapults loosed another round, flame streaming through the air and striking their ship's flank. Fire bloomed, a thunderous boom drowning out the crowd. Men fell screaming to the deck, wailing into the water, drakes' teeth flashing and gnashing in the foaming red. Black smoke drifted among the dancing sparks, the stench of burning oil and meat. And Mia raised her sword and struck again at her foe.

The man stumbled, just a touch drunk from the Swoon, but it was enough to give her the edge. A whistling slash from Mia's blade opened up his windpipe, just as Furian ended his foe with a short, deadly thrust. Despite the carnage, despite the fear, she felt elated, her blood thrilling, her skin prickling. And as she glanced down to the deck, Mia realized her shadow was moving of its own accord, creeping like molasses across the blood-slick wood toward Furian's. And more, his own was reaching out to hers.

Like lovers parted.

Like a puzzle, searching for missing pieces of themselves.

Mia shook her head. Breathless. Hungry. The deck around them had erupted into chaos, gladiatii turning on each other as the Lions attacked Mia and Furian and their brief allegiance collapsed. Steel crashed against steel, agonized cries splitting the air, another barrel of burning pitch exploding overhead and raining liquid fire down onto the deck. The Lions were beset from behind, Furian and Mia fighting for their lives up against the bow. She realized the Gold ship had reached the fort, the gladiatii seizing control of the mekwerk catapults. The White galley was almost entirely ablaze, the Blue ship almost as bad, timber shrieking and men screaming as it crashed headlong into the keep. The Blues charged with a bloody cry, scrambling up the rope ladders and onto the battlements, the Golds meeting them head-on.

Another fire barrel hit the Red galley, this time onto the aft deck, immolating the gladiatii at the helm. The oarsmen rowed hard, desperate to reach the fort and escape their burning coffin. But with none to steer and the helm ablaze, the ship sailed wide, oars crushed to kindling against the plinth. The vessel shook, Furian stumbling to his knees, Mia almost following.

"Come on!" Mia cried, sheathing her blades and taking a running leap over the rails. Hands outstretched, she clutched a rope ladder hanging from the battlements, dangling precariously over the water. Furian followed, leaping onto a ladder beside her, oarsmen and other gladiatii following swift suit. A Lion made a desperate leap, seizing the ladder below Furian, only to have the Unfallen's boot send him down into the churning waters with a scream. Smoke burning her eyes, Mia scrambled up the rope, onto the keep's walls, the stink of burning oil and sundered guts almost overpowering.

The crowd was chanting, cheering, awestruck at the slaughter and spectacle. Mia blinked the sweat from her eyes, felt Furian leap over the battlements behind without turning to look at him. Just as when they fought in his room, Mia felt the pull in her own shadow, the hunger inside her swelling like a living thing.

And looking to her feet, she saw their shadows were completely entwined.

"What the 'byss is happening?" she gasped.

Leonides spat a black curse, on his feet and roaring. It was difficult to tell through the pall of smoke, but it seemed the great sanguila had very few warriors left in the battle at all. Leona watched as the Red and White galleys began sinking, oarsmen leaping over the side to take their chances with the drakes rather than burn to death. The water was a churning soup of dorsal fins and forked tails and wails, the crowd baying as the tiny ocean turned red.

Leona watched the Crow through narrowed eyes. A wrongness chewing at her insides. There was something about the girl . . . something amiss that she couldn't quite place. Watching her move among the Lions, she'd proved herself every bit the champion Leona had named her. But there was something off about the way she fought. Hacking, slashing, punching, kicking . . .

. . . *but never stabbing* . . .

Leona rose to her feet, squinting through the black haze, watching the Crow fight upon the battlements alongside Furian. The pair were devastating, cutting down all before them and slowly advancing from the fortification's edge. But her suspicion was right. Even when presented an opening for a thrust with her dagger, the Crow was only using it to block her opponent's strikes. She'd used the smaller blade with bloody abandon in the execution bout, but now the *magni* was under way . . .

"She only strikes with her gladius . . . ," she whispered.

Magistrae turned to her mistress. "Domina?"

Leona felt a chill in her belly. Remembering the turn she presented Crow with her armor, the gladius and dagger of black Liisian steel to match it. Watching the sunslight flash on the silvered blade in the Crow's hand, and knowing with dread certainty . . .

". . . That is not the dagger I gifted her."

A shlinn and Mercurio walked through the arena's belly, down wending corridors and beneath archways of stone, following the trail of sticky scarlet. They passed patrols of soldiers, cleaners, attendants, but almost anyone with eyes was upstairs watching the *magni*. They could hear the sounds of the conflict raging above, hollow booms and the howls of the crowd.

At the end of the hall, they saw a set of broad wooden doors, a pair of distinctly frustrated legionaries standing watch, heads tilted as they listened to the carnage upstairs. The taller one straightened as he saw Mercurio approach, looking the old man up and down before fixing Ashlinn in his stare.

"You hav—"

Ashlinn bent low and sent a small white glass globe bouncing across the stone. The pair had time enough to register the wyrdglass before it popped with a hollow bang, a cloud of pale gas filling the end of the hall. Ash and Mercurio waited to see if any came running at the sound, but the volume of the crowd and the conflict above seemed to have successfully drowned out the explosion.

Tying heavy kerchiefs about their faces, the pair entered the room, sealing it behind them, the carved plaque on the doors now clearly visible.

MORTUARY.

B lood on her hands and on her tongue.

Blood on her blades and in her eyes.

Mia fought atop the battlements, the stone slippery with gore. Knots of gladiatii hacked and stabbed at one another, steel ringing on steel, war cries filling the air. Worldeater, Champion of the Phillipi, was drenched head to foot in red, swinging a mighty two-handed mattock and crushing armor and shields like paper. Ragnar of the Tacitus Collegium was still standing, howling like a madman as he bent low and flipped a charging gladiatii over his shoulder, down into the water below.

The carnage was awful, the bodies piled high, perhaps only twenty gladiatii remaining where almost three hundred had begun. Mia had never seen blood-shed like it in her life. Furian fought beside her, painted to the armpits.

Their shadows were fully entwined now, all four of them, Mia, Mister Kindly, Furian, Eclipse, coalescing in the black beneath their feet. She could hear the crowd dimly, watched her blades dancing in the air almost as if they had minds of their own. But more, she could hear Furian, his heartbeat, his breathing, and beneath that, beneath the blood and the smoke and the deaf-ening roar of the slaughter-drunk crowd, she realized she could hear . . .

. . . *not his thoughts, but* . . .

His hunger. His longing. His thoughts for Leona, edged with sorrow and bitterness. His desire for the victor's laurel, echoing in every beat of his heart. For a moment, she felt it so truly, so much a part of herself, that she was tempted to simply throw down her sword and let him best her. For his own part, Furian seemed to feel her, also, sparing a glance for the consul's box, the grand cardinal among his craven flock, his jaw clenching with hatred.

"Almighty Aa," he breathed. "Those bastards . . ."

Her breath was burning, eyes stinging with sweat, pulse drumming be-neath her skin. Her blade sang in the air, her arms aching, and somewhere in the distance, ever so faint, beneath the roar of the crowd, the roar of the flames, the roar of those three suns burning the sky blind overhead, she heard it.

The darkness.

Beneath the water.

Beneath her skin.

Beneath the marble crust over this city's bones. Her shadow entwining with Furian's, bleeding into his own like the gore slicked across the stone.

"*. . . mia . . .*"

"Do you feel it?" she breathed.

Furian buried his blade in another chest, blood slick on his hands.

"I feel *you*," he gasped.

Twisting and turning, feinting and striking, time crawling.

"I feel *us* . . ."

"*. . . MIA, WHAT IS HAPPENING . . . ?*"

"I don't know," she whispered.

She felled another gladiatii, ducking beneath his strike and slicing his ham-string clean through. "Black Mother help me, I don't know . . ."

Worldeater raised his mattock and charged at Mia, feet pounding on the stone. From behind, she could feel Ragnar and Furian locked together, blade to blade. Even with the Swoon in their veins, the men were champions, veterans of a dozen slaughters, hard as steel. But Mia could still sense Furian, their shadows utterly enmeshed, coiling across the stone, dancing in the blood. It was as if she had two sets of eyes, two hearts, two minds, twice the strength, twice the will, twice the fury. Worldeater swung his mattock at her head and she felt Furian's hand on her own, guiding her counter. Furian struck at Ragnar, and he felt Mia's grip on his blade. Coalescing, unending, no sense of where she ended and he began. There beneath those burning suns, if only for a moment, the puzzle seemed to have found its missing piece.

Her gladius sliced the flesh behind Worldeater's knee, severing tendon to the bone. Furian disarmed Ragnar with a lightning thrust, but the Vaanian crash-tackled the Unfallen to the ground, the pair clawing and punching on the red-slicked stone. As Ragnar's hands closed about Furian's throat, Mia felt her own windpipe constrict. She gasped, choking, felt Worldeater's mattock crash against her ribs. Both she and Furian cried out in pain. Mia lost her grip on her dagger, the blade ringing bright as it skidded across the stone, coming to rest beside Furian and Ragnar.

Ragnar's hands tightened on Furian's throat, Mia gasping for breath. Worldeater dragged the girl to the ground, slammed his fist into her head, knocking her helm loose, her gladius flying. She couldn't breathe, couldn't see, Ragnar's grip on Furian making her choke. Reaching out across the stone, the crowd roaring at the top of their lungs, Furian's fingers scrabbled at the hilt of Mia's fallen knife. Worldeater slammed Mia's head into the ground, again, again, again, sunlight burning in her eyes.

Furian's fingers closed on the hilt of Mia's dagger.

"Furian," Mia gasped. "It won't—"

With a desperate cry, the Unfallen drew back the knife and plunged it into the gap between Ragnar's breastplate and spaulders.

The crowd gasped.

Furian cried out in triumph.

And Mia's spring-loaded blade slid right up into the hilt.

O i."

Sidonius felt a light kick to his arm. His belly lurched sideways, but the gladiatii kept his eyes closed, holding his breath.

Another kick from a particularly bony toe.

"I can still see your slavemark, deadman. Good thing the folks who dragged your corpse down here didn't bother to pull off your helmets. Time to go."

Sidonius opened his eye the tiniest crack, saw an old man in tattered rags leaning over him. He had bright blue eyes, a shock of gray hair, a lit cigarillo on his lips.

"You're . . . Mercurio?" he whispered.

"No, I'm the grand cardinal's mistress. Now get up."

Sidonius sat up on the mortuary floor, surrounded by hundreds of dead bodies. He could see a slender girl in guard's armor leaning over Wavewaker's "corpse," tapping him on the shoulder.

"You're Ashlinn," Sidonius whispered.

"Pleased to meet you," the girl nodded. "Now seriously, get the fuck up."

Bladesinger was standing, dragging off her helmet, still drenched in gore. With a grimace, Sidonius pulled off his own helm, reached behind his neck, pulled the punctured bladder out from under his breastplate. He could feel the chicken's blood down his back, coagulating into a slick, greasy mess.

"Bucket's in the wheelbarrow," Mercurio said. "Get washed, get dressed. We need to be gone before the *magni*'s done. And that won't be long."

The Falcons of Remus collegium took turns, scrubbing off the blood as best they could and changing into the outfits they were given. Armor from the unconscious doormen, rags for the rest of them. Sidonius pulled on a guard's steel helm, leather breastplate, looking to the stone above as the crowd roared in delight.

"How you suppose she's doing up there?" he murmured.

Wavewaker patted him on the shoulder. "Have faith, brother. She got us this far."

"With more than a little help from you." Bryn grinned.

"Aye, but did it have to be chicken's blood?" Butcher grimaced. "It stinks."

Wavewaker shrugged. "That's the way they taught me back in the theater."

Mercurio scowled, stubbed out his cigarette.

"I realize the odds of the administratii sending out a search party to look for a pack of dead gladiatii are slim, but if you lot are finished chatting, we have a daring escape to undertake." The old man gestured toward the door. "So if you wouldn't fucking mind . . . ?"

"Apologies," Ashlinn muttered. "He's always like this."

Straightening his helm, Sidonius squared his shoulders. His comrades behind him, he marched out into the corridor. The arena's innards were virtually empty, all eyes on the spectacle above. They made their way swiftly through the hallways, Ashlinn out in front, until they came to a small servants' entrance, locked and barred.

Ashlinn opened the door onto a small alleyway. Two guards were slumped outside it, dead or sleeping, Sid couldn't tell. But he also saw a small merchant's wagon, and a pretty blond girl sitting in the driver's seat. She looked at them and smiled.

"This is Belle," Mercurio said. "She'll take you across the aqueduct. A slaver named Teardrinker is waiting for you on the mainland."

"A slaver?" Bladesinger growled.

"She owes Mia a favor," Ashlinn said. "The largest kind of favor there is. She has the papers verifying that you've purchased your freedom. And contacts with the administratii to get your brands removed. Now go."

"Mia . . . ," Sid began.

"Go."

Bryn and the others were already in the wagon. Wavewaker clasped Sidonius's arm, hauled him up into the flatbed. The girl snapped the reins and they were moving, bouncing across the cobbles and off through the Godsgrave streets.

"Fine horses," Bryn said, nodding at the beasts leading the wagon.

"The black stallion is Onyx," the girl smiled. "The white mare is Pearl."

Sidonius climbed into the driver's seat beside her, trying to look officious in his uniform. But he found his hands were shaking, his knees weak, the ordeal leaving him hollow. After weeks of plotting, playing the part, praying they might somehow pull it off, the adrenaline was souring in his veins, leaving him exhausted and . . .

"Don't be afraid," the girl said, squeezing his hand. "All will be well."

Sidonius looked her up and down. Dark, wide eyes. Barely more than a child.

". . . How do you know?" he scoffed.

"Because the voices in your head that say otherwise are just fear talking. Never listen to fear."

The girl smiled, turned her eyes back to the open road.

"Fear is a coward."

Mia gasped as Worldeater cracked her skull back into the stone again, his thumbs pressed into her eyes. And slipping her gravebone dagger out from the bracer at her wrist, she slammed the blade up under the champion's chin, right into his brain.

Worldeater gurgled, toppled aside. Rolling to her feet, she snatched up her gladius and charged across the battlement, lips peeled back in a snarl. Ragnar had his hands about Furian's throat, looking up as the girl ran him down. He raised arms to ward off her blow, but the Swoon still hummed in his veins and her blade of Liisian steel sheared through his wrist, cleaving his helmet and splitting the flesh and bone beyond. Mia tore the blade free, the champion's body falling back in a spray of red.

Furian kicked free of the corpse, rolled up to his feet. Mia's spring-loaded dagger was still clutched in his hand, dark eyes burning into hers. The crowd was roaring with bloodlust. Of the hundreds of men and women who'd taken to the sand, only two now remained. Though they couldn't hear the words the Falcons spoke over the distance, the howls of their fellows, the blood pounding in their veins, all knew the match would soon be ended. The fact that these two were comrades from the same collegium made no difference. There was only one way this could end.

"*All must fall so one may stand!*" came the cry.

Mia and Furian stared at each other across the carnage, shadows seething at their feet. Where once they'd been entwined, coalescing to a perfect black, now they were coiled, writhing, clawing at each other with fury.

"So," Furian spat, hurling the false dagger at Mia's feet. "A liar to the last."

The crowd was a distant roar. The arena a faded backdrop, pale and translucent. Mia could feel the city of Godsgrave around them, sweltering beneath those awful suns. Feel it like a living thing, feel the rage and hatred nestled in its bones, like the truedark so long ago when she'd failed to kill Scaeva in the Basilica Grande.

Feel it like she felt herself.

"Furian . . . ," she began.

"You've learned *nothing* of honor, have you? I thought you claimed you weren't a hero? That if they needed help, they could help themselves?"

"They *did* help themselves, Furian," Mia replied. "We helped each other."

"And why?"

"Because they're my friends. And they didn't deserve to die."

"But die they will," he spat. "Like the traitors they are. When I am named victor, the first thing I will do is tell the editorii of your ploy. And all your lies will be for naught."

He stooped and picked up a bloody sword from the carnage about them.

"You can't wash your hands clean with more blood, Furian," Mia said.

"I give myself to the Everseeing."

"Furian, can't you feel it? Look at our shadows! Listen!"

"I hear nothing," he spat. "Save the witch I am about to kill."

"Don't!"

The Unfallen charged across the stone, bloody sword raised high. The roar of the crowd came crashing back down around her, a deafening tidal wave ringing in her skull. Time crawled, second by second, Furian's mouth open in a roar, his blade raised high.

She didn't want to kill him.

But she didn't want to die.

"... *mia*...?"

"All must fall so one may stand!" came the cry.

"... MIA...!"

All must fall so one may stand.

And so she moved, gentlefriends. Moved like wind. Like silver. Like shadows. Slipping beneath the blow scything toward her throat, steel whistling past her skin. The dark beneath them clawed and tore at each other, ink black upon the bloody stone, hate and hunger and something close to sorrow. The shadowcat hissed and the shadowwolf growled and the girl, the Blade, the gladiatii struck, the tip of her sword catching the Unfallen in the neck as he rushed past.

A spray of red. A breathless gasp. She felt pain, hand pressed to her throat as if she'd been dealt the blow herself. No bladders filled with chicken's blood now. No ploy. No play. His blood as real as the sunlight on her skin.

Furian looked to her, eyes wide with surprise. Clutching his throat, he turned to the sanguila's box, looking toward his domina. Mia felt it all. Regret. Sorrow. Bidding Mister Kindly and Eclipse to reach out across the stone, and in his final breath, to take his fear away.

And with a final gasp, the Unfallen fell.

A hammerblow to Mia's spine. A rush of blood in her veins, skin crawling, every nerve ending on fire. She fell to her knees, hair billowing about her as if in some phantom breeze, her shadow scrawled in maddened, jagged lines beneath her, Mister Kindly and Eclipse and a thousand other forms scribbled among the shapes it drew upon the stone. The hunger inside her sated, the longing gone, the emptiness suddenly, violently filled. A severing. An awakening. A communion, painted in red and black. And face upturned to the sky, for a moment, just for a breath, she saw it. Not an endless field of blinding blue, but of bottomless black. Black and whole and perfect.

Filled with tiny stars.

Hanging above her in the heavens, Mia saw a globe of pale light shining. Like a sun almost, but not red or blue or gold or burning with furious heat. The sphere was ghostly white, shedding a pale luminance and casting a long shadow at her feet.

"THE MANY WERE ONE."

"*Crow! Crow! Crow! Crow!*"

"AND WILL BE AGAIN."

A scream ripped up and out of her lungs, long and thin and keening. The sky crashed closed, the scorch of the suns bringing burning tears to her eyes. She was on her knees on the bloody stone, the arena ringing, the crowd on their feet, "*Crow! Crow! Crow! Crow!*" arkemical current dancing on her skin, sweeping her up on their wave of euphoria. Blood on her hands. Blood on her tongue.

Furian dead on the stone before her.

She hung her head. Gasping. Breath burning in her lungs. Full and empty all at once. Triumphant. All the miles, all the years, all the pain, and she'd done it.

She'd won.

But something . . .

. . . something was different.

And looking down, she saw her shadow, now still as a millpond, pooled on the bloodstained stone beneath her.

Dark enough for four.

CHAPTER 35
GONE

Leona cried out with the rest, heart in her throat. Something between elation and agony, watching Furian topple and the Crow fall to her knees over his corpse, triumphant. She'd done it. She'd won. Victory for the Remus Collegium. All Leona's dreams realized. All her sacrifice vindicated.

But the dagger the Crow used during the *magni* was wrong.

Which meant the execution bout . . .

"Mi Dona, a glass?"

Leona blinked, turned to a slave who'd materialized beside her. An old man with a silver tray, goblets, and a bottle of top-shelf goldwine. He was one of a dozen bondsmen now roaming the sanguila boxes, handing the blood masters fresh drinks as they stood and offered Leona grudging applause. The *magni* had been hard fought, but it had been glorious, and it was time for the men who profited most to honor the games and their victor with a traditional and well-earned drink.

The old man's circular brand looked fresh, a touch too dark on his cheek. His blue eyes twinkled like razors, and something about him put Leona distinctly ill at ease. She looked to the goblet he offered, shook her head.

"No," she murmured. "My thanks."

Leona turned her eyes back to the arena's heart, saw the Crow standing amid the carnage. The girl held aloft her bloody gladius, and the audience erupted. Everyone was on their feet—from the ministers of Aa's church to the commonfolk, all the way up to the consul's box. Scaeva himself was standing, his boychild on his shoulders, cheering loud.

Could none of them see?

Were they all blind?

"Mi Dona?" the old man asked again.

"I said no," Leona snapped. "I am not thirsty, begone!"

"I'm not suggesting you drink, Dona," he said, forcing a goblet into her hands.

The dona snarled, ready to berate the old fool for his temerity. But then she caught sight of the vintage on his bottle. A label she recognized from her childhood, the memory burned into her mind's eye. That bottle clutched in her father's hand, splashed blood red as her mother screamed.

"Albari," she whispered. "The seventy-four."

"Fine drop, that one," the old man replied.

"Be off!" Magistrae snapped. "Before I have you beaten for your impertinence!"

The old man turned to the magistrae, fixed her in his ice-blue stare. He pushed his laden tray into the woman's arms as she blustered, and, reaching into his tunic, he pulled out an expensive clove cigarillo, propped it on his lips.

"You know," he growled, "there's a special place in the abyss reserved for those who murder little girls."

Leona's heart stilled. She looked to Anthea, then to her father. Never the type to waste a fine vintage, the man was raising his glass of Albari seventy-four with the rest, glittering blue eyes locked on her as he and his colleagues drank deep. Perhaps he thought it chance. Perhaps he simply didn't care. But after he'd drunk deep from his cup, he looked at his daughter and gifted her a dark smile.

Leona stared at the goblet the old man had given her. A thin strip of parchment was nestled in the bottom, six words scribed in black ink.

"All the thanks I can muster."

Below it, she saw a sketch of a crow in flight above two crossed swords. The sigil of the Familia Corvere.

Leona looked up into the old man's eyes. Her own wide with realization. The old man pulled out a flintbox, lit his cigarillo, and dragged deep.

"Should you want him, you'll find Arkades in Blackbridge," he said. "I'd not return to Crow's Nest if you value your pretty neck. They'll take everything from you. Your house. Your collegium. Your wealth. And you'll have to leave your name behind. But you'll still have your life if you scamper away now. That's all she was willing to leave you, I'm afraid."

The old man scowled once more at Anthea, then turned and shuffled away, up through the sanguilas' boxes and down the stairs. Leona looked again to her father, turning to her magistrae. The perfume of a funeral pyre in her nostrils. Mia's voice echoing in her head.

Look to those closest to you . . .

". . . I need to use the privy," she said. "I feel ill."

"But, Domina . . . ," Magistrae began. "Your honors? They will be presen—"

". . . I'll only be a moment. Wait here until I return."

Magistrae frowned, but bowed low. "Your whisper, my will."

Leona nodded to her houseguards, gathered up her dress, and began marching up the stairs. Pausing, she turned back to her magistrae.

"O, and Anthea?" She nodded to the tray in the woman's arms. "Pour yourself a drink while I'm gone."

"Yes, Domina," the woman frowned. ". . . Thank you, Domina."

"Not at all," Leona replied, turning away. "I believe you've earned it."

P*atience.*

Mia stood on the central plinth, steady as the stone around her. The memory of that single, softly glowing orb in the heavens etched in her mind. That voice, echoing in her skull. Despite the three suns burning overhead, her grip on the dark felt stronger with Furian dead. Deeper, *richer* somehow, the shadow at her feet rippling, rolling, bleeding out across the flagstones toward . . .

Scaeva.

Duomo.

"... THEY COME ..."

"... *ever the observant one* ..."

She could see them, making their way down to the arena's edge. The crowd about them parting like a sea before the wave of Luminatii preceding them. Mia heard a mekwerk groan, the drake-infested waters churning as a large stone archway surfaced from the arena floor. Seawater pouring from its flanks, it slid into place, forming a broad bridge from the arena's edge to the central plinth. Scaeva stood on one side, his son on his shoulders, raising three fingers to bless the adoring crowd.

"... *he brings the boy* ..."

"... AND? HE THOUGHT NOTHING OF MURDERING MIA'S FATHER IN FRONT OF HER ..."

"... *so thirsty for blood, dear mongrel* ..."

"... GIRD YOURSELF, CUR. TIME FOR YOUNG LUCIUS TO LEARN LIFE'S HARSH REALITIES ..."

Mia fixed her eyes on Scaeva in his rich purple toga, Duomo behind him in his blood-red cardinal's robes. As she watched, a half-dozen attendants took the cardinal's staff from his hands, slipped off his vestments. Beneath, the great holy man was clad in a shift made of threadbare sackcloth, barefooted. He removed his rings, his golden bracelets, and finally, the blessed trinity of Aa hanging about his neck.

Stripped bare.

The holiest man in the Republic. The Hand of God himself, reduced to a beggar, just as the Father of Light had been in the old parable when he granted the generous slave his freedom. And soon, the champion of the *magni* would know that same freedom, bestowed by the voice of the Everseeing upon this earth.

But first came the Luminatii and a bevy of arena attendants. Marching across the stone span, fat and sated stormdrakes cruising below. An entire century of soldiers, clad in gravebone armor, their sunsteel blades rippling with holy flame. Reaching the fortifications, they surrounded Mia, the attendants setting to work, tipping the bodies of the slaughtered gladiatii off the battlements and into the churning waters below. She spared a glance for Furian's body, watching it tumble and splash down into the blue, the black at her feet rippling. A Luminatii centurion stood before Mia, wordlessly held out his hand, glancing to her bloody gladius. Mia gave over the blade without blinking.

As the crowd chanted, cheered, the attendants quickly washed away the blood, gathered the fallen weapons and tossed them into the water beside the corpses of their owners, and scurried back across the bridge. Mia was left surrounded by Luminatii, flanking her on all sides, a hundred to her one.

"Kneel, slave," the centurion commanded.

Mia did as she was told, knee and knuckles pressed to the stone, head bowed. Her gravebone dagger hidden back inside the iron bracer at her wrist.

Trumpets rang. The procession began, Duomo first, his broad shoulders squared, beard bristling, three fingers raised as he marched across the bridge surrounded by yet more legionaries. Next came Scaeva, waving to the jubilant crowd, his son atop his shoulders holding the golden victor's wreath. Mia kept her head down, glaring through her lashes as the cardinal approached, the Luminatii around her parting to allow him through.

Duomo stopped before her, looked down with a gentle smile. It had been years since he'd seen her last. She had a new face and new scars to show for her time. But looking up into his eyes, she searched for recognition. Some sliver of understanding about who it was kneeling before him. Some acknowledgment of all he'd done.

Nothing.

He doesn't even know me.

More Luminatii, Scaeva marching behind, taking his time. Waving with his son to the crowd. And as he and his retinue drew nearer, closer, above the stubborn butterflies flitting about her belly, Mia felt it. A now familiar sensation.

Hunger.

Want.

The longing of a puzzle, searching for a piece of itself.

Maw's teeth . . .

Her eyes widened. Mouth dry as ashes.

Someone here is darkin . . .

She searched among the soldiers, felt no hint of hunger. Heart hammering, she looked to Duomo, but no . . . that would be impossible. She'd seen him wielding a blessed trinity in his hand—if he were darkin, sanctified sigils of Aa would repel him, just as she . . .

O, Black Mother . . .

. . . Scaeva?

Her stomach sank. Eyes wide. But again, she'd seen him the truedark she attacked the Basilica Grande. There among the pews in Aa's holy house, no ill effects among the Light Father's faithful or his blessed symbols. But . . .

O, Black Mother . . .

The boy . . .

Scaeva's son.

She looked at him, found him looking back, brow creased in puzzlement. He was dark of hair, dark of eye, just like her. And as her stomach sank toward her toes, in his face, the line of his cheeks, or perhaps the shape of his lips, she saw . . .

"Luminus Invicta, heretic," Remus said, raising the blade above her head. "I will give your brother your regards."

. . . she *saw.*

"You have what is yours," Alinne said. "Your hollow victory. Your precious Republic. I trust it keeps you warm in the nevernight."

Consul Julius looked down at Mia, his smile dark as bruises. "Would you like to know what keeps me warm in the nevernight, little one?"

No . . .

Mia blinked in the gloom. Eyes searching the cell beyond.

"Mother, where's Jonnen?"

The Dona Corvere mouthed shapeless words. She clawed her skin, dug her hands into her matted hair. Gritting her teeth and closing her eyes as tears spilled down her cheeks.

"Gone," she breathed. "With his father. Gone."

Not "dead."

Only "gone."

With his . . .

. . . no.

O, mother, please no . . .

"Father," the boy on Scaeva's shoulders asked.

"Yes, my son?" the consul replied.

The child narrowed his ink-black eyes. Looking right at Mia.

"I'm hungry . . ."

Mia turned her eyes to the stone. Her heart was thundering now, despite all Mister Kindly's and Eclipse's efforts. Pulse rushing beneath her skin. The thought was too repulsive to believe, too awful, too horrifying, but glancing up again into the boy's face, she saw it. The shape of her mother's eyes. The bow of her lips. Memories of the babe she'd played with as a child, six years and a lifetime ago, flooding back into her mind and threatening to spill from her throat in a scream.

Jonnen.

O, sweet little Jonnen.

My brother lives . . .

Mind racing. Heart pounding. Sweat burning. Mia curled her hands into fists and pressed her knuckles into the stone as Cardinal Duomo stood before her and spread his arms wide, face upturned to the sky.

Patience.

"Father of Light!" Duomo called. "Creator of fire, water, storm and earth! We call you to bear witness, on this, your holy feast! Through right of combat and trial before your everseeing eyes, we name this slave a free woman, and beg you grant her the honor of your grace! Stand and speak your name, child, that all may know our victor!"

Patience.

"Crow!" the crowd roared. "CROW!"

The name echoed on the arena walls.

Reverberation.

Admonition.

Benediction.

"Crow! Crow! Crow! Crow!"

The girl rose slowly, standing like a mountain beneath those burning suns.

"My name is Mia," she said softly.

Hand slipping to the gravebone blade at her wrist.

"Mia Corvere."

Duomo's eyes widened. Scaeva's brow creased. The blade whistled as it came, slicing through the cardinal's throat, ear to bloody ear. He staggered back, dark blood fountaining from the wound, fingers to his severed carotid and jugular. The spray hit her face, thick and red, warm on her lips as she moved, as the Luminatii moved, as everything around her moved. The crowd roaring in horror. The cardinal collapsing to the stone. The Luminatii crying out, raising their blades. And the girl. The Blade. The gladiatii. The daughter of a murdered house, child of a failed rebellion, victor of the greatest bloodsport the Republic had ever seen . . . she charged.

Right at Julius Scaeva.

Fear bleached his handsome features, his dark eyes wide with horror. The Luminatii moved to intercept her, but she was quick as shadows, sharp as razors, hard as steel. Scaeva cried out, lifting the boy off his shoulders, the child's eyes wide with fear. And as Mia's belly rolled, the consul held his son out like a shield, and coward among cowards, he threw the boy at Mia's face.

She cried out, hand outstretched, the child's arms pinwheeling as he flew. The world slowed to a crawl, the suns pounding at her back, the heat of sunsteel flame rippling on her skin. She caught the boy, clutching him tight in her free arm, pulling him close. And rising up on her toes, she spun like a dancer, long dark hair streaming, arm outstretched in a glittering arc.

Perfection.

Her blade sank into Scaeva's chest, buried all the way to the hilt. The consul gasped, eyes open wide. Mia's face twisted, scar tissue pulling at her cheek, hatred like acid in her veins. All the miles, all the years, all the pain, coalescing in the muscles of her arm, corded and pulled tight as she dragged her blade sideways, splitting his ribs and cutting his heart in two. She left the gravebone blade quivering in his chest, the crow on the hilt smiling with its amber eyes, dark blood fountaining from the wound. And with the boy clutched tight to her chest, still spinning like poetry, like a picture, she twisted backward, over the edge of the battlements.

And she fell.

In turns to come, the next few moments would be the topic of countless taverna tales, dinner table debates, and barroom brawls across the city of Godsgrave.

The confusion arose for a number of reasons. Firstly, it was around this moment when Magistrae, Leonides, Tacitus, Phillipi, and virtually every other sanguila and executus in the ringside boxes began vomiting blood from the poisoned goldwine they'd drunk, which proved more than a little distracting. The central plinth was a fair distance from even ringside seats, so it was difficult for many in the audience to see. And last, and most important, the grand cardinal and the consul had just been brutally murdered by the champion of the *magni*, which left everyone in the crowd a little shocked.

Some said the girl fell, the boy in her arms, right into the mouth of a hungry stormdrake. Some said she hit the water, but avoided the drakes, making her escape through the pipes that had vented the ocean out onto the arena floor. And then there were those—discounted as madmen and drunks, for the most part—who swore by the Everseeing and all four of his Holy Daughters that this little slip of a girl, this daemon wrapped in leather and steel who'd just murdered the two highest officials in the Republic, simply *disappeared*. One moment falling toward the water in the long shadow of the battlements, the next, completely vanished.

The arena was in an uproar, fury, dismay, terror. The blood masters collapsed in their seats, or fell to the stone, Leonides and Magistrae dead among them, every gladiatii stable in the Republic beheaded with a single stroke. Duomo lay on the battlements, his face bled white, throat cut to the bone.

And beside the grand cardinal, his purple robe drenched with dark heart's blood, lay the savior of the Republic.

Julius Scaeva, the People's Senator, the man who had bested the King-makers and rescued Itreya from calamity, had been assassinated.

CHAPTER 36
GODSGRAVE

Ashlinn stole through the City of Bridges and Bones like a knife through a consul's chest. The sounds of panic were swelling in the arena behind them, the girl's heart singing as cathedrals all over the city began ringing a death knell.

"Black Mother, she did it."

She chewed her lip, stifling a fierce grin.

"She *did* it."

Ash moved quicker, over canals and through the twisting thoroughfares of the marrowborn district. The three suns blazed above, the heat relentless, sweat soaking her through. She would have stopped for a breather, but truth was, she had no time to breathe. From the sounds of chaos rising from the distant arena, word of Scaeva's death was spreading across the city like a brush fire. Soon the Red Church would know their beloved patrons were dead, and all the fury of the acolytes of Our Lady of Blessed Murder would be raining down on their heads.

She had to meet Mercurio at the necropolis, then Mia in the harbor. From there, they could slip out into the blue where no Blade or member of the Ministry could find them. Then she could rest. Breathe. Sink into Mia's arms and never, ever let go again.

Ashlinn made her way in the shadow of the Ribs, over a broad marble span to the Sword Arm. The air was slowly filling with the song of tolling bells, panicked shouts ringing through the city behind her. A boy ran past, eyes wide, waving his cap and yelling in a shrill voice.

"The consul and cardinal slain!"

"Assassin!" came another distant shout. "*Assassin!*"

She reached the wrought-iron fences surrounding the houses of Godsgrave's dead. Slipping through the tall gates, Ashlinn made her way to a door carved with a relief of human skulls, and down into the dank shadows of the necropolis. Swift and silent, she stole through the twisted tunnels of femurs and ribs, to the tomb of some long-forgotten senator. Pulling a small lever to reveal a hidden door in a stack of dusty bones, and finally, slipping into the corridors of the Red Church chapel.

Dark.

Quiet.

Safe at last.

She dashed to Mia's sparse bedchamber, snatched up a small leather pack and Mia's precious gravebone longsword. The crow's eyes on the hilt glittered red in the low light, Ash sparing a glance for the empty bed, the empty walls, the empty dark. And turning on her heel, she dashed back down the corridor to Mercurio's office.

"Are you ready t—"

Ashlinn's heart stilled in her chest. Sitting behind Mercurio's desk, fingers steepled at her chin, was an elderly woman with curling gray hair. She seemed a kindly old thing, eyes twinkling as she looked Ashlinn up and down. Though she sat in the bishop's chair, she wouldn't have seemed out of place beside a happy hearth, grandchildren on her knee and a cup of tea by her elbow.

"Revered Mother Drusilla," Ashlinn breathed.

"O, no, young Dona Järnheim," the old woman said. "I've not been Revered Mother since your treachery saw Lord Cassius murdered. Now, I am Lady of Blades."

Ashlinn looked about the room. Four other figures, swathed in gloom—the entire Red Church Ministry, waiting for her. Aalea with her death-black stare and blood-red lips. Spiderkiller, glowering in a gown of emerald green. Mouser with his old man's eyes and his young man's smile. And finally, Solis, blind gaze upturned to the ceiling, glowering at her nonetheless.

Ashlinn's grip tightened on Mia's gravebone sword.

". . . Where's Mercurio?" she demanded.

"The bishop of Godsgrave is already back at the Quiet Mountain," Solis said.

"He put up some resistance," Mouser said. "We had to hurt him, I'm afraid."

Spiderkiller looked at Ashlinn with black, glittering eyes. "There are some among us who are dearly hoping the same can be said of you, child."

"Please," Drusilla waved to the chair in front of her. "Sit."

"Or what?" Ashlinn said, her anger rising. "You can't kill me like you killed my da, you old bitch. The map's branded on my skin. If I die, it's lost forever."

"Please sit, Dona Järnheim," said a voice.

A man stepped out from Mercurio's bedchamber, and Ashlinn's belly filled with cold ice. He was tall, painfully handsome, dark hair shot through with the faintest streaks of gray. He wore a long toga of rich purple, a golden laurel at his brow.

"No . . . ," Ashlinn breathed.

"If we wanted you dead, you'd have been so long ago," Consul Scaeva said. "So please, sit before we are forced to resort to . . . unpleasantness."

"You're dead," Ashlinn whispered. "I *saw* you die . . ."

"No," Scaeva said. "Although I admit the likeness *was* uncanny."

Ashlinn's eyes grew wide as realization sank home . . .

"The Weaver," Ash whispered. "Marielle. She gave someone else your face . . ."

"You always were a clever one, Ashlinn," Aalea smiled.

"You'll forgive the appertaining drama, I hope," Consul Scaeva said. "But such subterfuge is necessary for a man with as many enemies as I."

Ashlinn searched their faces, mind awhirl.

They'd known.

They'd known this whole fucking time . . .

But why would they let us . . .

. . . Unless they wanted *us . . .*

Like a puzzle box with no more missing pieces.

All of them falling into place.

"You wanted Cardinal Duomo dead," she whispered. "But you couldn't just have the Church kill him. He was protected by the Red Promise. Only a Blade would be good enough to end him . . . but it had to be a Blade willing to betray the Ministry. That way, the Church's reputation stays intact, and you still see your enemy dead."

"And once I reveal myself miraculously alive to Godsgrave's adoring citizens . . ."

". . . They'll adore you all the more."

"And be left with *no doubt* of the continuing danger our Republic faces."

"Buying you a fourth term as consul . . ."

"O, no," Scaeva said, smiling wide. "That laurel is already bought. But the brutal assassination of a grand cardinal in front of the entire capital on Aa's most holy feast? Say it with me, young Dona Järnheim. Perpetual. Emergency. Powers."

Ashlinn's lips curled in derision.

The ego on this tosser . . .

The girl tossed her pack away with an almost casual contempt, plopped herself into the offered chair, and put her feet on Mercurio's desk, right in Drusilla's face. The old woman glowered, but Mia's gravebone blade was still in Ash's hand, her fingers drumming on the hilt.

"Foresaw everything, neh?" she asked the consul.

"I foresaw enough."

"Except the part where Mia stole your son?"

The smile slowly faded from Scaeva's lips.

"That was . . . unfortunate," the consul said, a muscle twitching at his jaw. "The boy should never have been allowed to accompany my doppelgänger to the presentation. My wife . . . she cannot have children, you see. So she indulges, perhaps too much." Scaeva's lips curled in a smile again, small and deadly. "But no matter. I have the beloved teacher. And now I have the beloved. And cold as she is, I think not even my daughter would harm her own brother."

The floor dropped away from beneath Ashlinn's feet.

". . . Daughter?"

Ashlinn felt movement behind her. A quick glance showed a thin, pale boy with stunning blue eyes in the chamber doorway, dressed in a dark velvet doublet. He was mute as always, but the knife in his hands looked sharp enough to cut the sunlight in six. The last time she'd seen him, he'd been trussed up in Luminatii chains, thanks to her betrayal. She'd wager he was the type to bear a grudge.

"All right, Hush?" Ashlinn asked.

She saw other figures behind him, scowling, glowering—Blades, all, no doubt.

"Time to go, Ashlinn," Drusilla said.

"O, no," Ashlinn mewled. "Can't I stay a little longer and listen to the consul gloat? I do *so* enjoy hearing the wanker tell me how he's thought of everything."

"You disagree, Dona Järmheim?" Scaeva smiled.

"I fear I must, Consul Scaeva," Ashlinn smiled in reply. "Because a person who'd thought of everything might have thought to look in my pack before I dropped it. And a person not so fond of his own fucking voice might have heard the fuse on the tombstone bomb inside."

Drusilla's eyes widened. Ashlinn threw herself aside as her pack exploded with an earsplitting boom. Solis was blasted across the room, smashing into the wall. The Ministry were caught in the arkemical fireball. Hush was smashed out through the chamber doors, his doublet aflame, the rest of the Blades tossed about like straw.

Ashlinn was up and running, ears bleeding, clothes smoking, head swimming from the blast. Mia's gravebone sword in hand, she dashed through the necropolis, at least three Church Blades on her heels. Sprinting through the twisting labyrinth, she made it to the upper levels, bursting out into the graveyard, suns beating down on her back. She had to make it to the harbor, had to—

The dagger took her in the back of her thigh, scraping the bone. She screamed and stumbled, mincing her palms and knees on the flagstones as she hit the ground. Teeth gritted, she rolled over, tore the dagger loose. Staggering to her feet, she saw four Church Blades bearing down on her. Silent and grim, dark eyes hardened to flint. Killers one, killers all. Each a storm, with no pity for the one they were to drown.

Ashlinn raised Mia's gravebone sword.

Looking among the killers and smiling dark.

"I'm guessing you're supposed to take me alive," she grinned. "Apologies in advance . . ."

"Aye," said the woman leading them. "We're sorry too."

Ashlinn blinked. Vision swimming. World spinning. Looking at the blood on her shaking fingers, spilling over her wounded thigh, down to the dagger that had struck her, and finally noticing the discoloration on the steel.

Poison.

"S'pose I should've expected that . . . ," she muttered.

A chill stole over her, dark and hollow. Goosebumps rippling on her bloodied skin. The suns burned high overhead, but here in the necropolis, the shadows were dark, almost black. A shape rose up behind the Blades, hooded and cloaked, swords of what could only have been gravebone in its hands. It lashed out at the closest killer, hacked his head almost off his shoulders. The other Blades turned quick as flies, raised their steel, but the figure moved like lightning, striking with its gravebone once, twice, three times. And almost faster than Ashlinn could blink, all four Blades were left dead and bleeding on the flagstones.

"Maw's teeth," she whispered.

It wasn't human. That much was clear. O, it was shaped like a man beneath that cloak—tall and broad shouldered. But its hands . . .'byss and blood, the hands wrapped about its sword hilts were black. Tenebrous and semitranslucent, fingers coiled about the hilts like serpents. Ashlinn couldn't see its face, but small, black tentacles writhed and wriggled from within the hollows of its hood, pulling the cowl lower over its features. And though it was truelight, three suns burning high in the sky, its breath hung in white clouds before its lips, Ash's whole body shivering at the chill.

". . . Who are you?"

The thing peeled back its hood. Pallid skin. Saltlocks writhing like living things. Pitch-black and hollow eyes. But even with the poison swimming in her veins, all the world around her fading to black, Ashlinn would recognize his face anywhere.

"Hello, Ashlinn," he said.

" 'Byss and blood," she breathed.

The darkness closing in.

". . . Tric?"

DICTA ULTIMA

No.

    I hear you say the word, as if I sat in the room beside you. I see you, bent over the tome in your hand with a frown on your face and a curse on your lips, as if I were puddled in the shadow at your feet. The realization that there are no more pages is sinking in now. I hear it. I see it.

    No, *you say again.*

    What of Mia and Jonnen? Of Scaeva? Mercurio and Ashlinn and Tric? The secrets of the darkin? The Crown of the Moon? I promised ruins in her wake. Pale light glittering on waters that drank a city of bridges and bones. All these questions unanswered, and yet the book is at its end?

    No, *you say.* It cannot *end like that.*

    Fear not, little mortal. The song is not yet sung. This is but the calm before the crescendo. This tale is only two of three.

    Birth. And life. And death.

    So patience, gentlefriends.

    Patience.

    Close your eyes.

    Take my hand.

    And walk with me.

ACKNOWLEDGMENTS

Thanks as deep as the Dark to the following:

Amanda, Pete, Jennifer, Paul, Joseph, Hector, Young, Steven, Justin, Rafal, Cheryl, Martin, and all at St. Martin's Press; Natasha, Katie, Emma, Jaime, Dom, and all at Harper Voyager UK; Rochelle, Alice, Sarah, Andrea, and all at Harper Australia; Mia, Matt, LT, Josh, Tracey, Samantha, Stefanie, Steven, Steve, Jason, Kerby, Megasaurus, Virginia, Vilma, Kat, Stef, Wendy, Marc, Molly, Tovo, Orrsome, Tsana, Lewis, Shaheen, Soraya, Amie, Jessie, Caitie, Nic, Ursula, Louise, Tori, Siân, Caz, Marie, Marc, Tina, Maxim, Zara, Ben, Clare, Jim, Rowie, Weez, Sam, Eli, Rafe, AmberLouise, Caro, Melanie, Barbara, Judith, Rose, Tracy, Aline, Louise, Adele, Jordi, Kylie, Iryna, Joe, Andrea, Piéra, Julius, Antony, Antonio, Emily, Robin, Drew, William, China, David, Aaron, Terry (RIP), Douglas (RIP), George, Margaret, Tracy, Ian, Steve, Gary, Mark, Tim, Matt, George, Ludovico, Philip, Randy, Oli, Corey, Maynard, Zack, Pete (RIP), Robb, Ian, Marcus, Tom (RIP), Trent, Winston, Andy (RIP), Tony, Kath, Kylie, Nicole, Kurt, Jack, Max, Poppy, and every reader, blogger, vlogger, bookstagrammer, and other breed of bookpimp who has helped spread the word about this series.

The people and city of Rome.

The people and city of Venice.

And you.

Turn the page for a sneak peek at
Jay Kristoff's next novel

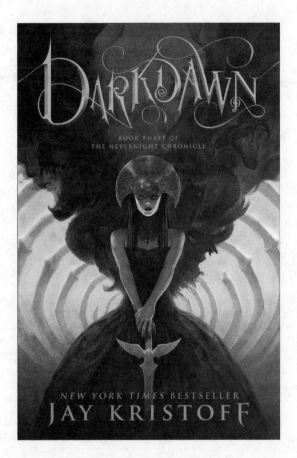

Available September 2019

BROTHER

Salt burning in her eyes.

Breath burning in her lungs.

Crowd still roaring in her ears.

She'd fallen so far, her little brother in her arms, fingers still sticky with blood. The light of the three suns above, burning and blinding. The mob howling, bewildered and outraged at the murders of their grand cardinal, their beloved consul, both at the hands of their revered champion. The greatest games in Godsgrave's history had ended with the most audacious murders in the history of the Republic. The entire arena was in chaos. But through it all, the screams, the roars, the rage, Mia Corvere had known only triumph. After seven years of blood and sweat and death.

Seven years of poison and murder and shit.

Seven fucking years.

Mother.

Father.

I did it.

I killed them for you.

She hit the water hard, the sights and sounds of Godsgrave arena swallowed up as she plunged beneath the surface. Her little brother, Jonnen, was struggling, punching, wriggling in her arms like a landed fish. She could sense the shadows of stormdrakes, serpentine and dark, cruising toward her through the blue.

Razor smiles and dead black eyes.

Truelight was so bright, even here beneath the surface. But even with those awful suns in the sky, even with all the outrage of the Everseeing pouring down upon her, her own shadows were with her. Dark enough for four. And Mia reached toward the outflow in the arena floor—the wide spout from which all that salt and water flowed

and she

Stepped

into the

shadows

inside it.

It left Mia dizzied and sick—she could still feel that blinding sunslight in the sky above. She sank like a stone in her armor, weighed down by black iron and sodden falcon's wings. Pulling Jonnen down with her, she hit the bottom of the outflow pipe with a dull clunk. She had only moments, only the breath she'd brought with her. And she'd not planned to have a struggling child in her arms when she did this.

Dragging herself and the boy along the pipe, she found a pocket of air inside the pressure valve, just as Ashlinn had promised. Standing up with a ragged gasp, she pulled her brother up beside her. The boy sputtered in her arms, wailing, struggling, flailing at her face.

"Unhand me, wench!" he cried.

"Stop it!" Mia gasped.

"Let me *go*!"

"Jonnen, stop it, please!"

She wrapped the boy up, pinning his arms so he couldn't punch anymore. His cries echoed on the pipe above her head. Struggling with her armor's clasps and straps with her free hand, she dragged the pieces away, one by one. Shedding the skin of the gladiatii, the assassin, the daughter of vengeance, sloughing those seven years all the way off her bones. It'd been worth it. All of it. Duomo dead. Scaeva dead. And Jonnen, her blood, the babe she'd thought long buried in his grave . . .

My little brother lives.

The boy kicked, thrashed, bit. There were no tears for his murdered da, only fury, rippling and red. Mia had thought the boy dead years ago—swallowed up inside the Philosopher's Stone with her mother and the last of her hope. But if she'd had any lingering doubts he could be a Corvere, that he could be her mother's son, the boy's bloody rage put them all to the sword.

"Jonnen, listen to me!"

"My name is Lucius!" he shrieked, his voice echoing on the iron.

"Lucius, then, listen!"

"I won't!" he shouted. "You k-killed my father! You *killed* him!"

Pity swelled inside her. A soft horror rising in her breast as she saw herself reflected in the boy's eyes. She remembered her own version of this moment, years past. Looking at the ones who hanged her own da in the forum. Her vow of vengeance ringing in her head, the hatred boiling like white-hot acid in her veins.

Did Jonnen now feel the same way about her?

. . . *Am I his Scaeva?*

"I'm sorry, Jonnen," she said. "But your father . . ." The girl shook her head, hardening her heart. "Listen, we need to get out of this pipe before they start draining the arena. The stormdrakes will come back this way, do you understand?"*

"Let them come, I hope they *eat* you!"

". . . *O, I LIKE HIM* . . ."

". . . *why does that not surprise me* . . ."

The boy turned to the dark shapes coalescing on the wall beside them, the air around them growing chill. A cat made of shadows and a wolf of the same, staring at him with their not eyes. Mister Kindly's tail twitched side to side as he studied the child. Eclipse simply tilted her head, shivering slightly. Jonnen fell silent, wide dark eyes looking first to Mia's passengers, then to the girl who held him.

"You hear them, too . . ." he breathed.

"I'm like you," Mia nodded. "We're the same."

---

*Of the three breeds of drake found in Itreyan waters—white, saber, and storm—the stormdrake is by far the stupidest. The beasts eat virtually anything that will fit inside their mouths, including fellow stormdrakes and their own young. A complete list of oddities found in stormdrake bellies is kept in the zoology archives of the Iron Collegium, and includes, in no particular order:

- A full suit of plate armor
- A leather chaise lounge
- A six-foot-long timber saw
- An entire family of (presumably enraged) porcupines

This habit of eating anything vaguely interesting has earned them the moniker "sewers of the sea" among Itreyan fishermen, since upon catching one and cutting it open, you're likely to find all kinds of strange . . .

Well, yes.

You get the idea.

The boy stared at her, perhaps feeling the same sickness, hunger, *longing* she did. Mia looked him over, tears welling in her eyes. All the miles, all the years . . .

"You don't remember me," she whispered, her voice shaking. "You were only a baby when they t-took you away from us. But I remember you."

She was almost overcome for a moment. Burning tears in her lashes and a sob caught in her throat. Recalling the boy wrapped in swaddling on her mother's bed the turn her father died. Staring up at her with his big, dark eyes. Envying him that he was too young to know their father had ended, and all their world besides.

But he wasn't Jonnen's father at all, was he?

Mia shook her head, blinked back those hateful tears.

O, Mother, how could you . . .

Looking at the boy now, she could barely speak. Barely force her jaw to move, her lungs to breath, her lips to form the words burning in her chest. He had the same flint-black eyes as she, the same ink-black hair. She could see their mother in him so clearly, it was like peering into a looking glass. But beyond the Corvere in him, something in the shape of Jonnen's little nose, the line of his puppy-fat cheeks . . .

She could see him.

Scaeva.

"My name is Mia," she finally managed. "I'm your sister."

"I have no sister," the boy spat.

"Jonn . . ." Mia caught herself. Licked her lips and tasted salt. "Lucius, we have to go. I'll explain everything, I swear it. But it's dangerous here. Please, come with me."

"*. . . ALL WILL BE WELL, CHILD . . .*"

"*. . . breathe easy . . .*"

Mia watched as her daemons slipped into the boy's shadow, eating away at his fear as they'd always done for her. His breath came easier, the rage in his eyes eased, the bunched muscles in his little arms relaxed. Mia propped Jonnen against the pipe as she finished working at the buckles on her armor, slipping off her breastplate and spaulders, dropping them to the floor of the valve. She kept her boots, her studded leather skirt, the threadbare, blood-stained tunic beneath. And gathering the boy into her arms, she held him tight.

"I need you to hold your breath," she said. "We have to swim."

Dark eyes locked on hers, his lips pressed thin. But now utterly fearless, the boy complied. And dragging a deep breath into her lungs, Mia pulled them below and swam for their lives.

They surfaced in sapphire water a half hour later to the sound of pealing bells.

With Jonnen in her arms, Mia had swum through the vast storage tanks below the arena, through the echoing dark of the mekwerk outflow pipes, spilling finally out into the sea a few hundred feet north of the Sword Arm harbor. Her brother had glared at her all the while. But though she could see anger swimming in Jonnen's stare, he seemed sedated after his earlier outburst. Sullen and silent.

Perhaps it was shock. Perhaps the passengers riding in his shadow. Either way, Mia was thankful. She couldn't possibly have left him up there on the victor's plinth with the cooling corpses of Duomo and his da. Couldn't ever have left him behind. But in all her planning with Ashlinn and Mercurio, she'd not bargained on having to wrangle an eight-year-old child after having murdered his father right in from of him.

. . . *His father.*

The thought swam behind her eyes, too dark and heavy to look at for long. She pushed it aside, focusing on getting them into shallower waters. Ash and Mercurio were waiting for her aboard a swift galley named the *Siren's Song,* berthed at the Sword Arm. The sooner they were out of Godsgrave, the better. Word would be spreading across the metropolis about Scaeva's assassination, and if they didn't already, the Red Church would soon know their richest and most powerful patron was dead. A storm of knives and shit was about to start raining down on Mia's head.

As she swam toward the Sword Arm docks, she saw the streets of the metropolis beyond were in chaos. Cathedrals were ringing a death knell across the City of Bridges and Bones. Folk were emerging from taverna and tenements, bewildered, outraged, terrified as rumor of Scaeva's murder uncoiled through the city like blood in the water. Legionaries were everywhere, armor glinting under that awful sunlight.

With all the fuss and bother, precious few folk noticed the bedraggled and bleeding slavegirl paddling slowly toward the shore with a boy in her arms. Picking her way carefully through the gondolas and dinghies bobbing about the Sword Arm jetties, Mia reached the shadows beneath a long timber boardwalk.

"I'm going to hide us for a moment," she murmured to her brother. "You won't be able to see for a while, but I need you to be brave."

The boy only glared, dark curls hanging in his eyes. Stretching out her fingers, Mia dragged her mantle of shadows about her and Jonnen's shoulders. It took real effort with truelight blazing above her—the sunlight scorching and bright. But even with her passengers now riding with her brother, the shadow beneath Mia was twice as dark as it had been before Furian's death. Her grip on the dark felt stronger. Tighter. Closer.

She remembered the vision she'd seen as she slew the Unfallen before the adoring crowd. The sky above her, not bright and blinding, but pitch-black and flooded with stars. And shining high above her head, a pale and perfect orb.

Like a sun, but somehow . . . not.

"*THE MANY WERE ONE. AND WILL BE AGAIN.*"

Or so the voice she'd heard had said. Echoing the message from that hearthless wraith with the gravebone blades who'd saved her skin in Galante.

Mia didn't know what it meant. She'd never had a mentor to show her what it was to be darkin, never found an answer to the riddle of what she was. She didn't know. *Couldn't* know. But she knew this, sure as she knew her own name: since the moment Furian had died at her hands, a newfound strength was flowing in her veins.

Somehow, she was . . . *more.*

The world fell into muzzy blackness as she threw on her shadowcloak, and she and her brother became faint smudges on the watercolors of the world. Jonnen squinted in the gloom beneath her mantle, watching her with suspicious eyes. Mia followed Mister Kindly and Eclipse's whispered directions, slowly climbing a barnacle-encrusted ladder and up to the jetty proper. And there, in the shadow of a shallow-bottomed trawler, she curled down to wait, cross-legged, dripping wet, arms around her brother.

Mister Kindly coalesced in the shadow at Jonnen's feet, licking at a translucent paw. Eclipse melted from the boy's shadow, outlined black against the trawler's hull.

". . . *I WILL RETURN* . . ." the not-wolf growled.

". . . *you will be missed* . . ." the not-cat yawned.

". . . *WILL YOU MISS YOUR TONGUE AS MUCH, WHEN I TEAR IT FROM YOUR SKULL* . . . ?"

"Enough, the pair of you," Mia hissed. "Be swift, Eclipse."

". . . *AS IT PLEASES YOU* . . ."

The shadowwolf shivered and was gone, flitting along the cracks in the jetty's boards and off along the harbor wall. Mister Kindly continued with his pointless ablutions and Mia sat cradling her brother for long minutes, muscles aching, salt water stinging in her cuts as the suns blazed overhead. She was tired, beaten, bleeding from a dozen wounds after her ordeals in the arena. The adrenaline of her victory was wearing off, leaving a bone-deep fatigue in its wake. She'd fought two major battles earlier in the turn, helped her fellow gladiatii from the Remus Collegium escape their bondage, slaughtered dozens including Duomo and Scaeva, won the greatest contest in the history of the Republic, seen all her plans come to fruition.

An emptiness was slowly creeping in to replace her elation.

An exhaustion that left her hands shaking.

She wanted a soft bed and a cigarillo and to savor the taste of goldwine on Ashlinn's lips. To feel their bones collide, then sleep for a thousand years. But more, beneath it all, beneath the longing and the fatigue and the pain, looking down at her brother, she realized she felt . . .

. . . hungry.

It was similar to what she'd felt in the presence of Lord Cassius. Of Furian. Not mingled with same sense of burning desire, Mother, no. This was her baby brother, after all. But Mia felt a sameness to it. A sickening kinship. She'd felt it when she first saw the boy on his father's shoulders at the victor's plinth. She felt it as she glanced at him, now.

The longing of a puzzle, searching for a piece of itself.

She wondered if Jonnen felt the same.

But what does it mean?

". . . *i have an ill feeling, mia* . . ."

Mister Kindly's whisper dragged her eyes from the back of her brother's head. The shadowcat had stopped pretending to clean his paw, instead staring out at the City of Bridges and Bones from within Jonnen's shadow.

"What's to fear?" she murmured. "The deed is done. And all things considered, nothing went too badly tits up."

". . . *what difference does it make, the direction your breasts are pointing . . . ?*"

"Spoken like someone who's never owned a pair."

Mister Kindly glanced at the boy he was riding.

". . . *we seem to have some unexpected luggage* . . ."

"You worry too much."

". . . *and you not enough* . . ."

"And whose fault is that?"

The daemon tilted his head, but before he could give reply, Mia felt a cool shiver down her spine. Goosebumps prickled on her skin, and her shadow grew darker as she heard a low growl from the boards beneath her feet.

"... *THEY ARE NOT THERE* ..." Eclipse said.

Mia blinked, her belly lurching a little to the left. Squinting in the glare, she peered at the murky blur of the *Siren's Song*, rocking gently at berth a few jetties down.

"You're certain?" she asked.

"... *I SEARCHED FROM BOW TO STERN. MERCURIO AND ASHLINN ARE NOT ABOARD* ..."

Mia swallowed hard, her tongue thick with salt. The plan had been for Ash and her old teacher to meet at the Godsgrave Chapel, gather their belongings, then make their way to the harbor and await her aboard the *Song*. With the time it took for her to get from the arena to the ocean and out again ...

"They should be here by now," she whispered.

"... *shhhh* ..." came a murmur at her feet. "... *do you hear that* ... ?"

"... Hear what?"

"... *it appears to be the sound of* ... *breasts tilting skyward* ... ?"

Mia scowled at the jest, dragging her sopping hair over her shoulder. Her heart was beating faster, thoughts racing. There was simply no way Mercurio or Ash would have been late—not with all their lives at stake.

"Something's happened to them ..."

"... *I CAN SEARCH THE CHAPEL, REPORT BACK* ... ?"

"No. If she ... If they ..." Mia chewed her lip, dragged herself to her feet despite her fatigue. "We go together."

"... *even our new luggage* ... ?"

"We can't just leave him here, Mister Kindly," Mia snapped.

The not-cat sighed.

"... *and the tits continue to rise* ..."

Mia took Jonnen's hand, pulled him up. The boy was still sullen, shivering, silent. He was sopping wet, his lips pressed tight together, his dark eyes clouded with anger. But with Mister Kindly riding his shadow, Jonnen still allowed himself to be led by the hand. Moving slowly beneath Mia's shadowcloak, the unlikely quartet made their way down the jetty and onto the crowded boardwalk, gentle water lapping beneath them.

Following her passenger's whispered directions, carefully feeling her way between the dockside warehouses, creeping past the patrols of legionaries and Luminatii, Mia and her brother slipped into the Godsgrave streets beyond the harbor. The sounds of the city were muted beneath her cloak, the colors naught but dull white and terracotta blurs. But she could still hear tolling bells, running feet, panicked shouts.

"The consul and cardinal slain!"

"Assassin!" came the cry. *"Assassin!"*

She glanced to Jonnen, saw he was staring at her with unveiled malice.

"You really killed him," the boy said softly. "You killed my f-father."

"He imprisoned our mother, Jonnen," Mia replied. "Left her to die in agony inside the Philosopher's Stone. He killed my father, and hundreds more besides. Do you not remember him throwing you at me on the victor's plinth to save his own wretched skin?" She shook her head and sighed. "I'm sorry. I know it's hard to understand. But your father was a monster."

"They're going to kill you," he said softly. "For what you did."

Mia could only shrug.

"Well, they'll just have to take a number and join the queue."

Leading her brother by the hand, pawing near-blind along the walls, Mia made her way through the twisted alleys of Godsgrave backstreets. Her pulse was thumping in her veins, her belly turning slow, cold somersaults. Eclipse was prowling out ahead. Mister Kindly was still riding Jonnen. And without her passengers, Mia was left trying to fight off fearful thoughts about what might've delayed Mercurio and Ash.

Luminatii?

The Ministry?

What could have gone wrong?

Goddess, if anything has happened to them because of me . . .

Slipping through alleys and squeezeways and over little bridges and canals, the quartet finally reached the wrought-iron fences surrounding the city's necropolis. Mia's boots were near soundless on the gravel, one hand stretched out before her, groping blind. Almost inaudible beneath the peal of cathedral bells, Eclipse's whispers guided her through the twisted gates to the houses of the city's dead, down rows of grand mausoleums and moldy tombs. In a weed-choked corner of the necropolis's old quarter, she found a door carved with a relief of human skulls, leading down to the boneyards. Slipping through, down a flight of crumbling stairs, she finally stepped into the dank shadows beneath the city's skin.

It was sweet relief, being out of the light of those awful suns. Throwing aside her mantle, holding Jonnen close, Mia made her way through twisted tunnels of femurs and ribs—bones of the city's destitute and nameless, too poor to afford tombs of their own. Twisting a hidden lever, she opened a secret door in a stack of dusty bones, and finally, slipped into the Red Church chapel hidden beyond.

She crept down the twisting hallways, lined with the remains of those long dead. Jonnen was wide-eyed, gazing at the bones all around them, but Mister Kindly stayed coiled in his shadow, keeping the worst of his fear at bay.

The corridors were dark.

Silent.

Empty.

Wrong.

Mia felt it almost immediately. Smelled it in the air. The faint scent of blood wasn't out of place in a chapel to Our Lady of Blessed Murder, but the lingering aroma of a tombstone bomb and burned parchment certainly was.

The chapel was far too quiet, the air far too still.

Suspicion ever her watchword, Mia pulled her mantle of shadows back about their shoulders, and crept onward in near blindness. Jonnen's hand was clutched tightly in hers, her palm damp with sweat. Her ears strained for the slightest sound, but the chapel seemed completely deserted.

Mia stopped in a bone-lined hallway, the hair on back of her neck prickling. She knew, even before she heard Eclipse's warning growl.

"... BEHIND ..."

The dagger flashed from out of the darkness, gleaming silver, poison-dark. Mia twisted, damp hair whipping in a long black ribbon behind her, spine bent in a perfect arch. The blade sailed over her chin, missing her by a breath. Her free hand touched the ground, pushed her back up to standing, her heart hammering.

Her mind was racing, brow creased in confusion. Beneath her cloak of shadows, she was almost blind, aye—but the world should have been just as blind to her.

Blind ...

... O, Goddess ...

He stepped from dark, silent despite his bulk. His gray leathers were stretched taut across the barn-broad span of his shoulders. His ever-empty scabbard hung at his waist, dark leather embossed with a pattern of concentric circles. Thirty-six small scars were etched into his forearm—one for every life he'd taken in the Red Church's name. His eyes were milky white, but Mia saw his eyebrows were gone entirely. The once-blonde stubble on his head was crisped black as if burned, and the four sharp spikes of his beard were charred nubs.

"Solis ..."

His face was swathed in shadows, blind eyes fixed on the ceiling. He drew two short, double-edged blades from his back, both darkened by poison. And, hidden as Mia was beneath her mantle, he still spoke directly to her.

"Treacherous fucking quim," he growled.

Mia reached for the gravebone dagger at her wrist.

Heart sinking as she realized she'd left it buried in Consul Scaeva's chest.

"O, shit . . ." she whispered.